Comdex®

Tally.ERP 9 Course Kit

With GST & MS Excel

VIKAS GUPTA
BE, DPPS, MBA (PGPMAX)

Published by:

dreamtech PRESS

ISBN: 978-93-86052-43-8

Reprint: 2024

Printed at: Srk Graphics

Table of Contents

TALLY.ERP 9 WITH GST

MS EXCEL

Tally.ERP 9 with GST

CHAPTER

1

Basics of Accounting

In this Chapter:

- Need for Accounting
- Definitions of Accounting
- Important Terms in Accounting
- Concept of Accounting
- Conventions of Accounting
- Classification of Accounts
- Rules of Debit and Credit
- Journal
- Ledger
- Trial Balance
- Financial Statements

In a business, many transactions take place everyday and it is nearly impossible to remember all of them. Therefore, you need to keep the record of each transaction. Accounting is used to record, report, summarize, and interpret the financial data. With the help of accounting records, a businessman is able to determine the profit or loss and the financial position of the business at a particular accounting period. It also helps to communicate the accounting information to all the interested parties whose decisions and actions are related to its performance. The accounting records help in knowing whether the income has increased or the expenditure has increased and how much we owe to others and how much others owe to us.

In this chapter, you learn about the basic needs and definitions of accounting. Next, you learn key terms, concepts, and conventions in accounting. Further, the chapter discusses the different types of accounts. After this, you learn the rules of debit and credit in accounting. In addition, you learn about the journal, ledger, and trial balance. At the end of the chapter, you learn about the financial statements.

Let us start the chapter by learning about the need for accounting.

Need for Accounting

In early days, business transactions were small and easily manageable by the owner of the business. During this time, most of the business concerns worked as a company type of transaction. A transaction involves transfer of money, goods or services from one person to another and it is not possible for the owner to remember all the transactions. Therefore, it is necessary to record all the transactions properly to their respective books of accounts. Accounting is used to maintain records of all the financial transactions. It also helps to determine the net results in terms of profit or loss and provide the information about the financial status of the business to the owners of a business. It is also useful for the employees and customers in order to know the condition of the business entity. Accounting is needed in a business to provide the information which is useful for planning, controlling and decision-making process.

After learning about the need for accounting, let us learn about the definitions of accounting.

Definitions of Accounting

Accounting is the backbone of any business, and it forms a clear financial image of a business. Accounting is a method or a system used to record and control the financial status of a person. It is the process of keeping and examining the records of every transaction and preparing the financial reports for a business. In other words, we can say that accounting is the process of recording, identifying, measuring, and communicating the economic activities of a business to make smart and informed decisions.

Some other definitions of Accounting are as follows:

- According to **American Accounting Association (AAA)**, "Accounting is the process of identifying, measuring and communicating economic information to permit informed judgments and decisions by the users of the information."
- According to **American Institute of Certified Public Accountants (AICPA)**, "Accounting is the art of recording, classifying and summarizing in a significant manner in terms of money, transactions and events, which are, in part at least, of financial character, and interpreting the results thereof."
- According to **A.W. Johnson**, "Accounting may be defined as the collection, compilation and systematic recording of business transactions in terms of money, the preparation of financial reports, the analysis and interpretation of these reports and the use of these reports for the information and guidance of management."
- According to **Weygandt, Kieso and Kimmel**, "Accounting is an information system that identifies records and communicates the economic events of an organization to the interested users."
- According to **Smith and Ashburne**, "Accounting is the science of recording and classifying business transactions and events, primarily of a financial character and the art of making significant summaries, analysis and interpretations of those transactions and events and communicating the results to persons who must take decisions or form judgments."

After learning about the definition of accounting, let us learn about the important terms in accounting.

Important Terms in Accounting

It is necessary to understand the basic accounting terms which are used in the business. These terms are parts of the basic accounting terminology. The important accounting terms are as follows:

- **Assets:** Refer to anything with economic value that an individual, organisation or country holds with an expectation to produce benefit in future. In other words, an organisation owns or controls an asset to generate cash flow, reduce expenses and/or improve sales in future. According to the **Finny and Miller,** "Assets are future economic benefits, the rights, which are owned or controlled by an organization or individual."

  Assets can be categorized into:
  - **Fixed Assets:** Refer to those assets which are purchased for the purpose of business operation and not for resale. For example land, building, and machinery.
  - **Current Assets:** Refer to those assets which are purchased for the short term and then convert them into cash o for resale. For example debtors, unsold goods, bank balance, and bills receivables.
  - **Tangible Assets:** Refer to those assets which have physical assistance means they can be seen and touched. For example land, building, plant and machinery, and computer.
  - **Intangible Assets:** Refer to those assets which do not have any physical assistance and they cannot be seen and touched. For example goodwill, trademarks, patent, and copyright.
  - **Wasting Assets:** Refer to those assets which are consumed natural resource during the process of use. For example mines and quarries.
- **Liabilities:** Refer to the financial responsibilities of a business other than owner's fund. These consist of an obligation to pay money, assets, or render services to another person or persons. According to the Finny and Miller, "Liabilities are debts, they are amounts owed to creditors."

  Liabilities can be categorized into:
  - **Long-Term Liabilities:** Refer to those liabilities which are owed after a long-term, generally more than one year. For example, long-term loans and debentures.
  - **Short-Term Liabilities:** Refer to those liabilities which are owed in the near future. For example, creditors, bank overdrafts, bills payable and short-term loans.
- **Capital:** Refers to the amount which the owner has invested in the business. It is treated as owners' equity which is claim against assets.
- **Incomes:** Refer to the profits earned accruing over a given period of time.
- **Expenses:** Refer to the amount expended to produce and sell the goods and services which producc the profits.
- **Debtors:** Refer to the persons, entities, or firms to whom goods have been sold on credit or who pay a certain amount to the business unit.
- **Creditors:** Refer to the persons or other entities that have to be paid an amount by an enterprise or firm for providing the enterprises goods and services on credit.
- **Purchases:** Refer to the goods which are purchased by a business for selling purpose or producing the finished product which are also to be sold.
- **Sales:** Refer to the goods which are sold out by the business or firm. When the goods are sold in cash, they are cash sales, but if the goods are sold on credit, they are credit sales.
- **Revenue:** Refers to the amount of income before any deduction, such as interest, dividends, and royalties.
- **Transaction:** Refers to the business activities involving transfer of money, goods or services between two persons or accounts. A transaction is a financial activity that is entered into by the parties and is recorded in the books of accounts.
- **Discount:** Allows any type of reduction in the prices of goods. The discounts are of two types: trade discount and cash discount. An amount that the retailer or manufacturer reduces from the total

prices of the sold goods is called trade discount. A cash discount is the amount that the seller or retailer gives to his customer for the timely payment of sold goods.

- **Debit:** Refers to a book-keeping entry that results in increasing the assets and in decreasing the liability or owner equity. If an account is to be debited, then the entry is posted to the debit side of the account.
- **Credit:** Refers to a book-keeping entry that results in increasing the liability or owner equity and in decreasing the assets. If an account is to be credited, then the entry is posted to the credit side of the account.
- **Profit:** Refers to the benefit of an individual or a company on the financial level, which is earned when the revenue generated from a business exceeds the total cost, expenses and taxes needed to sustain the business.
- **Loss:** Refers to the decrease in the revenue of a company. It is always less than the capital invested.
- **Bad debts:** Refer to the amount that is considered unrecovered. It is a loss for the business and debited to the profit and loss account.
- **Drawing:** Refers to the amount of money or quantity of goods that a proprietor takes from a business for his/her domestic or personal use. It reduces the investment of the owner.
- **Depreciation:** Refers to the decrement in the value of assets due to their usage or with the passage of time.
- **Wages:** Refer to the amount paid to the labourers.

After learning about the important terms of accounting, let us discuss about the accounting concept.

Concept of Accounting

Accounting is the language of every business. The financial transactions are recorded and reported to a number of interested parties and outsiders. In the absence of systematic approach, accountants may use their own language and it will not be necessary to understand these languages by the other business concerns. Therefore, the language used to record transactions is uniform, which helps in conveying the same meaning to all the stakeholders and interested parties. Generally, the accountants have agreed on certain accounting concepts or principles and followed them to maintain the uniformity. These principles or concepts are general guidelines for comprehensive accounting practices. These concepts are known as **'Generally Accepted Accounting Principles (GAAP)'**. Thus, GAAP includes a set of rules, principles, and concept for preparing financial accounting reports.

The list of accounting concepts is as follows:

- Business entity concept
- Dual aspect concept
- Accounting period concept
- Cost concept
- Money measurement concept
- Going concern concept
- Accrual concept
- Matching concept

Let us learn about these accounting concepts one by one.

Business Entity Concept

The business entity concept holds the business to be separate and distinct from its owners who control the business. According to this concept, the transactions are recorded in the books of accounts from the business perspective rather than the owner perspective. The owners of the firm are considered as creditors of the business to the extent of their capital. It means that the capital invested by the owner is the liability of the business. For example, when the proprietor contributes his capital in the business, the cash account and bank account are debited and the capital account is credited. The amount in the credit of the capital is a liability of the business towards the proprietor.

Dual Aspect Concept

According to the dual aspect concept, each transaction has two effects, namely debit and credit. This means that whenever a transaction takes place, it affects at least two accounts.

For example, Mr. Ajay borrows ₹ 20,000 from Bank for the purpose of business. In this case, in the accounting books of Ajay, his cash/bank balance for business will be ₹ 20,000; but, on the other side, he has created a liability as payable to Bank to the extent of ₹ 20,000. Therefore, the cash-in-hand/bank account is debited and loans account is credited as payable.

Accounting Period Concept

Accounting period refers to the period for which an organization realizes revenue and assesses its financial position. Usually, an accounting period is a period of one year. This concept helps to measure the progress of the business on a consistent basis and facilitates the comparison of the progress of the business.

For example, the accounting period 1st April to 31st March indicates the financial year of the Indian Government. Some of the other accounting periods applicable in India are 1st January to 31st December (calendar year), and the Diwali year.

Cost Concept

According to the cost concept, assets are recorded in the books of account at the price paid (cost incurred) to acquire them. By the concept, the value of an asset does not change with the market value of the asset.

For example, suppose three years ago a building was purchased for ₹ 25,00,000 and now its market value is ₹ 40,00,000. In this case, when the financial statements are prepared, the purchase value of the building will be considered.

Money Measurement Concept

The money measurement concept implies that the events and transactions that can be measured in terms of money are recognized in financial statements. Transactions that cannot be measured in money terms are not recorded in the books of accounts. However, it is important to the business or enterprise. For example, human resources with enterprise or business are important to them, but are not reflected in the financial statements because their worth cannot be measured in terms of money.

Going Concern Concept

According to this concept, a business entity will continue to exist for an indefinite time period and it will not be liquidated in the immediate future. According to **Kohler's Dictionary for Accountants**, "Going concern is defined as the enterprises which are expected to continue operating indefinitely in the future".

By the going concern concept, an organization is able to achieve its pre-defined objectives and contractual duties through the resources available to it. These resources include plant, machinery, land, and building, which are the assets of an organization and are required to carry out its business.

For example, if a machine is purchased and its useful life is expected to be 5 years, then the total cost of the machine is allocated over that period of 5 years.

Accrual Concept

According to this concept, the incomes and expenses are recognized by the enterprise or business when they are earned or incurred irrespective of whether the actual money is received or paid. For example, if a company sells anything on credit, then it will enter the revenue (income) on the income statement, regardless of the fact that the enterprise or business has received the payment (cash) or not.

Matching Concept

Matching concept is based on the accounting period concept and accrual concept of accounting. Every business is run to earn profit and the profit is calculated by the business during an accounting period. To compare a profit or loss of an accounting period, it is necessary to match or compare all the expenses incurred in an accounting year with the revenues earned during the year.

After learning about the accounting concepts, let us learn about the accounting conventions.

Conventions of Accounting

Accounting conventions refer to the guidelines or behavior that are followed by an accountant for preparing a financial statement. By following these conventions, we make accounting information more clear and meaningful. The basic accounting conventions are listed as follows:

- Convention of Full Disclosure
- Convention of Materiality
- Convention of Consistency
- Convention of Conservatism

Let us discuss these accounting conventions one by one.

Convention of Full Disclosure

According to this convention, all the important information of the business and the material information must be disclosed for the various purposes of its users. In other words, this convention specifies the complete and full disclosure of important information related to the financial activities of a business. The main objective of disclosing the information is that any person who wants to analyse the financial activities should not be unfair by hiding any facts. So, it is necessary that the information must be fair and satisfactory to make impartial conclusion.

Convention of Materiality

This convention refers to the relative importance of an item or an event that makes financial statements meaningful. Only the important and relevant information related to the material is supplied to the users in the business enterprises. According to the American Accounting Association, "An item should be regarded as material if there is a reason to believe that knowledge of it would influence the decision of informed investors." According to the users of financial statements, trivial information should not be recorded and reported in the business enterprises.

Convention of Consistency

This convention is based on the different accounting periods. According to this convention, a particular set of the selected and adopted accounting principles and rules applied in an accounting period should not be changed in another accounting period. In other words, the adopted accounting principles and rules should be applied consistently year after year. The primary objective of this convention helps in better understanding of the accounting information and makes it comparable with the previous year. However, the adopted accounting principles and rules are not changed, but if in case the change is desirable, then it is necessary that the changes and its effects are mentioned in the financial statement.

Convention of Conservatism

This convention is based on the policy of 'playing safe' and it is also known as convention of prudence. This convention is described using the phrase: "Do not anticipate a profit, but provide for all the possible losses." Due to business doubts and risks, it is important to account for the possible losses. According to **Kohler**, "Conservatism is a guideline which chooses between acceptable accounting alternatives for recording events or transactions so that the least favorable immediate effect on assets, income and owner's equity is reported." This convention leaves all prospective profits as it is uncertain to earn such profit and considers all prospective losses.

After learning about the accounting conventions, let us learn about the classification of accounts.

Classification of Accounts

The individual transaction record of a person, firm, and an item of income and expense is called accounts. An account is a concise record of significant transactions at one place relating to a particular head, such as person, furniture, bank, income, and expense. It records the transaction amount and its effect and direction. According to Kohler's dictionary for accountants, "An account is a formal record of a particular type of transaction expressed in terms of money or other units of measurement and kept in a ledger."

The transaction of a business is categorised into three categories:

- Related to persons and individuals
- Related to properties and assets
- Related to incomes and expenses

Corresponding to these three categories of transactions, the accounts are classified into two categories: personal account and impersonal account. Classification of accounts can be exhibited in Fig.AC-1.1:

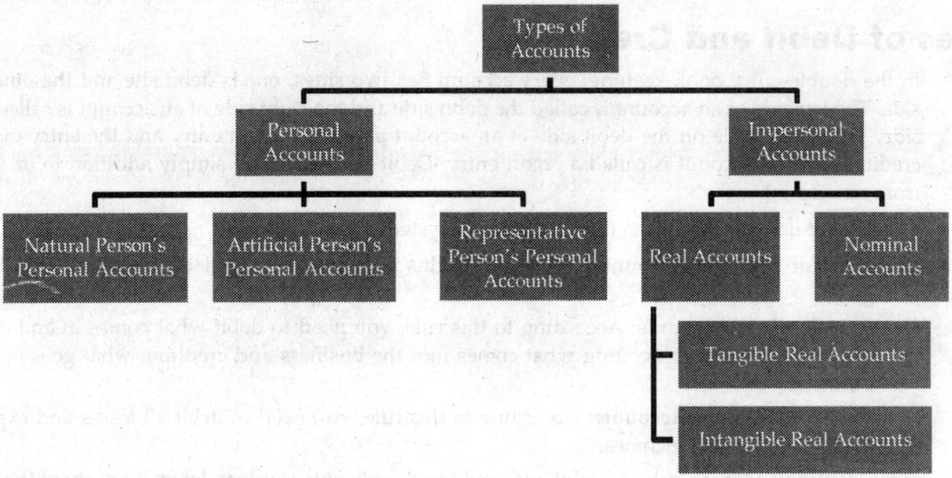

Fig.AC-1.1

Personal Accounts

Personal Accounts are the accounts which record the transactions related to the individuals, companies, banks, and organizations. Examples of Personal Accounts are Ramesh A/c, Outstanding Salary A/c, and Mohan & Co. A/c.

There are three types of personal accounts. These are as follows:

- **Natural Person's Personal Accounts:** Refer to those accounts which record the transactions related to human beings. For example, Rahul's account and Kavita's account.
- **Artificial Person's Personal Accounts:** Refer to those accounts which record the transactions related to the non-living beings or human beings who have some existence as per the law. For example, D.A.V. College A/c, Institution Club A/c, and M/s Ram and Bros. A/c.
- **Representative Person's Personal Accounts:** Refer to those accounts which represent a certain person or a group of persons. For example, Outstanding Rent A/c.

After learning about the personal accounts, let us learn about the impersonal accounts.

Impersonal Accounts

Those accounts that do not come under the personal accounts are called impersonal accounts, such as furniture account, cash account, and salary account. There are two types of impersonal accounts. These are as follows:

- **Real Accounts:** Refer to those accounts which record the transactions related to the property and assets. For example, furniture, land and building, and machinery accounts. Real account is also classified into two accounts:
  - **Tangible Real Accounts:** Refer to those accounts which can be touched, seen, felt, measured, purchased, and sold. For example, Land & Building A/c, Cash A/c, and Stock A/c.

- **Intangible Real Accounts:** Refer to those accounts which cannot be seen and touched in the physical manner, but measured in terms of value. For example, Goodwill A/c, Trademarks A/c, and Patent A/c.

- **Nominal Accounts:** Refer to those accounts which record the transactions related to the expenses, losses, profits, and revenues. These accounts are used to define the nature of transactions. For example, Purchases A/c, Sales A/c, Salary A/c, Rent A/c, Commission A/c, and Discount A/c.

After learning about the impersonal accounts, let us learn about the rules of debit and credit in double-entry book-keeping.

Rules of Debit and Credit

In the double-entry book-keeping, every account has two sides, one is debit site and the other is credit side. The left side of an account is called the debit side and the right side of an account is called the credit side. The entry made on the debit side of an account is called a debit entry and the entry made on the credit side of an account is called a credit entry. Debit and credit are simply addition to or subtraction from an account.

The rules of debit and credit in the double-entry system are as follows:

- **Rule for Personal Accounts**: According to this rule, you need to debit the receiver and credit the giver.
- **Rule for Real Accounts**: According to this rule, you need to debit what comes in and credit what goes out. It refers to debiting what comes into the business and crediting what goes out from the business.
- **Rule for Nominal Accounts**: According to this rule, you need to debit all losses and expenses and credit all gains and incomes.

After learning about the rules of debit and credit in double-entry system, let us learn about the journal.

Journal

Journal is the primary book of account in which all transactions are recorded in the form of entries. The journal is the chronological (in order of date) record of the transactions of a business. The process of recording a transaction in a journal is known as journalizing.

According to **Cropper**, "A journal is a book used to record, classify or sort out transactions in a convenient form to record their subsequent entry in ledger."

According to the **Carter**, "The 'Journal' or 'Daily Record', as originally used, was a book of prime entry in which transactions were copied in order of date from a memorandum or waste book. The entries, as they were copied, were classified into debits and credits, so as to facilitate their being correctly posted afterwards in the ledger."

A format of the journal is shown here:

Journal

Date	Particulars	L.F.	Debit Amount (₹)	Credit Amount (₹)
	Name of the debited account Name of the credited account (Narration)			

The terms used in journal are as follows:

- **Date:** It refers to recording the date of the transaction.
- **Particulars:** It refers to recording the names of the accounts in which the debit amount and credit amount are written. The debit account is written at the left side of the particulars column and **Dr.** is

written at the right side of the particulars column. The credit account is written in the next line with a prefix **To**. The narration is a brief description of the transaction.

- **Ledger Folio (L.F.):** It refers to recording the page number of the ledger on which the debit and credit accounts are posted.
- **Debit Amount:** It refers to recording the debited amount.
- **Credit Amount:** It refers to recording the credited amount.

After learning about the basics of a journal, let us learn how to record transactions in a journal.

Recording Transactions in a Journal

On the basis of double-entry rules of debit and credit, transactions are recorded in the journal.

Transaction 1: Hari Mohan started business with ₹ 50,00,000.

In transaction 1, the two accounts being affected are: Cash Account and Hari Mohan's Capital Account. The cash account is a real account and rule for the real account is 'debit what comes in and credit what goes out'. Here the cash comes into the business. Hence, the cash account is to be debited. Hari Mohan's capital account is a personal account and the rule for the personal account is 'debit the receiver and credit the giver'. Here Hari Mohan has given cash to the business. Hence, Hari Mohan's capital account is to be credited.

The transaction will be recorded in the journal as follows:

Date	Particulars	L.F.	Debit Amount (₹)	Credit Amount (₹)
	Cash A/c Dr. To Hari Mohan's Capital A/c (Being money invested in the business)		50,00,000	50,00,000

Transaction 2: Purchase building from Swati Builders in cash ₹ 2,00,0000.

In transaction 2, the two accounts being affected are: Building Account and Cash Account. Both Building and Cash accounts are real accounts and the rule for real account is 'debit the receiver and credit the giver'. Here the Building is coming in the business. Hence, the Building account is to be debited and the cash goes out of the business. Hence, the cash account is to be credited. The transaction will be recorded in the journal as follows:

Date	Particulars	L.F.	Debit Amount (₹)	Credit Amount (₹)
	Building A/c Dr. To Cash A/c (Being building purchased by cash)		50,000	50,000

Transaction 3: Paid cartage to Harish & Co. ₹ 5,000.

In transaction 3, the two accounts being affected are: Cartage Account and Cash Account. The Cartage account is a nominal account and the rule for the nominal account is 'debit all expenses and losses and credit all incomes and gains'. Here the cartage is the expense. Hence, the cartage account is to be debited. The cash account is a real account and the rule for the real account is 'debit what comes in and credit what goes out'. Here the cash goes out of the business. Hence, the cash account is to be credited. The transaction will be recorded in the journal as follows:

Date	Particulars	L.F.	Debit Amount (₹)	Credit Amount (₹)
	Cartage A/c Dr. To Cash A/c (Being cartage paid)		5,000	 5,000

Illustration 1: Journalize the following transaction of Dreamtech Press for the month of March 2017:

2017

March 1 Dreamtech Press started business with ₹ 4,00,000 in cash.

3 Purchases goods for ₹ 2,50,000 on account from Yogesh.

5 Purchases furniture for ₹ 30,000 on account from Ramesh.

8 Pays Ramesh ₹ 59,000.

10 Pays Yogesh ₹ 35,000.

15 Cash sales ₹ 50,000.

18 Sells goods to Rahul on credit ₹ 27,000.

27 Pays salary in cash ₹ 12,000.

30 Pays rent to owner ₹ 6,000.

Solution:

Books of Dreamtech Press

Journal

Date	Particulars	L.F.	Debit Amount (₹)	Credit Amount (₹)
2017 March 1	Cash A/c Dr. To Dreamtech Press's Capital A/c (Being capital invested in cash)		4,00,000	 4,00,000
March 3	Purchase A/c Dr. To Yogesh (Being goods purchased on credit)		2,50,000	 2,50,000
March 5	Furniture A/c Dr. To Ramesh (Being furniture purchased on credit)		30,000	 30,000
March 8	Ramesh Dr. To Cash A/c (Being cash paid to Ramesh against purchase of furniture)		59,000	 59,000
March 10	Yogesh Dr. To Cash A/c (Being cash paid to Ramesh against purchase of goods)		35,000	 35,000

Date	Particulars		L.F.	Debit Amount (₹)	Credit Amount (₹)
March 15	Cash A/c	Dr.		50,000	
	To Sales A/c				50,000
	(Being goods sold for cash)				
March 18	Rahul	Dr.		27,000	
	To Sales A/c				27,000
	(Being goods sold on credit to Rahul)				
March 27	Salary A/c	Dr.		12,000	
	To Cash A/c				12,000
	(Being salary paid)				
March 30	Rent A/c	Dr.		6,000	
	To Cash A/c				6,000
	(Being rent paid)				
	Grand Total			8,69,000	8,69,000

After learning about recording the transactions in a journal, let us learn about compound journal entry.

Defining Compound Journal Entry

In compound journal entry, when two or more transactions of the same nature occur on the similar date, such transactions are recorded in one journal entry instead of separate entry for each transaction. There are three ways to record the compound journal entries.

1. To record one account to be credited and two or more accounts to be debited. For example, on 28th March 2017, ₹ 5000 is paid for rent and ₹ 3500 is paid for freight. The transaction will be recorded in the journal as follows:

Date	Particulars		L.F.	Debit Amount (₹)	Credit Amount (₹)
2017	Rent A/c	Dr.		5,000	
Mar 28	Freight A/c	Dr.		3,500	
	To Cash A/c				8,500
	(Being rent and freight paid)				

2. To record two or more accounts to be credited and one account to be debited. For example, on 29th March 2017, paid to Ram & Co. ₹ 50,000 and discount allowed by him was ₹ 3,000. The transaction will be recorded in the journal as follows:

Date	Particulars		L.F.	Debit Amount (₹)	Credit Amount (₹)
2017	Ram & Co.	Dr.		50,000	
Mar 29	To Çash A/c				47,000
	To Discount A/c				3,000
	(Being payment made by cash and discount received)				

3. To record two or more accounts to be debited and two or more accounts to be credited. For example, on 30 March 2017, purchased goods from Ram & Co. for ₹ 40,000 and paid cartage on these goods amounting to ₹ 2000. The transaction will be recorded in the journal as follows:

Date	Particulars		L.F.	Debit Amount (₹)	Credit Amount (₹)
2017	Purchases A/c	Dr.		40,000	
Mar 30	Cartage A/c	Dr.		2,000	
	To Ram & Co.				40,000
	To Cash A/c				2,000
	(Being goods purchased from Ram & Co. and paid cartage)				

After learning about compound journal entry, let us learn about the ledger.

Ledger

Ledger is a book or register in which transactions are permanently recorded in a summarized and classified form. In other words, ledger is a book of accounts in which the transactions are arranged under the suitable headings. Ledger helps to prepare the trial balance and after preparing the trial balance, we prepare a final account. Hence, the ledger is also known as Principle Book.

According to the **L.C. Cropper**, "The book in which a trader's all transactions are recorded in a classified permanent form is called the ledger."

According to **William Pickles**, "A ledger is the most important book of accounts and is the (final) distinction of entries made in the subsidiary books."

In a ledger, personal accounts show how much money the enterprise or firm owes to its creditors and the amount to be recovered from its debtors Real accounts show the value of properties and the value of stock. And the nominal accounts reflect the sources of income and also the amount expended on various items.

The format of the Ledger is as shown below:

Dr. **Name of the Account** **Cr.**

Date	Particulars	J.F.	Amount (₹)	Date	Particulars	J.F.	Amount (₹)

In the ledger, each account id divided into two sides – debit side and credit side. The left side of the ledger is called debit side and the right side is called credit side. Both the sides are further divided into four columns. The brief descriptions of these columns are as follows:

- **Date:** It refers to recording the date of the transaction.
- **Particulars:** It refers to recording the names of the accounts to be credited on the debit side and the amount of the debited on the credit side.
- **Journal Folio (J.F.):** It refers to recording the page number of the ledger on which the posting of ledger takes place.
- **Amount:** It refers to recording the amount of the each transaction.

Let us now learn about the rules of posting the transactions in a ledger.

Guiding Rules for Ledger Posting

Posting is the method of moving the transactions from the journal to the ledger. Posting the transactions into the ledger is done periodically, maybe weekly or monthly, according to the convenience. The rules for posting transactions are as follows:

1. Open a separate account in a ledger for posting the transactions that are related to the accounts recorded in the journal.
2. Enter the date of the transaction in the date column.
3. Write the name of the account which has been credited in the respective entry in the particular column on the debit side of the account. Entries in the debit side of the ledger begin with the word **To**.
4. Write the name of the account which has been debited in the respective entry in the particular column on the credit side of the account. Entries in the credit side of the ledger begin with the word **By**.
5. Enter the page number of the journal from where the entry is transferred to the ledger.
6. Enter the same amount in the debit and credit columns, which is entered in the journal.

For example, on 2 April 2017, paid salary ₹ 15,000. Journalize this transaction and post it to the ledger.

The transaction will be recorded in the journal as follows:

Journal

Date	Particulars	L.F.	Debit Amount (₹)	Credit Amount (₹)
2017 Apr 2	Salary A/c Dr. To Cash A/c (Being paid salary)		15,000	 15,000

The above entry will be posted into the ledger as follows:

Dr. Cash Account Cr.

Date	Particulars	J.F.	Amount (₹)	Date	Particulars	J.F.	Amount (₹)
				2017 Apr 2	By Salary A/c		15,000

Dr. Salary Account Cr.

Date	Particulars	J.F.	Amount (₹)	Date	Particulars	J.F.	Amount (₹)
2017 Apr 2	To Cash A/c		15,000				

In the preceding example, two accounts are opened in a ledger – Salary Account and Cash Account. The Salary account which is debited in the journal entry is debited in the ledger and the Cash account which is credited in the journal entry is credited in the ledger. The Salary account shows the debited amount and Cash account shows the credited amount.

Balancing the Account

After knowing the process of posting and recording all the transactions, it is necessary to balance each account. Balancing an account means totaling the amount of both the sides of the account. The difference of the sides is written to the side whose total is short. For example, if the total of the credit side is more than the debit side, then the difference of the sides will be recorded on the debit side and vice versa. The procedure for balancing an account is as follows:

1. Calculate the amount of both debit and credit sides of the account separately.
2. Calculate the difference between both the sides. If there is no difference, then the balance is nil. If the debit total of the account is greater than the credit total, then the difference is written on the credit side. If the credit total of the account is greater than the debit total, then the difference is written on the debit side.
3. Write against the balance as **To Balance c/d** if the difference is placed on the debit side. The word **c/d** refers **to carry down to the next period**. Similarly, write against the balance as **To Balance b/d**, if the difference is placed on the credit side. The word **b/d** refers **to bring down from the earlier period**.
4. Put the total of both the sides at the bottom of each side.
5. Please note that the closing balance of the previous account will appear as the opening balance of the current period in the opposite side of the account as **To Balance b/d** or **By Balance b/d**.

Illustration 2: Prepare the ledger of the journal prepared in Illustration 1.

Solution: Illustration 1 has 10 different accounts in the journal; therefore, 10 ledger accounts are opened.

Dr. Dreamtech Press' Capital Account Cr.

Date	Particulars	J.F.	Amount (₹)	Date	Particulars	J.F.	Amount (₹)
2017				2017			
Mar 31	To Balance c/d		4,00,000	Mar 1	By Cash A/c		4,00,000
			4,00,000				4,00,000
				2017			
				Apr 1	By Balance b/d		4,00,000

Dr. Cash Account Cr.

Date	Particulars	J.F.	Amount (₹)	Date	Particulars	J.F.	Amount (₹)
2017				2017			
Mar 1	To Dreamtech Press Capital A/c		4,00,000	Mar 8	By Ramesh		59,000
Mar 15	To Sales A/c		50,000	Mar 10	By Yogesh		35,000
				Mar 27	By Salary A/c		12,000
				Mar 30	By Rent A/c		6,000
				Mar 31	By Balance c/d		3,38,000
			4,50,000				4,50,000
2017							
Apr 1	To Balance b/d		3,38,000				

Dr. **Purchase Account** Cr.

Date	Particulars	J.F.	Amount (₹)	Date	Particulars	J.F.	Amount (₹)
2017 Mar 3	To Yogesh		2,50,000	2017 Mar 31	By Balance c/d		2,50,000
			2,50,000				2,50,000
2017 Apr 1	To Balance b/d		2,50,000				

Dr. **Yogesh Account** Cr.

Date	Particulars	J.F.	Amount (₹)	Date	Particulars	J.F.	Amount (₹)
2017 Mar 10	To Cash A/c		35,000	2017 Mar 3	By Purchase A/c		2,50,000
Mar 31	To Balance c/d		2,15,000				
			2,50,000				2,50,000
				2017 Apr 1	By Balance b/d		2,15,000

Dr. **Furniture Account** Cr.

Date	Particulars	J.F.	Amount (₹)	Date	Particulars	J.F.	Amount (₹)
2017 Mar 5	To Ramesh		30,000	2017 Mar 31	By Balance c/d		30,000
			30,000				30,000
2017 Apr 1	To Balance b/d		30,000				

Dr. **Ramesh Account** Cr.

Date	Particulars	J.F.	Amount (₹)	Date	Particulars	J.F.	Amount (₹)
2017 Mar 8	To Cash A/c		59,000	2017 Mar 5	By Furniture A/c		30,000
				Mar 31	By Balance c/d		29,000
			59,000				59,000
2017 Apr 1	To Balance b/d		29,000				

Sales Account

Dr. | Cr.

Date	Particulars	J.F.	Amount (₹)	Date	Particulars	J.F.	Amount (₹)
2017				2017			
Mar 31	To Balance c/d		77,000	Mar 15	By Cash A/c		50,000
				Mar 18	By Rahul		27,000
			77,000				77,000
				2017			
				Apr 1	By Balance b/d		77,000

Rahul Account

Dr. | Cr.

Date	Particulars	J.F.	Amount (₹)	Date	Particulars	J.F.	Amount (₹)
2017				2017			
Mar 18	To Sales A/c		27,000	Mar 31	By Balance c/d		27,000
			27,000				27,000
2017							
Apr 1	To Balance b/d		27,000				

Salary Account

Dr. | Cr.

Date	Particulars	J.F.	Amount (₹)	Date	Particulars	J.F.	Amount (₹)
2017				2017			
Mar 27	To Cash A/c		12,000	Mar 31	By Balance c/d		12,000
			12,000				12,000
2017							
Apr 1	To Balance b/d		12,000				

Rent Account

Dr. | Cr.

Date	Particulars	J.F.	Amount (₹)	Date	Particulars	J.F.	Amount (₹)
2017				2017			
Mar 30	To Cash A/c		6,000	Mar 31	By Balance c/d		6,000
			6,000				6,000
2017							
Apr 1	To Balance b/d		6,000				

After learning about the ledger, let us now learn about the concept of trial balance.

Trial Balance

After posting the transactions in the ledger accounts and balancing them, a statement is prepared to show the debit and credit balances of each account separately. Such a statement is called a trial balance. If the total of the debit amount and credit amount columns of the trial balance is equal, it is recognized that the posting of the transaction to the ledger is complete and accurate.

According to **Spicer and Pegler**, "A trial balance is a list of all the balances standing in the ledger and the cash book of a concern at any given time."

According to **Carter (1937)**, "Trial balance is the list of debit and credit balances taken out from ledger."

According to **J.R. Batliboi**, "A trial balance is a statement of debit and credit balances extracted from the ledger with a view to listing the arithmetical accuracy of books."

According to **Pickles**, "A trial balance is a statement prepared with the help of ledger balances at the end of financial year (or at any other date) to find out whether the debit total agrees with the credit total."

The format of the trial balance is shown as below:

Name of the Firm ....
Trial Balance as on ....

S. No.	Name of the Account	L.F.	Dr. Amount (₹)	Cr. Amount (₹)

The trial balance is prepared on a particular date; therefore, the term **as on** is used. Trial balance is further divided into five columns. The brief description of these columns is as follows:

- **S. No.:** Records the serial number of the transaction
- **Name of the Account:** Records the names of the accounts that are prepared in the ledger
- **Ledger Folio (L.F.):** Records the page number of the ledger
- **Debit Amount:** Records the debit amount of the transaction
- **Credit Amount:** Records the credit amount of the transaction

Now, let us learn about the objective of preparing the trial balance.

Objective of Preparing the Trial Balance

Trial balance is a list of debit and credit balances standing on the ledger account of a firm at any given point of time. The important objectives and purpose of preparing the trial balance are:

- **To check arithmetical accuracy of ledger accounts:** This provides the facility to check the arithmetic accuracy of the ledger. If the total of the both the debit column and credit column amounts of the trial balance is the same, it is assumed that the trial balance is arithmetically correct and posting the transaction to the ledger is accurate.
- **To comply with the double-entry system:** This verifies the dual aspect of each transaction. If the trial balance is correct, then it is presumed that every transaction followed the rule of double-entry system.
- **To summarize the ledger:** This summarizes the balance of each ledger account in the form of a statement.
- **To detect errors:** This provides the facility to detect the error in recording or posting transactions to the journal and the ledger and then rectify those errors.
- **To help in preparing final accounts:** This contains the list of balances of all the accounts at one place. This also provides the facility to prepare the trading account, profit and loss account, and the balance sheet which is used to define the financial position of the business.

Now, let us learn about the limitation of trial balance.

Limitations of a Trial Balance

A trial balance is not the final proof of the absolute correctness of the account books. If the total of both debit and credit sides of the trial balance is the same, it does not mean that now there are absolutely no errors in account books. Even if the trial balance appears to be correct, some errors may remain undetected and will not be disclosed by the trial balance. This is the main limitation of the trial balance. Some other limitations of the trial balance are as follows:

- **Not a conclusive proof of accuracy:** It does not show the final proof of the exact correctness of the account books. Some errors may remain undetected while preparing the trial balance.
- **Incomplete information about the ledger:** It does not provide the complete information about the account books. It only shows the balances of both the debit and credit sides of each account.
- **Not a substitute of final accounts:** It does not give information about the profit and loss made by the business in the accounting period.

After learning about the limitations of the trial balance, let us learn about the method of preparing a trial balance.

Method of Preparing a Trial Balance

Trial balance is prepared to check the arithmetic accuracy of the account books and provide the facility to prepare the trading account, profit and loss account, and balance sheet of the particular accounting period. There are two methods of preparing the trial balance, which are as follows:

1. Total Method
2. Balancing Method

Let us learn about these methods one by one.

1. **Total Method:** In this method, the trial balance is prepared by totaling the amount of debit and credit sides of the ledger accounts. This method is also known as gross trial balance. The debit total amount of each account is noted down on the debit side of the trial balance and the credit total amount is noted down on the credit side of the trial balance. After noting down all the total debit and credit amounts of the ledger accounts, the trial balance is totaled. If the sum of the debit and credit sides of the trial balance is equal, then it is said that the trial balance is correct.

Illustration 3: Prepare the trial balance of the ledger accounts of illustration 2 under the Total Method.

Solution:

Dreamtech Press' Books

Trial Balance as on March 31, 2017

S. No.	Name of the Account	L.F.	Dr. Amount (₹)	Cr. Amount (₹)
1.	Dreamtech Press' capital account			4,00,000
2.	Cash account		4,50,000	1,12,000
3.	Purchase account		2,50,000	
4.	Yogesh		35,000	2,50,000
5.	Furniture		30,000	
6.	Ramesh		59,000	30,000
7.	Sales			77,000
8.	Rahul		27,000	
9.	Salary		12,000	
10.	Rent		6,000	
			8,69,000	8,69,000

After learning how to prepare the trial balance using Total Method, let us learn how to prepare the trial balance using the Balance Method.

2. **Balancing Method:** In this method, the debit balance and credit balance amounts of the ledger accounts are recorded separately into debit and credit columns in the trial balance. The total of balances in the debit column of the trial balance must be equal to the total of balances in the credit column of the trial balance. This is a commonly used method of preparing the trial balance because it facilitates the preparation of final accounts.

Illustration 4: Prepare the trial balance of the ledger accounts of illustration 2 under the Balance Method.

Solution:

Dreamtech Press' Books

Trial Balance as on March 31, 2017

S. No.	Name of Account	L.F.	Dr. Amount (₹)	Cr. Amount (₹)
1.	Dreamtech Press' capital account			4,00,000
2.	Cash account		3,38,000	
3.	Purchase account		2,50,000	
4.	Yogesh			2,15,000
5.	Furniture		30,000	
6.	Ramesh		29,000	
7.	Sales			77,000
8.	Rahul		27,000	
9.	Salary		12,000	
10.	Rent		6,000	
			6,92,000	6,92,000

Illustration 5: Prepare a trial balance in the books of Pranav Associates by using the following balances of the ledger accounts:

Capital ₹ 1,28,000; Purchase ₹ 30,000; Discount Allowed ₹ 1,200; Carriage Inwards ₹ 6700; Carriage Outwards ₹ 2300; Sales ₹ 48,500; Return Inwards ₹ 300; Return Outwards ₹ 700; Rent and Taxes ₹ 1,200; Plant and Machinery ₹ 72,200; Stock (April 1, 2016) ₹ 13,500; Sundry Debtors ₹ 17,200; Sundry Creditors ₹ 12,000; Investments ₹ 3,600; Commission Received ₹ 1,800; Cash in Hand ₹ 1,700; Cash at Bank ₹ 7000; Motor Cycle ₹ 34,100.

Solution: The trial balance of Pranav Associates is shown as follows:

Pranav Associates' Books

Trial Balance as on March 31, 2017

S. No.	Name of Account	L.F.	Dr. Amount (₹)	Cr. Amount (₹)
1.	Capital			1,28,000
2.	Purchase		30,000	
3.	Discount Allowed		1,200	
4.	Carriage Inwards		6,700	
5.	Carriage Outwards		2,300	
6.	Sales			48,500
7.	Return Inwards		300	
8.	Return Outwards			700
9.	Rent and Taxes		1,200	
10.	Plant and machinery		72,200	
11.	Stock (April 1, 2016)		13,500	
12.	Sundry Debtors		17,200	
13.	Sundry Creditors			12,000

S. No.	Name of Account	L.F.	Dr. Amount (₹)	Cr. Amount (₹)
14.	Investments		3,600	
15.	Commission received			1,800
16.	Cash in Hand		1,700	
17.	Cash at Bank		7,000	
18.	Motor Cycle		34,100	
			1,91,000	1,91,000

After learning about the methods of preparing a trial balance, let us learn about the suspense account.

Suspense Account

If in the trial balance, amounts of both sides are not same and the error cannot be rectified after performing the considerable efforts, then, ultimately it results in the delay in the preparation of final accounts. This issue can be resolved by preparing the suspense account. It shows the difference in the trial balance and will be used temporarily in the trail balance to prepare the final accounts.

If the credit side is short, the suspense account will be credited, and if the debit side is short, the suspense account will be debited. With the inclusion of this account in the trial balance, the trial balance appears to agree. However, the errors in the trial balance still remain and have to be located and rectified.

Rectification of Errors

A trial balance is prepared to check the arithmetical accuracy of transactions recorded in a journal, post them into the ledger and balance the ledger accounts. If a trial balance agrees, it is assumed that recording, posting, and balancing are done correctly. However, if it does not agree, efforts are made to locate the errors. The errors in a trial balance may occur at the time of recording, classifying, or summarizing the financial transactions.

Even when the trial balance is correct, some errors may remain in the accounting records. For example, if the credit purchases are not recorded in the purchase book, it would not affect the agreement of the trial balance because the entry is not made in either sides of the book. Therefore, the errors can be of two types, namely the errors that affect the trial balance, and the errors that do not affect the trial balance. However, both the types of errors should be identified and rectified. The process of rectifying the errors and correcting the accounting records is termed as rectification of errors.

All the errors can be classified into four categories, which are shown in Fig.AC-1.2:

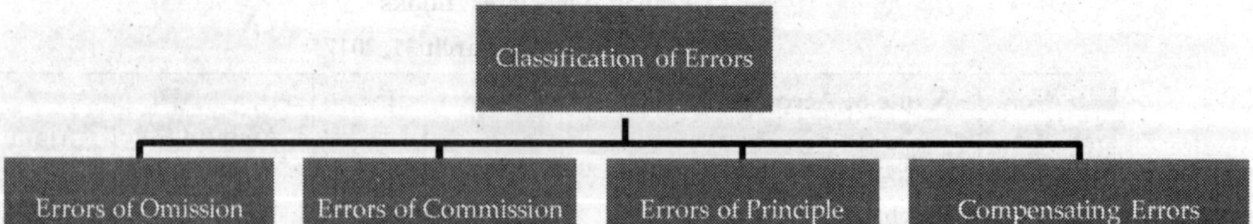

Fig.AC-1.2

Let us discuss the classification of accounting errors in detail in the next section.

Errors of Omission

An error of omission occurs when a transaction is omitted to be recorded in the books of accounts. An error of omission could be completely or partially in nature. The errors of partial recording of transactions are different from the errors of complete recording of the transactions, as the errors of partial recording result in improper trail balance, but the errors of complete recording do not.

For example, the recording of goods worth ₹ 1,000 purchased on credit from Mohan Lal is omitted from the purchase book. In such a case, it would be omitted from being posted in the ledger as well. Consequently, the transaction is not found in the trial balance. Thus, the accuracy of accounts is diminished. Therefore, it is quite difficult to locate such errors. These types of transactions are generally noticed when the statement of account is sent or received from the debtor or creditor. Such errors can be rectified by correcting the normal journal entry that was supposed to be made for the transaction, which is omitted. After recording the omitted entry in the journal, it would be posted in the concerned ledger account for making correction in the ledger account.

Let us understand the rectification process of errors of omission with the help of an illustration.

Illustration 6: Pass the journal entries to rectify the following errors:

1. A credit sale of ₹ 50,000 to Krish omitted to be recorded in the books.
2. Goods (cost ₹ 20,000 and sales price ₹ 24,000) taken by the proprietor were not recorded anywhere.
3. Goods worth ₹ 3,500 sold to Ravi on credit were omitted from the accounts. Although, cash received subsequently from him stands posted to his credit.
4. A credit sale of old furniture to Rajesh for ₹ 5,000 omitted to be posted.
5. The goods worth ₹ 30,000 were returned by Ram and were taken into stock on the same date, but no entry was passed in the books.

Solution: The journal entries after rectification of errors are shown as follows:

Date 2017	Particulars	L.F.	Dr. Amount (₹)	Cr. Amount (₹)
1.	Krish Dr. To Sales A/c (Being a credit sale omitted to be recorded, now recorded)		50,000	50,000
2.	Drawing A/c Dr. To Purchase A/c (Being goods taken away by the proprietor omitted to be recorded, now recorded)		20,000	20,000
3.	Ravi Dr. To Sales A/c (Being the rectification of goods sold to Ravi not recorded in the books)		3,500	3,500
4.	No journal entry is to be posted as it has already been correctly passed in the journal, merely posting in both the accounts in the ledger is required			
5.	Sales Return A/c Dr. To Ram (Being entry of goods returned by him taken into stock omitted from records)		30,000	30,000

Errors of Commission

Errors of commission arise due to wrong recording, wrong posting, wrong carrying forward, wrong casting of subsidiary books, or wrong balancing. Such errors may occur due to the negligence of the accountant and are clerical in nature.

Errors of commission can occur due to the following reasons:

- By entering a wrong amount in the correct subsidiary books
- By recording a correct amount in the wrong subsidiary book

For example, Ram paid an amount of ₹ 15,000 to Raghav and the amount is correctly recorded in the cash book, but while posting to the ledger, Raghav A/c is debited with ₹ 1,500. Such type of error is termed as error of commission. Most of the errors of commission affect the trial balance. Such errors are rectified only by means of a suitable rectification entry.

Let us learn the rectification process of errors of commission with the help of an example.

Illustration 7: Rectify the following entries:

1. A credit sale of old machinery to Krish for ₹ 17,000 was entered in the sales book for ₹ 71,000.
2. A credit sale of old furniture to Ravi for ₹ 1,000 is recorded as ₹ 10,000.

Solution: The rectified entries are shown as follows:

Date 2017	Particulars		L.F.	Dr. Amount (₹)	Cr. Amount (₹)
1.	Sales A/c	Dr.		71,000	
	To Krish				54,000
	To Machinery A/c				17,000
	(Being credit sale of machinery to Krish for ₹ 17,000 entered in the sales book as ₹ 71,000, now rectified)				
2.	Furniture A/c	Dr.		1,000	
	To Ravi				1,000
	(Being credit sale of old furniture to Ravi for ₹ 1,000 posted as ₹ 10,000, now rectified)				

Errors of Principle

The accounting transactions should be recorded according to the generally accepted accounting principles. When a transaction is recorded as an infringement of the accounting principle, it is known as an error of principle. Such errors do not affect the trial balance as the entry of transaction is made on the correct side of the account, but the value of entry or the amount of transaction is incorrect. The rectification of such errors is very important as they directly affect financial statements. Such errors may occur due to the following reasons:

Lack of discrepancy between the revenue and capital items. The revenue receipt may be taken as capital receipt or vice versa.

Lack of distinction between the business expenses and personal expenses.

Lack of distinction between the productive expenses and non-productive expenses.

Let us comprehend the process of rectification of errors of principle with the help of an example. Cartage

Illustration 8: Rectify the following errors:

1. Paid wages for the construction of office debited to wages account ₹ 2,000.
2. Paid freight for the newly purchased furniture ₹ 500, posted to freight account.
3. Paid ₹ 5,000 for the installation of machinery debited to wages account.

Solution: The rectified entries are shown as follows:

Date 2017	Particulars		L.F.	Dr. Amount (₹)	Cr. Amount (₹)
1.	Building A/c	Dr.		2,000	
	To Wages A/c				2,000
	(Being wages paid for construction of office wrongly debited to wages A/c, now rectified)				
2.	Furniture A/c	Dr.		500	
	To Freight A/c				500
	(Being freight paid for newly purchased furniture wrongly posted to Freight A/c, now rectified)				

Date 2017	Particulars	L.F.	Dr. Amount (₹)	Cr. Amount (₹)
3.	Machinery A/c Dr. To Wages A/c (Being amount paid for installation of machinery wrongly debited to wages A/c, now rectified)		5,000	5,000

Compensating Errors

Compensating errors are those that are nullified by errors of equal proportion. It means that one accounting error is compensated by another error. It may happen that an error in an account has occurred, and the same kind of error has taken place in another account. In such a case, it is hard to detect that error. For example, Ravi's A/c was debited with ₹ 1000 instead of ₹ 10,000 while Krish's A/c was debited with ₹ 10,000 instead of ₹ 1,000. Therefore, Ravi's A/c, which was debited by ₹ 9,000, was compensated by another error in Krish's A/c, whose account was debited excess of ₹ 9,000. Such errors do not affect the trail balance.

Locating the Errors

When trial balance is prepared, there can be two possibilities – either the total of the balance tallies or does not tally. If the balance does not tally, it indicates that at least one error has occurred. In such a case, the errors must be located and corrected before the preparation of the financial statements. The errors can be located by implementing the following steps:

1. Determine the summation of the debit and credit balances of the trial balance again.
2. Determine whether the account title and the amount appearing in the trial balance are agreeing with that posted to the ledger. This helps in detecting the incorrect figures or omissions of an account.
3. Compare the present-year trial balance with that of the previous years so as to check if there is any unexpected increment or decrement in the amounts.
4. Determine the accuracy of the balances of individual accounts in the ledger by rechecking them.
5. Determine the accuracy of the posting of transactions from the journal to the ledger by rechecking them.
6. Determine the differences between the debit and credit balances. If the difference is divisible by two, then it means that half of the difference amount is posted on the wrong side of another ledger account. In addition, it would also indicate the occurrence of error of omission.

However, if the difference between the balances is divisible by nine, the error can be due to a transposition of the amount. For example, the number 954 may have been posted as 945 in the books of accounts.

Illustration 9: Rectify the following errors by giving journal entries:

1. On sale of machinery, an amount of ₹ 5,000 is received. This amount is credited to the Sales A/c from the cash book.
2. An item worth ₹ 800 was sold on credit to Rajesh. This amount is correctly recorded in the sales book, but wrongly posted in the ledger book as ₹ 80.
3. An amount of ₹ 400 spent on repair of machinery was debited to the Machinery A/c.
4. A credit sale of old furniture to Satish for ₹ 24,000 was entered in the sales book for ₹ 42,000.
5. An amount of ₹ 500 drawn by the proprietor for his/her personal use is recorded as trade expenses.
6. An amount of ₹ 900 due from Dhoni, which was written down as bad debt last year, has been recovered and is posted to the personal account of Dhoni.

Solution: The rectified entries are shown as follows:

S. No.	Particulars	Debit Amount (₹)	Credit Amount (₹)
1.	Error of Principle:		
	Sales A/c Dr.	5,000	
	To Machinery A/c		5,000
	(Correction of error in crediting sales A/c for sales of machinery)		
2.	Error of Commission:		
	Rajesh's A/c should be further debited with an amount of ₹ 720		
	(No Journal entry is required in this error)		
3.	Error of Principle:		
	Repairs A/c Dr.	400	
	To Machinery A/c		400
	(Rectification of wrong debit in Machinery A/c instead of Repairs A/c)		
4.	Error of Commission:		
	Sales A/c Dr.	42000	
	To Satish		18000
	To Furniture A/c		24000
	(Being credit sale of furniture to Satish for ₹ 24,000 entered in the sales book as ₹ 42,000, now rectified)		
5.	Error of Principle:		
	Drawings A/c Dr.	500	
	To Trade Expenses A/c		500
	(Correction of wrong debit given to Trade Expenses A/c for the amount withdrawn for personal use)		
6.	Error of Principle		
	Dhoni's Dr.	900	
	To Bad Debt Recovered A/c		900
	(Correction of wrong credit to Personal A/c for recovery of bad debt)		

After learning about the suspense account, let us learn about the financial statement.

Financial Statements

After preparing the trial balance, a businessman assures that the books of accounts are accurate. Now, the businessman is interested in knowing about the financial position of the business. It is determined by calculating the profit he has made and loss he has sustained for a particular accounting period. The trading and profit and loss accounts are prepared to show the profit and loss of the business and the balance sheet is prepared to show the financial position of the particular accounting period. The two statements – trading account and profit and loss account – and balance sheet are called the financial statements. These are also known as the final accounts.

Note

The trading and profit and loss accounts are divided into two sections – the first section is called trading account and the second section is called profit and loss account.

Now, let us learn about the trading account.

Trading Account

The first stage of preparing the final account is to prepare a trading account. This account is based on matching the selling price of the goods and services with the cost of goods sold and service condensed. According to **Batliboi**, "The trading account shows the results of buying and selling of goods. In preparing this account, the general establishment charges are ignored and only the transactions in goods are included."

Trading account is prepared to calculate the gross profit or gross loss of a business in a particular accounting period. The trading account also shows the information about all the direct expenses and the comparisons of the closing stock with the opening stock. It also helps to take effective steps to safeguard against the future losses.

The format and content of the trading account are as follows:

(Name of the Firm)

Trading Account

Dr. **for the year ending** **Cr.**

Particulars		Amount (₹)	Particulars		Amount (₹)
To Opening Stock		....	By Sales	....	
To Purchase	....		Less: Return Inwards	....	....
Less: Return Outwards	......	....	By Abnormal Loss of Stock		
To Direct Expenses		....	By Closing Stock		....
To Wages and Salaries		....			
To Freight Outwards		....	By Gross Loss (transferred to Profit & Loss A/c)		....
To Carriage Inwards		....			
To Cartage Inwards		....			
To Gas, Fuel and Power		....			
To Octori		....			
To Manufacturing Expenses		....			
To Gross Profit (transferred to Profit & Loss A/c)		....			
		....			....

As you know, the trading account is prepared to calculate the gross profit and gross loss. The trading account shows the gross loss if the total amount of the debit side is more than that of the credit side. The trading account shows the gross profit if the total amount of the credit side is more than that of the debit side. The gross profit is transferred to the credit side of the profit and loss account, whereas the gross loss is transferred to the debit side of the profit and loss account.

After learning about the trading account, let us learn about the profit and loss account.

Profit and Loss Account

After preparing the trading account, profit and loss account is the second stage in the process of preparing the final account. According to **Carter**, "A Profit and Loss Account is an account into which all the gains and losses are collected in order to ascertain the excess of gains over the losses or vice versa." Profit and Loss Account is prepared to measure the net profit or net loss of the business at a particular accounting period. The remaining expenses and losses are put on the debit side of the Profit and Loss Account and the remaining profits and gains are put on the credit side of the Profit and Loss Account. The net profit or net loss directly affects the capital of the proprietor.

Profit and Loss Account tells the net profit or net loss of the business. It controls the unnecessary expenses of the business and helps to prepare a balance sheet. It also helps to compare the net profit or net loss of the accounting period with the net profit or loss of the previous years. The format and the contents of the Profit and Loss Account are:

Profit and Loss Account

Dr. **for the year ending** **Cr.**

Particulars	Amount (₹)	Particulars	Amount (₹)
To Gross Loss (transferred from Trading A/c)	....	By Gross Profit (transferred from Trading A/c)	....
To Office Salaries and Wages	....	By Rent Received	....
To Office Rent, Rates and Taxes	....	BY Discount Received	....
To Printing and Stationery	....	By Commission Earned	....
To Postage and Telegram	....	By Interest	....
To Legal Expenses	....	By Bad Debts Recovered	....
To Trade Expenses	....	By Income from Investment	....
To Audit Fees	....	By Dividends on Shares	....
To General Expenses	....	By Miscellaneous Revenue Gains	....
To Telephone Expenses	....	By Income from Other Sources	....
To Interest on Capital	....		
To Interest of Loans	....	By Net Loss (transferred to Capital A/c)	....
To Conveyance	....		
To Charity	....		
To Insurance Premium	....		
To Repairs and Renewals	....		
To Commission	....		
To Advertisement	....		
To Freight and Carriage Outward	....		
To Travelling Expenses	....		
To Bad Debts	....		
To Packing Expenses	....		
To Discount Allowed	....		
To License Fee	....		
To Brokerage	....		
To Depreciation	....		
To Loss by Fire, Theft	....		
To Bank Charges	....		
To Net Profit (transferred to Capital A/c)	....		
	....		....

As you know, the Profit and Loss Account is prepared to represent the net profit or net loss. The profit and loss account shows the net loss if the total amount of the debit side is more than that of the credit side. The profit and loss account shows the net profit if the total amount of the credit side is more than that of the debit side. Net profit is added in the capital of the proprietor in the balance sheet, whereas net loss is deducted from the capital of the proprietor in the balance sheet.

After learning about the Profit and Loss Account, let us learn about the Balance Sheet.

Balance Sheet

After preparing the Profit and Loss account, the Balance Sheet is prepared and it is the final stage in the process of preparing the final accounts. A balance sheet is the summarized statement of assets and liabilities of the business. Generally, the balance sheet is prepared at the end of the accounting period and shows the financial position of the business.

According to **Francis R. Stead**, "A balance sheet is a screen picture of the financial position of a going business at a certain moment."

According to **Karlson**, "A business form showing what is owed and what is the proprietor's worth is called a balance sheet."

According to **Pamer**, "The balance sheet is a statement at a particular date showing on one side the trader's property and possession and, on the other side, the liabilities."

According to **J. R. Batliboi**, "A balance sheet is a statement prepared with a view to measure the exact financial position of a business on a certain fixed date."

The format and contents of the balance sheet are as follows:

Balance Sheet of ....

as on ....

Liabilities	Amount (₹)	Assets	Amount (₹)
Capital		Cash in Hand	....
Add: Interest on Capital		Cash in Bank	....
Net Profit		Bills Receivable	....
Less: Drawing		Sundry Debtors	....
Income Tax		Loans (Dr.)	....
Interest on Drawing	....	Loose Tools	....
Net Loss	....	Investments	....
Sundry Creditors	....	Furniture and Fittings	....
Bills Payable	....	Plant and Machinery	....
Bank Overdraft	....	Land and Buildings	....
Loans (Cr.)	....	Patents and Trademarks	....
Mortgage	....	Goodwill	....
Reserve Fund		Closing Stock	....
	....		....

Illustration 10: Prepare the final account for the year ending 31st March, 2017 from the trial balance of illustration 4.

Solution:

Trading and Profit and Loss Accounts

Dr. **for the year ending 31st March, 2017** **Cr.**

Particulars	Amount (₹)	Particulars	Amount (₹)
To Purchase	2,50,000	By Sales	77,000
		By Gross Loss (transferred to Profit and Loss A/c)	1,73,000
	2,50,000		2,50,000

Particulars	Amount (₹)	Particulars	Amount (₹)
To Gross Loss (transferred from Trading A/c)	1,73,000	By Net Loss (transferred to Capital A/c)	1,91,000
To Salary	12,000		
To Rent	6,000		
	1,91,000		1,91,000

Balance Sheet of Dreamtech Press

as on 31st March, 2017

Liabilities		Amount (₹)	Assets	Amount (₹)
Capital	4,00,000		Cash in Hand	3,38,000
Less: Net Loss	1,91,000	2,09,000	Sundry Debtors	56,000
			Furniture	30,000
Sundry Creditors		2,15,000		
		4,24,000		4,24,000

In our Trial Balance, Yogesh is the creditor and Ramesh and Rahul are the debtors.

Working Note:

Total Sundry Creditors: Yogesh A/c = ₹ 2,15,000

Total Sundry Debtors:

Ramesh A/c + Rahul A/c

= ₹ 29,000 + ₹ 27,000

= ₹ 56,000

With this, we come to the end of the chapter, Let us summarize the key points discussed in this chapter.

Summary

In this chapter, you have learned about the need and definition of accounting. After this, you have learned about the important terms, concepts, and conventions used in accounting. In addition, you have learned about the different categories of accounts. Next, you have learned about the rules of debit and credit or double-entry rules in accounting. Further, the chapter discussed the journal, ledger, and trial balance. At the end of the chapter, you have learned about the financial statements.

CHAPTER

2

Computerized Accounting

In this Chapter:

* Exploring Computerized Accounting
* Computerized Accounting Software

Introduction

The business transactions of an organization have to be recorded and analyzed accurately so that the actual financial position of the organization can be determined. Earlier, the financial reports and statements of a business organization were prepared manually. Manual accounting system lacked accuracy at times and was time-consuming. These two factors hampered the decision-making process in the management of an organization. The problems related to manual accounting were solved with the introduction of computerized accounting, which provided quick and error-free accounting data.

The chapter begins with the description of computerized accounting, wherein you learn the need of computerized accounting as well as the merits and demerits of this system. The chapter further describes accounting software, such as Tally, Busy, SAP, Zoho Books, Sage 50 Accounting, and QuickBooks.

Let us begin the chapter with a discussion on computerized accounting.

Exploring Computerized Accounting

Accounting is a systematic way of recording and analyzing the financial information. This involves measuring, identifying, and presenting the financial growth of a company. When accounting is done with the help of computers, it is known as computerized accounting. The software used in computerized accounting helps a user in maintaining the accounts payable and accounts receivable, recording of invoices, and calculating tax.. Nowadays, accounting has numerous sophisticated tools to handle functions, such as book-keeping, raising invoices, and billing vendors for balance due. Various low-cost and user-friendly accounting software applications, such as Tally, Busy and SAP are available in the market. We will discuss these software as the chapter progresses.

Computerized accounting has a number of features that makes it so popular. Hence, the organizations of all types and sizes today prefer computerized accounting to manual accounting.

Fig.AC-2.1 displays the features of computerized accounting:

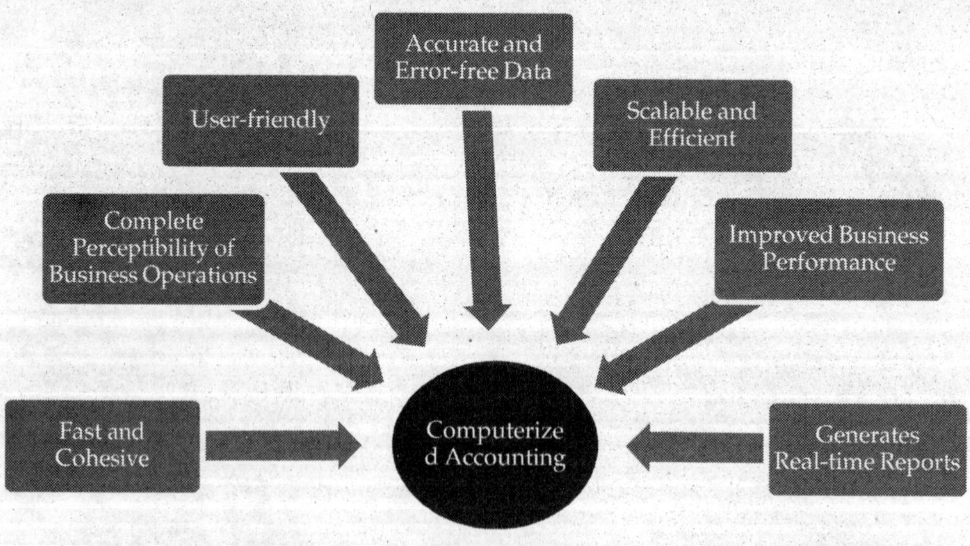

Fig.AC-2.1

Let us discuss these features in brief.

- **Fast and cohesive:** Computerized accounting provides a user with accurate and up-to-date business information. It is suitable for all business operations, such as manufacturing, purchase, and finance. The enhanced features of computerized accounting help an organization to simplify the business process.

- **Complete perceptibility of business operations:** It facilitates an organization with greater visibility of day-to-day business operations by retrieving the updated financial reports at any stage. This helps the management in taking decisions accordingly.
- **User-friendly:** It allows an organization to work more easily and efficiently and make the working atmosphere more pleasant. It reduces conflict between co-workers and management by providing them a single platform to work.
- **Accurate and error-free data:** It allows a user to work on user-defined templates that are fast and accurate. A user does not need to record the transactions repeatedly. Once the changes have been made in one of the books of accounts, the changes are updated in the other related books of accounts.
- **Scalable and efficient:** It facilitates a user to handle millions of transactions without affecting the speed and efficiency of the computing process.
- **Improved business performance:** It facilitates a user in transforming the business processes with performance-enhancing features, such as accounting, inventory, reporting and statutory processes. It gives the facility for real-time optimization of operations and enhanced communication.

Computerized accounting system works on two aspects. First, the system works within a well-defined set of rules. Second, accounting software maintains records and generates reports as per the guidelines and requirements of the user.

Let us now discuss the need of computerized accounting.

Need of Computerized Accounting

Before the advent of computerized accounting, the manual recording of entries in the books of the company and verification of mathematical calculations was time-consuming. The accountant had to maintain many types of account books, such as journals, ledgers, balance sheets, and financial statements. It was a tedious and laborious process and the chances of errors were high. Computerized accounting streamlined and simplified the accounting process and eliminated the errors of manual accounting. It became easier to prepare financial reports, keep a track of inflow and outflow of cash with the help of updated financial reports, and maintain transparency in business.

Due to its advantages over manual accounting, computerized accounting is now applicable in various financial processes.

Some areas where computerized accounting is applicable are as follows:

- **Financial statement:** Facilitates the quick preparation of financial reports, such as income statements, cash flow statements, and balance sheets with full accuracy.
- **Inventory:** Facilitates the recording of each sale and purchase of goods and helps in determining the closing stock of various goods in inventory.
- **Billing:** Allows the generation of cash memos and credit invoices.
- **Banking:** Allows the bankers to manage bank accounts easily. Due to computerized accounting, an account gets updated automatically when a customer deposits or withdraws money from his account.
- **Ticket reservation:** Facilitates booking railway tickets and flight tickets from any part of the world.
- **Standard Costing:** Allows the accountants to record variations between the expected and actual costs of a particular unit.
- **Budgetary Control:** Allows the preparation of several budgets quickly, such as production budget, expense budget, sales budget, and cash budget. Control ratio reports are also prepared by analyzing the results of the previous budgets.

Now, let us discuss the factors that make computerized accounting more effective than manual accounting.

Fig.AC-2.2 displays the factors making computerized accounting accurate and effective:

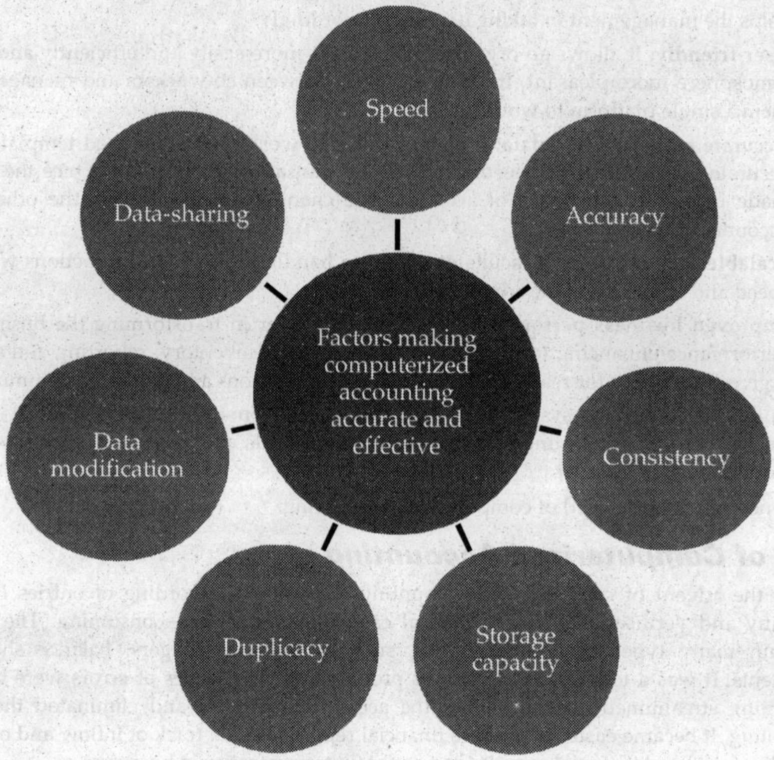

Fig.AC-2.2

The description of these features is as follows:

- **Speed:** Refers to the ability of computers to perform millions of instructions per second at high speed. Thus, the time taken to create and record a report is very less compared to manual accounting.
- **Accuracy:** Allows a user to receive zero-error data, if instructions are provided to the computer accurately.
- **Consistency:** Refers to the performance of a computerized system that never slows down and remains constant, compared to manual working.
- **Storage:** Refers to the computer memory that can store a large amount of data.
- **Duplicacy:** Refers to the features in computerized accounting that allow a user to recognize redundancy in data easily.
- **Modification of data:** Refers to the addition, deletion or modification of the existing data at any stage in a computerized accounting process.
- **Data-sharing:** Allows a user to share data and other information in the network through the Internet or LAN.

Let us now learn about the merits of computerized accounting.

Merits of Computerized Accounting

Accounting is an indispensable part of all the organizations as it records the incomes, expenses and other business transactions accurately. The data generated and stored help in analyzing the financial health of an organization. Computerized accounting also streamlines the accounting process by reducing the lengthy procedure of manual accounting.

The advantages of computerized accounting are as follows:

- **Increased production:** Allows a user to make changes in the accounting books more easily and quickly. Auto-updating helps a user to update the changes in the overall reports in just one click. Data tools help a user to find the specific data without searching every page to correct the data.
- **Increased accuracy:** Facilitates a user to retrieve data, which is free from or has few errors. Computerized accounting removes errors that are part of manual accounting and provides accurate data.
- **Backup availability:** Allows a user to retrieve a specific piece of data when required. Computerized accounting software keeps backup data of the accomplished tasks. This backup data can be retrieved in the event of system failure or security breach.
- **Cost saving:** Reduces labor and paper work that is expended in manual accounting. It also helps management keep track of the company's financial position in "real time" and make adjustments to the business strategy as needed.
- **Time saving:** Allows a user to record and maintain entries more easily and more quickly in different accounting books. Documents such as invoices, purchase orders and payroll can be collated more quickly and with perfect accuracy.
- **Up-to-date information:** Computerized accounting automatically updates the records and thus provides up-to-date information.
- **Efficiency:** Increases the efficiency of business by producing error-free data quickly.
- **Reduced workload:** Eliminates the lengthy data-entry process of manual accounting, thereby reducing workload.

Let us discuss the demerits of computerized accounting in brief.

Demerits of Computerized Accounting

Computerized accounting also has a few demerits. These demerits or disadvantages are related to the use of software, their application, complexity and the vulnerability that accompany the usage of a computer.

The demerits of computerized accounting are as follows:

- **Power failure:** Refers to the functional problems of a computer that arise due to power cut.
- **Computer viruses:** Refers to the programs that harm a computer by corrupting the operating system and stealing or erasing data.
- **Unauthorized access:** Refers to the unauthorized access to confidential data, thus breaching an authorized user's privacy.
- **Improper installation of accounting system:** Refers to the operating problems that arise when software is not installed properly. In case of software like Tally, improper installation might lead to errors in calculation, deletion of data or even data theft.

Let us now discuss the accounting software and its utility in business operations.

Computerized Accounting Software

Computerized accounting is an essential part of all businesses today, as the use of accounting software eliminates the errors involved in manual accounting. Accounting software provides a systematic and accurate process of recording, calculating, and updating the financial data. These software applications are generally easy to use and can be customized to meet the needs of different businesses.

Let us discuss a few widely used accounting software applications, starting with Tally.

Exploring Tally

Tally is financial accounting software used by small, medium, and large-scale business organizations. Tally is used to maintain the records of all the business transactions and provides various services, such as government-defined report and challan formats, taxation support, and online transaction processing for small as well as large businesses. Tally.ERP 9 enables you to view the information of any period, compare data across companies and financial periods, maintain account details, and generate reports. It provides data protection through the use of specific passwords for different documents. Data can also be customized as per the user's needs.

Let us have an overview of the general and accounting features of Tally.

General Features of Tally Software

Tally provides a wide range of easy-to-use dynamic features. These features are designed to simplify the day-to-day business activities.

A list of these general features is as follows:

- Tally is a Windows-based application software, which makes it user-friendly.
- Data can be easily created, modified or deleted using Tally.
- Data can be modified at any stage as per the requirements of the user.
- Modification made at a single place updates every concerned report and book.
- It allows you to print the various reports in government-prescribed format.
- Many crucial reports are available in well-organized formats, such as balance sheet, funds flow statements, and trial balance.
- It provides the option of protecting data through passwords.
- It automatically backs up all the completed tasks.
- It provides a simple interface and simple menus.
- It is easy to import and export data in Tally.
- It is available for both single as well as multiple users.

Accounting Features of Tally Software

A list of the accounting features of Tally software is given as follows:

- **Complete accounting software:** Allows you to record different types of vouchers in Tally, such as journals, debit notes, sale and purchase receipts. Data can be retrieved as per the user's choice. For example, a user can get information bill-wise, group-wise, or party-wise.
- **Classification of accounts:** Provides flexibility to choose a group from 28 predefined groups, which are further divided into 15 primary groups and 13 sub-groups. The software allows the user to manipulate and alter any of the groups and also create new groups when required.
- **Wide range of inventory options:** Provides simple and advanced inventory options, such as multiple stock valuation methods, purchase and sales orders, stock query, and allow multiple price level.
- **Diverse protocol support:** Supports various protocols, such as HTTP, HTTPS, FTP, SMTP, and ODBC, to provide data reliability and security.
- **Extracting reports:** Allows users to retrieve a report for a particular date or for any date range.
- **Data synchronization:** Allows used to synchronize and update data across multiple locations.

After learning about the features of Tally, let us discuss the types of Tally software.

Types of Tally Accounting Software

Tally offers two versions of its accounting software.

Fig.AC-2.3 displays the two Tally software applications:

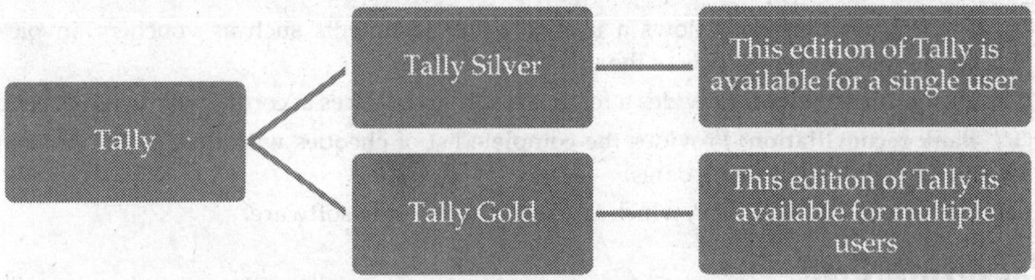

Fig.AC-2.3

The description of these versions is as follows:

- **Tally Silver:** Tally Silver can be installed on only one computer and can be activated online or offline. However, it is possible to use the same version on another system. To do this, the software license has to be granted from the first computer and then reactivated on the second computer. For offline activation, one can take a request filed to a computer with Internet connectivity and then activate the copy of this version on the computer easily.
- **Tally Gold:** Tally Gold has multi-user licensing feature. It can be installed on many computers connected with each other through a local area network (LAN). LAN connectivity allows the license to be activated online or offline. The multi-user license is activated on one of the computers in the LAN as the license server. The other computers connected to the network act as license clients. The software is then installed in all the computers in the same manner as Tally Silver.

Let us now learn about another accounting software called Busy.

Exploring Busy

Busy is an accounting software used mostly by micro, small and medium enterprises in India. Basic, Standard and Enterprise are the initial versions offered by Busy. The Basic version of Busy is available in single-user type while the Standard and Enterprise versions are available in single-user, multi-user, and client-server type.

The general features of Busy are as follows:

- **Completely codeless:** In Busy, the accounts of parties can be saved by their proper names instead of codes. This prevents the confusion created by using codes.
- **Self-explanatory home page:** It provides an easy and understandable main menu and intuitive sub-menus on the home page that guide a user to complete a task.
- **Flexible numbering system for vouchers:** It provides an option to enable or disable the numbering system for vouchers. A user can set the numbering on vouchers as automatic or manual according to his choice.
- **Flexibility of defining fields in vouchers:** It provides an option to define up to 10 fields of choice in vouchers. A user can generate filtered reports based on these reports.
- **Grouping of the same types of files:** It allows a user to group the same types of ledgers, items and parties.
- **Multi-company accounting:** It allows a user to create any number of companies in Busy.
- **Operating environment:** It is available on MS-DOS and LAN platforms.

Accounting features of Busy are as follows:

- **Outstanding reports and analysis:** Allows a user to generate bill-wise receivables and payables, bill-wise statements of accounts, pending bills and overdue bills statements.
- **Calculating interest:** Facilitates a user with the option of calculating interest on overdue bills.

- **Calculating depreciation:** Allows a user to calculate depreciation on fixed assets and print depreciation charts.
- **Determining the cost center:** Provides a feature to determine the profit made by the organization department-wise, product-wise or project-wise.
- **Printing documents:** Allows a user to print documents such as vouchers, invoices, debit notes, credit notes and price lists of the items at any stage.
- **Designing invoices:** Provides a feature to design invoices according to the user's need.
- **Bank reconciliation:** Provides the complete list of cheques with their status (cleared or uncleared) along with their clearing dates.

Let us now take a look at SAP, which is another accounting software.

Exploring SAP

Systems, Applications and Products in Data Processing (SAP) is a business software that integrates more than one business application, with each application representing a particular business area. This integration helps in transferring data easily between applications and provides the correct information about an organization. The integration also helps in automatically updating the business processes in the SAP system.

SAP provides functional and technical modules. The functional modules, such as Sales and Distribution (SD), Materials Management (MM), and Production Planning (PP) help in accomplishing day-to-day business transactions; whereas, the technical modules, such as Advanced Business Application Programming (ABAP) help in making different queries according to business requirements.

SAP provides a centralized location for all modules to execute business activities. Due to centralized location of modules and communication between them, the changes made in a module are communicated to other modules. The SAP system was developed as an Enterprise Resource Planning (ERP) software. The ERP software is designed to organize all the resources, information, and activities related to automate business processes.

SAP Products

SAP provides various products that make managing a business easier. Some of these products are described as follows:

- **Customer Relationship Management (CRM):** Provides end-to-end solution for all your customer front-end applications. SAP CRM covers marketing, sales, service, contact center, e-commerce, and IT services.
- **Supplier Relationship Management (SRM):** Deals with end-to-end solution for overall vendor-relationship management. This essentially covers the Procure to Pay Business Cycle (P2P). SRM includes supplier collaboration, supplier evaluation, centralized contract management, centralized sourcing, and catalog management.
- **Product Lifecycle Management (PLM):** Deals with the complexity of developing a new product. Organizations frequently launch new products to stay ahead in the market. But developing a new product is a complex process. SAP's Product Lifecycle Management handles such complexities. It covers all the aspects of product development, such as life-cycle data management, program and project management, life-cycle collaboration, quality management, enterprise asset management, and environment, health, and safety.
- **Supply Chain Management (SCM):** Handles all the activities related to collaboration, execution, and planning of the supply chain. An organization's success depends on how efficiently, quickly, and economically it can deliver goods to customers. Therefore, the entire process of supply chain has assumed great importance in modern times. SCM includes supply-chain planning and collaboration, supply-chain execution, and supply-chain visibility design and analytics.
- **Business Intelligence (BI):** Handles all aspects of management reporting. In management reporting, the slicing and dicing of information is unique and generates large data volume. It is not possible for transaction-based systems to handle such huge volumes of data. Therefore, a business data

warehouse is built to generate such information. SAP's BI supports data warehousing, business planning, business insights, measurement and management, information broadcasting, and accelerated business intelligence.

Let us learn about Zoho Books.

Zoho Books

Zoho Books is a cloud-based, smart and a pliable online Accounting software that was developed to suit the needs of any type of business or company. It was launched in the year 2011 and it is the 26th productivity application developed by Zoho Corporation. The monthly subscription of Zoho Books costs between $9 and $29. However, a trial version of 14 days is also offered to the customers. Zoho Books has a designated mobile application which is freely downloadable from Google App store.

Zoho Corporation defines Zoho Books as "accounting for rest of us". It lets us create invoices, manage inventory, filing Goods and Services Tax (GST), keeping a track of our bank account transactions and generating financial reports. It has a very simple and easy-to-use interface. The users get accustomed to its interface very fast. This software comes at a very affordable cost. It integrates deeply with other Zoho productivity applications like Zoho CRM and Zoho Invoice that enhances the functionality of the software.

The striking key features of Zoho Books are listed below:

- **Professional invoicing:** It enables us to create invoices for the business clients in multiple currencies. It comes with an in-built payment gateway that accepts payments from clients.
- **Inventory management:** It lets us track the inventory flow of the business. In addition to this, it helps us to manage the stocks of the business.
- **Banking:** It incorporates banking features into the interface as well. You can fetch your banking transactions and manage multiple bank accounts.
- **Multi-user environment:** It provides a multi-user environment, where you can work along with other accountants and fellow workers, without having to pay an additional cost.
- **GST:** The new added feature in this software which is vital to its functionality is the compliance to GST. You can file GST directly from the GST portal in the application.
- **Financial reports:** It lets us create strong financial and accounting reports which help in future predictions relating to the company.

There are many irresistible reasons to use Zoho Books for the accounting needs of your software or your company. They are listed below:

- **Scalability:** Zoho Books enables the users to expand their business around the world with the automated payment options available in all currencies.
- **GST compatibility:** The GST-filing option incorporated in the software lets the users adapt to the GST policies.
- **Functional Extensibility**: The functionality of this software is extended by integrating other Zoho productivity applications.
- **Multiple user interface:** It lets you work in a multi-user environment, where more than one user can work on the same project at the same time.
- **Clean interface:** It has a sleek design and clean interface where you can work with minimal to nil confusion and complexities.
- **Minimalistic pricing:** The pricing of this accounting software is kept as economical as possible.
- **Free online support:** An online support is provided for this software by Zoho Corporation, which is available round the clock.

Merits of Zoho Books

Zoho Books overcomes the drawbacks usually found in other accounting software applications available in the market. The advantages of using Zoho Books for accounting are as follows:

- **Client focus:** It provides a different portal for the clients where they can login and view their invoice receipts and transactions they made.
- **Project management:** When you plan to expand your business or you are managing many projects at the same time, this software helps you in logging time manually and creating widget timers.
- **Automated rules set-up:** This enables us to set the rules that automate the flow of the work in a business.
- **Information library:** There is a specific section reserved for the documentation and tutorials related to the software usage. You may refer to it when needed. A 24 x 7 support is also provided through email, chat and phone whenever any issue arises.

Demerits of Zoho Books

Although Zoho Books caters to the needs of almost every type of user, but there are a few areas where Zoho Books lacks. These are listed as below:

- **Limited number of advisors**: As the tenure of this product is not long enough in the market, it has less number of advisors available. You may only find very few people to hire to work on Zoho Books.
- **No recurring payment**: There is no option available for charging the client's bank account or credit cards for the same amount. However, you can regenerate and send the invoice of the recurring amount every month.
- **No Balance Sheet**: There is no option to create a balance sheet in this application. Neither does it let you create an income statement report.
- **Limited third-party integration**: It does not offer many third-party connections, if your business requires selling products online.

Zoho Books faces competition from other popular names in the list of accounting software applications like Tally, Xero and QuickBooks, but it is a robust accounting software which comes with numerous functionalities to offer like automated rules and client portal, which sets it apart from others.

Let us learn about Sage 50 Accounting.

Sage 50 Accounting

Sage 50 Accounting is the accounting software developed by Sage Software, aimed at providing the solution to all your accounting needs. It was formerly known as Peachtree. The simplification of your everyday business tasks is the main key factor that leads to the development of this software. It provides the feature that enables the users to save big on money. It is packed with all the security features that ensure the safety and integrity of your financial data. It tracks your invoices, expenses, payments, cash flow, and inventory. It creates a budget plan to give you an overview of where you are spending and how you are getting paid. It organizes all your financial data in a single place so that you do not have to look for the past records elsewhere.

Sage 50 Accounting is released in different versions, namely Pro, Premium and Quantum to suit the needs of different types of users. Every version of Sage 50 Accounting has some features that are common to all versions and some features that are version-specific. The pricing of these versions ranges between $439 and $1729 on yearly basis. You can use the trial version free of cost for a limited time period with limited functionality to have an idea about the software.

It also provides cloud access to your accounts that gives you freedom from anywhere in the world. Furthermore, it has a deep integration with Microsoft Office 365 to provide flexibility in working.

Features of Sage 50 Accounting

Sage 50 Accounting is bulked with striking key features. These are listed as follows:

- **Reliability:** You can rely on this software for many of your financial needs like generating reports.
- **Accessibility:** You can access your data anywhere through the cloud service provided with this software. It also keeps your data secure.
- **Flexibility:** It provides you with the ease of choosing the number of employees and selecting your business needs as per your requirements.
- **Security:** It allows the user to track the entering and editing of the data by any user. It also lets us track the access of the functions of the software.

Benefits of Sage 50 Accounting

- **Payments:** It provides an in-built payment gateway called Sage Payment Solutions that enables the user to accept the payment anywhere and anytime.
- **Check and norm security:** It enables the user to perform the transactions that are secured using the checks guaranteed 100% safe by Sage. It incorporates a monitoring service that is absolutely fraud-free.
- **Simplified payroll:** The Sage Payroll service enables the employer to process the payrolls of the employees in a hassle-free and time-saving manner.

Now, let us learn about QuickBooks.

QuickBooks

QuickBooks is an accounting software that was developed by Intuit Inc. for small business owners and freelancers for saving their time and efforts. It was designed to aim at working in real-time on clients' accounts and make future predictions based on it. Initially, the QuickBooks was released in a DOS version. Over a period of time, QuickBooks evolved as a strong and impactful accounting software which is very popular among small businesses. Intuit offers a cloud-based service called QuickBooks Online (QBO) that enables the users to access the software by paying a nominal subscription fees. The subscription fees for Quick Books ranges from $9.99 to $29.99. In other words, it gives you the flexibility of being available for the customers from anywhere and anytime in the world whenever the client demands. It has a user-friendly interface that focuses on the cash flows, invoicing and account management. It incorporates the encryption security technique, which ensures the safety of the data of the clients. It also provides some mobile tools meant for iOS and Android devices. Furthermore, Intuit keeps releasing various upgrades for QuickBooks time to time for better functionality and adding new features.

There are a variety of features offered by QuickBooks to the accountants. These are listed as follows:

- **Collaborating in real-time:** It provides the feature of logging in to the application across various devices and platforms that enables the user to co-ordinate with other team members and clients.
- **Integrating banking transactions:** It enables the application to download all your banking transactions. Additionally, it categorizes the types of transactions according to the transactions usually done in your account.
- **Sharing of documents:** If you need to send a document to the client or receive a document from the client, QuickBooks provides a hassle-free share through an in-built document center.
- **Viewing of financial reports:** It lets you view the client's reports about his financial health along with viewing the accountant's side financial reports like balance sheets, profit-loss report and trial balance.
- **Complying of GST (Goods and Services Tax):** It is well-versed with the GST policies. It enables you to create taxation reports in accordance with GST that are needed for filing the tax.

- **Expert training:** It provides free training and support from the QuickBooks experts and through dedicated helpline for accountants, whenever you need help with anything related to it. Intuit offers certifications for QuickBooks.

QuickBooks also offers a wide variety of features for the clients as well. These are listed as follows:

- **Invoicing:** It lets the client create, print and email professional invoices. It also keeps a track of the unpaid orders.
- **Tracking the money:** It enables a user to collect and organize the entire financial information in one application like bills paid and card payments. It keeps a track of everything that comes in and goes out of the business.
- **Automated report generation:** It gives you an insight of the status of your business through the automated financial reports it generates. It helps you to make better business decisions.
- **Automatic bank integration:** It creates a link to your bank account automatically and downloads all the transactions, which reduces the risk of entering data manually. It is completely secure just like your banking transactions.
- **Multiple access anywhere:** It allows you to access your QuickBooks account from anywhere in the world. You can modify the access controls and put restrictions on the users of the account.
- **Real-time connection:** It offers your accountant the access to your data and documents whenever required. You do not have to run after your accountant for any sort of financial information.
- **Integrated payroll:** It gives you the flexibility of managing your payroll account from anywhere.

With this, we come to the end of this chapter. Let us now summarize the main topics covered so far.

Summary

In this chapter, you have learned about computerized accounting. You have also learned about the need of computerized accounting as well as the merits and demerits of computerized accounting. Towards the end of the chapter, you have learned about different accounting software applications, such as Tally, Busy, SAP, Zoho Books, Sage 50 Accounting, and QuickBooks.

CHAPTER

3

Tally.ERP 9 & Elemental Features

In this Chapter:

* Opening the Tally.ERP 9 Application
* Understanding the Components of the Tally.ERP 9 Application Window
* Mouse and Keyboard Conventions
* Managing the Screen Area
* Closing the Tally.ERP 9 Application
* Creating a Company in Tally.ERP 9
* Selecting a Company
* Shutting a Company
* Altering Company Details
* Company Features
* Configurations of Tally

Introduction

Tally is the accounting software that is designed to integrate and automate all types of business transactions. Every business has various processes, ranging from simple to complex. As your business grows, acquires new customers, and ventures into newer markets, you need to maintain accurate and updated accounting and inventory records. Tally is a cost-effective accounting software that allows you to simplify, integrate, and streamline all your business transactions. Tally.ERP 9 is the latest version of Tally, which comes with various enhancements. It can handle the accounts of more than one company simultaneously. In addition, Tally.ERP 9 enables you to view information of any period, compare data across companies and financial periods, maintain account details, and generate reports. Tally.ERP 9 enables quick and correct decisions, thus, providing a better control over the business.

In this chapter, you learn about the procedure to open the Tally.ERP 9 application. After this, you learn about the components of Tally.ERP 9 application window. Then, you learn about the mouse and keyboard conventions and the procedure to manage the screen area. You also learn about the procedure to close the Tally.ERP 9 application. Further, the chapter discusses the process to create, select, and shut a company in Tally. You also learn about the procedure to alter the details of a company. Toward the end of the chapter, you learn about the company features and configurations of Tally.

Let us start the chapter by learning about the procedure to open the Tally.ERP 9 application.

Opening the Tally.ERP 9 Application

To be able to work on Tally.ERP 9, you first need to install the software successfully and then open it on your computer system.

Perform the following steps to open the Tally.ERP 9 application:

1. *Click* the **Start** button on the taskbar (Fig.TL-3.1).

   The **Start** menu appears with a list of installed programs and apps (Fig.TL-3.1).
2. *Click* the **Tally.ERP 9** folder. A list of options appears (Fig.TL-3.1).
3. *Select* the **Tally.ERP 9** option, as shown in Fig.TL-3.1:

Fig.TL-3.1

The Tally.ERP 9 application window opens on your screen, as shown in Fig.TL-3.2:

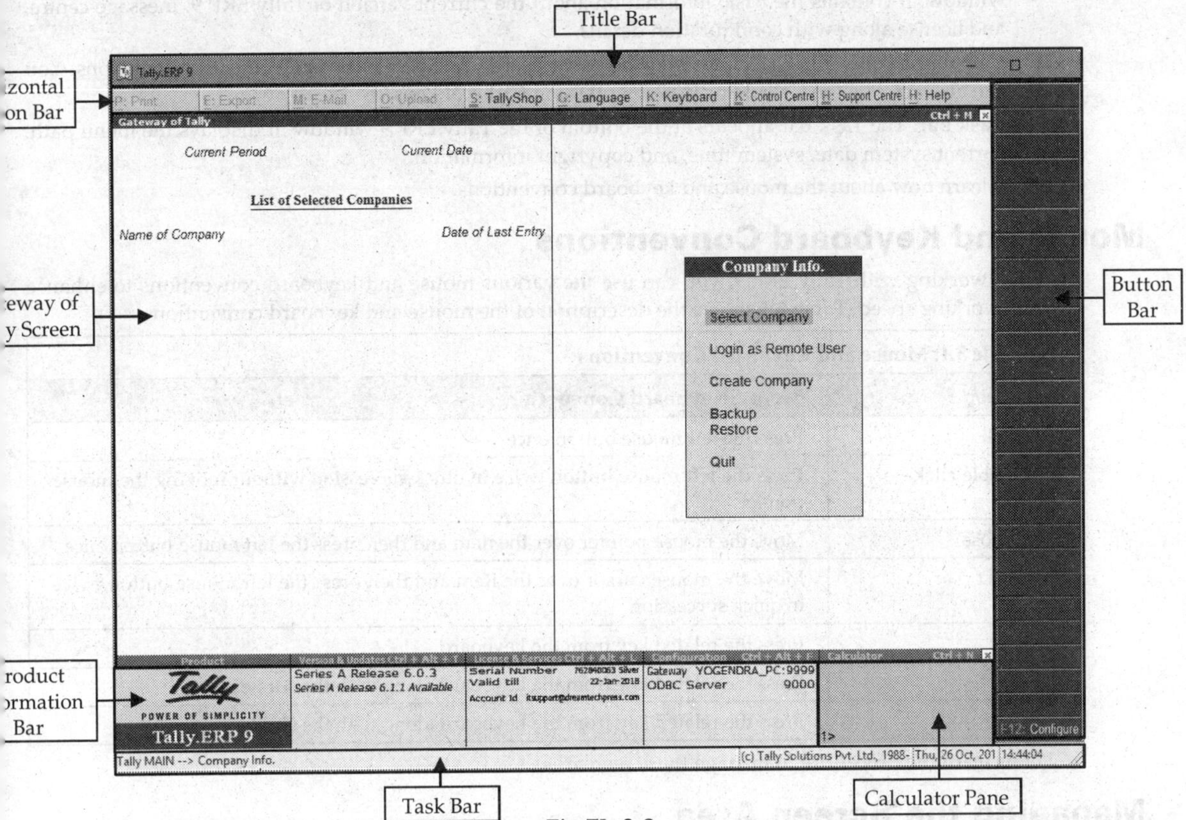

Fig.TL-3.2

After learning the procedure to open the Tally.ERP 9 application, let us now learn about the components of the Tally.ERP 9 application window in the next section.

Understanding the Components of the Tally.ERP 9 Application Window

The Tally.ERP 9 window (Fig.TL-3.2) contains various components that can be used to perform various functions. The following are the major components present in this application window:

- **Title Bar:** The Title Bar is located at the top of the Tally.ERP 9 window. It displays the version number of Tally.
- **Horizontal Button Bar:** The Horizontal Button Bar is located below the Title Bar in the Tally.ERP 9 window. It contains buttons that are used to perform various tasks.
- **Gateway of Tally Screen:** The Gateway of Tally screen appears just below the Horizontal Button Bar and occupies most of the Tally.ERP 9 window. This screen is divided into two parts – left side and right side. The left side displays the name of the currently opened company and its details, such as the last entry made into the company and the current period of the company. On the right side of the screen, you will find different menus. This is the entry point for navigating to the location of Tally.ERP 9 where you want to work.
- **Button Bar:** The Button Bar is located at the extreme right side of the Tally.ERP 9 application window. It displays various buttons that provide a quick and direct access to several options and tasks. The buttons that do not correspond to the currently selected options are displayed in the inactive state.

- **Product Information Bar:** The Product Information Bar appears at the bottom of the Tally.ERP 9 window. It contains the basic information about the current version of Tally.ERP 9, message centre, and license along with configuration details.
- **Calculator Pane**: The Calculator Pane allows a user to calculate basic and complex calculations. You can also activate the Calculator Pane by pressing **Ctrl + N** keys.
- **Task Bar:** The Task Bar appears at the bottom of the Tally.ERP 9 window. It displays the menu path, current system date, system time, and copyright information.

Let us learn now about the mouse and keyboard conventions.

Mouse and Keyboard Conventions

While working with Tally.ERP 9, you can use the various mouse and keyboard conventions to enhance your working speed. Table 3.1 shows the description of the mouse and keyboard conventions.

Table 3.1: Mouse and Keyboard Conventions

Action	Mouse/Keyboard Convention
Click	Press the left mouse button once
Double-click	Press the left mouse button twice in quick succession without moving the mouse pointer
Choose	Move the mouse pointer over the item and then press the left mouse button once
Select	Move the mouse cursor over the item and then press the left mouse button twice in quick succession
Fn	Press the related key from the keyboard
Fn	Press the related key from the keyboard along with the Alt key
Fn	Press the related key from the keyboard along with the Ctrl key

Let us learn the procedure to manage the screen area.

Managing the Screen Area

In Tally.ERP 9, you can manage the screen area by collapsing or restoring the elements of the Tally.ERP 9 window. For example, if you want to view some detailed information that is not fitting in the default window size, you can collapse or close the Product Information Bar along with the Calculator Pane. To do so, click the Close button present on the top-right side of the Product Information Bar. To restore the Product Information Bar, click the up arrow (^) on the center of the screen. Similarly, press the **Ctrl + M** keys to collapse the Calculator Pane and the **Ctrl + N** keys to restore the Calculator Pane.

Let us now learn to close the Tally.ERP 9 application.

Closing the Tally.ERP 9 Application

You can close the Tally.ERP 9 application in different ways, which are as follows:

- Press the **Esc** key until the **Quit ?** message box appears. Then, click the **Yes** button in the **Quit ?** message box or press the **Y** key.
- Press the **Ctrl + Q** keys in the **Gateway of Tally** screen to close the Tally.ERP 9 application without any confirmation.
- Double-click the **Quit** option in the **Gateway of Tally** screen. The **Quit ?** message box appears. Now, click the **Yes** button in the **Quit ?** message box or press the **Y** key.
- Press the **Enter** key when the **Quit** option is selected in the **Gateway of Tally** screen. The **Quit ?** message box appears. Now, click the **Yes** button in the **Quit ?** message box or press the **Y** key.

Let us learn about the procedure to create a company in Tally.ERP9.

Creating a Company in Tally.ERP 9

After installing the Tally.ERP 9 application, the first task you need to carry out is to create a company. In Tally, the term company signifies an entity for which an independent set of accounts is maintained. Tally.ERP 9 is used to create and manage accounts-related information and data of a company. Therefore, creating a company in Tally.ERP 9 means providing the basic information about the company whose accounts are to be maintained.

Perform the following steps to create a company in Tally:

1. *Double-click* the **Create Company** option from the **Company Info.** menu, as shown in Fig.TL-3.3:

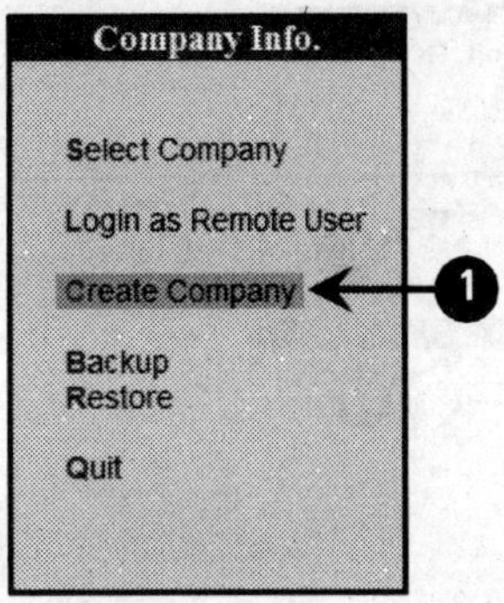

Fig.TL-3.3

The **Company Creation** screen appears (Fig.TL-3.4).

> **Note:** **In the Company Creation screen, you are required to fill the company information. While filling information on the screen, you can press the Tab key, the Enter key, or the down-arrow key to go to the next option, or you can press the Shift + Tab key or up-arrow key to go to the previous option.**

The first option to be filled in the Company Creation screen is Directory. This option shows the path of your computer where the company's entire information will be saved. It is recommended not to modify the directory path, unless it is required.

2. *Enter* the name of the company whose account books are to be opened beside the **Name** option. In our case, we have entered **Trinity Soft. Del** as the company's name (Fig.TL-3.4).
3. *Press* the **Enter** key to move to the **Mailing name** option.
4. *Enter* the mailing name of the company beside the **Mailing name** option. In our case, we have entered **Trinity Soft. Del** (Fig.TL-3.4).
5. *Press* the **Enter** key to move to the **Address** option.
6. *Enter* the address of the company beside the **Address** option. In our case, we have entered **19-A, Rama Garden** (Fig.TL-3.4).
7. *Press* the **Enter** key to move to the next line.
8. *Enter* the remaining address of the company. In our case, we have entered **Karawal Nagar** (Fig.TL-3.4).
9. *Press* the **Enter** key twice to move to the **Country** option.
   The **List of Countries** menu appears.

> **Note:** **By default, the Country option displays the country name, India, which was selected during the installation of the Tally.ERP 9 software.**

10. *Double-click* the desired country name from the **List of Countries** menu for the **Country** option. In our case, we have retained the default option, i.e. **India** (Fig.TL-3.4).

11. *Press* the **Enter** key to move to the **State** option.

    The **List of States** menu appears on the screen.
12. *Double-click* the desired state name from the **List of States** menu for the **State** option. In our case, we have double-clicked **Delhi** (Fig.TL-3.4).
13. *Enter* the pin code beside the **Pincode** option. In our case, we have entered **110094**, as shown in Fig.TL-3.4:

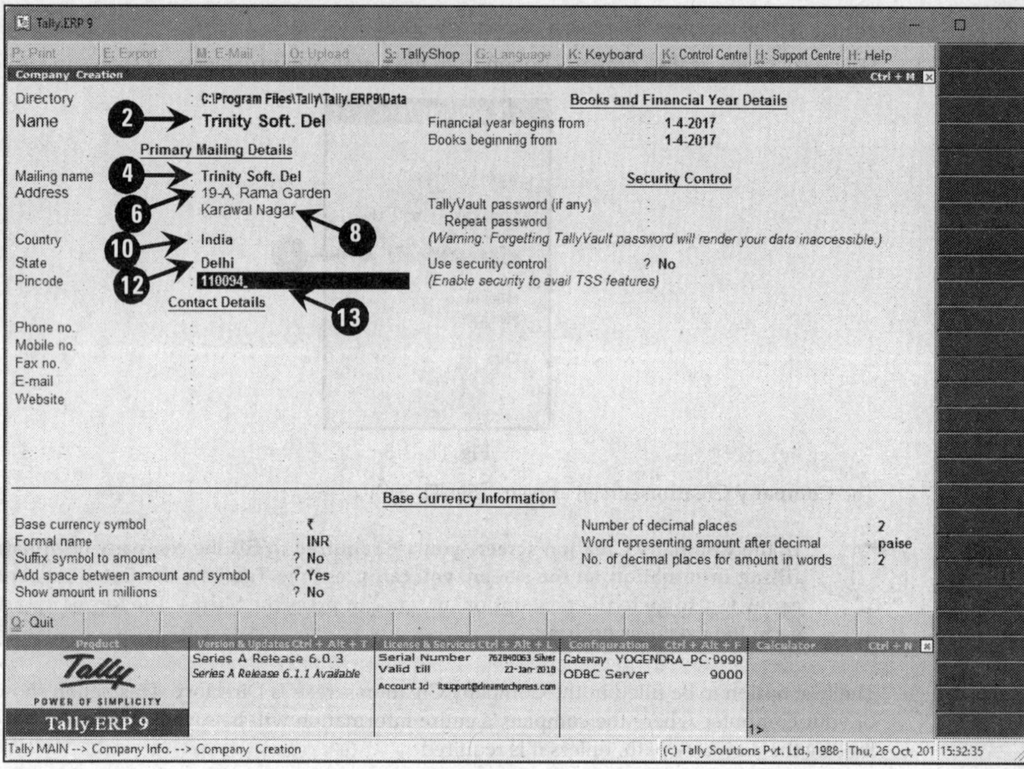

Fig.TL-3.4

14. *Press* the **Enter** key to move to the **Phone no.** option.
15. *Enter* the telephone number of the company beside the **Phone no.** option. In our case, we have entered **011-23568914** (Fig.TL-3.5).
16. *Press* the **Enter** key to move to the **Mobile no.** option.
17. *Enter* the mobile number of the company beside the **Mobile no.** option. In our case, we have entered **8281114341** (Fig.TL-3.5).
18. *Press* the **Enter** key twice to move to the **E-mail** option.
19. *Enter* the e-mail address of the company beside the **E-mail** option. In our case, we have entered **info@trinitysoftdel.com** (Fig.TL-3.5).
20. *Press* the **Enter** key twice to move to the **Financial year begins from** option.
21. *Enter* the date beside the **Financial year begins from** option. In our case, we have retained the default date, **1-4-2017** (Fig.TL-3.5).
22. *Press* the **Enter** key to move to the **Books beginning from** option.
23. *Enter* the date beside the **Books beginning from** option. In our case, we have retained the default date, **1-4-2017** (Fig.TL-3.5).
24. *Press* the **Enter** key until the **Accept ?** message box appears (Fig.TL-3.5).

25. *Click* **Yes** in the **Accept ?** message box to create the company and save the information, as shown in Fig.TL-3.5:

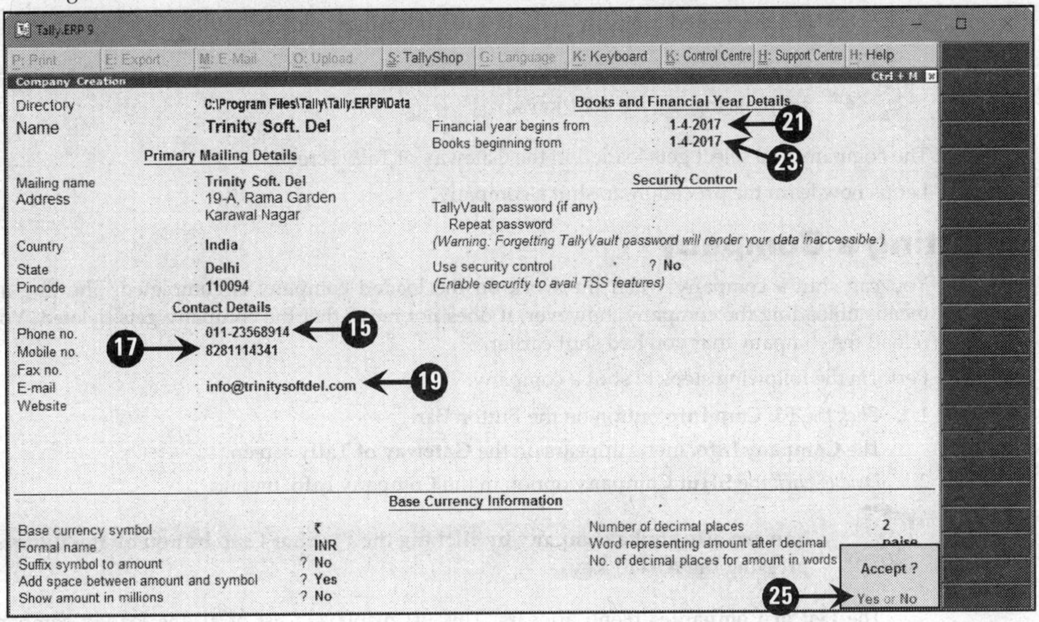

Fig.TL-3.5

The company named **Trinity Soft. Del** is created.

Similarly, you can create other companies.

After learning about the process to create a company, let us now learn the procedure to select a company in Tally.ERP 9.

Selecting a Company

Once you have created a company in Tally, you need to select the company stored in Tally to work on it. Perform the following steps to select a company:

1. *Click* the **F3: Cmp Info** button on the Button Bar.
   The **Company Info.** menu appears on the **Gateway of Tally** screen (Fig.TL-3.6).
2. *Double-click* the **Select Company** option in the **Company Info.** menu, as shown in Fig.TL-3.6:

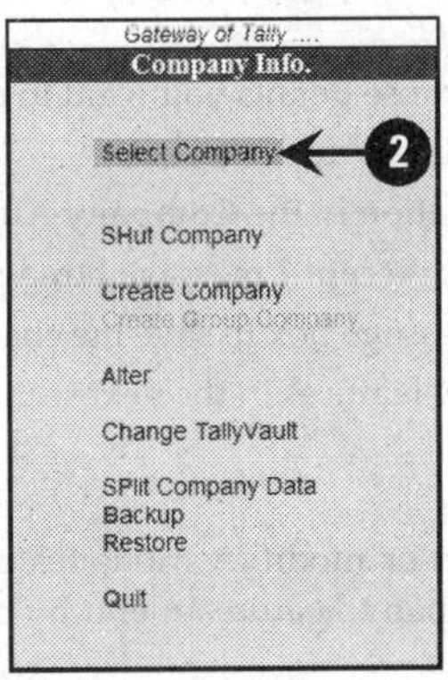

Fig.TL-3.6

The **List of Companies** menu appears. This list displays a list of all the companies available in the database of Tally.

3. *Double-click* the desired company in the **List of Companies** menu.

Note: **You can also select a company by clicking the F1: Select Cmp button on the Button Bar or by pressing the Alt + F1 keys.**

The company you select gets loaded in the Gateway of Tally screen.

Let us now learn the procedure to shut a company.

Shutting a Company

You can shut a company when the work on the loaded company is completed. Shutting a company means unloading the company; however, it does not mean that the company gets deleted. You can also reload the company that you had shut earlier.

Perform the following steps to shut a company:

1. *Click* the **F3: Cmp Info** button on the Button Bar.

   The **Company Info.** menu appears on the **Gateway of Tally** screen.

2. *Double-click* the **SHut Company** option in the **Company Info.** menu.

Note: **You can also shut a company by clicking the F1: Shut Cmp button on the Button Bar or by pressing the Alt+F1 keys.**

The **List of Companies** menu appears. This list displays a list of all the loaded companies in the Tally database.

3. *Double-click* the desired company in the **List of Companies** menu.

The company you select gets unloaded.

Let us now learn the procedure to alter company details.

Altering Company Details

You can alter the details of a company as per the requirement.

Perform the following steps to alter the details of a company:

1. *Click* the **F3: Cmp Info** button on the Button Bar.

   The **Company Info.** menu appears on the **Gateway of Tally** screen.

2. *Double-click* the **Alter** option in the **Company Info.** menu.

   The **List of Companies** menu appears. This list displays a list of all the loaded companies in the Tally database.

3. *Double-click* the company whose details you want to modify from the **List of Companies** menu.

   The **Company Alteration** screen appears.

4. *Make* the necessary modification in the **Company Alteration** screen.
5. *Press* the **Enter** key until the **Accept ?** message box appears.
6. *Click* **Yes** in the **Accept ?** message box to save the changes.

Let us now learn about company features in the next section.

Company Features

Tally.ERP 9 allows you to select or modify various features of a company with the Company Features menu. You can access the Company Features menu by clicking the F11: Features button on the Button Bar.

The Company Features menu appears on the Gateway of Tally screen, as shown in Fig.TL-3.7:

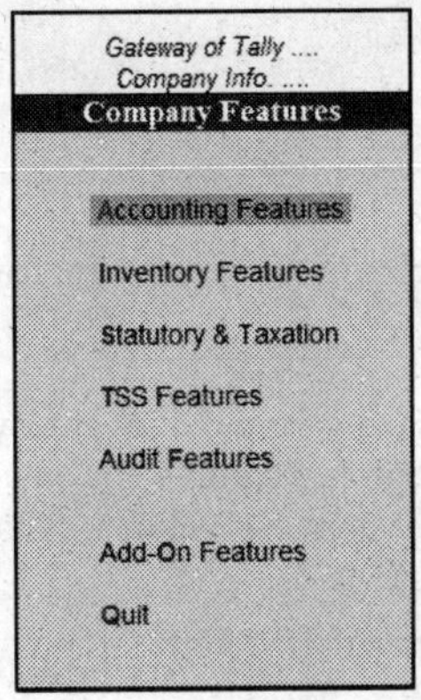

Fig.TL-3.7

The Company Features menu consists of various features, namely, Accounting Features, Inventory Features, Statutory & Taxation, TSS Features, Audit Features, and Add-On Features.

Let us discuss these features one by one in the following sections.

Accounting Features

Accounting features are required for maintaining the accounts of a company. You can access the accounting features by double-clicking the Accounting Features option in the Company Features menu. The Company Operations Alteration screen displays the accounting features of the selected company, as shown in Fig.TL-3.8:

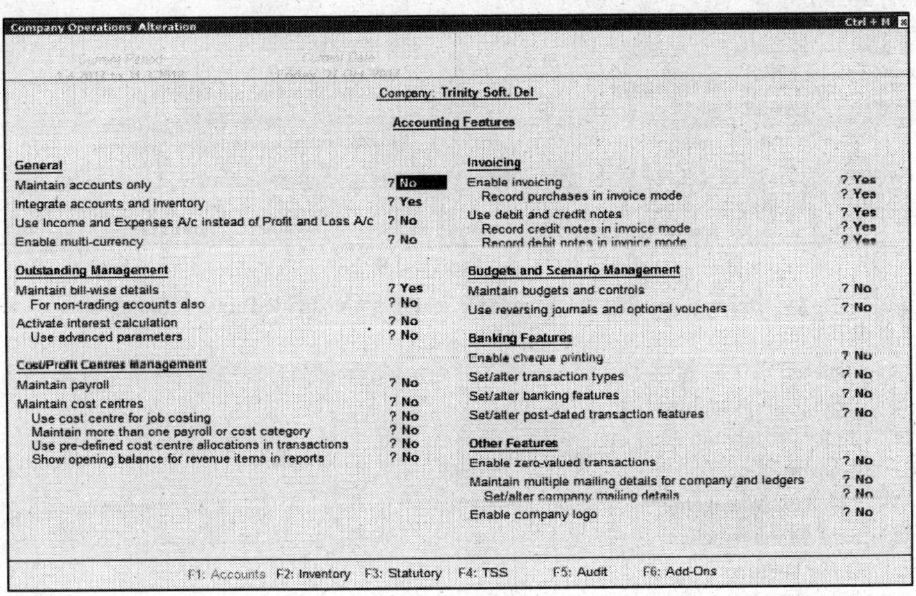

Fig.TL-3.8

In Fig.TL-3.8, you can see that the accounting features are divided into various sections, which are as follows:

- General
- Outstanding Management

- Cost/Profit Centres Management
- Invoicing
- Budgets and Scenario Management
- Banking Features
- Other Features

To enable/disable the required feature in the accounting features, you can set it to Yes/No.

Inventory Features

Inventory features are required for managing the inventory of a company. You can access the inventory features by double-clicking the Inventory Features option in the Company Features menu. The Company Operations Alteration screen displays the inventory features of the selected company, as shown in Fig.TL-3.9:

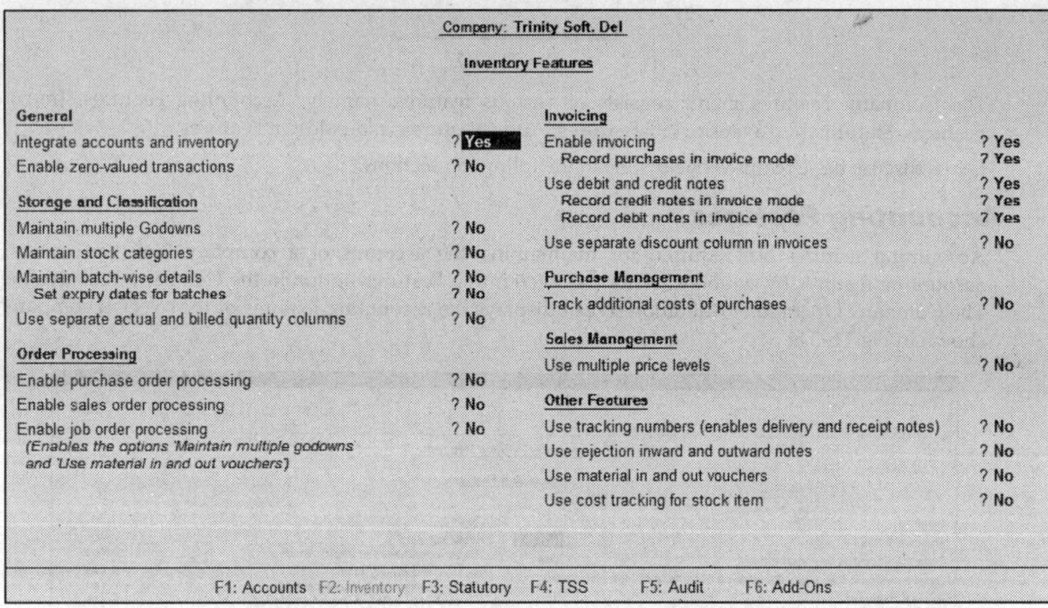

Fig.TL-3.9

In Fig.TL-3.9, you can see that the inventory features are divided into various sections, which are as follows:

- General
- Storage and Classification
- Order Processing
- Invoicing
- Purchase Management
- Sales Management
- Other Features

To enable the required feature in the inventory features, you need to set it to Yes.

Statutory & Taxation

Statutory & Taxation features are related to the statutory compliances. These features vary from one country to another. You can access the Statutory & Taxation features by double-clicking the Statutory & Taxation option in the Company Features menu. The Company Operations Alteration screen displays the statutory and taxation features, as shown in Fig.TL-3.10:

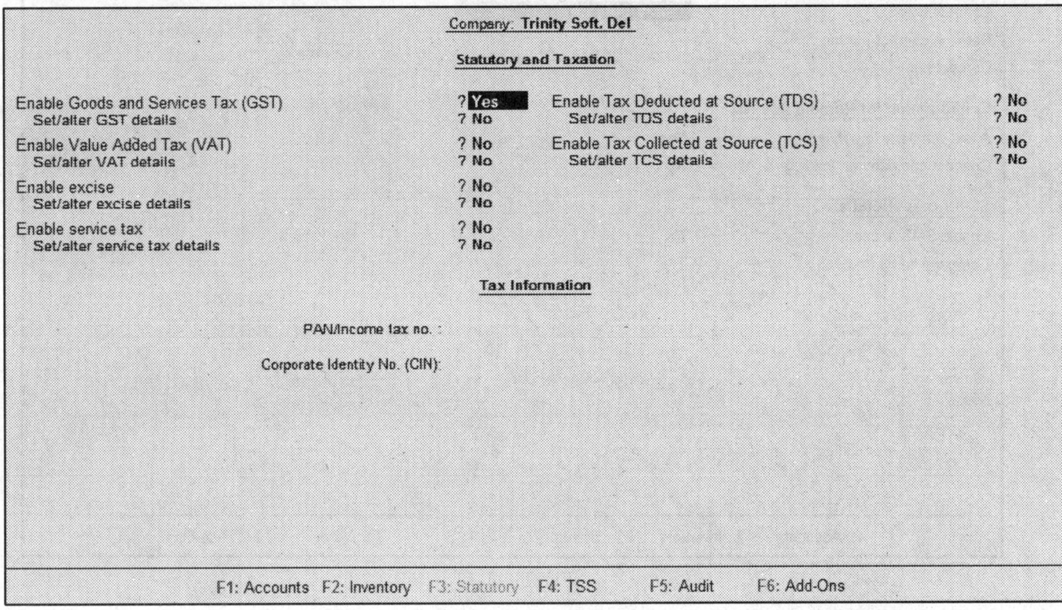

Fig.TL-3.10

In Fig.TL-3.10, you can see the various statutory & taxation features, which are as follows:

- Goods and Services Tax (GST)
- Value Added Tax (VAT)
- Excise
- Service Tax
- Tax Deducted at Source (TDS)
- Tax Collected at Source (TCS)

Tally Software Services (TSS) Features

Tally Software Services (TSS) features are related to remote connectivity, SMS access details, banking services, and center location (secure server) to store data of all branch offices. This features appear on the Company Features menu when you enable the Use security control option in the Company Creation screen. You can access the TSS features by double-clicking the TSS Features option in the Company Features menu.

The Company Operations Alteration screen displays the TSS features, as shown in Fig.TL-3.11:

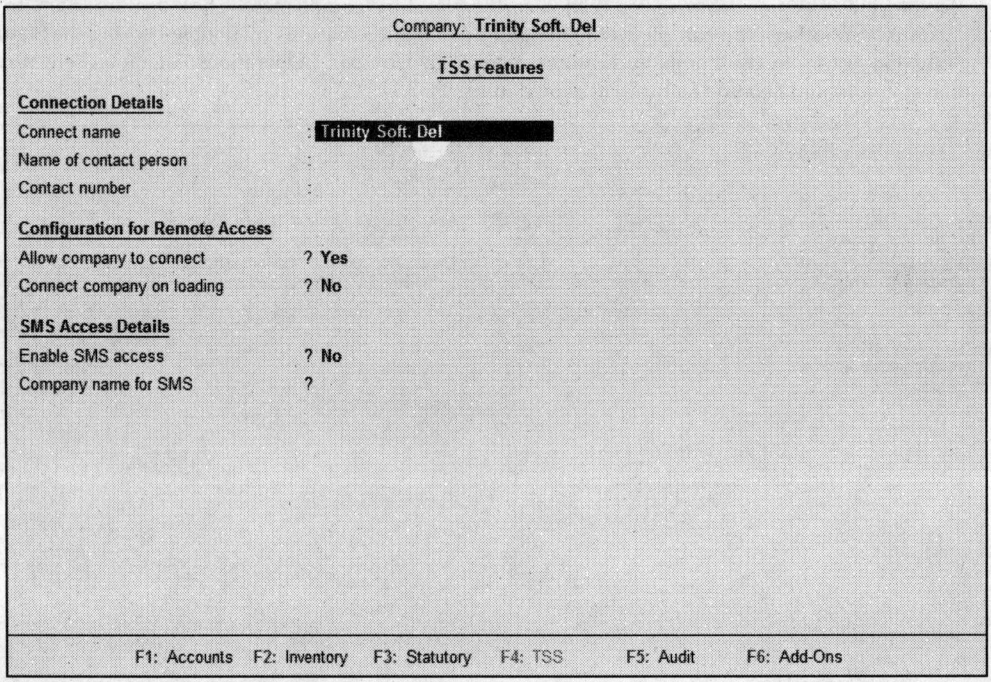

Fig.TL-3.11

In Fig.TL-3.11, you can see the various TSS features, which are as follows:

- Connection Details
- Configuration for Remote Access
- SMS Access Details

Audit Features

Audit features that are related to use audit services. This features appear on the Company Features menu when you enable the Use security control option in the Company Creation screen. You can access the Audit features by double-clicking the Audit Features option in the Company Features menu. The Company Operations Alteration screen displays the audit features, as shown in Fig.TL-3.12:

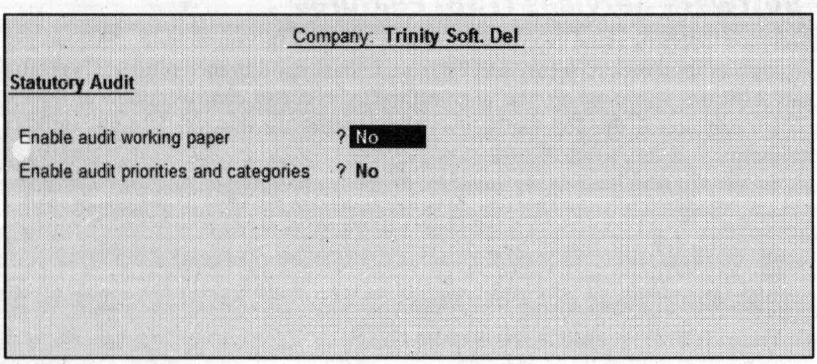

Fig.TL-3.12

Add-On Features

Add-On features are required from time to time for carrying out the transactions of a company smoothly. These features allow users to purchase customized solutions from authorized Tally.ERP 9 partners or directly from the manufacturer and distributors of Tally.

Let us learn about the configurations of Tally.

Configurations of Tally

Tally allows you to change the configuration options of various features, such as accounting, inventory, payroll, and banking, according to the requirement. When you set the configuration option of the company, it is applicable to all the companies that reside in the same data directory.

The configuration options may vary depending on the screen currently appearing on the Tally.ERP 9 window. You can access the general configuration options by clicking the F12: Configure button on the Button Bar. When you click the F12: Configure button, the Configuration menu appears, as shown in Fig.TL-3.13:

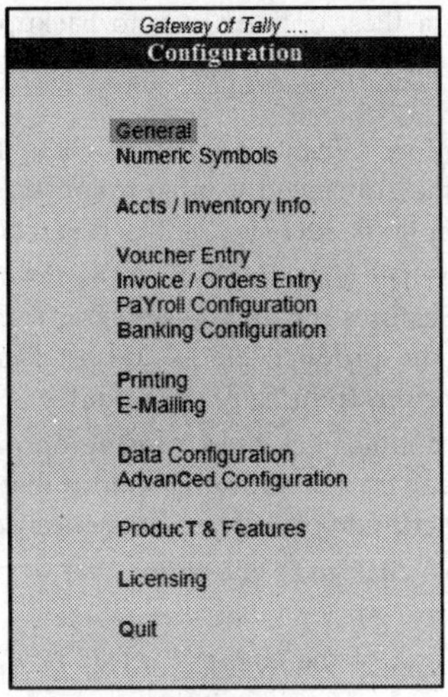

Fig.TL-3.13

The description of the options present in the Configuration menu are as follows:

- **General:** When you double-click the General option in the Configuration menu, the General Configuration screen appears. This screen allows users to configure various options, such as country details, style of name that appears on reports, date format, import and export options, and table configuration.
- **Numeric Symbols:** When you double-click the Numeric Symbols option in the Configuration menu, the Configuration of Numeric Symbols screen appears. This screen allows you to set the number style and the symbol style that is used to define the positive, negative, debit, and credit amounts.
- **Accts / Inventory Info.:** When you double-click the Accts / Inventory Info. option in the Configuration menu, the Master Configuration screen appears. This screen allows you to set the additional features and options related to accounting and inventory masters.
- **Voucher Entry:** When you double-click the Voucher Entry option in the Configuration menu, the Voucher Configuration screen appears. This screen allows you to set the additional features and options for accounting and inventory vouchers.
- **Invoice / Orders Entry:** When you double-click the Invoice / Orders Entry option in the Configuration menu, the Invoice Configuration screen appears. This screen allows you to configure invoices, delivery notes, sales and purchase orders, and the options related to exporters.

- **PaYroll Configuration:** When you double-click the PaYroll Configuration option in the Configuration menu, the Payroll Configuration screen appears. This screen allows users to enable the statutory details, passport and visa details, contact details, and resigned or retired details.
- **Banking Configuration:** When you double-click the Banking Configuration option in the Configuration menu, the Banking Configuration screen appears. This screen allows users to set the Bank Reconciliation Statement (BRS) report, alter the reconciled vouchers, and specify the location of bank statement files.
- **Printing:** When you double-click the Printing option in the Configuration menu, the Printing menu appears. This menu contains various options that are used to set the print setting of vouchers, invoices, statements, and reminder letters.
- **E-Mailing:** When you double-click the E-Mailing option in the Configuration menu, the E-Mail Configuration screen appears. This screen allows users to specify various settings related to e-mail, such as e-mail server, server address, sender name and e-mail address, and authentication details.
- **Data Configuration:** When you double-click the Data Configuration option in the Configuration menu, the Data Configuration screen appears. This screen allows users to specify various settings, such as location of data files, options to auto backup copy of data files, location of export files, options to load a company when you start the Tally.ERP 9 application, and location of the language and configuration files.
- **AdvanCed Configuration:** When you double-click the AdvanCed Configuration option in the Configuration menu, the Advanced Configuration screen appears. This screen allows users to set various configuration options, such as client/server, connection, log, and proxy.
- **ProducT & Features:** When you double-click the ProducT & Features option in the Configuration menu, the Product & Features screen appears. This screen shows the new Tally live updates. Users can install or update the product, Stat, add-ons, local and account Tally Definition Languages (TDLs), and Tally extensions from Tally live updates.
- **Licensing:** When you double-click the Licensing option in the Configuration menu, the Licensing menu appears. This menu contains various options that are used to update the license, surrender the license, extend the subscription of Tally, reset the license, and configure the existing license.
- **Quit:** When you double-click the Quit option, the Configuration menu closes and the Gateway of Tally screen appears.

With this, we come to the end of the chapter. Let us now summarize the key points discussed in the chapter.

Summary

In this chapter, you have learned about the procedure to open the Tally.ERP 9 application. Next, you have learned about various compounts of Tally.ERP 9 window. Then, you became acquainted with the mouse and keyboard conventions and the procedure to manage the screen area. You have also learned about the procedure to close the Tally.ERP 9 application. Next, the chapter discussed the process to create, select, and shut a company in Tally. After this, you have learned about the procedure to alter the details of a company. Toward the end of the chapter, you have learned about company features and configurations of Tally.

CHAPTER

4

Creating Masters in Tally.ERP 9

In this Chapter:

- Understanding Chart of Accounts
- Creating Accounting Masters in Tally.ERP 9
- Creating Inventory Masters in Tally.ERP 9

Introduction

To run a business smoothly, an organization needs to maintain its complete account details and inventory of goods and services. In Tally.ERP 9, accounting information is given in terms of groups and ledgers and inventory is maintained by means of stock groups, stock categories, godowns, units of measure, and stock items. A ledger represents assorted, summarized, and balanced transactions of similar nature, while the account groups organize ledger of accounts into hierarchical levels. Stock groups are used for grouping common stock items, while stock categories are used for storing these items. Godowns are places to store stock items. Units of measure are the units in which the quantities of items are expressed. Stock items are the goods that are manufactured, such as a monitor, book, and table.

The chapter begins with a discussion of the chart of accounts. It also discusses accounting masters, which include groups and ledgers. The chapter also describes the procedure to create single as well as multiple groups and ledgers. Toward the end, the chapter describes how to create, display, and alter stock groups, stock categories, godowns, units of measure, and stock items.

Let us begin the chapter by learning about the chart of accounts.

Understanding Chart of Accounts

As you know, Tally.ERP 9 is used to record accounting transactions. Based on the nature of a transaction, you can debit or credit accounts (ledgers and groups). Tally.ERP 9 provides 15 pre-defined parent groups and 13 pre-defined sub-groups and contains two pre-defined ledgers: Cash and Profit & Loss A/c.

In addition, Tally.ERP 9 allows you to set up groups and ledgers into a chart of accounts. You can view the chart of accounts by clicking **Gateway of Tally→Display→List of Accounts**. The List of Accounts screen appears, displaying the chart of accounts.

Let us now learn the procedure to create accounting masters in Tally.ERP 9.

Creating Accounting Masters in Tally.ERP 9

Account details of a company are required to be maintained for making accurate financial transactions. Tally.ERP 9 allows the same with the help of its accounting masters, such as groups and ledgers.

Let us now learn about groups.

Groups

Groups (also known as account groups) are a collection of ledgers of the same nature, for example, the indirect expenses group contains the expense ledgers. A group helps in organizing ledger accounts into a tree-structured hierarchy. A group is created under the parent group to maintain the hierarchy of information in Tally. As already mentioned, Tally.ERP 9 provides 15 pre-defined parent groups and 13 pre-defined sub-groups. You can also divide the primary group into the following two sub-categories:

- Primary group in Capital nature
- Primary group in Revenue nature

Note: **Primary groups cannot be deleted in Tally.ERP 9.**

Let us first learn to create a single group.

Creating a Single Group

Perform the following steps to create a single group:

1. *Double-click* the **Accounts Info.** option in the **Gateway of Tally** menu (Fig.TL-4.1).

   The **Accounts Info.** menu appears (Fig.TL-4.2).

2. *Double-click* the **Groups** option in the **Accounts Info.** menu (Fig.TL-4.2).

   The **Groups** menu appears (Fig.TL-4.3).

3. *Double-click* the **Create** option under the **Single Group** section in the **Groups** menu, as shown in Fig.TL-4.3:

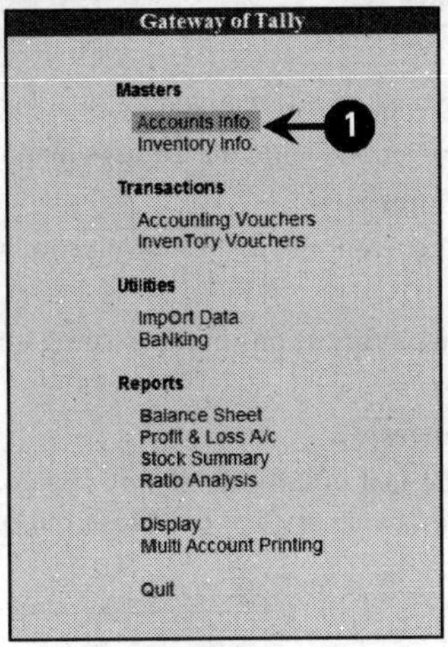

Fig.TL-4.1

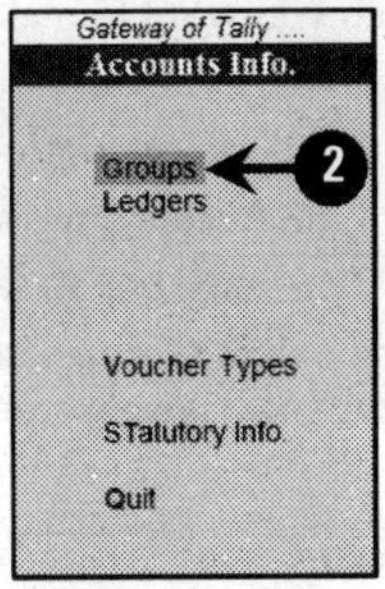

Fig.TL-4.2

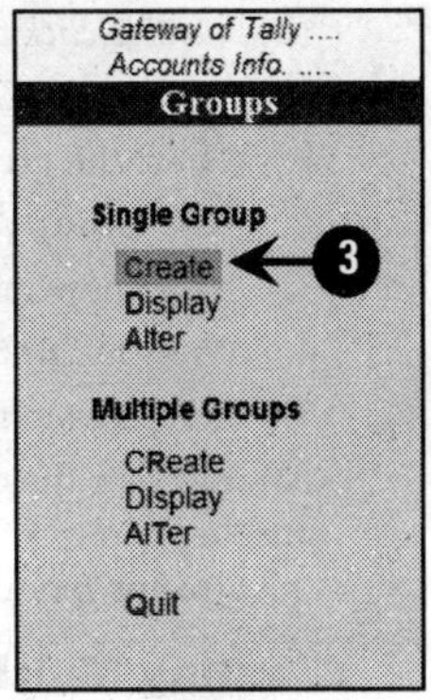

Fig.TL-4.3

The **Group Creation** screen appears (Fig.TL-4.4).

4. *Type* the name of the group that you want to create beside the **Name** option. In our case, we have typed **Office Expenses** (Fig.TL-4.4).
5. *Press* the **Enter** key to go to the **(alias)** option.
6. *Enter* an alias (additional name apart from the primary name) beside the **(alias)** option to access the group. In our case, we are not assigning any alias to the group, and therefore, we have left the **(alias)** option blank (Fig.TL-4.4).
7. *Press* the **Enter** key to go to the **Under** option.

   The **List of Groups** menu appears.
8. *Double-click* the desired parent group in the **List of Groups** menu for the **Under** option. In our case, we have double-clicked the **Indirect Expenses** group (Fig.TL-4.4).

   The **Accept ?** message box appears (Fig.TL-4.4).
9. *Click* **Yes** in the **Accept ?** message box to create the group (Office Expenses) under the selected parent group (Indirect Expenses), as shown in Fig.TL-4.4:

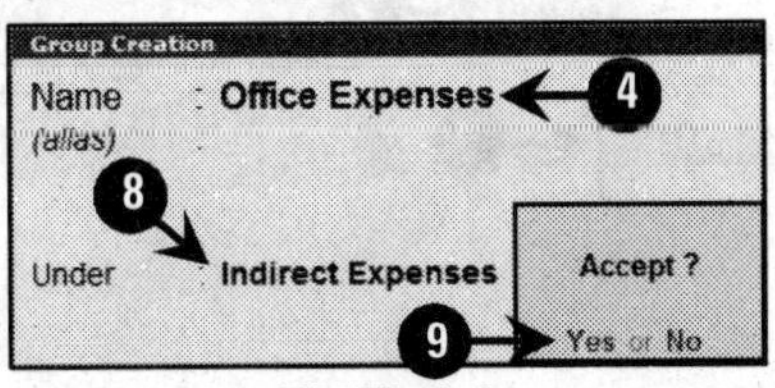

Fig.TL-4.4

Display a Single Group

After creating a single group, you can view the details of the group. You need to perform the following steps to display a single group:

1. *Double-click* the **Display** option under the **Single Group** section in the **Groups** menu.

   The **Select Group** screen appears with the **List of Groups** menu.
2. *Select* a group you want to display from the **List of Groups** menu.

   The **Group Display** screen appears with details of the selected group.

You cannot make any changes, such as altering the name and selecting a new parent, to a group in the Group Display screen.

Alter a Single Group

You can make changes in any single group by performing the procedure given in the following steps:

1. *Double-click* the **Alter** option under the **Single Group** section inside the **Groups** menu.

   The **Select Group** screen appears with the **List of Groups** menu.
2. *Select* the group in which you want to make the changes from the **List of Groups** menu.

   The **Group Alteration** screen appears.
3. *Enter* new information for the selected group or make modifications in the existing information.
4. *Press* the **Enter** key until the **Accept?** message box appears.
5. *Click* **Yes** in the **Accept ?** message box to save the changes.

After saving the changes, the **Select Group** screen with the **List of Groups** menu appears. You can select another group for alternation; otherwise, press the **Esc** key twice or click the **Close** button to go back to the **Groups** menu.

Creating Multiple Groups

In multiple groups, the groups inherit the features of their parent group automatically. You need to specify group information, such as the name of the group and parent group, for creating multiple groups.

Perform the following steps to create multiple groups in Tally:

1. *Double-click* the **CReate** option under the **Multiple Groups** section in the **Groups** menu.

   The **Multi Group Creation** screen appears, displaying the **List of Groups** menu.
2. *Double-click* the parent group under which you want to create new groups, in the **List of Groups** menu for the **Under Group** option. In our case, we have double-clicked **Indirect Expenses** (Fig.TL-4.5).
3. *Type* the name of sub-groups under the **Name of Group** column. In our case, we have typed **Administrative Expenses** and **Electricity Expenses** (Fig.TL-4.5).

   The name of the parent group appears automatically beneath the **Under** column (Fig.TL-4.5).
4. *Press* the **Enter** key until the **Accept ?** message box appears (Fig.TL-4.5).
5. *Click* **Yes** in the **Accept ?** message box to create the multiple group, as shown in Fig.TL-4.5:

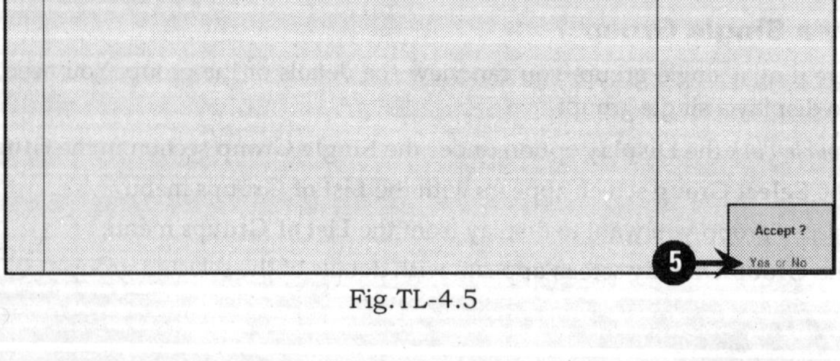

Fig.TL-4.5

After you click Yes in the Accept ? message box, the multiple group is created, and the Groups menu reappears.

Note: If you insert any group other than the All Items group for the Under Group option, the Under column is filled automatically with the selected group name, and the cursor skips the column. However, if you select the All Items group for the Under Group option, the cursor does not skip the Under column and allows you to insert the parent group of each group that you have created.

Display a Multiple Group

After creating a multiple group, you can view its details. Perform the following steps to display the details of a multiple group:

1. *Double-click* the **DIsplay** option under **Multiple Groups** of the **Groups** menu.

   The **Select Group** screen appears with the **List of Groups** menu.

2. *Select* a group from the **List of Groups** menu, you want to display.

   After selecting the group name, the **Multi Group Display** screen appears

The **Multi Group Display** screen shows a list of sub-groups under the **Name of Group** column.

Alter Multiple Groups

Sometimes after creating a multiple group, you need to alter/modify its details. You can make changes in a multiple group by performing the following simple steps:

1. *Double-click* the **AlTer** option under **Multiple Groups** inside the **Groups** menu.

   The **Select Group** screen appears with the **List of Groups** menu.

2. *Select* a group in which you want to make changes from the **List of Groups** menu.
3. *Click* **Yes** in the **Accept?** message box to save the changes.

   The **Select Group** screen with the **List of Groups** menu reappears.

4. *Press* the **Esc** key or click the **Close** button to go back to the **Groups** menu.

Let us now learn about ledgers.

Ledgers

A ledger is the most important part of a company's financial records. It constitutes the records of each transaction, such as withdrawal or deposit of money through vouchers. Tally.ERP 9 contains the following pre-defined ledgers:

- **Cash:** Refers to the ledger that is created under the Cash-in-hand group. In this ledger, you can specify the opening balance on the basis of the beginning date on the account books of the company.
- **Profit & Loss A/c:** Refers to the ledger that is created under the Primary group. The profit and loss of the previous financial year is considered as the opening balance for this ledger.

Note: The name of the Cash ledger can be altered and deleted, whereas the Profit & Loss A/c ledger can be modified but cannot be deleted.

You can create single as well as multiple ledgers in Tally.

Creating a Single Ledger

To create a single ledger, you need to specify information such as the name of the parent group as well as the name, alias, mailing details, and opening balance of the ledger.

Perform the following steps to create a single ledger:

1. *Double-click* the **Accounts Info.** option in the **Gateway of Tally** menu.

   The **Accounts Info.** menu appears.

2. *Double-click* the **Ledgers** option in the **Accounts Info.** menu.

   The **Ledgers** menu appears (Fig.TL-4.6).

3. *Double-click* the **Create** option under the **Single Ledger** section in the **Ledgers** menu, as shown in Fig.TL-4.6:

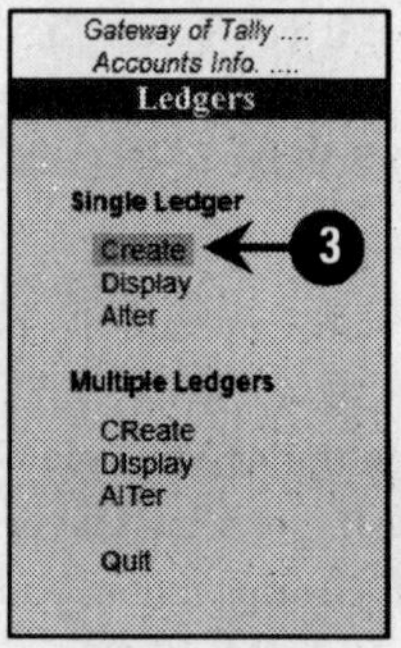

Fig.TL-4.6

   The **Ledger Creation** screen appears (Fig.TL-4.7).

4. *Type* the name of the ledger beside the **Name** option. In our case, we have typed **Trinity Soft. Del's Capital** (Fig.TL-4.7).
5. *Type* an alias for the ledger beside the **(alias)** option. In our case, we have typed **TSD Capital** (Fig.TL-4.7).
6. *Press* the **Enter** key twice. The **List of Groups** menu appears (Fig.TL-4.7).
7. *Double-click* the desired parent group in the **List of Groups** menu for the **Under** option. In our case, we have double-clicked the **Capital Account** group, as shown in Fig.TL-4.7:

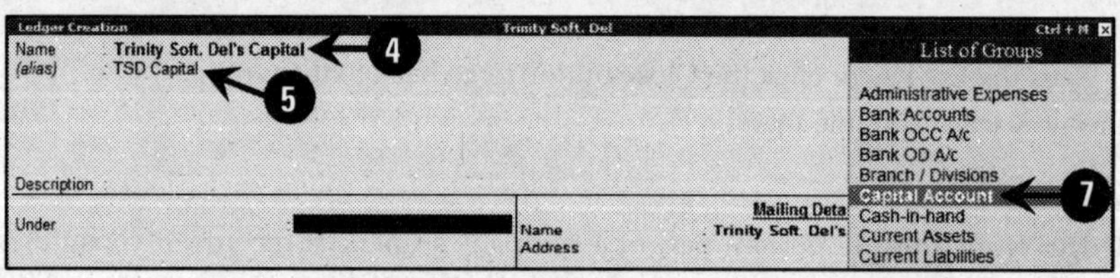

Fig.TL-4.7

8. *Type* the correspondence name beside the **Name** option under the **Mailing Details** section. You can type either the name of the ledger or some different name as per your requirement. In our case, we have typed the name of the ledger, i.e., **Trinity Soft. Del's Capital** (Fig.TL-4.8).
9. *Type* the mailing address beside the **Address** option. In our case, we have typed **19-A, Rama Garden, Karawal Nagar** (Fig.TL-4.8).
10. *Press* the **Enter** key twice. The **List of Countries** menu appears.
11. *Double-click* the country in the **List of Countries** menu for the **Country** option. In our case, we have double-clicked the **India** option (Fig.TL-4.8).

    The **List of States** menu appears.

12. *Double-click* the state in the **List of States** menu for the **State** option. In our case, we have double-clicked the **Delhi** option (Fig.TL-4.8).
13. *Type* the pin code beside the **Pincode** option. In our case, we have typed **110094** (Fig.TL-4.8).
14. *Enter* the amount beside the **Opening Balance** option. In our case, we have entered **75,000.00 Cr** (Fig.TL-4.8).
15. *Press* the **Enter** key. The **Accept ?** message box appears (Fig.TL-4.8).

16. *Click* **Yes** in the **Accept ?** message box to create the ledger with the specified information, as shown in Fig.TL-4.8:

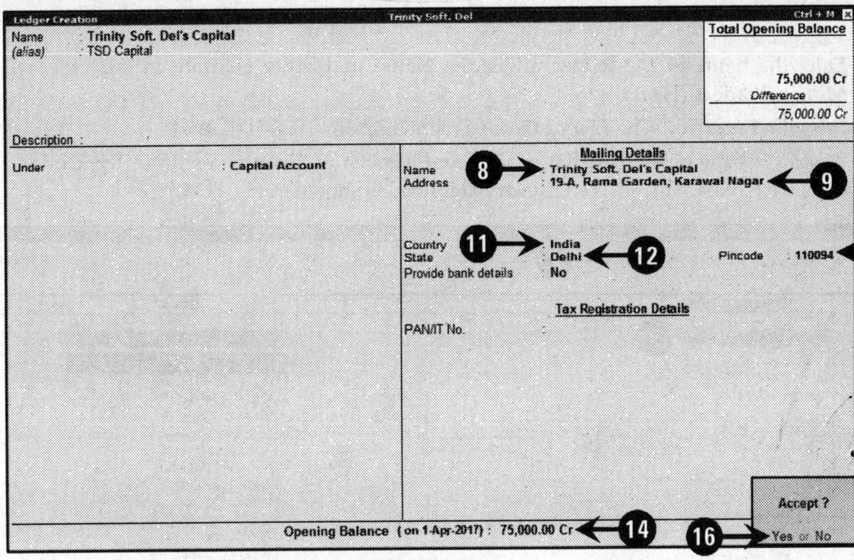

Fig.TL-4.8

Display a Single Ledger

You can view the name of the parent account group and name, alias, mailing details, and opening balance of the ledger. Perform the following steps to display a single ledger created in Tally:

1. *Double-click* the **Display** option under the **Single Ledger** section in the **Ledgers** menu.
   The **Select Ledger** screen appears with the list of created ledgers.
2. *Select* the ledger that you want to display from the **List of Ledgers** menu.
   The **Ledger Display** screen appears with information pertaining to the selected ledger.

Alter a Single Ledger

Sometimes after creating a ledger, you need to modify its details. Perform the following steps to alter a single ledger:

1. *Double-click* the **Alter** option under the **Single Ledger** section in the **Ledgers** menu.
   The **Select Ledger** screen appears with the list of created ledgers.
2. *Select* the ledger that you want to alter from the **List of Ledgers** menu.
   The **Ledger Alteration** screen for the selected ledger appears.
3. *Make* some changes in the ledger.
4. *Press* the **Enter** key until the **Accept ?** message box appears.
5. *Click* **Yes** in the **Accept ?** message box to save the changes.

Creating Multiple Ledgers

To create multiple ledgers, you need to specify information such as the name of the parent group, name of the ledger, and opening balance.

Perform the following steps to create multiple ledgers:

1. *Double-click* the **CReate** option under the **Multiple Ledgers** section in the **Ledgers** menu.
   The **Multi Ledger Creation** screen appears (Fig.TL-4.9).
2. *Double-click* the desired group in the **List of Groups** menu for the **Under Group** option. In our case, we have double-clicked the **All Items** group (Fig.TL-4.9).

Note: If you have selected the group name in the Under Group option, the Under column is automatically skipped. If the All Items group is selected from the List of Groups menu for the Under Group option, you need to enter the group name for the Under column.

3. *Enter* the name of the ledger under the **Name of Ledger** column. In our case, we have entered **Mohan Traders** (Fig.TL-4.9).
4. *Press* the **Enter** key. The **List of Groups** menu appears (Fig.TL-4.9).
5. *Double-click* the desired parent group from the **List of Groups** menu for the **Under** column. In our case, we have double-clicked **Sundry Debtors**, as shown in Fig.TL-4.9:

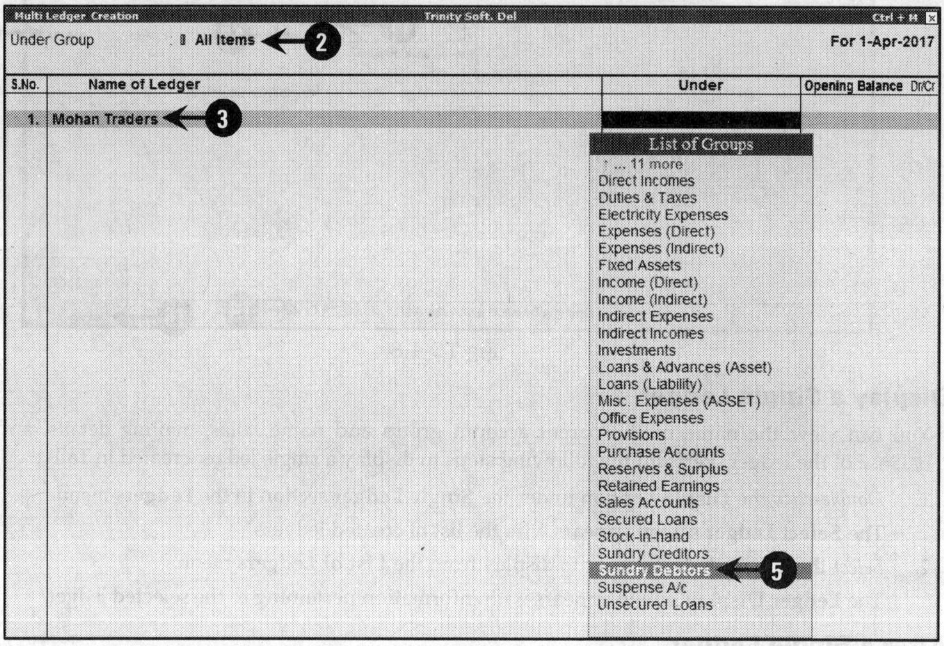

Fig.TL-4.9

6. *Enter* the opening balance under the **Opening Balance** column. In our case, we have entered **20,000.00** (Fig.TL-4.10).
7. *Specify* whether the opening balance of the ledger is debited or credited under the **Dr/Cr** column. In our case, we have specified **Dr** (Fig.TL-4.10).
8. *Repeat* steps 3-7 for creating more ledgers. In our case, we have created the following ledgers, listed in Table 4.1:

Table 4.1: Ledger Information

Ledger Name	Parent Group	Opening Balance	Dr/Cr
Land & Building	Fixed Assets	1,80,000.00	Dr
SBI Bank	Bank Accounts	80,000.00	Dr
Yash Traders	Sundry Creditors	40,000.00	Cr

9. *Press* the **Enter** key until the **Accept ?** message box appears (Fig.TL-4.10).

10. *Click* **Yes** in the **Accept ?** message box to create multiple ledgers, as shown in Fig.TL-4.10:

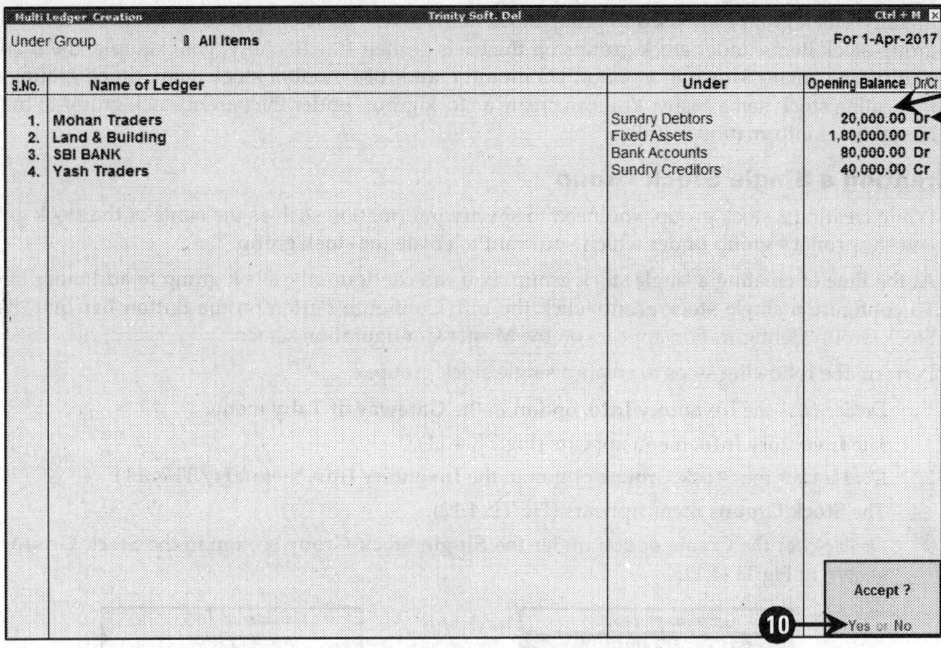

Fig.TL-4.10

Display Multiple Ledgers

Perform the following steps to display multiple ledgers in Tally:

1. *Click* the **DIsplay** option under the **Multiple Ledger** section in the **Ledgers** menu.
   The **Select Group** screen appears with the **List of Groups** menu.
2. *Select* the group whose ledgers you want to display from the **List of Groups** menu.
   The **Multi Ledger Display** screen appears with information pertaining to the selected group.

Alter Multiple Ledger

Perform the following steps to alter multiple ledgers:

1. *Click* the **AlTer** option under the **Multiple Ledger** in the **Ledgers** menu.
   The **Select Group** screen appears with the **List of Groups** menu.
2. *Select* the group whose ledgers you want to alter from the **List of Groups** menu.
   The **Multi Ledger Alteration** screen appears with information pertaining to the selected group.
3. *Make* some changes in the ledgers.
4. *Press* the **Enter** key until the **Accept ?** message box appears.
5. *Click* **Yes** in the **Accept ?** message box to save the changes.

Let us now learn to create inventory masters in Tally.ERP 9 in the next section.

Creating Inventory Masters in Tally.ERP 9

Tally.ERP allows you to manage goods and services of a business with the help of inventory masters. Inventory is the quantity of goods or materials that are stored at any given time and held for some purpose and use. In other words, inventory simply means the goods and services that a business holds in stock. In Tally, you can define the inventory by creating stock groups, stock categories, godowns, units of measure, and stock items.

Let us learn about all these in the following sections, starting with stock groups.

Stock Groups

In Tally, stock groups are used to group stock items on the basis of their common behavior. You can also group stock items under stock groups on the basis of their functionality. For example, the monitor stock group can contain Samsung monitor, LG monitor, and IBM monitor stock items. Stock groups are useful in locating stock items easily. You can create a stock group under the parent stock group to maintain the hierarchy of information in Tally.

Creating a Single Stock Group

While creating a stock group, you need to specify information such as the name of the stock group, alias, and the primary group under which you want to create the stock group.

At the time of creating a single stock group, you can configure the stock group to add more information. To configure a single stock group, click the F12: Configure button on the Button Bar that displays the Stock Group Configuration appears on the Master Configuration screen.

Perform the following steps to create a single stock group:

1. *Double-click* the **Inventory Info.** option in the **Gateway of Tally** menu.

   The **Inventory Info.** menu appears (Fig.TL-4.11).
2. *Double-click* the **Stock Groups** option in the **Inventory Info.** menu (Fig.TL-4.11).

   The **Stock Groups** menu appears (Fig.TL-4.12).
3. *Double-click* the **Create** option under the **Single Stock Group** section in the **Stock Groups** menu, as shown in Fig.TL-4.12:

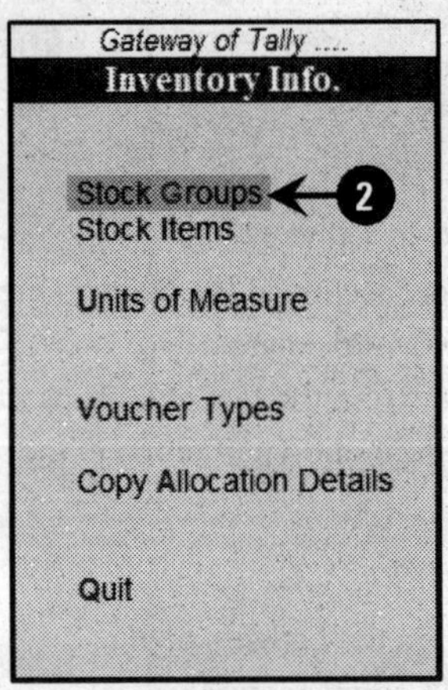

Fig.TL-4.11

Fig.TL-4.12

   The **Stock Group Creation** screen appears (Fig.TL-4.13).
4. *Type* the name of the stock group beside the **Name** option. In our case, we have typed **Computer** (Fig.TL-4.13).
5. *Type* an alias for the group beside the **(alias)** option. In our case, we have left it blank (Fig.TL-4.13).
6. *Press* the **Enter** key to go to the **Under** option. The **List of Groups** menu appears.
7. *Double-click* the desired parent stock group in the **List of Groups** menu. In our case, we have double-clicked the **Primary** group (Fig.TL-4.13).
8. *Set* the **Should quantities of items be added** option to **Yes** (Fig.TL-4.13).
9. *Press* the **Enter** key until the **Accept ?** message box appear (Fig.TL-4.13).

10. *Click* **Yes** in the **Accept ?** message box to create the stock group, as shown in Fig.TL-4.13:

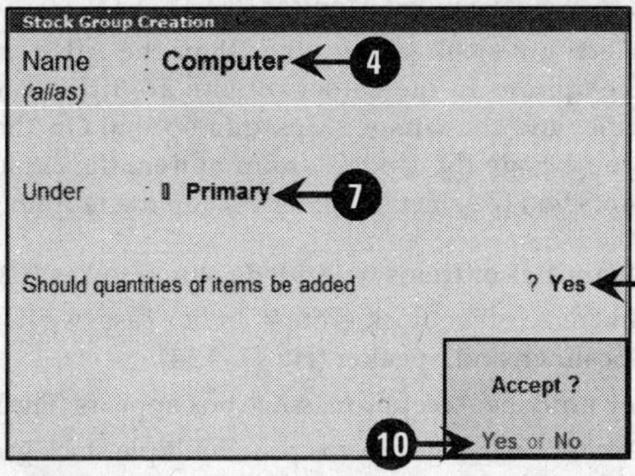

Fig.TL-4.13

A blank Stock Group Creation screen appears where you can create another stock group, if required.

Displaying a Single Stock Group

After creating a single stock group, you can display its details, such as the name and alias of the stock group.

Perform the following steps to display a single stock group:

1. *Double-click* the **Display** option under the **Single Stock Group** section in the **Stock Groups** menu. The **Select Stock Group** screen appears with the **List of Stock Groups** menu.
2. *Double-click* the stock group whose details you want to display in the **List of Stock Groups** menu. The **Stock Group Display** screen appears, displaying the details of the selected stock group.
3. *Press* the **Esc** key to close the **Stock Group Display** screen.

Altering a Single Stock Group

You can also alter the details of a single stock group by using the Alter option in the Stock Groups menu.

Perform the following steps to alter a single stock group:

1. *Double-click* the **Alter** option under the **Single Stock Group** section in the **Stock Groups** menu. The **Select Stock Group** screen appears with the **List of Stock Groups** menu.
2. *Double-click* the stock group whose details you want to alter, in the **List of Stock Groups** menu. The **Stock Group Alteration** screen appears.
3. *Make* the required changes in the screen.
4. *Press* the **Enter** key until the **Accept ?** message box appears.
5. *Click* **Yes** in the **Accept ?** message box to save the changes.

Note

You can delete a stock group by pressing the Alt+D keys in the single alteration mode.

Creating Multiple Stock Groups

In multiple stock groups, new stock groups are created under a single parent group.

Perform the following steps to create multiple stock groups:

1. *Double-click* the **CReate** option under the **Multiple Stock Groups** section in the **Stock Groups** menu. The **Multi Stock Group Creation** screen appears.
2. *Double-click* the desired parent stock group in the **List of Groups** menu for the **Under Group** option. In our case, we have double-clicked the **Computer** stock group (Fig.TL-4.14).

3. *Type* the name of the sub-stock group that you want to create under the **Name of Stock Group** column. In our case, we have typed **Monitor** (Fig.TL-4.14).

Note: **If you select any stock group other than the All Items group beside the Under Group option, the options in the Under column are filled automatically with the selected stock group name, and the cursor skips this option. On the other hand, if you select the All Items group beside the Under Group option, the cursor does not skip the Under column and prompts you to select the parent group name from the List of Groups menu.**

4. *Set* the **Should Quantities of Items be Added** column to **Yes** (Fig.TL-4.14).

   Similarly, you can create other stock groups. In our case, we have created three more stock groups, namely, **Printer**, **Scanner**, and **Speaker** (Fig.TL-4.14).

5. *Press* the **Enter** key until the **Accept ?** message box appears (Fig.TL-4.14).
6. *Click* **Yes** in the **Accept ?** message box to create multiple stock groups, as shown in Fig.TL-4.14:

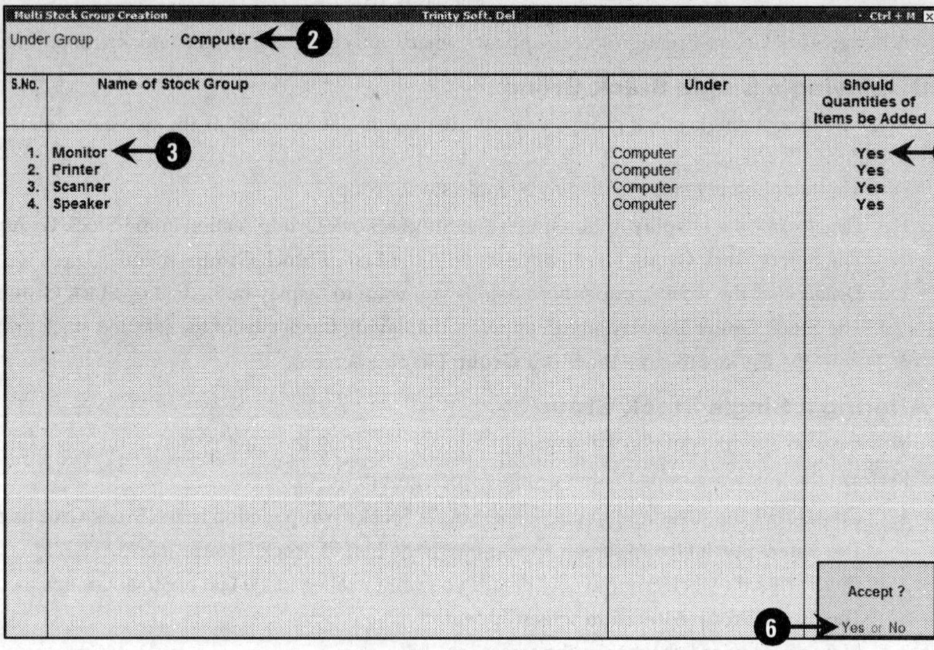

Fig.TL-4.14

Displaying Multiple Stock Groups

Perform the following steps to display multiple stock groups:

1. *Double-click* the **DIsplay** option under the **Multiple Stock Groups** section in the **Stock Groups** menu.

   The **Select Stock Group** screen appears with the **List of Stock Groups** menu.

2. *Double-click* the group whose details you want to display, in the **List of Stock Groups** menu.

   The **Multi Stock Group Display** screen appears, displaying the details of the selected group.

Altering Multiple Stock Groups

Similar to altering a single stock group, you can also alter the details of multiple stock groups.

Perform the following steps to alter multiple stock groups:

1. *Double-click* the **AlTer** option under the **Multiple Stock Groups** section in the **Stock Groups** menu.

   The **Select Stock Group** screen appears with the **List of Stock Groups** menu.

2. *Double-click* the stock group whose details you want to alter in the **List of Stock Groups** menu.

   The **Multi Stock Group Alteration** screen appears.
3. *Make* the desired changes in the screen as per the requirements.
4. *Press* the **Enter** key until the **Accept ?** message box appears.
5. *Click* **Yes** in the **Accept ?** message box to save the changes.

Note: **You cannot delete a stock group in the multiple alteration mode.**

After learning about stock groups, let us now learn about stock categories.

Stock Categories

Stock categories are used to store similar types of stock items. In Tally, you can create single as well as multiple stock categories. For example, the Samsung monitor stock category can contain Samsung 15 inches and Samsung 17 inches monitors. To create a stock category, you need to enable the Maintain stock categories option.

Perform the following steps to enable the Maintain stock categories option:

1. *Click* the **F11: Features** button on the Button Bar.

   The **Company Features** menu appears.
2. *Double-click* the **Inventory Features** option in the **Company Features** menu.

   The **Company Operations Alteration** screen appears with **Inventory Features** (Fig.TL-4.15).
3. *Set* the **Maintain stock categories** option to **Yes** under the **Storage and Classification** section (Fig.TL-4.15).
4. *Press* the **Enter** key until the **Accept ?** message box appears (Fig.TL-4.15).
5. *Click* **Yes** in the **Accept ?** message box to save the changes, as shown in Fig.TL-4.15:

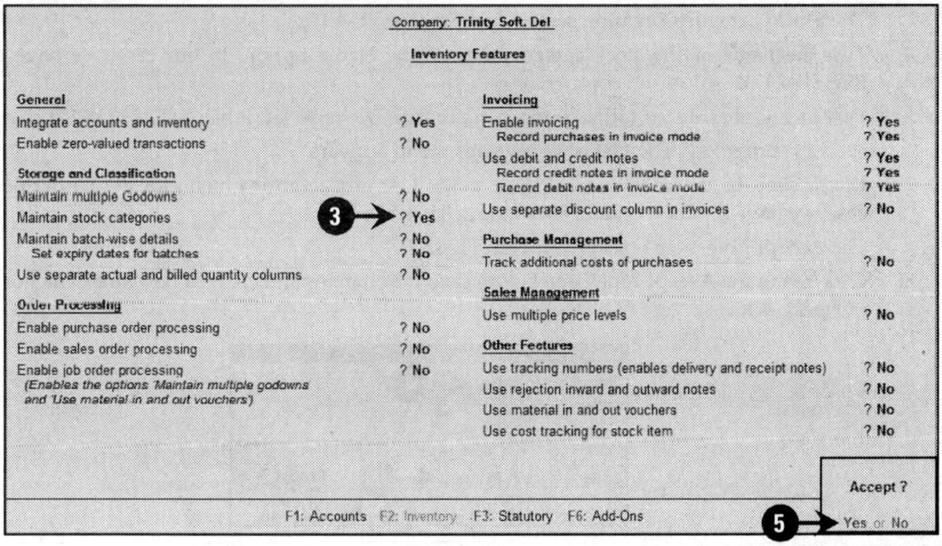

Fig.TL-4.15

Creating a Single Stock Category

While creating a stock category, you need to specify information such as the name of the stock category, alias, and the primary or sub-category under which you want to create a stock category. While creating a single stock category, you can click the F12: Configure button on the Button Bar to configure the stock category for adding more information.

Perform the following steps to create a single stock category:

1. *Double-click* the **Inventory Info.** option in the **Gateway of Tally** menu.

   The **Inventory Info.** menu appears.

2. *Double-click* the **StoCk Categories** option in the **Inventory Info.** menu, as shown in Fig.TL-4.16:

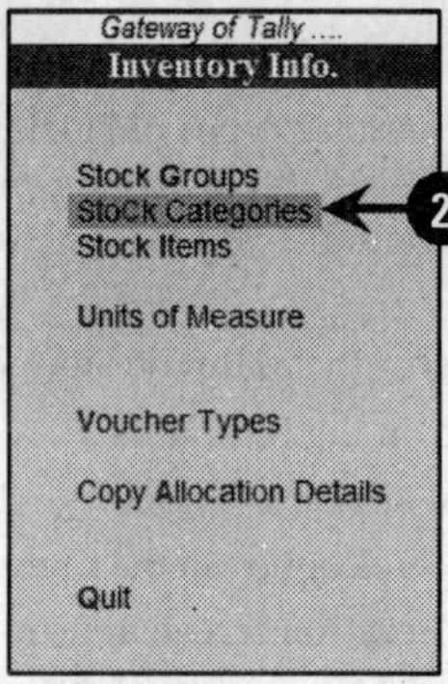

Fig.TL-4.16

   The **Stock Categories** menu appears.

3. *Double-click* the **Create** option under the **Single Stock Category** section in the **Stock Categories** menu.

   The **Stock Category Creation** screen appears (Fig.TL-4.17).

4. *Type* the name of the stock category beside the **Name** option. In our case, we have typed **Intex** (Fig.TL-4.17).
5. *Type* an alias beside the **(alias)** option. In our case, we have left it blank (Fig.TL-4.17).
6. *Press* the **Enter** key. The **List of Categories** menu appears.
7. *Double-click* the desired stock category in the **List of Categories** menu for the **Under** option. In our case, we have double-clicked **Primary** (Fig.TL-4.17).

   The **Accept ?** message box appears (Fig.TL-4.17).

8. *Click* **Yes** in the **Accept ?** message box to save the changes and create a new stock category, as shown in Fig.TL-4.17:

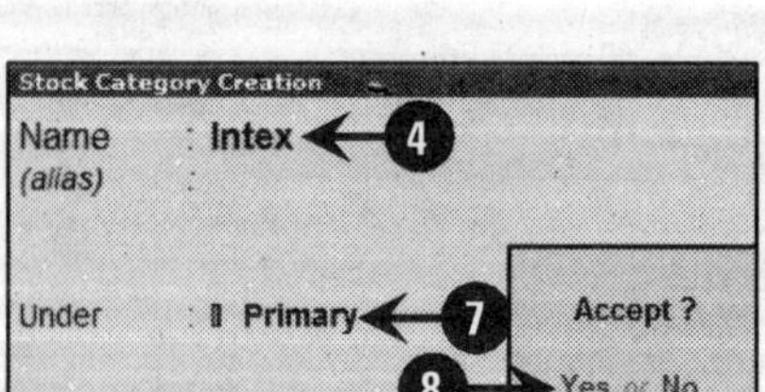

Fig.TL-4.17

Displaying a Single Stock Category

After creating a stock category, you can also display its details by using the Display option.

Perform the following steps to display a stock category:

1. *Double-click* the **Display** option under the **Single Stock Category** section in the **Stock Categories** menu.

   The **Select Stock Category** screen appears with the **List of Stock Categories** menu.

2. *Double-click* the stock category whose details you want to display in the **List of Stock Categories** menu.

   The **Stock Category Display** screen appears, displaying the details of the selected stock category.

Altering a Single Stock Category

You can alter or modify the details of an existing stock category by using the Alter option.

Perform the following steps to alter the details of a single stock category:

1. *Double-click* the **Alter** option under the **Single Stock Category** section in the **Stock Categories** menu.

   The **Select Stock Category** screen appears with the **List of Stock Categories** menu.

2. *Double-click* the stock category whose details you want to alter in the **List of Stock Categories** menu.

   The **Stock Category Alteration** screen appears.

3. *Make* the desired changes in the **Stock Category Alteration** screen as per your requirements.
4. *Press* the **Enter** key. The **Accept ?** message box appears.
5. *Click* **Yes** in the **Accept ?** message box to save the changes.

Note

You can delete a stock category by pressing the Alt + D keys in the single alteration mode.

Creating Multiple Stock Categories

As already discussed, multiple stock categories are created under a single parent stock category.

Perform the following steps to create multiple stock categories:

1. *Double-click* the **CReate** option under the **Multiple Stock Categories** section in the **Stock Categories** menu.

   The **Multi Stock Category Creation** screen appears (Fig.TL-4.18).

2. *Double-click* the desired parent stock category in the **List of Categories** menu for the **Under Category** option. In our case, we have double-clicked **All Items** (Fig.TL-4.18).
3. *Type* the name of the stock category under the **Name of Category** column. In our case, we have typed **LG** (Fig.TL-4.18).
4. *Press* the **Enter** key.

   The **List of Categories** menu appears.

5. *Double-click* the desired stock category in the **List of Categories** menu for the **Under** column. In our case, we have double-clicked **Primary** (Fig.TL-4.18).

   Similarly, you can create more stock categories. In our case, we have created two more stock categories, namely, **Samsung** and **Canon** (Fig.TL-4.18).

6. *Press* the **Enter** key until the **Accept ?** message box appears (Fig.TL-4.18).

7. *Click* **Yes** in the **Accept ?** message box to create multiple stock categories, as shown in Fig.TL-4.18:

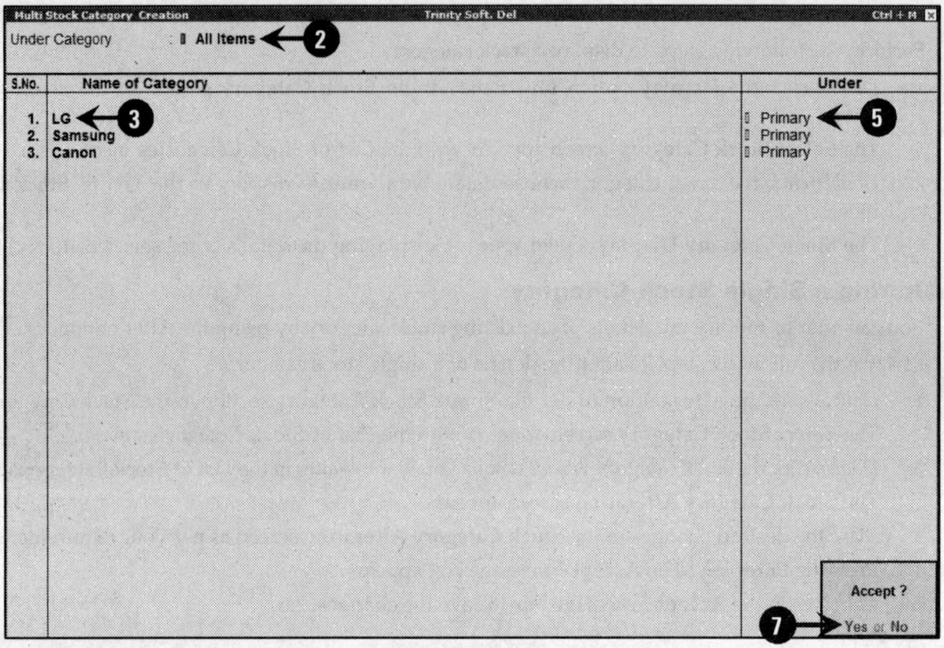

Fig.TL-4.18

Displaying Multiple Stock Categories

Perform the following steps to display multiple stock categories:

1. *Double-click* the **DIsplay** option under the **Multiple Stock Categories** section in the **Stock Categories** menu.

   The **Select Stock Category** screen appears with the **List of Stock Categories** menu.

2. *Double-click* the stock category whose details you want to display in the **List of Stock Categories** menu.

   The **Multi Stock Category Display** screen appears, displaying the details of the selected stock category.

Altering Multiple Stock Categories

After creating multiple stock categories, you can alter their details, if required. Perform the following steps to alter multiple stock categories:

1. *Double-click* the **AlTer** option under the **Multiple Stock Categories** section in the **Stock Categories** menu.

   The **Select Stock Category** screen appears with the **List of Stock Categories** menu.

2. *Double-click* the parent stock category that you want to alter in the **List of Stock Categories** menu.

   The **Multi Stock Category Alteration** screen appears.

3. *Make* the required changes in the **Multi Stock Category Alteration** screen as per the requirements.
4. *Press* the **Enter** key until the **Accept ?** message box appears.
5. *Click* **Yes** in the **Accept ?** message box to save the changes.

After learning about stock categories, let us now learn about godowns.

Godowns

Godowns are places, such as warehouses, where stock items are stored. In Tally, you can keep track of stock items in a godown. Godowns also provide the current stock position at any time, because Tally updates every inventory transaction automatically. Before creating a godown, you need to activate the Maintain multiple Godowns option.

Perform the following steps to activate the Godowns option:

1. *Click* the **F11: Features** button on the Button Bar of the **Gateway of Tally** screen.
   The **Company Features** menu appears.
2. *Double-click* the **Inventory Features** option in the **Company Features** menu.
   The **Company Operations** Alteration screen appears with Inventory Features (Fig.TL-4.19).
3. *Set* the **Maintain multiple Godowns** option to **Yes** under the **Storage and Classification** section (Fig.TL-4.19).
4. *Press* the **Enter** key until the **Accept** ? message box appears (Fig.TL-4.19).
5. *Click* **Yes** in the **Accept** ? message box, as shown in Fig.TL-4.19:

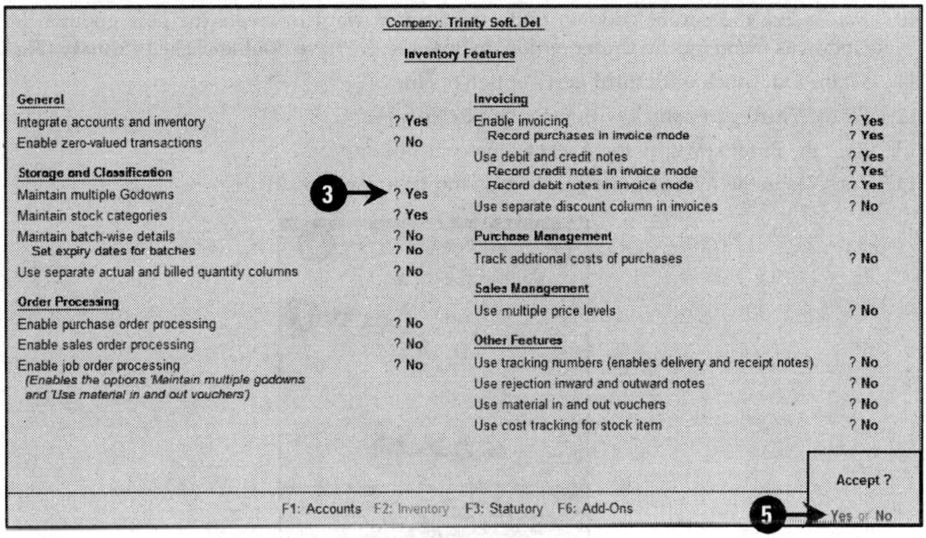

Fig.TL-4.19

Creating a Single Godown

While creating a single godown, you can configure it to add more information. To configure a single godown, you need to click the F12: Configure button on the Button Bar.

Perform the following steps to create a single godown:

1. *Double-click* the **GoDowns** option in the **Inventory Info.** menu.
   The **Godowns** menu appears.
2. *Double-click* the **Create** option under the **Single Godown** section to create a single godown
   The **Godown Creation** screen appears.
3. *Click* the **F12: Configure** button on the **Button Bar**
   The **Master Configuration** screen appears and shows **Godown Configuration** (Fig.TL-4.20).

4. *Set* the **Provide address for Godowns** option to **Yes**, as shown in Fig.TL-4.20:

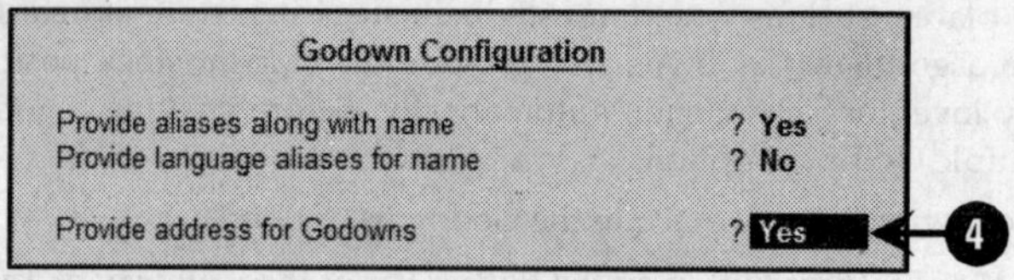

Fig.TL-4.20

5. *Press* the **Enter** key. The **Godown Creation** screen reappears (Fig.TL-4.21).
6. *Type* the name of the godown beside the **Name** option. In our case, we have typed **Moti Bagh Godown** (Fig.TL-4.21).
7. *Type* an alias beside the **(alias)** option. In our case, we have left it blank (Fig.TL-4.21).
8. *Type* the address of the godown beside the **Address** option. In our case, we have typed **F-6. Moti Bagh New Delhi** (Fig.TL-4.21).
9. *Press* the **Enter** key until the **List of Godowns** menu appears.
10. *Double-click* the parent godown under which you want to create the new godown in the **List of Godowns** menu for the **Under** option. In our case, we have double-clicked **Primary** (Fig.TL-4.21).
11. *Set* the **Our Stock with third party** option to **No.**
12. *Set* the **Third party stock with us** option to **No.**
13. *Press* the **Enter** key until the **Accept ?** message box appears.
14. *Click* **Yes** in the **Accept ?** message box, as shown in Fig.TL-4.21:

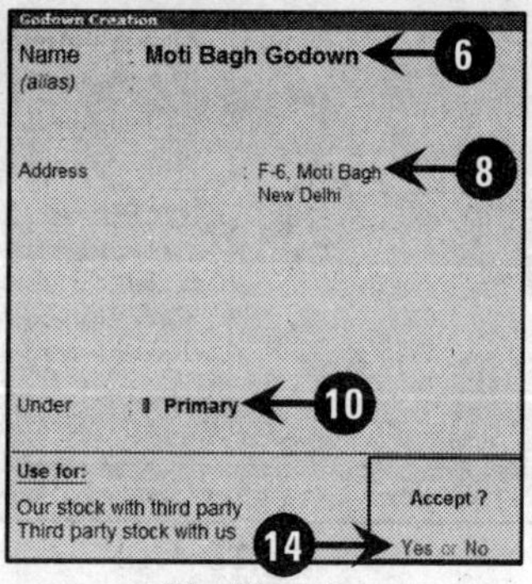

Fig.TL-4.21

A blank Godown Creation screen reappears. Now, you can create more godowns or press the Esc key to exit the screen.

Displaying a Single Godown

After creating a godown, you can display its details.

Perform the following steps to display a single godown:

1. *Double-click* the **Display** option under the **Single Godown** section in the **Godowns** menu. The **Select Godown** screen appears with the **List of Godowns** menu.
2. *Double-click* the godown whose details you want to display, in the **List of Godowns** menu. The **Godown Display** screen appears, displaying the details of the selected godown.

Altering a Single Godown

You can also alter the details of an existing godown by using the Alter option.

Perform the following steps to alter the details of a single godown:

1. *Double-click* the **Alter** option under the **Single Godown** section in the **Godowns** menu.

The **Select Godown** screen appears with the **List of Godowns** menu.

2. *Double-click* the godown that you want to alter in the **List of Godowns** menu.

   The **Godown Alteration** screen appears.
3. *Make* the required changes in the details of the godown as per the requirements.
4. *Press* the **Enter** key until the **Accept ?** message box appears.
5. *Click* **Yes** in the **Accept ?** message box to save the changes.

Creating Multiple Godowns

In Tally, apart from creating a single godown, you can also create multiple godowns by specifying the name of the parent group.

Perform the following steps to create multiple godowns:

1. *Double-click* the **CReate** option under the **Multiple Godowns** section in the **Godowns** menu.

   The **Multi Godown Creation** screen appears with the **List of Godowns** menu (Fig.TL-4.22).
2. *Double-click* the desired parent godown in the **List of Godowns** menu for the **Under Godown** option. In our case, we have double-clicked **Moti Bagh Godown** (Fig.TL-4.22).
3. *Type* the name of the sub-godown under the **Name** column. In our case, we have typed **Branch One** (Fig.TL-4.22).

Note: **When you specify the name of a sub-godown, the name of the parent godown automatically appears under the Under column.**

Similarly, you can enter more sub-godowns. In our case, we have entered **Branch Two, Branch Three,** and **Branch Four** (Fig.TL-4.22).

4. *Press* the **Enter** key until the **Accept ?** message box appears.
5. *Click* **Yes** in the **Accept ?** message box to save multiple godowns, as shown in Fig.TL-4.22:

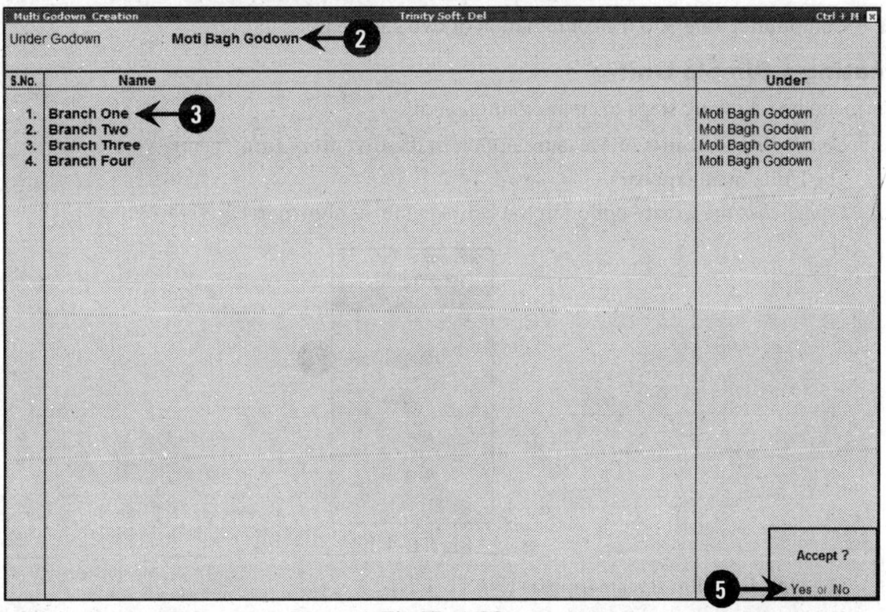

Fig.TL-4.22

Displaying Multiple Godowns

After creating multiple godowns, you can display their details.

Perform the following steps to display multiple godowns:

1. *Double-click* the **DIsplay** option under the **Multiple Godowns** section in the **Godowns** menu.
   The **Select Godown** screen appears with the **List of Godowns** menu.
2. *Double-click* the godown whose details you want to display in the **List of Godowns** menu.
   The **Multi Godown Display** screen appears, displaying the details of the selected godown.

Altering Multiple Godowns

Perform the following steps to alter the details of multiple godowns:

1. *Double-click* the **AlTer** option under the **Multiple Godowns** section in the **Godowns** menu.
   The **Select Godown** screen appears with the **List of Godowns** menu.
2. *Double-click* the godown that you want to alter in the **List of Godowns** menu.
   The **Multi Godown Alteration** screen appears.
3. *Make* the required alterations in the screen as per the requirements.
4. *Press* the **Enter** key until the **Accept ?** message box appears.
5. *Click* **Yes** in the **Accept ?** message box to save the changes.

After learning about godowns, let us now learn about units of measure.

Units of Measure

The quantity of stock items is measured in units. You need to create units for stock items because stock items are purchased or sold on the basis of quantity. For example, monitors, books, and chairs are measured in number; therefore, in this case, number is the measurement unit. Tally provides two types of units, which are as follows:

- **Simple:** Refers to a single unit, such as pieces, numbers, kilograms, and grams
- **Compound:** Refers to the combination of two simple units

Creating a Simple Unit

Perform the following steps to create a simple unit:

1. *Double-click* the **Units of Measure** option in the **Inventory Info.** menu.
   The **Units** menu appears.
2. *Double-click* the **Create** option in the **Units** menu, as shown in Fig.TL-4.23:

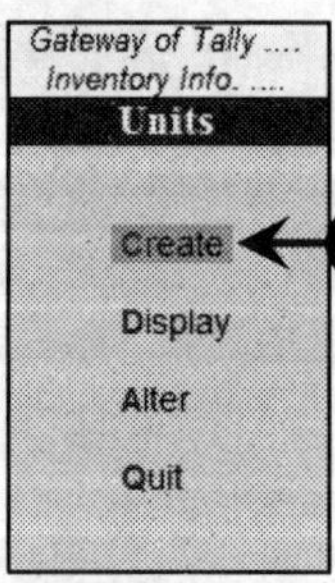

Fig.TL-4.23

   The **Unit Creation** screen appears (Fig.TL-4.24).
3. *Double-click* the type of unit that you want to create, in the **Types of Units** menu for the **Type** option. In our case, we have double-clicked **Simple** (Fig.TL-4.24).

4. *Type* the unit symbol beside the **Symbol** option. In our case, we have typed **doz** (Fig.TL-4.24).
5. *Type* the formal name for the unit beside the **Formal Name** option. In our case, we have typed **Dozen** (Fig.TL-4.24).
6. *Type* the desired number in the **Number of Decimal Places** option if you want to display the unit along with the decimal place. In our case, we have left it blank (Fig.TL-4.24).
7. *Press* the **Enter** key. The **Accept ?** message box appears (Fig.TL-4.24).
8. *Click* **Yes** in the **Accept ?** message box to save the unit, as shown in Fig.TL-4.24:

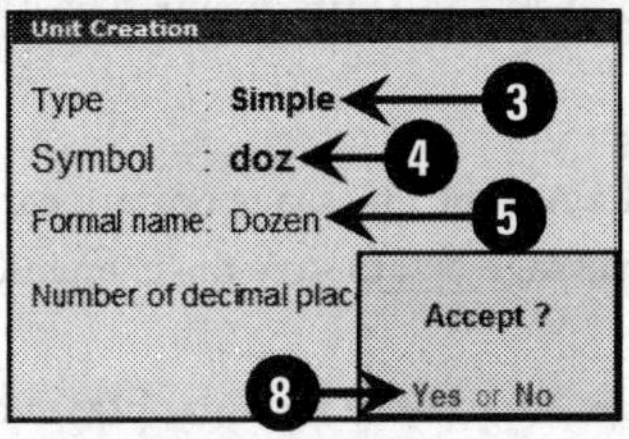

Fig.TL-4.24

Creating a Compound Unit

Perform the following steps to create a compound unit:

1. *Double-click* the **Units of Measure** option in the **Inventory Info.** menu. The **Units** menu appears.
2. *Double-click* the **Create** option in the **Units** menu.
   The **Unit Creation** screen appears.
3. *Double-click* the **Compound** option in the **Types of Units** menu (Fig.TL-4.25).
   The **Units** menu appears.
4. *Double-click* the desired option in the **Units** menu for the **First unit** option. In our case, we have double-clicked **MTR** (Fig.TL-4.25).
5. *Enter* the conversion factor under the **Conversion** option. In our case, we have entered **100** (Fig.TL-4.25).
6. *Double-click* the desired unit in the **Units** menu for the **Second unit** option. In our case, we have double-clicked **CM** (Fig.TL-4.25).
   The **Accept ?** message box appears (Fig.TL-4.26).
7. *Click* **Yes** in the **Accept ?** message box to save the compound unit, as shown in Fig.TL-4.26:

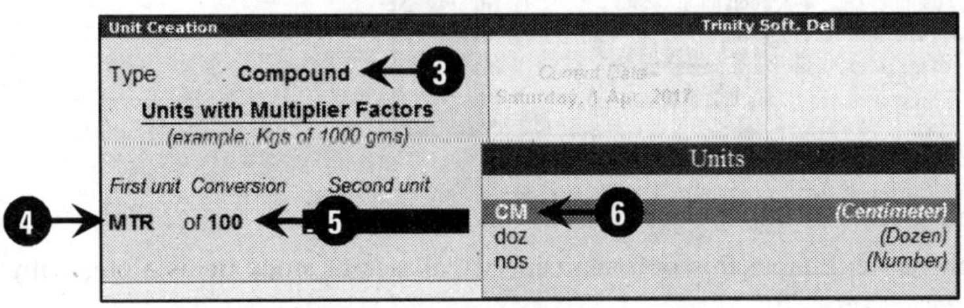

Fig.TL-4.25

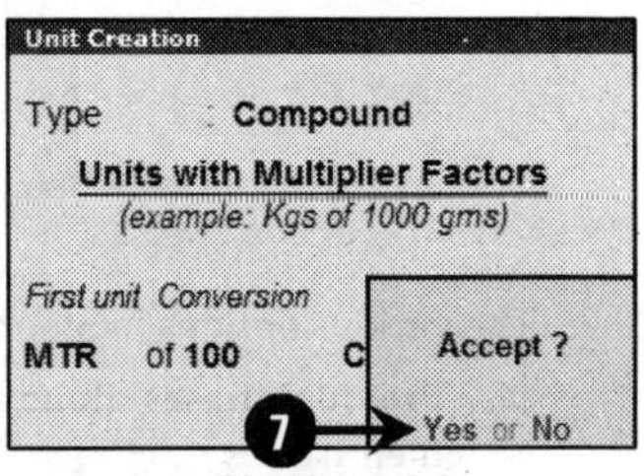

Fig.TL-4.26

A blank **Unit Creation** screen reappears. Press the **Esc** key to quit the screen.

Displaying a Unit

Perform the following steps to display a unit:

1. *Double-click* the **Display** option in the **Units** menu.
   The **Select Unit** screen appears with the **Units** menu.

2. *Double-click* the unit that you want to display in the **Units** menu.

   The **Unit Display** screen appears, displaying the details of the selected unit.

Altering Units

Perform the following steps to alter a unit:

1. *Double-click* the **Alter** option in the **Units** menu.

   The **Select Unit** screen appears with the **Units** menu.
2. *Double-click* the desired unit in the **Units** menu. The **Unit Alteration** screen of the selected unit appears.
3. *Make* the required changes.
4. *Press* the **Enter** key until the **Accept ?** message box appears.
5. *Click* **Yes** in the **Accept ?** message box to save the changes.

Note: **You cannot alter the Number of Decimal places option in the alteration mode.**

After learning about units of measure, let us now learn about stock items.

Stock Items

Stock items are the goods that you manufacture or trade, such as a monitor, table, pen, and book. These stock items can be bought, sold, or issued for production purpose.

Creating a Single Stock Item

While creating a single stock item, you can configure it to add more information. To configure the stock item, you need to click the F12: Configure button on the Button Bar. The Master Configuration screen appears and displays various Stock Item Configuration options, as shown in Fig.TL-4.27:

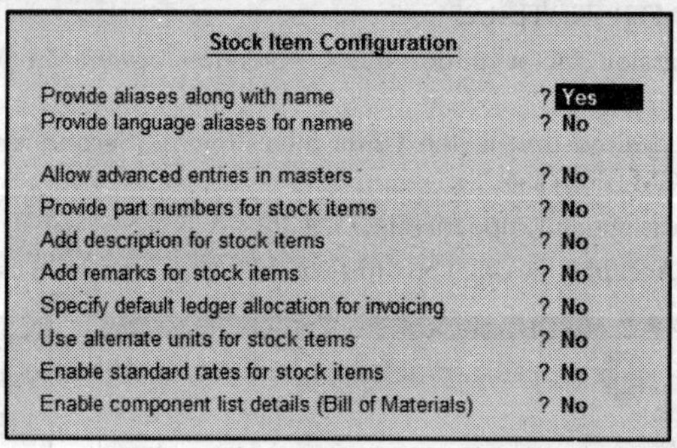

Fig.TL-4.27

The various options in Stock Item Configuration are described as follows:

- **Provide aliases along with name:** Enable this option to specify aliases of stock items along with their names
- **Provide language aliases along for names:** Enable this option to select the language of aliases of stock items along with their names
- **Allow advanced entries in masters:** Enable this option to specify advance masters entries in the stock item
- **Provide part numbers for stock items:** Enable this option to specify the part number of the stock item
- **Add description for stock items:** Enable this option to specify the description of the stock item
- **Add remarks for stock items:** Enable this option to specify remarks about the stock item

- **Specify default ledger allocation for invoicing:** Enable this option to specify the default ledger allocation for invoicing in the stock item
- **Use alternate units for stock items:** Enable this option to use alternative units for the stock item
- **Enable standard rates for stock items:** Enable this option to specify the standard rate of the stock item
- **Enable component list details (Bill of Materials):** Enable this option to specify the details of the stock item (Bill of Material)

Perform the following steps to create a stock item:

1. *Double-click* the **Stock Items** option in the **Inventory Info.** menu.
   The **Stock Items** menu appears.
2. *Double-click* the **Create** option under the **Single Stock Item** section in the **Stock Items** menu.
   The **Stock Item Creation** screen appears.

Note

The Rate of Duty option is visible when you set the Allow Invoicing option to Yes in Inventory Features.

3. *Type* the name of the stock item beside the **Name** option. In our case, we have typed **19 Inches Monitor** (Fig.TL-4.28).
4. *Type* an alias beside the **(alias)** option. In our case, we have left it blank.
5. *Press* the **Enter** key. The **List of Groups** menu appears.
6. *Double-click* the stock group under which you want to create a new stock item in the **List of Groups** menu for the **Under** option. In our case, we have double-clicked **Monitor** (Fig.TL-4.28).
   The **List of Categories** menu appears.
7. *Double-click* the stock category under which you want to create a new stock item in the **List of Categories** menu for the **Category** option. In our case, we have double-clicked **LG** (Fig.TL-4.28).
   The **Units** menu appears.
8. *Double click* the measurement unit for the stock item in the **Units** menu for the **Units** option. In our case, we have double-clicked **nos** (Fig.TL-4.28).
9. *Press* the **Enter** key to go to the **Quantity** option.
10. *Type* the quantity of the stock item under the **Quantity** option. In our case, we have entered **50**, as shown in Fig.TL-4.28:

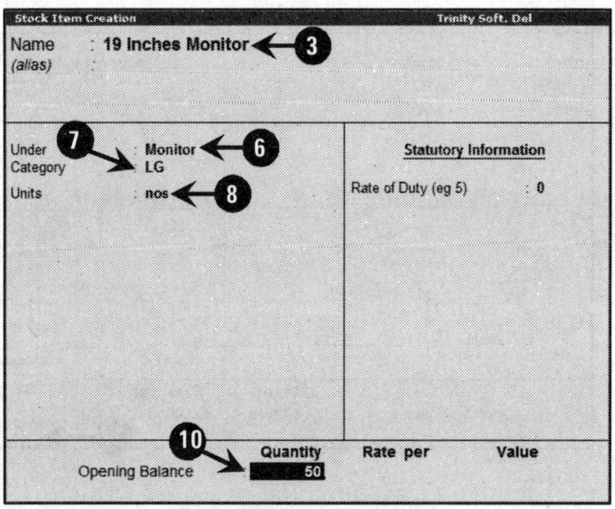

Fig.TL-4.28

11. *Press* the **Enter** key. The **Stock Item Allocation** screen appears with the **List of Godowns** menu.
12. *Double-click* the desired godown in the **List of Godowns** menu for the **Godown** option. In our case, we have double-clicked **Moti Bagh Godown** (Fig.TL-4.29).
13. *Enter* the quantity of the stock item equal to the quantity that you entered in the **Stock Item Creation** screen under the **Quantity** option. In our case, we have retained the same quantity, i.e. **50**, which was entered in the **Stock Item Creation** screen (Fig.TL-4.29).
14. *Enter* the price of the stock item under the **Rate** column. In our case, we have entered **5,000** (Fig.TL-4.29).
15. *Enter* the unit of the stock item under the **per** column. In our case, we have entered **nos** (Fig.TL-4.29).

    After entering all the values, Tally automatically performs the calculation and displays the total amount of the item under the **Amount** column, as shown in Fig.TL-4.29:

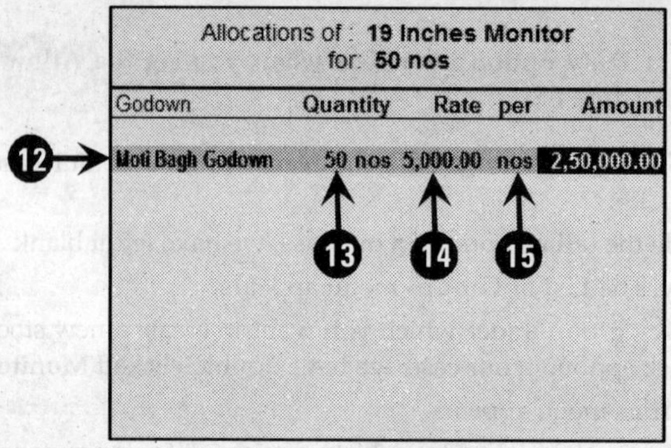

Fig.TL-4.29

16. *Press* the **Enter** key to go back to the **Stock Item Creation** screen.

    The **Accept ?** message box appears (Fig.TL-4.30).
17. *Click* **Yes** in the **Accept ?** message box to create the stock item, as shown in Fig.TL-4.30:

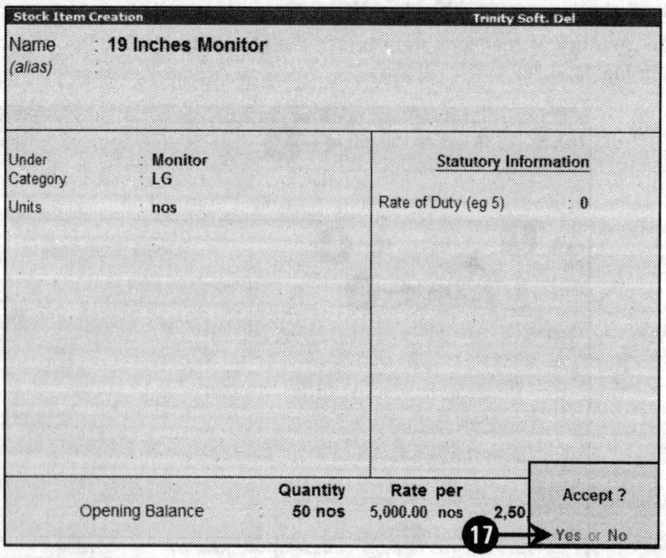

Fig.TL-4.30

Displaying a Single Stock Item

After creating a stock item, you can display its details by using the Display option.

Perform the following steps to display a single stock item:

1. *Double-click* the **Display** option under the **Single Stock Item** section in the **Stock Items** menu.
   The **Select Stock Item** screen appears with the **List of Stock Items** menu.
2. *Double-click* the stock item whose details you want to display, in the **List of Stock Items** menu.
   The **Stock Item Display** screen appears, displaying the details of the selected stock item.

Altering a Single Stock Item

After creating a stock item, you can alter its details by using the Alter option.

Perform the following steps to alter a single stock item:

1. *Double-click* the **Alter** option under the **Single Stock Item** section in the **Stock Items** menu.
   The **Select Stock Item** screen appears with the **List of Stock Items** menu.
2. *Double-click* the desired stock item in the **List of Stock Items** menu.
   The **Stock Item Alteration** screen appears.
3. *Make* the required changes in the screen.
4. *Press* the **Enter** key until the **Accept ?** message box appears.
5. *Click* **Yes** in **Accept ?** message box to save the changes.

Creating Multiple Stock Items

Perform the following steps to create multiple stock items:

1. *Double-click* the **CReate** option under the **Multiple Stock Items** section in the **Stock Items** menu.
   The **Multi Stock Item Creation** screen appears (Fig.TL-4.31).
2. *Double-click* the stock group under which you want to create multiple stock items in the **List of Groups** menu for the **Under Group** option. In our case, we have double-clicked **Monitor** (Fig.TL-4.31).
3. *Type* the name of the stock item under the **Name of Item** column. In our case, we have typed **21 Inches Monitor** (Fig.TL-4.31).

Note: **As you type the name of the stock item under the Name of Item column, the name of the stock group appears automatically under the Under column.**

4. *Press* the **Enter** key. The **List of Categories** menu appears.
5. *Double-click* the desired category in the **List of Categories** menu for the **Category** column. In our case, we have double-clicked **LG** (Fig.TL-4.31).
   The **Units** menu appears.
6. *Double-click* the desired unit in the **Units** menu for the **Units** column. In our case, we have double-clicked **nos** (Fig.TL-4.31).

7. *Enter* the opening quantity in the **Opening Qty** column. In our case, we have entered **25**, as shown in Fig.TL-4.31:

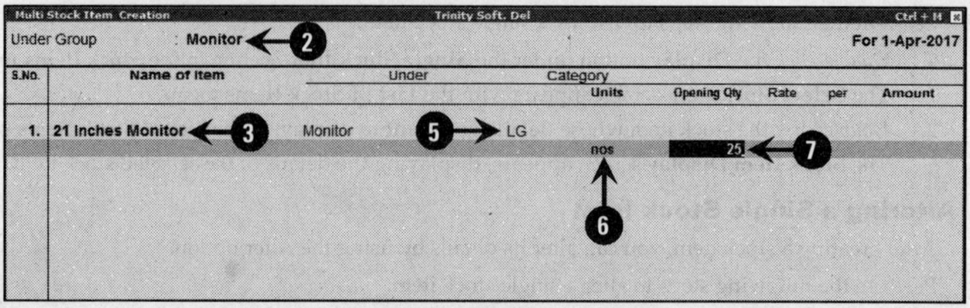

Fig.TL-4.31

8. *Press* the **Enter** key.

   The **Stock Item Allocation** screen appears with the **List of Godowns** menu.
9. *Double-click* the desired godown in the **List of Godowns** menu for the **Godown** column. In our case, we have double-clicked **Moti Bagh Godown** (Fig.TL-4.32).
10. *Enter* the quantity of the stock item equal to the quantity that you entered in the **Stock Item Creation** screen, under the **Quantity** column. In our case, we have retained the same quantity, i.e. **25**, which was entered in the **Stock Item Creation** screen (Fig.TL-4.32).
11. *Enter* the price of the stock item under the **Rate** column. In our case, we have entered **8800** (Fig.TL-4.32).
12. *Enter* the unit of the stock item under the **per** column. In our case, we have entered **nos** (Fig.TL-4.32).

    After entering all the values, Tally automatically performs the calculation and displays the total amount of the item under the **Amount** column, as shown in Fig.TL-4.32:

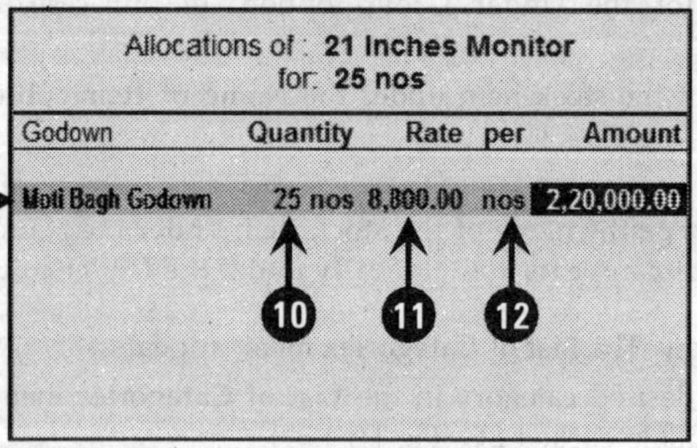

Fig.TL-4.32

13. *Press* the **Enter** key to open the **Multi Stock Item Creation** screen (Fig.TL-4.33).
14. *Repeat* steps 3-13 to enter another stock item. In our case, we have entered one more stock item, i.e., **17 Inches Monitor** of **Samsung** category (Fig.TL-4.33).
15. *Press* the **Enter** key until the **Accept ?** message box appears.

16. *Click* **Yes** in the **Accept ?** message box to create multiple stock items, as shown in Fig.TL-4.33:

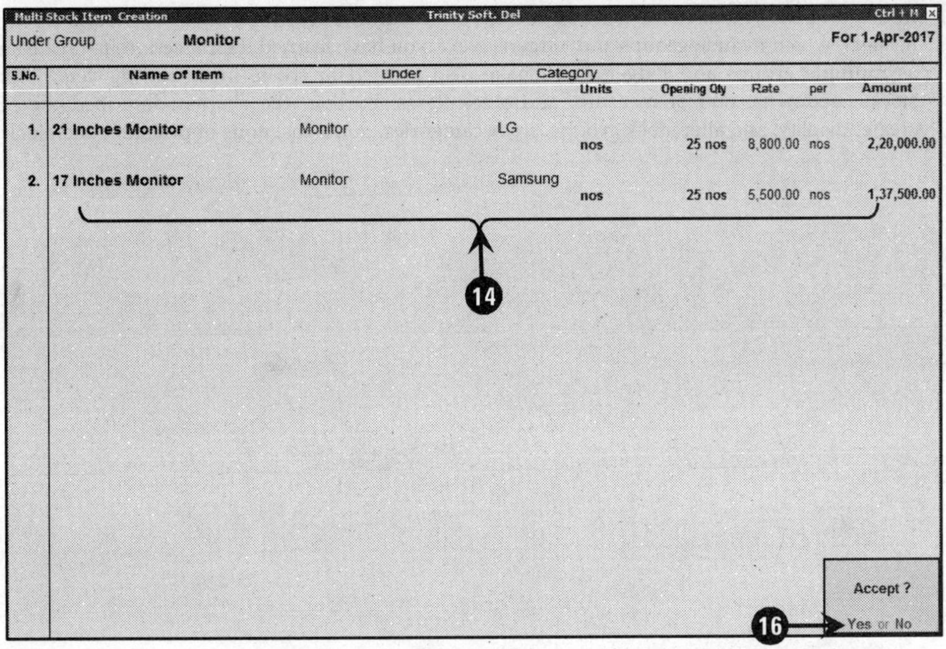

Fig.TL-4.33

Displaying Multiple Stock Items

Perform the following steps to display multiple stock items:

1. *Double-click* the **DIsplay** option under the **Multiple Stock Items** section in the **Stock Items** menu.

   The **Select Stock Group** screen appears with the **List of Stock Groups** menu.
2. *Double-click* the stock item that you want to display in the **List of Stock Groups** menu.

   The **Multi Stock Item Display** screen appears, displaying the details of the selected item.

Altering Multiple Stock Items

You can also alter the details of the existing multiple stock items.

Perform the following steps to alter multiple stock items:

1. *Double-click* the **AlTer** option under the **Multiple Stock Items** section in the **Stock Items** menu.

   The **Select Stock Group** screen appears with the **List of Stock Groups** menu.
2. *Double-click* the desired stock item in the **List of Stock Groups** menu.

   The **Multi Stock Item Alteration** screen appears.
3. *Make* the required changes.
4. *Press* the **Enter** key until the **Accept ?** message box appears.
5. *Click* **Yes** in the **Accept ?** message box to save the changes.

With this, we come to the end of the chapter. Let us summarize the key points discussed in the chapter.

Summary

In this chapter, you have learned about chart of accounts. Then, you have a learned to create accounting masters, which include groups and ledgers. Next, you have learned the procedure to create single as well as multiple groups and ledgers. You have also learned to create inventory masters, which includes stocks, godowns, unit of measure, and stock items. Further, the chapter described the procedure to create, display, and alter stock groups, stock categories, godowns, units of measure, and stock items.

CHAPTER

5

Working with Vouchers

In this Chapter:

- Creating a Voucher Type
- Accounting Vouchers
- Inventory Vouchers
- Order Processing
- Optional and Non-Accounting Vouchers

Introduction

A voucher is a document that records the details of the financial transactions of a company. When you record a transaction of a company in Tally, you need to specify the transaction's ledger name as well. This helps in maintaining consistency in accounts-related information. Tally provides different types of vouchers for different types of transactions. You can use the suitable voucher to enter details into ledgers for each transaction. The types of vouchers that Tally provides are accounting voucher, inventory voucher, and payroll voucher.

In this chapter, you learn about the concept of vouchers. You also learn about the process to create, display, and alter a voucher type. In addition, the chapter discusses the concept of accounting vouchers and the procedure to create them. You also learn about inventory vouchers and the procedure to create them. Further, you learn about order-processing vouchers and the procedure to create them. Towards the end of the chapter, you learn about the optional and non-accounting vouchers and the procedure to create them.

Creating a Voucher Type

While creating a voucher type, you need to specify information, such as the name of the voucher, alias of the voucher, name of the parent voucher, method of numbering the voucher, and effective dates of the voucher.

Perform the following steps to create a voucher type:

1. *Double-click* the **Accounts Info.** option in the **Gateway of Tally** menu. The **Accounts Info.** menu appears.
2. *Double-click* the **Voucher Types** option in the **Accounts Info.** menu. The **Voucher Types** menu appears.
3. *Double-click* the **Create** option in the **Voucher Types** menu. The **Voucher Type Creation** screen appears, which is divided into three sections—**General**, **Printing**, and **Name of Class** (Fig.TL-5.1).
4. *Enter* the name of the voucher beside the **Name** option. In our case, we have entered **Purchase Invoice** (Fig.TL-5.1).
5. *Type* the alias for the voucher beside the **(alias)** option. In our case, we have left it blank (Fig.TL-5.1). The **List of Voucher Types** menu appears.
6. *Double-click* the desired parent voucher type in the **List of Voucher Types** menu for the **Select type of voucher** option, to specify the category under which the voucher type is to be created. In our case, we have double-clicked **Purchase** (Fig.TL-5.1).

   When you select the type of voucher, the abbreviation for the selected voucher type appears beside the **Abbreviation** option as well as the **Enable default accounting allocations** and **Set/Alter Default Accounting Entries** options enable.
7. *Press* the **Enter** key. The **Methods of Numbering** menu appears.
8. *Double-click* the **Automatic** option from the **Methods of Numbering** menu for the **Method of voucher numbering** option (Fig.TL-5.1). When you select the **Automatic** option as the method of voucher numbering, the **Use advanced configuration** option gets enabled.
9. *Set* the remaining options under the **General** section as per your requirements (Fig.TL-5.1).
10. *Set* the **Print voucher after saving** option to No (Fig.TL-5.1).

Note

If you set the 'Print voucher after saving' option to Yes, each time you make changes to a voucher and save them, Tally will automatically send the voucher for printing.

11. *Enter* the name of the class under the **Name of Class** section. If you have a voucher class, specify it, otherwise you can skip it. In our case, we have skipped it (Fig.TL-5.1).
12. *Press* the **Enter** key. The **Accept ?** message box appears (Fig.TL-5.1).
13. *Click* **Yes** in the **Accept ?** message box to create the voucher, as shown in Fig.TL-5.1:

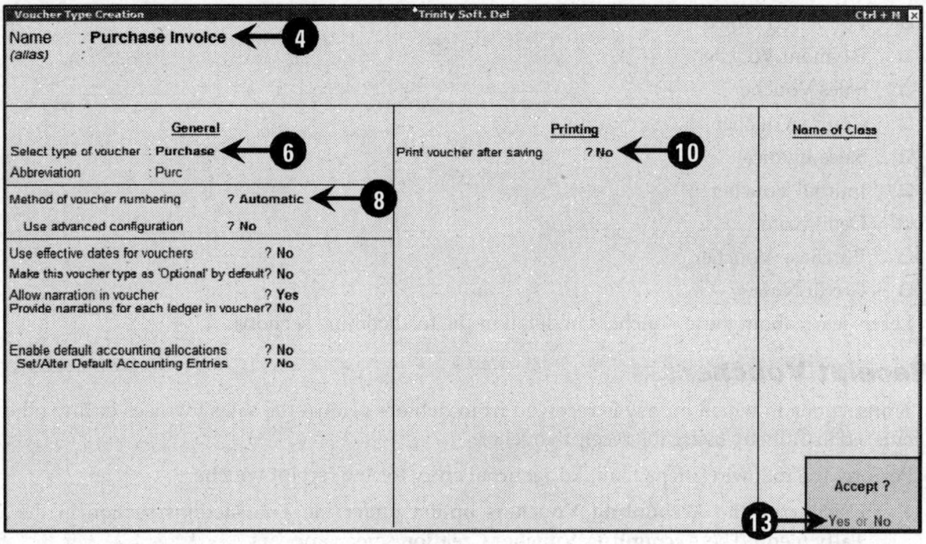

Fig.TL-5.1

Let us now learn how to display a voucher type.

Displaying a Voucher Type

After creating a voucher type, you can view its details. Perform the following steps to display a voucher type:

1. *Double-click* the **Display** option in the **Voucher Types** menu.
   The **Select Voucher Type** screen appears with the **List of Voucher Types** menu.
2. *Double-click* the voucher type, whose details you want to display, in the **List of Voucher Types** menu.
   The **Voucher Type Display** screen appears with the relevant information related to the selected voucher type.

Let us now learn how to alter a voucher type.

Altering a Voucher Type

After creating a voucher type, you might need to modify its details. You can easily do so by using the Voucher Types menu. Perform the following steps to alter/change a voucher type:

1. *Double-click* the **Alter** option in the **Voucher Types** menu.
   The **Select Voucher Type** screen appears with the **List of Voucher Types** menu.
2. *Double-click* the voucher type that you want to alter, in the **List of Voucher Types** menu. The **Voucher Type Alteration** screen appears.
3. *Change* the options in the **Voucher Type Alteration** screen as per your requirements.
4. *Press* the **Enter** key until the **Accept ?** message box appears.
5. *Click* **Yes** in the **Accept ?** message box to save the changes.

Let us now learn about the accounting vouchers.

Accounting Vouchers

Accounting vouchers are those vouchers that are used to record all accounts-related transactions. Some commonly used accounting vouchers are as follows:

- Receipt Voucher
- Purchase Invoice
- Payment Voucher
- Sales Voucher
- Contra Voucher
- Sales Invoice
- Journal Voucher
- Debit Note
- Purchase Voucher
- Credit Note

Let us learn about these vouchers in detail in the forthcoming sections.

Receipt Voucher

Transactions in which money is received from debtors against the sales invoices or any other source are entered in Tally by using the receipt voucher.

Perform the following steps to make a journal entry for the receipt voucher:

1. *Double-click* the **Accounting Vouchers** option under the **Transactions** section in the **Gateway of Tally** menu. The **Accounting Voucher Creation** screen appears.
2. *Click* the **F6: Receipt** button on the **Button Bar** to view the receipt voucher.
   The **Accounting Voucher Creation** screen appears with the receipt voucher.
3. *Click* the **F12: Configure** button on the **Button Bar**. The **Voucher Configuration** screen appears with Receipt Configuration.
4. *Set* Yes/No to the **Use single entry mode for payment/receipt/contra vouchers** option. In our case, we have set **No**.
5. *Set* Yes/No to the **Use Cr/Dr instead of To/By during entry** option. In our case, we have set **No**.
6. *Press* the **Enter** key until the **Accounting Voucher Creation** screen reappears with the **List of Ledger Accounts** menu.
7. *Double-click* the desired ledger account in the **List of Ledger Accounts** menu for the **Particulars** column. In our case, we have double-clicked **Mohan Traders** (Fig.TL-5.2).
8. *Enter* the amount for the selected ledger under the **Credit** column. In our case, we have entered **10,000** (Fig.TL-5.2).
9. *Press* the **Enter** key twice. The **List of Ledger Accounts** menu appears.
10. *Double-click* the desired ledger account in the **List of Ledger Accounts** menu for the **Particulars** column. In our case, we have double-clicked **Cash** (Fig.TL-5.2).
11. *Press* the **Enter** key.
12. *Enter* the narration under the **Narration** option. In our case, we have entered **Cash received from Mohan Traders** (Fig.TL-5.2).
13. *Press* the **Enter** key. The **Accept ?** message box appears (Fig.TL-5.2).

14. *Click* **Yes** in the **Accept ?** message box to create the receipt voucher, as shown in Fig.TL-5.2:

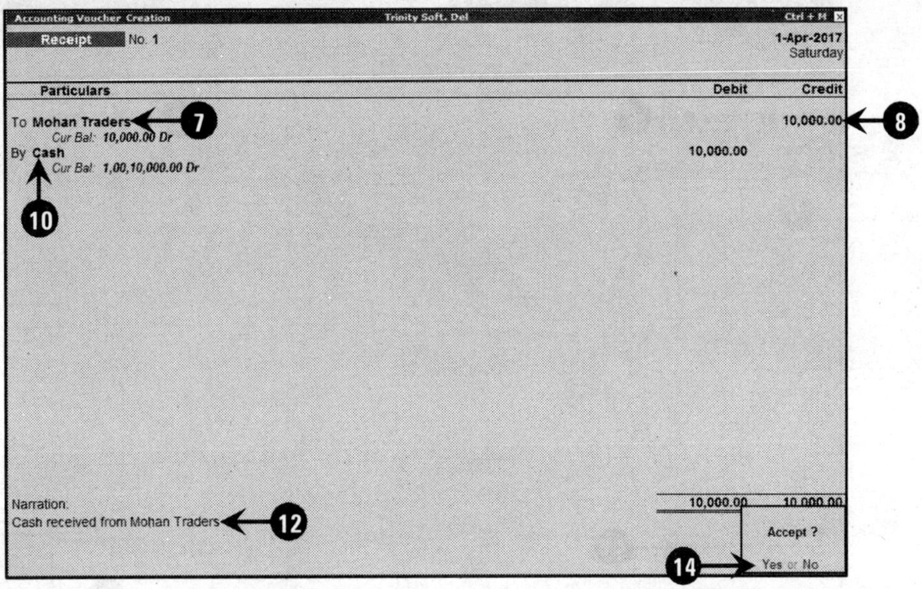

Fig.TL-5.2

Let us now learn about a payment voucher.

Payment Voucher

Payment voucher is used when you make payment by cheque or cash. You can create a journal entry for payment in two modes: single entry mode and double entry mode.

Perform the following steps to make a journal entry for the payment voucher:

1. *Double-click* the **Accounting Vouchers** option under the **Transactions** section in the **Gateway of Tally** menu.
2. *Click* the **F5: Payment** button on the Button Bar to view the voucher. The **Accounting Voucher Creation** screen appears with the payment voucher.
3. *Click* the **F12: Configure** button on the Button Bar. The **Voucher Configuration** screen appears with **Payment Configuration**.
4. *Set* Yes/No to the **Use single entry mode for payment/receipt/contra vouchers** option. In our case, we have set **No**.
5. *Press* the **Enter** key until the **Accounting Voucher Creation** screen reappears with the **List of Ledger Accounts** menu.
6. *Double-click* the desired ledger account in the **List of Ledger Accounts** menu for the **Particulars** column. In our case, we have double-clicked **Radhey Traders** (Fig.TL-5.3).
7. *Enter* the amount for the selected ledger under the **Debit** column. In our case, we have entered **5,000** (Fig.TL-5.3).
8. *Press* the **Enter** key twice. The **List of Ledger Accounts** menu appears.
9. *Double-click* the desired cash/bank ledger account in the **List of Ledger Accounts** menu for the **Particulars** column. In our case, we have double-clicked **Cash** (Fig.TL-5.3).
10. *Press* the **Enter** key.
11. *Enter* the narration under the **Narration** option. In our case, we have entered **Paid to Radhey Traders** (Fig.TL-5.3).
12. *Press* the **Enter** key. The **Accept ?** message box appears (Fig.TL-5.3).

13. *Click* **Yes** in the **Accept ?** message box to create the voucher, as shown in Fig.TL-5.3:

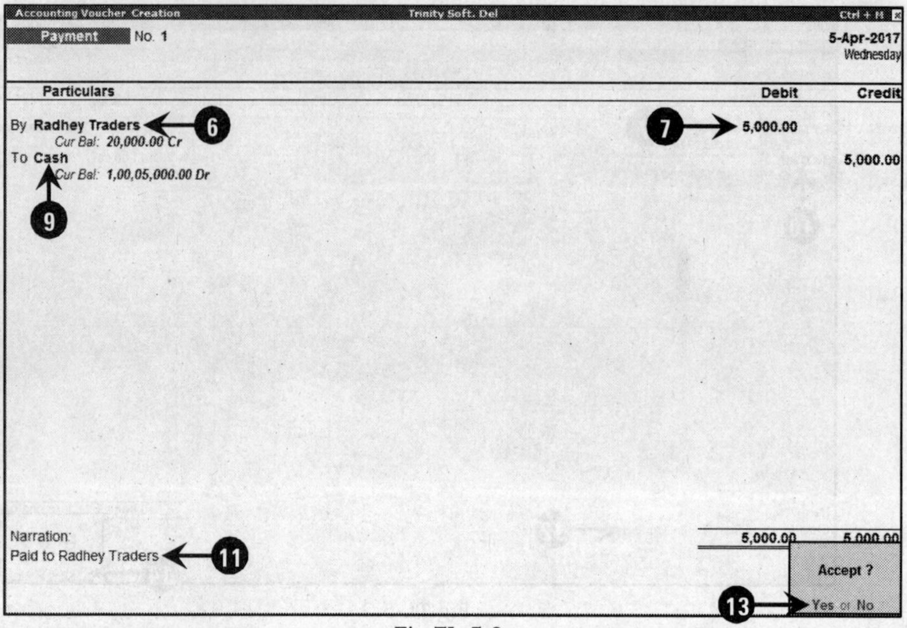

Fig.TL-5.3

Let us now learn about a contra voucher.

Contra Voucher

Contra voucher is a transaction that is used for fund transfer from a cash account to a bank account, a bank account to a cash account, a bank account to a bank account, and a cash account to a petty cash account.

Perform the following steps to make a contra entry for payment in the double entry mode:

1. *Double-click* the **Accounting Vouchers** option under the **Transactions** section in the **Gateway of Tally** menu. The **Accounting Voucher Creation** screen appears.
2. *Click* the **F4: Contra** button on the Button Bar to view the contra voucher.
3. *Click* the **F12: Configure** button on the Button Bar. The **Voucher Configuration** screen appears with **Contra Configuration.**
4. *Set* Yes/No to the **Use single entry mode for payment/receipt/contra vouchers** option. In our case, we have set **No**.
5. *Set* Yes/No to the **Use Cr/Dr instead of To/By during entry** option. In our case, we have set **Yes**.
6. *Press* the **Enter** key until the **Accounting Voucher Creation** screen reappears with the **List of Ledger Accounts** menu.
7. *Double-click* the ledger account that is to be credited in the **List of Ledger Accounts** menu for the **Particulars** column. In our case, we have double-clicked **Cash** (Fig.TL-5.4).
8. *Enter* the amount for the selected ledger under the **Credit** column. In our case, we have entered **5,000** (Fig.TL-5.4).
9. *Press* the **Enter** key twice.

10. *Double-click* the desired cash/bank ledger account that is to be debited in the **List of Ledger Accounts** menu for the **Particulars** column. In our case, we have double-clicked **SBI BANK**, as shown in Fig.TL-5.4:

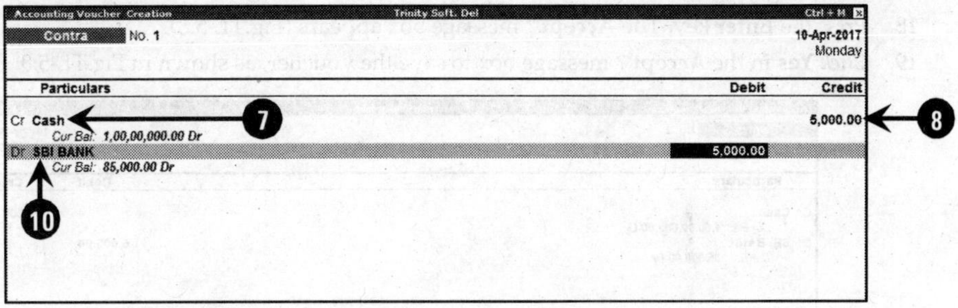

Fig.TL-5.4

11. *Press* the **Enter** key. The **Bank Allocations** screen appears (Fig.TL-5.5).

Note: **If more than one bank is used for transferring cash, a separate Cash Denominations screen will appear for each bank.**

12. *Press* the **Enter** key. The **Cash Denominations** screen appears (Fig.TL-5.6).
13. *Enter* the cash denomination details, as shown in Fig.TL-5.6:

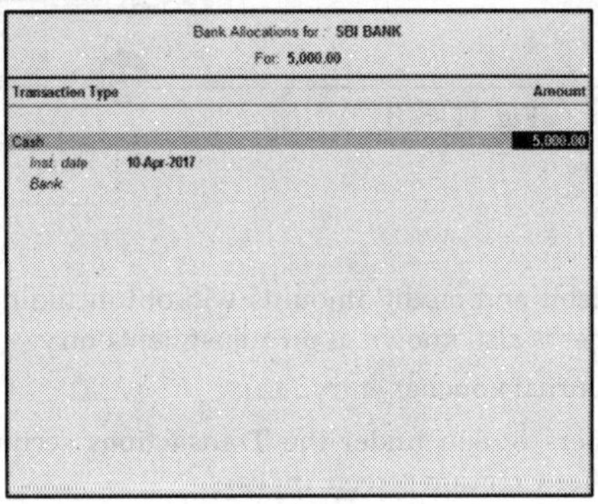

Fig.TL-5.5

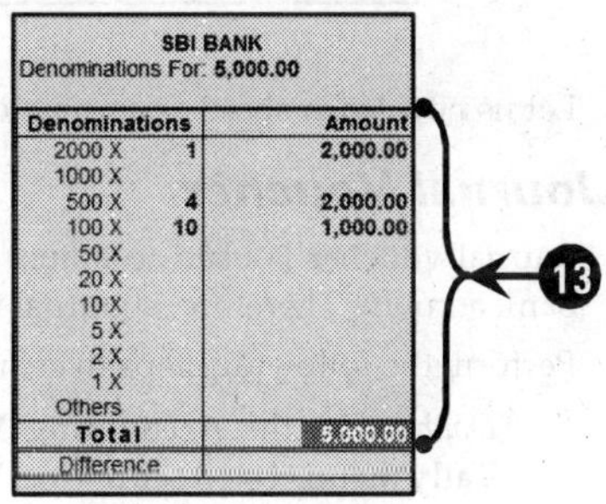

Fig.TL-5.6

14. *Press* the **Enter** key. The **Bank Allocations** screen reappears with the **List of Banks** menu (Fig.TL-5.7).
15. *Double click* the desired bank from the **List of Banks** menu for the **Bank** option. In our case, we have selected the **State Bank of India (India)** option, as shown in Fig.TL-5.7:

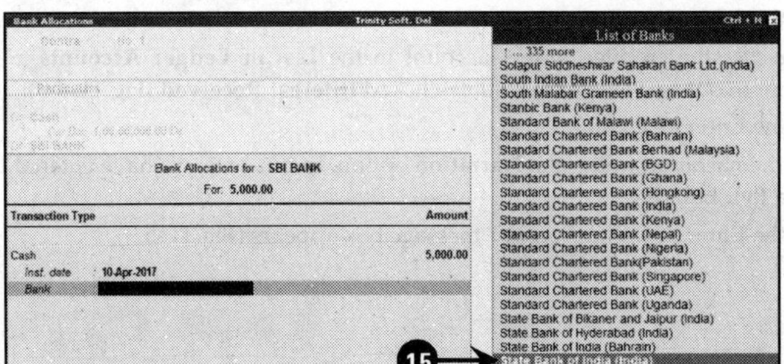

Fig.TL-5.7

16. *Press* the **Enter** key.
17. *Enter* the narration under the **Narration** option. In our case, we have entered **Transfer cash to SBI Bank** (Fig.TL-5.8).
18. *Press* the **Enter** key. The **Accept ?** message box appears (Fig.TL-5.8).
19. *Click* **Yes** in the **Accept ?** message box to save the voucher, as shown in Fig.TL-5.8:

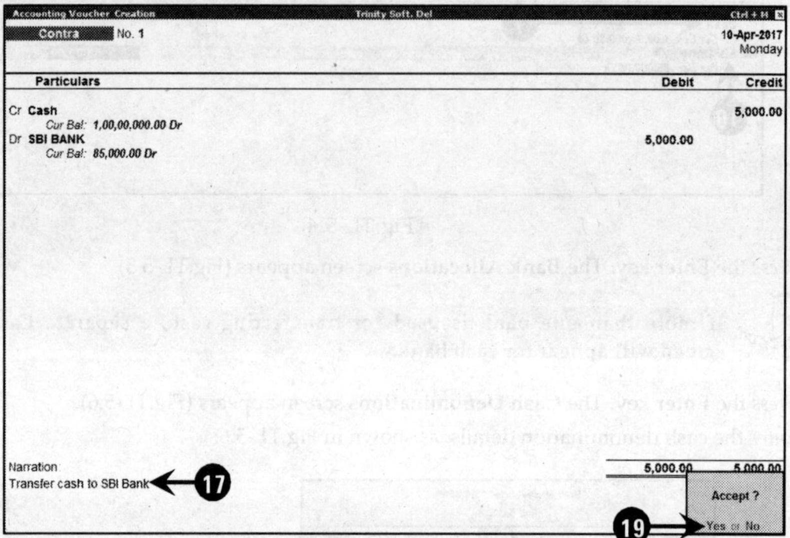

Fig.TL-5.8

Let us now learn about a journal voucher.

Journal Voucher

Journal voucher is used to adjust the debit and credit amounts without including the cash account or bank account. Therefore, a journal voucher is also known as an adjustment entry.

Perform the following steps to create a journal voucher entry:

1. *Double-click* the **Accounting Vouchers** option under the **Transactions** section in the **Gateway of Tally** menu. The **Accounting Voucher Creation** screen appears.
2. *Click* the **F7: Journal** button on the Button Bar to view the journal voucher.
3. *Double-click* the debited ledger account in the **List of Ledger Accounts** menu for the **Particulars** column. In our case, we have double-clicked **Gupta Pvt. Ltd.** (Fig.TL-5.9).
4. *Enter* the amount for the selected ledger under the **Debit** column. In our case, we have entered **2,000** (Fig.TL-5.9).
5. *Press* the **Enter** key twice.
6. *Double-click* the credited ledger account in the **List of Ledger Accounts** menu for the **Particulars** column. In our case, we have double-clicked **Interest Received** (Fig.TL-5.9).
7. *Press* the **Enter** key.
8. *Enter* the narration under the **Narration** option. In our case, we have entered **Interest Received from Gupta Pvt. Ltd.** (Fig.TL-5.9).
9. *Press* the **Enter** key. The **Accept ?** message box appears (Fig.TL-5.9).

10. *Click* **Yes** in the **Accept ?** message box to save the voucher, as shown in Fig.TL-5.9:

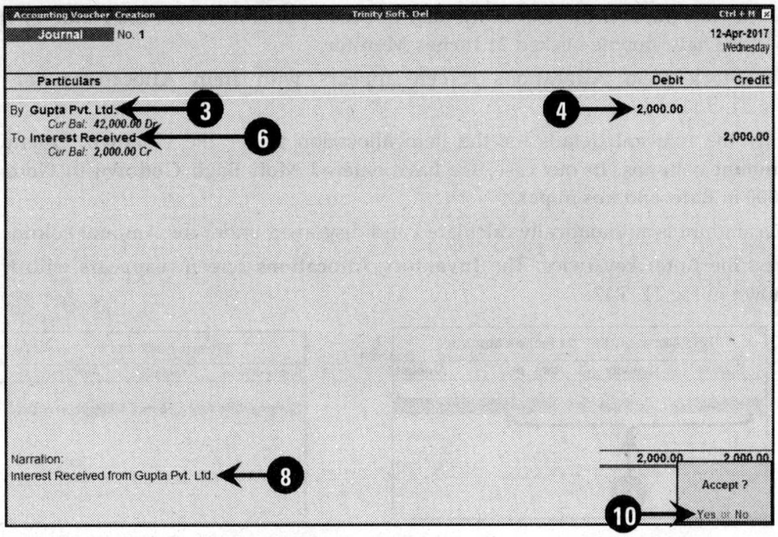

Fig.TL-5.9

Let us now learn about a purchase voucher.

Purchase Voucher

Purchase voucher is used to record purchase-related transactions in a company. Perform the following steps to create a purchase voucher:

1. *Double-click* the **Accounting Vouchers** option under the **Transactions** section in the **Gateway of Tally** menu. The **Accounting Voucher Creation** screen appears.
2. *Click* the **F9: Purchase** button on the Button Bar. The **Accounting Voucher Creation** screen of the purchase voucher appears.
3. *Click* the **V: As Voucher** button on the Button Bar.
4. *Enter* the supplier invoice number beside the **Supplier invoice no.** option. In our case, we have entered **1** (Fig.TL-5.10).
5. *Press* the **Enter** key.
6. *Enter* the date of invoice beside the **Date** option. In our case, we have entered **14-Apr-2017** (Fig.TL-5.10).
7. *Press* the **Enter** key. The **List of Ledger Accounts** menu appears.
8. *Double-click* the desired supplier in the **List of Ledger Accounts** menu for the **Particulars** column. In our case, we have double-clicked **Yash Traders** (Fig.TL-5.10).
9. *Enter* the amount under the **Credit** column. In our case, we have entered **44,000**.
10. *Press* the **Enter** key.
11. *Double-click* the desired purchase ledger in the **List of Ledger Accounts** menu for the **Particulars** column. In our case, we have double-clicked **Purchase**, as shown in Fig.TL-5.10:

Fig.TL-5.10

The **Inventory Allocations** screen appears with the **List of Stock Items** menu.

12. *Double-click* the desired item in the **List of Stock Items** menu for the **Name of Item** column. In our case, we have double-clicked **21 Inches Monitor**.

    The **Stock Item Allocations** screen appears with **Item Allocations for** the selected item (Fig.TL-5.11).

13. *Enter* the relevant details for the item allocation under the **Godown, Quantity, Rate, per,** and **Amount** columns. In our case, we have entered **Moti Bagh Godown** in **Godown, 5** in **Quantity 8,800** in **Rate,** and **nos** in **per**.

    The amount is automatically calculated and displayed under the **Amount** column (Fig.TL-5.11).

14. *Press* the **Enter** key twice. The **Inventory Allocations** screen reappears with the defined item, as shown in Fig.TL-5.12:

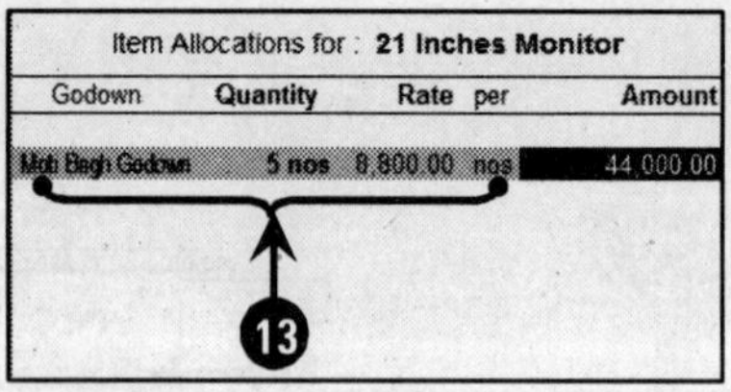

Fig.TL-5.11

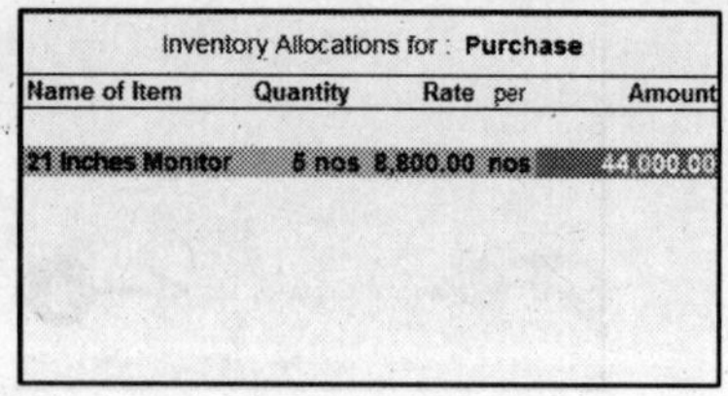

Fig.TL-5.12

15. *Press* the **Enter** key twice.

    The **Accounting Voucher Creation** screen reappears (Fig.TL-5.13).

16. *Enter* the narration under the **Narration** option. In our case, we have entered **Purchase 21 Inches Monitor from Yash Traders** (Fig.TL-5.13).

17. *Press* the **Enter** key. The **Accept ?** message box appears (Fig.TL-5.13).

18. *Click* **Yes** in the **Accept ?** message box to create the purchase voucher, as shown in Fig.TL-5.13:

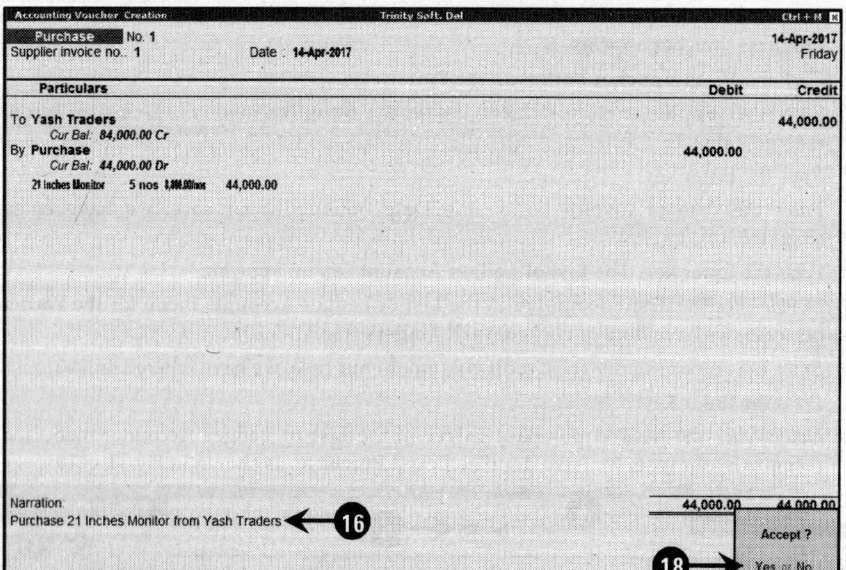

Fig.TL-5.13

Let us now learn about a purchase invoice.

Purchase Invoice

A document that contains the details of a purchase transaction is called a purchase invoice. This document should be given to buyers or debtors as a proof of purchase. Tally.ERP 9 offers the following two ways of making invoices:

- **Account invoice:** Refers to the invoice in which you directly select the ledger account. This invoice is useful when you want to record the service bill.
- **Item invoice:** Refers to an invoice in which you need to define the item first and then allocate the same item in the related ledger account.

Perform the following steps to make a purchase account invoice:

1. *Double-click* the **Accounting Vouchers** option under the **Transactions** section in the **Gateway of Tally** menu. The **Accounting Voucher Creation** screen appears.
2. *Click* the **F9: Purchase** button on the Button Bar. The **Accounting Voucher Creation** screen of the purchase voucher appears as invoice.

> Note: **If the purchase voucher does not appear as invoice, click the V: As Invoice button on the Button Bar or press the Ctrl+V keys to view the purchase voucher as invoice.**

3. *Click* the **I: Accounting Invoice** button on the Button Bar.

   The **Accounting Voucher Creation** screen of the purchase account invoice appears (Fig.TL-5.14).
4. *Enter* the supplier invoice number beside the **Supplier invoice no.** option.

   In our case, we have entered **2** (Fig.TL-5.14).
5. *Press* the **Enter** key.
6. *Enter* the date of invoice beside the **Date** option. In our case, we have entered **5-May-2017** (Fig.TL-5.14).
7. *Press* the **Enter** key. The **List of Ledger Accounts** menu appears.
8. *Double-click* the desired party name in the **List of Ledger Accounts** menu for the **Party A/c name** option. In our case, we have double-clicked **Gupta Courier Services** (Fig.TL-5.14). The **List of Ledger Accounts** menu appears.
9. *Double-click* the desired ledger in the **List of Ledger Accounts** menu for the **Particulars** column. In our case, we have double-clicked **Courier Charges** (Fig.TL-5.14).
10. *Enter* the service amount under the **Amount** column.

    In our case, we have entered **5,000** (Fig.TL-5.14).
11. *Press* the **Enter** key thrice to move to the **Narration** option.
12. *Enter* the narration under the **Narration** option.

    In our case, we have entered **Courier Charges of April 2017** (Fig.TL-5.14).
13. *Press* the **Enter** key. The **Accept ?** message box appears (Fig.TL-5.14).

14. *Click* **Yes** in the **Accept ?** message box to save the purchase account invoice, as shown in Fig.TL-5.14:

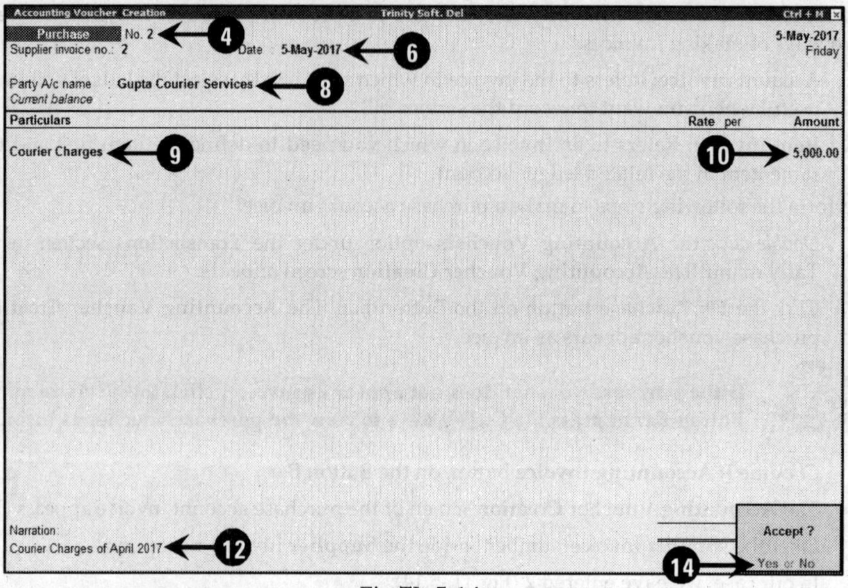

Fig.TL-5.14

The **Accounting Voucher Creation** screen of the purchase account invoice appears.

Now, perform the following steps to make a purchase item invoice:

1. *Double-click* the **Accounting Vouchers** option under the **Transactions** section in the **Gateway of Tally** menu. The **Accounting Voucher Creation** screen appears.
2. *Click* the **F9: Purchase** button on the Button Bar. The **Accounting Voucher Creation** screen of the purchase voucher appears as invoice.
3. *Click* the **I: Item Invoice** button on the Button Bar to view the Item invoice. The **Accounting Voucher Creation** screen of the purchase item invoice appears.
4. *Click* the **F12: Configure** button on the Button Bar to view the configuration of the voucher. The **Voucher Configuration** screen appears.
5. *Set* the **Use common ledger account for item allocation** option to Yes.

   The **Purchase ledger** option enables on the **Accounting Voucher Creation** screen of the purchase item invoice.
6. *Enter* the supplier invoice number beside the **Supplier invoice no.** option. In our case, we have entered **3** (Fig.TL-5.15).
7. *Press* the **Enter** key.
8. *Enter* the date of invoice beside the **Date** option. In our case, we have entered **6-May-2017** (Fig.TL-5.15).
9. *Press* the **Enter** key. The **List of Ledger Accounts** menu appears.
10. *Double-click* the desired party name in the **List of Ledger Accounts** menu for the **Party A/c name** option. In our case, we have double-clicked **Yash Traders** (Fig.TL-5.15). The **List of Ledger Accounts** menu appears.
11. *Double-click* the desired purchase ledger in the **List of Ledger Accounts** menu for the **Purchase ledger** option. In our case, we have double-clicked **Purchase** (Fig.TL-5.15). The **List of Stock Items** menu appears (Fig.TL-5.15).

12. *Double-click* the desired item in the **List of Stock Items** menu for the **Name of Item** column. In our case, we have double-clicked **21 Inches Monitor**, as shown in Fig.TL-5.15:

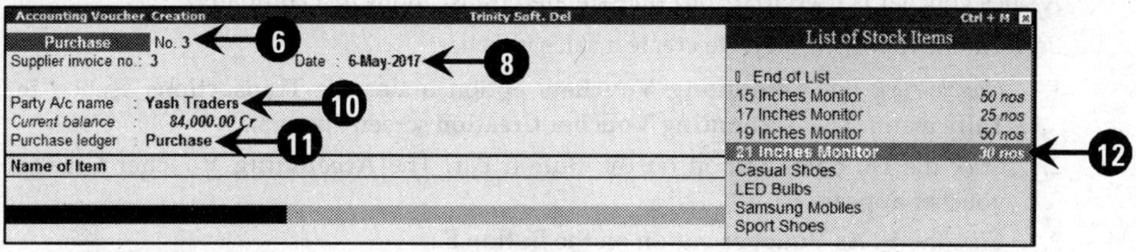

Fig.TL-5.15

The **Stock Item Allocations** screen appears (Fig.TL-5.16).

13. *Enter* the details of the item under their respective columns. In our case, we have entered **Moti Bagh Godown** under **Godown, 5** under **Quantity, 8,800** under **Rate**, and **nos** under **per** columns (Fig.TL-5.16). The **Amount** column is automatically filled, as shown in Fig.TL-5.16:

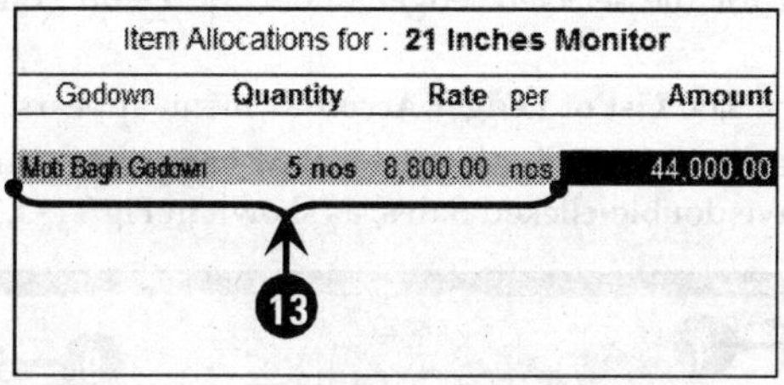

Fig.TL-5.16

14. *Press* the **Enter** key twice. The **Accounting Voucher Creation** screen reappears (Fig.TL-5.17).
15. *Press* the **Enter** key until the **Narration** option appears.
16. *Enter* the narration under the **Narration** option. In our case, we have entered **Purchase 21 Inches Monitor from Yash Traders** (Fig.TL-5.17).
17. *Press* the **Enter** key. The **Accept ?** message box appears (Fig.TL-5.17).
18. *Click* **Yes** in the **Accept ?** message box to save the purchase item invoice, as shown in Fig.TL-5.17:

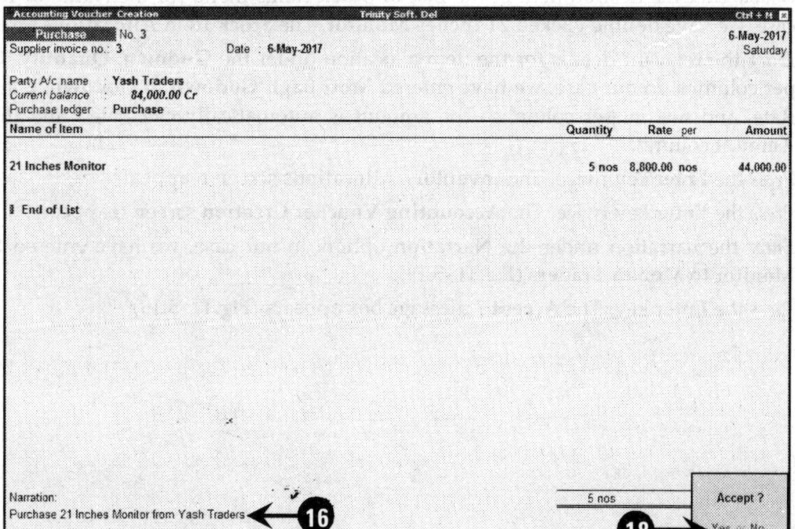

Fig.TL-5.17

Let us now learn about a sales voucher.

Sales Voucher

A sales voucher is used to record sales-related transactions in a company.

Perform the following steps to create a sales voucher:

1. *Double-click* the **Accounting Vouchers** option under the **Transactions** section in the **Gateway of Tally** menu. The **Accounting Voucher Creation** screen appears.
2. *Click* the **F8: Sales** button on the Button Bar. The **Accounting Voucher Creation** screen of sales voucher appears.
3. *Click* the **V: As Voucher** button on the Button Bar.
4. *Enter* the desired reference number beside the **Reference no.** option. In our case, we have entered **1** (Fig.TL-5.18).
5. *Press* the **Enter** key. The **List of Ledger Accounts** menu appears.
6. *Double-click* the desired party name in the **List of Ledger Accounts** menu for the **Particulars** column. In our case, we have double-clicked **Mohan Traders** (Fig.TL-5.18).
7. *Enter* the amount for the selected ledger under the **Debit** column. In our case, we have entered **18,000**.
8. *Press* the **Enter** key. The **List of Ledger Accounts** menu appears.
9. *Double-click* the desired sales ledger in the **List of Ledger Accounts** menu for the **Particulars** option. In our case, we have double-clicked **Sales**, as shown in Fig.TL-5.18:

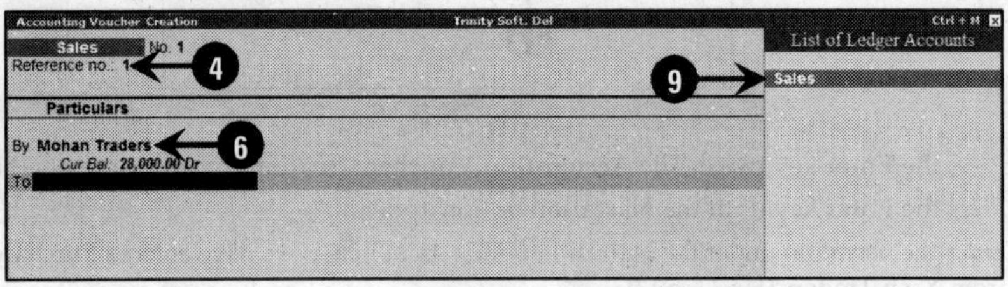

Fig.TL-5.18

The **Inventory Allocations** screen appears with the **List of Stock Items** menu.

10. *Double-click* the desired item in the **List of Stock Items** menu for the **Name of Item** column. In our case, we have double-clicked **21 Inches Monitor**. The **Stock Item Allocations** screen appears.
11. *Enter* the relevant details for the item allocation under the **Godown, Quantity, Rate, Amount,** and **per** columns. In our case, we have entered **Moti Bagh Godown** in **Godown, 2** in **Quantity, 9,000** in **Rate,** and **nos** in **per** columns. The amount is automatically calculated and displayed under the **Amount** column.
12. *Press* the **Enter** key twice. The **Inventory Allocations** screen reappears.
13. *Press* the **Enter** key twice. The **Accounting Voucher Creation** screen reappears.
14. *Enter* the narration under the **Narration** option. In our case, we have entered **Sales of 21 Inches Monitor to Mohan Traders** (Fig.TL-5.19).
15. *Press* the **Enter** key. The **Accept ?** message box appears (Fig.TL-5.19).

16. *Click* **Yes** in the **Accept ?** message box to create the sales voucher, as shown in Fig.TL-5.19:

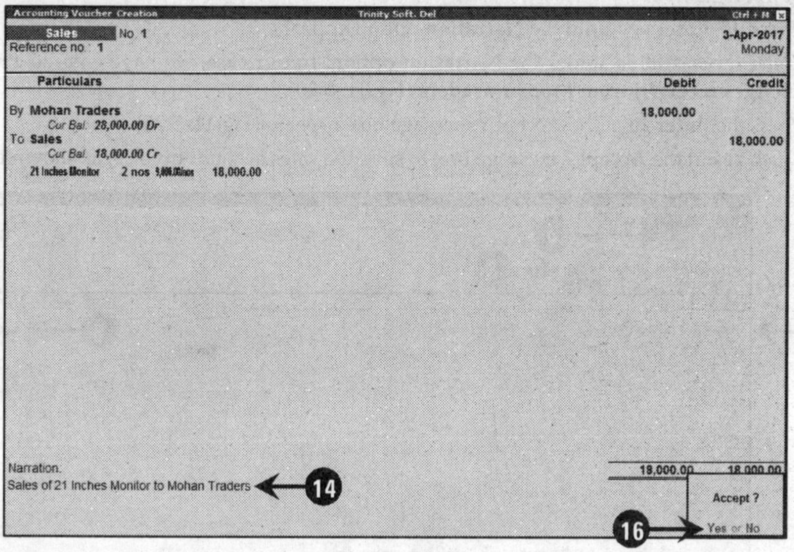

Fig.TL-5.19

Let us now learn about a sales invoice.

Sales Invoice

A document that contains the details of a sales transaction is called a sales invoice or bill. This document should be given to buyers or debtors as a proof of purchase by them. Tally.ERP 9 offers the following two ways of making invoices:

- **Account invoice:** Refers to the invoice that is used by specialists who need to issue an invoice for providing certain services, such as consultancy charges or professional fees.
- **Item invoice:** Refers to the invoice that is used for the sale of stock. This invoice lists the details of sold items.

Perform the following steps to make a sales account invoice:

1. *Double-click* the **Accounting Vouchers** option under the **Transactions** section in the **Gateway of Tally** menu. The **Accounting Voucher Creation** screen appears.
2. *Click* the **F8: Sales** button on the Button Bar. The **Accounting Voucher Creation** screen of the sales voucher appears as invoice.

Note: **If the sales voucher does not appear as invoice, click the V: As Invoice button on the Button Bar or press the Ctrl+V keys to view the sales voucher as invoice.**

3. *Click* the **I: Accounting Invoice** button on the Button Bar. The **Accounting Voucher Creation** screen of the sales account invoice appears (Fig.TL-5.20).
4. *Enter* the reference number beside the **Reference no.** option. In our case, we have entered **2** (Fig.TL-5.20).
5. *Press* the **Enter** key. The **List of Ledger Accounts** menu appears.
6. *Double-click* the desired party name in the **List of Ledger Accounts** menu for the **Party A/c name** option. In our case, we have double-clicked **Mohan Traders** (Fig.TL-5.20). The **List of Ledger Accounts** menu appears.
7. *Double-click* the desired ledger in the **List of Ledger Accounts** menu for the **Particulars** column. In our case, we have double-clicked **Professional Service Charges** (Fig.TL-5.20).

8. *Enter* the service amount under the **Amount** column. In our case, we have entered **10,000** (Fig.TL-5.20).
9. *Press* the **Enter** key until the **Narration** option appears.
10. *Enter* the narration under the **Narration** option. In our case, we have entered **Professional service charges received from Mohan Traders** (Fig.TL-5.20).
11. *Press* the **Enter** key. The **Accept ?** message box appears (Fig.TL-5.20).
12. *Click* **Yes** in the **Accept ?** message box to save the sales account invoice, as shown in Fig.TL-5.20:

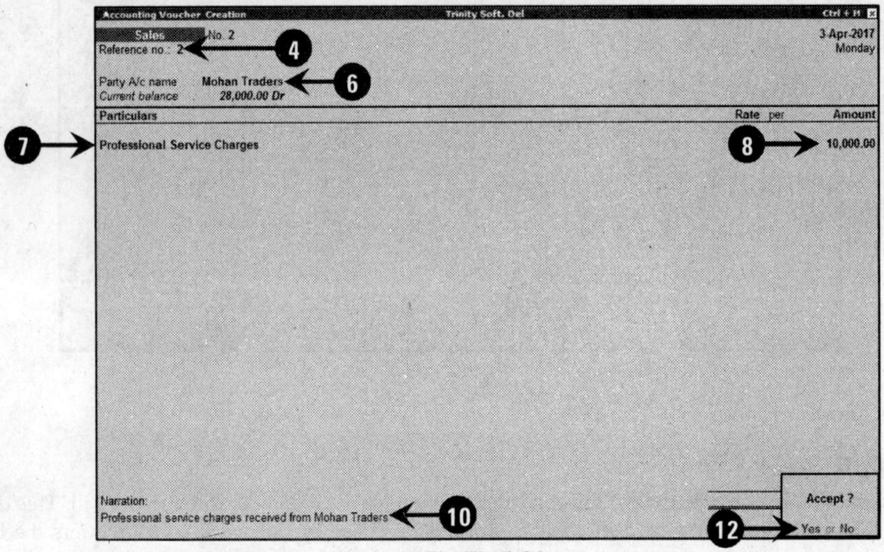

Fig.TL-5.20

The **Accounting Voucher Creation** screen of the sales account invoice reappears.

Now, perform the following steps to make a sales item invoice:

1. *Double-click* the **Accounting Vouchers** option under the **Transactions** section in the **Gateway of Tally** menu. The **Accounting Voucher Creation** screen appears.
2. *Click* the **F8: Sales** button on the Button Bar.

   The **Accounting Voucher Creation** screen of the sales voucher appears as invoice.
3. *Click* the **I: Item Invoice** button on the Button Bar. The **Accounting Voucher Creation** screen of the sales item invoice appears (Fig.TL-5.21).
4. *Click* the **F12: Configure** button on the Button Bar to view the configuration of the voucher. The **Voucher Configuration** screen appears.
5. *Set* the **Use common ledger account for item allocation** option to **Yes**.

   The **Sales ledger** option enables on the **Accounting Voucher Creation** screen of the sales item invoice.
6. *Enter* the reference number beside the **Reference no.** option. In our case, we have entered **3** (Fig.TL-5.21).
7. *Press* the **Enter** key. The **List of Ledger Accounts** menu appears.
8. *Double-click* the desired party name in the **List of Ledger Accounts** menu for the **Party A/c name** option. In our case, we have double-clicked **Manish Co.** (Fig.TL-5.21). The **List of Ledger Accounts** menu appears.
9. *Double-click* the desired sales ledger in the **List of Ledger Accounts** menu for the **Sales ledger** option. In our case, we have double-clicked **Sales** (Fig.TL-5.21). The **List of Stock Items** menu appears.

10. *Double-click* the desired item in the **List of Stock Items** menu for the **Name of Item** column. In our case, we have double-clicked **15 Inches Monitor**, as shown in Fig.TL-5.21:

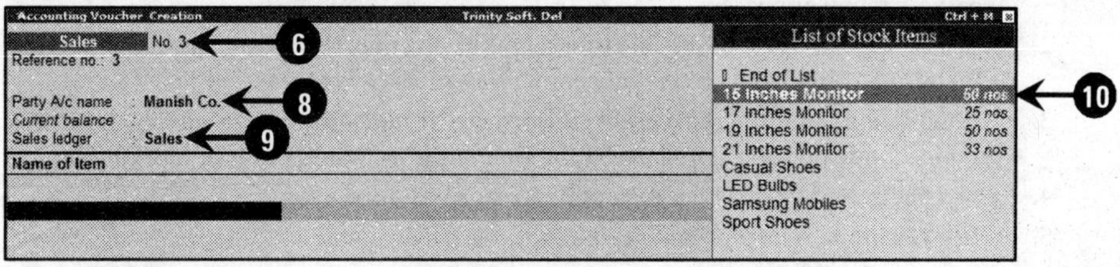

Fig.TL-5.21

The **Stock Item Allocations** screen appears with **Item Allocations for** the selected item.

11. *Enter* the details of the item under their respective columns. In our case, we have entered **Moti Bagh Godown** under **Godown**, **5** under **Quantity**, **4,400** under **Rate**, and **nos** under **per** columns. The **Amount** column is automatically filled.
12. *Press* the **Enter** key twice. The **Accounting Voucher Creation** screen appears (Fig.TL-5.22).
13. *Press* the **Enter** key until the **Narration** option appears.
14. *Enter* the narration under the **Narration** option. In our case, we have entered **Sales of 15 Inches Monitor to Manish Co.** (Fig.TL-5.22).
15. *Press* the **Enter** key. The **Accept ?** message box appears (Fig.TL-5.22).
16. *Click* **Yes** in the **Accept ?** message box to save the sales item invoice, as shown in Fig.TL-5.22:

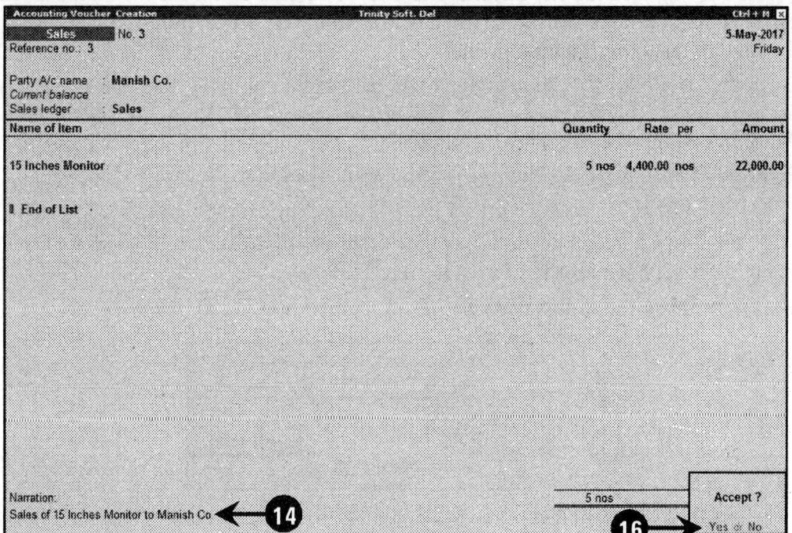

Fig.TL 5.22

Let us now learn about a debit note.

Debit Note

A debit note is a document that is issued by the buyer to the supplier. It contains all the details of goods returned with a specific reason. This document is mainly used in case of purchase returns or an increase/decrease in the price of items.

Perform the following steps to enable a debit note:

1. *Click* the **F11: Features** button on the Button Bar in the **Gateway of Tally** screen. The **Company Features** menu appears.
2. *Double-click* the **Inventory Features** option in the **Company Features** menu. The **Company Operations Alteration** screen appears with **Inventory Features.**
3. *Set* the **Use debit and credit notes, Record credit notes in invoice mode,** and **Record debit notes in invoice mode** options to **Yes** under the **Invoicing** section in the **Inventory Features.**
4. *Press* the **Enter** key until the **Accept ?** message box appears.
5. *Click* **Yes** in the **Accept ?** message box to save the changes.

Now, perform the following steps to create a debit note:

1. *Double-click* the **Accounting Vouchers** option under the **Transactions** section in the **Gateway of Tally** menu. The **Accounting Voucher Creation** screen appears.
2. *Click* the **F9: Debit Note** button on the Button Bar to view the debit note voucher. The **Accounting Voucher Creation** screen appears with the **List of Ledger Accounts** menu.
3. *Enter* the **invoice** number beside the **Original invoice no** option. In our case, we have entered **3.**
4. *Press* the **Enter** key.
5. *Enter* date beside the **Date** option. In our case, we have entered **6-May-2017.**
6. *Press* the **Enter** key.
7. *Double-click* the desired supplier in the **List of Ledger Accounts** menu for the **Party A/c name** option. In our case, we have double-clicked **Yash Traders.** The **List of Stock Items** menu appears.
8. *Double-click* the desired item in the **List of Stock Items** menu for the **Name of Item** column. In our case, we have double-clicked **21 Inches Monitor.** The **Stock Item Allocations** screen appears with the **List of Tracking Numbers** menu.
9. *Enter* the details of the item under their respective columns. In our case, we have entered **Main Location** under **Godown, 2** under **Quantity, 8,800** under **Rate,** and **nos** under **per** columns. The **Amount** column is automatically filled.
10. *Press* the **Enter** key twice. The **Accounting Voucher Creation** screen reappears.
11. *Press* the **Enter** key. The **Accounting Details** screen appears (Fig.TL-5.23).
12. *Select* the desired ledger account from the **List of Ledger Accounts** menu for the **Particulars** column. In our case, we have selected **Purchase** (Fig.TL-5.23).

    The amount column is automatically filled, as shown in Fig.TL-5.23:

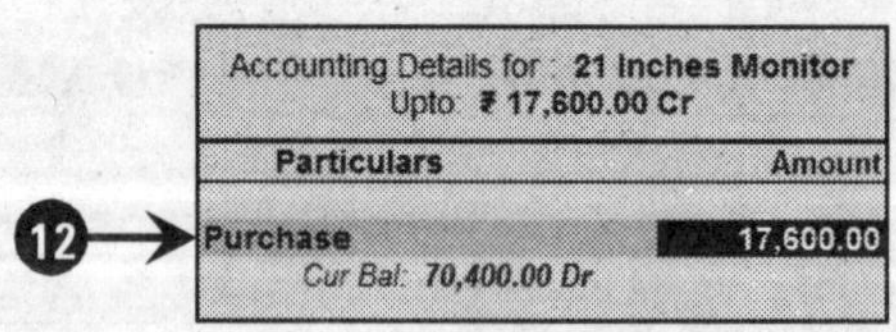

Fig.TL-5.23

13. *Press* the **Enter** key. The **Accounting Voucher Creation** screen reappears.
14. *Press* the **Enter** key until the **Narration** option appears.
15. *Enter* the narration under the **Narration** option. In our case, we have entered **Purchase Return of 21 Inches Monitor to Yash Traders** (Fig.TL-5.24).
16. *Press* the **Enter** key. The **Accept ?** message box appears (Fig.TL-5.24).

17. *Click* **Yes** in the **Accept ?** message box to save the debit note voucher, as shown in Fig.TL-5.24:

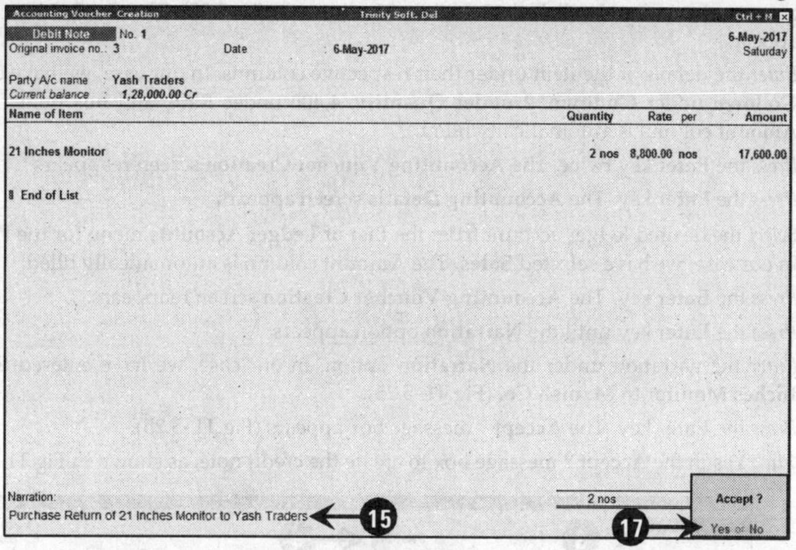

Fig.TL-5.24

Let us now learn about the procedure to create a credit note.

Credit Note

A credit note is a document issued by the seller to the buyer if the buyer returns the goods purchased from the seller with a specific reason. This document is mainly used in case of sales returns or an increase/decrease in the prices of items. You need to create a customer or party ledger (account) for creating a credit note. The customer ledger is created under the Sundry Debtors group.

Perform the following steps to enable a credit note:

1. *Click* the **F11: Features** button on the Button Bar in the **Gateway of Tally** screen. The **Company Features** menu appears.
2. *Double-click* the **Inventory Features** option in the **Company Features** menu. The **Company Operations Alteration** screen appears with **Inventory Features**.
3. *Set* the **Use debit and credit notes, Use credit notes in invoice mode,** and **Use debit notes in invoice mode** options to **Yes** under the **Invoicing** section in **Inventory Features**.
4. *Press* the **Enter** key until the **Accept ?** message box appears.
5. *Click* **Yes** in the **Accept ?** message box to save the changes.

Now, perform the following steps to create a credit note:

1. *Double-click* the **Accounting Vouchers** option under the **Transactions** section in the **Gateway of Tally** menu.
2. *Click* the **F8: Credit Note** button on the Button Bar to view the credit note voucher. The **Accounting Voucher Creation** screen appears with the **List of Ledger Accounts** menu.
3. *Enter* the desired invoice number beside the **Original invoice no.** option. In our case, we have entered **3** (Fig.TL-5.25).
4. *Enter* date beside the **Date** option. In our case, we have entered **6-May-2017** (Fig.TL-5.25).
5. *Double-click* the desired customer in the **List of Ledger Accounts** menu for the **Party A/c name** option. In our case, we have double-clicked **Manish Co.** (Fig.TL-5.25). The **List of Stock Items** menu appears (Fig.TL-5.25).

6. *Double-click* the desired item in the **List of Stock Items** menu for the **Name of Item** column. In our case, we have double-clicked **15 Inches Monitor** (Fig.TL-5.25). The **Stock Item Allocations** screen appears.
7. *Enter* the details of the item under their respective columns. In our case, we have entered **Moti Bagh Godown** under **Godown, 2** under **Quantity, 4,400** under **Rate,** and **nos** under **per columns**. The **Amount** column is automatically filled.
8. *Press* the **Enter** key twice. The **Accounting Voucher Creation** screen reappears.
9. *Press* the **Enter** key. The **Accounting Details** screen appears.
10. *Select* the desired ledger account from the **List of Ledger Accounts** menu for the **Particulars** column. In our case, we have selected **Sales.** The **Amount** column is automatically filled.
11. *Press* the **Enter** key. The **Accounting Voucher Creation** screen reappears.
12. *Press* the **Enter** key until the **Narration** option appears.
13. *Enter* the narration under the **Narration** option. In our case, we have entered **Sales Return of 15 Inches Monitor to Manish Co.** (Fig.TL-5.25).
14. *Press* the **Enter** key. The **Accept ?** message box appears (Fig.TL-5.25).
15. *Click* **Yes** in the **Accept** ? message box to create the credit note, as shown in Fig.TL-5.25:

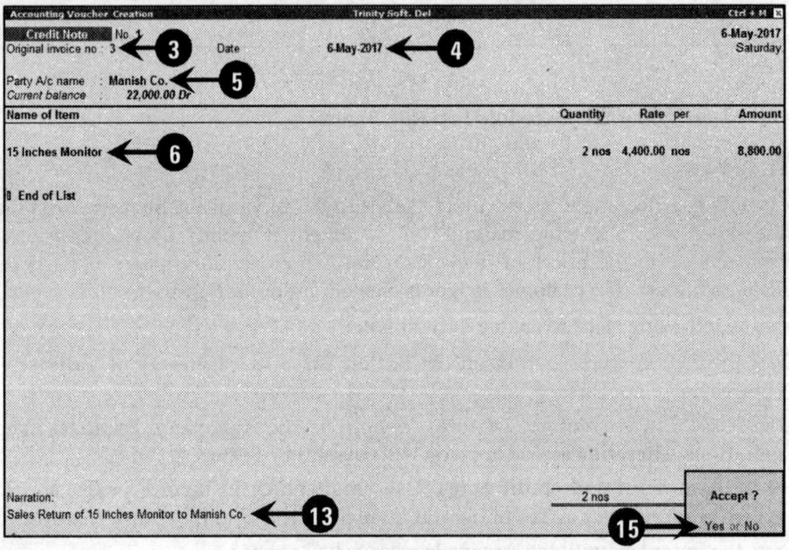

Fig.TL-5.25

Inventory Vouchers

Inventory vouchers are those vouchers that are used to record all inventory-related transactions. In Tally.ERP 9, there are various types of inventory vouchers, which are as follows:

- Receipt Note Voucher
- Rejections In Voucher
- Rejections Out Voucher
- Stock Journal
- Delivery Note Voucher
- Physical Stock

Let us learn about these vouchers one by one in the following sections.

Receipt Note Voucher

A receipt note voucher is used to record transactions related to received goods. To create a receipt note, you need to first enable the Use tracking numbers (enables delivery and receipt notes) option under Inventory Features.

Perform the following steps to enable the Use tracking numbers (enables delivery and receipt notes) option:

1. *Click* the **F11: Features** button on the Button Bar in the **Gateway of Tally** screen. The **Company Features** menu appears.
2. *Double-click* the **Inventory Features** option in the **Company Features** menu. The **Company Operations Alteration** screen appears with **Inventory Features.**
3. *Set* the **Use tracking numbers (enables delivery and receipt notes)** option to **Yes** under the **Other Features** section.
4. *Press* the **Enter** key until the **Accept ?** message box appears.
5. *Click* **Yes** in the **Accept ?** message box to save the changes.

Now, perform the following steps to create a receipt note voucher:

1. *Double-click* the **InvenTory Vouchers** option under the **Transactions** section in the **Gateway of Tally** menu. The **Inventory Voucher Creation** screen appears.
2. *Click* the **F9: Receipt Note** button on the Button Bar to view the receipt note voucher. The **Inventory Voucher Creation** screen appears with the **Receipt Note** voucher (Fig.TL-5.26).
3. *Enter* the desired reference number beside the **Reference no.** option. In our case, we have entered **3** (Fig.TL-5.26).
4. *Press* the **Enter** key. The **List of Ledger Accounts** menu appears.
5. *Double-click* the desired supplier in the **List of Ledger Accounts** menu for the **Party A/c name** option. In our case, we have double-clicked **Yash Traders** (Fig.TL-5.26). The **List of Ledger Accounts** menu appears (Fig.TL-5.26).
6. *Double-click* the desired purchase ledger in the **List of Ledger Accounts** menu for the **Purchase ledger** option. In our case, we have double-clicked **Purchase** (Fig.TL-5.26). The **List of Stock Items** menu appears (Fig.TL-5.26).
7. *Double-click* the desired item in the **List of Stock Items** menu for the **Name of Item** column. In our case, we have double-clicked **21 Inches Monitor**, as shown in Fig.TL-5.26:

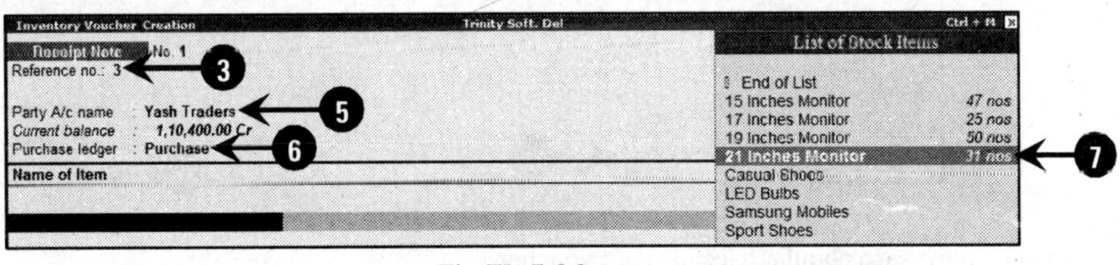

Fig.TL-5.26

The **Stock Item Allocations** screen appears with the **List of Tracking Numbers** menu.

8. *Double-click* the desired tracking number in the **List of Tracking Numbers** menu for the **Tracking No.** option. In our case, we have double-clicked **1** (Fig.TL-5.27).

9. *Enter* the details of the item under their respective columns. In our case, we have entered **Moti Bagh Godown** under **Godown**, **2** under **Quantity**, **8,800** under **Rate**, and **nos** under **per** columns (Fig.TL-5.27). The **Amount** column is automatically filled, as shown in Fig.TL-5.27:

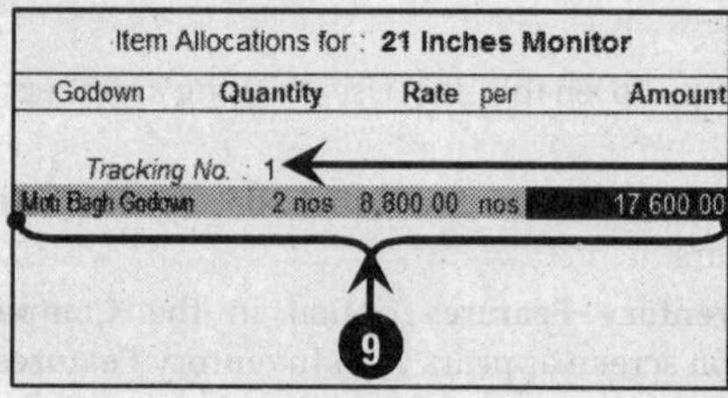

Fig.TL-5.27

10. *Press* the **Enter** key twice. The **Inventory Voucher Creation** screen reappears (Fig.TL-5.28).
11. *Press* the **Enter** key four times.
12. *Enter* the narration under the **Narration** option. In our case, we have entered **Receipt note of 21 Inches Monitor from Yash Traders** (Fig.TL-5.28).
13. *Press* the **Enter** key. The **Accept ?** message box appears (Fig.TL-5.28).
14. *Click* **Yes** in the **Accept ?** message box to create the voucher, as shown in Fig.TL-5.28:

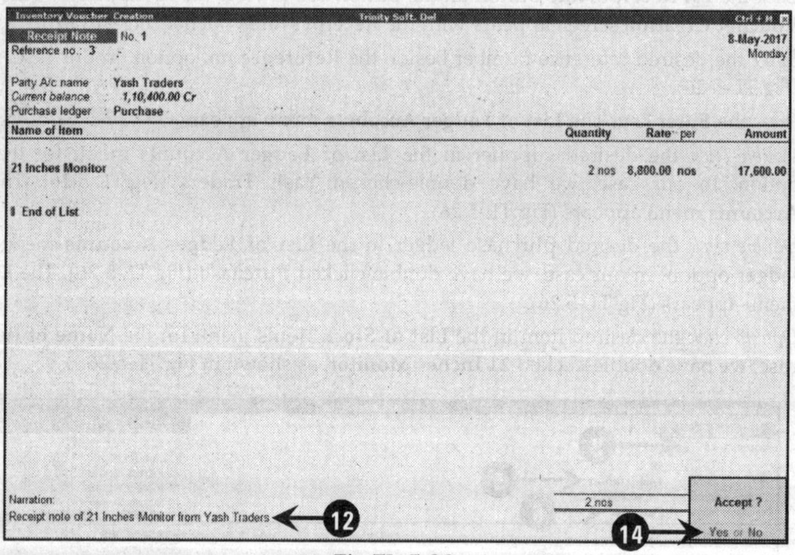

Fig.TL-5.28

Let us now learn about a rejections out voucher.

Rejections Out Voucher

A rejections out voucher is used for recording transactions related to goods that are rejected and returned to the supplier. To create a rejections out voucher, you need to first activate the Use rejection inward and outward notes option under Inventory Features.

Perform the following steps to activate the Use rejection inward and outward notes option:

1. *Click* the **F11: Features** button on the Button Bar in the **Gateway of Tally** screen.
   The **Company Features** menu appears.

2. *Double-click* the **Inventory Features** option in the **Company Features** menu. The **Company Operations Alteration** screen appears with **Inventory Features.**
3. *Set* the **Use rejection inward and outward notes** option to **Yes** under the **Other Features** section.
4. *Press* the **Enter** key until the **Accept ?** message box appears.
5. *Click* **Yes** in the **Accept ?** message box to save the changes.

Now, let us perform the following steps to create a rejections out voucher:

1. *Double-click* the **InvenTory Vouchers** option under the **Transactions** section in the **Gateway of Tally** menu. The **Inventory Voucher Creation** screen appears with the **Rejections Out** voucher.
2. *Click* the **F6: Rejections Out** button on the Button Bar to view the rejections out voucher.
3. *Double-click* the name of the party, to whom you want to return the goods, in the **List of Ledger Accounts** menu for the **Ledger Account** column. In our case, we have double-clicked **Yash Traders** (Fig.TL-5.29).

   The **Supplier's Name and Address** column will be filled automatically with the address of the supplier if the address is provided at the time of ledger creation (Fig.TL-5.29).
4. *Press* the **Enter** key until the **List of Stock Items** menu appears (Fig.TL-5.29).
5. *Double-click* the desired item in the **List of Stock Items** menu for the **Name of Item** column. In our case, we have double-clicked **21 Inches Monitor**, as shown in Fig.TL-5.29:

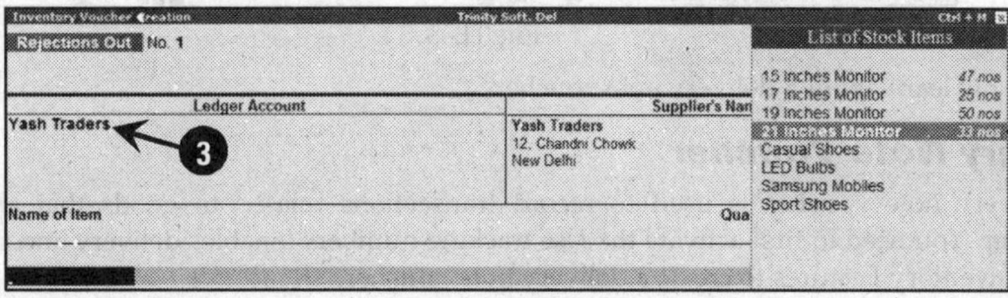

Fig.TL-5.29

   The **Stock Item Allocation** screen appears with the **List of Tracking Numbers** menu.
6. *Double-click* the desired tracking number in the **List of Tracking Numbers** menu for the **Tracking No.** option. In our case, we have double-clicked **1** (Fig.TL-5.30).
7. *Enter* the details of the item under their respective columns. In our case, we have entered **Moti Bagh** under **Godown, 2** under **Quantity, 8,800** under **Rate,** and **nos** under **per** columns. The **Amount** column is automatically filled, as shown in Fig.TL-5.30:

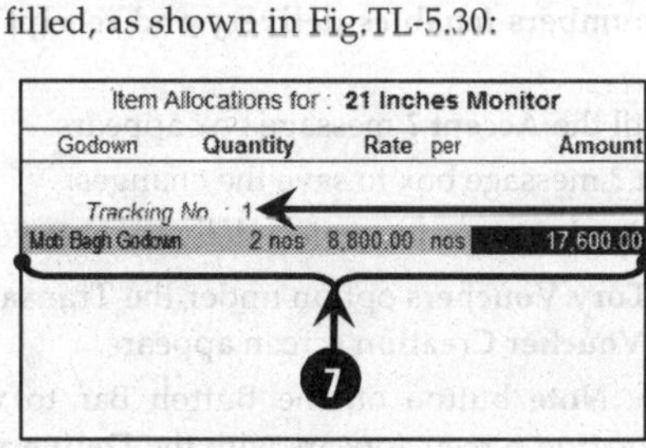

Fig.TL-5.30

8. *Press* the **Enter** key until the **Inventory Voucher Creation** screen reappears (Fig.TL-5.31).
9. *Enter* the narration under the **Narration** option. In our case, we have entered **Rejection Out of 21 Inches Monitor to Yash Traders** (Fig.TL-5.31).
10. *Press* the **Enter** key. The **Accept ?** message box appears (Fig.TL-5.31).

11. *Click* **Yes** in the **Accept ?** message box to create the voucher, as shown in Fig.TL-5.31:

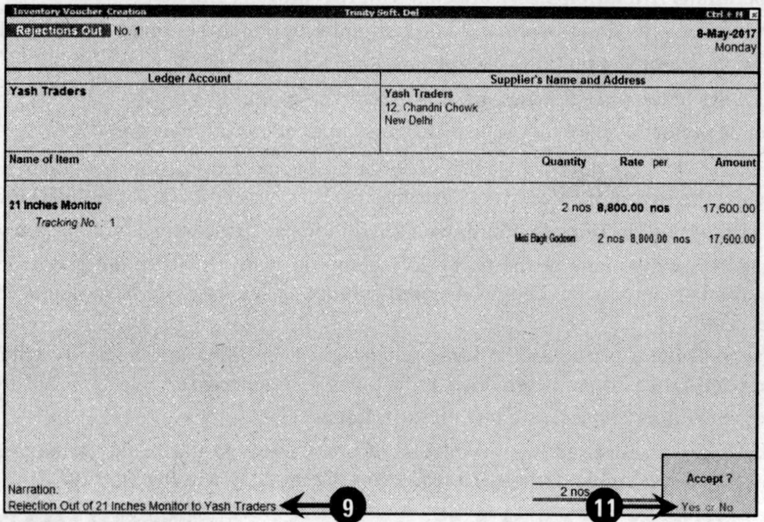

Fig.TL-5.31

Let us now learn about a delivery note voucher.

Delivery Note Voucher

A delivery note voucher is used to record transactions related to goods that are delivered to the customer. You need to first activate the Use tracking numbers (enables delivery and receipt notes) option under Inventory Features to create a delivery note voucher.

Perform the following steps to activate the Use tracking numbers (enables delivery and receipt notes) option:

1. *Click* the **F11: Features** button on the Button Bar in the **Gateway of Tally** screen. The **Company Features** menu appears.
2. *Double-click* the **Inventory Features** option in the **Company Features** menu. The **Company Operations Alteration** screen appears with **Inventory Features.**
3. *Set* the **Use tracking numbers (enables delivery and receipt notes)** option to **Yes** under the **Other Features** section.
4. *Press* the **Enter** key until the **Accept ?** message box appears.
5. *Click* **Yes** in the **Accept ?** message box to save the changes.

Now, let us perform the following steps to create a delivery note voucher:

1. *Double-click* the **InvenTory Vouchers** option under the **Transactions** section in the **Gateway of Tally** menu. The **Inventory Voucher Creation** screen appears.
2. *Click* the **F8: Delivery Note** button on the Button Bar to view the delivery note voucher. The **Inventory Voucher Creation** screen appears with the **Delivery Note** voucher (Fig.TL-5.32).
3. *Enter* the desired reference number beside the **Reference no.** option. In our case, we have entered **1** (Fig.TL-5.32).
4. *Press* the **Enter** key. The **List of Ledger Accounts** menu appears.
5. *Double-click* the desired supplier in the **List of Ledger Accounts** menu for the **Party A/c name** option. In our case, we have double-clicked **Manish Co.** (Fig.TL-5.32).
6. *Double-click* the desired sales ledger in the **List of Ledger Accounts** menu for the **Sales ledger** option. In our case, we have double-clicked **Sales** (Fig.TL-5.32). The **List of Stock Items** menu appears (Fig.TL-5.32).

7. *Double-click* the desired item in the **List of Stock Items** menu for the **Name of Item** column. In our case, we have double-clicked **15 Inches Monitor**, as shown in Fig.TL-5.32:

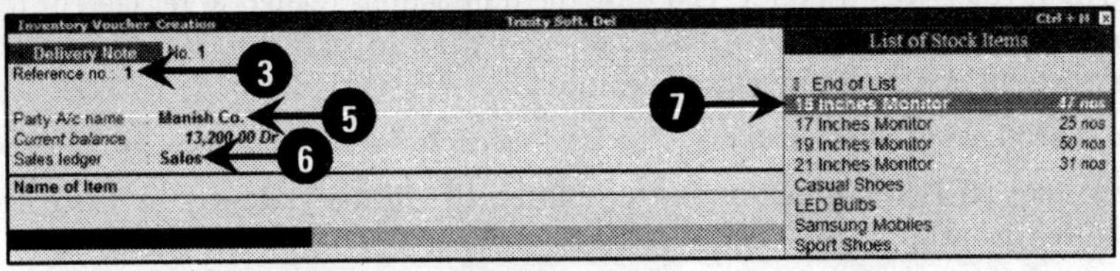

Fig.TL-5.32

The **Stock Item Allocations** screen appears with the **List of Tracking Numbers** menu.

8. *Double-click* the desired tracking number in the **List of Tracking Numbers** menu for the **Tracking No.** option. In our case, we have double-clicked **2** (Fig.TL-5.33).
9. *Enter* the details of the item under their respective columns. In our case, we have entered **Moti Bagh Godown** under **Godown**, **2** under **Quantity**, **4,400** under **Rate**, and **nos** under **per** columns (Fig.TL-5.33).

   The **Amount** column is automatically filled, as shown in Fig.TL-5.33:

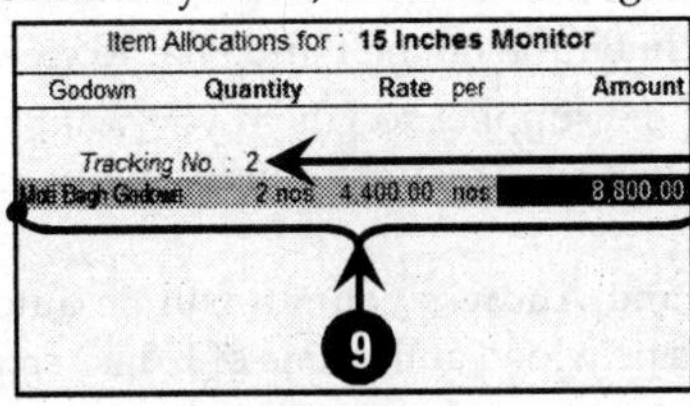

Fig.TL-5.33

10. *Press* the **Enter** key twice. The **Inventory Voucher Creation** screen reappears (Fig.TL-5.34).
11. *Press* the **Enter** key four times.
12. *Enter* the narration under the **Narration** option. In our case, we have entered **Delivery note of 15 Inches Monitor to Manish Co.** (Fig.TL-5.34).
13. *Press* the **Enter** key. The **Accept ?** message box appears (Fig.TL-5.34).
14. *Click* **Yes** in the **Accept ?** message box to create the voucher, as shown in Fig.TL-5.34:

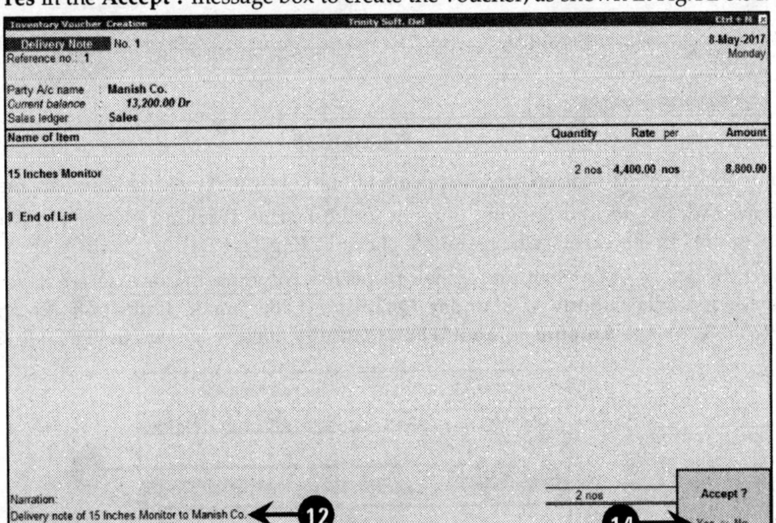

Fig.TL-5.34

Let us now learn about rejections in voucher.

Rejections In Voucher

A rejection in voucher is used for recording the transactions related to rejected or returned goods by the customer. To create a rejection in voucher, you need to first activate the Use rejection inward and outward notes option under Inventory Features.

Perform the following steps to activate the Use rejection inward and outward notes option:

1. *Click* the **F11: Features** button on the Button Bar in the **Gateway of Tally** screen. The **Company Features** menu appears.
2. *Double-click* the **Inventory Features** option in the **Company Features** menu. The **Company Operations Alteration** screen appears with **Inventory Features**.
3. *Set* the **Use rejection inward and outward notes** option to **Yes** under the **Other Features** section.
4. *Press* the **Enter** key until the **Accept ?** message box appears.
5. *Click* **Yes** in the **Accept ?** message box to save the changes.

Now, let us perform the following steps to create a rejection in voucher:

1. *Double-click* the **InvenTory Vouchers** option under the **Transactions** section in the **Gateway of Tally** menu. The **Inventory Voucher Creation** screen appears with the **Rejections In** voucher.
2. Click the **F6: Rejections In** button on the Button Bar to view the rejections in voucher.
3. *Double-click* the name of the supplier to whom you want to return the goods, in the **List of Ledger Accounts** menu for the **Ledger Account** column. In our case, we have double-clicked **Manish Co.** (Fig.TL-5.35).

   The **Customer's Name and Address** column will be automatically filled with the address of the supplier, if the address is provided at the time of ledger creation (Fig.TL-5.35).
4. *Press* the **Enter** key until the **List of Stock Items** menu appears.
5. *Double-click* the desired item in the **List of Stock Items** menu for the **Name of Item** column. In our case, we have double-clicked **15 Inches Monitor**, as shown in Fig.TL-5.35:

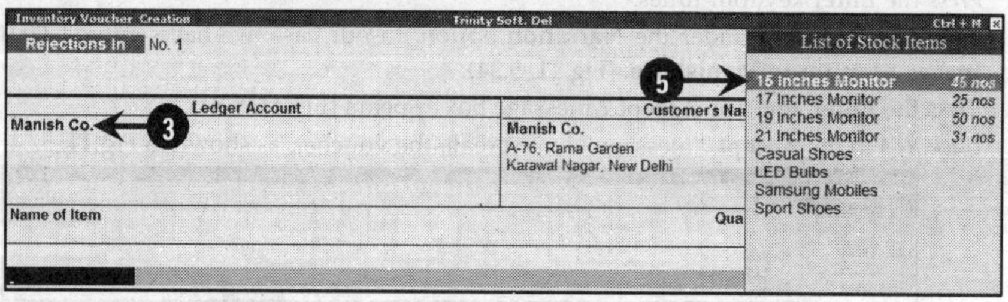

Fig.TL-5.35

The **Stock Item Allocation** screen appears with the **List of Tracking** Numbers menu.

6. *Double-click* the desired tracking number in the **List of Tracking Numbers** menu for the **Tracking No.** option. In our case, we have double-clicked 2 (Fig.TL-5.36).
7. *Enter* the details of the item under their respective columns. In our case, we have entered **Moti Bagh Godown** under **Godown**, **2** under **Quantity**, **4,400** under **Rate**, and **No** under **per** columns (Fig.TL-5.36). The **Amount** column is automatically filled, as shown in Fig.TL-5.36:

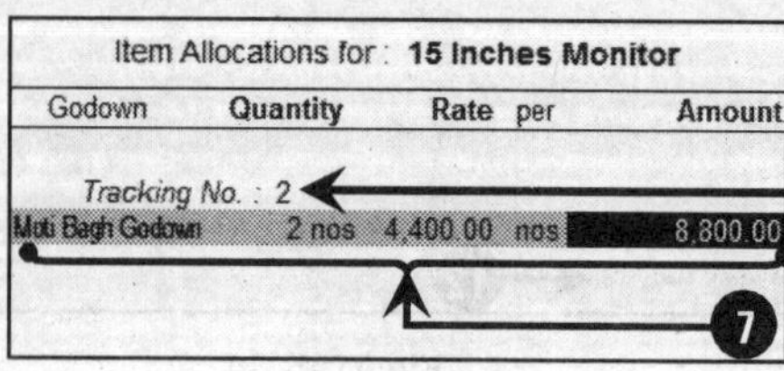

Fig.TL-5.36

8. *Press* the **Enter** key twice. The **Inventory Voucher Creation** screen reappears (Fig.TL-5.37).
9. *Press* the **Enter** key.
10. *Enter* the narration under the **Narration** option. In our case, we have entered **Rejection In of 15 Inches Monitor** (Fig.TL-5.37).
11. *Press* the **Enter** key. The **Accept ?** message box appears (Fig.TL-5.37)
12. *Click* **Yes** in the **Accept ?** message box to save the voucher, as shown in Fig.TL-5.37:

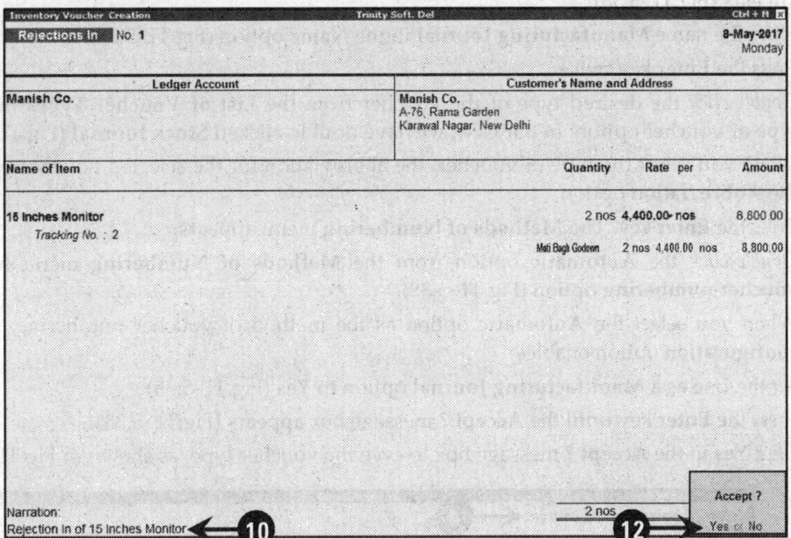

Fig.TL-5.37

Let us now learn about a stock journal.

Stock Journal

A stock journal allows you to track the movement of inventory. It is used to enter all types of stock adjustments that occur because of two reasons. These two reasons are as follows:

- **Consumption in manufacturing process:** Raw materials are used to produce finished products, reducing the stock in hand.
- **Inter-godown transfer:** Stock is transferred from one location to another while the quantity remains the same.

To create a stock journal, you need to prepare a manufacturing journal and a transfer journal.

Manufacturing journal is used by a company to keep a record of raw materials used for producing finished goods in the manufacturing process. To create a manufacturing journal, you need to enable Maintain multiple Godowns option and create a manufacturing voucher type.

Perform the following steps to enable the Maintain multiple Godowns option:

1. *Click* the **F11: Features** button on the Button Bar in the **Gateway of Tally** screen. The **Company Features** menu appears.
2. *Double-click* the **Inventory Features** option in the **Company Features** menu. The **Company Operations Alteration** screen appears with **Inventory Features.**
3. *Set* the **Maintain multiple Godowns** option to **Yes** under the **Storage and Classification** section in **Inventory Features.**
4. *Press* the **Enter** key until the **Accept ?** message box appears.
5. *Click* **Yes** in the **Accept ?** message box to save the changes.

Now, perform the following steps to create a manufacturing voucher type:

1. *Double-click* the **Inventory Info.** option under the **Masters** section in the **Gateway of Tally** menu. The **Inventory Info.** menu appears.
2. *Double-click* the **Voucher Types** option in the **Inventory Info.** menu. The **Voucher Types** menu appears.
3. *Double-click* the **Create** option in the **Voucher Types** menu. The **Voucher Type Creation** screen appears (Fig.TL-5.38).
4. *Enter* the name **Manufacturing Journal** in the **Name** option (Fig.TL-5.38).
5. *Press* the **Enter** key twice.
6. *Double-click* the desired type of the voucher from the **List of Voucher Types** menu for the **Select type of voucher** option. In our case, we have double-clicked **Stock Journal** (Fig.TL-5.38).

   When you select the type of voucher, the abbreviation for the selected voucher type appears beside the **Abbreviation** option.
7. *Press* the **Enter** key. The **Methods of Numbering** menu appears.
8. *Double-click* the **Automatic** option from the **Methods of Numbering** menu for the **Method of voucher numbering** option (Fig.TL-5.38).

   When you select the **Automatic** option as the method of voucher numbering, the **Use advanced configuration** option enables.
9. *Set* the **Use as a Manufacturing Journal** option to **Yes** (Fig.TL-5.38).
10. *Press* the **Enter** key until the **Accept ?** message box appears (Fig.TL-5.38).
11. *Click* **Yes** in the **Accept ?** message box to save the voucher type, as shown in Fig.TL-5.38:

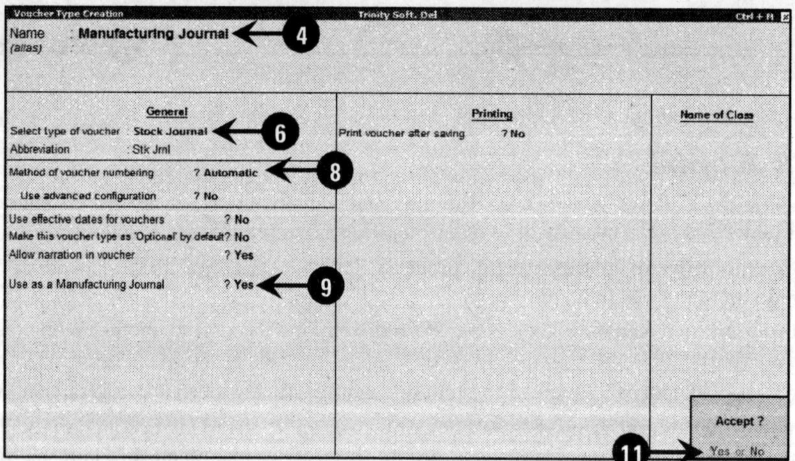

Fig.TL-5.38

After creating the manufacturing voucher type, perform the following steps to create a manufacturing journal:

1. *Double-click* the **InvenTory Vouchers** option under the **Transactions** section in the **Gateway of Tally** menu. The **Inventory Voucher Creation** screen appears.
2. *Click* the **F7: Stock Journal** button on the Button Bar. The **Change Voucher Type** screen appears with the **List of Types** menu.
3. *Double-click* the **Manufacturing Journal** option in the **List of Types** menu for the **Name** option to create a manufacturing journal. The **Inventory Voucher Creation** screen of the **Manufacturing Journal** appears.
4. *Double-click* the desired item in the **List of Stock Items** menu for the **Name of product** option. In our case, we have double-clicked **17 Inches Monitor** (Fig.TL-5.39). The **List of Godowns** menu appears.

5. *Double-click* the desired godown in the **List of Godowns** menu for the **Godown** option. In our case, we have double-clicked **Moti Bagh Godown** (Fig.TL-5.39).
6. *Enter* the desired quantity of the item beside the **Qty** option. In our case, we have entered **5** (Fig.TL-5.39).
7. *Press* the **Enter** key. The **List of Stock Items** menu appears (Fig.TL-5.39).
8. *Double-click* the desired item in the **List of Stock Items** menu for the **Name of Item** column. In our case, we have double-clicked **17 Inches Monitor** (Fig.TL-5.39).
9. *Press* the **Enter** key. The **List of Godowns** menu appears.
10. *Double-click* the desired godown in the **List of Godowns** menu for the **Godown** column. In our case, we have double-clicked **Moti Bagh Godown** (Fig.TL-5.39).
11. *Enter* the quantity and rate of the item under the **Quantity** and **Rate** columns. In our case, we have entered **5** in the **Quantity** column and **5,500** in the **Rate** column (Fig.TL-5.39). The **Amount** column is automatically filled (Fig.TL-5.39).
12. *Press* the **Enter** key three times. The **List of Ledger Accounts** menu appears (Fig.TL-5.39).
13. *Double-click* the desired ledger in the **List of Ledger Accounts** menu for the **Type of Additional Cost** column. In our case, we have double-clicked **Freight** (Fig.TL-5.39).
14. *Enter* the percentage of the freight in the **Percentage** column. In our case, we have entered **1%** (Fig.TL-5.39).
15. *Press* the **Enter** key thrice.
16. *Enter* the narration under the **Narration** option. In our case, we have left it blank (Fig.TL-5.39).
17. *Press* the **Enter** key. The **Accept ?** message box appears (Fig.TL-5.39).
18. *Click* **Yes** in the **Accept ?** message box to save the manufacturing journal, as shown in Fig.TL-5.39:

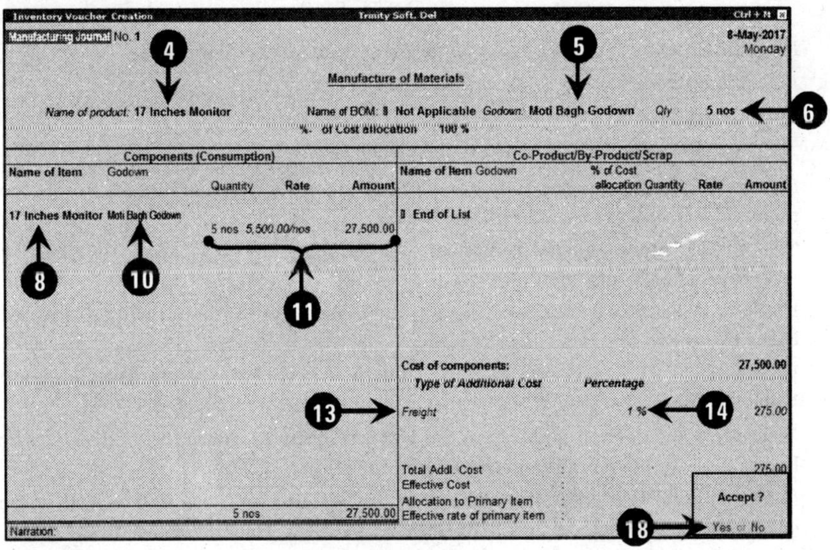

Fig.TL-5.39

Transfer journal is used by a company to keep a record of the movement of stock from one location (godown) to another. In this movement of stock, only the location changes while the quantity remains the same. To create a transfer journal, you need to enable the Maintain multiple Godowns option in Inventory Features.

Perform the following steps to enable the Maintain multiple Godowns option:

1. *Click* the **F11: Features** button on the Button Bar in the **Gateway of Tally** screen. The **Company Features** menu appears.

2. *Double-click* the **Inventory Features** option in the **Company Features** menu. The **Company Operations Alteration** screen appears with **Inventory Features.**
3. *Set* the **Maintain multiple Godowns** option to **Yes** under the **Storage and Classification** section in **Inventory Features.**
4. *Press* the **Enter** key until the **Accept ?** message box appears.
5. *Click* **Yes** in the **Accept ?** message box to save the changes.

Now, perform the following steps to alter the stock journal voucher type:

1. *Double-click* the **Inventory Info.** option under the **Masters** section in the **Gateway of Tally** menu. The **Inventory Info.** menu appears.
2. *Double-click* the **Voucher Types** option in the **Inventory Info.** menu. The **Voucher Types** menu appears.
3. *Double-click* the **Alter** option in the **Voucher Types** menu. The **Select Voucher Type** screen appears with the **List of Voucher Types** menu.
4. *Double-click* the **Stock Journal** option in the **List of Voucher Types** menu. The **Voucher Type Alteration** screen appears.
5. *Press* the **Enter** key until the **Name of Class** option appears.
6. *Enter* **Transfer** in the **Name of Class** option.
7. *Press* the **Enter** key. The **Voucher Type Class** screen appears (Fig.TL-5.40).
8. *Set* the **Use Class for Inter- Godown Transfers** option to **Yes**, as shown in Fig.TL-5.40:

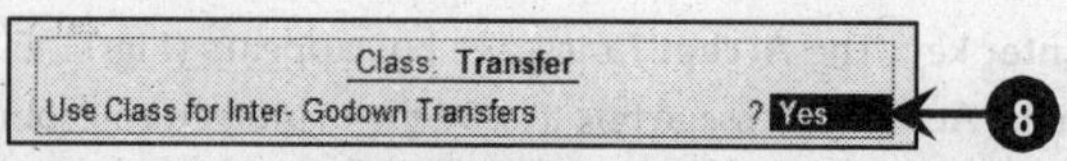

Fig.TL-5.40

9. *Press* the **Enter** key. The **Voucher Type Alteration** screen reappears.
10. *Press* the **Enter** key until the **Accept ?** message box appears.
11. *Click* **Yes** in the **Accept ?** message box to save the changes.

Now, perform the following steps to create a stock transfer journal:

1. *Double-click* the **InvenTory Vouchers** option under the **Transactions** section in the **Gateway of Tally** menu. The **Inventory Voucher Creation** screen appears.
2. *Click* the **F7: Stock Journal** button on the Button bar. The **Change Voucher Type** screen appears with the **List of Types** menu.
3. *Double-click* the **Stock Journal** option in the **List of Types** menu for the **Name** option. The **Voucher Class List** menu appears.
4. *Double-click* the **Transfer** option in the **Voucher Class List** menu for the **Class** option. The **Inventory Voucher Creation** screen of the Transfer Journal appears (Fig.TL-5.41).
5. *Double-click* the desired godown in the **List of Godowns** menu for the **Destination Godown** option. In our case, we have double-clicked **Main Location** (Fig.TL-5.41).
6. *Double-click* the desired item in the **List of Stock Items** for the **Name of Item** column. In our case, we have double-clicked **15 Inches Monitor** (Fig.TL-5.41). The **List of Godowns** menu appears.
7. *Double-click* the desired godown in the **List of Godowns** menu for the **Godown** column. In our case, we have double-clicked **Moti Bagh Godown** (Fig.TL-5.41).
8. *Enter* the quantity and rate of the item under the **Quantity** and **Rate** columns. In our case, we have entered **10** in the **Quantity** column and **4,200** in the **Rate** column (Fig.TL-5.41).

   The **Amount** column is automatically filled.

   Similarly, you can add more items and their relevant details in the **Inventory Voucher Creation** screen. Repeat steps 6 to 8. In our case, we have added **19 Inches Monitor** and entered details for it (Fig.TL-5.41).

9. *Press* the **Enter** key twice.
10. *Enter* the narration under the **Narration** option. In our case, we have entered **Transfer Journal of 15 Inches and 19 Inches Monitor** (Fig.TL-5.41).
11. *Press* the **Enter** key. The **Accept ?** message box appears.
12. *Click* **Yes** in the **Accept ?** message box to save the transfer journal, as shown in Fig.TL-5.41:

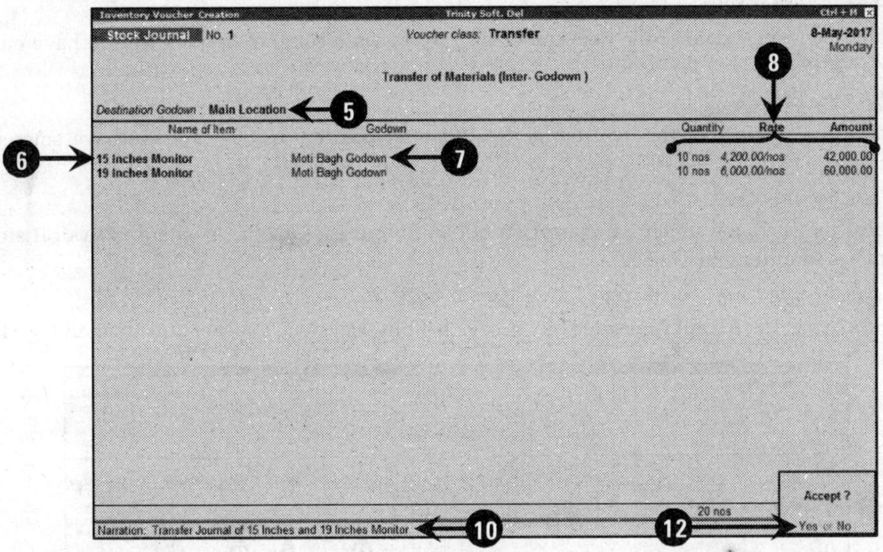

Fig.TL-5.41

Let us now learn about a physical stock voucher.

Physical Stock Voucher

A physical stock voucher is defined as a stock voucher that records the real stock in hand, which is physically counted and verified. Sometimes, a physical stock difference may arise between the actual stock and the stock shown by the computer. To avoid this difference, physical stock voucher is created. In case the configured voucher does not resolve the physical stock differences, then all the transactions subsequent to the physical stock voucher use the balance mentioned in it.

Perform the following steps to create a physical stock voucher:

1. *Double-click* the **InvenTory Vouchers** option under the **Transactions** section in the **Gateway of Tally** menu. The **Inventory Voucher Creation** screen appears.
2. *Click* the **F10: Physical Stock** button on the Button Bar. The **Inventory Voucher Creation** screen for the Physical Stock appears.
3. *Press* the **Enter** key. The **List of Stock Items** menu appears.
4. *Double-click* the desired item in the **List of Stock Items** menu for the **Name of Item** column. In our case, we have double-clicked **19 Inches Monitor** (Fig.TL-5.42). The **List of Godowns** menu appears.
5. *Double-click* the desired godown in the **List of Godowns** menu for the **Godown** column. In our case, we have double-clicked **Moti Bagh Godown** (Fig.TL-5.42). The **List of Active Batches** menu appears (Fig.TL-5.42).
6. *Double-click* the relevant batch number in the **List of Active Batches** menu for the **Batch/Lot No.** column. In our case, we have double-clicked **Batch 01** (Fig.TL-5.42).

Note **Batch-wise details will appear only if Batch-wise details are enabled during creation of Stock Item.**

7. *Enter* the manufacturing date of the selected item under the **Mfg Dt.** column. In our case, we have entered **Apr-2017** (Fig.TL-5.42).
8. *Press* the **Enter** key.
9. *Enter* the expiry date of the item under the **Expiry Date** column. In our case, we have entered **31-Mar-2019** (Fig.TL-5.42).
10. *Press* the **Enter** key.
11. *Enter* the quantity of the item under the **Quantity** column. In our case, we have entered **10 nos** (Fig.TL-5.42).
12. *Press* the **Enter** key.
13. *Enter* the narration under the **Narration** option. In our case, we have entered **Physical stock of 19 Inches Monitor** (Fig.TL-5.42).
14. *Press* the **Enter** key. The **Accept ?** message box appears.
15. *Click* **Yes** in the **Accept ?** message box to save the physical stock voucher, as shown in Fig.TL-5.42:

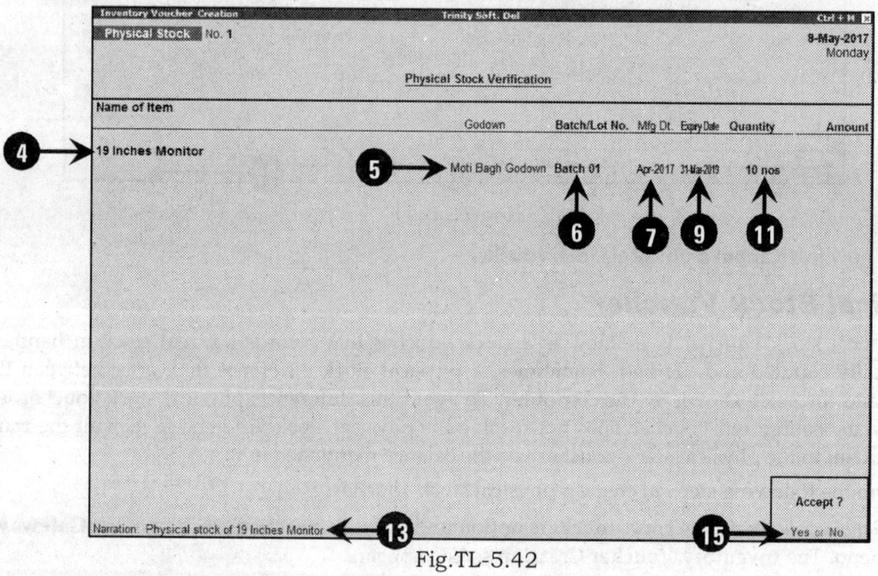

Fig.TL-5.42

Order Processing

Order processing can be defined as a procedure of placing purchase orders with traders or sales orders with customers. This procedure also covers tracking the receipt or delivery of the ordered materials or goods. Therefore, order processing is beneficial in the aspects such as tracking the stage of order, delivery of the ordered goods, and receipt of the goods ordered. In a nutshell, you can say that order processing is related to purchasing, selling, and tracking orders. In Tally, you can activate order processing by enabling the Enable purchase order processing, Enable sales order processing, and Use tracking numbers (enable delivery/receipt notes) options from the Inventory Features.

Purchase Order Processing

Purchase order is a type of order placed by a customer in order to procure goods from a supplier. To create a purchase order, you need to first enable the Enable purchase order processing option under Inventory Features in the Company Operations Alteration screen.

Perform the following steps to enable the Enable purchase order processing option:

1. *Click* the **F11: Features** button located on the Button Bar in the **Gateway of Tally** screen. The **Company Features** menu appears.
2. *Double-click* the **Inventory Features** option in the **Company Features** menu. The **Company Operations Alteration** screen appears with **Inventory Features**.
3. *Set* the **Enable purchase order processing** option to **Yes**.
4. *Press* the **Enter** key until you get the **Accept ?** message box.
5. *Click* **Yes** in the **Accept ?** message box to save the changes.

After enabling the **Enable purchase order processing** option, perform the following steps to create a purchase order:

1. *Double-click* the **OrdEr Vouchers** option in the **Transactions** section in the **Gateway of Tally** menu. The **Order Voucher Creation** screen appears.
2. *Click* the **F4: Purchase Order** button on the Button Bar to view the purchase order. The **Order Voucher Creation** screen of the purchase order appears with the **List of Ledger Accounts** menu (Fig.TL-5.43).
3. *Double-click* the name of supplier in the **List of Ledger Accounts** menu for the **Party A/c name** option. In our case, we have double-clicked **Yash Traders** (Fig.TL-5.43).
4. *Enter* the purchase order number beside the **Order no.** option. In our case, we have entered **2**.
5. *Press* the **Enter** key. The **List of Ledgers Accounts** menu appears (Fig.TL-5.43).
6. *Double-click* the name of purchase ledger in the **List of Ledger Accounts** menu for the **Purchase ledger** option. In our case, we have double-clicked **Purchase** (Fig.TL-5.43). The **List of Stock Items** menu appears (Fig.TL-5.43).
7. *Double-click* the name of item in the **List of Stock Items** menu for the **Name of Item** column. In our case, we have double-clicked **17 Inches Monitor** as shown in Fig.TL-5.43:

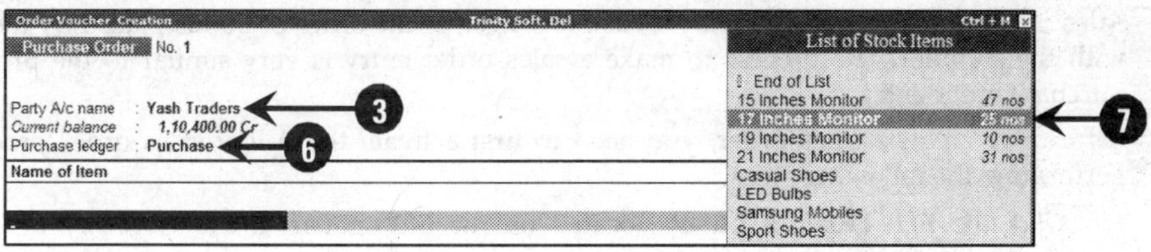

Fig.TL-5.43

The **Stock Item Allocations** screen appears (Fig.TL-5.44).

8. *Enter* the due date for receipt of the items beside the **Due on** option. In our case, we have entered **30-May-2017** (Fig.TL-5.44).
9. *Press* the **Enter** key. The **List of Godowns** menu appears.
10. *Double-click* the godown in the **List of Godowns** menu for the **Godown** column. In our case, we have double-clicked **Main Location** (Fig.TL-5.44).
11. *Enter* the relevant details for the item allocation in the **Quantity**, **Rate**, and **per**, columns. In our case, we have entered **25** under **Quantity**, **5,500** under **Rate**, and **nos** under **per** (Fig.TL-5.44).

    The amount is automatically calculated and displayed under **Amount**, as shown in Fig.TL-5.44:

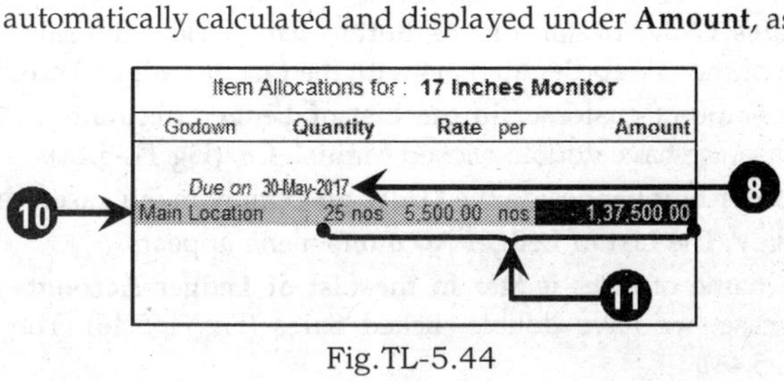

Fig.TL-5.44

12. *Press* the **Enter** key twice. The **Order Voucher Creation** screen reappears (Fig.TL-5.45).
13. *Press* the **Enter** key until the **Accept ?** message box appears (Fig.TL-5.45).
14. *Click* **Yes** in the **Accept ?** message box to create the purchase order, as shown in Fig.TL-5.45:

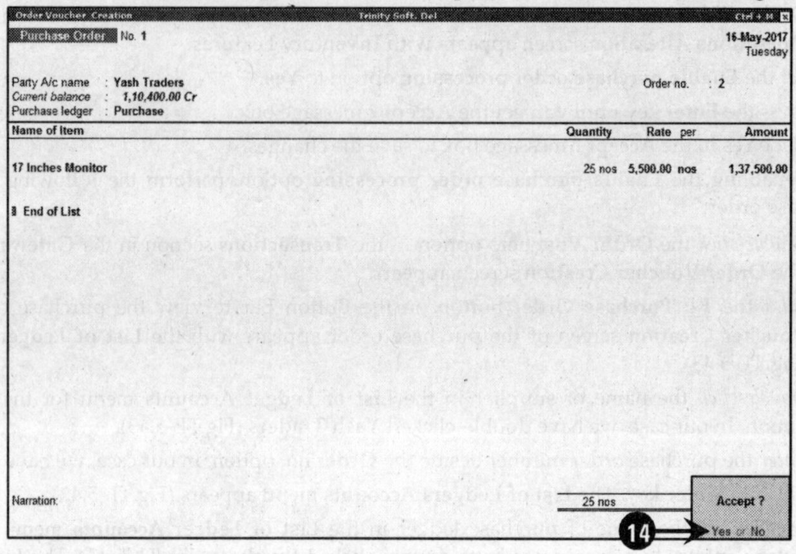

Fig.TL-5.45

Let us now learn about processing a sales order.

Sales Order Processing

Sales order is an order received by a customer against the order of goods placed by the customer earlier with the supplier. The process to make a sales order entry is very similar to the process of making a purchase order entry.

Before you create a sales order, you need to first activate the Allow sales order processing option by performing the following steps:

1. *Click* the **F11: Features** button located on the Button Bar in the **Gateway of Tally** screen. The **Company Features** menu appears.
2. *Double-click* the **Inventory Features** option in the **Company Features** menu. The **Company Operations Alteration** screen appears with **Inventory Features.**
3. *Set* the **Enable sales order processing** option to **Yes.**
4. *Press* the **Enter** key until you get the **Accept ?** message box.
5. *Click* the **Yes** option in the **Accept ?** message box to save the changes.

After activating the **Enable sales order processing** option, perform the following steps to create a sales order:

1. *Double-click* the **OrdEr Vouchers** option in the **Transactions** section in the **Gateway of Tally** menu. The **Order Voucher Creation** screen appears.
2. *Click* the **F5: Sales Order** button on the Button Bar to view the sales order. The **Order Voucher Creation** screen of the sales order appears with the **List of Ledger Accounts** menu (Fig.TL-5.46).
3. *Double-click* the name of customer in the **List of Ledger Accounts** menu for the **Party A/c name** option. In our case, we have double-clicked **Manish Co.** (Fig.TL-5.46).
4. *Enter* the sales order number beside the **Order no.** option. In our case, we have entered **5.**
5. *Press* the **Enter** key. The **List of Ledger Accounts** menu appears.
6. *Double-click* the name of sales ledger in the **List of Ledger Accounts** menu for the **Sales ledger** option. In our case, we have double-clicked **Sales** (Fig.TL-5.46). The **List of Stock Items** menu appears (Fig.TL-5.46).

7. *Double-click* the name of item in the **List of Stock Items** menu for the **Name of Item** column. In our case, we have double-clicked **15 Inches Monitor**, as shown in Fig.TL-5.46:

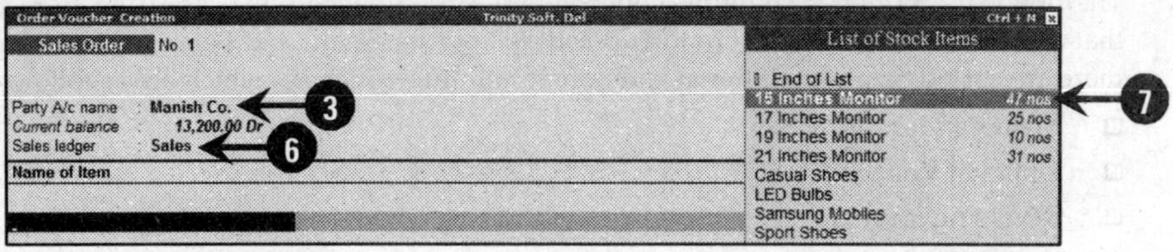

Fig.TL-5.46

The **Stock Item Allocations** screen appears (Fig.TL-5.47).

8. *Enter* the due date for delivery of the items beside the **Due on** option. In our case, we have entered **30-May-2017** (Fig.TL-5.47).
9. *Press* the **Enter** key. The **List of Godowns** menu appears.
10. *Double-click* the name of godown in the **List of Godowns** menu for the **Godown** column. In our case, we have double-clicked **Moti Bagh Godown** (Fig.TL-5.47).
11. *Enter* the relevant details for the item allocation in the **Quantity, Rate**, and **per** columns. In our case, we have entered **10** under **Quantity, 4,400** under **Rate**, and **nos** under **per** (Fig.TL-5.47).

    The amount is automatically calculated and displayed under **Amount**, as shown in Fig.TL-5.47:

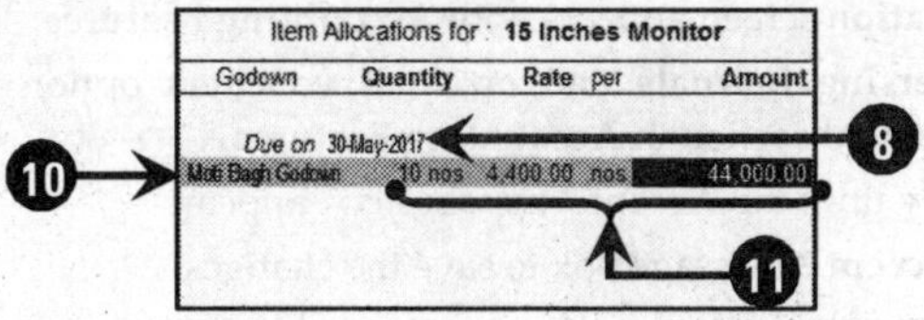

Fig.TL-5.47

12. *Press* the **Enter** key twice. The **Order Voucher Creation** screen reappears (Fig.TL-5.48).
13. *Press* the **Enter** key until the **Accept ?** message box appears (Fig.TL-5.48).
14. *Click* **Yes** in the **Accept ?** message box to create the sales order, as shown in Fig.TL-5.48:

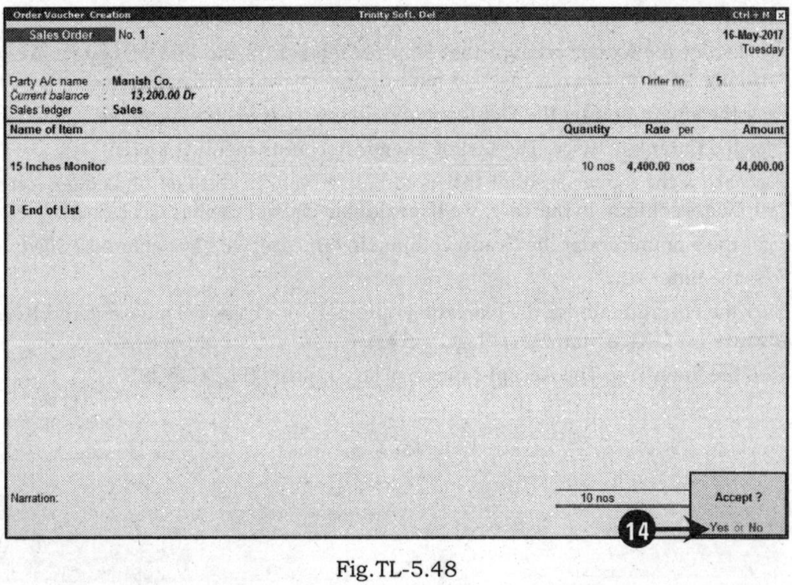

Fig.TL-5.48

Optional and Non-Accounting Vouchers

The optional and non-accounting vouchers are those vouchers that are used to record all transactions that do not affect the financial reports (Profit & Loss statement and Balance Sheet report). In Tally.ERP 9, there are various types of optional and non-accounting vouchers, which are as follows:

- Memorandum Voucher
- Optional Voucher
- Reversing Journal
- Post-Dated Voucher

Let us learn about these vouchers one by one in the following sections.

Memorandum Voucher

Memorandum vouchers are used for suspense payments, vouchers that are not verified at the time of entry, items given on approval, and reminder services. The entries made in the memorandum voucher do not affect the accounts.

Perform the following steps to enable a memorandum voucher:

1. *Click* the **F11: Features** button on the Button Bar in the **Gateway of Tally** screen. The **Company Features** menu appears.
2. *Double-click* the **Accounting Features** option in the **Company Features** menu. The **Company Operations Alteration** screen appears with **Accounting Features.**
3. *Set* the **Use reversing journals and optional vouchers** option to **Yes** under the **Budgets and Scenario Management** section in **Accounting Features.**
4. *Press* the **Enter** key until the **Accept ?** message box appears.
5. *Click* **Yes** in the **Accept ?** message box to save the changes.

Now, perform the following steps to create a memorandum voucher:

1. *Double-click* the **Accounting Vouchers** option under the **Transactions** section in the **Gateway of Tally** menu. The **Accounting Voucher Creation** screen appears.
2. *Click* the **F10: Memos** button on the Button Bar.

   The **Accounting Voucher Creation** screen of memorandum voucher appears with the **List of Ledger Accounts** menu.
3. *Double-click* the ledger account that is to be debited, in the **List of Ledger Accounts** menu for the **Particulars** column. In our case, we have double-clicked **Office Stationery** (Fig.TL-5.49).
4. *Enter* the amount under the **Debit** column. In our case, we have entered **2,500** (Fig.TL-5.49).
5. *Press* the **Enter** key twice. The **List of Ledger Accounts** menu appears.
6. *Double-click* the ledger account that is to be credited, in the **List of Ledger Accounts** menu for the **Particulars** column. In our case, we have double-clicked **Cash** (Fig.TL-5.49).
7. *Enter* the amount under the **Credit** column. In our case, we have entered **2,500** (Fig.TL-5.49).
8. *Press* the **Enter** key.
9. *Enter* the narration under the **Narration** option. In our case, we have entered **Received petty cash in advance for Office Stationery** (Fig.TL-5.49).
10. *Press* the **Enter** key. The **Accept ?** message box appears (Fig.TL-5.49).

11. *Click* **Yes** in the **Accept ?** message box to save the voucher, as shown in Fig.TL-5.49:

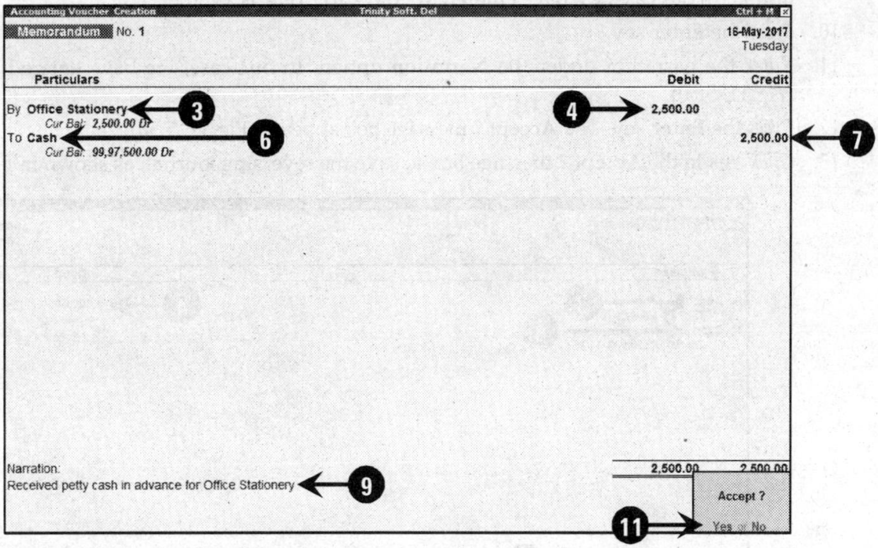

Fig.TL-5.49

Let us now learn about a reversing journal.

Reversing Journal

A reversing journal is a journal that is automatically reversed after a defined date. This type of journal will exist until the defined date and is used for making a provisional report on the progress of the financial year.

Perform the following steps to enable a reversing journal:

1. *Click* the **F11: Features** button on the Button Bar in the **Gateway of Tally** menu. The **Company Features** menu appears.
2. *Double-click* the **Accounting Features** option in the **Company Features** menu. The **Company Operations Alteration** screen appears with **Accounting Features**.
3. *Set* the **Use reversing journals and optional vouchers** option to **Yes** under the **Budgets and Scenario Management** section in **Accounting Features**.
4. *Press* the **Enter** key until the **Accept ?** message box appears.
5. *Click* **Yes** in the **Accept ?** message box to save the changes.

Now, perform the following steps to create a reversing journal:

1. *Double-click* the **Accounting Vouchers** option under the **Transactions** section in the **Gateway of Tally** menu. The **Accounting Voucher Creation** screen appears.
2. *Click* the **F10: Reversing Journal** button on the Button Bar. The **Accounting Voucher Creation** screen of reversing journal appears with the **List of Ledger Accounts** menu.
3. *Double-click* the ledger account that is to be debited, in the **List of Ledger Accounts** menu for the **Particulars** column. In our case, we have double-clicked **Rent** (Fig.TL-5.50).
4. *Enter* the amount under the **Debit** column. In our case, we have entered **5,000** (Fig.TL-5.50).
5. *Press* the **Enter** key twice. The **List of Ledger Accounts** menu appears.
6. *Double-click* the ledger account that is to be credited, in the **List of Ledger Accounts** menu for the **Particulars** column. In our case, we have double-clicked **Cash** (Fig.TL-5.50).
7. *Enter* the amount under the **Credit** column. In our case, we have entered **5,000** (Fig.TL-5.50).
8. *Press* the **Enter** key.

9. *Enter* the date from which the reversing journal will be applicable beside the **Applicable Upto** option. In our case, we have entered **31-May-2017** (Fig.TL-5.50).
10. *Press* the **Enter** key.
11. *Enter* the narration under the **Narration** option. In our case, we have entered **Reversing Journal** (Fig.TL-5.50).
12. *Press* the **Enter** key. The **Accept ?** message box appears (Fig.TL-5.50).
13. *Click* **Yes** in the **Accept ?** message box to save the reversing journal, as shown in Fig.TL-5.50:

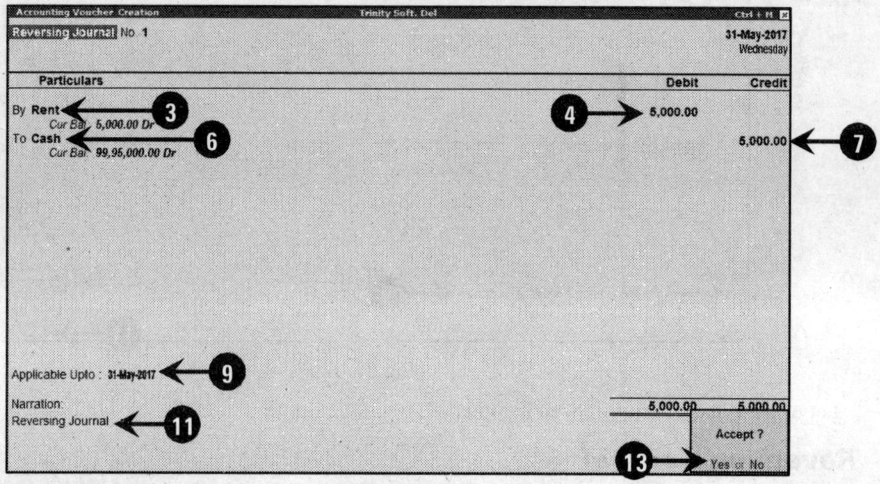

Fig.TL-5.50

Let us now learn about an optional voucher.

Optional Voucher

An optional voucher is used to view the effects of transactions without really posting the transactions. You can mark an existing voucher as optional by pressing the L: Optional button on the Button Bar. The entry made in the optional voucher is not posted anywhere, but it remains in the optional voucher register.

Perform the following steps to enable an optional voucher:

1. *Click* the **F11: Features** button on the Button Bar in the **Gateway of Tally** menu. The **Company Features** menu appears.
2. *Double-click* the **Accounting Features** option in the **Company Features** menu. The **Company Operations Alteration** screen appears with **Accounting Features**.
3. *Set* the **Use reversing journals and optional vouchers** option to **Yes** under the **Budgets and Scenario Management** section in **Accounting Features**.
4. *Press* the **Enter** key until the **Accept ?** message box appears.
5. *Click* **Yes** in the **Accept ?** message box to save the changes.

Now, perform the following steps to create an optional voucher:

1. *Double-click* the **Accounting Vouchers** option under the **Transactions** section in the **Gateway of Tally** menu. The **Accounting Voucher Creation** screen appears.
2. *Click* the **L: Optional** button on the Button Bar. The word **Optional** appears on the voucher (Fig.TL-5.51).
3. *Double-click* the ledger account that is to be debited, in the **List of Ledger Accounts** menu for the **Particulars** column. In our case, we have double-clicked **Salary** (Fig.TL-5.51).
4. *Enter* the amount under the **Debit** column. In our case, we have entered **25,000** (Fig.TL-5.51).

5. *Press* the **Enter** key twice.
6. *Double-click* the ledger account that is to be credited, in the **List of Ledger Accounts** menu for the **Particulars** column. In our case, we have double-clicked **Cash** (Fig.TL-5.51).
7. *Enter* the amount under the **Credit** column. In our case, we have entered **25,000** (Fig.TL-5.51).
8. *Press* the **Enter** key.
9. *Enter* the narration under the **Narration** option. In our case, we have entered **Optional Voucher of Salary of May 2017** (Fig.TL-5.51).
10. *Press* the **Enter** key. The **Accept ?** message box appears (Fig.TL-5.51).
11. *Click* **Yes** in the **Accept ?** message box to save the voucher, as shown in Fig.TL-5.51:

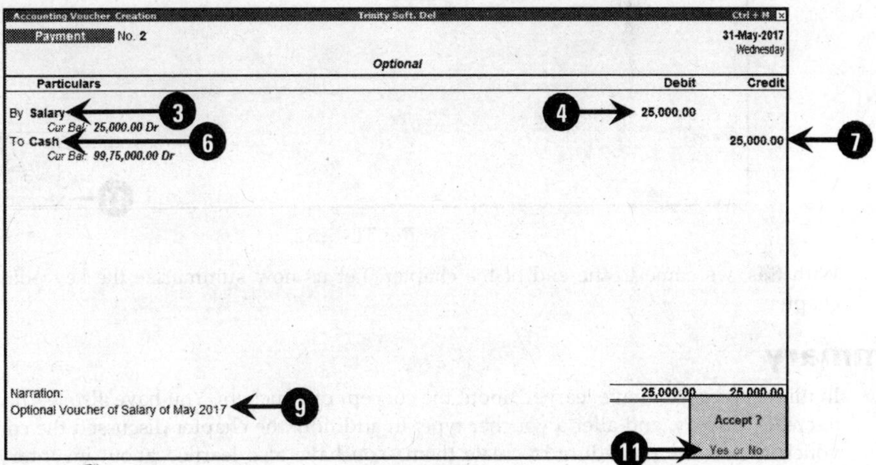

Fig.TL-5.51

Let us now learn about a post-dated voucher.

Post-Dated Voucher

A post-dated voucher is useful when the same transaction is posted on a regular basis. You can mark an existing voucher as post-dated by pressing the T: Post-Dated button on the Button bar. The entry made in the post-dated voucher will not be posted until the specified date.

Perform the following steps to create a post-dated voucher:

1. *Double-click* the **Accounting Vouchers** option under the **Transactions** section in the **Gateway of Tally** menu. The **Accounting Voucher Creation** screen appears.
2. *Click* the **T: Post-Dated** button on the Button Bar. The word **Post-Dated** appears on the voucher (Fig.TL-5.52).
3. *Double-click* the ledger account that is to be debited, in the **List of Ledger Accounts** menu for the **Particulars** column. In our case, we have double-clicked **Salary** (Fig.TL-5.52).
4. *Enter* the amount under the **Debit** column. In our case, we have entered **20,000** (Fig.TL-5.52).
5. *Press* the **Enter** key twice.
6. *Double-click* the ledger account that is to be credited, in the **List of Ledger Accounts** menu for the **Particulars** column. In our case, we have double-clicked **SBI BANK** (Fig.TL-5.52).
7. *Enter* the amount under the **Credit** column. In our case, we have entered **20,000** (Fig.TL-5.52).
8. *Press* the **Enter** key.
9. *Enter* the narration under the **Narration** option.
10. *Press* the **Enter** key. The **Accept ?** message box appears.

11. *Click* **Yes** in the **Accept ?** message box to save the voucher, as shown in Fig.TL-5.52:

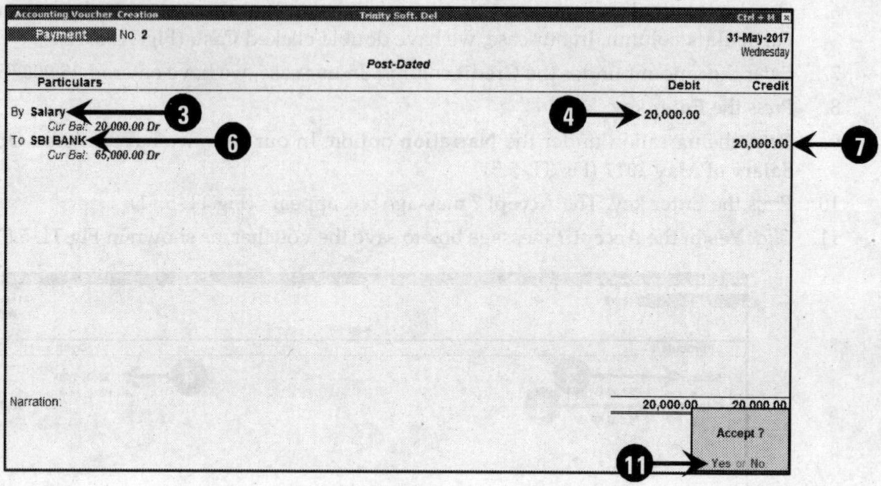

Fig.TL-5.52

With this, we come to the end of the chapter. Let us now summarize the key points discussed in the chapter.

Summary

In this chapter, you have learned about the concept of vouchers. You have also learned about the process to create, display, and alter a voucher type. In addition, the chapter discussed the concept of accounting vouchers and the procedure to create them. You have also learned about inventory vouchers and the procedure to create them. Further, you have learned about order-processing vouchers and the procedure to create them. Towards the end of the chapter, you have learned about the optional and non-accounting vouchers and the procedure to create them.

CHAPTER

6

Working with Advanced Accounting Features

In this Chapter:

* Cost Categories
* Cost Centre
* Budget
* Credit Limit
* Interest Calculation
* Basics of Banking

Introduction

Tally.ERP 9, apart from the basic accounting features and capabilities, offers advanced accounting features which allow you to generate and manage advanced accounting and MIS (Management Information System) reports in a better way. A few of the advanced accounting features in Tally.ERP 9 are cost categories, cost centres, budget, interest calculation, credit limit, cheque printing, cheque management, and bank reconciliation statement. These advanced features enable you to record and maintain your financial transactions in the books of accounts.

Cost categories specify the distribution of costs to general ledger. Cost centres enable you to view invoices and give extra information on sales and purchase orders. Budgets utilize funds and allow companies to meet their goals. Credit limit refers to the amount against the ledger in the Credit Limit option. Interest calculation lets you obtain reports on the specified interest. Cheque printing benefits businesses and users by providing the facility of configuring dimensions of cheques before getting them printed.

The chapter begins by explaining cost categories and then cost centres. Further, the chapter describes the concept of budget and credit limit. Next, the chapter discusses interest calculation. Towards the end, the chapter describes the basics of banking, such as cheque printing, cheque management, deposit slip, payment advice, and bank reconciliation statement.

Let us start the chapter by learning about cost categories.

Cost Categories

A cost category refers to a classification applied to item sites. This classification specifies the distribution of costs to general ledger. Cost categories are useful for those organizations that allocate resources to the parallel sets of cost centres.

Perform the following steps to enable the **Cost Category** feature in Tally:

1. *Click* the **F11: Features** button on the Button Bar. The **Company Features** menu appears.
2. *Double-click* the **Accounting Features** option on the **Company Features** menu. The **Company Operations Alteration** screen appears with **Accounting Features**.
3. *Set* the **Maintain cost centres** option to **Yes** under the **Cost/Profit Centres Management** section on the **Company Operations Alteration** screen.
4. *Set* the **Maintain more than one payroll or cost category** option to **Yes** under the **Cost/Profit Centres Management** section on the **Company Operations Alteration** screen.
5. *Press* the **Enter** key until the **Accept ?** message box appears.
6. *Click* **Yes** in the **Accept ?** message box to enable the **Cost Category** feature.

Creating a Single Cost Category

Perform the following steps to create a single cost category:

1. *Double-click* the **Accounts Info.** option under the **Masters** section on the **Gateway of Tally** menu. The **Accounts Info.** menu appears.
2. *Double-click* the **COst Categories** option on the **Accounts Info.** menu. The **Cost Categories** menu appears.
3. *Double-click* the **Create** option under the **Single Cost Category** section on the **Cost Categories** menu. The **Cost Category Creation** screen appears (Fig.TL-6.1).
4. *Type* the name of the cost category beside the **Name** option. In our case, we have entered **Pitam Pura** (Fig.TL-6.1).
5. *Press* the **Enter** key to move to the next option.
6. *Type* an alternative name for the cost category in the **(alias)** option.
7. *Press* the **Enter** key to move to the next option.
8. *Set* the **Allocate Revenue Items** option to **Yes** (Fig.TL-6.1).

9. *Press* the **Enter** key to move to the next option.
10. *Set* the **Allocate Non-revenue items** option to **No** (Fig.TL-6.1).
11. *Press* the **Enter** key. The **Accept ?** message box appears.
12. *Click* **Yes** in the **Accept ?** message box to create the cost category, as shown in Fig.TL-6.2:

Fig.TL-6.1

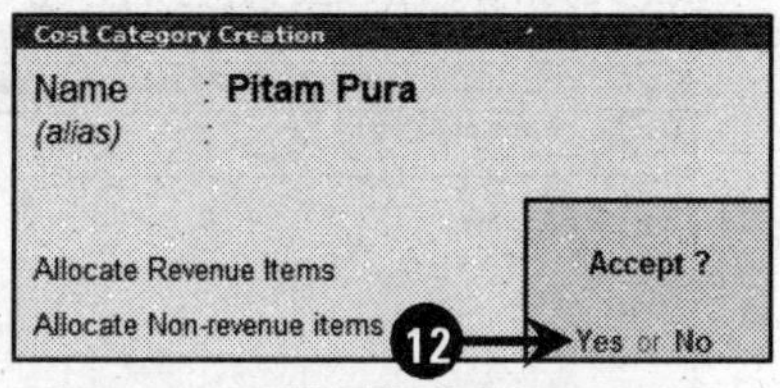

Fig.TL-6.2

Displaying a Cost Category

Perform the following steps to display a cost category:

1. *Double-click* the **Display** option under the **Single Cost Category** section on the **Cost Categories** menu. The **Select Cost Category** screen appears with a **List of Cost Categories** menu.
2. *Double-click* the cost category you want to display from the **List of Cost Categories** menu. The **Cost Category Display** screen appears with the details of the selected cost category.

Altering a Cost Category

You can alter or make changes in the details of a cost category by performing the following steps:

1. *Double-click* the **Alter** option under the **Single Cost Category** section on the **Cost Categories** menu. The **Select Cost Category** screen appears with the **List of Cost Categories** menu.
2. *Double-click* the cost category you want to alter from the **List of Cost Categories** menu. The **Cost Category Alteration** screen of the selected cost category appears.
3. *Enter* the new information for the selected cost category or make modifications in the existing information as per the requirement.
4. *Press* the **Enter** key until the **Accept ?** message box appears.
5. *Click* **Yes** in the **Accept ?** message box to save the cost category.

Creating Multiple Cost Categories

Perform the following steps to create multiple cost categories:

1. *Double-click* the **CReate** option under the **Multiple Cost Categories** section on the **Cost Categories** menu. The **Multi Cost Category Creation** screen appears (Fig.TL-6.3).
2. *Type* the name of the cost category you want to create under the **Name of Category** column. In our case, we have typed **Nirman Vihar** (Fig.TL-6.3).
3. *Press* the **Enter** key.
4. *Type* **Yes** under the **Revenue Items** column (Fig.TL-6.3).
5. *Press* the **Enter** key.
6. *Type* **No** under the **Non-Revenue Items** column, as shown in Fig.TL-6.3:

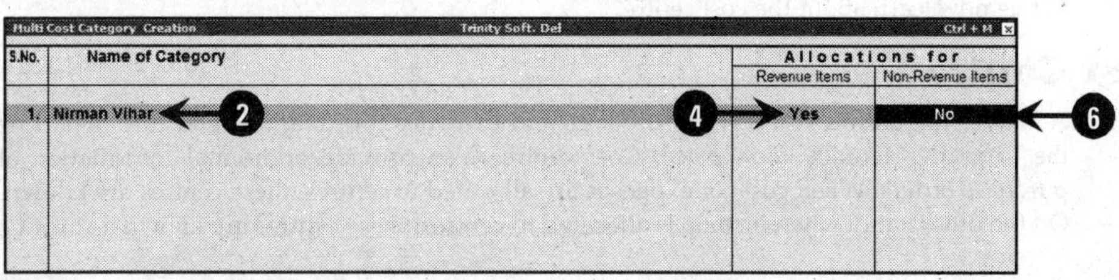

Fig.TL-6.3

7. *Press* the **Enter** key.

   Similarly, you can create another cost category. In our case, we have typed **Moti Bagh** under **Name of Category**, **Yes** under **Revenue Items**, and **No** under **Non-Revenue Items.**

8. *Press* the **Enter** key until the **Accept ?** message box appears.
9. *Click* **Yes** in the **Accept ?** message box to create the multiple cost category, as shown in Fig.TL-6.4:

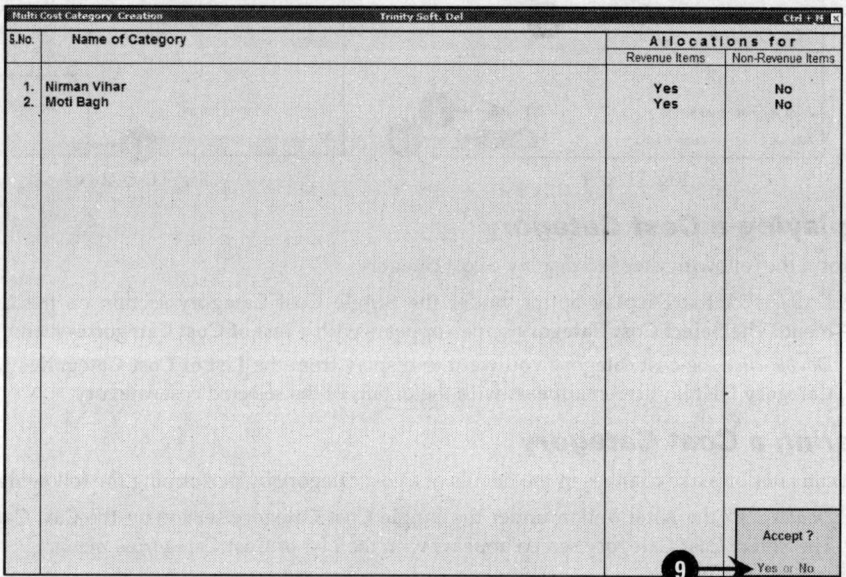

Fig.TL-6.4

Displaying Multiple Cost Categories

To display multiple cost categories, you can click the **DIsplay** option under the **Multiple Cost Categories** section on the **Cost Categories** menu. The **Multi Cost Category Display** screen appears with a list of all multiple cost categories. On this screen, you can view the details of the cost categories from the list of all multiple cost categories.

Altering Multiple Cost Categories

Perform the following steps to alter multiple cost categories:

1. *Double-click* the **AlTer** option under the **Multiple Cost Categories** section on the **Cost Categories** menu.

   The **Multi Cost Category Alteration** screen appears with a list of multiple cost categories.

2. *Enter* the new information for the selected cost category or make modifications in the existing information as per the requirements.
3. *Press* the **Enter** key until the **Accept ?** message box appears.
4. *Click* **Yes** in the **Accept ?** message box to save the changes.

Let us now learn about the cost centre.

Cost Centre

A cost centre allows you to view invoices and provides information about the department from where the invoicing actually took place. Cost centres also provide additional information about sales and purchase orders. When costs or expenses are allocated to centres, these centres are known as cost centres. On the other hand, when income is allocated to centres, these centres are known as profit centres.

Creating a Single Cost Centre

Perform the following steps to create a single cost centre:

1. *Double-click* the **Cost Centres** option on the **Accounts Info.** menu. The **Cost Centres** menu appears.
2. *Double-click* the **Create** option under the **Single Cost Centre** section in the **Cost Centres** menu. The **Cost Centre Creation** screen appears with the **List of Categories** menu.
3. *Double-click* a category on the **List of Categories** menu for the **Category** option. In our case, we have double-clicked **Moti Bagh** (Fig.TL-6.5).

Note: **By default, Tally creates a Primary Cost Category to which all cost centres are allocated. The Category option appears on the Cost Centre Creation screen if you activate the Maintain more than one payroll or cost category option under the Cost/Profit Centres Management section in Accounting Features.**

4. *Type* the name of the cost centre beside the **Name** option. In our case, we have typed **Account** (Fig.TL-6.5).
5. *Press* the **Enter** key.
6. *Enter* the alias name beside the **(alias)** option. In our case, we have left this option blank.
7. *Press* the **Enter** key. The **List of Cost Centres** menu appears.
8. *Double-click* the parent cost centres on the **List of Cost Centres** menu for the **Under** option. In our case, we have double-clicked **Primary** (Fig.TL-6.5).

   The **Accept ?** message box appears (Fig.TL-6.5).
9. *Click* **Yes** in the **Accept ?** message box to create the cost centre, as shown in Fig.TL-6.5:

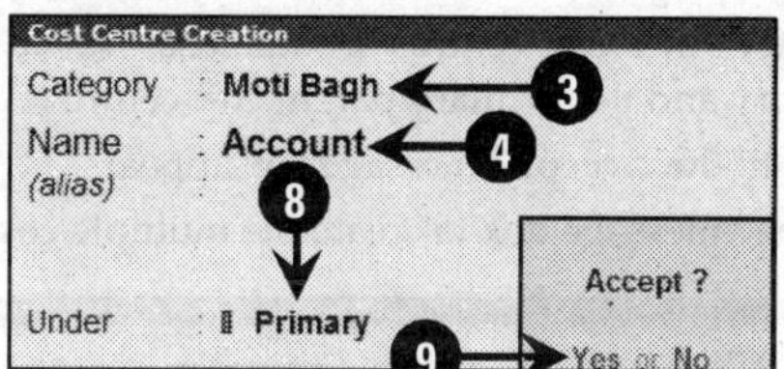

Fig.TL-6.5

Displaying a Single Cost Centre

Perform the following steps to display a single cost centre:

1. *Double-click* the **Display** option under the **Single Cost Centre** section on the **Cost Centres** menu. The **Select Cost Centre** screen appears displaying the **List of Cost Centres** menu.
2. *Double-click* the cost centre that you want to display from the **List of Cost Centres** menu. The **Cost Centre Display** screen appears with the details of the selected cost centre.

Altering a Single Cost Centre

You can easily alter or make changes in the details of a cost centre by performing the following steps:

1. *Double click* the **Alter** option under the **Single Cost Centre** section on the **Cost Centres** menu. The **Select Cost Centre** screen appears displaying the **List of Cost Centres** menu.
2. *Double-click* the cost centre that you want to alter from the **List of Cost Centres** menu. The details of the selected cost centre appear on the **Cost Centre Alteration** screen.
3. *Enter* the new information or make the required changes in the cost centre.
4. *Press* the **Enter** key until the **Accept ?** message box appears.
5. *Click* **Yes** in the **Accept ?** message box to save the changes.

Creating Multiple Cost Centres

Perform the following steps to create multiple cost centres:

1. *Double-click* the **CReate** option under the **Multiple Cost Centres** section on the **Cost Centres** menu. The **Multi Cost Centre Creation** screen appears with the **List of Cost Centres** menu (Fig.TL-6.6).
2. *Double-click* the parent cost centre on the **List of Cost Centres** menu for the **Under Cost Centre** option. In our case, we have double-clicked **All Items** (Fig.TL-6.6).
3. *Double-click* the category on the **List of Categories** menu for the **Category** column. In our case, we have double-clicked **Moti Bagh** (Fig.TL-6.6).
4. *Enter* the name of the cost centre for the **Name of Cost Centre** column. In our case, we have entered **Purchase** (Fig.TL-6.6).
5. *Press* the **Enter** key. The **List of Cost Centres** menu appears.
6. *Double-click* the parent cost centre on the **List of Cost Centres** menu for the **Under** column. In our case, we have double-clicked **Primary**, as shown in Fig.TL-6.6:

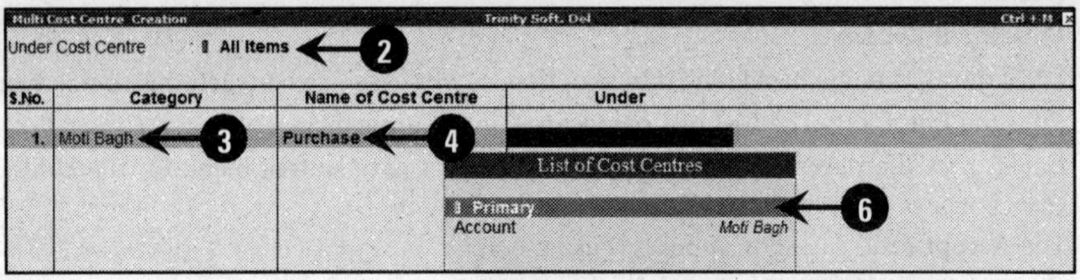

Fig.TL-6.6

Similarly, you can enter other cost centres. In our case, we have entered **Sales** cost centre under the **Moti Bagh** cost category and the **Primary** parent cost centre (Fig.TL-6.7).

7. *Press* the **Enter** key until the **Accept ?** message box appears.
8. *Click* **Yes** in the **Accept ?** message box to create the multiple cost centre, as shown in Fig.TL-6.7:

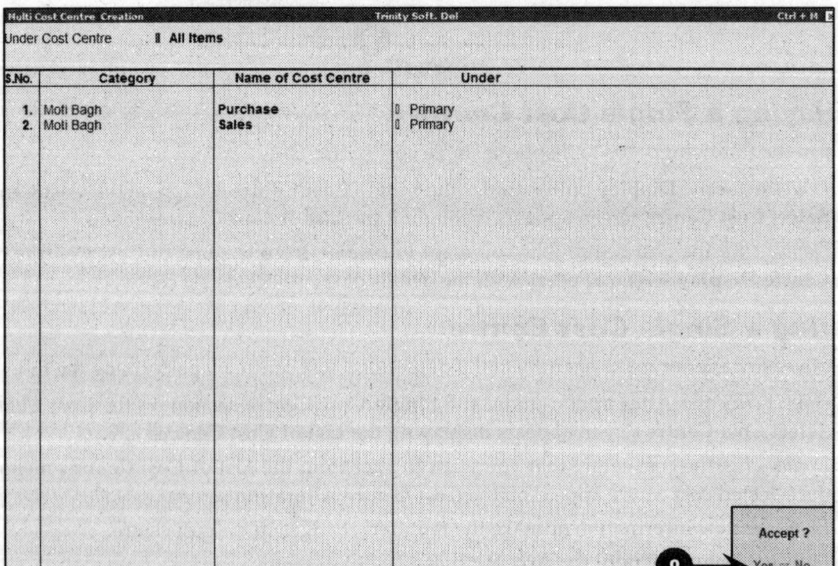

Fig.TL-6.7

Displaying Multiple Cost Centres

Perform the following steps to display multiple cost centres:

1. *Double-click* the **DIsplay** option under **Multiple Cost Centres** section on the **Cost Centres** menu. The **Select Cost Centre** screen appears with the **List of Cost Centres** menu.
2. *Double-click* the cost centre which you want to display on the **List of Cost Centres** menu. The **Multi Cost Centre Display** screen appears displaying the details of the selected multiple cost centre.

Altering Multiple Cost Centre

Perform the following steps to alter multiple cost centres:

1. *Double-click* the **AlTer** option under **Multiple Cost Centres** section on the **Cost Centres** menu. The **Select Cost Centre** screen appears with the **List of Cost Centres** menu.
2. *Double-click* the cost centre which you want to alter on the **List of Cost Centres** menu. The **Multi Cost Centre Alteration** screen appears.
3. *Make* the changes in the details of the multiple cost centre as per the requirements.
4. *Press* the **Enter** key until the **Accept?** message box appears.
5. *Click* **Yes** in the **Accept ?** message box to save the changes in the selected cost centre.

Creating a Voucher using Cost Centres

Perform the following steps to create a voucher using cost centres:

1. *Double-click* the **Accounting Vouchers** option under the **Transactions** section on the **Gateway of Tally** menu. The **Accounting Voucher Creation** screen appears.
2. *Click* the **F8: Sales** button on the Button Bar to open the sales voucher screen.
3. *Click* the **V: As Voucher** button located on the Button Bar. The **Accounting Voucher Creation** screen of sales invoice appears (Fig.TL-6.8).
4. *Enter* the reference number beside the **Reference no.** option. In our case, we have entered 5 (Fig.TL-6.8).
5. *Press* the **Enter** key. The **List of Ledger Accounts** menu appears (Fig.TL-6.8).
6. *Double-click* the debited party name on the **List of Ledger Accounts** menu for the **Particulars** column. In our case, we have double-clicked **Mohan Traders** (Fig.TL-6.8).
7. *Enter* the amount for the selected ledger under the **Debit** column. In our case, we have entered **27,000**, as shown in Fig.TL-6.8:

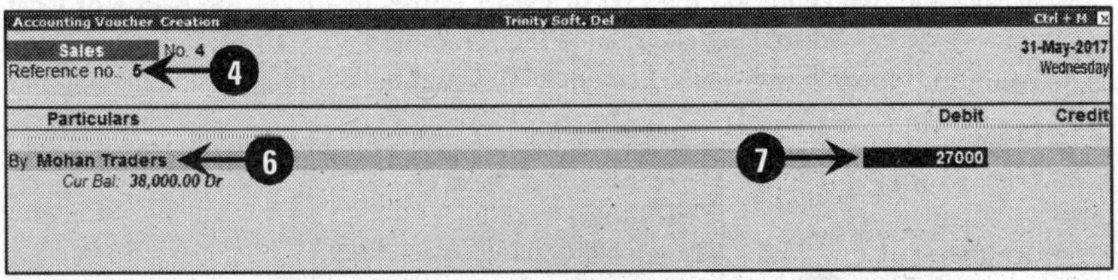

Fig.TL-6.8

8. *Press* the **Enter** key. The **List of Ledger Accounts** menu appears.
9. *Double-click* the desired sales ledger on the **List of Ledger Accounts** menu for the **Particulars** column. In our case, we have double-clicked **Sales**.

   The **Inventory Allocations** screen appears with the **List of Stock Items** menu (Fig.TL-6.9).

10. *Double-click* the name of items on the **List of Stock Items** menu for the **Name of Item** column. In our case, we have double-clicked **21 Inches Monitor**, as shown in Fig.TL-6.9:

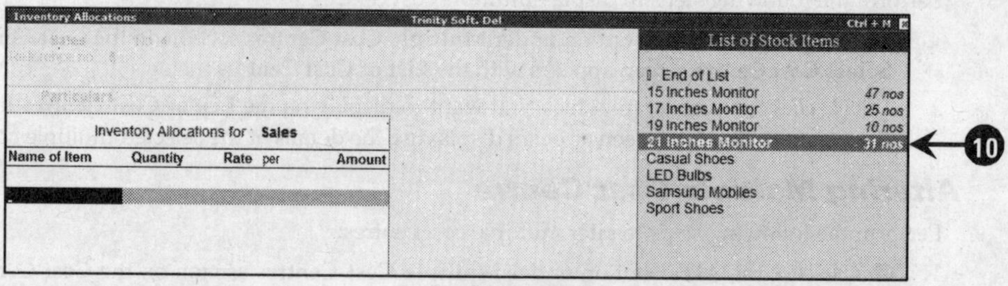

Fig.TL-6.9

The **Stock Item Allocations** screen appears with the **List of Godowns** menu.

11. *Select* the godown from the **List of Godowns** for the **Godown** column. In our case, we have double-clicked **Moti Bagh Godown** (Fig.TL-6.10).
12. *Enter* the relevant details for the item allocation under the **Quantity, Rate,** and **per** columns. In our case, we have entered **3** in **Quantity, 9000** in **Rate**, and **nos** in **per** (Fig.TL-6.10).

    The amount is automatically calculated and displayed under the **Amount** column, as shown in Fig.TL-6.10:

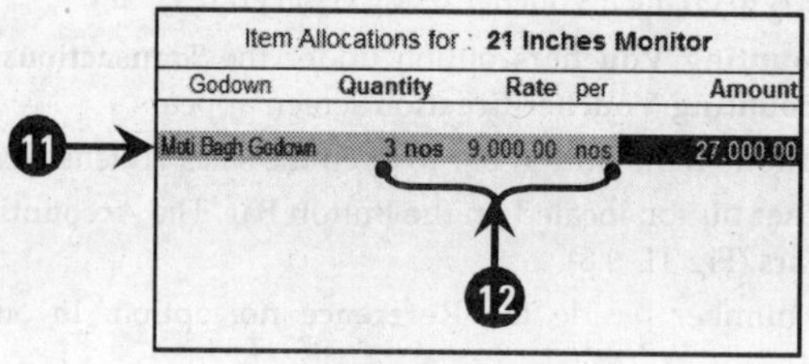

Fig.TL-6.10

13. *Press* the **Enter** key twice. The **Inventory Allocations** screen reappears with the items.
14. *Press* the **Enter** key.
15. *Double-click* the cost category on the **List of Categories** menu for the **Cost Category** column. In our case, we have double-clicked **Moti Bagh** (Fig.TL-6.11). The **List of Cost Centres** menu appears.
16. *Double-click* the cost centre on the **List of Cost Centres** menu for the **Name of Cost Centre** column. In our case, we have double-clicked **Sales** (Fig.TL-6.11).

    The **Amount** column is automatically filled, as shown in Fig.TL-6.11:

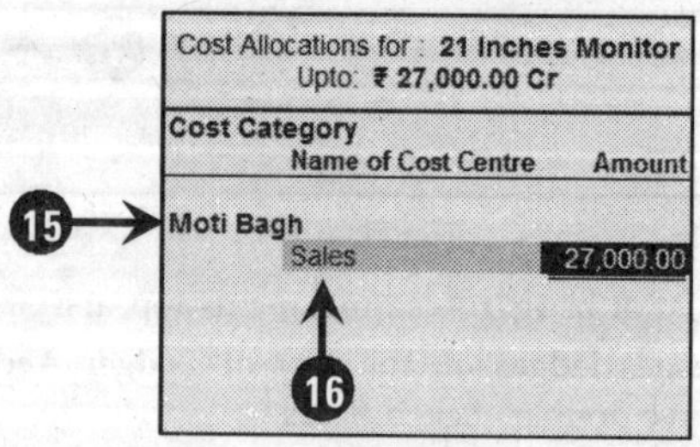

Fig.TL-6.11

17. *Press* the **Enter key** twice. The **Inventory Allocations** screen appears with the items.
18. *Press* the **Enter** key. The **Accounting Voucher Creation** screen reappears (Fig.TL-6.12).

19. *Enter* the narration under the **Narration** option. In our case, we have left it blank.
20. *Press* the **Enter** key. The **Accept?** message box appears (Fig.TL-6.12).
21. *Click* **Yes** in the **Accept ?** message box to save the sales voucher, as shown in Fig.TL-6.12:

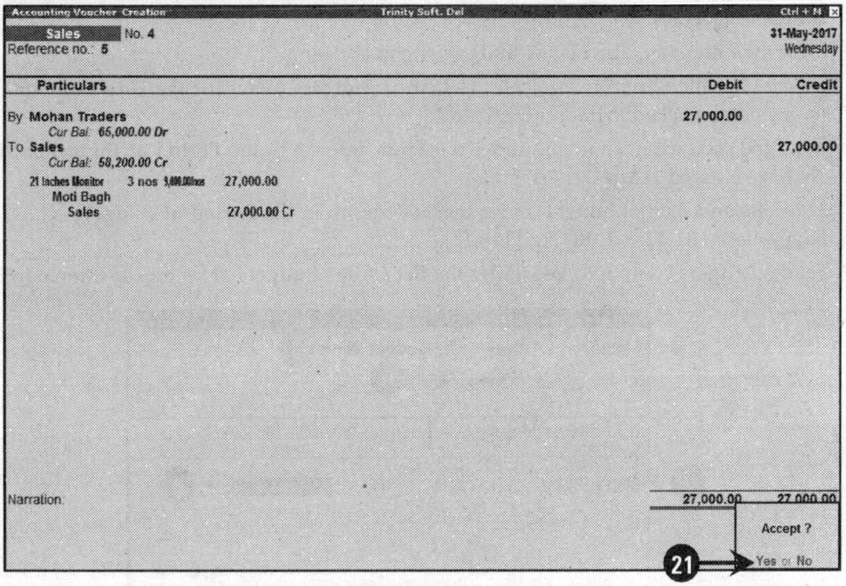

Fig.TL-6.12

After learning about cost centres, let us now discuss about a budget.

Budget

A budget is a strategy, which defines the flow of funds in a company. It covers all the financial strategies that provide the guidelines for the upcoming plan of action during a defined period of time. Budget assists in enhancing the goals of the company and utilizing the funds efficiently. It also helps in taking crucial financial decisions and provides a reference for future planning.

Creating a Budget

Tally allows you to create a budget for groups, ledger accounts, and cost centres. To create a budget, you need to first enable the budget by performing the following steps:

1. *Click* the **F11: Features** button on the Button Bar in the **Gateway of Tally** screen. The **Company Features** menu appears.
2. *Double-click* the **Accounting Features** option on the **Company Features** menu. The **Company Operations Alteration** screen appears with **Accounting Features**.
3. *Set* the **Maintain budgets and controls** option to **Yes** under the **Budgets and Scenario Management** section in **Accounting Features**.
4. *Press* the **Enter** key until the **Accept ?** message box appears.
5. *Click* **Yes** in the **Accept ?** message box to save the changes.

After enabling the **Maintain budgets and controls** option, let us perform the following steps to create the budget for a ledger account:

1. *Double-click* the **Accounts Info.** option under the **Masters** section on the **Gateway of Tally** menu. The **Accounts Info.** menu appears.

2. *Double-click* the **Budgets** option on the **Accounts Info.** menu. The **Budgets** menu appears.
3. *Double-click* the **Create** option on the **Budgets** menu. The **Budget Creation** screen appears (Fig.TL-6.13).
4. *Enter* the name of the budget beside the **Name** option. In our case, we have entered **Trinity Soft. Budget** (Fig.TL-6.13).
5. *Press* the **Enter** key. The **List of Budgets** menu appears.
6. *Double-click* the parent budget on the **List of Budgets** menu for the **Under** option. In our case, we have double-clicked **Primary** (Fig.TL-6.13).
7. *Enter* the start date of budget under the **From** column in the **Period of Budget** section. In our case, we have entered **1-Apr-2017** (Fig.TL-6.13).
8. *Enter* the end date of budget under the **To** column in the **Period of Budget** section. In our case, we have entered **31-Mar-2018** (Fig.TL-6.13).
9. *Set* the **Ledgers** column to **Yes** under the **Set / Alter Budgets of** section, as shown in Fig.TL-6.13:

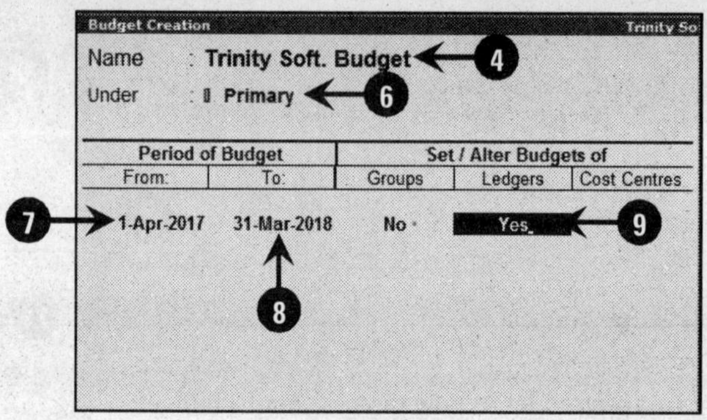

Fig.TL-6.13

10. *Press* the **Enter** key. The **Ledger Budget** screen appears with the **List of Ledgers** menu (Fig.TL-6.14).
11. *Enter* the ledger account on the **List of Ledgers** menu for the **Account Name** column. In our case, we have entered **Cash** (Fig.TL-6.14). The **List of Cost Centres** menu appears (Fig.TL-6.14).
12. *Double-click* the cost centre on the **List of Cost Centres** menu for the **Cost Centre** column. In our case, we have double-clicked **Sales** (Fig.TL-6.14). The **Budget Transaction Table** menu appears (Fig.TL-6.14).
13. *Double-click* the budget type on the **Budget Transaction Table** menu for the **Type of Budget** column. In our case, we have double-clicked **On Nett Transactions** (Fig.TL-6.14).
14. *Enter* the amount of the ledger account under the **Amount** column. In our case, we have entered **250000**, as shown in Fig.TL-6.14:

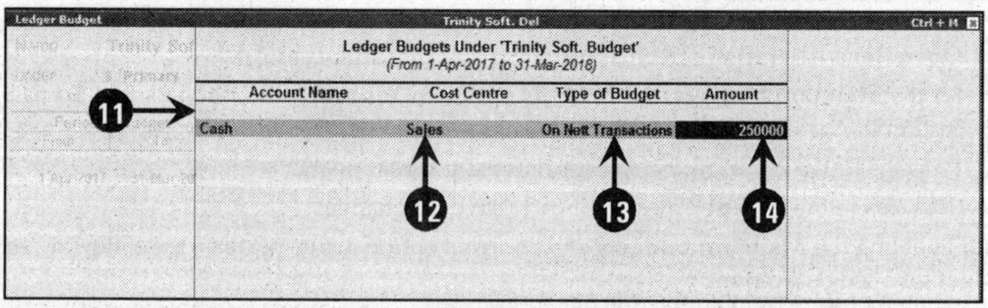

Fig.TL-6.14

15. *Press* the **Enter** key twice. The **Budget Creation** screen reappears (Fig.TL-6.15).
16. *Press* the **Enter** key twice. The **Accept ?** message box appears (Fig.TL-6.15).

17. *Click* **Yes** in the **Accept ?** message box to save the budget, as shown in Fig.TL-6.15:

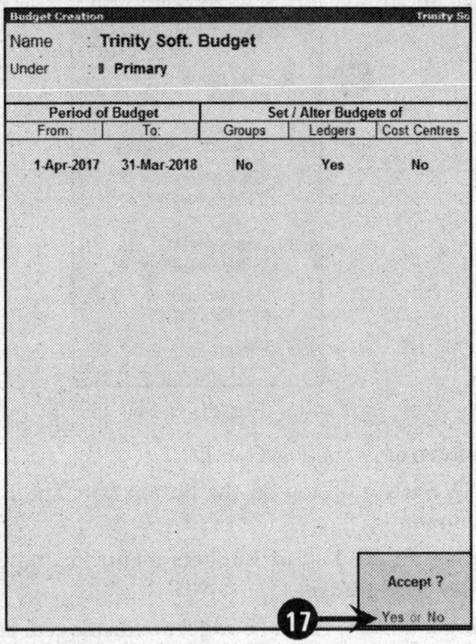

Fig.TL-6.15

Altering a Budget

You can alter or make changes in the details of a budget by performing the following steps:

1. *Double-click* the **Accounts Info.** option under the **Masters** section in the **Gateway of Tally** menu. The **Accounts Info.** menu appears.
2. *Double-click* the **Budgets** option on the **Accounts Info.** menu. A **Budgets** menu appears.
3. *Double-click* the **Alter** option on the **Budgets** menu. The **Select Budget** screen appears with the **List of Budgets** menu.
4. *Double-click* the budget, which you want to alter, on the **List of Budgets** menu. The **Budget Alteration** screen appears.
5. *Make* the changes in the budget as per the requirements.
6. *Press* the **Enter** key until the **Accept ?** message box appears.
7. *Click* **Yes** in the **Accept ?** message box to save the changes

Note

You have to set the Set/Alter Budget of option Budget Creation screen to Yes to alter a budget. This option is set to No by default.

Displaying a Budget Variance Report

Budget variance is the difference between the planned budget amount and the actual budget amount. The budget variance report displays the budget amount, the actual amount, and the variance of their differences. You can view the budget variance report through the trial balance and group summary. Perform the following steps to display the budget variance report through the trial balance:

1. *Double-click* the **Display** option under the **Reports** section in the **Gateway of Tally** menu. The **Display Menu** menu appears (Fig.TL-6.16).

2. *Double-click* the **Trial Balance** option on the **Display Menu** menu, as shown in Fig.TL-6.16:

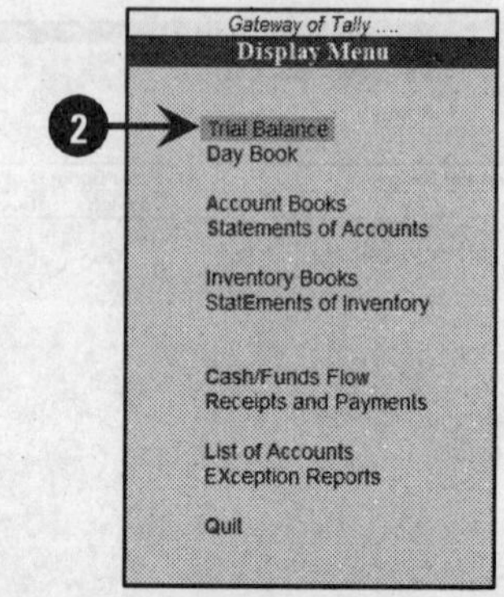

Fig.TL-6.16

The **Trial Balance** screen appears (Fig.TL-6.17).

3. *Click* the **B: Budget Variance** button on the Button Bar. The **Budget Analysis** screen appears with the **List of Budgets** menu.
4. *Double-click* the budget on the **List of Budgets** menu for the **Budget** option. In our case, we have double-clicked **Trinity Soft. Budget.**

The Trinity Soft. Budget and the Actual budget are displayed, as shown in Fig.TL-6.17:

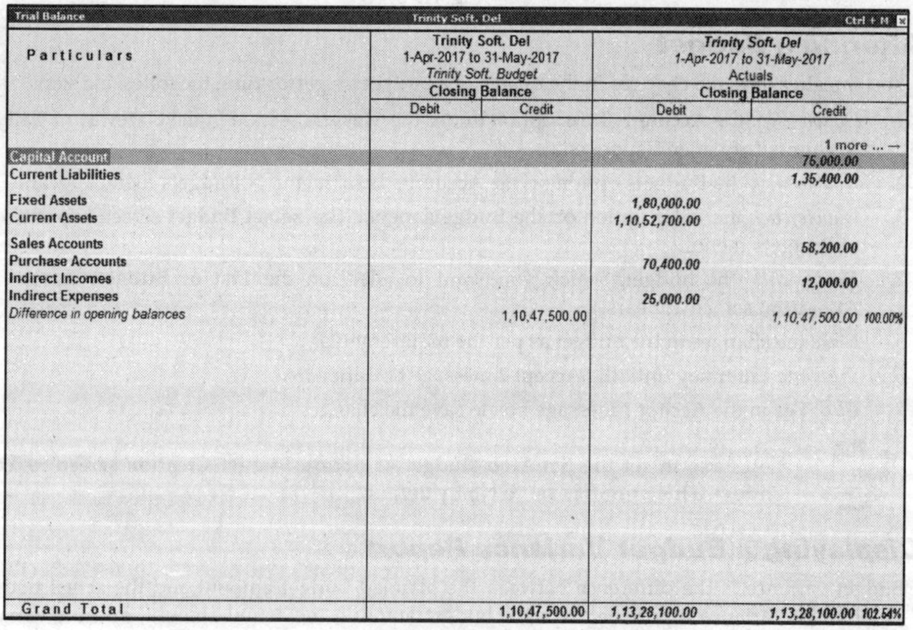

Trial Balance — Trinity Soft. Del — Ctrl + M

Particulars	Trinity Soft. Del 1-Apr-2017 to 31-May-2017 Trinity Soft. Budget Closing Balance		Trinity Soft. Del 1-Apr-2017 to 31-May-2017 Actuals Closing Balance		1 more ... →
	Debit	Credit	Debit	Credit	
Capital Account				75,000.00	
Current Liabilities				1,35,400.00	
Fixed Assets			1,80,000.00		
Current Assets			1,10,52,700.00		
Sales Accounts				58,200.00	
Purchase Accounts			70,400.00		
Indirect Incomes				12,000.00	
Indirect Expenses			25,000.00		
Difference in opening balances		1,10,47,500.00		1,10,47,500.00	100.00%
Grand Total		1,10,47,500.00	1,13,28,100.00	1,13,28,100.00	102.54%

Fig.TL-6.17

If the budget variance displays a negative value, the real expenditure value has surpassed the budgeted values.

Let us learn about credit limit.

Credit Limit

A seller and a buyer set a budgetary limit which is agreed upon by both of them for trading purposes. This mutually decided budgetary limit is known as credit limit. This limit can be specified for a ledger account, which falls under the Sundry Creditors and Sundry Debtors groups. The ledger accounts falling under Sundry Creditors can also define credit limits. This is done to ensure the two-way process of trade between the parties. Selling to Sundry Creditors and buying from Sundry Debtors is an instance of this two-way process.

Enabling Credit Limit Feature

In Tally.ERP 9, to activate the credit limit feature, perform the following steps:

1. *Click* the **F11: Features** button on the Button Bar on the **Gateway of Tally** screen. The **Company Features** menu appears.
2. *Double-click* the **Accounting Features** option on the **Company Features** menu. The **Company Operations Alteration** screen appears with **Accounting Features**.
3. *Set* the **Maintain budgets and controls** option to **Yes** in the **Budgets and Scenario Management** section in **Accounting Features.**
4. *Press* the **Enter** key until the **Accept ?** message box appears.
5. *Click* **Yes** in the **Accept ?** message box to save the changes.

Specifying Credit Limit for Single Ledger

To specify credit limit for a single ledger, perform the following steps:

1. *Double-click* the **Accounts Info.** option in the **Masters** section on the **Gateway of Tally** menu. The **Accounts Info.** menu appears.
2. *Double-click* the **Ledgers** option on the **Accounts Info**. menu. The **Ledgers** menu appears.
3. *Double-click* the **Create** option in the **Single Ledger** section on the **Ledgers** menu. The **Ledger Creation** screen appears (Fig.TL-6.18).
4. *Enter* the name of the ledger in the **Name** option. In our case, we have entered **Mohan Bros.** (Fig.TL-6.18).
5. *Press* the **Enter** key until the **List of Groups** menu appears.
6. *Double-click* a group on the **List of Groups** menu for the **Under** option. In our case, we have double-clicked **Sundry Debtors** (Fig.TL-6.18).
7. Set the **Maintain balances bill-by-bill** option to **Yes** (Fig.TL-6.18).
8. *Press* the **Enter** key until the **Default credit period** option appears.
9. *Enter* the relevant time period in the **Default credit period** option. In our case, we have entered **30 Days** (Fig.TL-6.18).
10. *Press* the **Enter** key.
11. *Set* the **Check for credit days during voucher entry** option to **Yes** (Fig.TL-6.18).
12. *Press* the **Enter** key.
13. *Enter* the relevant credit limit in the **Specify credit limit** option. In our case, we have entered **30,000.00 Dr** (Fig.TL-6.18).
14. *Press* the **Enter** key.
15. *Set* the **Override credit limit using post-dated transactions** option to **No** (Fig.TL-6.18).
16. *Enter* the mailing details in the **Mailing Details** sections (Fig.TL-6.18).
17. *Press* the **Enter** key until the **Accept ?** message box appears.

18. *Click* **Yes** in the **Accept ?** message box to specify the entered credit limit, as shown in Fig.TL-6.18:

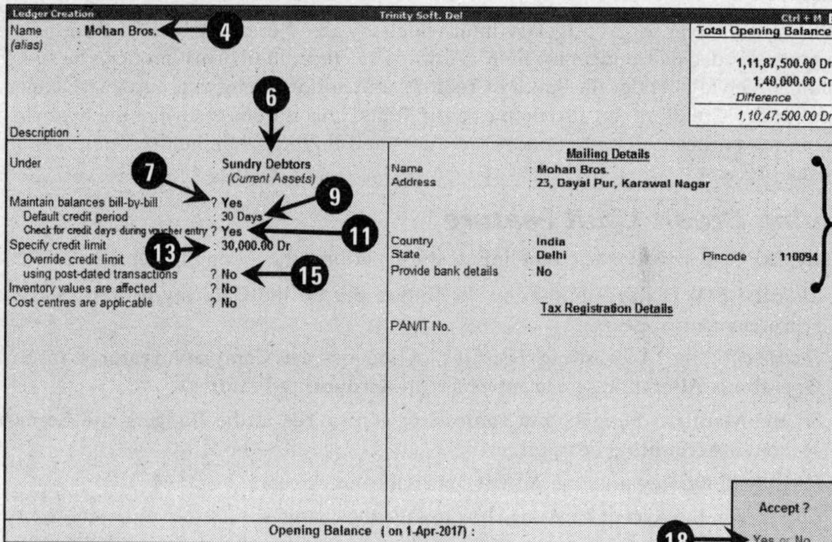

Fig.TL-6.18

Specifying Credit Limit for Multiple Ledgers

To specify credit limit for multiple ledgers, perform the following steps:

1. *Double-click* the **Accounts Info.** option in the **Masters** section on the **Gateway of Tally** menu. The **Accounts Info.** menu appears.
2. *Double-click* the **Ledgers** option on the **Accounts Info.** menu. The **Ledgers** menu appears.
3. *Double-click* the **Credit Limits** option in the **Multiple Ledgers** section on the **Ledgers** menu. The **Select Group** screen appears with the **List of Groups** menu (Fig.TL-6.19).
4. *Double-click* the desired group from the **List of Groups** menu. In our case, we have double-clicked **Sundry Debtors**, as shown in Fig.TL-6.19:

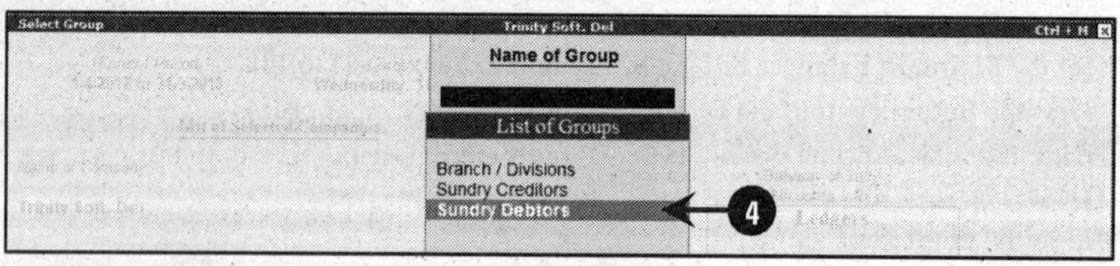

Fig.TL-6.19

The **Multi Ledger Limit Alteration** screen appears with the list of ledger accounts under the selected group (Fig.TL-6.20).

5. *Enter* the credit limit and credit period in the **Credit Limit**, **Credit Period**, and **Check for Credit Days during Voucher Entry** columns for the relevant ledger accounts. In our case, we have entered **35,000**, **30 Days**, and **Yes** respectively for **Gupta Pvt. Ltd.** (Fig.TL-6.20).

Note

You can specify credit limit and credit period for any number of ledger accounts available in the Multi Ledger Limit Alteration screen.

6. *Press* the **Enter** key until the **Accept ?** message box appears.

7. *Click* **Yes** in the **Accept ?** message box to specify the entered credit limit, as shown in Fig.TL-6.20:

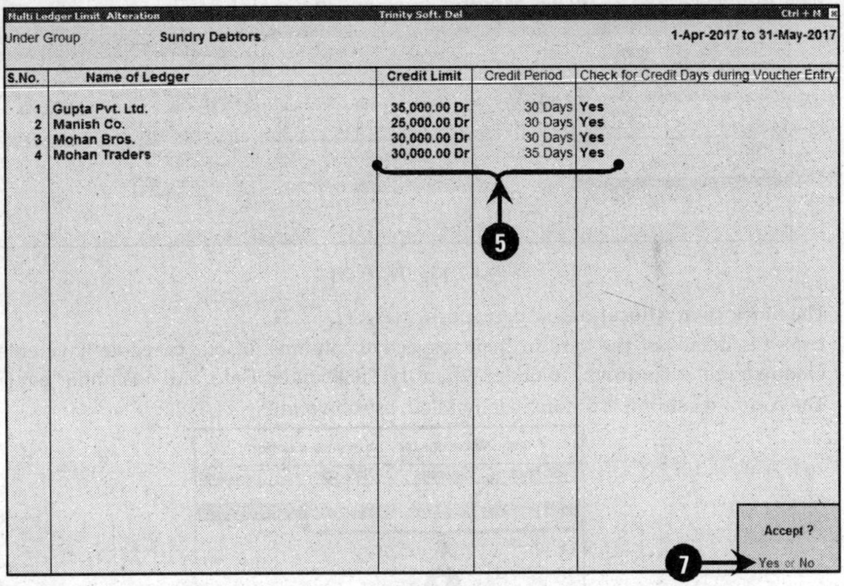

Fig.TL-6.20

Exceeding Credit Limit

Tally.ERP 9 shows an error prompt if the credit amount limit is exceeded while making an order or invoice entry. This situation is referred to as exceeding the credit limit, in which the amount above the specified credit limit is shown. To resolve this issue, you can insert a lower value, which lies within the specified credit limit. In addition, you can obtain permission to raise the credit limit on the **Multi Ledger Limit Alteration** screen after leaving the current entry.

Perform the following steps to create a voucher that shows exceeded credit limit message:

1. *Double-click* the **Accounting Vouchers** option in the **Transactions** section on the **Gateway of Tally** menu. The **Accounting Voucher Creation** screen appears.
2. *Click* the **F8: Sales** button on the Button Bar to view the voucher. The **Accounting Voucher Creation** screen appears with the sales voucher.
3. *Enter* the desired reference number beside the **Reference no.** option. In our case, we have entered **3** (Fig.TL-6.21).
4. *Press* the **Enter** key. The **List of Ledger Accounts** menu appears (Fig.TL-6.21).
5. *Double-click* the party name on the **List of Ledger Accounts** menu for the **Party A/c name** option. In our case, we have double-clicked **Mohan Traders** (Fig.TL-6.21).

   When you select the party account, the current balance and the credit limit of the party appears beside the **Current balance** and **Credit Limit** options (Fig.TL-6.21). The **List of Ledger Accounts** menu appears (Fig.TL-6.21).
6. *Double-click* the name of sales ledger on the **List of Ledger Accounts** menu for the **Sales ledger** option. In our case, we have double-clicked **Sales** (Fig.TL-6.21).

   The **List of Stock Items** menu appears (Fig.TL-6.21).

7. *Double-click* the item on the **List of Stock Items** menu for the **Name of Item** column. In our case, we have double-clicked **21 Inches Monitor**, as shown in Fig.TL-6.21:

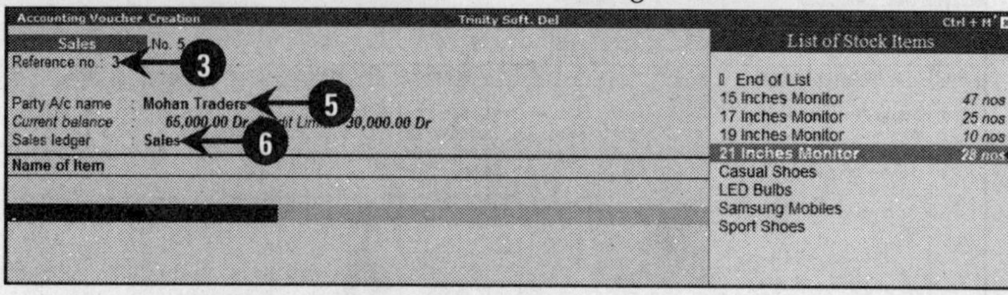

Fig.TL-6.21

The **Stock Item Allocations** screen appears (Fig.TL-6.22).

8. *Enter* the details of the item in their respective columns. In our case, we have entered **Moti Bagh Godown** under **Godown**, **10** under **Quantity**, **9,000** under **Rate**, and **nos** under **per** (Fig.TL-6.22). The **Amount** column is automatically filled, as shown in Fig.TL-6.22:

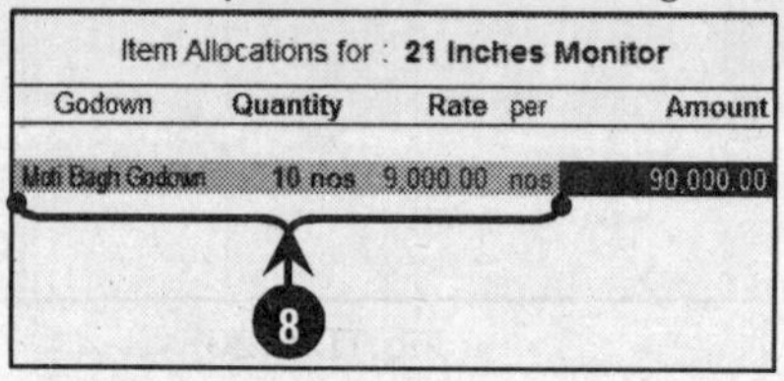

Fig.TL-6.22

9. *Press* the **Enter** key twice. The **Accounting Voucher Creation** screen appears (Fig.TL-6.23).
10. *Press* the **Enter** key until the **Narration** option appears.
11. *Enter* the narration beside the **Narration** option. In our case, we have entered **Sales of 21 Inches Monitor to Mohan Traders** (Fig.TL-6.23).
12. *Press* the **Enter** key.

An error message appears informing that the credit limit exceeded, as shown in Fig.TL-6.23:

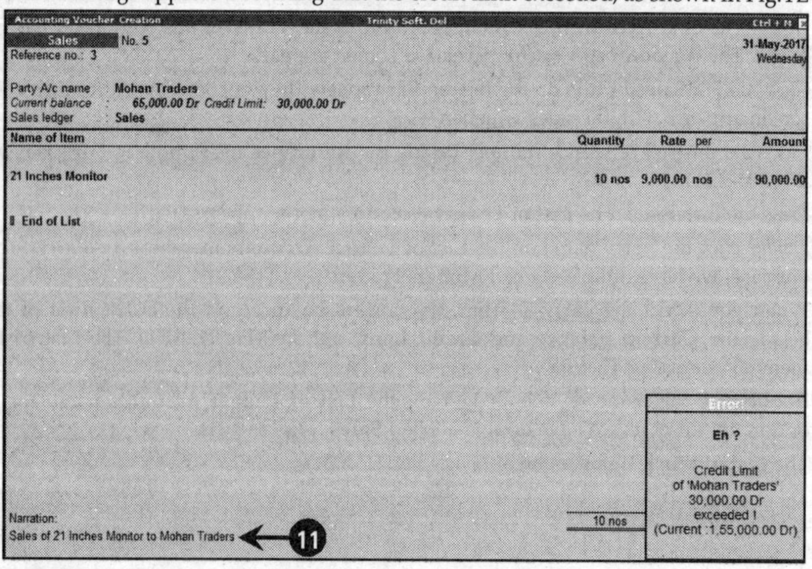

Fig.TL-6.23

Let us learn how to calculate interest in Tally.

Interest Calculation

In accounting, interest can be considered as an amount paid or earned on a fixed amount of cash. You pay interest in case you borrow money from the market or bank. On the other hand, when you deposit money in a bank or some financial institution, in the form of long-term savings, mutual bonds, or life insurance policy, you earn interest. Interest is calculated on the basis of pre-defined percentage, which is charged or paid annually or over a fixed period of time. The percentage of interest is governed according to the rules and regulations of the government. Tally allows you to compute interest in two ways: simple interest and advance interest.

In Tally, simple interest calculation is done on the basis of a fixed percentage that extends over a fixed period of time. Consider a scenario where you borrow ₹ 10000 from a bank for five years at the rate of 10%. At this rate, ₹ 1000 is calculated as interest for every year. So, when your loan ends, you need to pay a total of ₹ 5000 to the bank as interest. In order to compute simple interest in Tally, you need to enable the **Activate interest calculation** option.

In Tally, you can also compute floating interest. Unlike fixed interest rate, which remains constant throughout a fixed period of time, floating interest is a type of interest that keeps on changing according to the time period (measured in days). Consider a scenario where you have borrowed ₹ 10000 from the market for five years at the rate of 10%. For the first two years, the interest rate will remain 10% and for the remaining three years, the rate of interest will be 12%. Therefore, after five years, the total amount to be paid by you would be ₹ 2000 (for the first two years) + ₹ 3600 (for the remaining three years), which sums up to ₹ 5600. In order to compute advanced interest in Tally.ERP 9, you need to enable the **Use advanced parameters** option.

Enabling the Interest Calculation Feature

Perform the following steps to enable the Activate interest calculation option:

1. *Click* the **F11: Features** button on the Button Bar in the **Gateway of Tally** screen. The **Company Features** menu appears.
2. *Double-click* the **Accounting Features** option in the **Company Features** menu. The **Company Operations Alteration** screen appears with **Accounting Features**.
3. *Set* the **Activate interest calculation** and **Use advanced parameters** options under the **Outstandings Management** section to **Yes**.
4. *Press* the **Enter** key until the **Accept ?** message box appears.
5. *Click* **Yes** in the **Accept ?** message box to save the changes.

Creating Party Ledger

Perform the following steps to create a party ledger:

1. *Double-click* the **Accounts Info.** option under the **Masters** section in the **Gateway of Tally** menu. The **Account Info.** menu appears.
2. *Double-click* the **Ledgers** option in the **Account Info.** menu. The **Ledgers** menu appears.
3. *Double-click* the **Create** option under the **Single Ledger** section in the **Ledgers** menu. The **Ledger Creation** screen appears (Fig.TL-6.24).
4. *Type* the name of the ledger beside the **Name** option. In our case, we have typed **Vikas Bros.** (Fig.TL-6.24).
5. *Press* the **Enter** key.
6. *Type* an alias for the ledger beside the **(alias)** option. In our case, we have left it blank (Fig.TL-6.24).
7. *Press* the **Enter** key twice. The **List of Groups** menu appears.
8. *Double-click* the parent account group under which you want to create the ledger, in the **List of Groups** menu for the **Under** option. In our case, we have double-clicked **Sundry Debtors** (Fig.TL-6.24).

9. *Set* the **Maintain balances bill-by-bill** option to **Yes** (Fig.TL-6.24).
10. *Set* the **Activate interest calculation** option to **Yes**, as shown in Fig.TL-6.24:

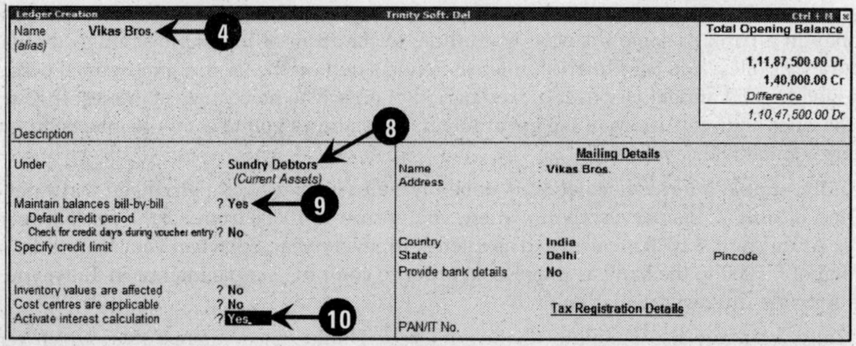

Fig.TL-6.24

11. *Press* the **Enter** key. The **Interest Parameters** screen appears (Fig.TL-6.25).
12. *Set* the **Calculate Interest Transaction-by-Transaction** option to **Yes** (Fig.TL-6.25).
13. *Enter* the desired percentage beside the **Rate** option. In our case, we have entered **10** (Fig.TL-6.25).
14. *Press* the **Enter** key. The **Interest Style** menu appears (Fig.TL-6.25).
15. *Double-click* the desired interest style for the **per** option in the **Interest Style** menu. In our case, we have double-clicked **365-Day Year** (Fig.TL-6.25). The **Interest Balances** menu appears (Fig.TL-6.25).
16. *Double-click* the desired interest balance on the **Interest Balances** menu for the **on** option. In our case, we have double-clicked **Debit Balances Only** (Fig.TL-6.25). The **Interest Applicable On** menu appears.
17. *Double-click* the desired applicability on the **Interest Balances** menu for the **Applicability** option. In our case, we have double-clicked **Always** (Fig.TL-6.25). The **Interest Appl From** menu appears.
18. *Double-click* the desired applicability on the **Interest Appl From** menu for the **Calculate From** option. In our case, we have double-clicked **Due Date of Invoice/Ref** (Fig.TL-6.25). The **Rounding Methods** menu appears.
19. *Double-click* the desired rounding method style in the **Rounding Method** menu for the **Rounding** option. In our case, we have double-clicked **Not Applicable**, as shown in Fig.TL-6.25:

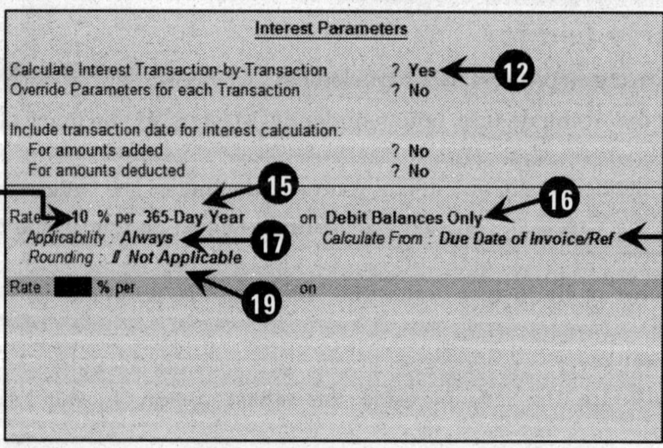

Fig.TL-6.25

20. *Press* the **Enter** key until the **Ledger Creation** screen reappears (Fig.TL-6.26).
21. *Enter* the required details under the **Mailing Details** section. In our case, we have entered the relevant details in the **Name, Address, Country, State,** and **Pincode** options (Fig.TL-6.26).

22. *Press* the **Enter** key until the **Accept ?** message box appears.
23. *Click* **Yes** in the **Accept ?** message box to create the ledger, as shown in Fig.TL-6.26:

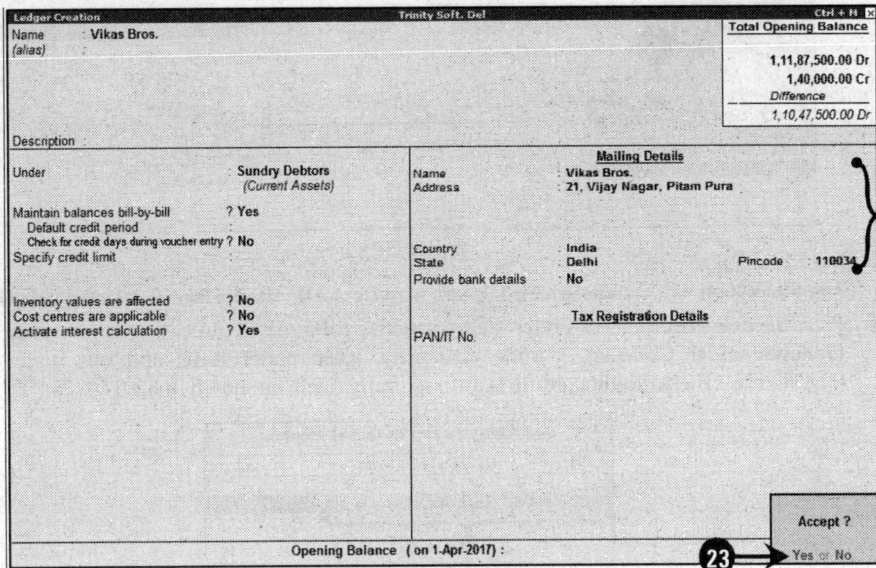

Fig.TL-6.26

Creating Sales Voucher

Now, perform the following steps to make a sales item invoice:

1. *Double-click* the **Accounting Vouchers** option under the **Transactions** section in the **Gateway of Tally** menu. The **Accounting Voucher Creation** screen appears.
2. *Click* the **F8: Sales** button on the Button Bar. The **Accounting Voucher Creation** screen of the sales voucher appears as invoice.
3. *Click* the **I: Item Invoice** button on the Button Bar. The **Accounting Voucher Creation** screen of the sales item invoice appears (Fig.TL-6.27).
4. *Click* the **F12: Configure** button on the Button Bar to view the configuration of the voucher. The **Voucher Configuration** screen appears.
5. *Set* the **Use common ledger account for item allocation** option to **Yes**. The **Sales ledger** option enables on the **Accounting Voucher Creation** screen of the sales item invoice.
6. *Enter* the reference number beside the **Reference no.** option. In our case, we have entered **5** (Fig.TL-6.27).
7. *Press* the **Enter** key. The **List of Ledger Accounts** menu appears.
8. *Double-click* the desired party name in the **List of Ledger Accounts** menu for the **Party A/c name** option. In our case, we have double-clicked **Vikas Bros.** (Fig.TL-6.27). The **List of Ledger Accounts** menu appears.
9. *Double-click* the desired sales ledger in the **List of Ledger Accounts** menu for the **Sales ledger** option. In our case, we have double-clicked **Sales** (Fig.TL-6.27). The **List of Stock Items** menu appears.

10. *Double-click* the desired item in the **List of Stock Items** menu for the **Name of Item** column. In our case, we have double-clicked **21 Inches Monitor**, as shown in Fig.TL-6.27:

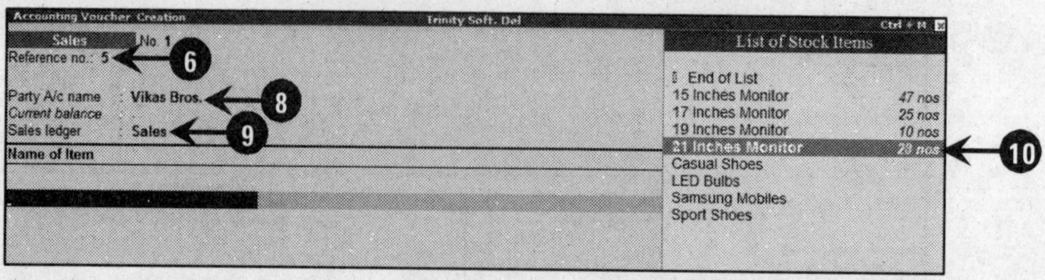

Fig.TL-6.27

The **Stock Item Allocations** screen appears with **Item Allocations for** the selected item (Fig.TL-6.28).

11. *Enter* the details of the item under their respective columns. In our case, we have entered **Moti Bagh Godown** under **Godown**, **5** under **Quantity**, **9,000** under **Rate**, and **nos** under **per** columns (Fig.TL-6.28). The **Amount** column is automatically filled, as shown in Fig.TL-6.28.

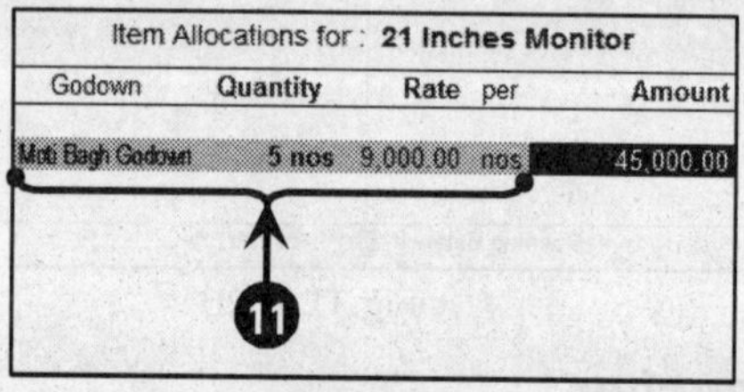

Fig.TL-6.28

12. *Press* the **Enter** key twice. The **Accounting Voucher Creation** screen appears (Fig.TL-6.29).
13. *Press* the **Enter** key four times. The **Bill-wise Details** screen appears with the **Method of Adj.** menu (Fig.TL-6.29).
14. *Double-click* the type of reference in the **Method of Adj.** menu for the **Type of Ref** column. In our case, we have double-clicked **New Ref** (Fig.TL-6.29).
15. *Enter* the name of the reference under the **Name** column. In our case, we have entered **5**, as shown in Fig.TL-6.29:

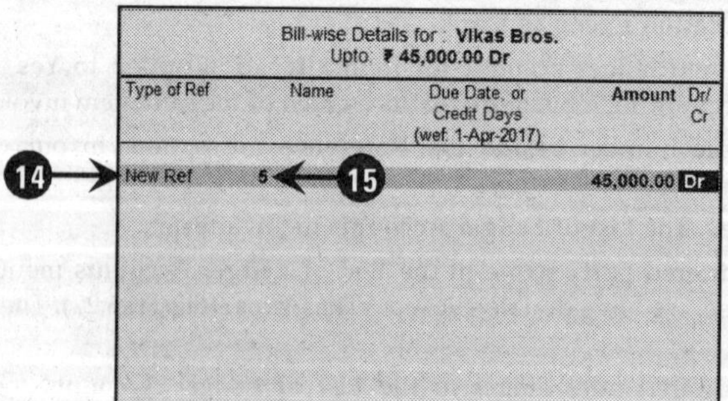

Fig.TL-6.29

16. *Press* the **Enter** key until the **Accounting Voucher Creation** screen appears (Fig.TL-6.30).
17. *Enter* the narration under the **Narration** option. In our case, we have entered **Sales of 21 Inches Monitor to Vikas Bros.** (Fig.TL-6.30).

18. *Press* the **Enter** key. The **Accept ?** message box appears (Fig.TL-6.30).
19. *Click* **Yes** in the **Accept ?** message box to save the sales item invoice, as shown in Fig.TL-6.30:

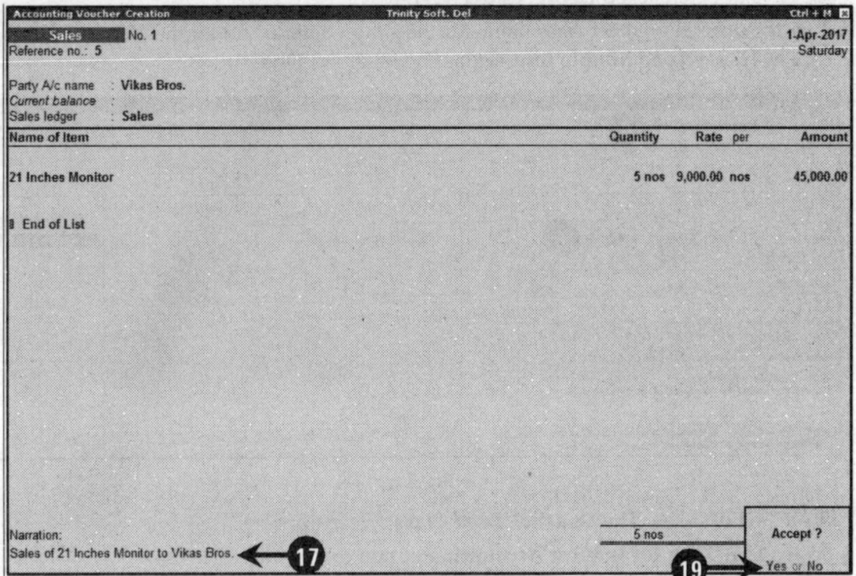

Fig.TL-6.30

Booking Interest to Ledger Accounts

To apply interest parameters to ledger accounts, you need to record the interest amount to the debit note or credit note vouchers. These vouchers must use the voucher class. You can use the debit note vouchers for interest receivable, whereas the credit note vouchers are used for interest payable. Tally allows you to compute simple as well as compound interest. Hence, you need to create two separate voucher classes for both simple and compound interest methods.

In order to apply interest parameters to ledger accounts, you need to create the following masters and vouchers:

- Debit note or credit note vouchers class
- Ledger
- Debit note or credit note voucher

Perform the following steps to create a debit note voucher class for simple interest and compound interest:

1. *Double-click* the **Accounts Info.** option in the **Gateway of Tally** menu. The **Accounts Info.** menu appears.
2. *Double-click* the **Voucher Types** option in the **Accounts Info.** menu. The **Voucher Types** menu appears.
3. *Double-click* the **Create** option in the **Voucher Types** menu. The **Voucher Type Creation** screen appears.
4. *Enter* the name of the voucher beside the **Name** option. In our case, we have entered **Interest** (Fig.TL-6.31).
5. *Press* the **Enter** key twice. The **List of Voucher Types** menu appears.

6. *Double-click* the desired parent voucher type in the **List of Voucher Types** menu for the **Select type of voucher** option to specify the category under which the voucher type is to be created. In our case, we have double-clicked **Debit Note** (Fig.TL-6.31).
7. *Type* the desired voucher class name for the simple interest under the **Name of Class** column. In our case, we have typed **Simple Interest**, as shown in Fig.TL-6.31:

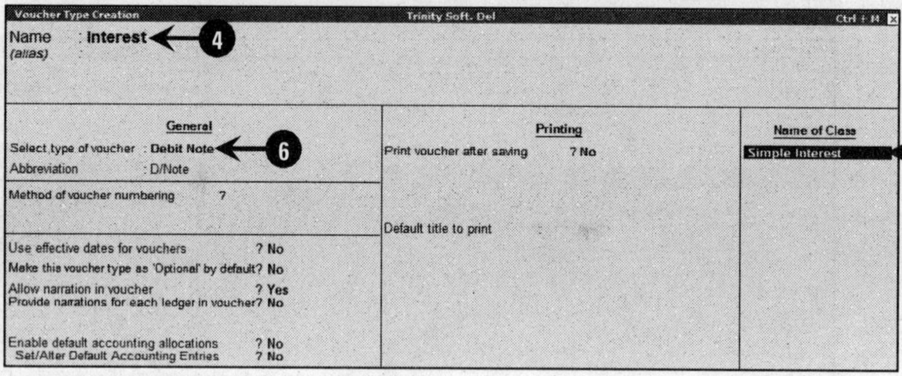

Fig.TL-6.31

8. *Press* the **Enter** key. The **Voucher Type Class** screen appears.
9. *Set* the **Use Class for Interest Accounting** option to **Yes** (Fig.TL-6.32).
10. *Set* the **Amounts to be treated as Compound Interest** option to **No**, as shown in Fig.TL-6.32:

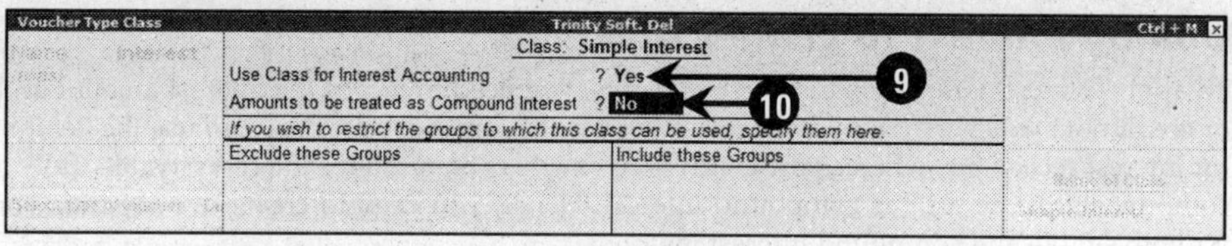

Fig.TL-6.32

11. *Press* the **Enter** key. The **Voucher Type Creation** screen reappears.
12. *Type* the desired voucher class name for the compound interest under the **Name of Class** column. In our case, we have typed **Compound Interest**.
13. *Press* the **Enter** key. The **Voucher Type Class** screen appears.
14. *Set* the **Use Class for Interest Accounting** option to **Yes** (Fig.TL-6.33).
15. *Set* the **Amounts to be treated as Compound Interest** option to **Yes**, as shown in Fig.TL-6.33:

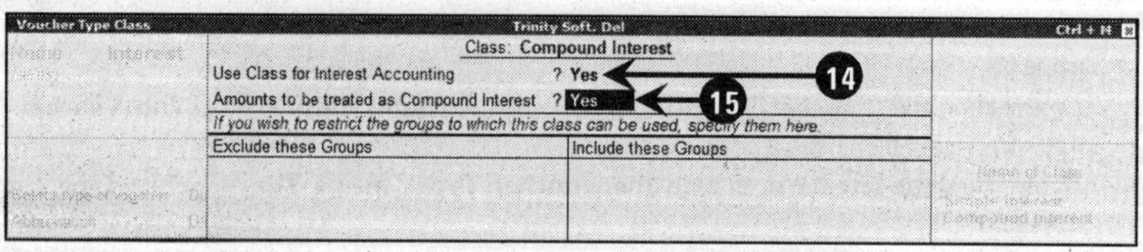

Fig.TL-6.33

16. *Press* the **Enter** key. The **Voucher Type Creation** screen reappears.
17. *Press* the **Enter** key. The **Accept ?** message box appears.

18. *Click* **Yes** in the **Accept ?** message box to save the changes, as shown in Fig.TL-6.34:

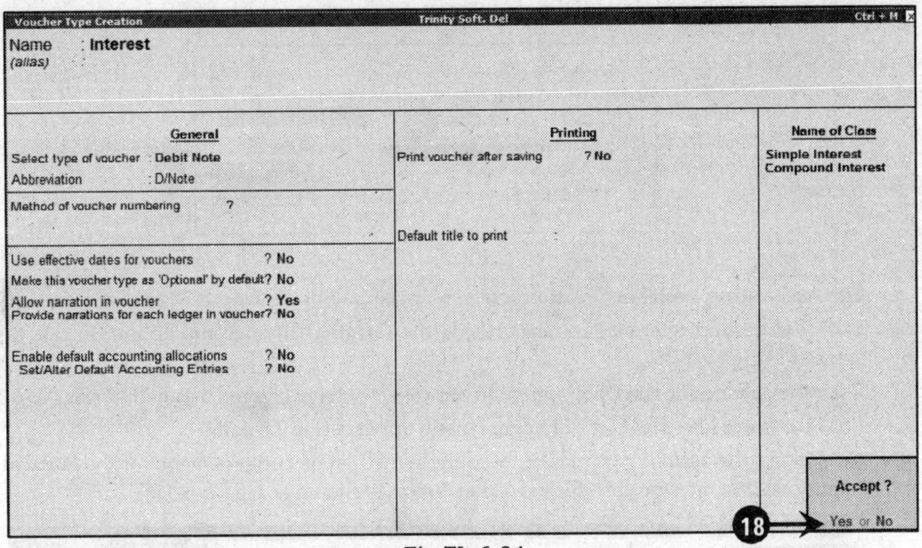

Fig.TL-6.34

Now, perform the following steps to create an interest ledger account:

1. *Double-click* the **Accounts Info.** option under the **Masters** section in the **Gateway of Tally** menu. The **Account Info.** menu appears.
2. *Double-click* the **Ledgers** option in the **Account Info.** menu. The **Ledgers** menu appears.
3. *Double-click* the **Create** option under the **Single Ledger** section in the **Ledgers** menu. The **Ledger Creation** screen appears.
4. *Type* the name of the ledger beside the **Name** option. In our case, we have typed **Interest Received**.
5. *Press* the **Enter** key.
6. *Type* an alias for the ledger beside the **(alias)** option.
7. *Press* the **Enter** key twice. The **List of Groups** menu appears.
8. *Double-click* the parent account group under which you want to create the ledger, in the **List of Groups** menu for the **Under** option. In our case, we have double-clicked **Indirect Incomes**.
9. *Press* the **Enter** key until the **Accept ?** message box appears.
10. *Click* **Yes** in the **Accept ?** message box to create the ledger.

Now, create the voucher that is used to record the transaction. In our case, we have created a debit note voucher.

Perform the following steps to create a debit note voucher:

1. *Double-click* the **Accounting Vouchers** option under the **Transactions** section in the **Gateway of Tally** menu. The **Accounting Voucher Creation** screen appears.
2. *Click* the **F9: Debit Note** button on the Button Bar to view the voucher. In the **Change Voucher Type** screen appears the **List of Types** menu.
3. *Double-click* the desired voucher type from the **List of Types** menu for the **Name** option. In our case, we have selected **Interest** (Fig.TL-6.35). The **Voucher Class List** menu appears.

4. *Double-click* the desired voucher class option from the **Voucher Class List** menu for the **Class** option. In our case, we have selected **Simple Interest**, as shown in Fig.TL-6.35:

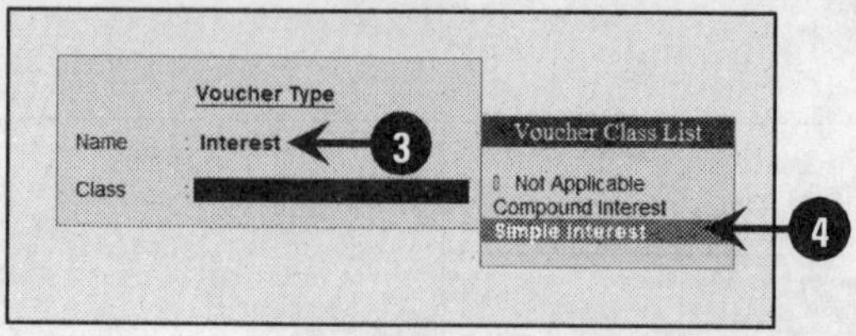

Fig.TL-6.35

The **Accounting Voucher Creation** screen reappears with the **Interest** voucher.

5. *Enter* the desired reference number beside the **Original invoice no.** option. In our case, we have entered **5** (Fig.TL-6.36).
6. *Enter* the date beside the **Date** option. In our case, we have entered **1-Jun-2017** (Fig.TL-6.36).
7. *Press* the **Enter** key. The **List of Ledgers** menu appears (Fig.TL-6.36).
8. *Double-click* the desired party ledger account in the **List of Ledgers** menu for the **Particulars** column. In our case, we have double-clicked **Vikas Bros.**, as shown in Fig.TL-6.36:

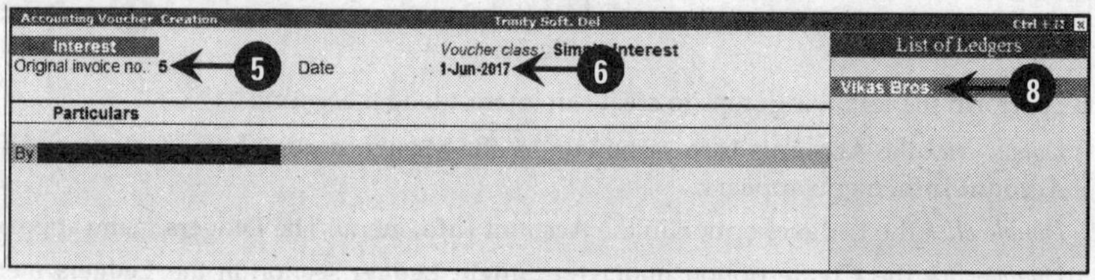

Fig.TL-6.36

The **Interest Details** screen appears with the **List of Interest Bills** menu (Fig.TL-6.37).

9. *Double-click* the desired interest bill from the **List of Interest Bills** menu for the **Name** column. In our case, we have double-clicked **5**, as shown in Fig.TL-6.37:

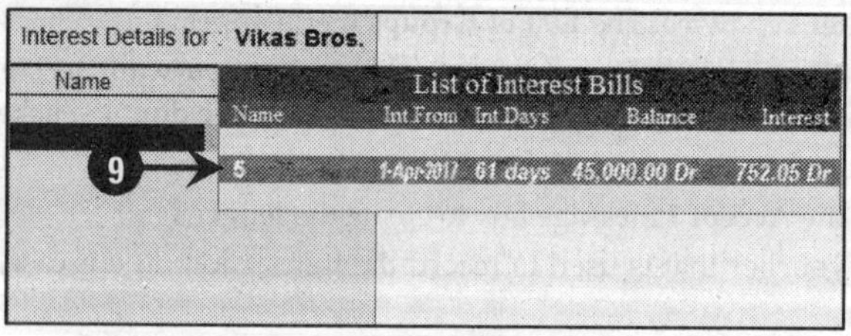

Fig.TL-6.37

10. *Press* the **Enter** key. The **Accounting Voucher Creation** screen appears.
11. *Press* the **Enter** key. The **List of Ledger Accounts** menu appears (Fig.TL-6.38).
12. *Double-click* the desired interest ledger account in the **List of Ledger Accounts** menu for the **Particulars** column. In our case, we have double-clicked **Interest Received** (Fig.TL-6.38).
13. *Press* the **Enter** key.
14. *Enter* the narration of the transaction beside the **Narration** option.
15. *Press* the **Enter** key. The **Accept ?** message box appears (Fig.TL-6.38).

16. *Click* **Yes** in the **Accept ?** message box, as shown in Fig.TL-6.38:

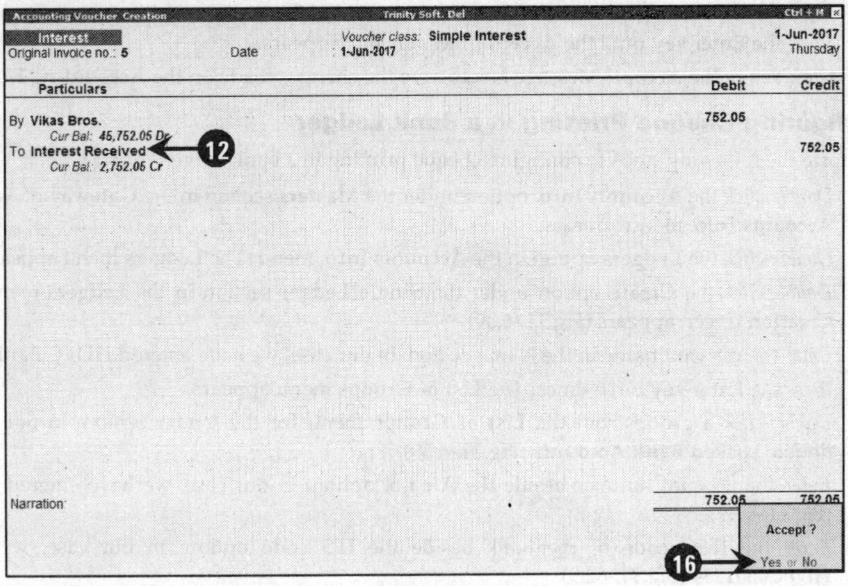

Fig.TL-6.38

Let us now learn about basics of banking.

Basics of Banking

As it is not possible for business without banking, organizations select banks for maintaining different accounts, such as savings, current, and overdraft. Banks maintain these accounts for fulfilling the business requirements and other economic needs of the organizations. Tally provides the various banking features, such as cheque printing, cheque management, deposit slip, payment advice, and bank reconciliation statement, as it covers all the functionalities of banking very comfortably. The cheque printing feature gives the facility of printing pending or already printed cheques. Any cash or cheque received has to be deposited into the bank with the help of the cheque deposit slip and cash deposit slip. The payment advice feature allows a user to send payment advice to a respective supplier or party. The bank reconciliation feature allows a user to reconcile the bank accounts.

Cheque Printing

Every bank keeps an exclusive cheque design for a native country and for other countries. These designing formats are considered for carrying out the process of cheque printing configuration in which the dimensions are used in terms of millimeters. A cheque is then printed on the basis of these specifications.

In this section, you learn how to enable cheque printing feature in Tally and how to configure cheque printing in a bank ledger.

Enabling Cheque Printing

Perform the following steps to enable cheque printing:

1. *Click* the **F11: Features** button on the Button Bar in the **Gateway of Tally** screen. The **Company Features** menu appears.
2. *Double-click* the **Accounting Features** option in the **Company Features** menu. The **Company Operations Alteration** screen appears with **Accounting Features**.

3. *Set* the **Enable cheque printing** option to **Yes** under the **Banking Features** section of the **Company Operations Alteration** screen.
4. *Press* the **Enter** key until the **Accept ?** message box appears.
5. *Click* **Yes** in the **Accept?** Message box to save the changes made on the **Accounting Features** screen.

Configuring Cheque Printing in a Bank Ledger

Perform the following steps to configure cheque printing in a bank ledger:

1. *Double-click* the **Accounts Info.** option under the **Masters** section in the **Gateway of Tally** menu. The **Accounts Info.** menu appears.
2. *Double-click* the **Ledgers** option in the **Accounts Info.** menu. The **Ledgers** menu appears.
3. *Double-click* the **Create** option under the **Single Ledger** section in the **Ledgers** menu. The **Ledger Creation** screen appears (Fig.TL-6.39).
4. *Enter* the relevant name in the **Name** option. In our case, we have entered **HDFC Bank** (Fig.TL-6.39).
5. *Press* the **Enter** key three times. The **List of Groups** menu appears.
6. *Double-click* a group from the **List of Groups** menu for the **Under** option. In our case, we have double-clicked **Bank Accounts** (Fig.TL-6.39).
7. *Enter* the account number beside the **A/c no.** option. In our case, we have entered **3152045374269** (Fig.TL-6.39).
8. *Enter* the IFSC code of the bank beside the **IFS code** option. In our case, we have entered **HDFC0001234** (Fig.TL-6.39).
9. *Press* the **Enter** key. The **List of Banks** menu appears.
10. *Double-click* the desired bank from the **List of Banks** menu for the **Bank name** option. In our case, we have double-clicked **HDFC Bank (India)** (Fig.TL-6.39).
11. *Enter* the branch name of the bank beside the **Branch name** option. In our case, we have entered **Karawal Nagar** (Fig.TL-6.39).
12. *Press* the **Enter** key.
13. *Set* the **Set cheque books** option to **Yes**, as shown in Fig.TL-6.39:

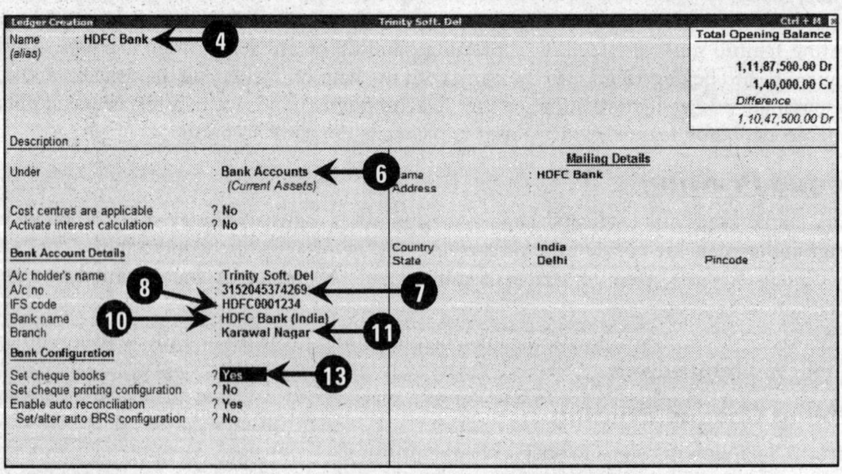

Fig.TL-6.39

14. *Press* the **Enter** key.

    The **Cheque Book Management** screen appears with the **Cheque Range for: HDFC Bank** section (Fig.TL-6.40).

15. *Enter* the relevant details in the **From Number** and **To Number** columns. In our case, we have entered **245001** and **245010,** respectively (Fig.TL-6.40).
16. *Press* the **Enter** key.

    The **Number of Cheques** is filled automatically.
17. *Enter* the relevant details in **Cheque Book Name** column. In our case, **General**, as shown in Fig.TL-6.40:

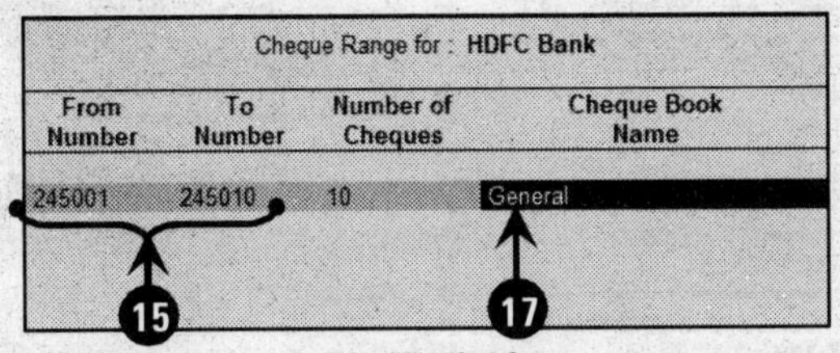

Fig.TL-6.40

18. *Press* the **Enter** key twice. The **Ledger Creation** screen reappears.
19. *Set* the **Set cheque printing configuration** option to **Yes**.
20. *Press* the **Enter** key. The **Cheque Format Selection** screen appears (Fig.TL-6.41).
21. *Click* the desired format for printing the cheque from the **List of Cheque Formats** menu. In our case, we have clicked **CTS Format 4**, as shown in Fig.TL-6.41:

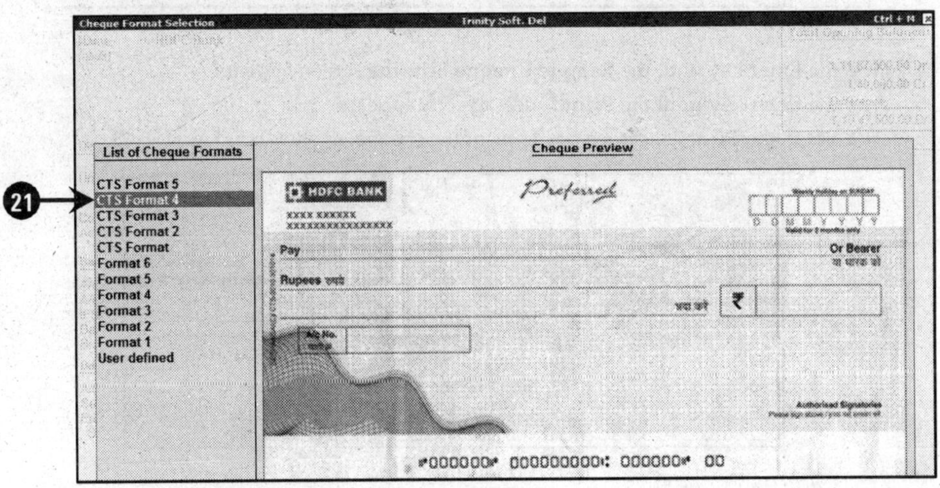

Fig.TL-6.41

> **You can also create your own format by double-clicking the User defined format from the List of Cheque Formats menu.**

22. *Press* the **Enter** key. The **Cheque Dimensions** screen appears (Fig.TL-6.42).

23. *Set* the dimensions of the cheque as per your requirements, as shown in Fig.TL-6.42:

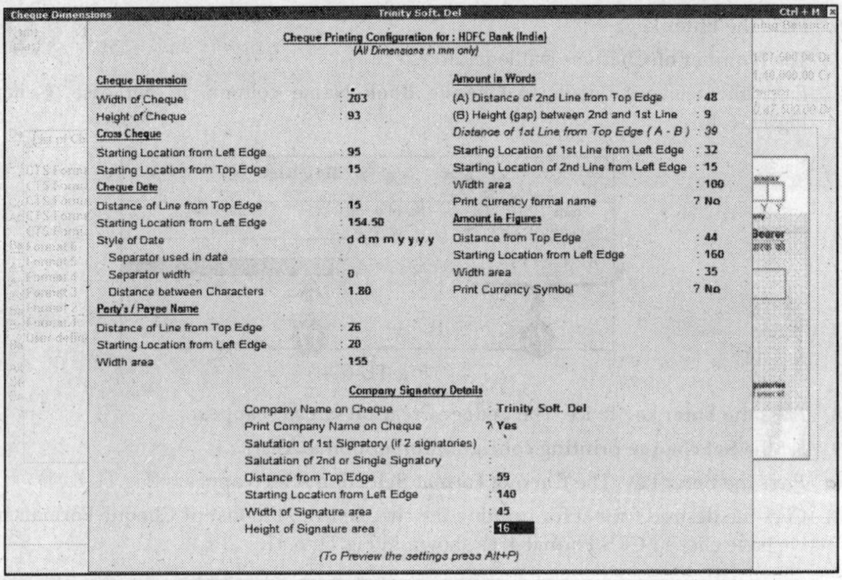

Fig.TL-6.42

24. *Press* the **Enter** key until the **Sample Cheque Printing** screen appears.
25. *Press* the **Enter** key until the **Print ?** message box appears.
26. *Click* **Yes** in the **Print ?** message box to print the cheque, as shown in Fig.TL-6.43:

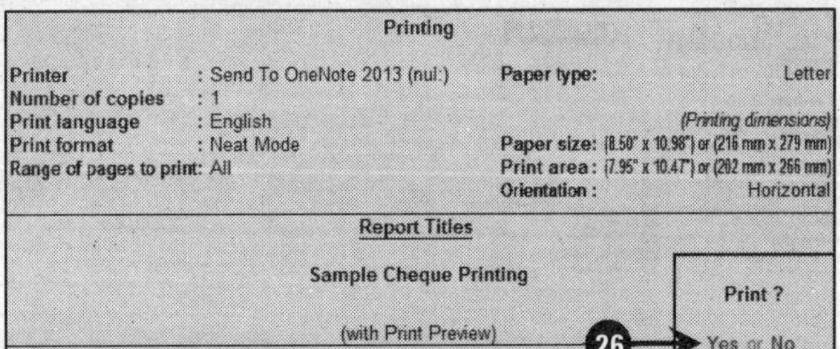

Fig.TL-6.43

The **Printed Sample Cheque** screen appears, as shown in Fig.TL-6.44:

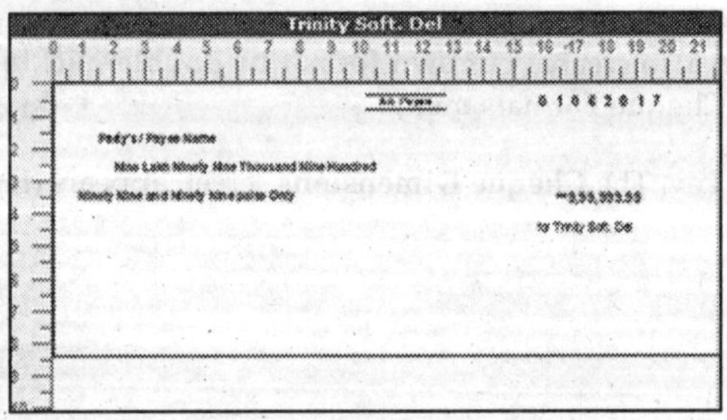

Fig.TL-6.44

27. *Click* the **Print** option in the **Printed Sample Cheque** screen. The **Ledger Creation** screen reappears (Fig.TL-6.45).

28. *Enter* the relevant mailing details in the **Mailing Details** section.
29. *Press* the **Enter** key until the **Accept ?** message box appears.
30. *Click* **Yes** in the **Accept?** Message box, as shown in Fig.TL-6.45:

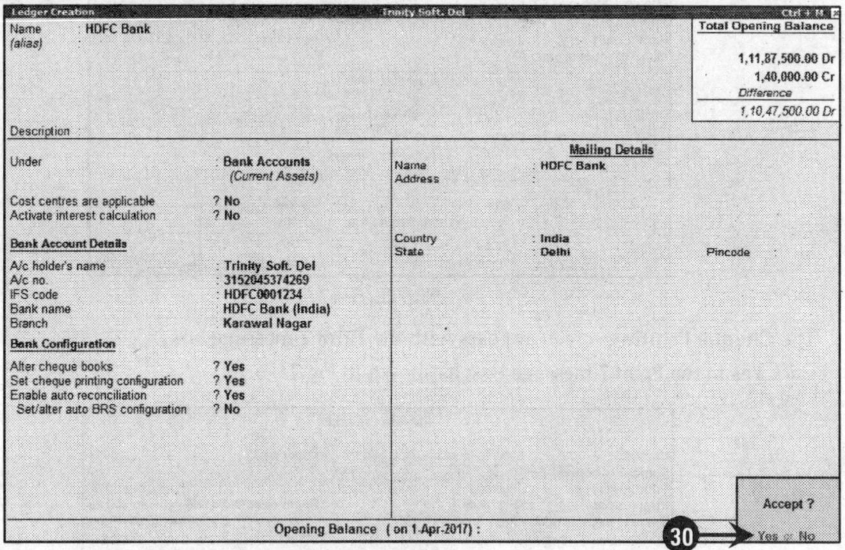

Fig.TL-6.45

Single or Multiple Cheque Printing

Tally allows you to print a single cheque or multiple cheques. To print single cheque, you need to select the cheques and press the **Spacebar** key or click the **Space: Select** button below the **Day Book** screen. To print multiple cheques, you need to select the **Space: Select All** button.

Perform the following steps to print a single cheque:

1. *Double-click* the **BaNking** option under the **Utilities** section in the **Gateway of Tally** menu. The **Banking** menu appears.
2. *Double-click* the **Cheque Printing** option from the **Banking** menu. The **Select bank** screen appears with the **List of Banks** menu.
3. *Double-click* the desired bank from the **List of Banks** menu whose cheque you want to print. In our case, we have double-clicked **HDFC Bank**. The **Cheque Printing** screen appears.
4. *Click* the **F6: Show All** button on the Button Bar. All transactions that are printed appears on the **Cheque Printing** screen.
5. *Click* the transaction that you want to print. In our case, we have clicked the **Courier Charges** transaction (Fig.TL-6.46).
6. *Press* the **Spacebar** key. The transaction is selected for printing.
7. *Click* the **P: Print** button on the Horizontal Button Bar, as shown in Fig.TL-6.46:

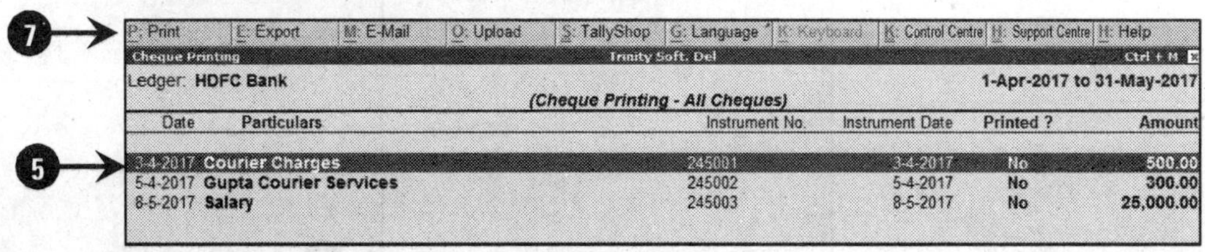

Fig.TL-6.46

The **Print Report** screen appears with the **Print ?** message box.

8. *Click* **Yes** in the **Print ?** message box, as shown in Fig.TL-6.47:

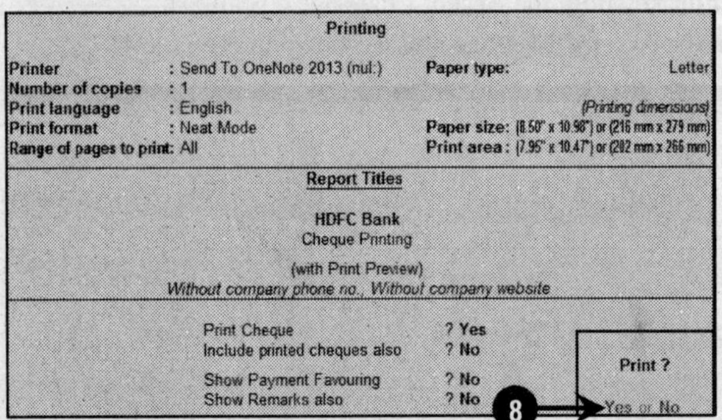

Fig.TL-6.47

The **Cheque Printing** screen appears with the **Print ?** message box.

9. *Click* **Yes** in the **Print ?** message box, as shown in Fig.TL-6.48:

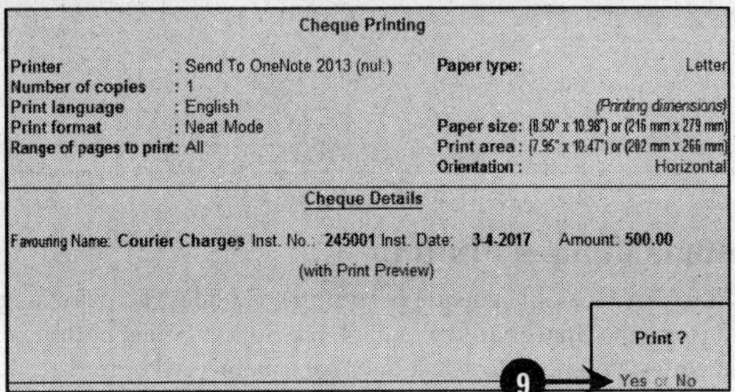

Fig.TL-6.48

The **Cheque** screen appears that shows the preview of the cheque (Fig.TL-6.49).

10. *Click* the **Zoom** option to zoom the preview, as shown in Fig.TL-6.49:

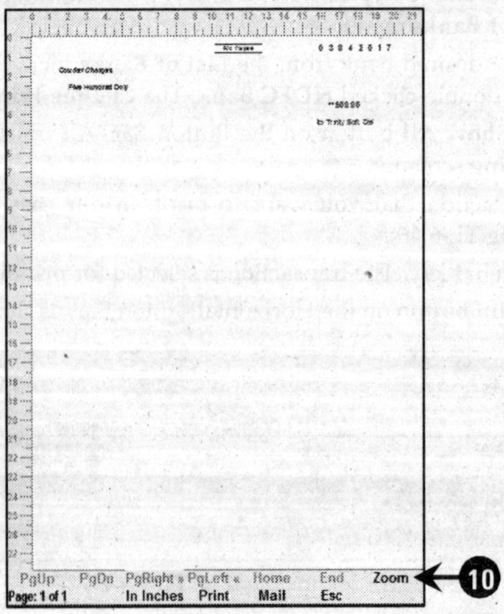

Fig.TL-6.49

The zoomed view is displayed as shown in Fig.TL-6.50:

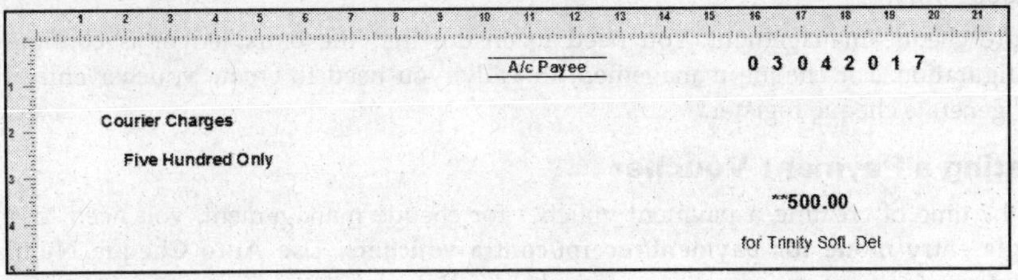

Fig.TL-6.50

11. *Press* the **Esc** key to return to the normal view.
12. *Click* the **Print** option in the **Cheque** screen to print the cheque.

Now, perform the following steps to print multiple cheques:

1. *Double-click* the **BaNking** option under the **Utilities** section in the **Gateway of Tally** screen. The **Banking** menu appears.
2. *Double-click* the **Cheque Printing** option from the **Banking** menu. The **Select bank** screen appears with the **List of Banks** menu.
3. *Double-click* the desired bank from the **List of Banks** menu whose cheque you want to print. In our case, we have double-clicked **HDFC Bank**. The **Cheque Printing** screen appears.
4. *Click* the **F6: Show All** button on the Button Bar. All transactions that are printed displays on the **Cheque Printing** screen.
5. *Click* the **Space: Select All** button. All transactions are selected for printing.
6. *Click* the **P: Print** button on the Horizontal Button Bar, as shown in Fig.TL-6.51:

Fig.TL-6.51

The **Print Report** screen appears with the **Print ?** message box

7. *Click* **Yes** in the **Print ?** message box. The **Cheque Printing** screen appears with the **Print ?** message box.
8. *Click* **Yes** in the **Print ?** message box. The **Cheque** screen that shows the preview of the cheque appears.
9. *Click* the **Zoom** option to zoom the preview. The zoomed view is displayed.
10. *Press* the **Esc** key to return to the normal view.
11. *Click* the **Print** option in the **Cheque** screen to print the cheque.
12. *Press* the **Esc** key until the **Cheque Printing** screen appears. The **Cheque Printing** screen displays the properties of the next cheque.
13. *Repeat* steps 8 to 11 to print all the cheques.

Cheque Management

Nowadays, cheques are used to make payment in the business world. Cheque gives significant value in day-to-day operations; hence, you need to effectively manage the cheques. Tally.ERP 9 gives you the facility to manage your cheque. It also allows you to create multiple cheque books with different ranges.

Tally.ERP 9 gives the facility to generate report that shows the status of all the cheques in the form of cheque format.

Before cheque management, you need to ensure that the bank ledger is configured with the bank configuration. For cheque management in Tally, you need to create voucher entry (payment voucher) and generate cheque register.

Creating a Payment Voucher

At the time of creating a payment voucher for cheque management, you need to ensure that the **Use single entry mode for payment/receipt/contra vouchers**, **Use Auto Cheque Numbering**, and **Allow selection of cheque range** options are enabled in the payment configuration options.

Perform the following steps to create a payment voucher:

1. *Double-click* the **Accounting Vouchers** option under the **Transactions** section in the **Gateway of Tally** menu.
2. *Click* the **F5: Payment** button on the Button Bar to view the voucher. An **Accounting Voucher Creation** screen appears with the payment voucher.
3. *Click* the **F12: Configure** button located on the Button Bar. The **Voucher Configuration** screen appears with the payment configuration (Fig.TL-6.52).
4. *Set* the **Use single entry mode for payment/receipt/contra vouchers** option to **Yes** (Fig.TL-6.52).
5. *Set* the **Use Auto Cheque Numbering** option to **Yes** (Fig.TL-6.52).
6. *Set* the **Allow selection of cheque range** option to **Yes**, as shown in Fig.TL-6.52:

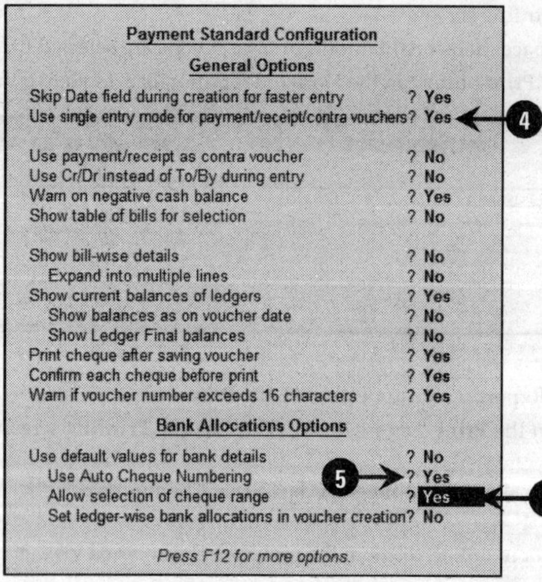

Fig.TL-6.52

7. *Press* the **Enter** key until the **Accounting Voucher Creation** screen reappears with the **List of Ledger Accounts** menu.
8. *Double-click* the bank ledger on the **List of Ledger Accounts** menu of the **Account** option. In our case, we have double-clicked **HDFC Bank** (Fig.TL-6.53). The **List of Ledger Accounts** menu appears.

9. *Double-click* the party ledger on the **List of Ledger Accounts** menu of the **Particulars** column. In our case, we have double-clicked **Rent** (Fig.TL-6.53).
10. *Enter* the amount for the selected ledger under the **Amount** column. In our case, we have entered **24000**, as shown in Fig.TL-6.53:

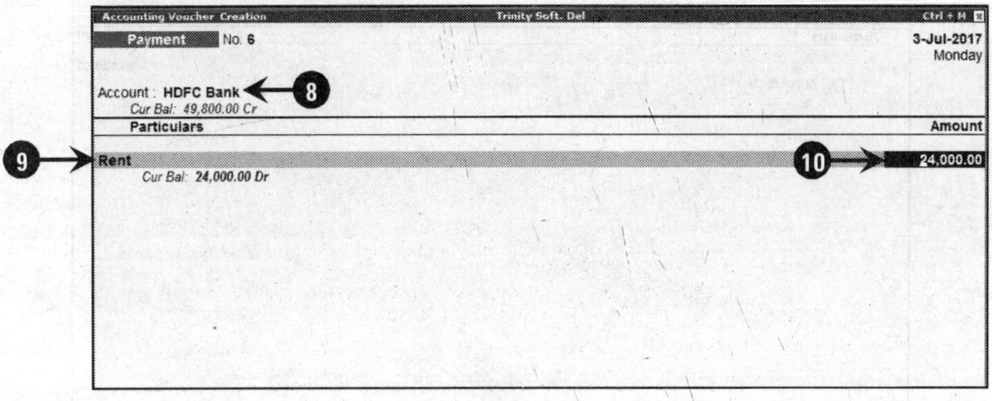

Fig.TL-6.53

11. *Press* the **Enter** key. The **Bank Allocations** screen appears (Fig.TL-6.54).
12. *Double-click* the desired transaction type in the **List of Transaction Types** menu under the **Transaction Type** column. In our case, we have double-clicked **Cheque** (Fig.TL-6.54).
13. *Enter* the amount under the **Amount** column. In our case, we have entered **8000** (Fig.TL-6.54).
14. *Enter* the cheque number beside the **Inst. No.** option. In our case, we have typed **245004** (Fig.TL-6.54).
15. *Enter* the date beside the **Inst. Date** option. In our case, we have entered **3-Jul-2017** (Fig.TL-6.54).

    Similarly, you can adjust the remaining amount, as shown in Fig.TL-6.54:

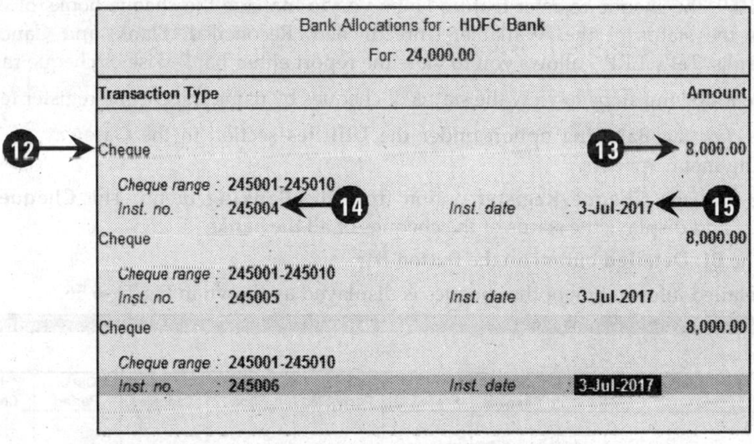

Fig.TL-6.54

16. *Press* the **Enter** key. The **Accounting Voucher Creation** screen reappears.
17. *Enter* the desired narration beside the **Narration** option.
18. *Press* the **Enter** key. The **Accept ?** message box appears (Fig.TL-6.55).

19. *Click* **Yes** in the **Accept?** message box to save the voucher, as shown in Fig.TL-6.55:

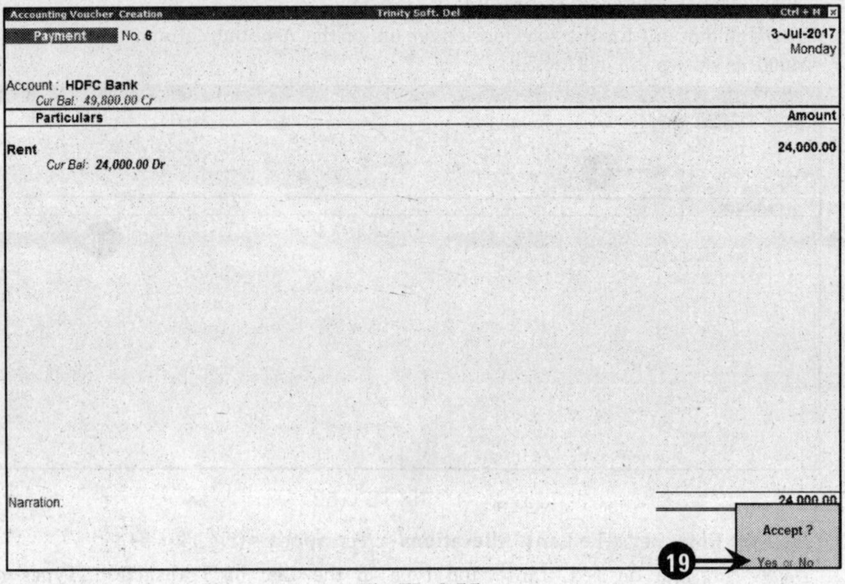

Fig.TL-6.55

Note: **If the Cheque Printing option is enabled for the bank configuration, then the Cheque Printing screen appears. If you want to print the voucher, then click Yes in the Print ? message box; otherwise, click No.**

Cheque Register

In Tally.ERP 9, the cheque register feature helps you to manage the cheque books of different banks. It also shows the status of the Available, Unreconciled, Reconciled, Blank, and Cancelled cheques of different banks. Tally.ERP 9 allows you to view the report either bank-wise or cheque range-wise.

Perform the following steps to view the status of cheques by using the cheque register feature:

1. *Double-click* the **BaNking** option under the **Utilities** section in the **Gateway of Tally** menu. The **Banking** menu appears.
2. *Double-click* the **Cheque Register** option from the **Banking** menu. The **Cheque Register** screen appears and displays the status of the cheques of all the banks.
3. *Click* the **F1: Detailed** button on the Button Bar.

   The detailed information of the cheques is displayed as shown in Fig.TL-6.56:

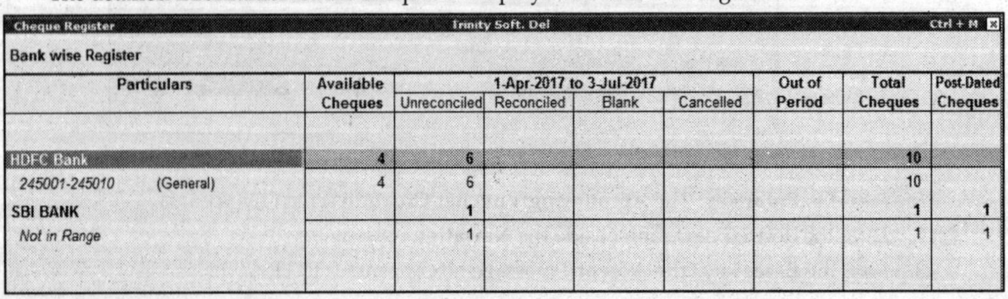

Cheque Register — Trinity Soft. Del — Ctrl + M

Bank wise Register

Particulars	Available Cheques	1-Apr-2017 to 3-Jul-2017 Unreconciled	Reconciled	Blank	Cancelled	Out of Period	Total Cheques	Post-Dated Cheques
HDFC Bank	4	6					10	
245001-245010 (General)	4	6					10	
SBI BANK		1					1	1
Not in Range		1					1	1

Fig.TL-6.56

Deposit Slip

Deposit slips are used as reference that the payment received through cheque or cash has to be deposited in the bank. In Tally.ERP 9, there are two types of deposit slip:

- Cheque deposit slip
- Cash deposit slip

Tally.ERP 9 allows you to print the cheque or cash deposit slip according to the requirement.

Cheque Deposit Slip

Any payment received through cheque has to be deposited in the bank by using the cheque deposit slip.

Perform the following steps to access and print the cheque deposit slip:

1. *Double-click* the **BaNking** option under the **Utilities** section on the **Gateway of Tally** menu. The **Banking** menu appears.
2. *Double-click* the **Deposit Slip** option from the **Banking** menu. The **Deposit Slip** menu appears.
3. *Double-click* the **Cheque Deposit Slip** option from the **Deposit Slip** menu. The **Select Bank** screen appears with the **List of Banks** menu.
4. *Double-click* the desired bank whose cheque deposit slip you want to view. In our case, we have double-clicked **HDFC Bank**. The **Cheque Deposit Slip** screen appears.
5. *Click* the **F12: Configure** button to configure the cheque deposit slip. The **Configuration** screen appears.
6. *Set* the **Show Received From** option to **Yes.**
7. *Press* the **Enter** key until the **Cheque Deposit Slip** screen reappears.
8. *Click* the **F7: Edit Ch. Details** button in the Button Bar.
9. *Enter* the name of the person or organization from which we received the cheque under the **Received From** column. In our case, we have retained with the default information (Fig.TL-6.57).
10. *Press* the **Enter** key until the **Accept ?** message box appears.
11. *Click* **Yes** in the **Accept ?** message box to save the changes, as shown in Fig.TL-6.57:

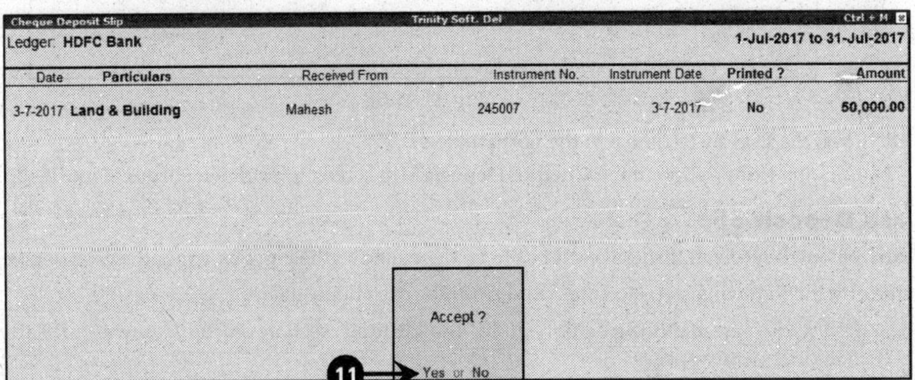

Fig.TL-6.57

12. *Click* the **P: Print** button in the Horizontal Button Bar. The **Print Report** screen appears with the **Print ?** message box.
13. *Click* **No** in the **Print ?** message box.
14. *Enter* date beside the **Date of Printing** option. In our case, we have entered **31-Jul-3017**.
15. *Press* the **Enter** key until the **Print ?** message box.

16. *Click* **Yes** in the **Print ?** message box. The **Cheque Deposit Slip** screen that shows the preview of the cheque deposit slip appears.
17. *Click* the **Zoom** option to zoom the preview. The zoomed view is displayed as shown in Fig.TL-6.58:

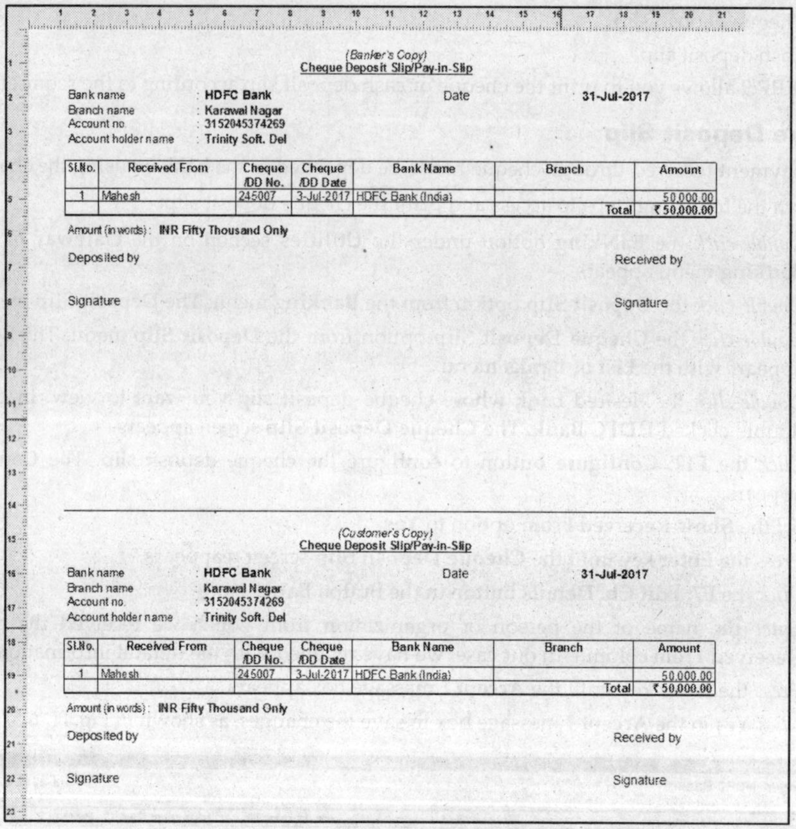

(Banker's Copy)
Cheque Deposit Slip/Pay-in-Slip

Bank name : HDFC Bank — Date 31-Jul-2017
Branch name : Karawal Nagar
Account no. : 3152045374269
Account holder name : Trinity Soft. Del

Sl.No.	Received From	Cheque /DD No.	Cheque /DD Date	Bank Name	Branch	Amount
1	Mahesh	245007	3-Jul-2017	HDFC Bank (India)		50,000.00
					Total	₹ 50,000.00

Amount (in words) : INR Fifty Thousand Only

Deposited by — Received by

Signature — Signature

(Customer's Copy)
Cheque Deposit Slip/Pay-in-Slip

Bank name : HDFC Bank — Date 31-Jul-2017
Branch name : Karawal Nagar
Account no. : 3152045374269
Account holder name : Trinity Soft. Del

Sl.No.	Received From	Cheque /DD No.	Cheque /DD Date	Bank Name	Branch	Amount
1	Mahesh	245007	3-Jul-2017	HDFC Bank (India)		50,000.00
					Total	₹ 50,000.00

Amount (in words) : INR Fifty Thousand Only

Deposited by — Received by

Signature — Signature

Fig.TL-6.58

18. *Press* the **Esc** key to return to the normal view.
19. *Click* the **Print** option in the **Cheque Deposit Slip** screen to print the cheque deposit slip.

Cash Deposit Slip

Any payment received through cash has to be deposited in the bank by using the cash deposit slip.

Perform the following steps to access and print the cash deposit slip:

1. *Double-click* the **BaNking** option under the **Utilities** section on the **Gateway of Tally** menu. The **Banking** menu appears.
2. *Double-click* the **Deposit Slip** option from the **Banking** menu. The **Deposit Slip** menu appears.
3. *Double-click* the **Cash Deposit Slip** option from the **Deposit Slip** menu. The **Select Bank** screen appears with the **List of Banks** menu.
4. *Double-click* the desired bank whose cash deposit slip you want to view. In our case, we have double-clicked **SBI BANK**. The **Cash Deposit Slip** screen appears.
5. *Click* the transaction that you want to print.

6. *Press* the **Spacebar** key. The transaction is selected for printing.
7. *Click* the **P: Print** button in the Horizontal Button Bar. The **Print Report** screen appears with the **Print ?** message box.
8. *Click* **No** in the **Print ?** message box.
9. *Enter* date beside the **Date of Printing** option. In our case, we have entered **31-Jul-2017.**
10. *Press* the **Enter** key until the **Print ?** message box.
11. *Click* **Yes** in the **Print ?** message box. The **Print Report** screen appears with the **Print ?** message box and shows the cash denomination.
12. *Click* **Yes** in the **Print ?** message box. The **Cash Deposit Slip Print** screen appears, showing the preview of the cash deposit slip with the Banker's copy and Customer's copy.
13. *Click* the **Zoom** option to zoom the preview. The zoomed view is displayed as shown in Fig.TL-6.59:

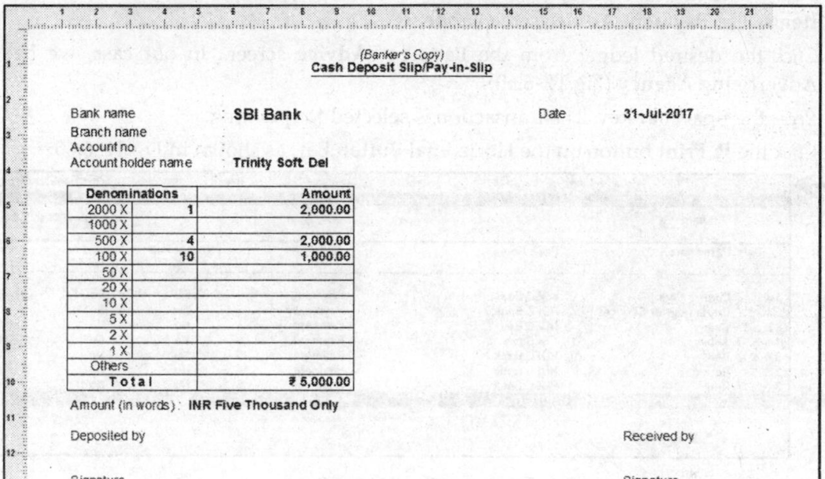

(Banker's Copy)
Cash Deposit Slip/Pay-in-Slip

Bank name : **SBI Bank** Date : **31-Jul-2017**
Branch name :
Account no :
Account holder name : **Trinity Soft. Del**

Denominations		Amount
2000 X	1	2,000.00
1000 X		
500 X	4	2,000.00
100 X	10	1,000.00
50 X		
20 X		
10 X		
5 X		
2 X		
1 X		
Others		
Total		**₹ 5,000.00**

Amount (in words) : **INR Five Thousand Only**

Deposited by Received by

Signature Signature

(Customer's Copy)
Cash Deposit Slip/Pay-in-Slip

Bank name : **SBI Bank** Date : **31-Jul-2017**
Branch name :
Account no :
Account holder name : **Trinity Soft. Del**

Denominations		Amount
2000 X	1	2,000.00
1000 X		
500 X	4	2,000.00
100 X	10	1,000.00
50 X		
20 X		
10 X		
5 X		
2 X		
1 X		
Others		
Total		**₹ 5,000.00**

Amount (in words) : **INR Five Thousand Only**

Deposited by Received by

Signature Signature

Fig.TL-6.59

14. *Press* the **Esc** key to return to the normal view.
15. *Click* the **Print** option in the **Cash Deposit Slip Print** screen to print the cash deposit slip.

Payment Advice

Tally.ERP 9 allows users to send generated payment advice to their respective suppliers or other parties. The payment advice contains the details of cheque or other instruments.

Perform the following steps to access and print payment advice:

1. *Double-click* the **BaNking** option under the **Utilities** section on the **Gateway of Tally** menu. The **Banking** menu appears.
2. *Double-click* the **Payment Advice** option from the **Banking** menu. The **Select Items** screen appears with the **List of Ledgers** menu.
3. *Double-click* the desired option from the **List of Ledgers** menu. In our case, we have selected **All Items**. The **Payment Advice** screen appears.
4. *Click* the desired ledger from the **Payment Advice** screen. In our case, we have clicked **Gupta Advertising Agency** (Fig.TL-6.60).
5. *Press* the **Spacebar** key. The transaction is selected for printing.
6. *Click* the **P: Print** button on the Horizontal Button Bar, as shown in Fig.TL-6.60:

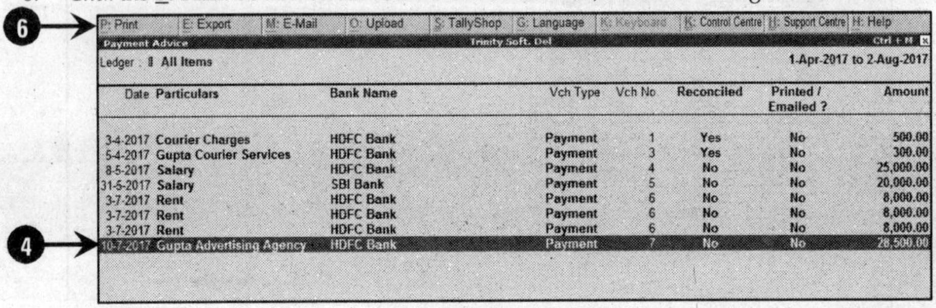

Fig.TL-6.60

The **Export Report** screen appears.

7. *Enter* the date beside the **Payment Advice Date** option. In our case, we have entered **31-Jul-2017** (Fig.TL-6.61).
8. *Press* the **Enter** key until the **Accept ?** message box appears (Fig.TL-6.61).
9. *Click* **Yes** in the **Accept ?** message box, as shown in Fig.TL-6.61:

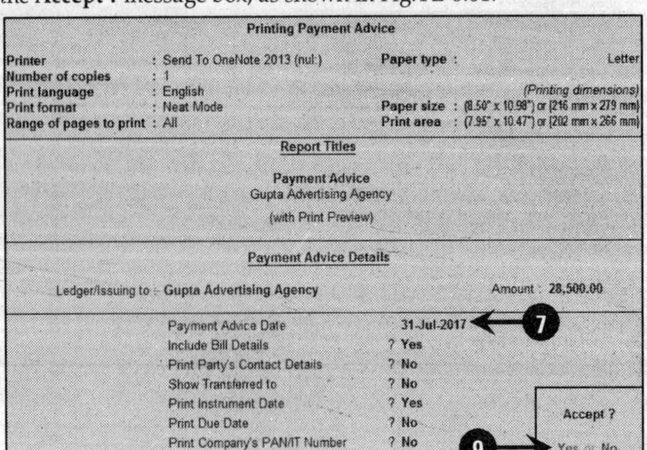

Fig.TL-6.61

The **Payment Advice** report displays.

10. *Click* the **Zoom** option to zoom the preview report.

    The zoomed view is displayed as shown in Fig.TL-6.62:

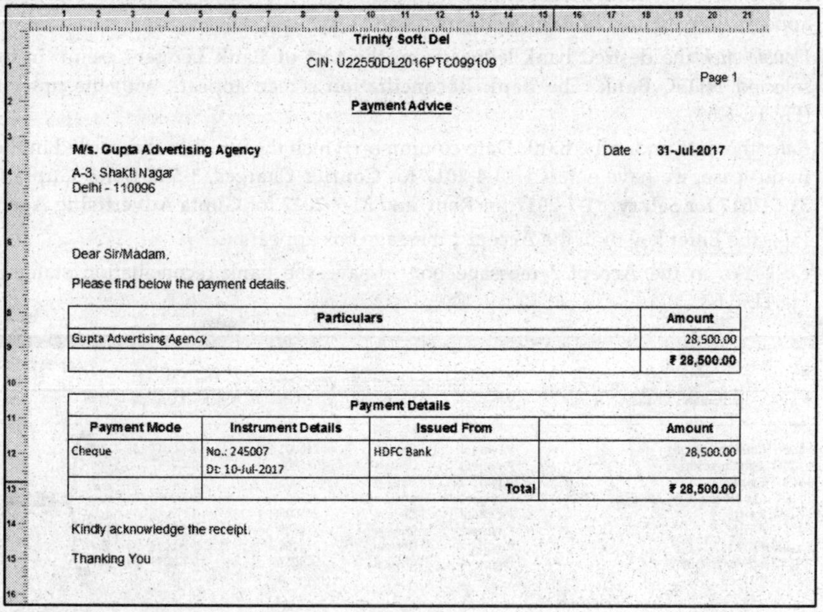

Trinity Soft. Del

CIN: U22550DL2016PTC099109

Page 1

Payment Advice

M/s. Gupta Advertising Agency Date : **31-Jul-2017**

A-3, Shakti Nagar
Delhi - 110096

Dear Sir/Madam,

Please find below the payment details.

Particulars	Amount
Gupta Advertising Agency	28,500.00
	₹ 28,500.00

Payment Details

Payment Mode	Instrument Details	Issued From	Amount
Cheque	No.: 245007 Dt: 10-Jul-2017	HDFC Bank	28,500.00
		Total	₹ 28,500.00

Kindly acknowledge the receipt.

Thanking You

Fig.TL-6.62

11. *Press* the **Esc** key to return to the normal view.
12. *Click* the **Print** option to print the payment advice.

Bank Reconciliation Statement

When money is deposited in a bank by a customer, the bank updates the account of the customer by recording the entry in the debit side of the cash book. Similarly, when money is withdrawn from the bank, it is recorded in the credit side of the cash book. The bank also maintains an account of the customer in its books of accounts. In the books of accounts, deposits made by the customer are recorded on the credit side of the customers' account and withdrawals on the debit side. A copy of it is also given to the customer for his/her knowledge in the form of a bank statement or a statement of account. As the same transactions relating to deposits and withdrawals made during a period are recorded in both the cash book and the bank statement, the balances shown by the two records at the end of a period (closing balance) should agree.

According to the **Institute of Chartered Accountants of India (ICAI)**, the bank reconciliation statement is defined as "the debit balance of bank account in the books of the concern should be equal to the credit balance of the concern's account in the books of the bank".

However, sometimes, the two balances differ. Consider a scenario where a cheque is deposited by the account-holder in the bank. However, it might be possible that the bank did not make entry for the same transaction. In such a situation, there would be a difference in the closing balance of the account-holder's cash book and bank statement. If the two balances differ, it becomes necessary to know the reason of difference. A statement showing the reasons of difference is prepared. This statement is termed as the bank reconciliation statement.

Perform the following steps to create a bank reconciliation statement:

1. *Double-click* the **BaNking** option under the **Utilities** section on the **Gateway of Tally** menu. The **Banking** menu appears.
2. *Double-click* the **Bank Reconciliation** option from the **Banking** menu. The **Select Banks** screen appears with the **List of Bank Ledgers** menu.
3. *Double-click* the desired bank ledger from the **List of Bank Ledgers** menu. In our case, we have selected **HDFC Bank**. The **Bank Reconciliation** screen appears with the unreconciled statement (Fig.TL-6.63).
4. *Enter* the date under the **Bank Date** column on which the voucher is recorded in the bank statement. In our case, we have entered **30-4-2017** for **Courier Charges, 3-5-2017** for **Gupta Courier Services, 31-5-2017** for **Salary, 31-7-2017** for **Rent**, and **31-7-2017** for **Gupta Advertising Agency** (Fig.TL-6.63).
5. *Press* the **Enter** key until the **Accept ?** message box appears.
6. *Click* **Yes** in the **Accept ?** message box to save the bank reconciliation statement, as shown in Fig.TL-6.63:

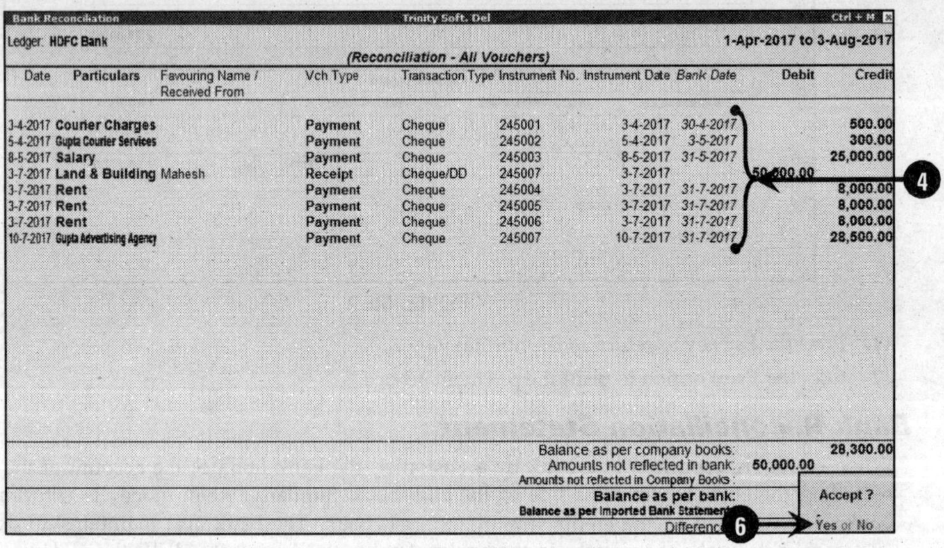

Fig.TL-6.63

The **Select Banks** screen appears with the **List of Bank Ledgers** menu.

7. *Double-click* the desired bank ledger from the **List of Bank Ledgers** menu. In our case, we have selected **HDFC Bank**. The **Bank Reconciliation** screen appears with the unreconciled statement.
8. *Click* the **F12: Configure** button on the Button Bar. The **Configuration** screen appears.
9. *Set* the **Show Reconciled Transactions also** option to **Yes.**

   All transactions that are reconciled or unreconciled are displayed on the Bank Reconciliation screen.
10. *Click* the **P: Print** button on the Horizontal Button Bar. The **Print Report** screen appears (Fig.TL-6.64).
11. *Click* the **I: With Preview** button on the Button Bar to view the report before printing.

12. *Click* **Yes** in the **Print ?** message box, as shown in Fig.TL-6.64:

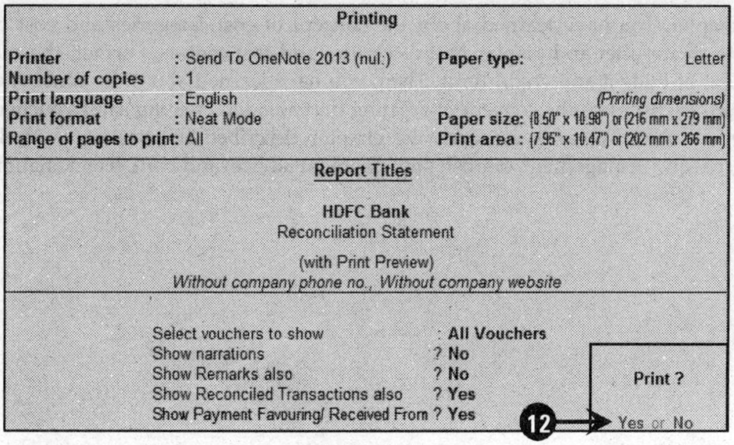

Fig.TL-6.64

The **Bank Reconciliation** screen appears.

13. *Click* the **Zoom** button to zoom the bank reconciliation statement.

The bank reconciliation statement is zoomed and displayed, as shown in Fig.TL-6.65:

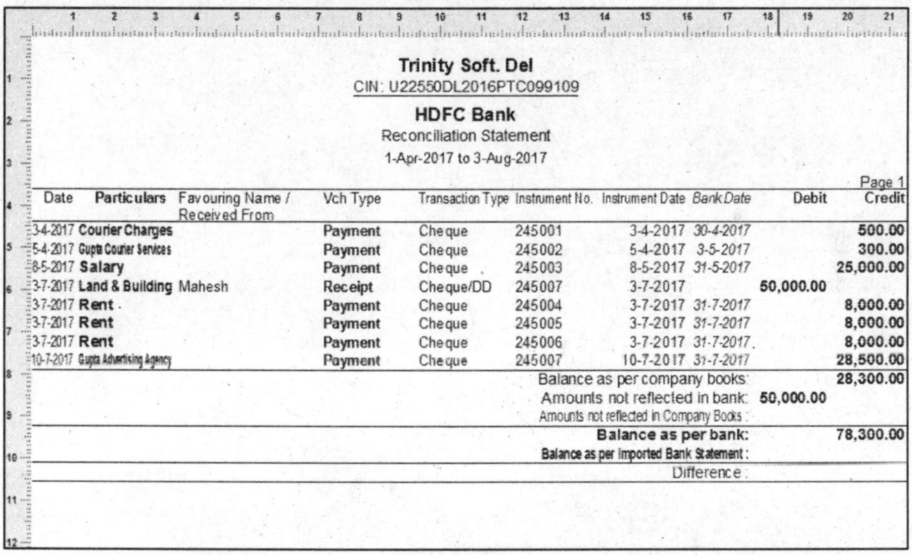

Trinity Soft. Del
CIN: U22550DL2016PTC099109
HDFC Bank
Reconciliation Statement
1-Apr-2017 to 3-Aug-2017

Page 1

Date	Particulars	Favouring Name / Received From	Vch Type	Transaction Type	Instrument No.	Instrument Date	Bank Date	Debit	Credit
3-4-2017	Courier Charges		Payment	Cheque	245001	3-4-2017	30-4-2017		500.00
5-4-2017	Gupta Courier Services		Payment	Cheque	245002	5-4-2017	3-5-2017		300.00
8-5-2017	Salary		Payment	Cheque	245003	8-5-2017	31-5-2017		25,000.00
3-7-2017	Land & Building	Mahesh	Receipt	Cheque/DD	245007	3-7-2017		50,000.00	
3-7-2017	Rent		Payment	Cheque	245004	3-7-2017	31-7-2017		8,000.00
3-7-2017	Rent		Payment	Cheque	245005	3-7-2017	31-7-2017		8,000.00
3-7-2017	Rent		Payment	Cheque	245006	3-7-2017	31-7-2017		8,000.00
10-7-2017	Gupta Advertising Agency		Payment	Cheque	245007	10-7-2017	31-7-2017		28,500.00
							Balance as per company books:		28,300.00
							Amounts not reflected in bank:	50,000.00	
							Amounts not reflected in Company Books :		
							Balance as per bank:		78,300.00
							Balance as per Imported Bank Statement :		
							Difference :		

Fig.TL-6.65

With this, we come to the end of the chapter. Let us summarize the key points discussed in the chapter.

Summary

In this chapter, you have learned about the concept of cost categories and cost centres. Where in you learned to create, after and display cost categories and cost centres. Further, the chapter discussed about the concept of budget and credit limit. Then, you have learned about the concept of interest calculation. Which further discusses the concept of creating party leader, creating sales voucher and booking interest to ledger account. Towards the end, the chapter described the basics for banking, such as cheque printing, cheque management, deposit slip, payment advice, and bank reconciliation statement.

CHAPTER

7

Working with Advanced Inventory Features

In this Chapter:

- Price Levels and Price Lists
- Actual and Billed Quantities
- Point of Sale (POS)

Introduction

In addition to the advanced accounting features and capabilities, Tally.ERP 9 provides advanced inventory features, such as advanced invoice features with inventory mode. A few of the advanced inventory features in Tally.ERP 9 are price level and price list, actual and billed quantities, and point of sale (POS).

Price level and price list enable you to make purchase and sales orders and invoices. Actual and billed quantities allow you to get correct stock values and correct position of accounts and inventory, respectively. POS is a place where the sale transaction occurs.

The chapter begins by explaining the price levels and price lists. Next, you learn about the concept of actual and billed quantities. Further more you learn about the concept of Point of Sale (POS). Towards the end, you learn to create a POS invoice by using a voucher class.

Let us start the chapter by learning how to create price levels and price lists.

Price Levels and Price Lists

Price lists are useful for making purchase and sales orders and invoices. A price list displays different pricing of the same item, depending upon the quantity and discount structure. When you generate a price list, you need to first create a price level. Tally.ERP 9 allows you to create different price levels and assign different price lists under these price levels.

Defining Price Levels

Perform the following steps to activate the **Use multiple price levels** option:

1. *Click* the **F11: Features** button on the Button Bar in the **Gateway of Tally** screen. The **Company Features** menu appears.
2. *Double-click* the **Inventory Features** option in the **Company Features** menu. The **Company Operations Alteration** screen appears with **Inventory Features**.
3. *Set* the **Use multiple price levels** option to **Yes** under the **Sales Management** section.
4. *Press* the **Enter** key. The **Company Price Levels** screen appears (Fig.TL-7.1).
5. *Enter* the name of the price level. In our case, we have entered **Company Retail Shop,** as shown in Fig.TL-7.1:

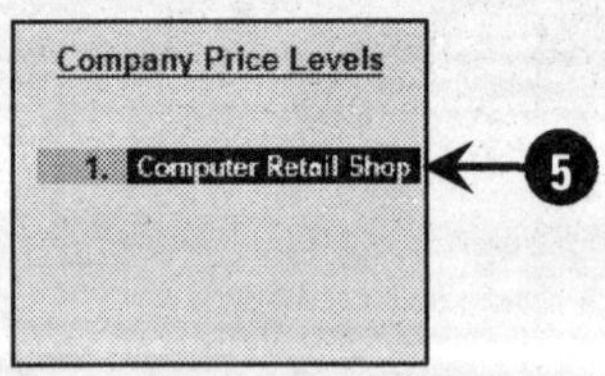

Fig.TL-7.1

6. *Press* the **Enter** key twice. The **Company Operations Alteration** screen reappears with **Inventory Features.**
7. *Press* the **Enter** key until the **Accept ?** message box appears.
8. *Click* **Yes** in the **Accept ?** message box to save the changes.

   Similarly, you can create other price levels.

Let us now learn how to create a price list.

Creating Price Lists

Perform the following steps to create a price list:

1. *Double-click* the **Inventory Info.** option in the **Masters** section in the **Gateway of Tally** menu. The **Inventory Info.** menu appears.

2. *Double-click* the **Price List** option. The **Price List** menu appears.
3. *Double-click* the **Stock Groups** option in the **Price List** menu. The **Price List** screen appears with the **List of Stock Groups** menu (Fig.TL-7.2).
4. *Double-click* the group, whose stock items price list you want to create, in the **List of Stock Groups** menu for the **Stock Group Name** option. In our case, we have double-clicked **All Items** (Fig.TL-7.2). The **List of Price Levels** menu appears.
5. *Double-click* the desired price level in the **List of Price Levels** menu for the **Price Level** option. In our case, we have double-clicked **Computer Retail Shop** (Fig.TL-7.2).
6. *Enter* the date from when the price list will be valid beside the **Applicable From** option. In our case, we have entered **3-Jul-2017**, as shown in Fig.TL-7.2:

Fig.TL-7.2

7. *Press* the **Enter** key. The **Price List** screen reappears with the **List Of Items** menu (Fig.TL-7.3).
8. *Double-click* the desired item in the **List Of Items** menu for the **Particulars** column. In our case, we have double-clicked **21 Inches Monitor**, as shown in Fig.TL-7.3:

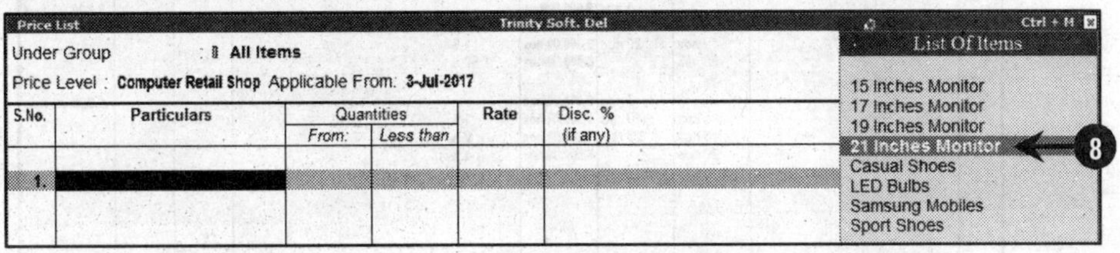

Fig.TL-7.3

9. *Enter* the quantity of the item in the **Less than** column. In our case, we have entered **5** (Fig.TL-7.4).
10. *Enter* the rate of each item in the **Rate** column. In our case, we have entered **9000** (Fig.TL-7.4).
11. *Enter* the discount rate over the price of each item in the **Disc. % (if any)** column. In our case, we have left it blank.

Note: **The Historical Details (Rate and Disc. %) column shows the previous price list defined for a stock group. The Cost Price column shows the cost price that is defined at the time of setting the costing method of an item. This column helps in fixing the prices of the item.**

12. *Press* the **Enter** key.
13. *Repeat* steps 9, 10, and 11. In our case, we have entered **10** in the **Less than** column, **9000** in the **Rate** column, and **2** in the **Disc. % (if any)** column (Fig.TL-7.4).
14. *Press* the **Enter** key.
15. *Repeat* steps 9, 10, and 11. In our case, we have entered **20** in the **Less than** column, **9000** in the **Rate** column, and **4** in the **Disc. % (if any)** column (Fig.TL-7.4).
16. *Press* the **Enter** key.

17. *Repeat* steps 10 and 11. In our case, we have entered **9000** in the **Rate** column, and **6** in the **Disc. % (if any)** column, as shown in Fig.TL-7.4:

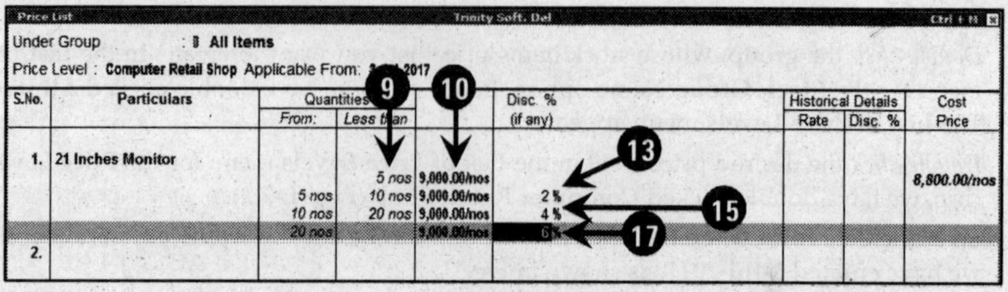

Fig.TL-7.4

Similarly, you can enter the details of quantity, rate, and discount for other items.

18. *Press* the **Enter** key until the **Accept ?** message box appears.
19. *Click* **Yes** in the **Accept ?** message box to save the price list, as shown in Fig.TL-7.5:

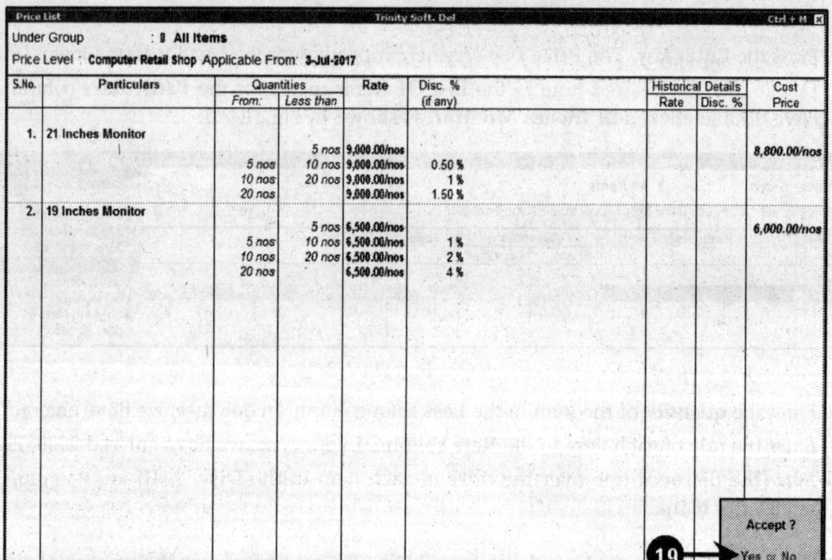

Fig.TL-7.5

Let us now learn how to use price lists.

Using Price Lists

You can use price list in a sales invoice. For this, you need to do the following tasks:

- Set the **Use separate discount column in invoices** option to **Yes**.
- Create a sales invoice.

Let us perform the following steps to enable the **Use separate discount column in invoices** option:

1. *Click* the **F11: Features** button on the Button Bar in the **Gateway of Tally** screen. The **Company Features** menu appears.
2. *Double-click* the **Inventory Features** option in the **Company Features** menu. The **Company Operations Alteration** screen appears with **Inventory Features**.
3. *Set* the **Use separate discount column in invoices** option to **Yes** in the **Invoicing** section.
4. *Press* the **Enter** key until the **Accept ?** message box appears.
5. *Click* **Yes** in the **Accept ?** message box to save the changes.

Now, let us perform the following steps to create a sales invoice:

1. *Double-click* the **Accounting Vouchers** option in the **Transactions** section in the **Gateway of Tally** menu. The **Accounting Voucher Creation** screen appears.
2. *Click* the **F8: Sales** button on the Button Bar. The **Accounting Voucher Creation** screen appears with the sales invoice.
3. *Enter* the desired date for the invoice. In our case, we have entered **6-Jul-2017** (Fig.TL-7.6).
4. *Press* the **Enter** key.
5. *Enter* the reference number for the sales invoice beside the **Reference no.** option. In our case, we have entered **12** (Fig.TL-7.6).
6. *Press* the **Enter** key. The **List of Ledger Accounts** menu appears (Fig.TL-7.6).
7. *Double-click* the desired ledger account in the **List of Ledger Accounts** menu for the **Party A/c name** option. In our case, we have double-clicked **Vikas Bros.** (Fig.TL-7.6).

   The **List of Price Levels** menu appears (Fig.TL-7.6).
8. *Double-click* the price level in the **List of Price Levels** menu for the **Price level** option. In our case, we have double-clicked **Computer Retail Shop**, as shown in Fig.TL-7.6:

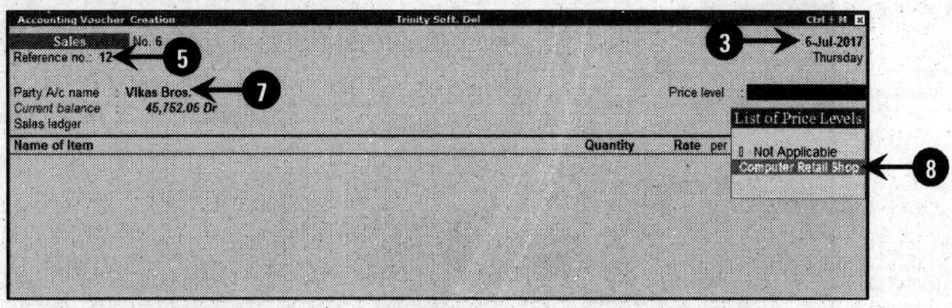

Fig.TL-7.6

   The **List of Ledger Accounts** menu appears (Fig.TL-7.7).
9. *Double-click* the desired sales ledger in the **List of Ledger Accounts** menu for the **Sales ledger** option. In our case, we have double-clicked **Sales**. (Fig.TL-7.7).

   The **List of Stock Items** menu appears for the **Name of Item** column (Fig.TL-7.7).
10. *Double-click* the desired stock item in the **List of Stock Items** menu for the **Name of Item** column. In our case, we have double-clicked **21 Inches Monitor**, as shown in Fig.TL-7.7:

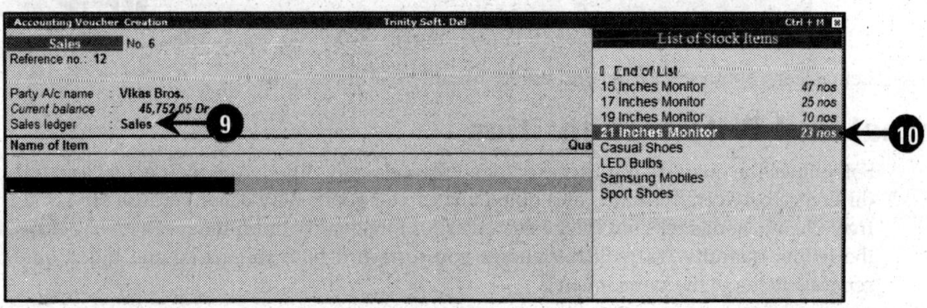

Fig.TL-7.7

   The **Stock Item Allocations** screen appears with the **List of Godowns** menu (Fig.TL-7.8).
11. *Double-click* the desired godown in the **List of Godowns** menu for the **Godown** column. In our case, we have double-clicked **Moti Bagh Godown** (Fig.TL-7.8).

12. *Enter* the desired quantity in the **Quantity** column. In our case, we have entered **15** (Fig.TL-7.8). The **Rate, per, Disc %**, and **Amount** columns are filled automatically, as shown in Fig.TL-7.8:

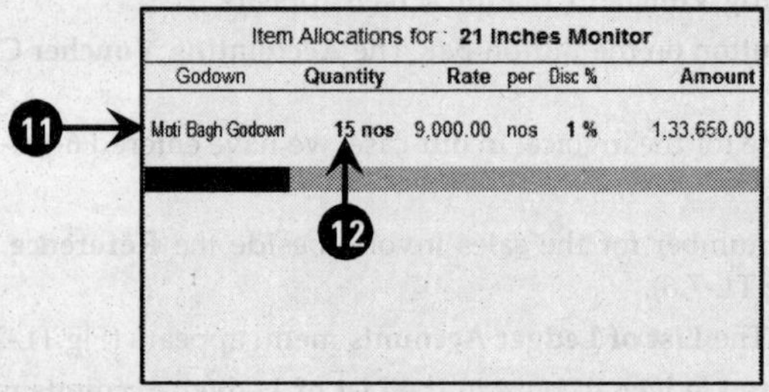

Fig.TL-7.8

13. *Press* the **Enter** key until the **Accept ?** message box appears.
14. *Click* **Yes** in the **Accept ?** message box to save the sales invoice, as shown in Fig.TL-7.9:

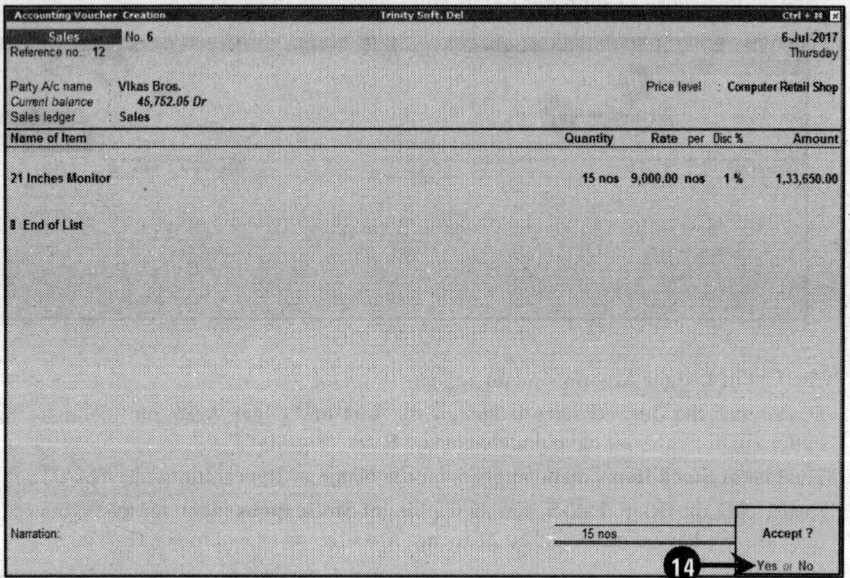

Fig.TL-7.9

Let us learn about the actual and billed quantity feature in Tally.

Actual and Billed Quantities

Sometimes the quantity of purchased or sold goods may differ from their actual and billed quantity. This difference between the actual and billed quantity of goods may occur because of various reasons, such as free scheme, goods rejected by the customer for low quality or on the grounds of defects, or rounding off the billing quantity. Tally.ERP 9 allows you to record both the actual and billed quantity of goods in separate fields in the same invoice.

Enabling the Actual and Billed Quantity Feature

Before recording the actual and billed quantity of goods in separate fields in an invoice, you need to first enable the Actual and Billed Quantity feature by performing the following steps:

1. *Click* the **F11: Features** button on the Button Bar in the **Gateway of Tally** screen. The **Company Features** menu appears.

2. *Double-click* the **Inventory Features** option in the **Company Features** menu. The **Company Operations Alteration** screen appears with **Inventory Features**.
3. *Set* the **Use separate actual and billed quantity columns** option to **Yes** under the **Storage and Classification** section in **Inventory Features**.
4. *Press* the **Enter** key until the **Accept ?** message box appears.
5. *Click* **Yes** in the **Accept ?** message box to save the changes.

Let us now learn how to create a purchase voucher.

Creating a Purchase Voucher

Perform the following steps to create a purchase voucher for actual and billed quantity:

1. *Double-click* the **Accounting Vouchers** option under the **Transactions** section in the **Gateway of Tally** menu. The **Accounting Voucher Creation** screen appears.
2. *Click* the **F9: Purchase** button on the Button Bar. The **Accounting Voucher Creation** screen of the **Purchase** voucher appears as item invoice (Fig.TL-7.10).
3. *Enter* the desired supplier invoice number beside the **Supplier invoice no.** option. In our case, we have entered **12** (Fig.TL-7.10).
4. *Press* the **Enter** key.
5. *Enter* the desired date of invoice beside the **Date** option. In our case, we have entered, **7-Jul-2017** (Fig.TL-7.10).
6. *Press* the **Enter** key. The **List of Ledger Accounts** menu appears.
7. *Double-click* the desired supplier in the **List of Ledger Accounts** menu for **Party A/c name** option. In our case, we have double-clicked **Yash Traders** (Fig.TL-7.10).

   The **List of Ledger Accounts** menu appears.
8. *Double-click* the desired purchase ledger in the **List of Ledger Accounts** menu for the **Purchase ledger** option. In our case, we have double-clicked **Purchase** (Fig.TL-7.10).

   The **List of Stock Items** menu appears (Fig.TL-7.10).
9. *Double-click* the desired item in the **List of Stock Items** menu for the **Name of Item** column. In our case, we have double-clicked **LED Bulbs**, as shown in Fig.TL-7.10:

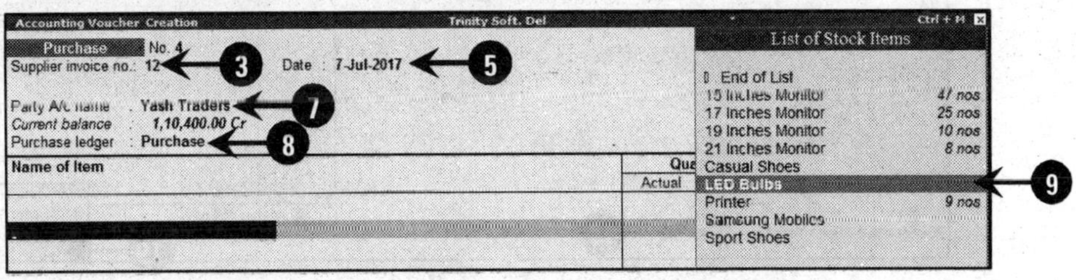

Fig.TL-7.10

   The **Stock Item Allocations** screen appears.

10. *Double-click* the desired godown in the **List of Godowns** menu for the **Godown** column. In our case, we have double-clicked **Moti Bagh Godown** (Fig.TL-7.11).
11. *Enter* the actual quantity of the item under the **Actual** column. In our case, we have entered **500** (Fig.TL-7.11).
12. *Enter* the billed quantity of the item under the **Billed** column. In our case, we have entered **450** (Fig.TL-7.11).
13. *Enter* the rate of the item under the **Rate** column. In our case, we have entered **90** (Fig.TL-7.11).

14. *Enter* **nos** under the **per** column (Fig.TL-7.11). The **Amount** column is filled automatically, as shown in Fig.TL-7.11:

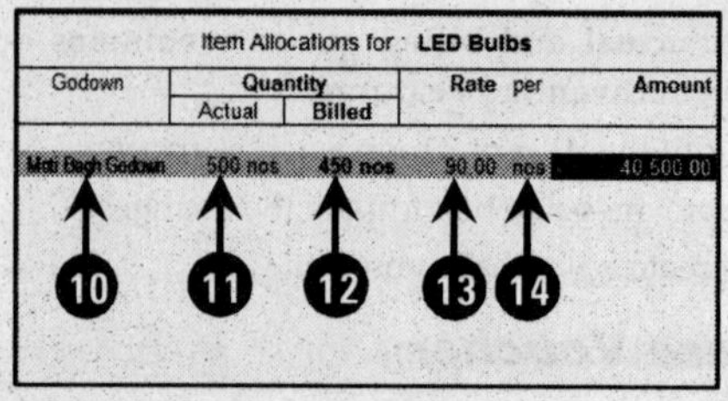

Fig.TL-7.11

15. *Press* the **Enter** key until the **Accounting Voucher Creation** screen reappears.
16. *Press* the **Enter** key until the **Narration** option appears.
17. *Enter* the narration under the **Narration** option. In our case, we have entered **Purchased LED Bulbs from Yash Traders** (Fig.TL-7.12).
18. *Press* the **Enter** key. The **Accept ?** message box appears.
19. *Click* **Yes** in the **Accept ?** message box to save the voucher, as shown in Fig.TL-7.12:

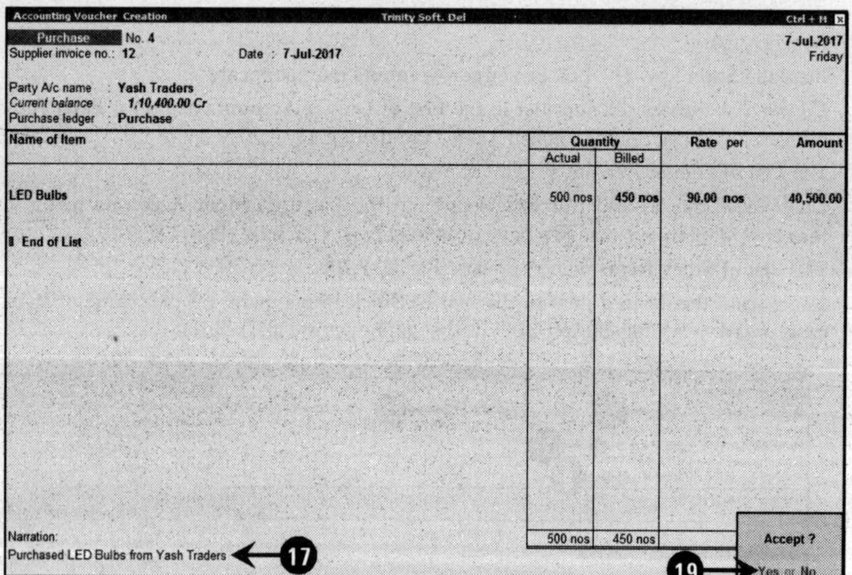

Fig.TL-7.12

Let us now learn how to create a sales voucher.

Creating a Sales Voucher

Perform the following steps to create a sales voucher for actual and billed quantity:

1. *Double-click* the **Accounting Vouchers** option under the **Transactions** section in the **Gateway of Tally** menu. The **Accounting Voucher Creation** screen appears.
2. *Click* the **F8: Sales** button on the Button Bar. The **Accounting Voucher Creation** screen of the **Sales** voucher appears (Fig.TL-7.13).
3. *Enter* the desired reference number beside the **Reference no.** option. In our case, we have entered **15** (Fig.TL-7.13).
4. *Press* the **Enter** key. The **List of Ledger Accounts** menu appears.

5. *Double-click* the desired customer in the **List of Ledger Accounts** menu for **Party A/c name** option. In our case, we have double-clicked **Vikas Bros.** (Fig.TL-7.13).

   The **List of Ledger Accounts** menu appears.

6. *Double-click* the desired sales ledger in the **List of Ledger Accounts** menu for the **Sales ledger** option. In our case, we have double-clicked **Sales** (Fig.TL-7.13). The **List of Stock Items** menu appears (Fig.TL-7.13).

7. *Double-click* the desired item in the **List of Stock Items** menu for the **Name of Item** column. In our case, we have double-clicked **LED Bulbs**, as shown in Fig.TL-7.13:

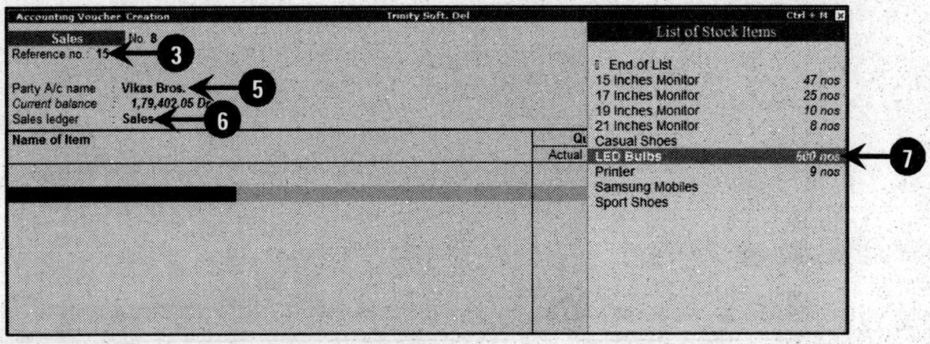

Fig.TL-7.13

The **Stock Item Allocations** screen appears.

8. *Double-click* the desired godown in the **List of Godowns** menu for the **Godown** column. In our case, we have double-clicked **Moti Bagh Godown** (Fig.TL-7.14).

9. *Enter* the actual quantity of the item under the **Actual** column. In our case, we have entered **400** (Fig.TL-7.14).

10. *Enter* the billed quantity of the item under the **Billed** column. In our case, we have entered **380** (Fig.TL-7.14).

11. *Enter* the rate of the item under the **Rate** column. In our case, we have entered **100** (Fig.TL-7.14).

12. *Enter* **nos** under the **per** column (Fig.TL-7.14). The **Amount** column is filled automatically, as shown in Fig.TL-7.14:

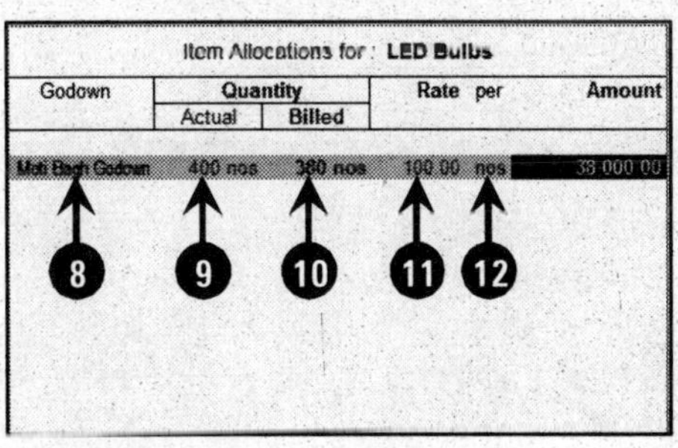

Fig.TL-7.14

13. *Press* the **Enter** key until the **Accounting Voucher Creation** screen reappears.

14. *Press* the **Enter** key until the **Narration** option appears.

15. *Enter* the narration under the **Narration** option. In our case, we have entered **Sold LED Bulbs to Vikas Bros.** (Fig.TL-7.15).

16. *Press* the **Enter** key. The **Accept ?** message box appears.

17. *Click* **Yes** in the **Accept ?** message box to save the voucher, as shown in Fig.TL-7.15:

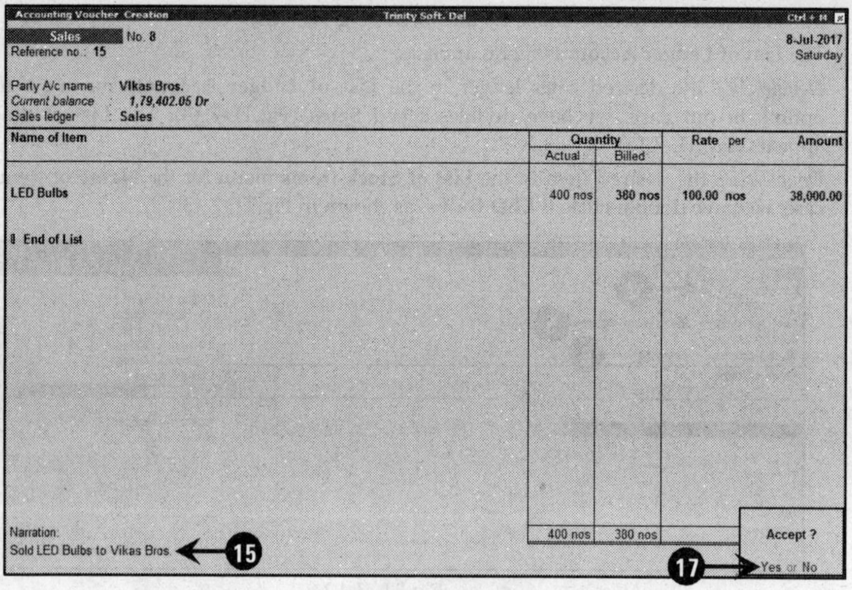

Fig.TL-7.15

Let us now learn how to display a stock summary report.

Displaying a Stock Summary Report

Perform the following steps to display a stock summary report:

1. *Double-click* the **Stock Summary** option under the **Reports** section in the **Gateway of Tally** menu. The **Stock Summary** screen appears (Fig.TL-7.16).
2. *Double-click* the desired stock group in the **Stock Summary** screen. In our case, we have double-clicked **LED Bulbs**, as shown in Fig.TL-7.16:

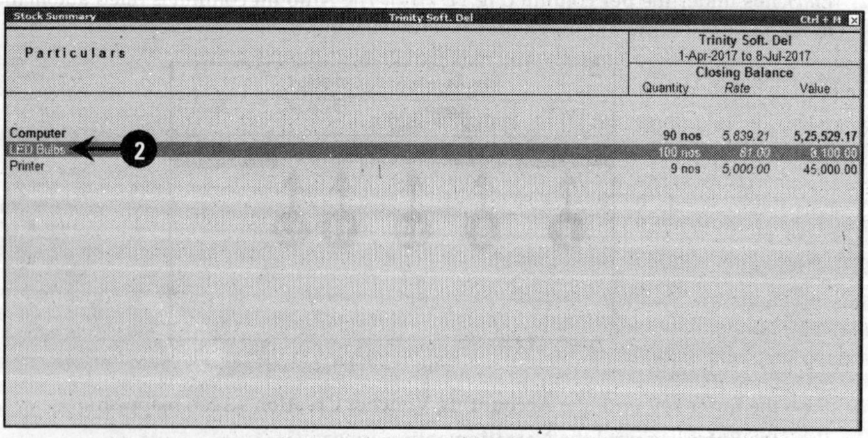

Fig.TL-7.16

The **Stock Item Monthly Summary** screen appears (Fig.TL-7.17).

3. *Double-click* the month, whose stock summary you want to view, in the **Stock Item Monthly Summary** screen. In our case, we have double-clicked **July**, as shown in Fig.TL-7.17:

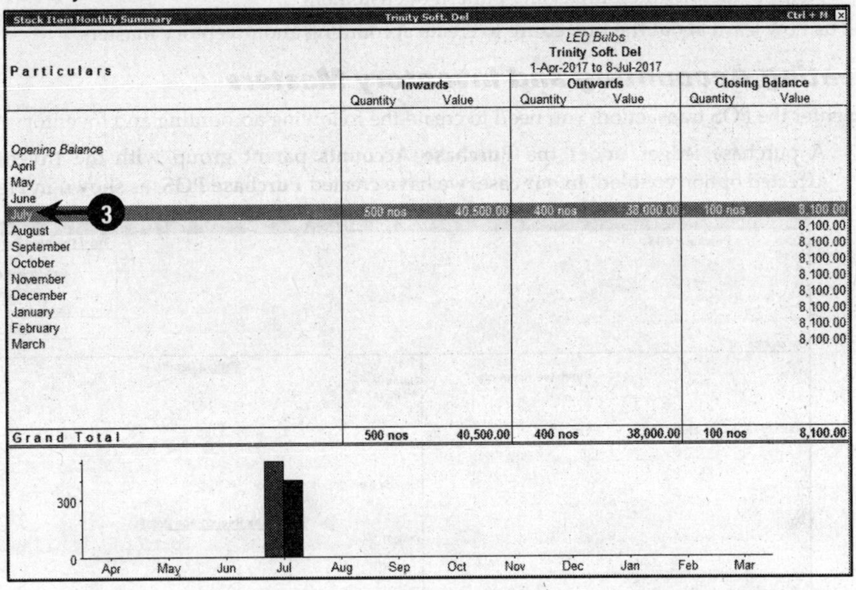

Fig.TL-7.17

The **Stock Vouchers** screen appears, displaying the stock item summary for the selected month, as shown in Fig.TL-7.18:

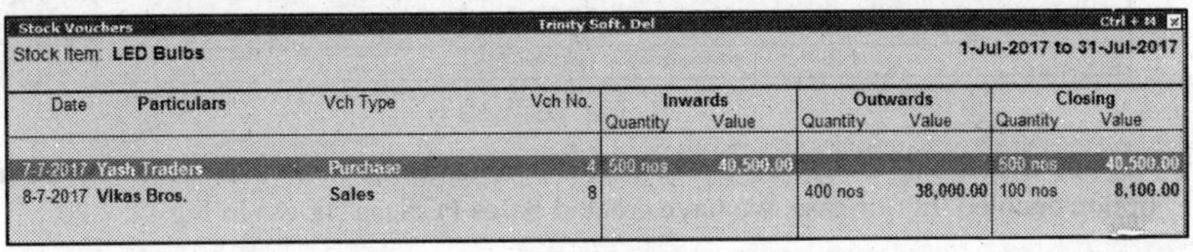

Fig.TL-7.18

Let us learn about the Point of Sale.

Point of Sale (POS)

Point of Sale (POS) (also known as the checkout counter) is the location where the sales transaction occurs. This concept is used in retail shops, which use computerized cash registers, card readers, and barcode readers. The card readers automatically calculate the total sale, compute the tax over the sales, and debit the inventory by the amount equal to the total inventory sold.

In Tally, two types of POS voucher types are created, one with a voucher class and one without a voucher class.

Features of POS

POS offers various features to users. These features are listed as follows:

- Helps to generate a POS invoice with date and time
- Allows to view or print a POS report
- Provides the facility of multiple mode of payment for a single POS invoice
- Gives the facility of bar code scanning of stock items
- Offers the facility of gift cards, gift vouchers, and discount

- Provides the facility to track the balance tendered to the customer
- Helps to identify the purchasing pattern of customers

Let us now learn about the procedure to create accounting and inventory masters.

Creating Accounting and Inventory Masters

To enter the POS transaction, you need to create the following accounting and inventory masters:

- A purchase ledger under the **Purchase Accounts** parent group with the **Inventory values are affected** option enabled. In our case, we have created **Purchase POS**, as shown in Fig.TL-7.19:

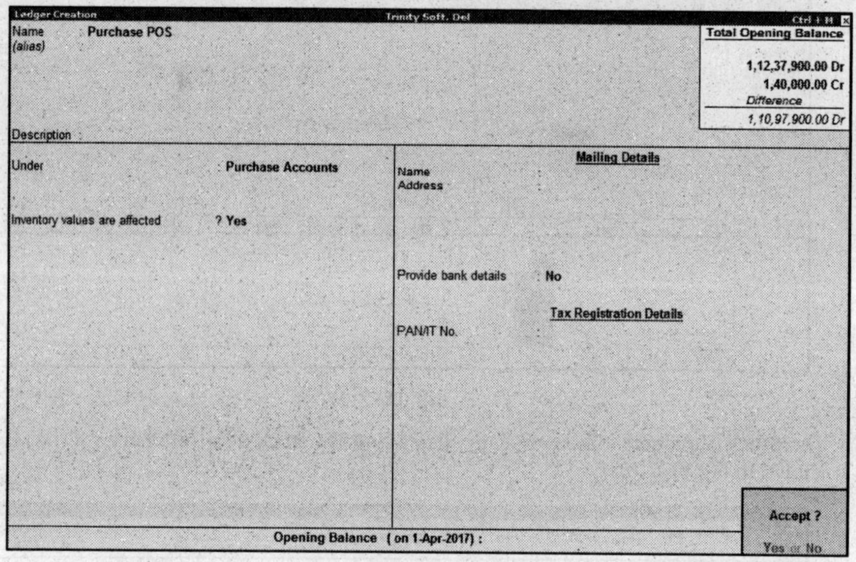

Fig.TL-7.19

- A sales ledger under the **Sales Accounts** parent group with the **Inventory values are affected** option enabled. In our case, we have created **Sales POS**, as shown in Fig.TL-7.20:

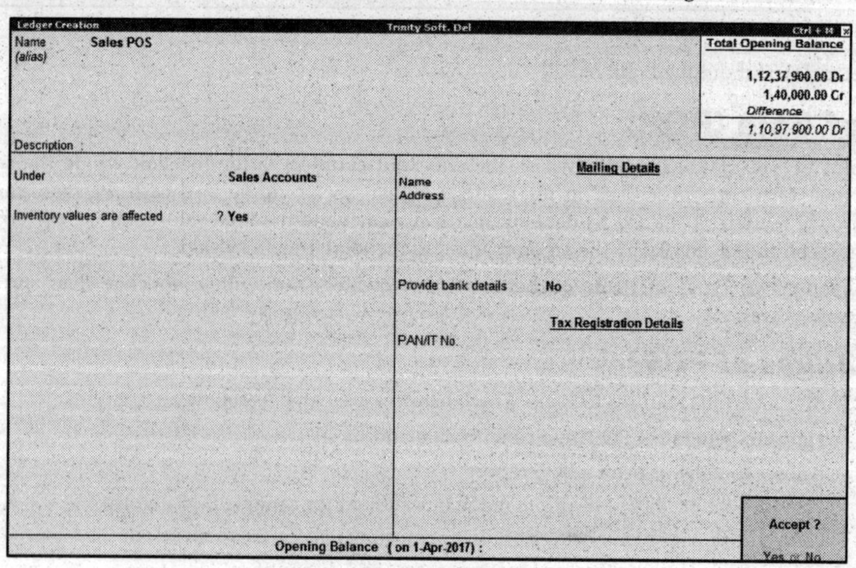

Fig.TL-7.20

- A stock group under the **Primary** parent group with the **should quantities of items be added** option enable. In our case, we have created **Hardware Devices** (Fig.TL-7.21):

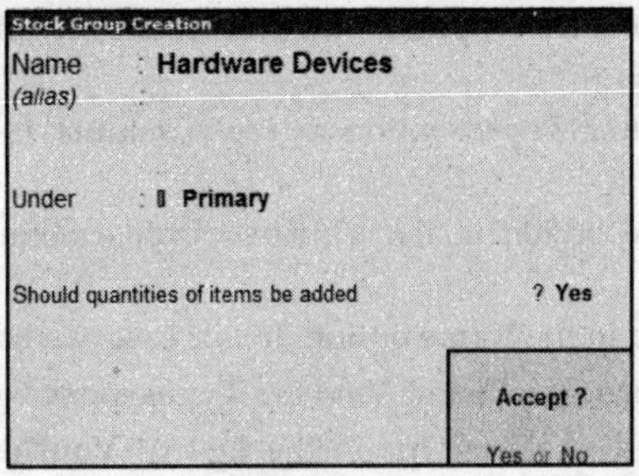

Fig.TL-7.21

- A unit with the name **Pieces**, as shown in Fig.TL-7.22:

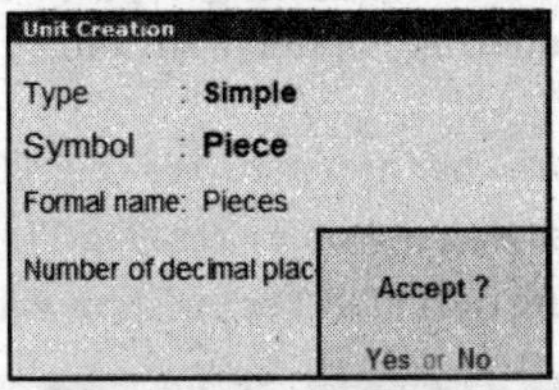

Fig.TL-7.22

- A stock item under the **Hardware Devices** stock group with the **Set standard rates** option enabled. The details of the standard rate are as follows:
  - Standard Cost is applicable from 1-Apr-2017 with the rate of ₹ 250.
  - Standard Selling Cost is applicable from 1-Apr-2017 with the rate of ₹ 300.

  In our case, we have created the **Keyboard** stock item, as shown in Fig.TL-7.23:

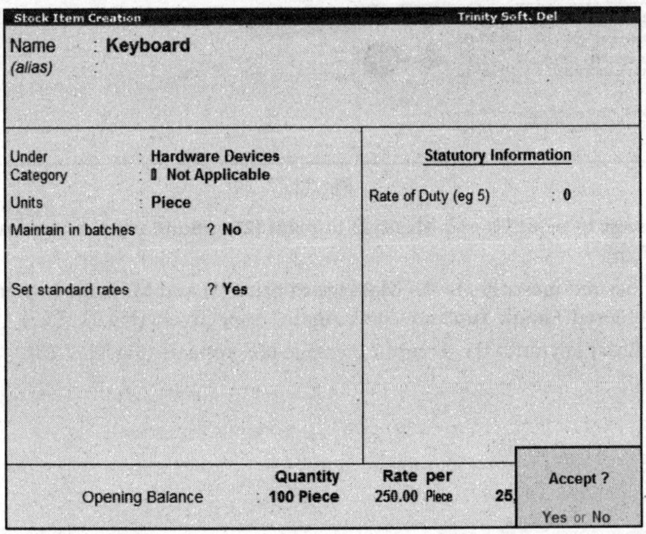

Fig.TL-7.23

Let us now learn about the procedure to create a POS voucher type without a voucher class.

Creating a POS Voucher Type without a Voucher Class

Perform the following steps to create a POS voucher type without a voucher class:

1. *Double-click* the **Accounts Info.** option under the **Masters** section in the **Gateway of Tally** menu. The **Accounts Info.** menu appears.
2. *Double-click* the **Voucher Types** option in the **Accounts Info.** menu. The **Voucher Types** menu appears.
3. *Double-click* the **Create** option in the **Voucher Types** menu. The **Voucher Type Creation** screen appears (Fig.TL-7.24).
4. *Enter* the desired name in the **Name** option. In our case, we have entered **POS** (Fig.TL-7.24).
5. *Press* the **Enter** key twice. The **List of Voucher Types** menu appears.
6. *Double-click* the desired voucher type in the **List of Voucher Types** menu for the **Select type of voucher** option. In our case, we have double-clicked **Sales** (Fig.TL-7.24).
7. *Press* the **Enter** key twice. The **Methods of Numbering** menu appears.
8. *Double-click* the desired voucher numbering type in the **Methods of Numbering** menu for the **Method of voucher numbering** option. In our case, we have double-clicked **Automatic** (Fig.TL-7.24).
9. *Set* the **Allow narration in voucher** option to **Yes** (Fig.TL-7.24).
10. *Set* the **Print voucher after saving** option to **Yes** (Fig.TL-7.24).
11. *Set* the **Use for POS invoicing** option to **Yes**, as shown in Fig.TL-7.24:

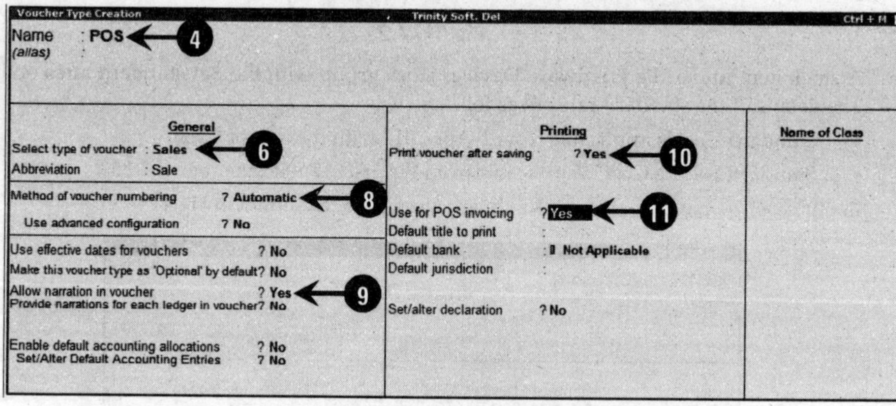

Fig.TL-7.24

The **Message to print (1)** and **Message to print (2)** options are displayed under the **Printing** section (Fig.TL-7.25).

12. *Enter* the desired messages in the **Message to print (1)** and **Message to print (2)** options. In our case, we have entered **Thank You** and **Come Again**, respectively (Fig.TL-7.25).
13. *Press* the **Enter** key until the **Accept ?** message box appears (Fig.TL-7.25).

14. *Click* **Yes** in the **Accept ?** message box to save the voucher type, as shown in Fig.TL-7.25:

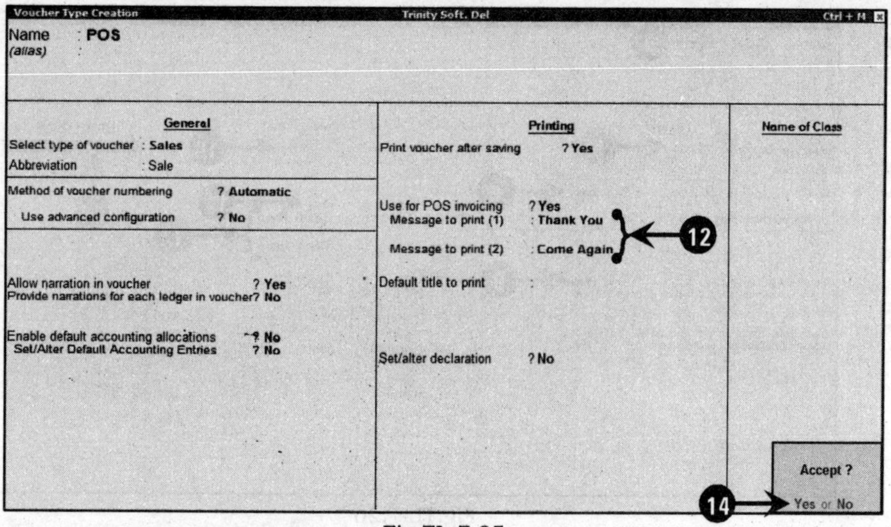

Fig.TL-7.25

Creating a POS Voucher Type with a Voucher Class

Perform the following steps to create a POS voucher type with a voucher class:

1. *Double-click* the **Accounts Info.** option under the **Masters** section in the **Gateway of Tally** menu. The **Accounts Info.** menu appears.
2. *Double-click* the **Voucher Types** option in the **Accounts Info.** menu. The **Voucher Types** menu appears.
3. *Double-click* the **Create** option in the **Voucher Types** menu. The **Voucher Type Creation** screen appears (Fig.TL-7.26).
4. *Enter* the desired name in the **Name** option. In our case, we have entered **POS 1** (Fig.TL-7.26).
5. *Press* the **Enter** key twice. The **List of Voucher Types** menu appears.
6. *Double-click* the desired voucher type in the **List of Voucher Types** menu for the **Select type of voucher** option. In our case, we have double-clicked **Sales** (Fig.TL-7.26).
7. *Press* the **Enter** key twice. The **Methods of Numbering** menu appears.
8. *Double-click* the desired voucher numbering type in the **Methods of Numbering** menu for the **Method of voucher numbering** option. In our case, we have double-clicked **Automatic** (Fig.TL-7.26).
9. *Set* the **Allow narration in voucher** option to **Yes** (Fig.TL-7.26).
10. *Set* the **Print voucher after saving** option to **Yes** (Fig.TL-7.26).
11. *Set* the **Use for POS invoicing** option to **Yes** (Fig.TL-7.26). The **Message to print (1)** and **Message to print (2)** options are displayed under the **Printing** section (Fig.TL-7.26).
12. *Enter* the desired messages in the **Message to print (1)** and **Message to print (2)** options. In our case, we have entered **Thank You** and **Come Again**, respectively (Fig.TL-7.26).
13. *Press* the **Enter** key three times.

14. *Enter* **POS Class** under the **Name of Class** column, as shown in Fig.TL-7.26:

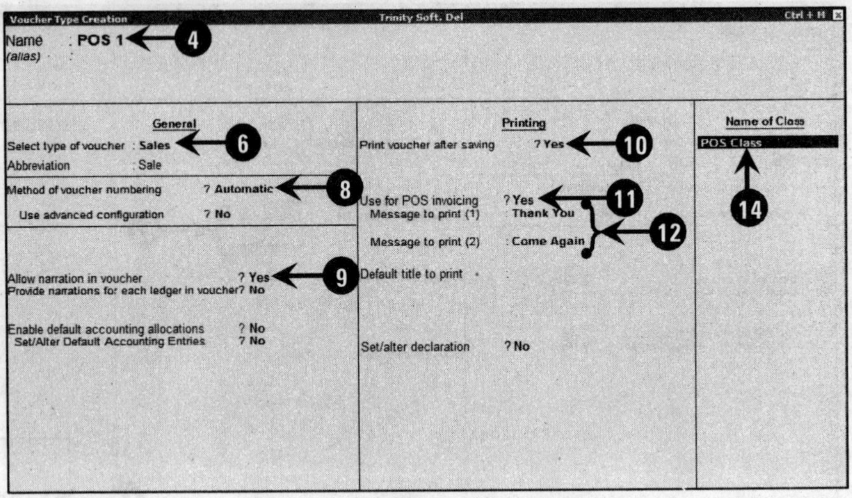

Fig.TL-7.26

15. *Press* the **Enter** key. The **Voucher Type Class** screen appears.
16. *Click* the **F12: Configure** button on the Button Bar. The **Configuration** screen appears.
17. *Set* the **Set accounting allocations for stockitem** option to **Yes.**
18. *Press* the **Enter** key. The **Voucher Type Class** screen reappears (Fig.TL-7.27).
19. *Enter* the relevant details as per the requirements in the **Default Ledger Accounts for POS Invoice** section (Fig.TL-7.27).
20. *Enter* the relevant details as per the requirements in the **Default Accounting Allocations for all items in Invoice** section (Fig.TL-7.27).
21. *Enter* the relevant details as per the requirements in the **Default Accounting Allocations for Stockitem** section, as shown in Fig.TL-7.27:

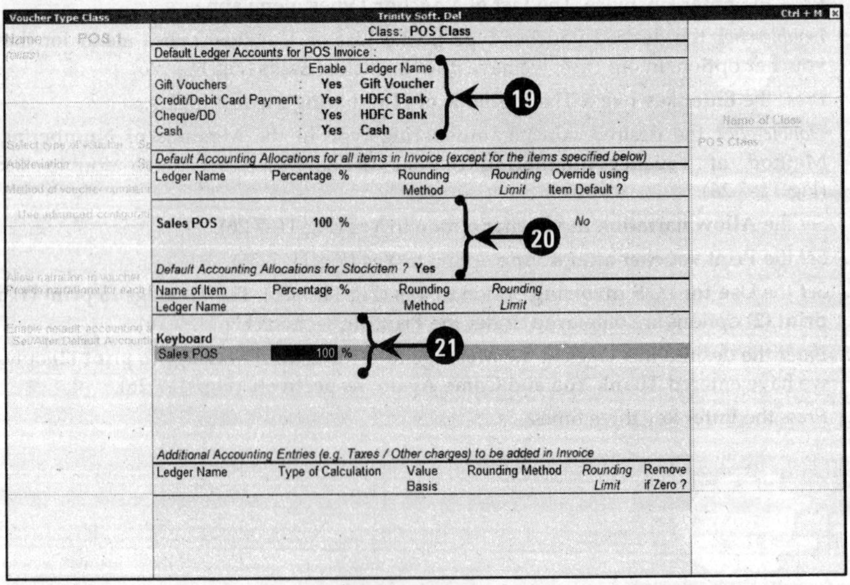

Fig.TL-7.27

22. *Press* the **Enter** key until the **Voucher Type Creation** screen reappears (Fig.TL-7.28).
23. *Press* the **Enter** key. The **Accept ?** message box appears (Fig.TL-7.28).
24. *Click* **Yes** in the **Accept ?** message box to save the voucher type, as shown in Fig.TL-7.28:

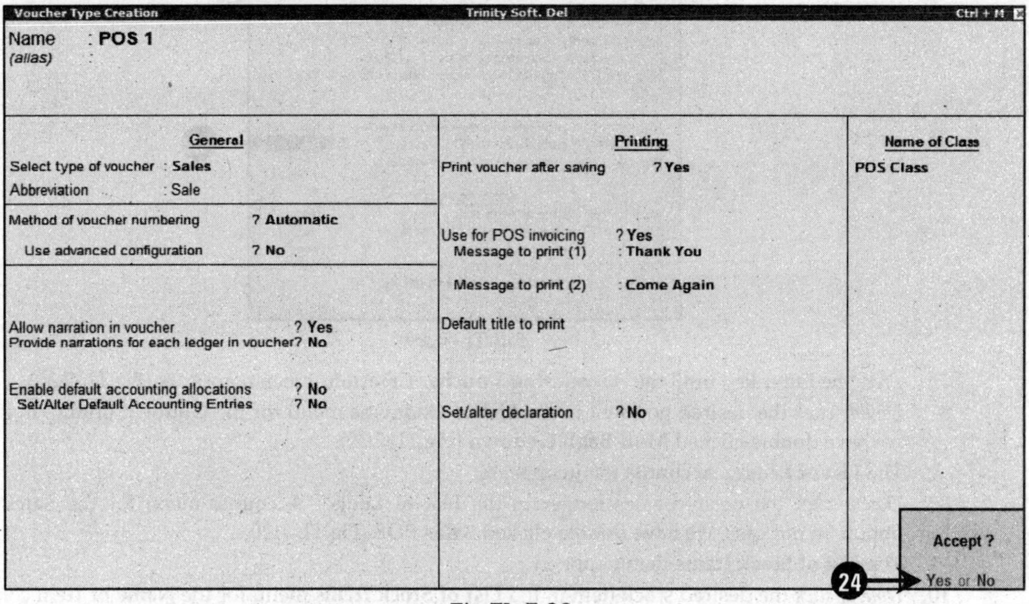

Fig.TL-7.28

Let us now learn how to create a POS invoice with the single payment mode.

Creating a POS Invoice with the Single Payment Mode

Perform the following steps to create a POS invoice with the single payment mode:

1. *Double-click* the **Accounting Vouchers** option under the **Transactions** section in the **Gateway of Tally** menu. The **Accounting Voucher Creation** screen appears.
2. *Click* the **F8: Sales** button on the Button Bar. The **Change Voucher Type** screen appears with the **List of Types** menu.
3. *Double-click* the **POS** option in the **List of Types** menu. The **Accounting Voucher Creation** screen appears with the POS invoice.
4. *Click* the **F12: Configure** button on the Button Bar. The **Voucher Configuration** screen appears with various options for POS invoice configuration.
5. *Set* the **Enable supplementary details** option to **No** (Fig.TL-7.29).

6. *Set* the **Enable entry of party details in POS invoice** to **No**, as shown in Fig.TL-7.29:

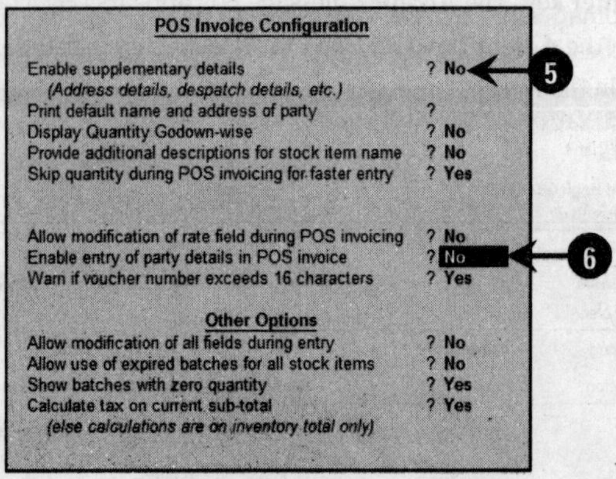

Fig.TL-7.29

7. *Press* the **Enter** key until the **Accounting Voucher Creation** screen reappears (Fig.TL-7.30).
8. *Double-click* the desired godown in the **List of Godowns** menu for the **Godown** option. In our case, we have double-clicked **Moti Bagh Godown** (Fig.TL-7.30).
   The **List of Ledger Accounts** menu appears.
9. *Double-click* the desired sales ledger in the **List of Ledger Accounts** menu for the **Sales Ledger** option. In our case, we have double-clicked **Sales POS** (Fig.TL-7.30).
   The **List of Stock Items** menu appears.
10. *Double-click* the desired stock item in the **List of Stock Items** menu for the **Name of Item** column. In our case, we have double-clicked **Keyboard** (Fig.TL-7.30).
    When you double-click the desired stock item, the **Quantity, Rate, per,** and **Amount** columns will be filled according to one quantity, as shown in Fig.TL-7.30:

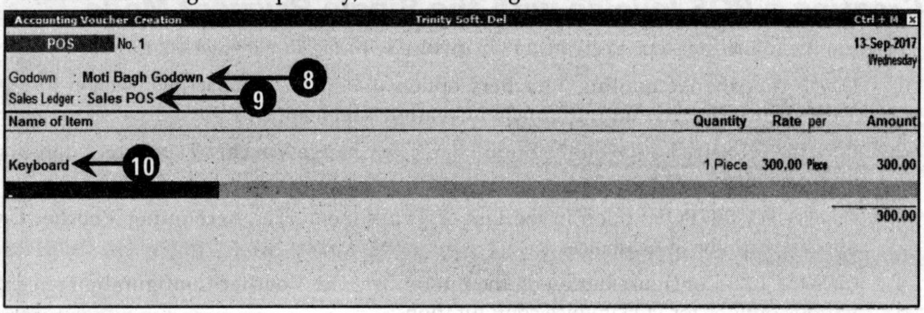

Fig.TL-7.30

11. *Press* the **Shift + Tab** keys to move backward to the **Quantity** column.
12. *Enter* the desired quantity under the **Quantity** column. In our case, we have entered **10** (Fig.TL-7.31).
13. *Press* the **Enter** key till the **Cash** option appears. The **List of Ledger Accounts** menu appears.
14. *Double-click* the desired cash ledger in the **List of Ledger Accounts** menu for the **Cash** option. In our case, we have double-clicked **Cash** (Fig.TL-7.31).
    The **Cash tendered** and **Balance** options are enabled and displayed on the voucher (Fig.TL-7.31).
15. *Enter* the amount that is received from the customer in the **Cash tendered** option. In our case, we have entered **3,200** (Fig.TL-7.31).

16. *Press* the **Enter** key.

    Tally automatically calculates the amount and shows the balance amount that is refunded to the customer beside the **Balance** option. The **Accept ?** message box appears.

17. *Click* **Yes** in the **Accept ?** message box to create the invoice, as shown in Fig.TL-7.31:

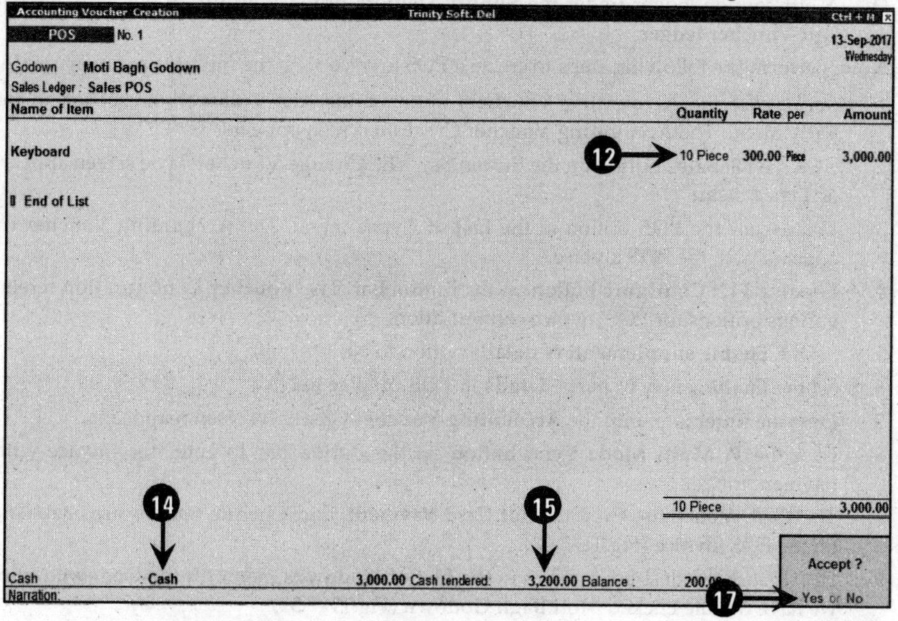

Fig.TL-7.31

The **Voucher Printing** screen appears, showing the message for a confirmation to print the invoice.

18. *Click* **Yes** in the **Print ?** message box to print the invoice. The **Accounting Voucher Display** screen appears that shows the POS invoice.

19. *Click* the **Zoom** button to zoom the POS invoice. The POS invoice is zoomed and displayed, as shown in Fig.TL-7.32:

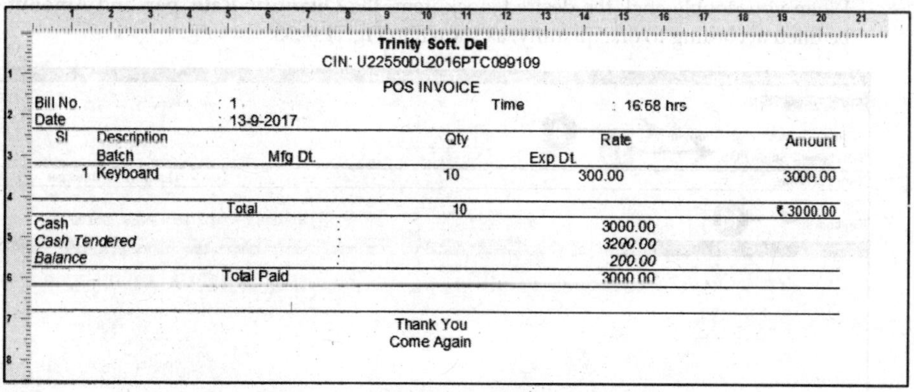

Fig.TL-7.32

Let us now learn how to create a POS invoice with the multiple payment mode.

Creating a POS Invoice with the Multiple Payment Mode

To create a POS invoice with the multiple payment mode, you need to create the following masters:

- A bank ledger under the **Bank accounts** primary group
- A gift coupon ledger under the **Sundry Debtors** primary group. In our case, we have created the **Gift Voucher ledger**.

Now, perform the following steps to create a POS invoice with the multiple payment mode:

1. *Double-click* the **Accounting Vouchers** option under the **Transactions** section in the **Gateway of Tally** menu. The **Accounting Voucher Creation** screen appears.
2. *Click* the **F8: Sales** button on the Button Bar. The **Change Voucher Type** screen appears with the **List of Types** menu.
3. *Double-click* the **POS** option in the **List of Types** menu. The **Accounting Voucher Creation** screen appears with the POS invoice.
4. *Click* the **F12: Configure** button on the Button Bar. The **Voucher Configuration** screen appears with various options for POS invoice configuration.
5. *Set* the **Enable supplementary details** option to **No.**
6. *Set* the **Enable entry of party details in POS invoice** to **No.**
7. *Press* the **Enter** key until the **Accounting Voucher Creation** screen reappears.
8. *Click* the **P: Multi Mode Pymt** button on the Button Bar to enter the invoice with the multiple payment mode.

   The **Cash Vouchers, Credit/Debit Card Payment,** and **Cheque** options are enabled and displayed on the POS invoice (Fig.TL-7.33).
9. *Double-click* the desired godown in the **List of Godowns** menu for the **Godown** option. In our case, we have double-clicked **Moti Bagh Godown** (Fig.TL-7.33).

   The **List of Ledger Accounts** menu appears.
10. *Double-click* the desired sales ledger in the **List of Ledger Accounts** menu for the **Sales Ledger** option. In our case, we have double-clicked **Sales POS** (Fig.TL-7.33).

    The **List of Stock Items** menu appears.
11. *Double-click* the desired stock item in the **List of Stock Items** menu for the **Name of Item** column. In our case, we have double-clicked **Keyboard** (Fig.TL-7.33).

    When you double-click the desired stock item, the **Quantity, Rate, per,** and **Amount** columns will be filled according to one quantity, as shown in Fig.TL-7.33:

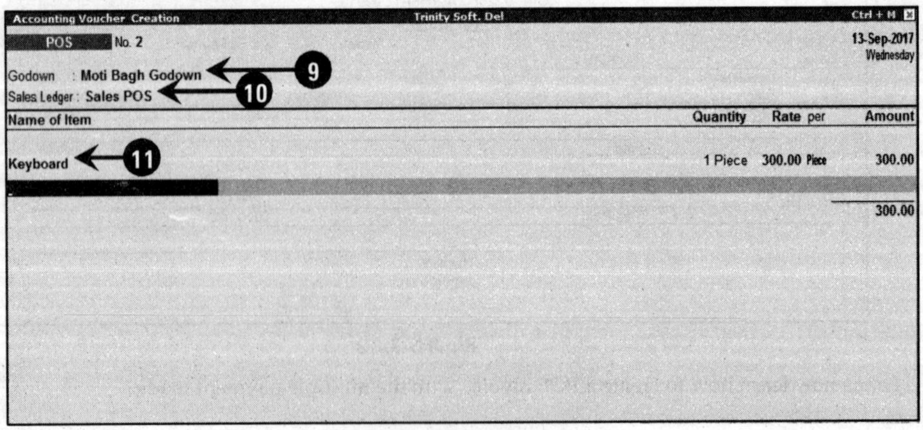

Fig.TL-7.33

12. *Press* the **Shift + Tab** keys to move backward to the **Quantity** column.
13. *Enter* the desired quantity under the **Quantity** column. In our case, we have entered **10** (Fig.TL-7.34).
14. *Press* the **Enter** key thrice to go to the **Gift Vouchers** option. The **List of Ledger Accounts** menu appears.
15. *Double-click* the desired gift ledger in the **List of Ledger Accounts** menu for the **Gift vouchers** option. In our case, we have double-clicked **Gift Voucher** (Fig.TL-7.34).
16. *Enter* the desired amount for the **Gift Vouchers** option. In our case, we have entered **1,500** (Fig.TL-7.34).
17. *Press* the **Enter** key. The **List of Ledger Accounts** menu appears.
18. *Double-click* the bank ledger whose credit or debit card is used for payment, in the **List of Ledger Accounts** menu for the **Credit/debit card** option. In our case, we have double-clicked **HDFC Bank** (Fig.TL-7.34).
19. *Enter* the desired amount for the **Credit/debit card** option. In our case, we have entered **1,200** (Fig.TL-7.34).
20. *Press* the **Enter** key.
21. *Enter* the credit or debit card number beside the **Card no.** option. In our case, we have entered **4527183729562356** (Fig.TL-7.34).
22. *Press* the **Enter** key twice to go to the **Cash** option.
23. *Double-click* the desired cash ledger in the **List of Ledger Accounts** menu for the **Cash** option. In our case, we have double-clicked **Cash** (Fig.TL-7.34). The **Cash tendered** and **Balance** options are enabled and displayed on the invoice.
24. *Enter* the amount that is received from the customer in the **Cash tendered** option. In our case, we have entered **400** (Fig.TL-7.34).
25. *Press* the **Enter** key.

    Tally automatically calculates the amount and shows the balance amount that is refunded to the customer beside the **Balance** option. The **Accept ?** message box appears.
26. *Click* **Yes** in the **Accept ?** message box to create the invoice, as shown in Fig.TL-7.34:

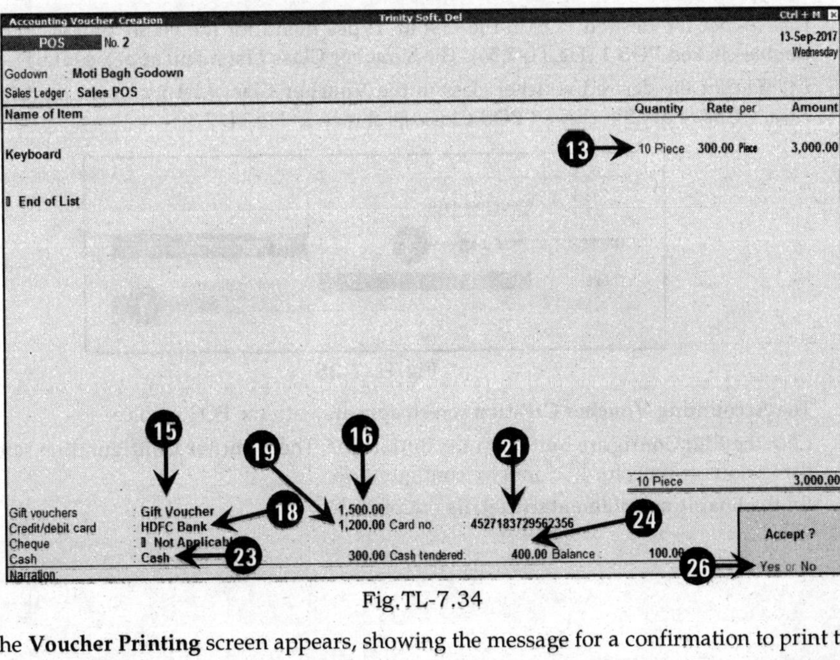

Fig.TL-7.34

The **Voucher Printing** screen appears, showing the message for a confirmation to print the invoice.

27. *Click* **Yes** in the **Print ?** message box to print the invoice. The **Accounting Voucher Display** screen appears that shows the POS invoice.
28. *Click* the **Zoom** button to zoom the POS invoice. The POS invoice is zoomed and displayed, as shown in Fig.TL-7.35:

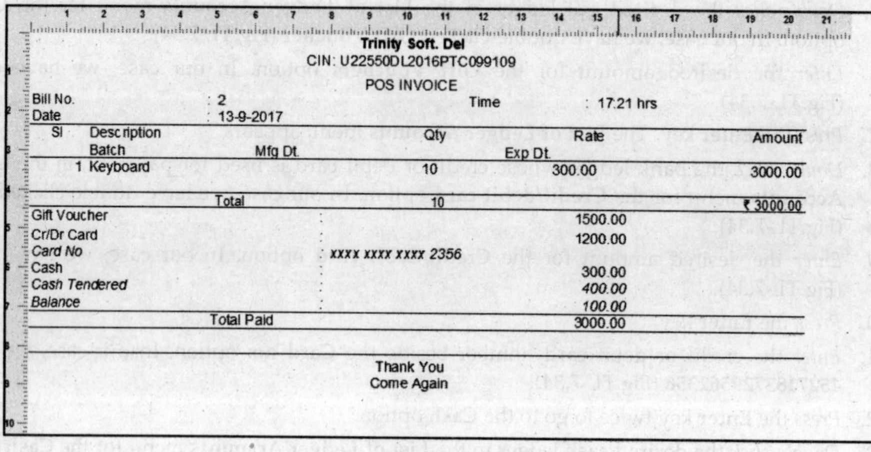

Fig.TL-7.35

Let us now learn how to create a POS invoice by using a voucher class.

Creating a POS Invoice by Using a Voucher Class

Perform the following steps to create a POS invoice by using a voucher class:

1. *Double-click* the **Accounting Vouchers** option under the **Transactions** section in the **Gateway of Tally** menu. The **Accounting Voucher Creation** screen appears.
2. *Click* the **F8: Sales** button on the Button Bar. The **Change Voucher Type** screen appears with the **List of Types** menu.
3. *Double-click* the desired POS in the **List of Types** menu for the **Name** option. In our case, we have double-clicked **POS 1** (Fig.TL-7.36). The **Voucher Class List** menu appears (Fig.TL-7.36).
4. *Double-click* the desired voucher class in the **Voucher Class List** menu for the **Class** option. In our case, we have double-clicked **POS Class**, as shown in Fig.TL-7.36:

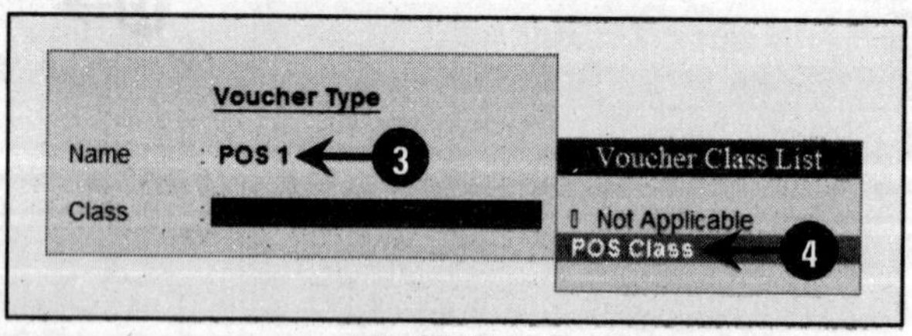

Fig.TL-7.36

The **Accounting Voucher Creation** screen appears with the POS invoice.

5. *Click* the **F12: Configure** button on the Button Bar. The **Voucher Configuration** screen appears with the various options for POS invoice configuration.
6. *Set* the **Enable supplementary details** option to **No**.

7. *Press* the **Enter** key until the **Accounting Voucher Creation** screen reappears (Fig.TL-7.37).
8. *Double-click* the desired godown in the **List of Godowns** menu for the **Godown** option. In our case, we have double-clicked **Moti Bagh Godown** (Fig.TL-7.37). The **List of Stock Items** menu appears.
9. *Double-click* the desired stock item in the **List of Stock Items** menu for the **Name of Item** column. In our case, we have double-clicked **Keyboard** (Fig.TL-7.37).

   When you double-click the desired stock item, the **Quantity**, **Rate**, **per**, and **Amount** columns will be filled according to one quantity, as shown in Fig.TL-7.37:

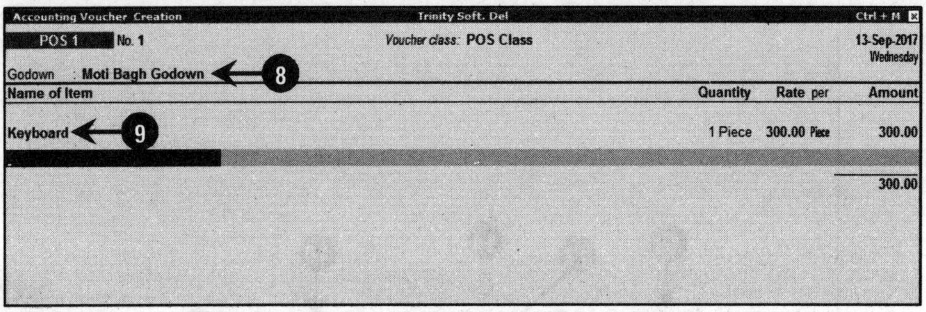

Fig.TL-7.37

10. *Press* the **Shift + Tab** keys to move backward to the **Quantity** column.
11. *Enter* the desired quantity under the **Quantity** column. In our case, we have entered **10** (Fig.TL-7.38).
12. *Press* the **Enter** key thrice to go to the **Gift Vouchers** option. The **List of Ledger Accounts** menu appears.
13. *Double-click* the desired gift ledger in the **List of Ledger Accounts** menu for the **Gift vouchers** option. In our case, we have double-clicked **Gift Voucher** (Fig.TL-7.38).
14. *Enter* the desired amount for the **Gift Vouchers** option. In our case, we have entered **1,200** (Fig.TL-7.38).
15. *Press* the **Enter** key. The **List of Ledger Accounts** menu appears.
16. *Double-click* the bank ledger whose credit or debit card is used for payment, in the **List of Ledger Accounts** menu for the **Credit/debit card** option. In our case, we have double-clicked **HDFC Bank** (Fig.TL-7.38).
17. *Enter* the desired amount for the **Credit/debit card** option. In our case, we have entered **1,400** (Fig.TL-7.38).
18. *Press* the **Enter** key.
19. *Enter* the credit or debit card number beside the **Card no.** option. In our case, we have entered **4578235646793869** (Fig.TL-7.38).
20. *Press* the **Enter** key twice to go to the **Cash** option.
21. *Double-click* the desired cash ledger in the **List of Ledger Accounts** menu for the **Cash** option. In our case, we have double-clicked **Cash** (Fig.TL-7.38). The **Cash tendered** and **Balance** options are enabled and displayed on the invoice.
22. *Enter* the amount that is received from the customer in the **Cash tendered** option. In our case, we have entered **500** (Fig.TL-7.38).
23. *Press* the **Enter** key.

    Tally automatically calculates the amount and shows the balance amount that is refunded to the customer beside the **Balance** option. The **Accept ?** message box appears.

24. *Click* **Yes** in the **Accept ?** message box to create the invoice, as shown in Fig.TL-7.38:

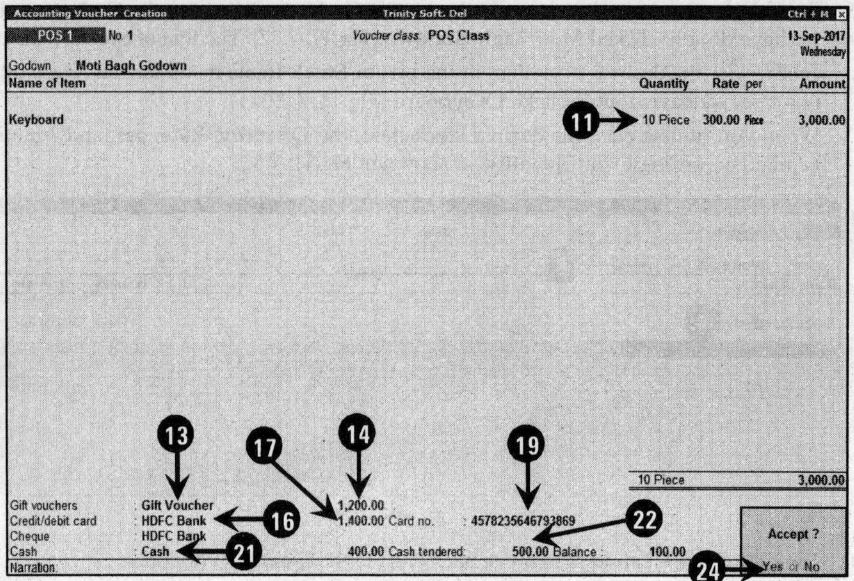

Fig.TL-7.38

The **Voucher Printing** screen appears, showing the message for a confirmation to print the invoice.

25. *Click* **Yes** in the **Print ?** message box to print the invoice. The **Accounting Voucher Display** screen appears that shows the POS invoice.
26. *Click* the **Zoom** button to zoom the POS invoice. The POS invoice is zoomed and displayed, as shown in Fig.TL-7.39:

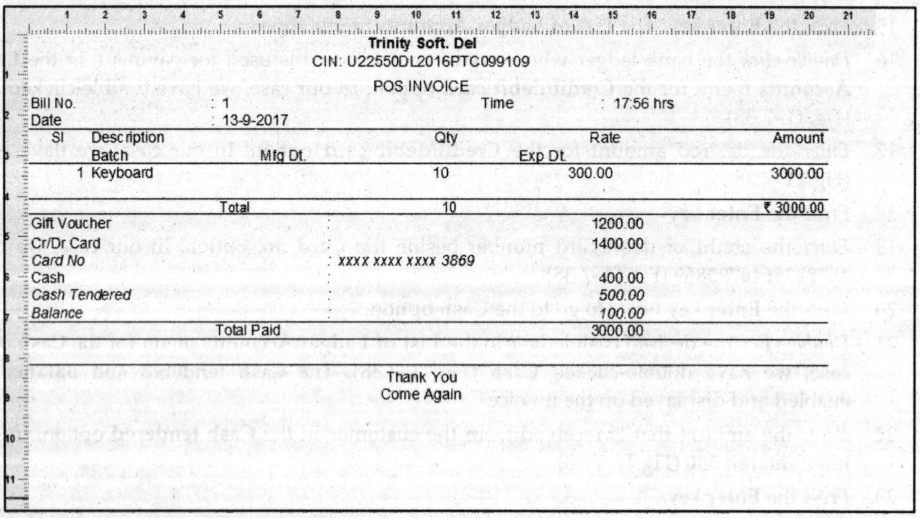

Fig.TL-7.39

Let us now learn how to view a POS report.

Viewing a POS Register Report

Perform the following steps to view and print a POS register report:

1. *Double-click* the **Display** option under the **Reports** section in the **Gateway of Tally** menu.

   The **Display Menu** menu appears.

2. *Double-click* the **Account Books** option in the **Display Menu** menu.

   The **Account Books** menu appears.

3. *Double-click* the **POS Register** option in **Account Books** menu.

   The **POS Register** screen appears.

4. *Click* the **F1: Detailed** button on the Button Bar.

   The **POS Register** screen appears with the detailed information, as shown in Fig.TL-7.40:

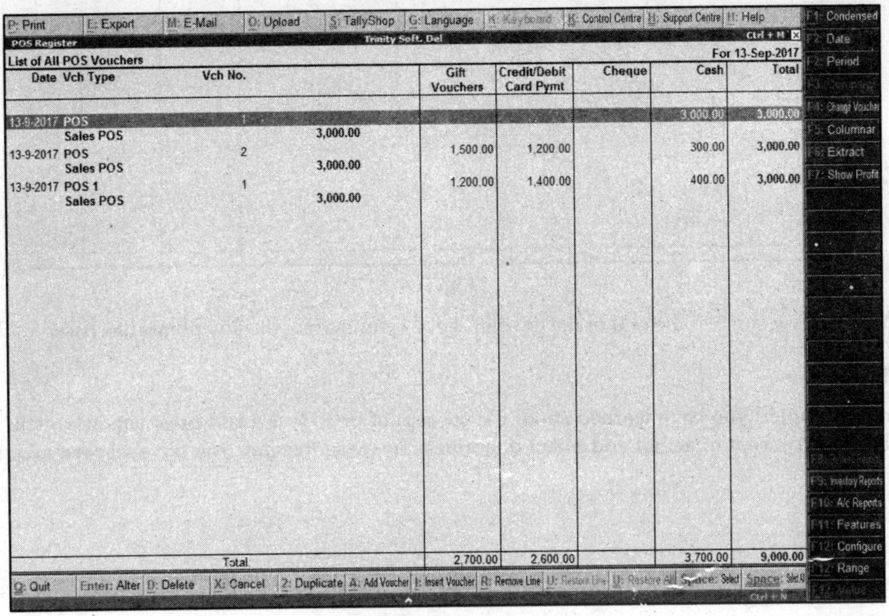

Fig.TL-7.40

5. *Click* the **F12: Configure** button on the Button Bar.

   The **Configuration** screen appears.

6. *Set* the **Show inventory details** option to **Yes**.

7. *Press* the **Enter** key until the **POS Register** screen reappears with the information of inventory, as shown in Fig.TL-7.41:

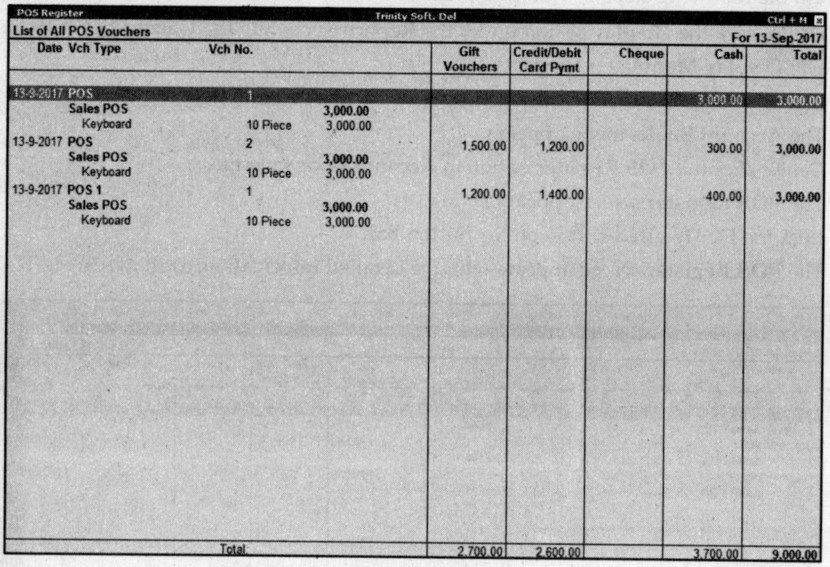

Fig.TL-7.41

With this, we come to the end of the chapter. Let us summarize the key points discussed in the chapter.

Summary

In this chapter, you have learned about the concept of price levels and price list. Next, you have learned about the concept of actual and billed quantities. Towards the end, you have learned about the Point of Sale.

CHAPTER

8

Bill-wise and Batch-wise Details

In this Chapter:

- Bill-wise Details
- Batch-wise Details

Introduction

Every business requires effective management of all transactions, debtors, and creditors. As your business grows, the count of transactions increases. Hence, managing all transactions, debtors, creditors, advance payment of goods, and pending bills becomes a complicated task. Tally.ERP 9 comes with a feature, named bill-wise details feature. This feature allows you to track the record of each transaction party-wise as well as group-wise.

Sometimes, you need to track the inventory movement in batches or lots, mainly in pharmaceutical industry. Tally.ERP 9 comes with a feature named Batch-wise Details feature. In batch-wise details, inventory is defined in batches or lots, where it is monitored on the manufacturing date, date of receipt, and expiry date.

In this chapter, you learn about the process to enable the Bill-wise Details feature. You also learn about the various methods to adjust bills. Then, you learn how to enable the Batch-wise Details feature in Tally. Further, you learn the procedure to create a stock item by using the Batch-wise Details feature. Toward the end of the chapter, you learn about the procedure to create a purchase and sales voucher with the help of the Batch-wise Details feature.

Let us start the chapter by learning about how to enable the bill-wise details feature.

Bill-wise Details

Bill-wise detail allows you to maintain transactions party-wise and group-wise. In addition, this feature manages the details of all payables and receivables. Using the feature, you can find out the outstanding amount and due date of each bill. The feature also provides the facility to keep bills in a systematic order, restrict users to make a duplicate bill entry, and help users track the bill payment date.

Enabling Bill-wise Details Feature

Before working with the **Bill-wise Details** feature, you need to enable it.

Perform the following steps to enable the **Bill-wise Details** feature:

1. *Click* the **F11: Features** button on the Button Bar on the **Gateway of Tally** screen. The **Company Features** menu appears.
2. *Double-click* the **Accounting Features** option on the **Company Features** menu. The **Company Operations Alteration** screen appears with **Accounting Features**.
3. *Set* the **Maintain bill-wise details** option to **Yes** in the **Outstanding Management** section in **Accounting Features** (Fig.TL-8.1).
4. *Press* the **Enter** key until the **Accept ?** message box appears.
5. *Click* **Yes** in the **Accept ?** message box to save the changes, as shown in Fig.TL-8.1:

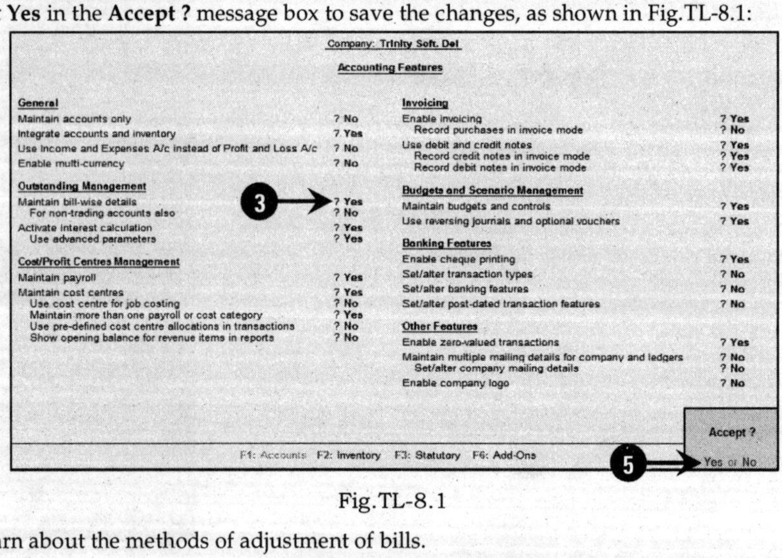

Fig.TL-8.1

Let us learn about the methods of adjustment of bills.

Methods of Bills Adjustment

At the time of creating a voucher entry, the **Maintain balances bill-by-bill** option is enabled, which allows the user to select the method of adjustment on the Bill-wise Details screen, as shown in Fig.TL-8.2:

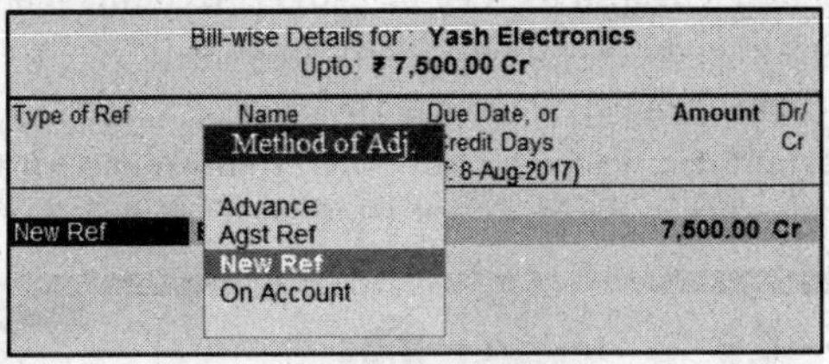

Fig.TL-8.2

In Tally.ERP 9, there are four methods of adjustment of bills:

- New ref
- Agst ref
- Advance
- On Account

Let us learn about these bill adjustment methods one-by-one in the following sections.

New Reference

The New Reference method of adjustment is used when you need to make new entries, as of purchase or sales. For example, recording a new purchase entry that uses a new reference method in the bill-wise details. This example specifies the proper use of New Reference method of adjustment.

To record a purchase entry, you need to create the following masters and vouchers:

- Create the party ledger in the Sundry Creditors parent group and enable the **Maintain balances bill-by-bill** option. In our case, we have created the **Infotech Pvt. Ltd.** party ledger.
- Create the purchase ledger in the **Purchase Accounts** parent group and enable the **Maintain balances bill-by-bill** option.
- Create a stock item. In our case, we have created the **RAM** stock item.
- Create a purchase voucher.

Perform the following steps to create a purchase invoice:

1. *Double-click* the **Accounting Vouchers** option under the **Transactions** section in the **Gateway of Tally** menu. The **Accounting Voucher Creation** screen appears.
2. *Click* the **F9: Purchase** button on the Button Bar. The **Accounting Voucher Creation** screen of the purchase voucher appears as invoice.

Note: **If the purchase voucher does not appear as invoice, click the V: As Invoice button on the Button Bar.**

3. *Click* the **I: Item Invoice** button on the Button Bar.

   The **Accounting Voucher Creation** screen of the purchase voucher appears as item invoice.
4. *Enter* the desired supplier invoice number beside the **Supplier invoice no.** option. In our case, we have entered **13** (Fig.TL-8.3).
5. *Press* the **Enter** key.
6. *Enter* the date of invoice beside the **Date** option. In our case, we have entered **10-Aug-2017** (Fig.TL-8.3).
7. *Press* the **Enter** key.

   The **List of Ledger** Accounts menu appears.

8. *Double-click* the desired party name in the **List of Ledger Accounts** menu for the **Party A/c name** option. In our case, we have double-clicked **Infotech Pvt. Ltd.** (Fig.TL-8.3).

   The **List of Ledger** Accounts menu reappears.

9. *Double-click* the desired ledger in the **List of Ledger Accounts** menu for the **Purchase ledger** option. In our case, we have double-clicked **Purchase** (Fig.TL-8.3).

   The **List of Stock Items** menu appears (Fig.TL-8.3).

10. *Double-click* the desired item in the **List of Stock Items** menu for the **Name of Item** column. In our case, we have double-clicked **RAM**, as shown in Fig.TL-8.3:

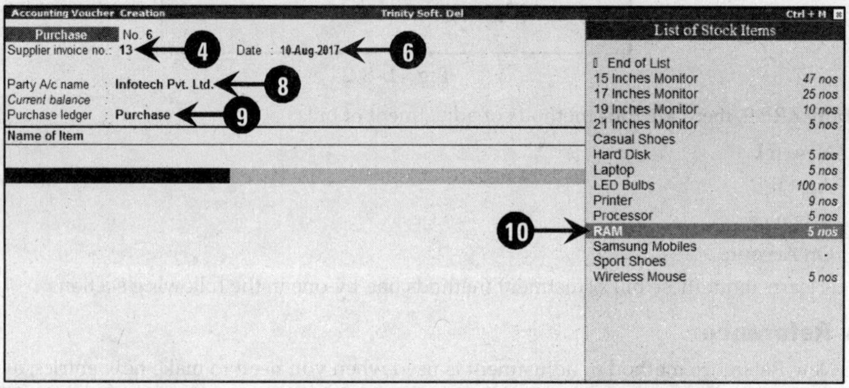

Fig.TL-8.3

The **Stock Item Allocations** screen appears with the **List of Godowns** menu (Fig.TL-8.4).

11. *Double-click* the desired godown in the **List of Godowns** menu for the **Godown** column. In our case, we have double-clicked **Moti Bagh Godown** (Fig.TL-8.4).

12. *Enter* the desired quantity and rate under the **Quantity** and **Rate** column respectively. In our case, we have entered **5** in the **Quantity** and **2500** in **Rate** columns respectively (Fig.TL-8.4).

    The **per** and **Amount** columns are also automatically filled, as shown in Fig.TL-8.4:

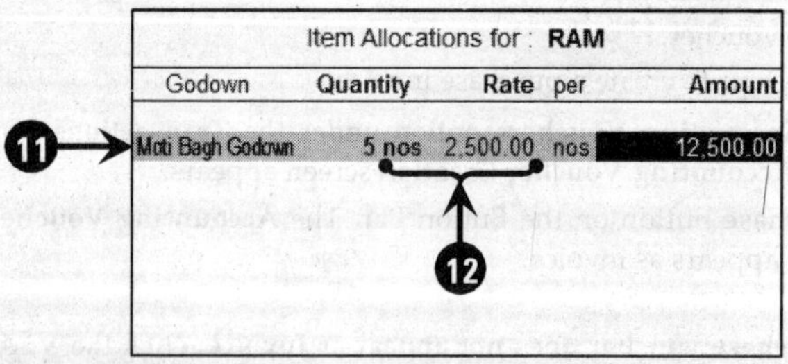

Fig.TL-8.4

13. *Press* the **Enter** key until the **Accounting Voucher Creation** screen reappears.

14. *Press* the **Enter** key until the **Bill-wise Details** screen appears.

15. *Double-click* the **New Ref** option on the **Method of Adj.** menu in the **Type of Ref** column (Fig.TL-8.5).

16. *Enter* the name of the bill in the **Name** column. In our case, we have entered **WA/13** (Fig.TL-8.5).

17. *Enter* the desired due date in the **Due Date, or Credit Days** column. In our case, we have entered **1-Sep-2017** (Fig.TL-8.5).

18. *Enter* the amount in the **Amount** column. In our case, we have entered **12500**, as shown in Fig.TL-8.5:

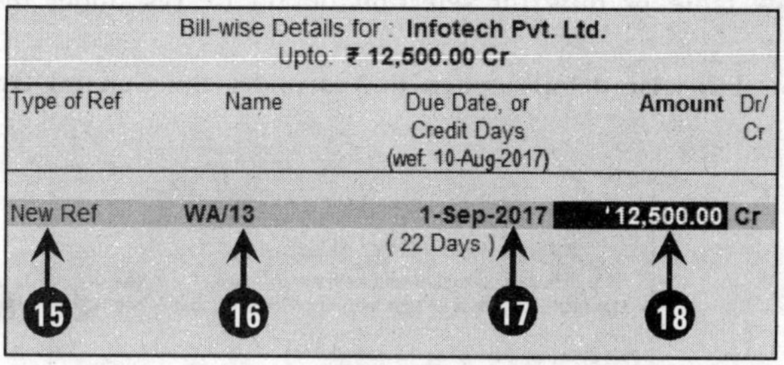

Fig.TL-8.5

19. *Press* the **Enter** key twice. The **Accounting Voucher Creation** screen reappears.
20. *Press* the **Enter** key until the **Accept ?** message box appears (Fig.TL-8.6).
21. *Click* **Yes** in the **Accept ?** message box to save the purchase item invoice, as shown in Fig.TL-8.6:

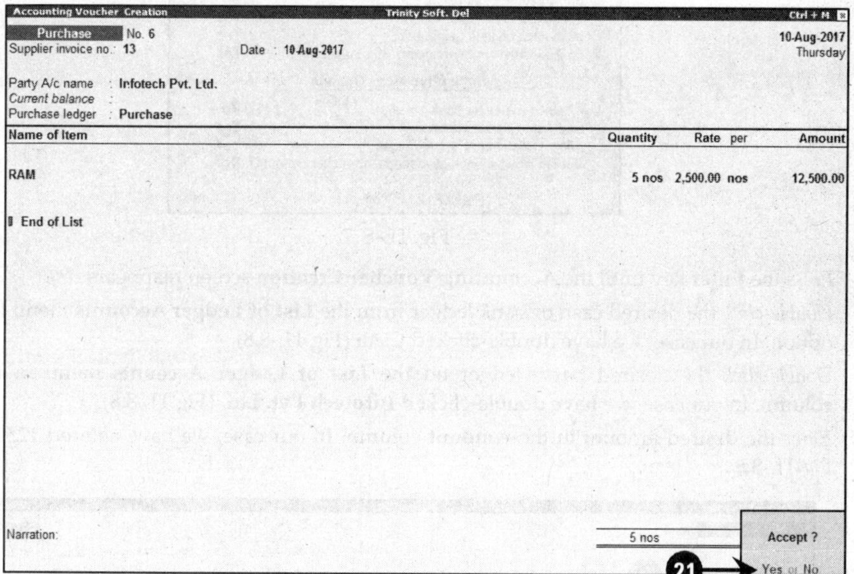

Fig.TL-8.6

Let us learn about the Against Reference method.

Against Reference

The Against Reference method of adjustment is used to track an existing recorded entry, which has a reference number. For example, recording a payment or receipt entry against the existing bill reference. This example specifies the proper use of Against Reference method of adjustment.

Perform the following steps to create a payment voucher:

1. *Double-click* the **Accounting Vouchers** option in the **Transactions** section on the **Gateway of Tally** menu. The **Accounting Voucher Creation** screen appears.
2. *Click* the **F5: Payment** button located on the Button Bar. The **Accounting Voucher Creation** screen appears with the payment voucher.
3. *Click* the **F12: Configure** button located on the Button Bar. The **Voucher Configuration** screen appears with the **Payment Standard Configuration** options (Fig.TL-8.7).

4. *Set* the **Use single entry mode for payment/receipt/contra vouchers** option to **Yes** under the **General Options** section (Fig.TL-8.7).
5. *Set* the **Show table of bills for selection** option to **Yes** under the **General Options** section (Fig.TL-8.7).
6. *Set* the **Show bill-wise details** option to **Yes** under the **General Options** section, as shown in Fig.TL-8.7:

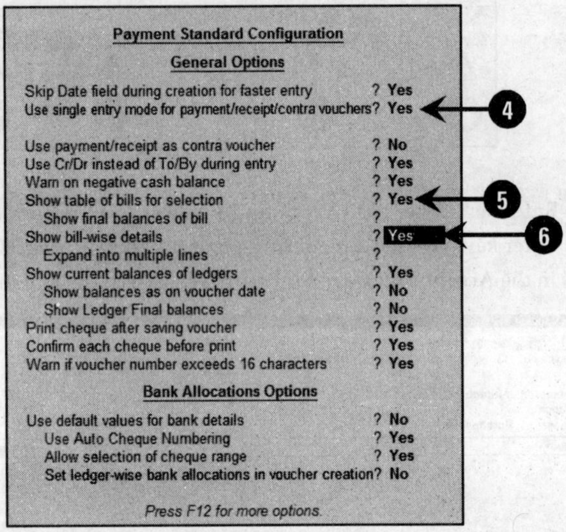

Fig.TL-8.7

7. *Press* the **Enter** key until the **Accounting Voucher Creation** screen reappears.
8. *Double-click* the desired cash or bank ledger from the **List of Ledger Accounts** menu for the **Account** option. In our case, we have double-clicked **Cash** (Fig.TL-8.8).
9. *Double-click* the desired party ledger on the **List of Ledger Accounts** menu in the **Particulars** column. In our case, we have double-clicked **Infotech Pvt. Ltd.** (Fig.TL-8.8).
10. *Enter* the desired amount in the **Amount** column. In our case, we have entered **12500**, as shown in Fig.TL-8.8:

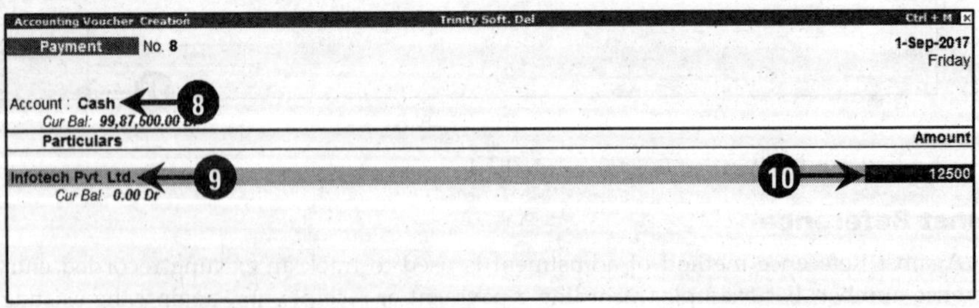

Fig.TL-8.8

11. *Press* the **Enter** key.

    The **Bill-wise Details** screen appears with the **Method of Adj.** menu (Fig.TL-8.9).
12. *Double-click* the **Agst Ref** option on the **Method of Adj.** menu in the **Type of Ref** column (Fig.TL-8.9). The **Pending Bills** menu appears.
13. *Double-click* the desired pending bill on the **Pending Bills** menu in the **Name** column. In our case, we have selected **WA/13** (Fig.TL-8.9).

When you select the pending bill on the **Pending Bills** menu, the **Due Date, or Credit Days** and **Amount** columns are filled automatically, as shown in Fig.TL-8.9:

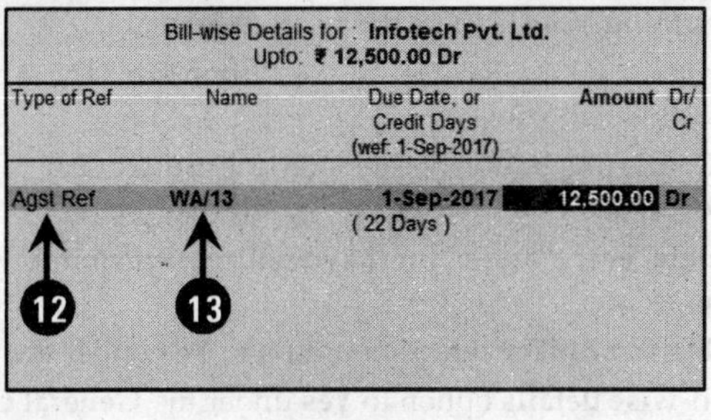

Fig.TL-8.9

14. *Press* the **Enter** key until the **Accounting Voucher Creation** screen reappears.
15. *Press* the **Enter** key until the **Accept ?** message box appears.
16. *Click* **Yes** in the **Accept ?** message box to save the payment voucher, as shown in Fig.TL-8.10:

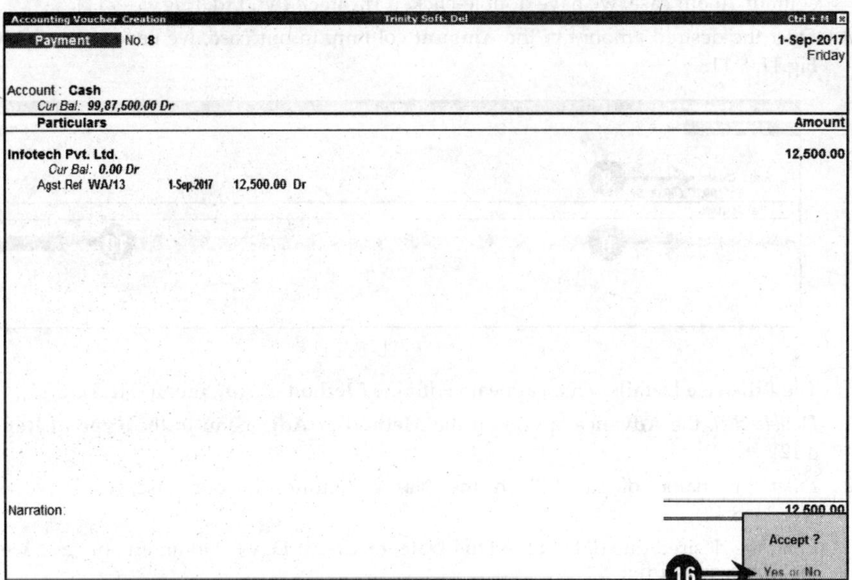

Fig.TL-8.10

Let us learn about the Advance method.

Advance

The Advance method of adjustment is used to indicate the amount paid or received in advance. For example, recording a payment entry that shows an advance payment and then adjusting the advance payment to a purchase.

To record a payment entry, you need to create the following masters and vouchers:

- Create the party ledger in the **Sundry Creditors** parent group and enable the **Maintain balances bill-by-bill** option.
- Create a stock item.
- Create a payment voucher.
- Create a purchase voucher.

Now perform the following steps to create a payment voucher:

1. *Double-click* the **Accounting Vouchers** option in the **Transactions** section on the **Gateway of Tally** menu. The **Accounting Voucher Creation** screen appears.
2. *Click* the **F5: Payment** button located on the Button Bar. The **Accounting Voucher Creation** screen appears with the payment voucher.
3. *Click* the **F12: Configure** button located on the Button Bar. The **Voucher Configuration** screen appears with the **Payment Standard Configuration** options.
4. *Set* the **Use single entry mode for payment/receipt/contra vouchers** option to **Yes** under the **General Options** section.
5. *Set* the **Show table of bills for selection** option to **Yes** under the **General Options** section.
6. *Set* the **Show bill-wise details** option to **Yes** under the **General Options** section.
7. *Press* the **Enter** key until the **Accounting Voucher Creation** screen reappears (Fig.TL-8.11).
8. *Double-click* the ledger on the **List of Ledger Accounts** menu for the **Account** option. In our case, we have double-clicked **Cash** (Fig.TL-8.11).
9. *Double-click* the desired party ledger on the **List of Ledger Accounts** menu in the **Particulars** column. In our case, we have double-clicked **Infotech Pvt. Ltd.** (Fig.TL-8.11).
10. *Enter* the desired amount in the **Amount** column. In our case, we have entered **20000**, as shown in Fig.TL-8.11:

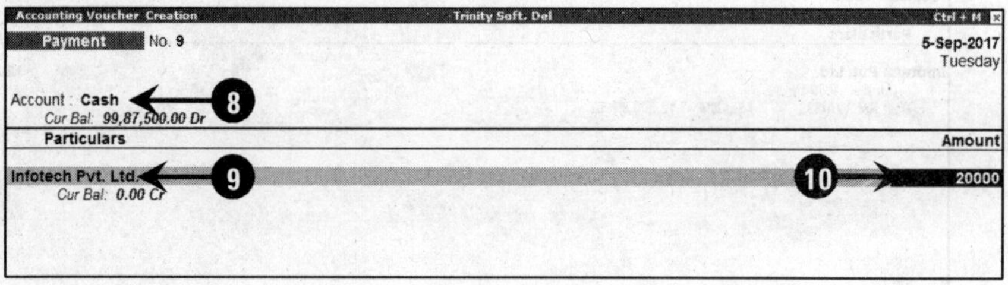

Fig.TL-8.11

The **Bill-wise Details** screen appears with the **Method of Adj.** menu (Fig.TL-8.12).

11. *Double-click* the **Advance** option on the **Method of Adj.** menu in the **Type of Ref** column (Fig.TL-8.12).
12. *Enter* the name of the bill in the **Name** column. In our case, we have entered **ADV/01** (Fig.TL-8.12).
13. *Enter* the desired due date in the **Due Date, or Credit Days** column. In our case, we have entered **15 Days** (Fig.TL-8.12).
14. *Enter* the amount in the **Amount** column. In our case, we have entered **20000**, as shown in Fig.TL-8.12:

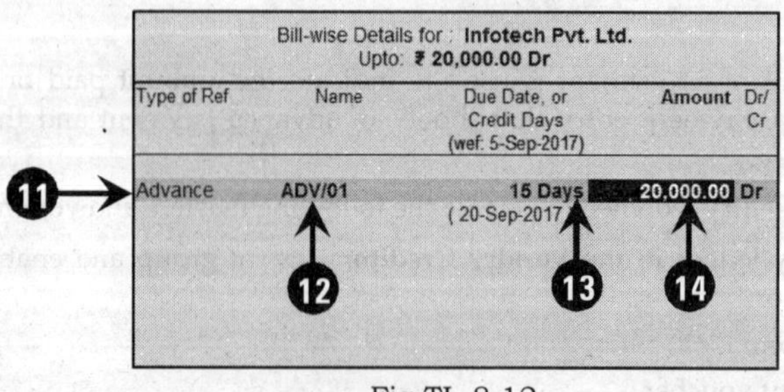

Fig.TL-8.12

15. *Press* the **Enter** key. The **Accounting Voucher Creation** screen reappears.
16. *Press* the **Enter** key until the **Accept ?** message box appears.

17. *Click* **Yes** in the **Accept ?** message box to save the payment voucher, as shown in Fig.TL-8.13:

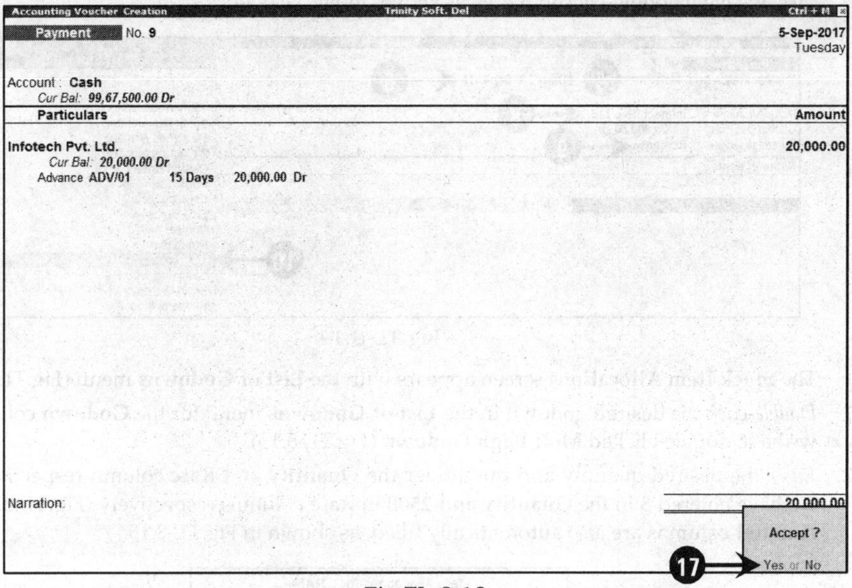

Fig.TL-8.13

Perform the following steps to create a purchase invoice:

1. *Double-click* the **Accounting Vouchers** option under the **Transactions** section in the **Gateway of Tally** menu.

   The **Accounting Voucher Creation** screen appears.
2. *Click* the **F9: Purchase** button on the Button Bar. The **Accounting Voucher Creation** screen of the purchase voucher appears as invoice.

Note

If the purchase voucher does not appear as invoice, click the V: As Invoice button on the Button Bar.

3. *Click* the **I: Item Invoice** button on the Button Bar. The **Accounting Voucher Creation** screen of the purchase voucher appears as item invoice.
4. *Enter* the desired supplier invoice number beside the **Supplier invoice no.** option. In our case, we have entered **14** (Fig.TL-8.14).
5. *Press* the **Enter** key.
6. *Enter* the date of invoice beside the **Date** option. In our case, we have entered **6-Sep-2017** (Fig.TL-8.14).
7. *Press* the **Enter** key. The **List of Ledger Accounts** menu appears.
8. *Double-click* the desired party name in the **List of Ledger Accounts** menu for the **Party A/c name** option. In our case, we have double-clicked **Infotech Pvt. Ltd.** (Fig.TL-8.14).

   The **List of Ledger Accounts** menu reappears.
9. *Double-click* the desired ledger in the **List of Ledger Accounts** menu for the **Purchase ledger** option. In our case, we have double-clicked **Purchase** (Fig.TL-8.14).

   The **List of Stock Items** menu appears (Fig.TL-8.14).

10. *Double-click* the desired item in the **List of Stock Items** menu for the **Name of Item** column. In our case, we have double-clicked **RAM**, as shown in Fig.TL-8.14:

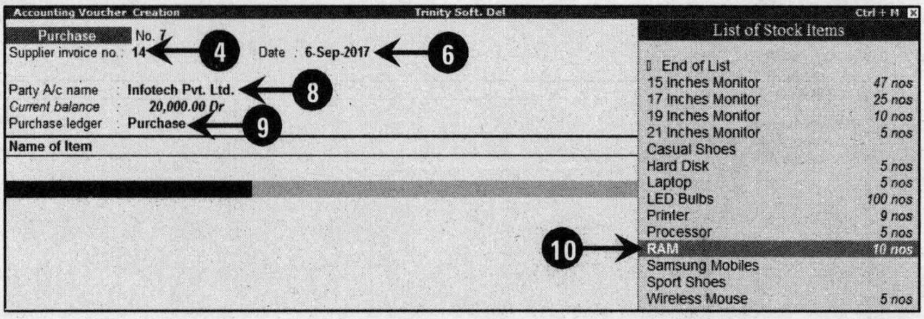

Fig.TL-8.14

The **Stock Item Allocations** screen appears with the **List of Godowns** menu (Fig.TL-8.15).

11. *Double-click* the desired godown in the **List of Godowns** menu for the **Godown** column. In our case, we have double-clicked **Moti Bagh Godown** (Fig.TL-8.15).
12. *Enter* the desired quantity and rate under the **Quantity** and **Rate** column respectively. In our case, we have entered **8** in the **Quantity** and **2500** in **Rate** columns respectively (Fig.TL-8.15). The **per** and **Amount** columns are also automatically filled, as shown in Fig.TL-8.15:

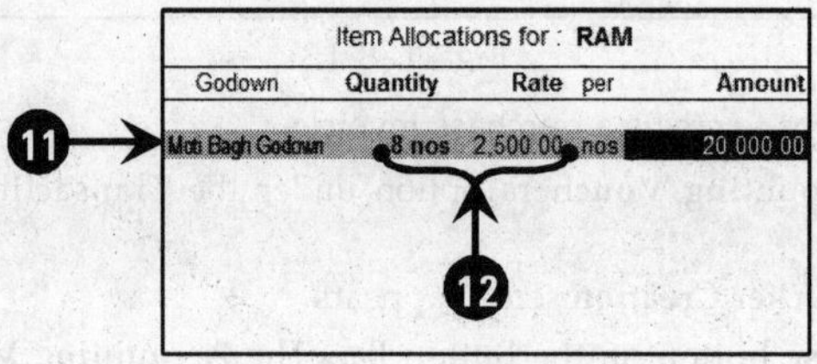

Fig.TL-8.15

13. *Press* the **Enter** key until the **Accounting Voucher Creation** screen reappears.
14. *Press* the **Enter** key until the **Bill-wise Details** screen appears.
15. *Double-click* the **Agst Ref** option on the **Method of Adj.** menu in the **Type of Ref** column (Fig.TL-8.16).
    The **Pending Bills** menu appears.
16. *Double-click* the desired pending bill on the **Pending Bills** menu in the **Name** column. In our case, we have selected **ADV/01** (Fig.TL-8.16).

    When you select the pending bill on the **Pending Bills** menu, the **Due Date, or Credit Days** and **Amount** columns are filled automatically, as shown in Fig.TL-8.16:

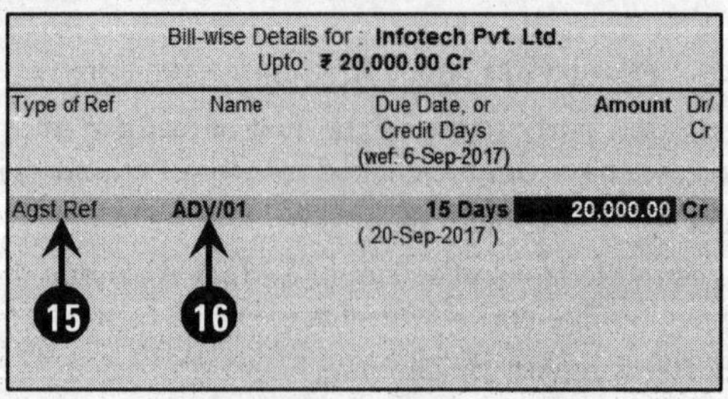

Fig.TL-8.16

17. *Press* the **Enter** key twice. The **Accounting Voucher Creation** screen reappears.
18. *Press* the **Enter** key until the **Accept ?** message box appears (Fig.TL-8.17).

19. *Click* **Yes** in the **Accept ?** message box to save the purchase invoice, as shown in Fig.TL-8.17:

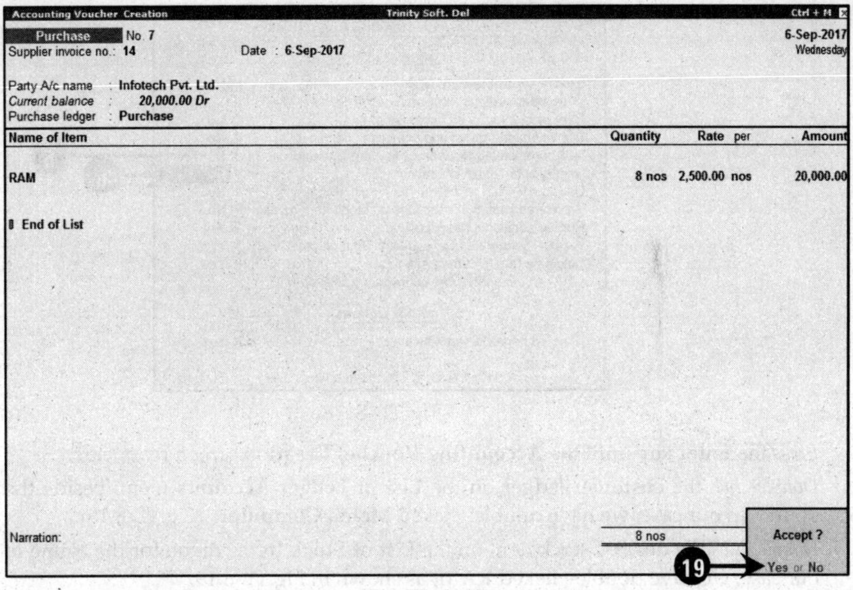

Fig.TL-8.17

Let us learn about the On Account method.

On Account

The On Account method of adjustment is used when you are unable to specify payment or receipt against the pending bills. For example, recording sales-related entries on different dates and receiving the payment by using the On Account method.

To record a sales entry, you need to create the following masters and vouchers:

- Create the party ledger in the **Sundry Debtor** parent group and enable the **Maintain balances bill-by-bill** option. In our case, we have created the **Mehta Computers** party ledger.
- Create a stock item.
- Create a sales voucher on different dates.
- Create a receipt voucher.

Now, perform the following steps to create a sales voucher:

1. *Double-click* the **Accounting Vouchers** option in the **Transactions** section on the **Gateway of Tally** menu. The **Accounting Voucher Creation** screen appears.
2. *Click* the **F8: Sales** button located on the Button Bar. The **Accounting Voucher Creation** screen appears with the sales voucher.
3. *Click* the **V: As Invoice** button located on the Button Bar. The **Accounting Voucher Creation** appears with the invoice mode.
4. *Click* the **F12: Configure** button located on the Button Bar. The **Voucher Configuration** screen appears.
5. *Set* the **Use common ledger account for item allocation** option to **No** (Fig.TL-8.18).

6. *Set* the **Use defaults for bill allocations** option to **No**, as shown in Fig.TL-8.18:

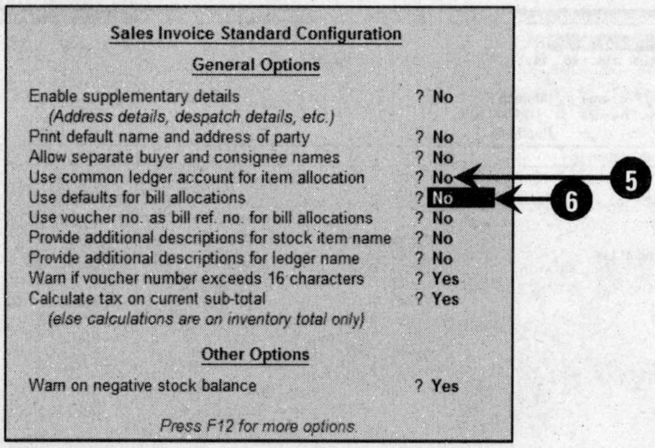

Fig.TL-8.18

7. *Press* the **Enter** key until the **Accounting Voucher Creation** screen reappears.
8. *Double-click* the customer ledger on the **List of Ledger Accounts** menu beside the **Party A/c name** option. In our case, we have double-clicked **Mehta Computers** (Fig.TL-8.19).
9. *Double-click* the desired stock item on the **List of Stock Items** menu for the **Name of Item** column. In our case, we have double-clicked **RAM,** as shown in Fig.TL-8.19:

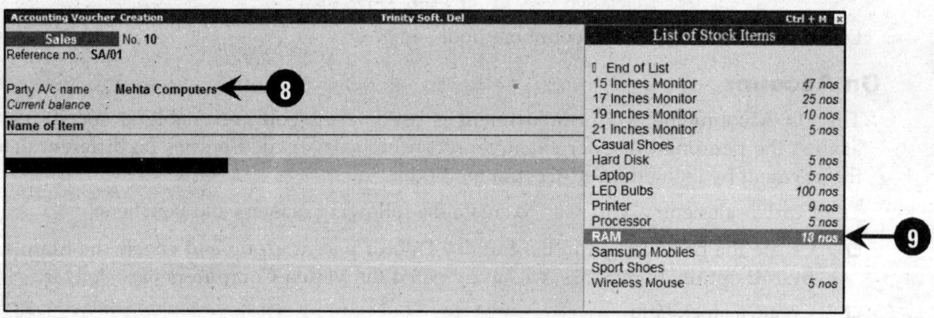

Fig.TL-8.19

The **Stock Item Allocation** screen appears with the **List of Godowns** menu.

10. *Double-click* the desired godown on the **List of Godowns** menu in the **Godown** column. In our case, we have double-clicked **Moti Bagh Godown** (Fig.TL-8.20).
11. *Enter* the desired quantity in the **Quantity** column. In our case, we have entered **4** (Fig.TL-8.20).
12. *Enter* the desired rate of stock item in the **Rate** column. In our case, we have entered **2750** (Fig.TL-8.20).

The **per** and **Amount** columns are automatically filled, as shown in Fig.TL-8.20:

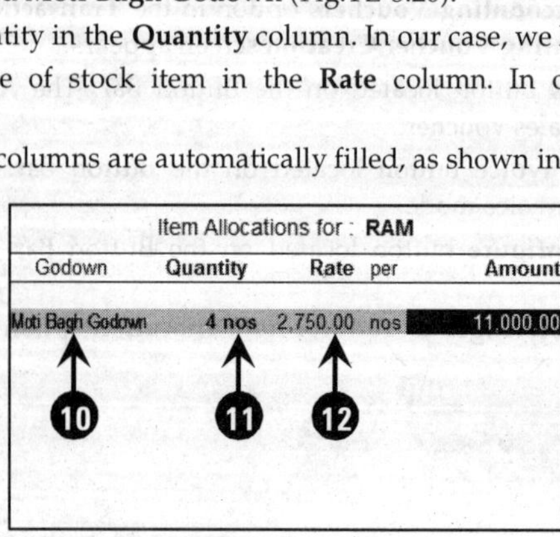

Fig.TL-8.20

13. *Press* the **Enter** key until the **Accounting Voucher Creation** screen reappears.
14. *Press* the **Enter** key. The **Accounting Details** screen appears with the **List of Ledger Accounts** menu.
15. *Double-click* the desired sales ledger on the **List of Ledger Accounts** menu in the **Particulars** column. In our case, we have double-clicked **Sales** (Fig.TL-8.21).

    The **Amount** column is filled automatically with the invoice amount, as shown in Fig.TL-8.21:

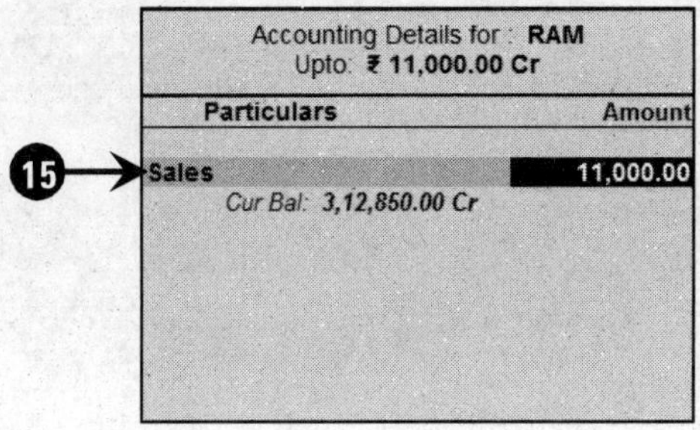

Fig.TL-8.21

16. *Press* the **Enter** key. The **Accounting Voucher Creation** screen appears.
17. *Press* the **Enter** key three times. The **Bill-wise Details** screen appears with the **Method of Adj.** menu (Fig.TL-8.22).
18. *Double-click* the **New Ref** option on the **Method of Adj.** menu in the **Type of Ref** column (Fig.TL-8.22).
19. *Enter* the name of the bill in the **Name** column. In our case, we have entered **SA/01** (Fig.TL-8.22).
20. *Enter* the desired due date in the **Due Date, or Credit Days** column. In our case, we have entered **15 Days** (Fig.TL-8.22).
21. *Enter* the amount in the **Amount** column. In our case, we have entered **11000**, as shown in Fig.TL-8.22:

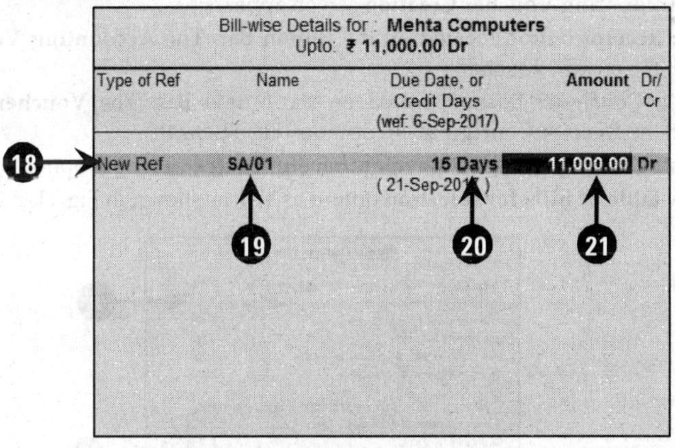

Fig.TL-8.22

22. *Press* the **Enter** key until the **Accounting Voucher Creation** screen reappears.
23. *Enter* the narration beside the **Narration** option.
24. *Press* the **Enter** key. The **Accept ?** message box appears (Fig.TL-8.23).

25. *Click* **Yes** in the **Accept ?** message box to save the purchase voucher, as shown in Fig.TL-8.23:

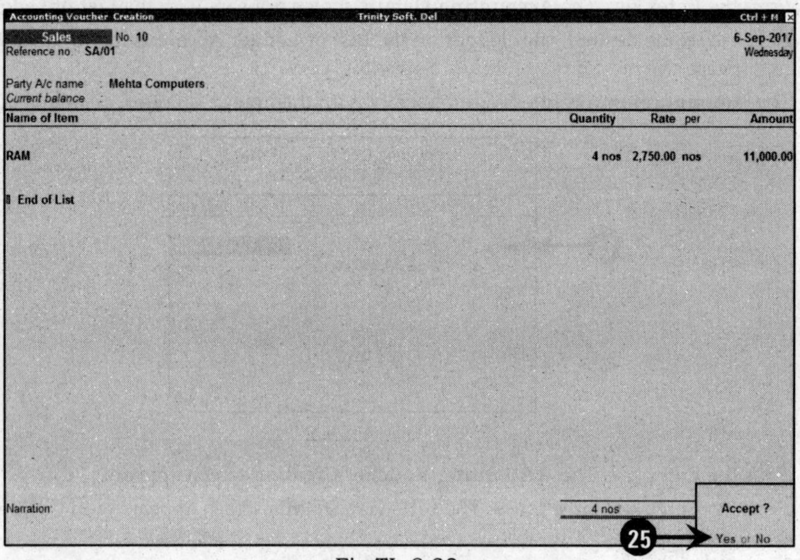

Fig.TL-8.23

Similarly, create the other sales invoices with the following details:

- On 8-Sep-2017, sales of 2 RAM @ 2725 with the bill reference SA/02
- On 9-Sep-2017, sales of 4 RAM @ 2800 with the bill reference SA/03
- On 11-Sep-2017, sales of 6 RAM @ 2775 with the bill reference SA/04

Now perform the following steps to create a receipt voucher:

1. *Double-click* the **Accounting Vouchers** option in the **Transactions** section on the **Gateway of Tally** menu. The **Accounting Voucher Creation** screen appears.
2. *Click* the **F6: Receipt** button located on the Button Bar. The **Accounting Voucher Creation** screen appears with the receipt voucher.
3. *Click* the **F12: Configure** button located on the Button Bar. The **Voucher Configuration** screen appears with the **Receipt Configuration** options (Fig.TL-8.24).
4. *Set* the **Use single entry mode for payment/receipt/contra vouchers** option to **No** (Fig.TL-8.24).
5. *Set* the **Show table of bills for selection** option to **Yes**, as shown in Fig.TL-8.24:

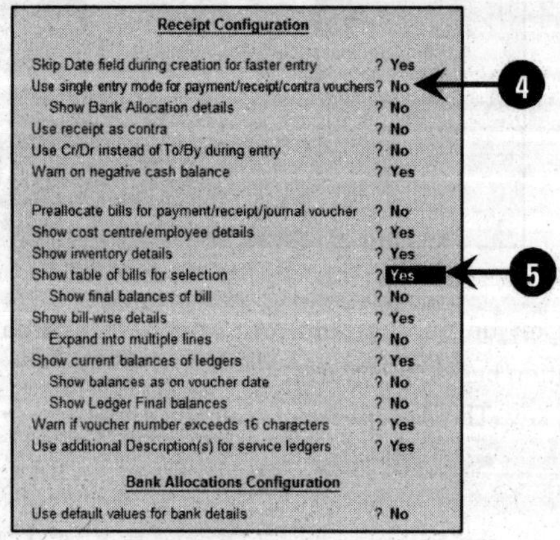

Fig.TL-8.24

6. *Press* the **Enter** key until the **Accounting Voucher Creation** screen reappears (Fig.TL-8.25).

7. *Double-click* the customer ledger on the **List of Ledger Accounts** menu in the **Particulars** column for the **To** field. In our case, we have double-clicked **Mehta Computers** (Fig.TL-8.25).
8. *Enter* the desired amount in the **Amount** column. In our case, we have entered **15000**, as shown in Fig.TL-8.25:

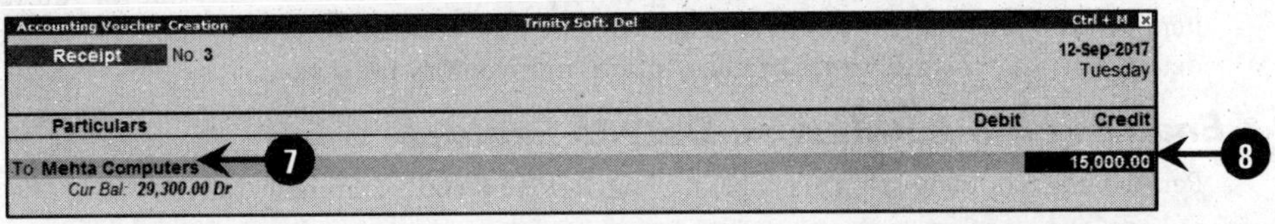

Fig.TL-8.25

9. *Press* the **Enter** key. The **Bill-wise Details** screen appears with the **Method of Adj.** menu (Fig.TL-8.26).
10. *Double-click* the **On Account** option on the **Method of Adj.** menu in the **Type of Ref** column (Fig.TL-8.26).

    When you select the **On Account** option from the **Method of Adj.** menu, the **Amount** column is filled automatically, as shown in Fig.TL-8.26:

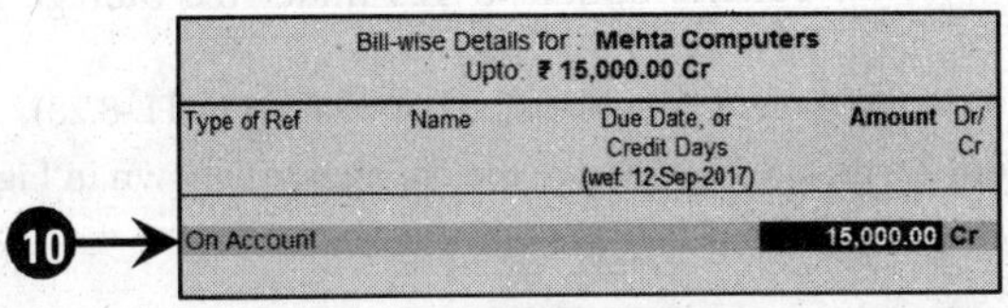

Fig.TL-8.26

11. *Press* the **Enter** key until the **Accounting Voucher Creation** screen reappears.
12. *Double-click* the bank or cash ledger on the **List of Ledger Accounts** menu in the **Particulars** column for the **By** field. In our case, we have double-clicked **Cash** (Fig.TL-8.27).

    The **Amount** column is filled automatically (Fig.TL-8.27).
13. *Press* the **Enter** key until the **Accept ?** message box appears.
14. *Click* **Yes** in the **Accept ?** message box to save the receipt voucher, as shown in Fig.TL-8.27:

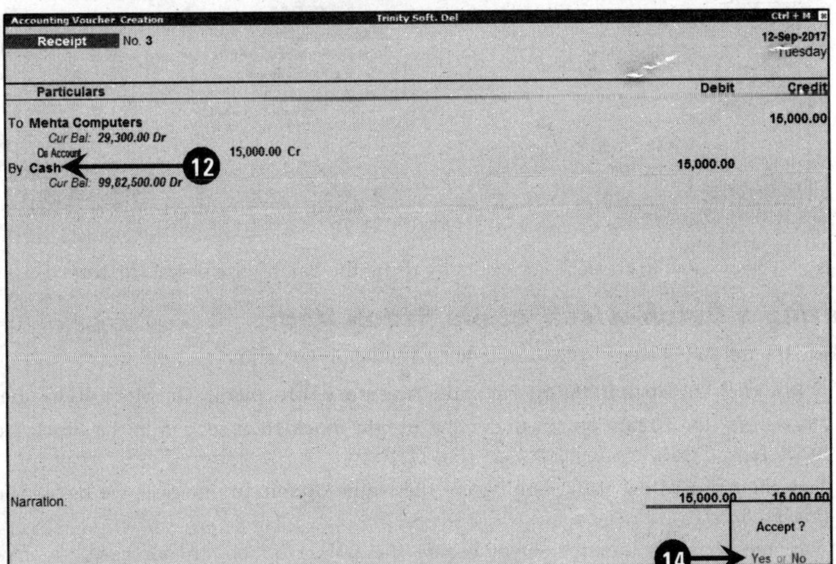

Fig.TL-8.27

Let us learn about the Batch-wise Details feature in Tally.

Batch-wise Details

In batch-wise details, stock items are maintained and monitored on the basis of their manufacturing date, date of receipt, and expiry date. Batch-wise details are maintained in the pharmacological industry or any other industry that keeps or manufactures perishable inventory. Tally allows you to create a stock item by using the Batch-wise Details feature. For this, you need to first enable the Maintain batch-wise details and Set expiry dates for batches options in Inventory Features.

Enabling the Batch-wise Details Feature

Perform the following steps to enable the **Batch-wise Details** feature in Tally:

1. *Click* the **F11: Features** button on the Button Bar of the **Gateway of Tally** screen. The **Company Features** menu appears.
2. *Double-click* the **Inventory Features** option in the **Company Features** menu. The **Company Operations Alteration** screen appears with **Inventory Features** (Fig.TL-8.28).
3. *Set* the **Maintain batch-wise details** option to **Yes** under the **Storage and Classification** section (Fig.TL-8.28).
4. *Set* the **Set expiry dates for batches** option to **Yes** under the **Storage and Classification** section (Fig.TL-8.28).
5. *Press* the **Enter** key until the **Accept ?** message box appears (Fig.TL-8.28).
6. *Click* **Yes** in the **Accept ?** message box to save the changes, as shown in Fig.TL-8.28:

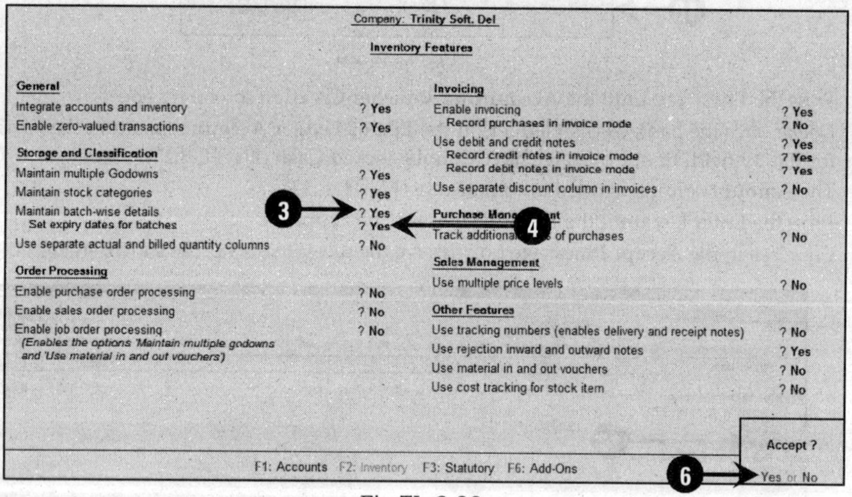

Fig.TL-8.28

Let us now learn how to create a stock item by using the Batch-wise Details feature.

Creating a Batch-wise Details Stock Item

Perform the following steps to create a batch-wise details stock item:

1. *Double-click* the **Stock Items** option in the **Inventory Info.** menu. The **Stock Items** menu appears.
2. *Double-click* the **Create** option under the **Single Stock Item** section in the **Stock Items** menu. The **Stock Item Creation** screen appears (Fig.TL-8.29).
3. *Type* the name of the stock item beside the **Name** option. In our case, we have typed **Paracetamol** (Fig.TL-8.29).
4. *Type* the alias for the stock item beside the **(alias)** option. In our case, we have left it blank (Fig.TL-8.29).

5. *Press* the **Enter** key. The **List of Groups** menu appears.
6. *Double-click* the stock group under which you want to create the new stock item, in the **List of Groups** menu for the **Under** option. In our case, we have double-clicked **Medicine** (Fig.TL-8.29). The **List of Categories** menu appears.
7. *Double-click* the stock category under which you want to create the new stock item, in the **List of Categories** menu for the **Category** option. In our case, we have double-clicked **Fever** (Fig.TL-8.29). The **Units** menu appears.
8. *Double-click* the desired measurement unit for the stock item in the **Units** menu for the **Units** option. In our case, we have double-clicked **Strip** (Fig.TL-8.29).
9. *Set* the **Maintain in batches** option to **Yes** (Fig.TL-8.29).
10. *Set* the **Track date of manufacturing** option to **Yes** (Fig.TL-8.29).
11. *Set* the **Use expiry dates** option to **Yes** (Fig.TL-8.29).
12. *Press* the **Enter** key twice.
13. *Type* the desired quantity for the stock item in the **Quantity** option. In our case, we have entered **10**, as shown in Fig.TL-8.29:

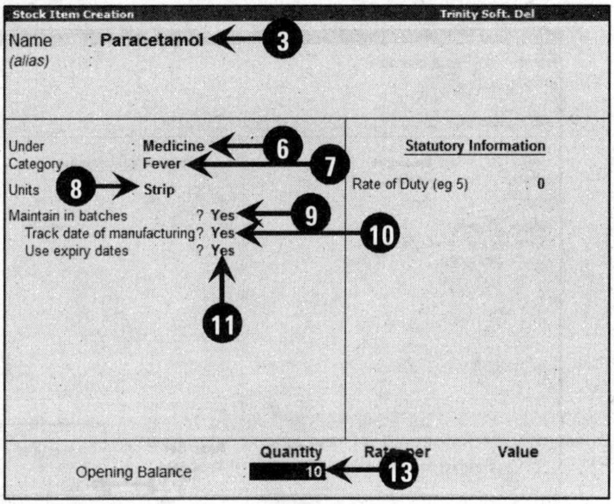

Fig.TL-8.29

14. *Press* the **Enter** key. The **Stock Item Allocation** screen appears with the **List of Godowns** menu.
15. *Double-click* the desired godown in the **List of Godowns** menu for the **Godown** column. In our case, we have double-clicked **Main Location** (Fig.TL-8.30).
16. *Enter* the batch detail under the **Batch** column. In our case, we have entered **PCM5H** (Fig.TL-8.30).
17. *Enter* the manufacturing date of the stock item under the **Mfg Dt.** Column. In our case, we have entered **Apr-2017** (Fig.TL-8.30).
18. *Enter* the expiry date of the stock item under the **Expiry Date** column. In our case, we have entered **31-Dec-2019** (Fig.TL-8.30).
19. *Enter* the quantity of the stock item under the **Quantity** column. In our case, we have entered **10** (Fig.TL-8.30).

20. *Enter* the price of the stock item under the **Rate** column. In our case, we have entered **40** (Fig.TL-8.30).

    The **per** and **Amount** columns are automatically filled, as shown in Fig.TL-8.30:

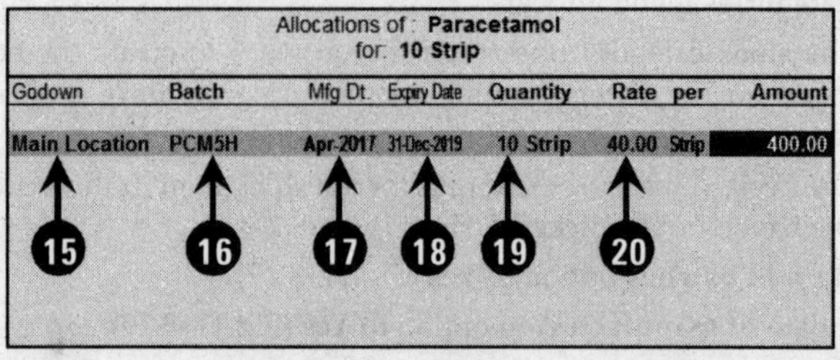

Fig.TL-8.30

21. *Press* the **Enter** key until the **Stock Item Creation** screen reappears. The **Accept ?** message box appears (Fig.TL-8.31).
22. *Click* **Yes** in the **Accept ?** message box to create the stock item, as shown in Fig.TL-8.31:

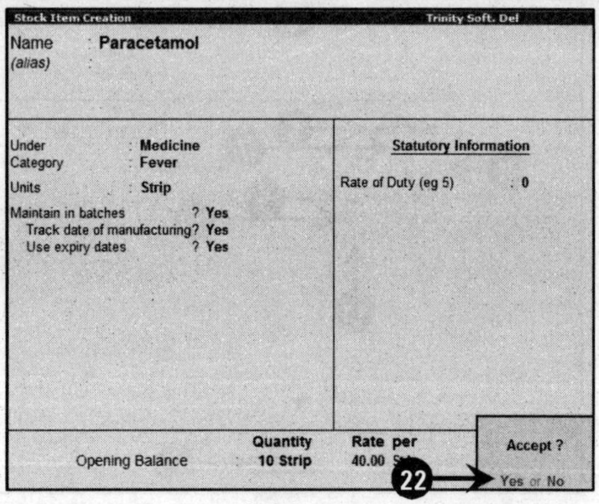

Fig.TL-8.31

Let us now learn how to create a purchase voucher by using the **Batch-wise Details** feature.

Creating a Purchase Voucher

Perform the following steps to create a purchase voucher by using the Batch-wise Details feature:

1. *Double-click* the **Accounting Vouchers** option under the **Transactions** section in the **Gateway of Tally** menu. The **Accounting Voucher Creation** screen appears.
2. *Click* the **F9: Purchase** button on the Button Bar. The **Accounting Voucher Creation** screen of the purchase voucher appears as item invoice (Fig.TL-8.32).
3. *Enter* the desired supplier invoice number beside the **Supplier invoice no.** option. In our case, we have entered **16** (Fig.TL-8.32).
4. *Press* the **Enter** key.
5. *Enter* the desired date of invoice beside the **Date** option. In our case, we have entered, **12-Sep-2017** (Fig.TL-8.32).
6. *Press* the **Enter** key. The **List of Ledger Accounts** menu appears.
7. *Double-click* the desired supplier in the **List of Ledger Accounts** menu for **Party A/c name** option. In our case, we have double-clicked **Yash Traders** (Fig.TL-8.32).

   The **List of Ledger Accounts** menu appears.

8. *Double-click* the desired purchase ledger in the **List of Ledger Accounts** menu for the **Purchase ledger** option. In our case, we have double-clicked **Purchase** (Fig.TL-8.32).

   The **List of Stock Items** menu appears (Fig.TL-8.32).

9. *Double-click* the desired item in the **List of Stock Items** menu for the **Name of Item** column. In our case, we have double-clicked **Paracetamol**, as shown in Fig.TL-8.32:

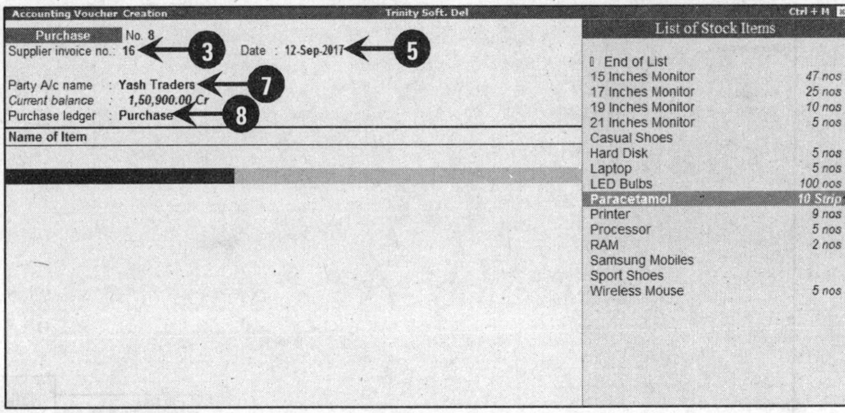

Fig.TL-8.32

   The **Stock Item Allocations** screen appears.

10. *Double-click* the desired godown in the **List of Godowns** menu for the **Godown** column. In our case, we have double-clicked **Main Location** (Fig.TL-8.33).

    The **List of Active Batches** menu appears (Fig.TL-8.33).

11. *Double-click* the desired batch from the **List of Active Batches** menu for the **Batch/Lot No.** column. In our case, we have double-clicked **PCM5H** (Fig.TL-8.33). The dates under the **Mfg Dt.** and **Expiry Date** columns are filled automatically.

12. *Enter* the quantity of the item under the **Quantity** column. In our case, we have entered **10** (Fig.TL-8.33).

13. *Enter* the rate of the item under the **Rate** column. In our case, we have entered **40** (Fig.TL-8.33).

14. *Enter* **Strip** under the **per** column (Fig.TL-8.33).

    The **Amount** column is filled automatically, as shown in Fig.TL 8.33:

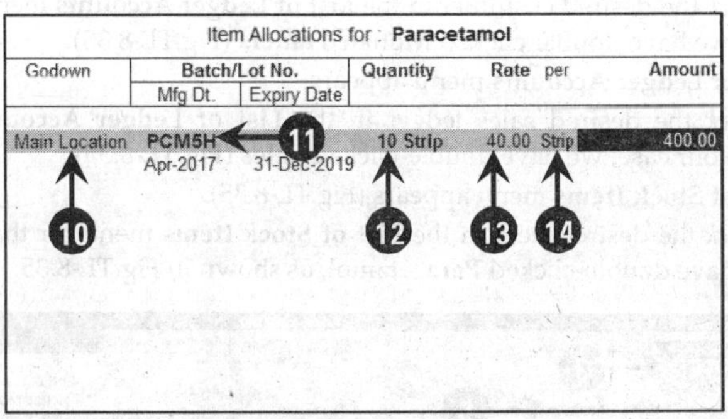

Fig.TL-8.33

15. *Press* the **Enter** key until the **Accounting Voucher Creation** screen reappears.

16. *Press* the **Enter** key until the **Accept ?** message box appears.

17. *Click* **Yes** in the **Accept ?** message box to save the voucher, as shown in Fig.TL-8.34:

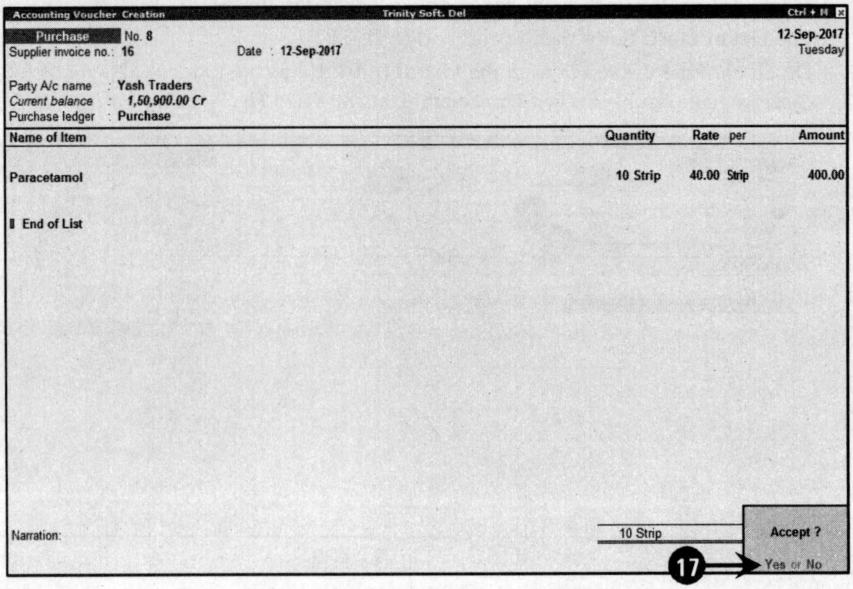

Fig.TL-8.34

Let us now learn how to create a sales voucher by using the Batch-wise Details feature.

Creating a Sales Voucher

Perform the following steps to create a sales voucher by using the Batch-wise Details feature:

1. *Double-click* the **Accounting Vouchers** option under the **Transactions** section in the **Gateway of Tally** menu. The **Accounting Voucher Creation** screen appears.
2. *Click* the **F8: Sales** button on the Button Bar. The **Accounting Voucher Creation** screen of the Sales voucher appears (Fig.TL-8.35).
3. *Enter* the desired reference number beside the **Reference no.** option. In our case, we have entered **12** (Fig.TL-8.35).
4. *Press* the **Enter** key. The **List of Ledger Accounts** menu appears.
5. *Double-click* the desired customer in the **List of Ledger Accounts** menu for **Party A/c name** option. In our case, we have double-clicked **Mohan Traders** (Fig.TL-8.35).
   The **List of Ledger Accounts** menu appears.
6. *Double-click* the desired sales ledger in the **List of Ledger Accounts** menu for the **Sales ledger** option. In our case, we have double-clicked **Sales** (Fig.TL-8.35).
   The **List of Stock Items** menu appears (Fig.TL-8.35).
7. *Double-click* the desired item in the **List of Stock Items** menu for the **Name of Item** column. In our case, we have double-clicked **Paracetamol**, as shown in Fig.TL-8.35:

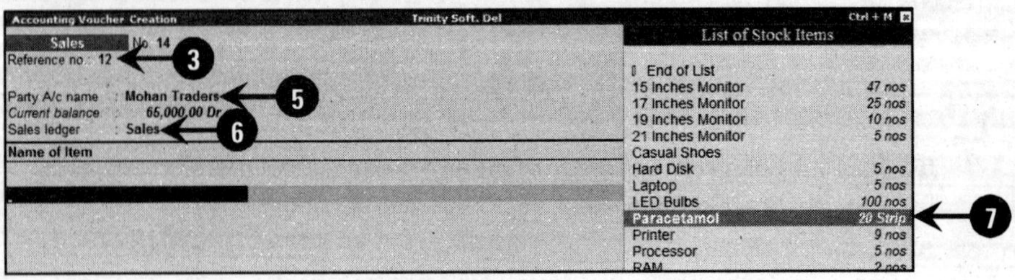

Fig.TL-8.35

The **Stock Item Allocations** screen appears.

8. *Double-click* the desired godown in the **List of Godowns** menu for the **Godown** column. In our case, we have double-clicked **Main Location** (Fig.TL-8.36).

   The **List of Active Batches** menu appears (Fig.TL-8.36).

9. *Double-click* the desired batch from the **List of Active Batches** menu for the **Batch/Lot No.** column. In our case, we have double-clicked **PCM5H** (Fig.TL-8.36).

   The date under the **Mfg Dt.** and **Expiry Date** columns are filled automatically.

10. *Enter* the quantity of the item under the **Quantity** column. In our case, we have entered **15** (Fig.TL-8.36).

11. *Enter* the rate of the item under the **Rate** column. In our case, we have entered **48** (Fig.TL-8.36).

12. *Enter* **Strip** under the **per** column (Fig.TL-8.36).

    The **Amount** column is filled automatically, as shown in Fig.TL-8.36:

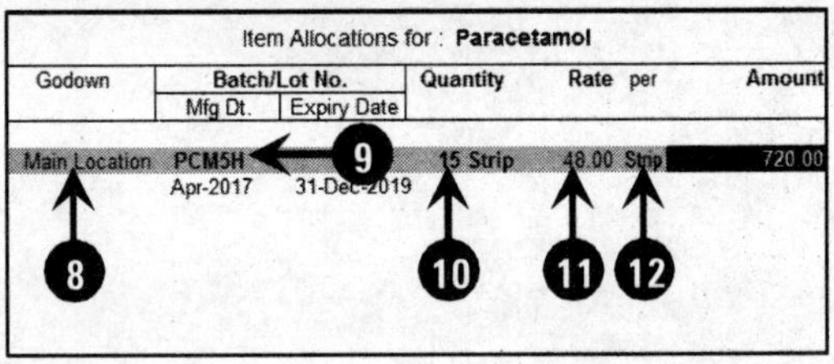

Fig.TL-8.36

13. *Press* the **Enter** key until the **Accounting Voucher Creation** screen reappears.
14. *Press* the **Enter** key until the **Accept ?** message box appears.
15. *Click* **Yes** in the **Accept ?** message box to save the voucher, as shown in Fig.TL-8.37:

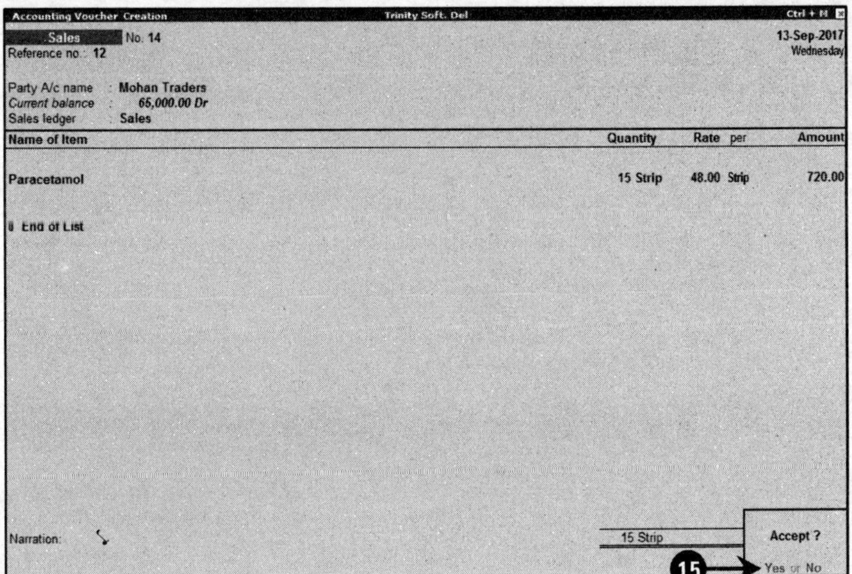

Fig.TL-8.37

With this, we come to the end of the chapter. Let us summarize the key points discussed in the chapter.

Summary

In this chapter, you have learned about the procedure to enable the Bill-wise Details feature. You have also learned about the way to use different methods to adjust bills. Next, you have learned about the procedure to enable the Batch-wise Details feature. Towards, the end of the chapter, you have learned about the procedure to create a stock item, purchase voucher, and sales voucher by using the Batch-wise Details feature.

CHAPTER

9

Bill of Materials

In this Chapter:

* Enabling the Bill of Materials Feature
* Creating a BOM

Introduction

A Bill of Materials (BOM) is a list of essential items with quantities that are required for manufacturing a particular product. This list allows the manufacturers to manage their physical stock and place orders for the new stock accordingly. You can create a BOM for items that are assembled in-house. Thus, you need to specify a BOM detail during the creation or alteration of stock item. By enabling the BOM feature in Tally, you can create a list of items that are needed to manufacture another item.

In this chapter, you will learn about the process to enable the bill of materials feature. You will also learn about the procedure to create a BOM for a stock item.

Let us start the chapter by learning the procedure to enable the bill of materials feature.

Enabling the Bill of Materials Feature

Perform the following steps to enable the bill of materials feature:

1. *Click* the **F12: Configure** button on the Button Bar in the **Gateway of Tally** screen. The **Configuration** menu appears.
2. *Double-click* the **Accts / Inventory Info.** option in the **Configuration** menu. The **Master Configuration** screen appears (Fig.TL-9.1).
3. *Set* the **Enable component list details (Bill of Materials)** option to **Yes** in the **Inventory** section, as shown in Fig.TL-9.1:

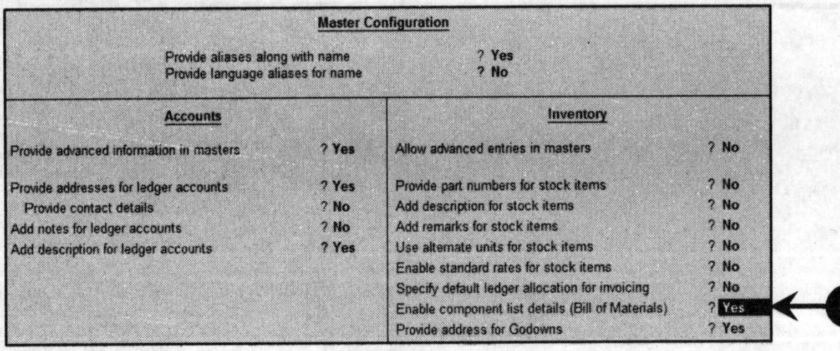

Fig.TL-9.1

4. *Press* the **Enter** key until **Configuration** menu reappears.

Let us now learn how to create a BOM.

Creating a BOM

You can create a BOM for any stock item. Usually, a BOM is created at the time of manufacturing the item.

Let us take a scenario to understand the procedure for creating a BOM for a stock item. Trinity Soft Del organization manufactures laptops. So, for this stock item, the organization creates and maintains a BOM.

To create a BOM for a stock item, you need to create the following masters and vouchers:

- A stock group with the name Laptop
- Stock items with the following details:

Stock Item Name	Stock Group	Stock Category	Units	Set components (BOM)	Set Standard Rates (in ₹)
RAM	Laptop	Electronics	nos.	No	2500
Processor	Laptop	Electronics	nos.	No	3200

Stock Item Name	Stock Group	Stock Category	Units	Set components (BOM)	Set Standard Rates (in ₹)
Wireless Mouse	Laptop	Electronics	nos.	No	800
Hard Disk	Laptop	Electronics	nos.	No	3000

Besides these stock items, create another stock item with the name **Laptop** under the **Primary** group. For the Laptop stock item, enable the **Set components (BOM)** option.

- A ledger account under the **Sundry Creditors** group with the **Maintain balances bill-by-bill** option enabled.
- A purchase invoice
- A manufacturing journal

Let us now learn how to create all these masters and vouchers one by one in the following sections.

Creating a Stock Group

Perform the following steps to create a single stock group:

1. *Double-click* the **Inventory Info.** option in the **Gateway of Tally** menu. The **Inventory Info.** menu appears.
2. *Double-click* the **Stock Groups** option in the **Inventory Info.** menu. The **Stock Groups** menu appears.
3. *Double-click* the **Create** option under the **Single Stock Group** section in the **Stock Groups** menu. The **Stock Group Creation** screen appears (Fig.TL-9.2).
4. *Type* the name of the stock group beside the **Name** option. In our case, we have typed **Laptop** (Fig.TL-9.2).
5. *Type* an alias for the group beside the **(alias)** option. In our case, we have left it blank.
6. *Press* the **Enter** key to go to the **Under** option. The **List of Groups** menu appears (Fig.TL-9.2).
7. *Double-click* the desired parent stock group in the **List of Groups** menu. In our case, we have double-clicked the **Primary** group (Fig.TL-9.2).
8. *Set* the **Should quantities of items be added** option to **Yes** (Fig.TL-9.2).
9. *Press* the **Enter** key. The **Accept ?** message box appears (Fig.TL-9.2).
10. *Click* **Yes** in the **Accept ?** message box to create the stock group, as shown in Fig.TL-9.2:

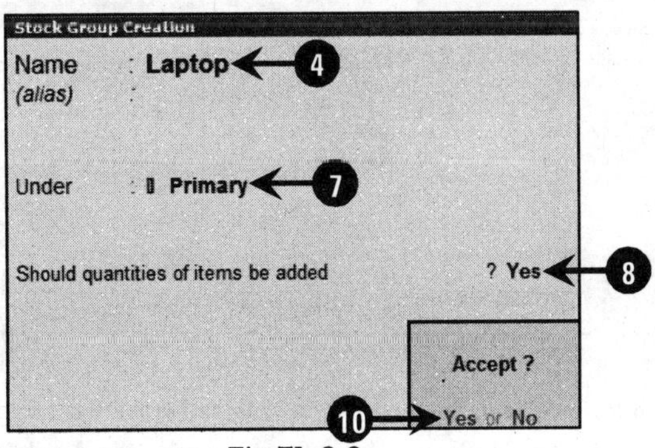

Fig.TL-9.2

Let us now learn how to create a stock item.

Creating a Stock Item

Perform the following steps to create a stock item by enabling the Set standard rates option:

1. *Double-click* the **Inventory Info.** option under the **Masters** section in the **Gateway of Tally** menu. The **Inventory Info.** menu appears.
2. *Double-click* the **Stock Items** option in the **Inventory Info**. menu. The **Stock Items** menu appears.
3. *Double-click* the **Create** option under the **Single Stock item** section in the **Stock Items** menu. The **Stock Item Creation** screen appears.
4. *Enter* the name of the item beside the **Name** option. In our case, we have entered **RAM** (Fig.TL-9.3).
5. *Press* the **Enter** key twice. The **List of Groups** menu appears.
6. *Double-click* the desired group in the **List of Groups** menu for the **Under** option. In our case, we have double-clicked **Laptop** (Fig.TL-9.3).
   The **List of Categories** menu appears.
7. *Double-click* the desired category in the **List of Categories** menu for the **Category** option. In our case, we have double-clicked **Electronics** (Fig.TL-9.3).
   The **Units** menu appears.
8. *Double-click* the desired unit in the **Units** menu for the **Units** option. In our case, we have double-clicked **nos** (Fig.TL-9.3).
9. *Set* the **Maintain in batches** option to **No** (Fig.TL-9.3).
10. *Set* the **Set components (BOM)** option to **No** (Fig.TL-9.3).
11. *Set* the **Set standard rates** option to **Yes**, as shown in Fig.TL-9.3:

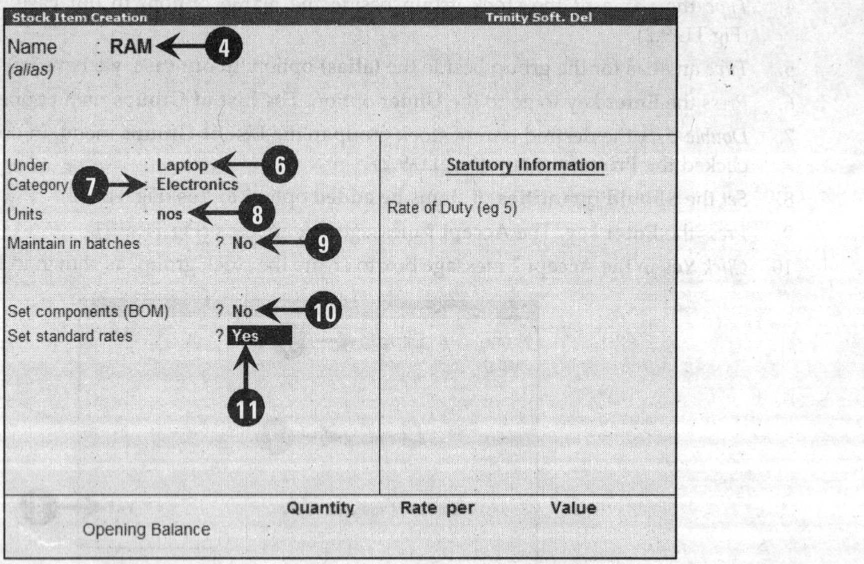

Fig.TL-9.3

The **Standard Rates** screen appears for the selected stock item (Fig.TL-9.4).

12. *Enter* the date from which the rate is applicable under the **Applicable From** column in the **Standard Cost** section. In our case, we have entered **1-Apr-2017** (Fig.TL-9.4).
13. *Enter* the desired amount under the **Rate** column in the **Standard Cost** section. In our case, we have entered **2,500** (Fig.TL-9.4).
14. *Press* the **Enter** key.

The **per** column is automatically filled by the specified unit, as shown in Fig.TL-9.4:

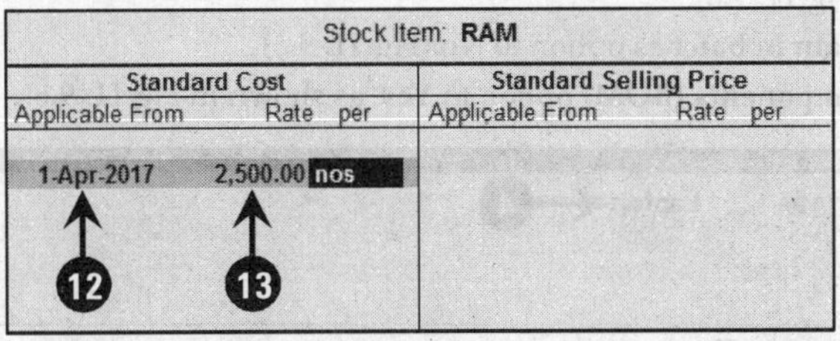

Fig.TL-9.4

15. *Press* the **Enter** key until the **Stock Item Creation** reappears.
16. *Press* the **Enter** key until the **Accept ?** message box appears.
17. *Click* **Yes** in the **Accept ?** message box to create the stock item, as shown in Fig.TL-9.5:

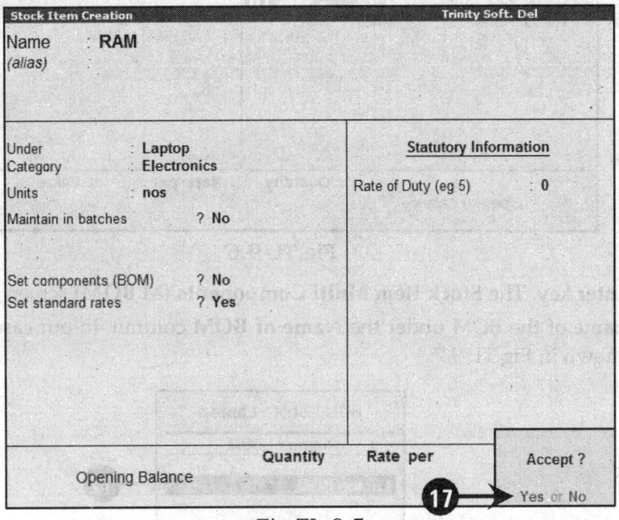

Fig.TL-9.5

Similarly, you can create the other stock items – Processor, Wireless Mouse, and Hard Disk.

Now, perform the following steps to create a stock item by enabling the **Set components (BOM)** option:

1. *Double-click* the **Inventory Info.** option under the **Masters** section in the **Gateway of Tally** menu. The **Inventory Info.** menu appears.
2. *Double-click* the **Stock Items** option in the **Inventory Info.** menu. The **Stock Items** menu appears.
3. *Double-click* the **Create** option under the **Single Stock item** section in the **Stock Items** menu. The **Stock Item Creation** screen appears (Fig.TL-9.6).
4. *Enter* the name of the item beside the **Name** option. In our case, we have entered **Laptop** (Fig.TL-9.6).
5. *Press* the **Enter** key twice. The **List of Groups** menu appears.
6. *Double-click* the desired group in the **List of Groups** menu for the **Under** option. In our case, we have double-clicked **Primary** (Fig.TL-9.6).

   The **List of Categories** menu appears.
7. *Double-click* the desired category in the **List of Categories** menu for the **Category** option. In our case, we have double-clicked **Electronics** (Fig.TL-9.6).

   The **Units** menu appears.

8. *Double-click* the desired unit in the **Units** menu for the **Units** option. In our case, we have double-clicked **nos** (Fig.TL-9.6).
9. *Set* the **Maintain in batches** option to **No** (Fig.TL-9.6).
10. *Set* the **Set components (BOM)** option to **Yes**, as shown in Fig.TL-9.6:

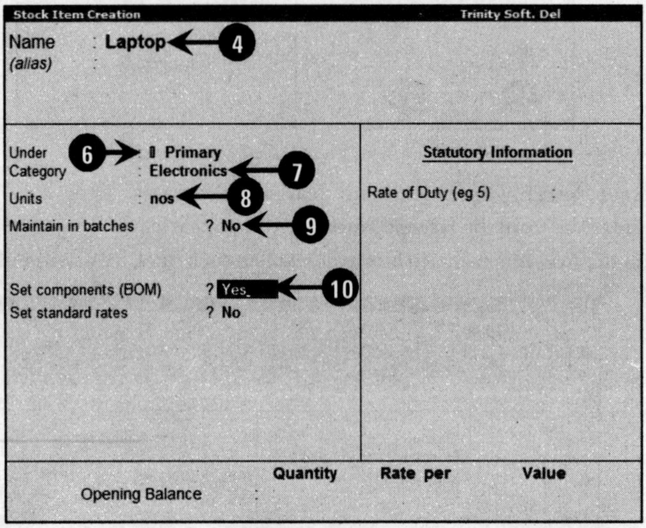

Fig.TL-9.6

11. *Press* the **Enter** key. The **Stock Item Multi Components (M BOM)** screen appears.
12. *Enter* the name of the BOM under the **Name of BOM** column. In our case, we have entered **Laptop BOM**, as shown in Fig.TL-9.7:

Fig.TL-9.7

13. *Press* the **Enter** key. The **Stock Item Components (BoM)** screen appears (Fig.TL-9.8).
14. *Enter* the quantity of the item to be manufactured beside the **Unit of manufacture** option. In our case, we have entered **1** (Fig.TL-9.8).
15. *Press* the **Enter** key. The **List of Stock Items** menu appears.
16. *Double-click* the desired stock item in the **List of Stock Items** menu for the **Item** column. In our case, we have double-clicked **RAM** (Fig.TL-9.8).

    The **List of Godowns** menu appears.
17. *Double-click* the desired godown in the **List of Godowns** menu for the **Godown** column. In our case, we have double-clicked **Moti Bagh Godown** (Fig.TL-9.8).

18. *Enter* the desired quantity under the **Quantity** column. In our case, we have entered **1**, as shown in Fig.TL-9.8:

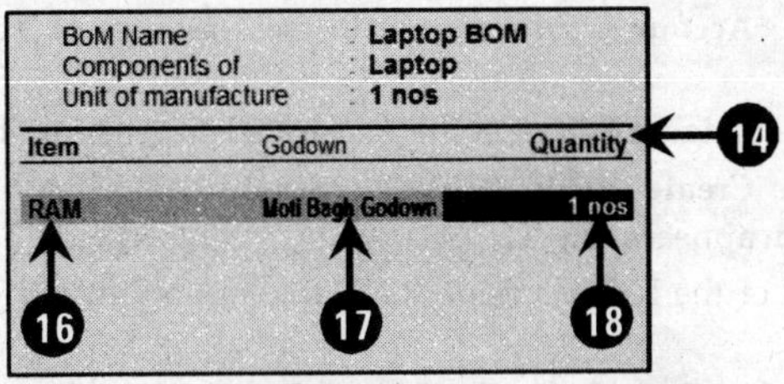

Fig.TL-9.8

19. *Press* the **Enter** key. The **List of Stock Items** menu appears.
20. *Repeat* steps 16, 17, 18, and 19 to add more items. In our case, we have added three more items, that is, **Processor, Wireless Mouse,** and **Hard Disk,** as shown in Fig.TL-9.9:

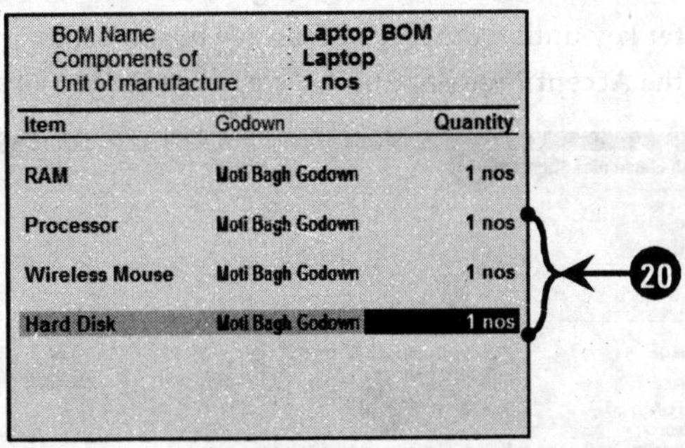

Fig.TL-9.9

21. *Press* the **Enter** key twice. The **Stock Item Multi Components (M BOM)** screen reappears.
22. *Press* the **Enter** key. The **Stock Item Creation** screen reappears.
23. *Set* the **Set standard rates** option to **No** (Fig.TL-9.10).
24. *Press* the **Enter** key until the **Accept ?** message box appears.
25. *Click* **Yes** in the **Accept ?** message box to save the stock item, as shown in Fig.TL-9.10:

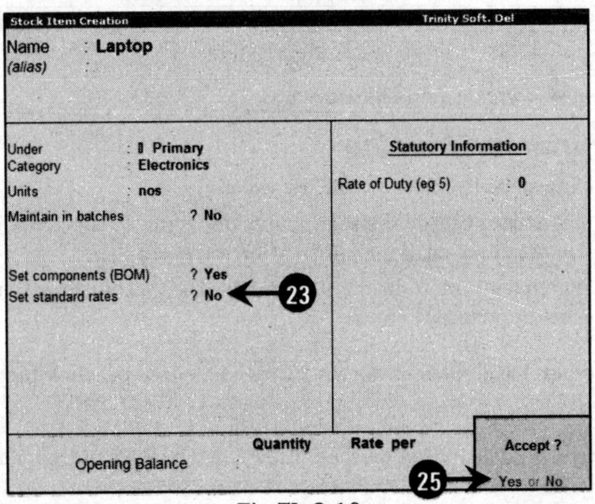

Fig.TL-9.10

Let us now learn how to create a ledger.

Creating a Ledger

Perform the following steps to create a ledger:

1. *Double-click* the **Accounts Info.** option in the **Gateway of Tally** menu. The **Accounts Info.** menu appears.
2. *Double-click* the **Ledgers** option in the **Accounts Info.** menu. The **Ledgers** menu appears.
3. *Double-click* the **Create** option under the **Single Ledger** section in the **Ledgers** menu. The **Ledger Creation** screen appears (Fig.TL-9.11).
4. *Type* the name of the ledger beside the **Name** option. In our case, we have typed **Yash Electronics** (Fig.TL-9.11).
5. *Press* the **Enter** key three times. The **List of Groups** menu appears.
6. *Double-click* the desired parent group in the **List of Groups** menu for the **Under** option. In our case, we have double-clicked **Sundry Creditors** (Fig.TL-9.11).
7. *Set* the **Maintain balances bill-by-bill** option to **Yes** (Fig.TL-9.11).
8. *Enter* the mailing details under the **Mailing Details** section (Fig.TL-9.11).
9. *Press* the **Enter** key until the **Accept ?** message box appears.
10. *Click* **Yes** in the **Accept ?** message box to create the ledger, as shown in Fig.TL-9.11:

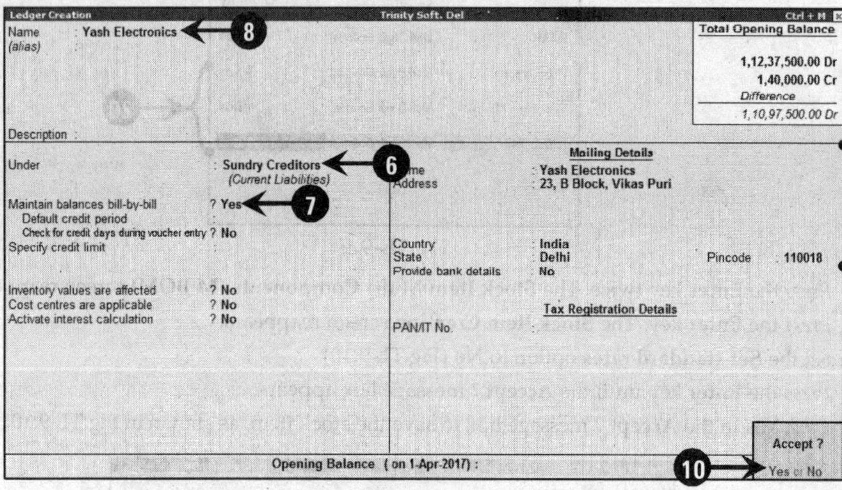

Fig.TL-9.11

Let us now learn how to create a purchase invoice.

Creating a Purchase Invoice

Perform the following steps to create a purchase invoice:

1. *Double-click* the **Accounting Vouchers** option under the **Transactions** section in the **Gateway of Tally** menu. The **Accounting Voucher Creation** screen appears.
2. *Click* the **F9: Purchase** button on the Button Bar. The **Accounting Voucher Creation** screen of the purchase voucher appears as invoice.

> Note: **If the purchase voucher does not appear as invoice, click the V: As Invoice button on the Button Bar.**

3. *Click* the **I: Item Invoice** button on the Button Bar. The **Accounting Voucher Creation** screen of the purchase voucher appears as item invoice.
4. *Enter* the desired supplier invoice number beside the **Supplier invoice no.** option. In our case, we have entered **12** (Fig.TL-9.12).

5. *Press* the **Enter** key.
6. *Enter* the date of invoice beside the **Date** option. In our case, we have entered **8-Aug-2017** (Fig.TL-9.12).
7. *Press* the **Enter** key. The **List of Ledger Accounts** menu appears.
8. *Double-click* the desired party name in the **List of Ledger Accounts** menu for the **Party A/c name** option. In our case, we have double-clicked **Yash Electronics** (Fig.TL-9.12).

   The **List of Ledger Accounts** menu reappears.
9. *Double-click* the desired ledger in the **List of Ledger Accounts** menu for the **Purchase ledger** option. In our case, we have double-clicked **Purchase** (Fig.TL-9.12).

   The **List of Stock Items** menu appears (Fig.TL-9.12).
10. *Double-click* the desired item in the **List of Stock Items** menu for the **Name of Item** column. In our case, we have double-clicked **RAM**, as shown in Fig.TL-9.12:

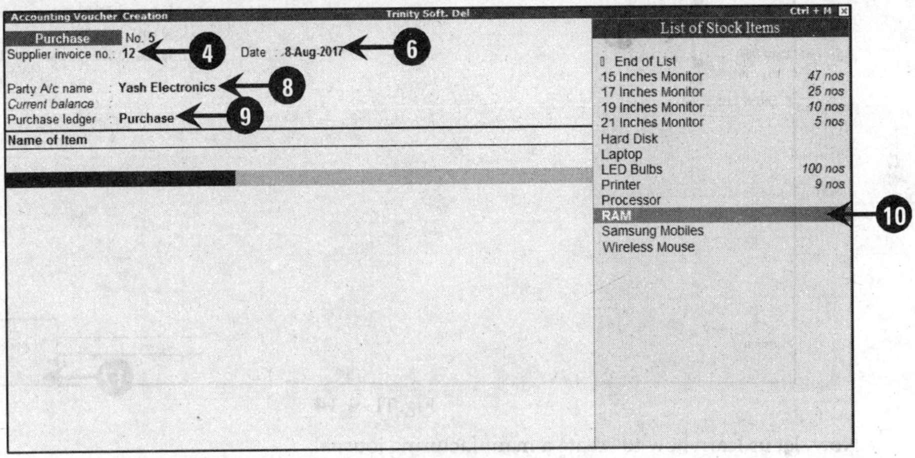

Fig.TL-9.12

The **Stock Item Allocations** screen appears with the **List of Godowns** menu (Fig.TL-9.13).

11. *Double-click* the desired godown in the **List of Godowns** menu for the **Godown** column. In our case, we have double-clicked **Moti Bagh Godown** (Fig.TL-9.13).
12. *Enter* the desired quantity under the **Quantity** column. In our case, we have entered **10** (Fig.TL-9.13).

    The **Rate** column is automatically filled by the defined standard rate. The **per** and **Amount** columns are also automatically filled, as shown in Fig.TL-9.13:

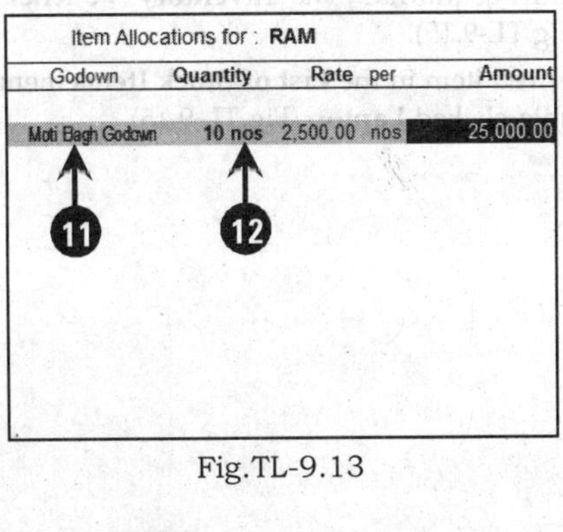

Fig.TL-9.13

13. *Press* the **Enter** key until the **Accounting Voucher Creation** screen reappears.
14. *Press* the **Enter** key.
15. *Repeat* steps 10 to 14 to add more stock items. In our case, we have added three more stock items, that is, **Processor**, **Wireless Mouse**, and **Hard Disk** (Fig.TL-9.14).
16. *Press* the **Enter** key until the **Accept ?** message box appears (Fig.TL-9.14).
17. *Click* **Yes** in the **Accept ?** message box to save the purchase invoice, as shown in Fig.TL-9.14:

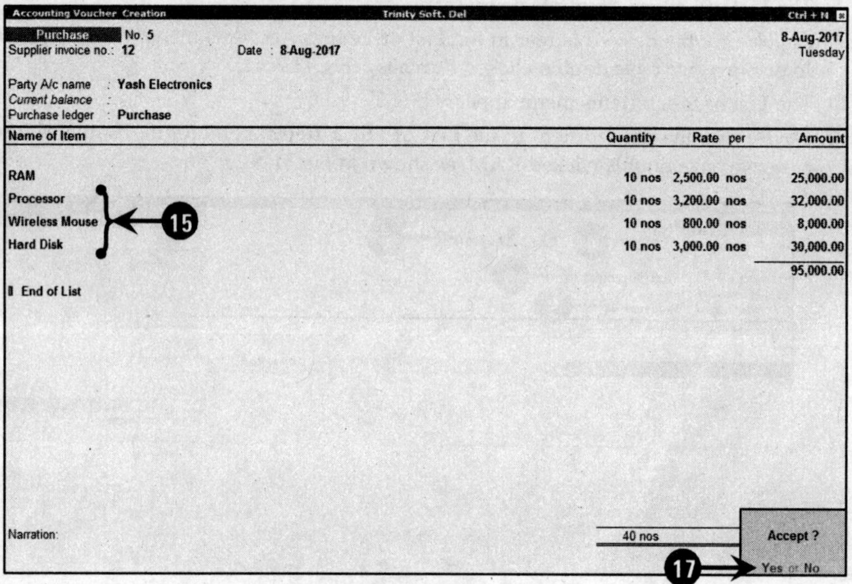

Fig.TL-9.14

Now, let us learn how to create a manufacturing journal.

Creating a Manufacturing Journal

Perform the following steps to create a manufacturing journal:

1. *Double-click* the **InvenTory Vouchers** option under the **Transactions** section in the **Gateway of Tally** menu. The **Inventory Voucher Creation** screen appears.
2. *Click* the **F7: Stock Journal** button on the Button Bar. The **Change Voucher Type** screen appears with the **List of Types** menu.
3. *Double-click* the **Manufacturing Journal** option in the **List of Types** menu for the **Name** option to create a manufacturing journal. The **Inventory Voucher Creation** screen of the manufacturing journal appears (Fig.TL-9.15).
4. *Double-click* the desired item in the **List of Stock Items** menu for the **Name of product** option. In our case, we have double-clicked **Laptop** (Fig.TL-9.15).

The **Name of BOM** option is automatically filled with the specified BOM name for the selected item. In our case, it is **Laptop BOM**. In addition, the stock items defined under the Laptop BOM are displayed in the **Name of Item** and **Godown** column under the **Components (Consumption)** section, as shown in Fig.TL-9.15:

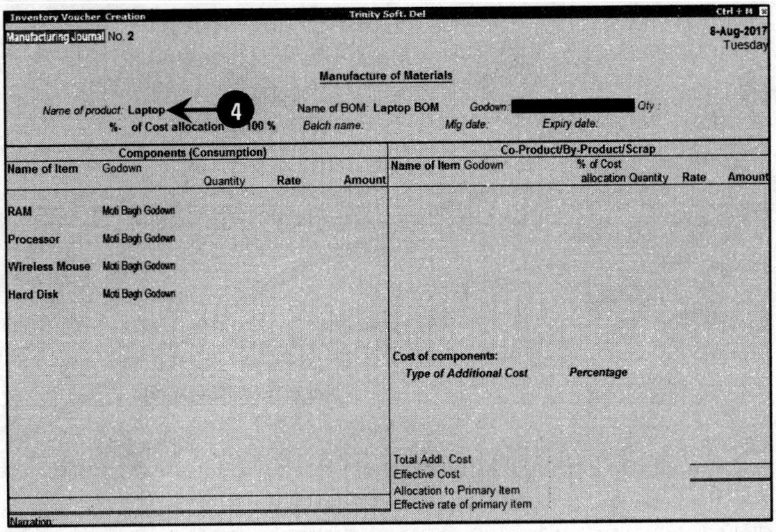

Fig.TL-9.15

5. *Double-click* the desired godown in the **List of Godowns** menu for the **Godown** option. In our case, we have double-clicked **Moti Bagh Godown** (Fig.TL-9.16).
6. *Enter* the quantity of the item beside the **Qty** option. In our case, we have entered **5** (Fig.TL-9.16).
7. *Press* the **Enter** key.

   The **Quantity**, **Rate**, and **Amount** columns are automatically filled according to the quantity specified for the **Qty** option, as shown in Fig.TL-9.16:

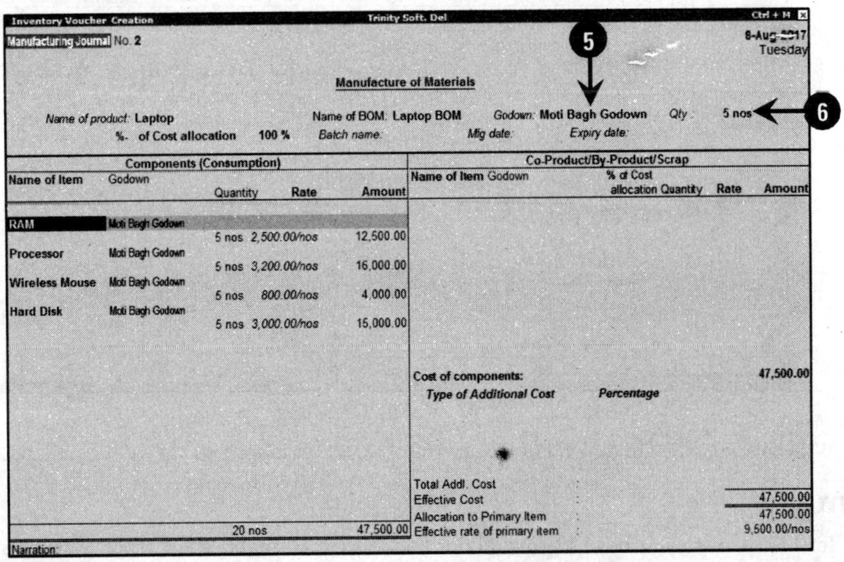

Fig.TL-9.16

8. *Press* the **Enter** key until the **List of Ledger Accounts** menu appears (Fig.TL-9.17).

9. *Double-click* the desired ledger in the **List of Ledger Accounts** menu for the **Type of Additional Cost** column. In our case, we have double-clicked **Freight**, as shown in Fig.TL-9.17:

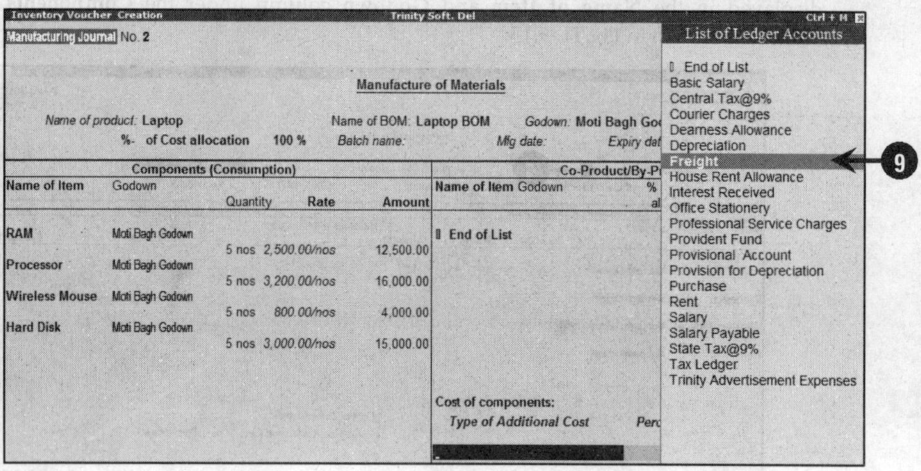

Fig.TL-9.17

10. *Enter* the amount for freight in the **Amount** column. In our case, we have entered **500** (Fig.TL-9.18).
11. *Press* the **Enter** key until the **Accept ?** message box appears.
12. *Click* **Yes** in the **Accept ?** message box to save the manufacturing journal, as shown in Fig.TL-9.18:

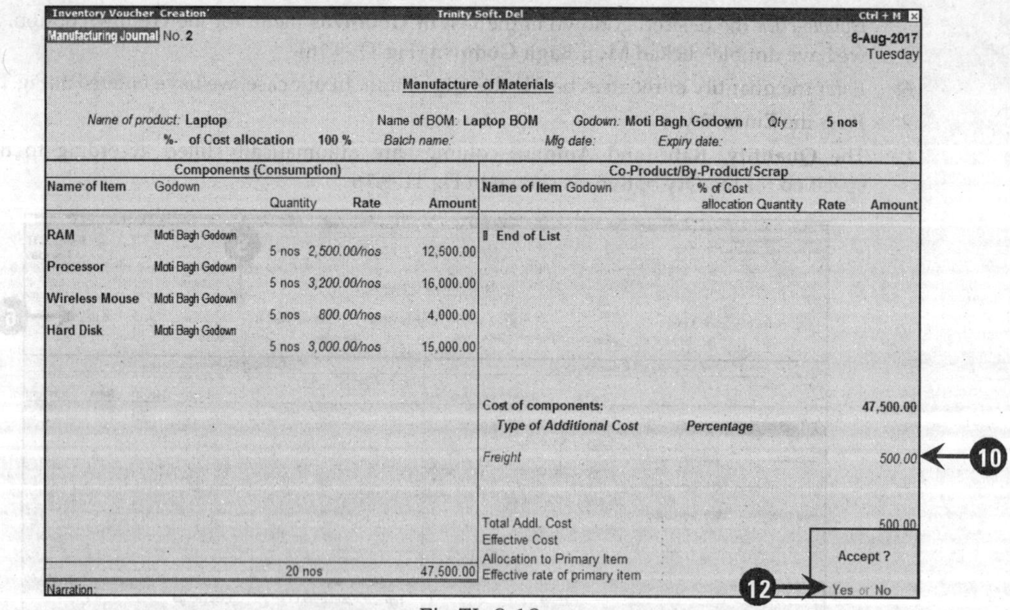

Fig.TL-9.18

With this, we come to the end of the chapter. Let us summarize the key points discussed in the chapter.

Summary

In this chapter, you have learned about the process to enable the **Bill of Materials** feature. Then, you have learned about the procedure to create a BOM for a stock item.

CHAPTER

10

Data Handling in Tally.ERP 9

In this Chapter:

- Taking the Backup of Data in Tally
- Restoring Data in Tally
- Exporting Data
- Importing Data
- Password Policy

Introduction

Tally.ERP 9 provides many important features to handle data, such as backup, restore, import, and export data. Backing up data refers to the process of storing a copy of a file or program at another location (i.e., other than that of the original file or program) of your computer or on an external storage medium, such as a CD/DVD or pen drive. The data stored in a computer is under constant threat of corruption or loss from several sources, such as bugs, malware, or natural disasters. If you do not take adequate precautions against such threats on time, your data may get lost forever! Backing up your data regularly ensures that any data that you lose is quickly restored. In Tally.ERP 9, this process is known as the restoration of data. Other important features of Tally are importing and exporting data. Exporting is the process of transferring data from a company (created in Tally) to multiple addresses. On the other hand, importing is the process of bringing in the data of other companies.

This chapter begins by explaining the procedure to take the backup of data. Further, you learn about the procedure to restore the backup data. Next, the chapter describes how to export and import data in Tally. Toward the end of the chapter, you learn about the password policy, wherein you learn about the procedure to set and apply the password policy.

Let us start the chapter by learning how to back up data in Tally.

Taking the Backup of Data in Tally

In Tally.ERP 9, you can take the backup of data. You can take this backup on a local drive or an external medium by providing the source and destination locations of the data. You can also create a main backup directory with subdirectories to take daily backups.

Perform the following steps to take the backup of data in Tally.ERP 9:

1. *Click* the **F3: Cmp Info** button on the Button Bar in the **Gateway of Tally** screen.

   The **Company Info.** menu appears.
2. *Double-click* the **Backup** option in the **Company Info.** menu.

   The **Backup Companies on Disk** screen appears.
3. *Type* the desired path beside the **Source** option to specify the location from where you want to take the backup. In our case, we have typed **C:\Program Files\Tally\Tally.ERP9\Data** (Fig.TL-10.1).
4. *Press* the **Enter** key.
5. *Type* the path beside the **Destination** option to specify the location where you want to save the backup. In our case, we have typed **D:\Tally Data** (Fig.TL-10.1).

> Note: **You can take the backup of data on the network by using the destination path: \\name of the system\name of the drive\name of the directory.**

6. *Press* the **Enter** key. The **List of Companies** menu appears (Fig.TL-10.1).
7. *Double-click* the company whose data you want to take as backup. In our case, we have double-clicked the **Trinity Soft. Del** company, as shown in Fig.TL-10.1:

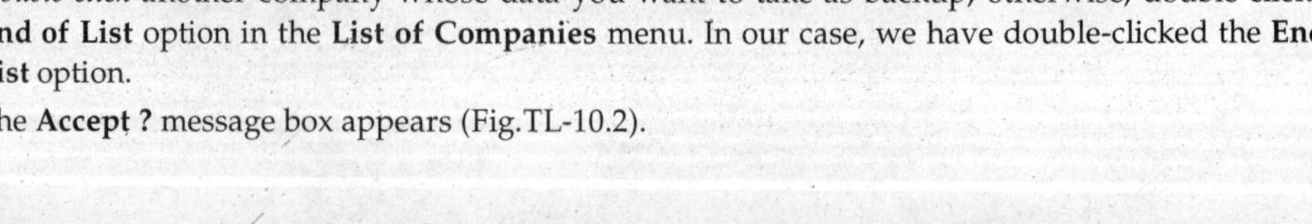

Fig.TL-10.1

8. *Double-click* another company whose data you want to take as backup; otherwise, double-click the **End of List** option in the **List of Companies** menu. In our case, we have double-clicked the **End of List** option.

   The **Accept ?** message box appears (Fig.TL-10.2).

9. *Click* **Yes** in the **Accept ?** message box to save the backup data of the company at the destination location, as shown in Fig.TL-10.2:

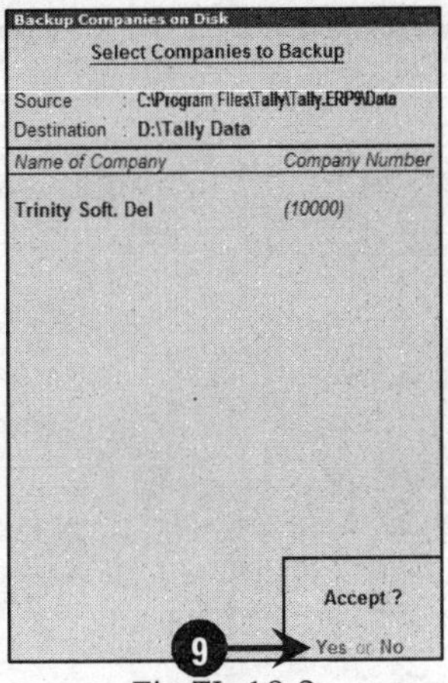

Fig.TL-10.2

Let us now learn how to restore data in Tally.

Restoring Data in Tally

Restoring data means bringing back the data whose backup you had taken to its original form. Tally.ERP 9 provides the Restore option to recover data from its backup copy and use it. However, it is advisable not to restore the backup data in the original data directory to avoid the data from being overwritten.

Perform the following steps to restore data in Tally.ERP 9:

1. *Click* the **F3: Cmp Info** button on the Button Bar in the **Gateway of Tally** screen.

   The **Company Info.** menu appears.

2. *Double-click* the **Restore** option in the **Company Info.** menu.

   The **Restore Companies** screen appears with the **List of Companies** menu. In this screen, **Destination** and **Source** option display the destination and source paths respectively that were set at the time of the last backup (Fig.TL-10.3).

3. *Double-click* the company in the **List of Companies** menu whose data you want to restore. The selected company along with its auto-generated number appears in the **Name of Company** and **Company Number** columns respectively in the **Backup** section. In our case, we have double-clicked the **Trinity Soft. Del** option, as shown in Fig.TL-10.3:

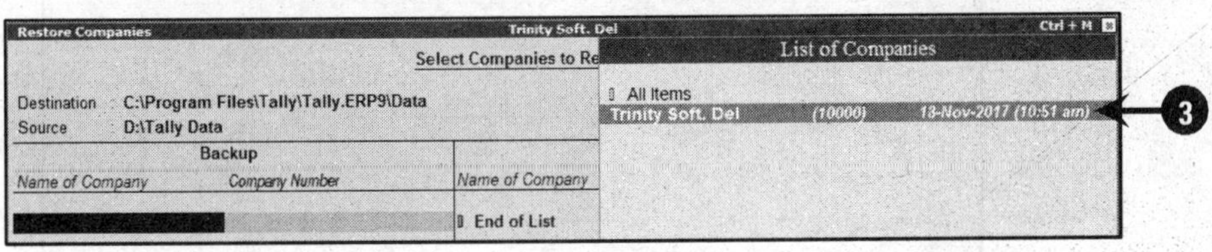

Fig.TL-10.3

4. *Double-click* another company whose data you want to restore; otherwise, double-click the **End of List** option in the **List of Companies** menu. In our case, we have double-clicked the **End of List** option.

   The **Accept ?** message box appears (Fig.TL-10.4).

5. *Click* **Yes** in the **Accept ?** message box to restore the data of the selected company/companies, as shown in Fig.TL-10.4:

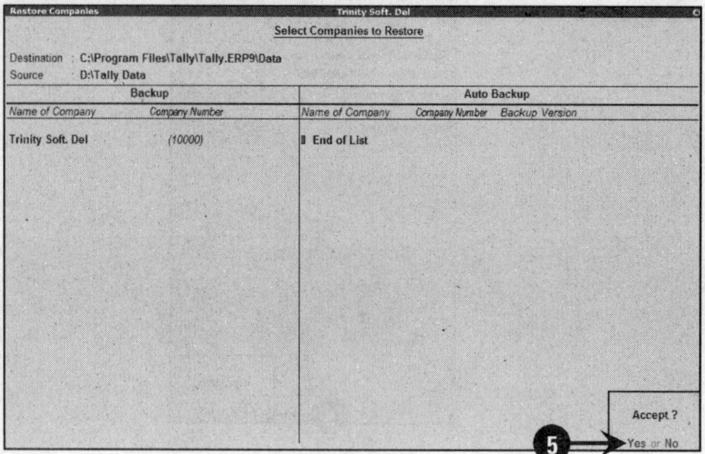

Fig.TL-10.4

Let us now learn how to export data in Tally.

Exporting Data

You may sometimes need to distribute reports and data of a company to creditors, debtors, shareholders, and partners for performing analyses. To do this, Tally allows you to export the formats, masters, vouchers, and reports of a company at a specified location.

Perform the following steps to export the data of a company:

1. *Double-click* the **Display** option in the **Reports** section in the **Gateway of Tally** menu.
   The **Display Menu** menu appears.
2. *Double-click* the **List of Accounts** option in the **Display Menu** menu for exporting masters.
   The **List of Accounts** screen appears (Fig.TL-10.5).
3. *Click* the **E: Export** button on the Horizontal Button Bar, as shown in Fig.TL-10.5:

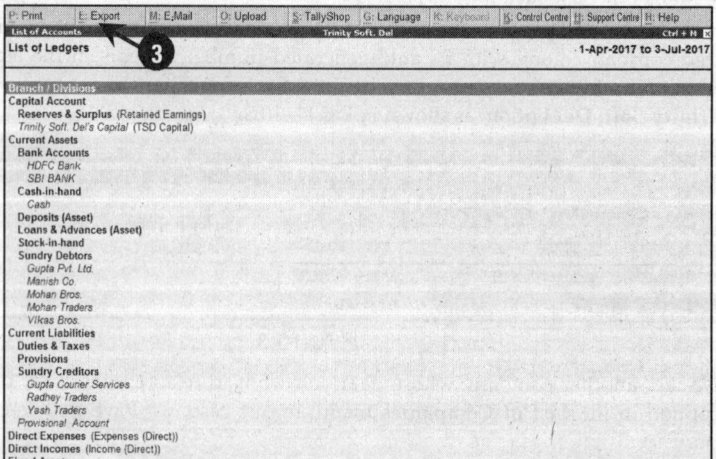

Fig.TL-10.5

The **Export Report** screen appears with the **Export?** message box (Fig.TL-10.6).

4. *Click* **No** in the **Export ?** message box, as shown in Fig.TL-10.6:

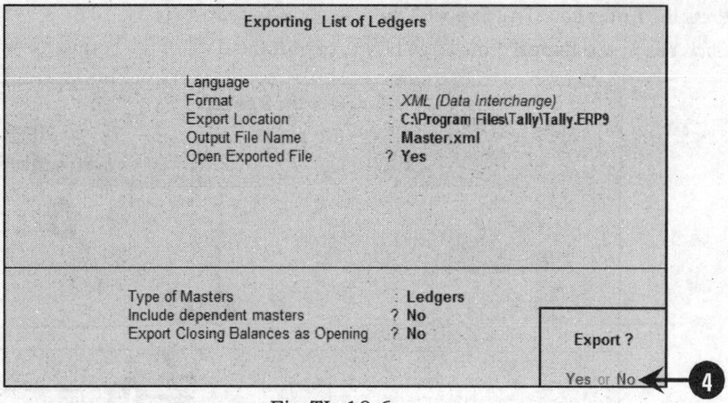

Fig.TL-10.6

The **Language** menu appears (Fig.TL-10.7).

5. *Double-click* the language from the **Language** menu in which you want to export the data or report(s) of the company for the **Language** option. In our case, we have double-clicked the **Default (All Languages)** option (Fig.TL-10.7).

   The **Format** menu appears (Fig.TL-10.7).

6. *Double-click* the format from the **Format** menu in which you want to export the data or report(s) of the company for the **Format** option. In our case, we have double-clicked the **XML (data interchange)** option, as shown in Fig.TL-10.7:

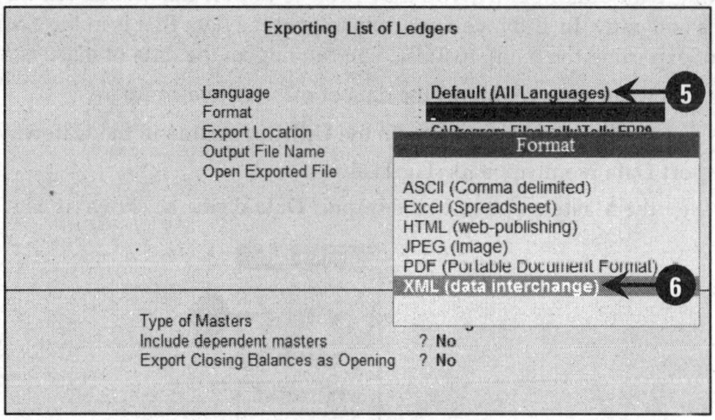

Fig.TL-10.7

7. *Type* the location where you want to store the exported file beside the **Export Location** option. In our case, we have typed **D:\Tally Export** (Fig.TL-10.8).
8. *Press* the **Enter** key.
9. *Type* the name of the output file beside the **Output File Name** option. In our case, we have typed **Ledgers.xml** (Fig.TL-10.8).
10. *Press* the **Enter** key.
11. *Set* the **Open Exported Folder** option to **Yes** (Fig.TL-10.8).
12. *Press* the **Enter** key. The **Type of Masters** menu appears (Fig.TL-10.8).
13. *Double-click* the type of master from the **Type of Masters** menu whose data you want to export for the **Type of Masters** option. In our case, we have double-clicked the **Ledgers** option (Fig.TL-10.8).
14. *Set* the **Include dependent masters** option to **No** (Fig.TL-10.8).

15. *Set* the **Export Closing Balances as Opening** option to **No** (Fig.TL-10.8).
16. *Press* the **Enter** key. The **Export ?** message box appears (Fig.TL-10.8).
17. *Click* **Yes** in the **Export ?** message box to export the data of the company, as shown in Fig.TL-10.8:

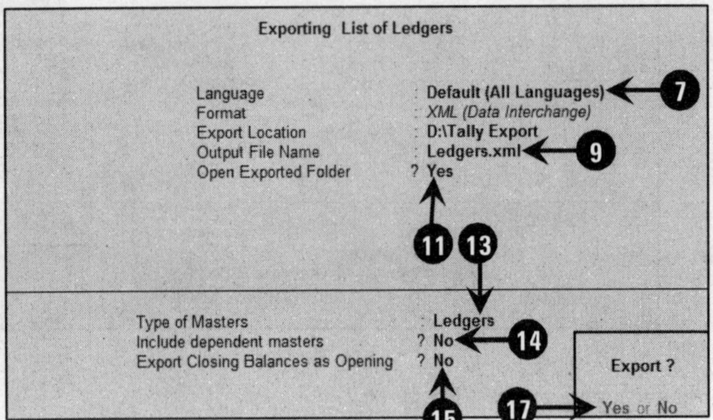

Fig.TL-10.8

As you click the **Yes** option, the folder containing the exported file opens. You can double-click the file to open it.

Let us now learn to import data in Tally.

Importing Data

While working with data in Tally, you may need to import data. Tally allows you to import the reports and data of a company. In Tally, you can only import the data that is in the XML format (which is created at the time of exporting the data). In Tally, you can import the data of masters as well as vouchers.

Perform the following steps to import the data of masters of a company:

1. *Double-click* the **ImpOrt Data** option in the **Utilities** section in the **Gateway of Tally** menu.
   The **Import Data** menu appears (Fig.TL-10.9).
2. *Double-click* the **Masters** option in the **Import Data** menu, as shown in Fig.TL-10.9:

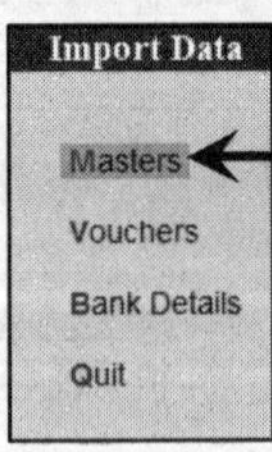

Fig.TL-10.9

   The **Import Data** screen appears (Fig.TL-10.10).
3. *Type* the desired filename beside the **Name of file to be imported (XML)** option. In our case, we have typed **Ledgers.xml** (Fig.TL-10.10).

Note: **If the file that you wish to import is located in the default folder, you need to specify only the filename.**

4. *Press* the **Enter** key.
   The **Behaviour** menu appears (Fig.TL-10.10).

5. *Double-click* the required behavior in the **Behaviour** menu for the **Treatment of entries already existing** option. In our case, we have double-clicked the **Combine Opening Balances** option, as shown in Fig.TL-10.10:

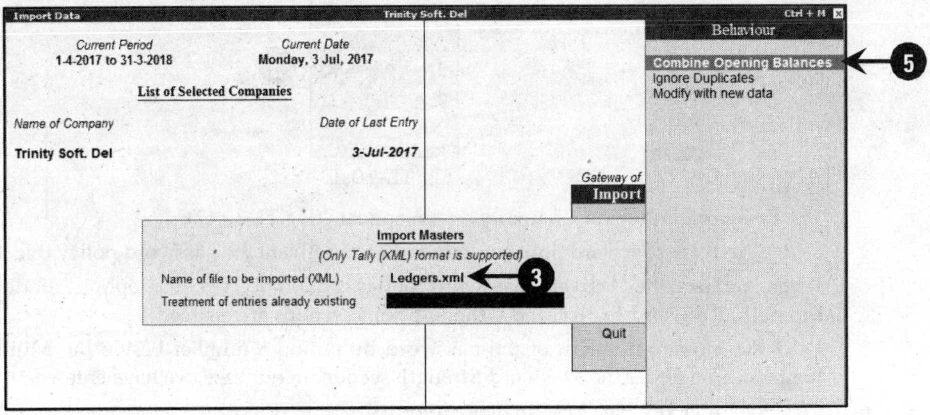

Fig.TL-10.10

6. *Press* the **Enter** key to import the masters.

In addition to importing masters, you can also import the vouchers of a company.

Perform the following steps to import the data of the vouchers of a company:

1. *Double-click* the **ImpOrt Data** option in the **Utilities** section in the **Gateway of Tally** menu. The **Import Data** menu appears.
2. *Double-click* the **Vouchers** option in the **Import Data** menu. The **Import Data** screen appears.
3. *Type* the desired filename beside the **Name of file to be imported (XML)** option. In our case, we have typed **Vouchers.xml**.
4. *Press* the **Enter** key to import the vouchers.

Let us now learn about the password policy.

Password Policy

The password policy in Tally.ERP 9 has three sections, which are as follows:

- **Password Strength:** This section contains options that allow you to define the complexity of a password by specifying the password length and the combination of alphabets, numerals, and special characters used in the password.
- **Password Expiry:** This section contains options that allow users to change their passwords on a regular basis for maintaining the secrecy of their passwords, notify a user that the password has expired after a particular time, and restrict a user to use an old password.
- **Other Options:** This section contains options for changing passwords.

Let us now learn how to set the password policy.

Setting the Password Policy

Perform the following steps to set the password policy for a company:

1. *Click* the F3: **Cmp Info** button on the Button Bar in the **Gateway of Tally** screen. The **Company Info.** menu appears.
2. *Double-click* the **SEcurity Control** option in the **Company Info.** menu. The **Security Control** menu appears.

3. *Double-click* the **Password Policy** option in the **Security Control** menu, as shown in Fig.TL-10.11:

Fig.TL-10.11

The **Password Policy for Company** screen appears (Fig.TL-10.12).

4. *Set* the **Activate password policy** option to **Yes** to activate the password policy (Fig.TL-10.12).

   When you set the **Activate password policy** option to **Yes**, the options under the **Password Strength, Password Expiry**, and **Other Options** sections are enabled.
5. *Enter* the minimum length of the password by typing a number beside the **Minimum password length** option under the **Password Strength** section. In our case, we have entered **10** (Fig.TL-10.12).
6. *Press* the **Enter** key. The **Yes/No** menu appears.
7. *Double-click* the **Yes** option in the **Yes/No** menu for the **Specify advanced parameters for password strength** option under the **Password Strength** section (Fig.TL-10.12).

   When you double-click the **Yes** option, the **Minimum number of alphabetic characters, Minimum number of numeric characters**, and **Minimum number of special characters** options are enabled and displayed on the **Password Policy for Company screen** (Fig.TL-10.12).
8. *Enter* the minimum number of alphabets to be used in the password beside the **Minimum number of alphabetic characters** option. In our case, we have entered **6** (Fig.TL-10.12).
9. *Enter* the minimum number of numerals to be used in the password beside the **Minimum number of numeric characters** option. In our case, we have entered **3** (Fig.TL-10.12).
10. *Enter* the minimum number of special characters to be used in the password beside the **Minimum number of special characters** option. In our case, we have entered **1** (Fig.TL-10.12).
11. *Enter* the desired number of days beside the **Password expires after** option under the **Password Expiry** section. In our case, we have entered **180** (Fig.TL-10.12).
12. *Press* the **Enter** key. The **Yes/No** menu appears.
13. *Double-click* the **Yes** option in the **Yes/No** menu for the **Notify users before password expires** option under the **Password Expiry** section, as shown in Fig.TL-10.12:

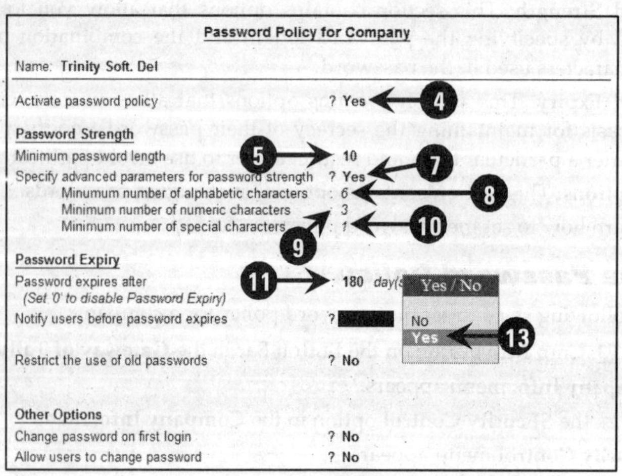

Fig.TL-10.12

When you set the **Notify users before password expires** option to **Yes**, the **Notify before** option is enabled and displayed (Fig.TL-10.13).

14. *Enter* the desired number of days beside the **Notify before** option. In our case, we have entered **10** (Fig.TL-10.13).
15. *Press* the **Enter** key. The **Yes/No** menu appears.
16. *Double-click* the **Yes** option in the **Yes/No** menu for the **Restrict the use of old passwords** option under the **Password Expiry** section (Fig.TL-10.13).

    When you set the **Restrict the use of old passwords** option to **Yes**, the **Number of old passwords to be restricted** option is enabled and displayed (Fig.TL-10.13).
17. *Enter* the desired number beside the **Number of old passwords to be restricted** option under the **Password Expiry** section. In our case, we have entered **3** (Fig.TL-10.13).
18. *Press* the **Enter** key. The **Yes/No** menu appears.
19. *Double-click* the **Yes** option in the **Yes/No** menu for the **Change password on first login** option under the **Other Options** section (Fig.TL-10.13). The **Yes/No** menu appears.
20. *Double-click* the **Yes** option in the **Yes/No** menu for the **Allow users to change password** option under the **Other Options** section (Fig.TL-10.13).

    The **Accept ?** message box appears (Fig.TL-10.13).
21. *Click* **Yes** in the **Accept ?** message box to set the password policy for the selected company, as shown in Fig.TL-10.13:

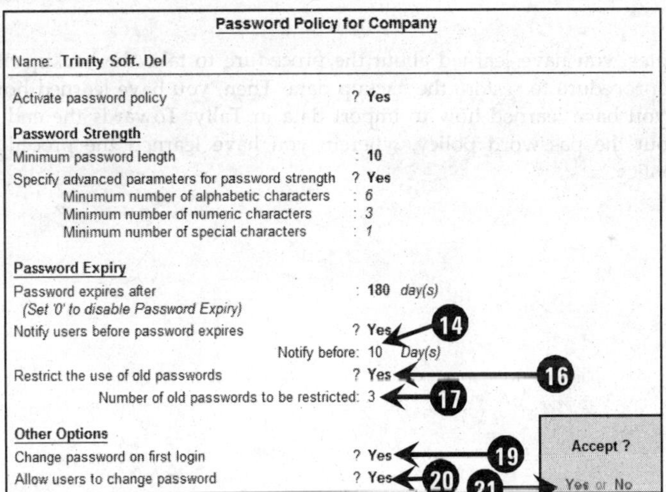

Fig.TL-10.13

Let us now learn how to apply the password policy.

Applying the Password Policy

Perform the following steps to apply the password policy to a user:

1. *Click* the F3: **Cmp Info** button on the Button Bar in the **Gateway of Tally** screen.

   The **Company Info.** menu appears.
2. *Double-click* the **SEcurity Control** option in the **Company Info.** menu.

   The **Security Control** menu appears.
3. *Double-click* the **Users and Passwords** option in the **Security Control** menu.

   The **Users for Company** screen appears.
4. *Click* the **F12: Configure** button on the Button Bar.

   The **Configuration** screen appears (Fig.TL-10.14).

5. *Set* the **Apply password policy** option to **Yes**, as shown in Fig.TL-10.14:

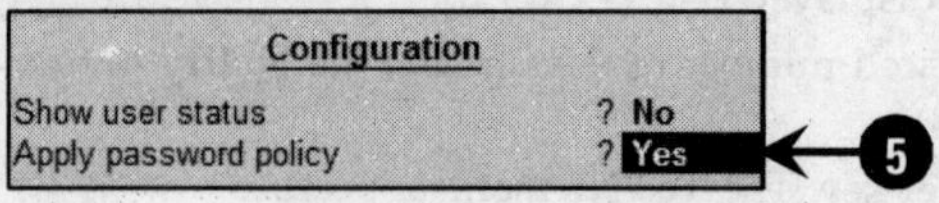

Fig.TL-10.14

The **Apply Password Policy** column is displayed on the **Users for Company** screen, as shown in Fig.TL-10.15:

List of Users for Company

Name: **Trinity Soft. Del**

Security Level	Username	Password (if any)	Apply Password Policy	Allow Remote Access	Allow Local TDL Files	Allow SMS Access
Data Entry	**Yash Gupta**	********	**Yes**	**No**	**No**	**No**

Fig.TL-10.15

The Password policies apply to the specified users.

With this, we come to the end of the chapter. Let us summarize the key points discussed in the chapter.

Summary

In this chapter, you have learned about the procedure to take the backup of data. Further, you have studied the procedure to restore the backup data. Then, you have learned how to export data in Tally. After this, you have learned how to import data in Tally. Towards the end of the chapter, you have learned about the password policy, wherein you have learned the procedure to set and apply the password policy.

CHAPTER

11

Reports in Tally.ERP 9

In this Chapter:

* Financial Statements
* Day Book
* Accounting Books and Registers
* Inventory Books and Registers
* Statements of Accounts
* Statements of Inventory
* Management Information System (MIS) Reports
* Exception Reports

Introduction

A report is an organized data in the form of text and calculations, which you have entered in Tally. Reports show a holistic picture of the data, which is helpful for taking decisions by the top management of an organization. By using the data entered in Tally, you can view various types of reports, such as Profit & Loss A/c, Stock Summary, and Ratio Analysis. In Tally, you can access all these reports by using the Gateway of Tally menu. Tally also allows you to print a report for taking its hard copy.

In this chapter, you learn about the financial statements. Then, you learn about displaying Day Book report. You also learn about displaying accounting books and registers; and inventory books and registers. You also learn about the Statements of Accounts reports. As the chapter progresses, you learn about the Statements of Inventory reports. Towards the end, you learn to view MIS reports and Exception Reports.

Let us start this chapter by learning about the financial statements.

Financial Statements

A statement that shows an overall summary of accounts spanning a specific accounting period to specify the financial status of a business is called financial statement. Financial statements are categorized into three statements, which are as follows:

- Balance Sheet
- Profit & Loss Account
- Trial Balance

Let us now learn about these statements one by one in the following section.

Balance Sheet

A Balance Sheet is a financial reporting tool that shows the financial position of an organization as on a particular date, by showing the assets and liabilities of the organization. This tool displays the exact financial position of the business on the last date of the financial year.

To view a Balance Sheet, you need to double-click the **Balance Sheet** option in the **Reports** section on the **Gateway of Tally** menu, as shown in Fig.TL-11.1:

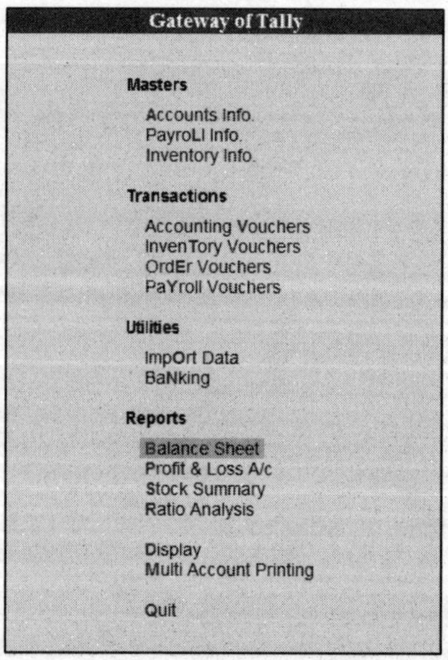

Fig.TL-11.1

The **Balance Sheet** screen appears displaying the Balance Sheet of the company, as shown in Fig.TL-11.2:

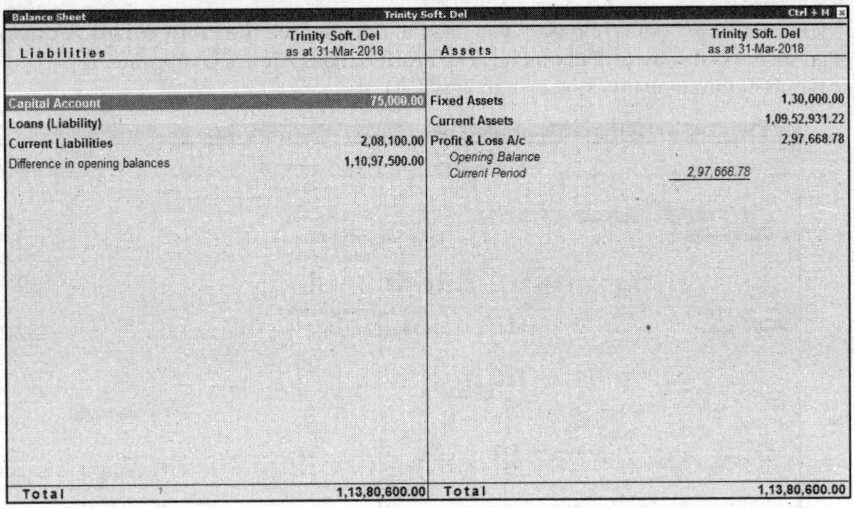

Balance Sheet — Trinity Soft. Del — Ctrl + M

Liabilities		Trinity Soft. Del as at 31-Mar-2018	Assets		Trinity Soft. Del as at 31-Mar-2018
Capital Account		75,000.00	Fixed Assets		1,30,000.00
Loans (Liability)			Current Assets		1,09,52,931.22
Current Liabilities		2,08,100.00	Profit & Loss A/c		2,97,668.78
Difference in opening balances		1,10,97,500.00	*Opening Balance*		
			Current Period	2,97,668.78	
Total		1,13,80,600.00	**Total**		1,13,80,600.00

Fig.TL-11.2

Tally also allows you to have a detailed view of a Balance Sheet. To do so, you need to click the **F1: Detailed** button on the Button Bar. The detailed view of the Balance Sheet is displayed, as shown in Fig.TL-11.3:

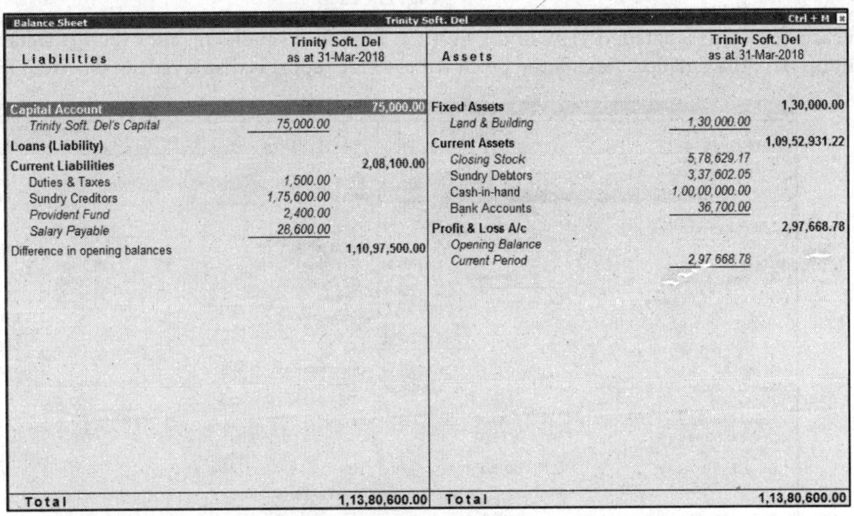

Balance Sheet — Trinity Soft. Del — Ctrl + M

Liabilities		Trinity Soft. Del as at 31-Mar-2018	Assets		Trinity Soft. Del as at 31-Mar-2018
Capital Account		75,000.00	Fixed Assets		1,30,000.00
Trinity Soft. Del's Capital	75,000.00		*Land & Building*	1,30,000.00	
Loans (Liability)			Current Assets		1,09,52,931.22
Current Liabilities		2,08,100.00	*Closing Stock*	5,78,629.17	
Duties & Taxes	1,500.00		Sundry Debtors	3,37,602.05	
Sundry Creditors	1,75,600.00		Cash-in-hand	1,00,00,000.00	
Provident Fund	2,400.00		Bank Accounts	36,700.00	
Salary Payable	28,600.00		Profit & Loss A/c		2,97,668.78
Difference in opening balances		1,10,97,500.00	*Opening Balance*		
			Current Period	2,97,668.78	
Total		1,13,80,600.00	**Total**		1,13,80,600.00

Fig.TL-11.3

The Condensed/Detailed button is a single button. It appears as the F1: Condensed button when the detailed view of the Balance Sheet is open and as the F1: Detailed button when the Balance Sheet is in condensed mode.

Let us learn about Profit & Loss A/c report.

Profit & Loss A/c

A Profit & Loss A/c is a report prepared to ascertain the net profit earned or net loss suffered by a business over an accounting period, depicting the financial performance of that organization. In other words, the Profit & Loss A/c report displays the expenditures, revenues, and net income of an organization.

To view a Profit & Loss A/c report, you need to double-click the **Profit & Loss A/c** option in the **Reports** section on the **Gateway of Tally** menu. The **Profit & Loss A/c** screen appears displaying the Profit & Loss A/c report of the company, as shown in Fig.TL-11.4:

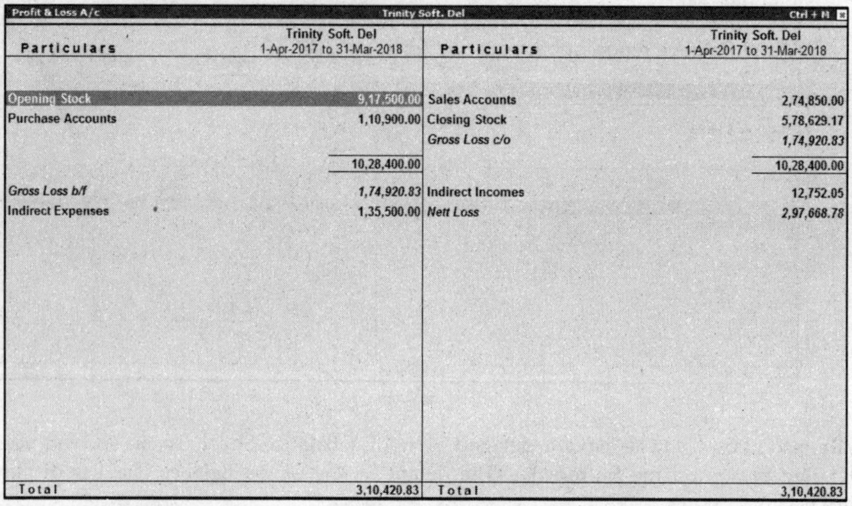

Profit & Loss A/c — Trinity Soft. Del — Ctrl + M

Particulars	Trinity Soft. Del 1-Apr-2017 to 31-Mar-2018	Particulars	Trinity Soft. Del 1-Apr-2017 to 31-Mar-2018
Opening Stock	9,17,500.00	Sales Accounts	2,74,850.00
Purchase Accounts	1,10,900.00	Closing Stock	5,78,629.17
		Gross Loss c/o	*1,74,920.83*
	10,28,400.00		10,28,400.00
Gross Loss b/f	*1,74,920.83*	Indirect Incomes	12,752.05
Indirect Expenses	1,35,500.00	*Nett Loss*	*2,97,668.78*
Total	3,10,420.83	Total	3,10,420.83

Fig.TL-11.4

In case you want a detailed view of the Profit & Loss A/c statement, click the **F1: Detailed** button on the Button Bar. The detailed view of the Profit & Loss A/c report is displayed, as shown in Fig.TL-11.5:

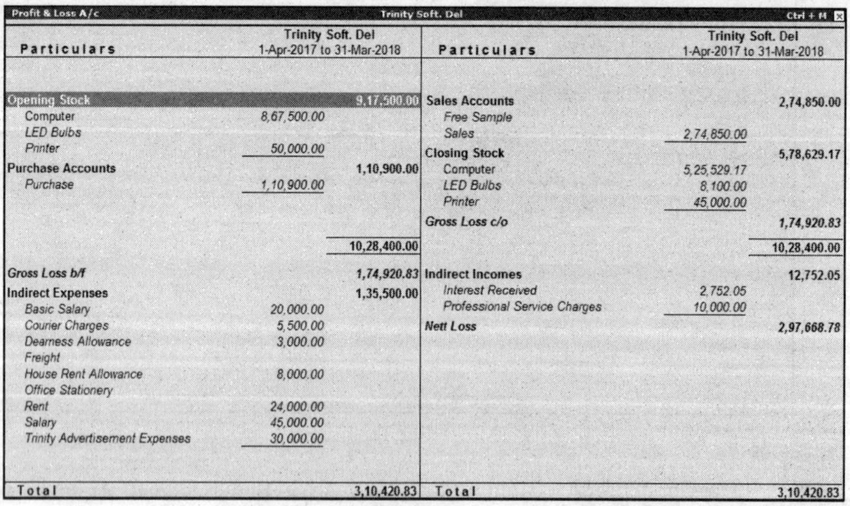

Profit & Loss A/c — Trinity Soft. Del — Ctrl + M

Particulars		Trinity Soft. Del 1-Apr-2017 to 31-Mar-2018	Particulars		Trinity Soft. Del 1-Apr-2017 to 31-Mar-2018
Opening Stock		9,17,500.00	Sales Accounts		2,74,850.00
Computer	8,67,500.00		*Free Sample*		
LED Bulbs			*Sales*	2,74,850.00	
Printer	50,000.00		Closing Stock		5,78,629.17
Purchase Accounts		1,10,900.00	Computer	5,25,529.17	
Purchase	1,10,900.00		*LED Bulbs*	8,100.00	
			Printer	45,000.00	
			Gross Loss c/o		*1,74,920.83*
		10,28,400.00			10,28,400.00
Gross Loss b/f		*1,74,920.83*	Indirect Incomes		12,752.05
Indirect Expenses		1,35,500.00	*Interest Received*	2,752.05	
Basic Salary	20,000.00		*Professional Service Charges*	10,000.00	
Courier Charges	5,500.00		*Nett Loss*		*2,97,668.78*
Dearness Allowance	3,000.00				
Freight					
House Rent Allowance	8,000.00				
Office Stationery					
Rent	24,000.00				
Salary	45,000.00				
Trinity Advertisement Expenses	30,000.00				
Total		3,10,420.83	Total		3,10,420.83

Fig.TL-11.5

Let us learn how to view the Trial Balance report.

Trial Balance

A Trial Balance is a report in which the closing balances of each ledger on a particular date are classified into two columns, sorted by groups. The two columns are named Debit and Credit. A Trial Balance is prepared in each of the financial periods as a summary of the closing of the previous ledger. In the ledger, the total debts of transactions should be equal to the total credits. This is called a double-entry system. The main purpose of a Trial Balance is to check the arithmetic accuracy of the accounts.

To view a Trial Balance report, you need to perform the following steps:

1. *Double-click* the **Display** option in the **Reports** section on the **Gateway of Tally** menu. The **Display Menu** menu appears.
2. *Double-click* the **Trial Balance** option on the **Display Menu** menu.

   The **Trial Balance** report appears, as shown in Fig.TL-11.6:

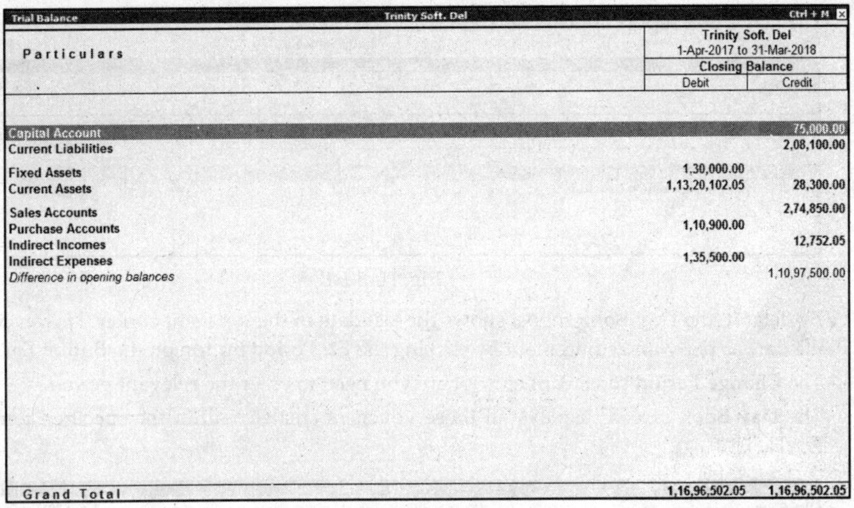

Trial Balance — Trinity Soft. Del — Ctrl + M

Particulars	Trinity Soft. Del 1-Apr-2017 to 31-Mar-2018 Closing Balance	
	Debit	Credit
Capital Account		75,000.00
Current Liabilities		2,08,100.00
Fixed Assets	1,30,000.00	
Current Assets	1,13,20,102.05	28,300.00
Sales Accounts		2,74,850.00
Purchase Accounts	1,10,900.00	
Indirect Incomes		12,752.05
Indirect Expenses	1,35,500.00	
Difference in opening balances		1,10,97,500.00
Grand Total	1,16,96,502.05	1,16,96,502.05

Fig.TL-11.6

In case you want a detailed view of the Trial Balance report, click the **F1: Detailed** button on the Button Bar. The detailed view of the Trial Balance report is displayed, as shown in Fig.TL-11.7:

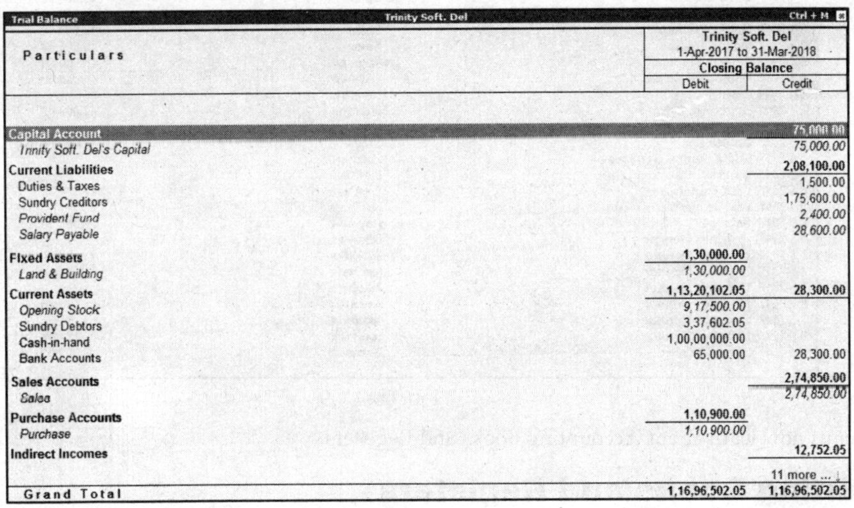

Trial Balance — Trinity Soft. Del — Ctrl + M

Particulars	Trinity Soft. Del 1-Apr-2017 to 31-Mar-2018 Closing Balance	
	Debit	Credit
Capital Account		75,000.00
Trinity Soft. Del's Capital		75,000.00
Current Liabilities		2,08,100.00
Duties & Taxes		1,500.00
Sundry Creditors		1,75,600.00
Provident Fund		2,400.00
Salary Payable		28,600.00
Fixed Assets	1,30,000.00	
Land & Building	1,30,000.00	
Current Assets	1,13,20,102.05	28,300.00
Opening Stock	9,17,500.00	
Sundry Debtors	3,37,602.05	
Cash-in-hand	1,00,00,000.00	
Bank Accounts	65,000.00	28,300.00
Sales Accounts		2,74,850.00
Sales		2,74,850.00
Purchase Accounts	1,10,900.00	
Purchase	1,10,900.00	
Indirect Incomes		12,752.05
		11 more ...
Grand Total	1,16,96,502.05	1,16,96,502.05

Fig.TL-11.7

Let us learn about Day Book.

Day Book

A Day Book is a report that shows the list of day-to-day business transactions that take place in an organization.

To display a day book report, undertake the following steps:

1. *Double-click* the **Display** option in the **Reports** section on the **Gateway of Tally** menu. The **Display Menu** menu appears.
2. *Double-click* the **Day Book** option on the **Display Menu** menu.

   The **Day Book** report appears, as shown in Fig.TL-11.8:

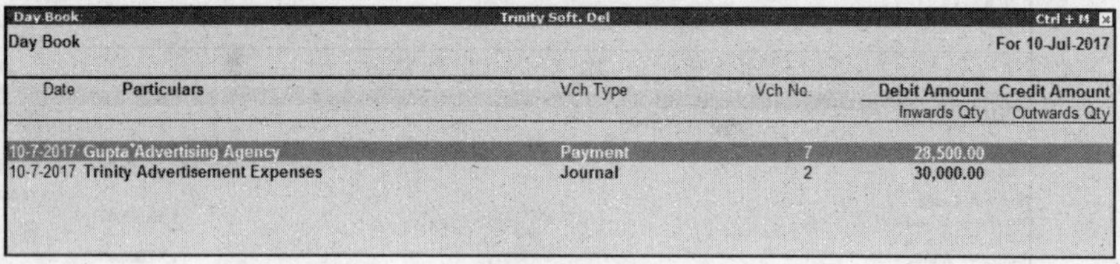

Day Book — Trinity Soft. Del — Ctrl + M

Day Book — For 10-Jul-2017

Date	Particulars	Vch Type	Vch No.	Debit Amount / Inwards Qty	Credit Amount / Outwards Qty
10-7-2017	Gupta Advertising Agency	Payment	7	28,500.00	
10-7-2017	Trinity Advertisement Expenses	Journal	2	30,000.00	

Fig.TL-11.8

By default, the **Day Book** report shows the last date in the top right corner. However, you can change the date as per your requirement by clicking the **F2: Period** button on the Button Bar.

The **Change Period** screen appears where you need to enter the relevant period.

The **Day Book** screen displays all those vouchers created within the specified period, as shown in Fig.TL-11.9:

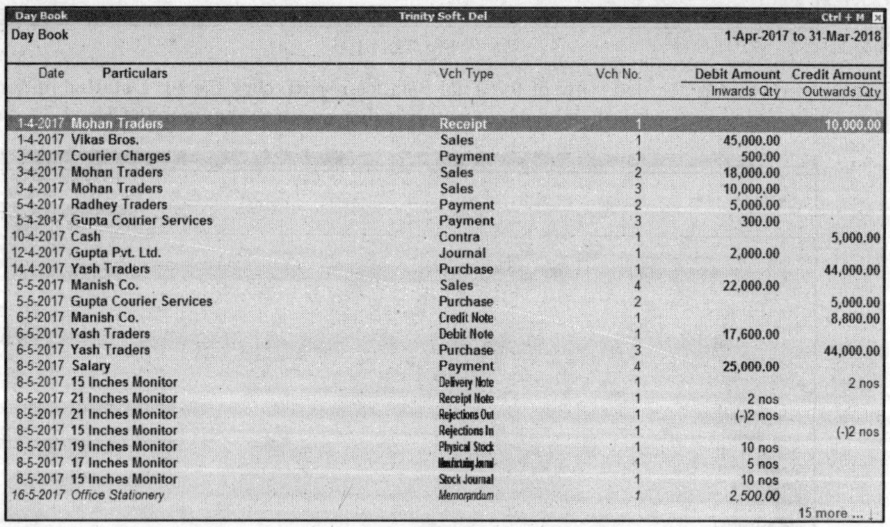

Day Book — Trinity Soft. Del — Ctrl + M

Day Book — 1-Apr-2017 to 31-Mar-2018

Date	Particulars	Vch Type	Vch No.	Debit Amount / Inwards Qty	Credit Amount / Outwards Qty
1-4-2017	Mohan Traders	Receipt	1		10,000.00
1-4-2017	Vikas Bros.	Sales	1	45,000.00	
3-4-2017	Courier Charges	Payment	1	500.00	
3-4-2017	Mohan Traders	Sales	2	18,000.00	
3-4-2017	Mohan Traders	Sales	3	10,000.00	
5-4-2017	Radhey Traders	Payment	2	5,000.00	
5-4-2017	Gupta Courier Services	Payment	3	300.00	
10-4-2017	Cash	Contra	1		5,000.00
12-4-2017	Gupta Pvt. Ltd.	Journal	1	2,000.00	
14-4-2017	Yash Traders	Purchase	1		44,000.00
5-5-2017	Manish Co.	Sales	4	22,000.00	
5-5-2017	Gupta Courier Services	Purchase	2		5,000.00
6-5-2017	Manish Co.	Credit Note	1		8,800.00
6-5-2017	Yash Traders	Debit Note	1	17,600.00	
6-5-2017	Yash Traders	Purchase	3		44,000.00
8-5-2017	Salary	Payment	4	25,000.00	
8-5-2017	15 Inches Monitor	Delivery Note	1		2 nos
8-5-2017	21 Inches Monitor	Receipt Note	1	2 nos	
8-5-2017	21 Inches Monitor	Rejections Out	1	(-)2 nos	
8-5-2017	15 Inches Monitor	Rejections In	1		(-)2 nos
8-5-2017	19 Inches Monitor	Physical Stock	1	10 nos	
8-5-2017	17 Inches Monitor	Manufacturing Journal	1	5 nos	
8-5-2017	15 Inches Monitor	Stock Journal	1	10 nos	
16-5-2017	*Office Stationery*	*Memorandum*	*1*	*2,500.00*	

15 more ...

Fig.TL-11.9

Let us now learn about Accounting Books and Registers.

Accounting Books and Registers

In Tally.ERP 9, the transactions you record are related to a particular book or register of accounts. Tally.ERP 9 allows you to view or print any particular books or registers of accounts. For example, the Purchase Book contains the records related to all purchase transactions. Some commonly used books and registers of accounts are as follows:

- Cash Book

- Bank Book
- Purchase Register
- Sales Register
- Debit Note Register
- Credit Note Register

Let us now learn about each of these account books and registers in the following section.

Cash Book

A Cash Book gives you the complete information regarding cash payments and receipts.

Perform the following steps to view a Cash Book report:

1. *Double-click* the **Display** option in the **Reports** section on the **Gateway of Tally** menu. The **Display Menu** menu appears.
2. *Double-click* the **Accounts Books** option on the **Display Menu** menu. The **Accounts Books** menu appears.
3. *Double-click* the **Cash/Bank Book(s)** option on the **Accounts Books** menu. The **Cash/Bank Summary** screen appears.
4. *Select* the desired cash ledger on the **Cash/Bank Summary** screen. The **Ledger Monthly Summary** screen appears.
5. *Select* the month for which you require the cash book.

   The **Ledger Vouchers** screen appears displaying all transactions in cash of the selected month, as shown in Fig.TL-11.10:

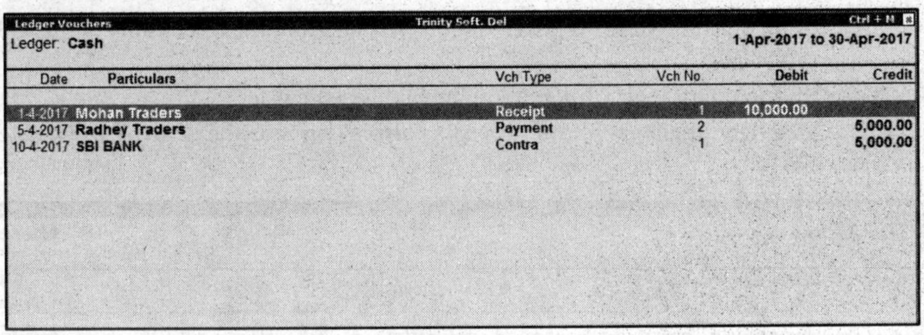

Fig.TL-11.10

Let us learn how to view the Bank Book report.

Bank Book

A Bank Book gives you the complete information regarding bank payments and receipts.

Perform the following steps to view a bank book report:

1. *Double-click* the **Display** option in the **Reports** section on the **Gateway of Tally** menu. The **Display Menu** menu appears.
2. *Double-click* the **Accounts Books** option on the **Display Menu** menu. The **Accounts Books** menu appears.
3. *Double-click* the **Cash/Bank Book(s)** option on the **Accounts Books** menu. The **Cash/Bank Summary** screen appears.
4. *Select* the desired bank ledger on the **Cash/Bank Summary** screen. The **Ledger Monthly Summary** screen appears.
5. *Select* the month for which you require the Bank Book.

The **Ledger Vouchers** screen appears displaying all transactions of the bank of the selected month, as shown in Fig.TL-11.11:

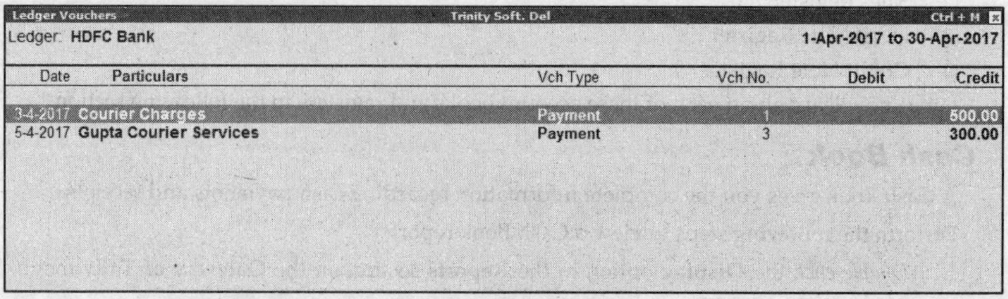

Fig.TL-11.11

Let us learn how to view the Purchase Register report.

Purchase Register

A Purchase Register gives you complete information of the goods purchased for a specified period. Perform the following steps to view a Purchase Register report:

1. *Double-click* the **Display** option in the **Reports** section on the **Gateway of Tally** menu. The **Display Menu** menu appears.
2. *Double-click* the **Accounts Books** option on the **Display Menu** menu. The **Accounts Books** menu appears.
3. *Double-click* the **Purchase Register** option on the **Accounts Books** menu. The **Purchase Register** screen appears.
4. *Select* the month for which you require the Purchase Register.

   The **Voucher Register** screen appears displaying all the Purchase Registers, as shown in Fig.TL-11.12:

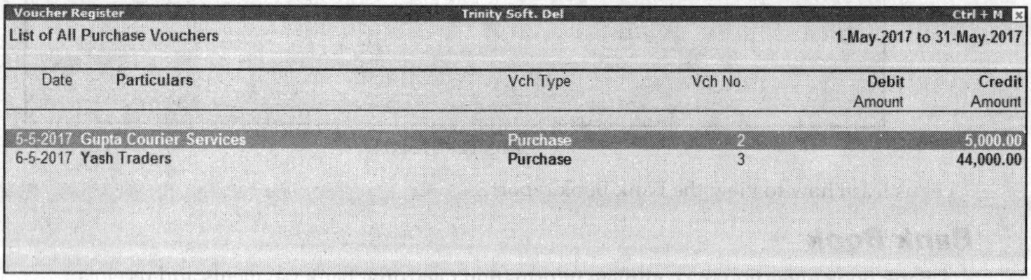

Fig.TL-11.12

Let us learn how to view the Sales Register report.

Sales Register

A Sales Register gives you complete information on sales turnover achieved for a specified period.

Perform the following steps to view a Sales Register report:

1. *Double-click* the **Display** option in the **Reports** section on the **Gateway of Tally** menu. The **Display Menu** menu appears.
2. *Double-click* the **Accounts Books** option on the **Display Menu** menu. The **Accounts Books** menu appears.
3. *Double-click* the **Sales Register** option on the **Accounts Books** menu.

   The **Sales Register** screen appears.

4. *Select* the month for which you require the Sales Register.

   The **Voucher Register** screen appears displaying all Sales Registers, as shown in Fig.TL-11.13:

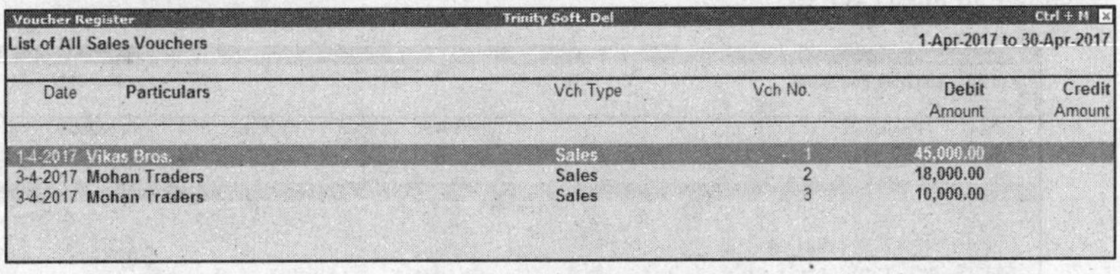

Fig.TL-11.13

Let us now learn how to view Debit Note Register report.

Debit Note Register

A Debit Note Register report displays the entries made as a Debit Note.

Perform the following steps to view Debit Note Register report:

1. *Double-click* the **Display** option in the **Reports** section on the **Gateway of Tally** menu. The **Display Menu** menu appears.
2. *Double-click* the **Accounts Books** option on the **Display Menu** menu. The **Accounts Books** menu appears.
3. *Double-click* the **Journal Register** option on the **Accounts Books** menu. The **Journal Register** menu appears
4. *Double-click* the **Debit Note Register** option on the **Journal Register** menu.

   The **Debit Note Register** screen appears.
5. *Select* the month for which you want to display the debit note register.

   The **Voucher Register** screen appears displaying all debit note vouchers of the selected month, as shown in Fig.TL-11.14:

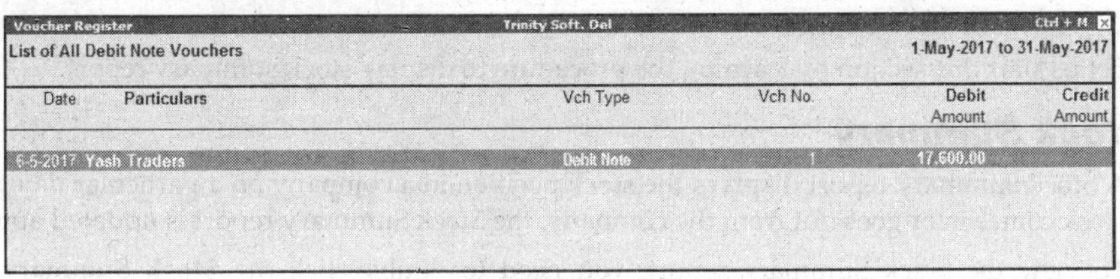

Fig.TL-11.14

Let us now learn how to view Credit Note Register report.

Credit Note Register

A Credit Note Register report displays all the entries made as a Credit Note.

Perform the following steps to view Credit Note Register report:

1. *Double-click* the **Display** option in the **Reports** section on the **Gateway of Tally** menu. The **Display Menu** menu appears.
2. *Double-click* the **Accounts Books** option on the **Display Menu** menu. The **Accounts Books** menu appears.
3. *Double-click* the **Journal Register** option on the **Accounts Books** menu. The **Journal Register** menu appears.
4. *Double-click* the **Credit Note Register** option on the **Journal Register** menu.

   The **Credit Note Register** screen appears.

5. *Select* the month for which you want to display the Credit Note Register.

   The **Voucher Register** screen appears displaying all credit note vouchers of the selected month, as shown in Fig.TL-11.15:

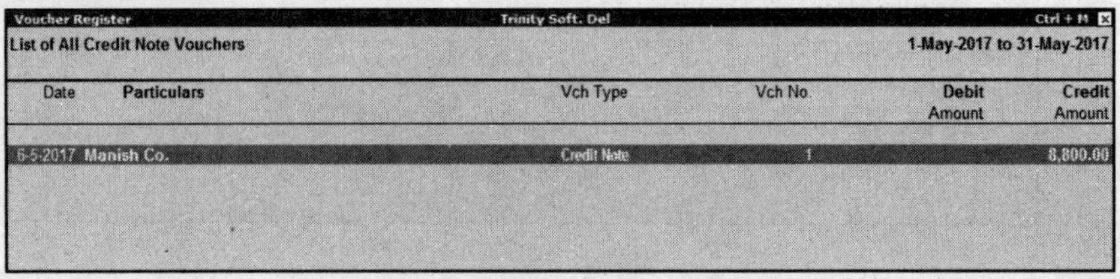

Fig.TL-11.15

After learning about displaying different types of accounting books and registers, let us now learn about displaying inventory books and registers.

Inventory Books and Registers

In Tally.ERP 9, the same process is used for displaying, modifying and printing accounting reports as well as inventory reports. The inventory reports are generated on the basis of the vouchers entered till date. In Tally.ERP 9, several inventory books and register reports can be viewed including the following:

- Stock Summary
- Stock Item Summary
- Stock Group Summary
- Sales Order Book
- Purchase Order Book
- Stock Transfer Register
- Movement Analysis Report
- Stock Ageing Analysis
- Physical Stock Register

Let us start this section by learning the procedure to display stock summary report.

Stock Summary

A Stock Summary report displays the stock position in a company on a particular date. In Tally, when the stock comes in or goes out from the company, the Stock Summary report is updated automatically.

To view the Stock Summary report, you need to double-click the **Stock Summary** option under the **Reports** section on the **Gateway of Tally** menu. The **Stock Summary** screen appears and displays the stock summary of the company, as shown in Fig.TL-11.16:

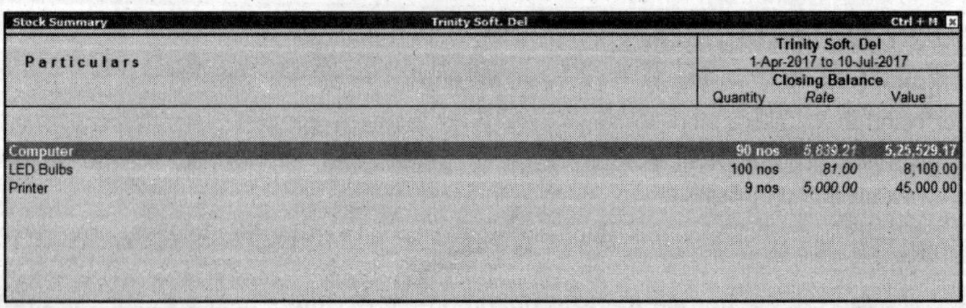

Fig.TL-11.16

If you want a detailed view of the Stock Summary, click the **F1: Detailed** button on the Button Bar. The detailed view of the stocks of the company is displayed.

Let us now learn about Stock Item Summary.

Stock Item Summary

A Stock Item Summary report shows stock summary of the selected items.

Perform the following steps to view Stock Item Summary:

1. *Double-click* the **Display** option in the **Reports** section on the **Gateway of Tally** menu. The **Display Menu** menu appears.
2. *Double-click* the **Inventory Books** option on the **Display Menu** menu. The **Inventory Books** menu appears.
3. *Double-click* the **Stock Item** option on the **Inventory Books** menu.
   The **Select Item** screen with the **List of Stock Items** menu appears (Fig.TL-11.17).
4. *Double-click* the desired stock item from the **List of Stock Items** menu, as shown in Fig.TL-11.17:

List of Stock Items
15 Inches Monitor
17 Inches Monitor
19 Inches Monitor
21 Inches Monitor
Casual Shoes
LED Bulbs
Printer
Samsung Mobiles
Sport Shoes

Fig.TL-11.17

The **Stock Item Monthly Summary** screen appears displaying summary for the selected item, as shown in Fig.TL-11.18:

Stock Item Monthly Summary — Trinity Soft. Del — Ctrl + M

15 Inches Monitor
Trinity Soft. Del
1-Apr-2017 to 10-Jul-2017

Particulars	Inwards		Outwards		Closing Balance	
	Quantity	Value	Quantity	Value	Quantity	Value
Opening Balance					50 nos	2,10,000.00
April					50 nos	2,10,000.00
May	10 nos	42,000.00	13 nos	55,200.00	47 nos	1,97,400.00
June					47 nos	1,97,400.00
July					47 nos	1,97,400.00
August						1,97,400.00
September						1,97,400.00
October						1,97,400.00
November						1,97,400.00
December						1,97,400.00
January						1,97,400.00
February						1,97,400.00
						1 more ...
Grand Total	10 nos	42,000.00	13 nos	55,200.00	47 nos	1,97,400.00

Fig.TL-11.18

Let us now learn how to view Stock Group Summary.

Stock Group Summary

A Stock Group Summary report displays stock summary report of a group.

Perform the following steps to view Stock Group Summary:

1. *Double-click* the **Display** option in the **Reports** section on the **Gateway of Tally** menu. The **Display Menu** menu appears.
2. *Double-click* the **Inventory Books** option on the **Display Menu** menu. The **Inventory Books** menu appears.
3. *Double-click* the **Group Summary** option on the **Inventory Books** menu.
   The **Select Item** screen with the **List of Stock Groups** menu appears.
4. *Double-click* the desired stock item from the **List of Stock Groups** menu.

The **Stock Summary** screen appears displaying summary for the selected group, as shown in Fig.TL-11.19:

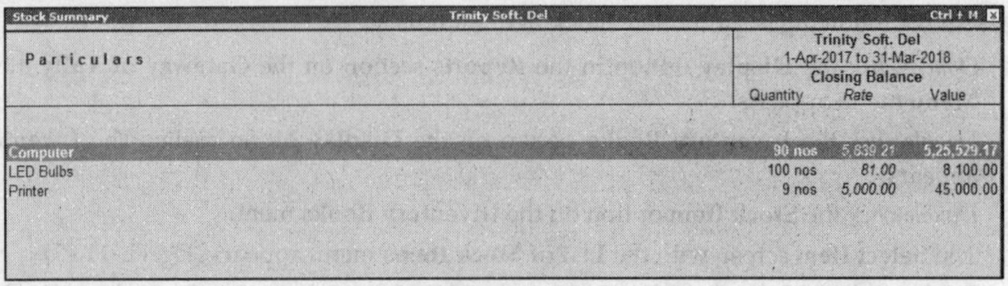

Fig.TL-11.19

Let us now learn how to view Sales Orders Book.

Sales Order Book

A Sales Order Book displays a list of all sales orders where a sales order is made when a buyer places an order for purchasing goods.

Perform the following steps to view the Sales Order Book:

1. *Double-click* the **Display** option in the **Reports** section on the **Gateway of Tally** menu. The **Display Menu** menu appears.
2. *Double-click* the **Inventory Books** option on the **Display Menu** menu. The **Inventory Books** menu appears.
3. *Double-click* the **Sales Orders Book** option on the **Inventory Books** menu.

   The **Sales Orders Book** screen appears.
4. *Select* the desired month whose Sales Order Book you want to view.

   The **Voucher Register** screen appears with the list of all sales order vouchers, as shown in Fig.TL-11.20:

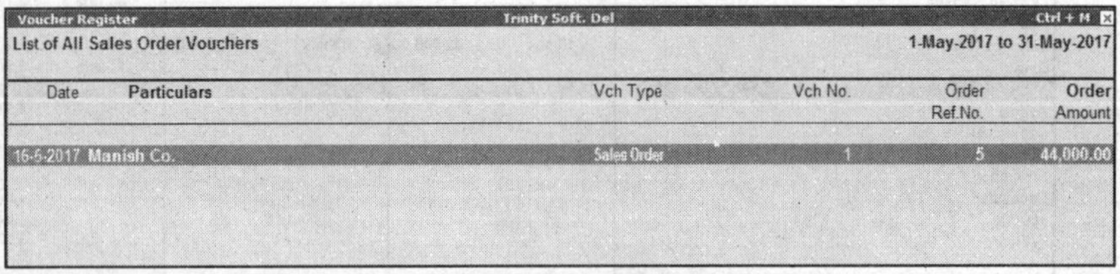

Fig.TL-11.20

Let us now learn how to view Purchase Order Book.

Purchase Order Book

A Purchase Order Book shows the list of all purchase orders where a purchase order is made when there is a request for material.

Perform the following steps to view the Purchase Order Book:

1. *Double-click* the **Display** option in the **Reports** section on the **Gateway of Tally** menu. The **Display Menu** menu appears.
2. *Double-click* the **Inventory Books** option on the **Display Menu** menu. The **Inventory Books** menu appears.
3. *Double-click* the **Purchase Orders Book** option on the **Inventory Books** menu.

   The **Purchase Orders Book** screen appears.
4. *Select* the desired month whose Purchase Order Book you want to view.

The **Voucher Register** screen appears with the list of all purchase order vouchers, as shown in Fig.TL-11.21:

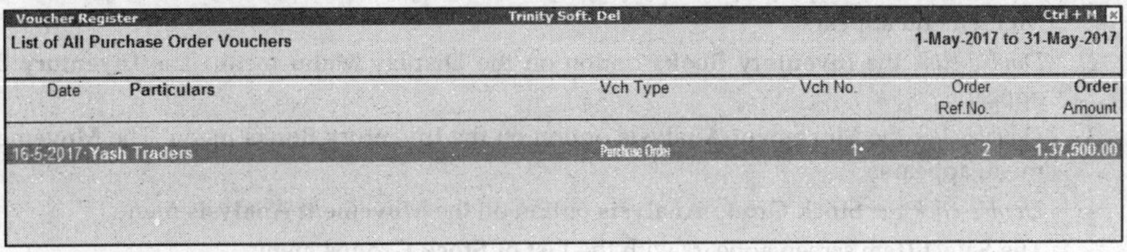

Fig.TL-11.21

Let us learn how to view the Stock Transfers Register.

Stock Transfers Register

A Stock Transfers Register displays all Stock Journal Vouchers that are used for stock adjustments due to shortage or wastage of stock, recording inter-godown transfers of stock, etc.

Perform the following steps to view stock transfers register:

1. *Double-click* the **Display** option in the **Reports** section on the **Gateway of Tally** menu. The **Display Menu** menu appears.
2. *Double-click* the **Inventory Books** option on the **Display Menu** menu. The **Inventory Books** menu appears.
3. *Double-click* the **STock Transfers** option on the **Inventory Books** menu. The **Stock Journal Register** screen appears.
4. *Select* the month for which you want to display Stock Journal Vouchers. The **Voucher Register** screen appears with the list of all Stock Journal Vouchers of the selected month, as shown in Fig.TL-11.22:

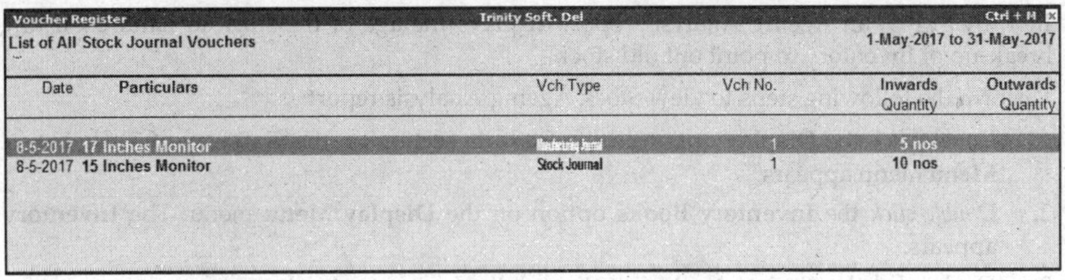

Fig.TL-11.22

Let us now learn how to view Movement Analysis report.

Movement Analysis

The analysis of the inventory transactions, which are incorporated with accounts are shown through Movement Analysis, i.e., inventories recoded in the accounts book. The stocks affected by the quantity of vouchers is not considered while preparing the analysis report.

The analysis report is mainly aimed at obtaining comparative studies. They give a deep understanding of the characteristics of the stock flow in a firm. It helps in recognition of items in the stock that affect the working capital of the firm by their slow movement.

The movement analysis can be identified on the basis of different parameters including the following:

- Stock Group
- Category
- Stock Item
- Group
- Ledger
- Transfer

Let us perform the following steps to identify Movement Analysis on the basis of the stock group:

1. *Double-click* the **Display** option in the **Reports** section on the **Gateway of Tally** menu. The **Display Menu** menu appears.
2. *Double-click* the **Inventory Books** option on the **Display Menu** menu. The **Inventory Books** menu appears.
3. *Double-click* the **Movement Analysis** option on the **Inventory Books** menu. The **Movement Analysis** menu appears.
4. *Double-click* the **Stock Group Analysis** option on the **Movement Analysis** menu.
   The **Select Item** screen appears with the **List of Stock Groups** menu.
5. *Select* the desired stock group from the **List of Stock Groups** menu. The **Movement Analysis** screen appears, as shown in Fig.TL-11.23:

Movement Analysis — Trinity Soft. Del — Ctrl + M

Particulars	Trinity Soft. Del 1-Apr-2017 to 31-Mar-2018					
	Inward			Outward		
	Quantity	*Eff. Rate*	Value	Quantity	*Eff. Rate*	Value
Computer	33 nos	*6,065.91*	2,00,175.00	53 nos	*6,912.26*	3,66,350.00
LED Bulbs	500 nos	*81.00*	40,500.00	400 nos	*95.00*	38,000.00

Fig.TL-11.23

Let us now learn how to view Stock Ageing Analysis report.

Stock Ageing Analysis

In Tally.ERP 9, an Ageing Analysis report displays the age of the stock in hand by listing the age-wise break-up of Inventory to point out old stock.

Perform the following steps to view Stock Ageing Analysis report:

1. *Double-click* the **Display** option in the **Reports** section on the **Gateway of Tally** menu. The **Display Menu** menu appears.
2. *Double-click* the **Inventory Books** option on the **Display Menu** menu. The **Inventory Books** menu appears.
3. *Double-click* the **Ageing Analysis** option on the **Inventory Books** menu.
   The **Select Item** screen appears with the **List of Stock Groups** menu.
4. *Select* the desired stock group from the **List of Stock Groups** menu. The **Stock Ageing Analysis** screen appears, as shown in Fig.TL-11.24:

Stock Ageing Analysis — Trinity Soft. Del — Ctrl + M

Items Under : **Primary** — **as at 10-Jul-2017**

All Batches (Aged by Date of Purchase) — *Valued based on actual purchase*

Particulars	Expiry Date	Total	(< 45 days)		45 to 90 days		90 to 180 days	
		Quantity	Quantity	Value	Quantity	Value	Quantity	Value
								2 more ... →
15 Inches Monitor		47 nos			10 nos	42,000.00	37 nos	1,55,400.00
17 Inches Monitor		25 nos					25 nos	1,37,500.00
19 Inches Monitor		10 nos			10 nos	60,000.00	10 nos	60,000.00
21 Inches Monitor		8 nos			8 nos	70,400.00		
LED Bulbs		100 nos	100 nos	8,100.00				
Printer		9 nos					9 nos	45,000.00

Fig.TL-11.24

Let us now learn how to view Physical Stock Register.

Physical Stock Register

A Physical Stock Register reports shows the physical stock vouchers that are used for recording the actual stock of a stock item. The actual balance of stock in hand as on the date of voucher entry is displayed in the inventory books while the differences in stocks are added as inward or outward.

Perform the following steps to view Physical Stock Register:

1. *Double-click* the **Display** option in the **Reports** section on the **Gateway of Tally** menu. The **Display Menu** menu appears.
2. *Double-click* the **Inventory Books** option on the **Display Menu** menu. The **Inventory Books** menu appears.
3. *Double-click* the **Physical Stock Register** option on the **Inventory Books** menu. The **Physical Stock Register** screen appears displaying the number of physical stock vouchers month-wise.
4. *Select* the desired month for which you want to view physical stock vouchers. The **Voucher Register** screen appears displaying a list of all physical stock vouchers, as shown in Fig.TL-11.25:

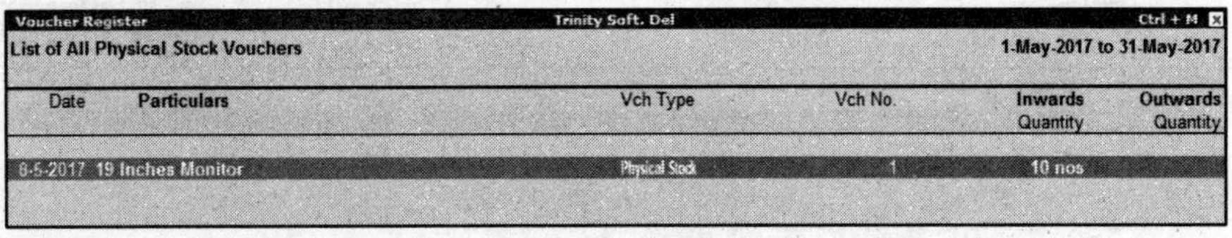

Fig.TL-11.25

Let us now learn about the statements of accounts reports.

Statements of Accounts

Statements of Accounts reports are those reports that display the accounts or transactions recorded in the books of accounts. In Tally.ERP 9, they are generated for cost centres and outstanding accounts. An outstanding report shows you the receivable and payable of a business. Both receivable and payable need to be controlled effectively for financial reliability of a business. Two commonly used outstanding reports are Receivable and Payable.

Bills Receivable

Bills Receivable are those bills whose payment is expected to be received on a later date. The receivable report displays all the outstanding receivable bills for a particular period.

You can view a Bills Receivable report by performing the following steps:

1. *Double-click* the **Display** option in the **Reports** section on the **Gateway of Tally** menu. The **Display Menu** menu appears.
2. *Double-click* the **Statements of Accounts** option on the **Display Menu** menu. The **Statements of Accounts** menu appears.
3. *Double-click* the **Outstandings** option on the **Statements of Accounts** menu. The **Outstandings** menu appears.
4. *Double-click* the **Receivables** option on the **Outstandings** menu. The **Bills Outstanding** screen with **Bills Receivable** appears, as shown in Fig.TL-11.26:

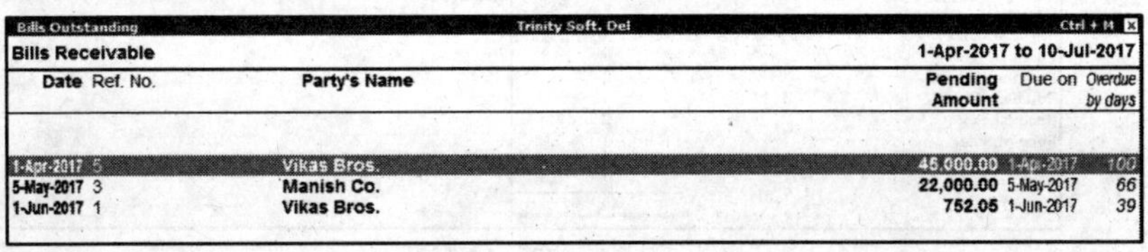

Fig.TL-11.26

Let us now learn how to view Bills Payable report.

Bills Payable

They are those bills whose due payment is to be paid on a future date. The payable report displays all the outstanding payable bills for a particular period.

You can view a Bills Payable report by performing the following steps:

1. *Double-click* the **Display** option in the **Reports** section on the **Gateway of Tally** menu. The **Display Menu** menu appears.
2. *Double-click* the **Statements of Accounts** option on the **Display Menu** menu. The **Statements of Accounts** menu appears.
3. *Double-click* the **Outstandings** option on the **Statements of Accounts** menu. The **Outstandings** menu appears.
4. *Double-click* the **Payables** option on the **Outstandings** menu.

The **Bills Outstanding** screen with **Bills Payable** appears, as shown in Fig.TL-11.27:

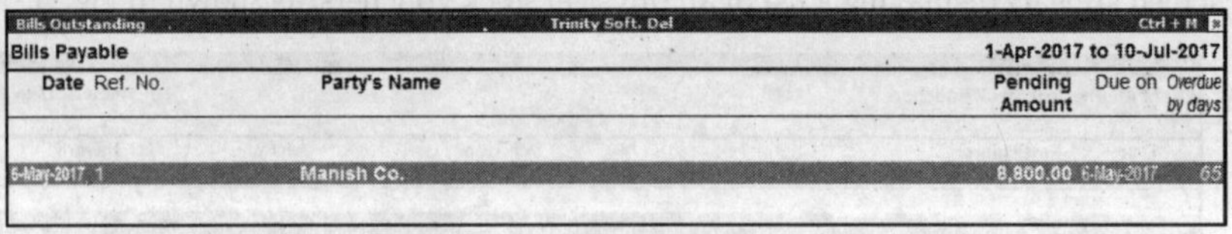

Fig.TL-11.27

Let us learn how to view Statistics report.

Statistics

The Statistics report shows the information about the types of accounts you created and types of vouchers you used for recording transactions.

Perform the following steps to view statistics report:

1. *Double-click* the **Display** option under the **Reports** section on the **Gateway of Tally** menu. The **Display Menu** menu appears.
2. *Double-click* the **Statements of Accounts** option in the **Display Menu** menu. The **Statements of Accounts** menu appears.
3. *Double-click* the **Statistics** option in the **Statements of Accounts** menu. The **Statistics** screen appears, as shown in Fig.TL-11.28:

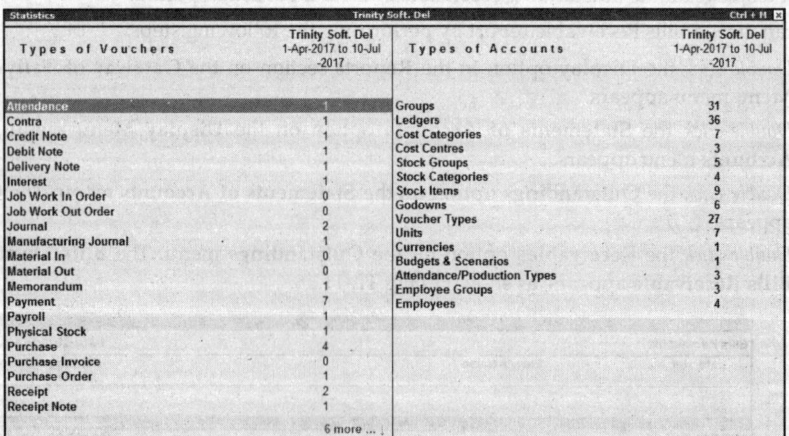

Fig.TL-11.28

Let us now learn about Statements of Inventory reports.

Statements of Inventory

Similar to accounting statements, inventory reports in Tally.ERP 9 are displayed, modified and printed. Inventory reports can be generated in Tally.ERP 9 on the basis of the inventory vouchers entered till date.

Let us learn how to view Godown Summary report.

Godown Summary

The Godown Summary report is used for displaying the stock summary at different godowns.

Perform the following steps to view Godown Summary report:

1. *Double-click* the **Display** option under the **Reports** section on the **Gateway of Tally** menu. The **Display Menu** menu appears.
2. *Double-click* the **StatEments of Inventory** option in the **Display Menu** menu. The **Statements of Inventory** menu appears.
3. *Double-click* the **Godowns** option in the **Statements of Inventory** menu.
   The **Select Item** screen appears with the **List of Godowns** menu.
4. *Double-click* the desired godown from the **List of Godowns** menu.
   The **Godown Summary** screen appears, as shown in Fig.TL-11.29:

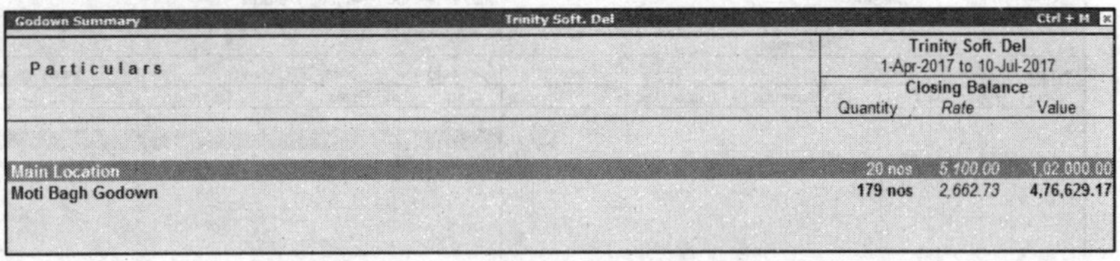

Fig.TL-11.29

Let us learn how to view Stock Categories Summary report.

Stock Category Summary

The Stock Category Summary report displays the closing balances of all stock items related to the selected stock category.

Perform the following steps to view Stock Category Summary report:

1. *Double-click* the **Display** option under the **Reports** section on the **Gateway of Tally** menu. The **Display Menu** menu appears.
2. *Double-click* the **StatEments of Inventory** option in the **Display Menu** menu. The **Statements of Inventory** menu appears.
3. *Double-click* the **Categories** option in the **Statements of Inventory** menu.
   The **Select Item** screen appears with the **List of Stock Categories** menu.
4. *Double-click* the desired item from the **List of Stock Categories** menu.
   The **Stock Category Summary** screen appears, as shown in Fig.TL-11.30:

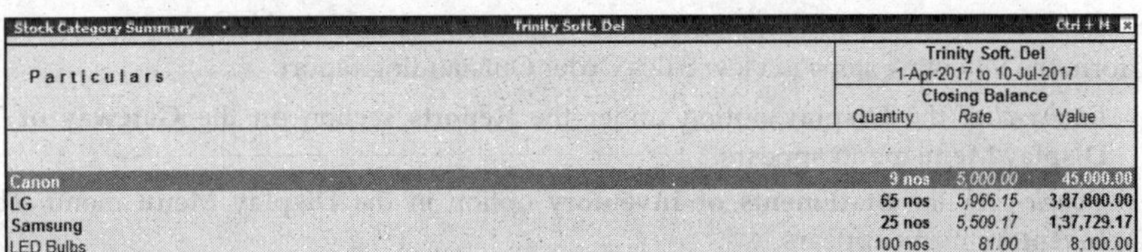

Fig.TL-11.30

Let us learn how to view Stock Query report.

Stock Query

In Tally.ERP9, the Stock Query report displays complete information about a specific stock item including Part No., Stock Group, Stock Category, available Closing Balance and Value, Cost Price, Standard Selling Price, Costing Method, Market Valuation Method, and so on.

Perform the following steps to view the stock query report:

1. *Double-click* the **Display** option under the **Reports** section on the **Gateway of Tally** menu. The **Display Menu** menu appears.
2. *Double-click* the **StatEments of Inventory** option in the **Display Menu** menu. The **Statements of Inventory** menu appears.
3. *Double-click* the **STock Query** option in the **Statements of Inventory** menu.

   The **Select Item** screen appears with the **List of Stock Items** menu.
4. *Double-click* the desired item from the **List of Stock Items** menu.

   The **Stock Query** screen appears, as shown in Fig.TL-11.31:

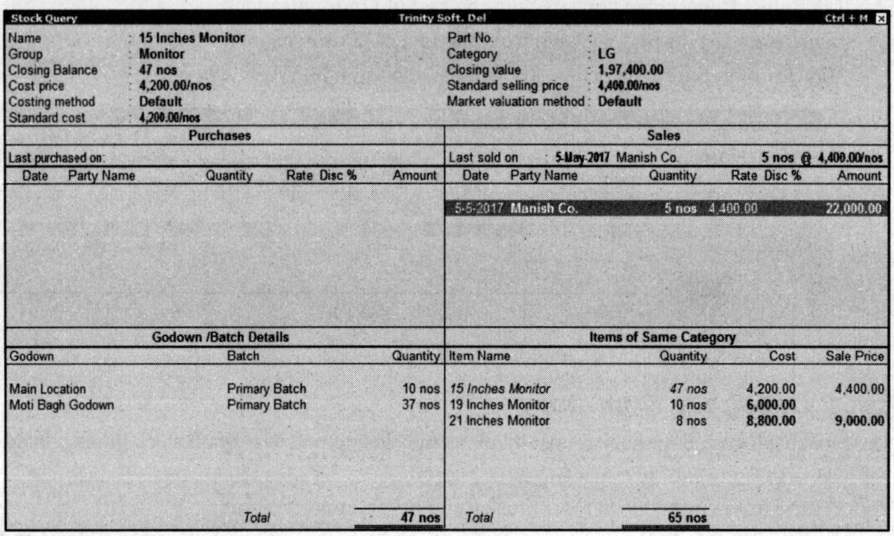

Fig.TL-11.31

Let us learn how to view Sales Order Outstanding report.

Sales Order Outstanding

Sales Order summary statement provides complete information related to the outstanding sales orders. The outstanding orders can be viewed according to the following:

- Stock Groupwise
- Stock Categorywise
- Stock Itemwise
- Groupwise
- Ledgerwise
- All Orders

Perform the following steps to view Sales Order Outstanding report:

1. *Double-click* the **Display** option under the **Reports** section on the **Gateway of Tally** menu. The **Display Menu** menu appears.
2. *Double-click* the **StatEments of Inventory** option in the **Display Menu** menu. The **Statements of Inventory** menu appears.
3. *Double-click* the **SAles Order Outstandings** option in the **Statements of Inventory** menu. The **Sales Order** menu appears.
4. *Double-click* the **All Orders** option in the **Sales Order** menu to view all orders.

The **Order Details** screen with **Sales Orders** appears, as shown in Fig.TL-11.32:

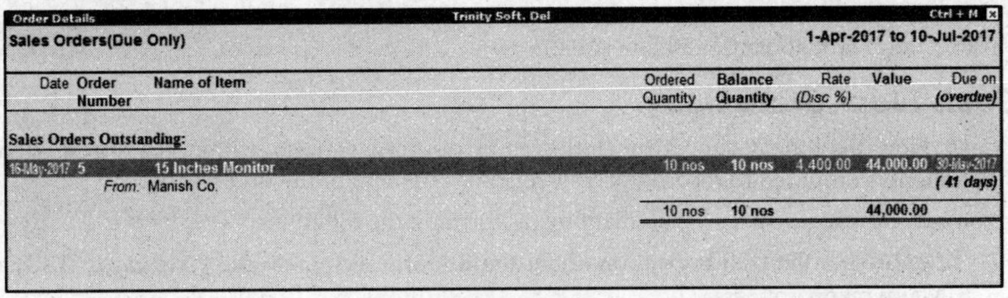

Fig.TL-11.32

Let us learn how to view Purchase Order Outstanding report.

Purchase Order Outstanding

Purchase Order Outstanding statement provides complete information related to the outstanding purchase orders. The outstanding orders can be viewed according to the following:

- Stock Groupwise
- Stock Categorywise
- Stock Itemwise
- Groupwise
- Ledgerwise
- All Orders

Perform the following steps to view Sales Order Outstanding report:

1. *Double-click* the **Display** option under the **Reports** section on the **Gateway of Tally** menu. The **Display Menu** menu appears.
2. *Double-click* the **StatEments of Inventory** option in the **Display Menu** menu. The **Statements of Inventory** menu appears.
3. *Double-click* the **Purchase Order Outstandings** option in the **Statements of Inventory** menu. The **Purchase Order** menu appears.
4. *Double-click* the **All Orders** option in the **Purchase Order** menu to view all orders.

   The **Order Details** screen with **Purchase Orders** appears, as shown in Fig.TL-11.33:

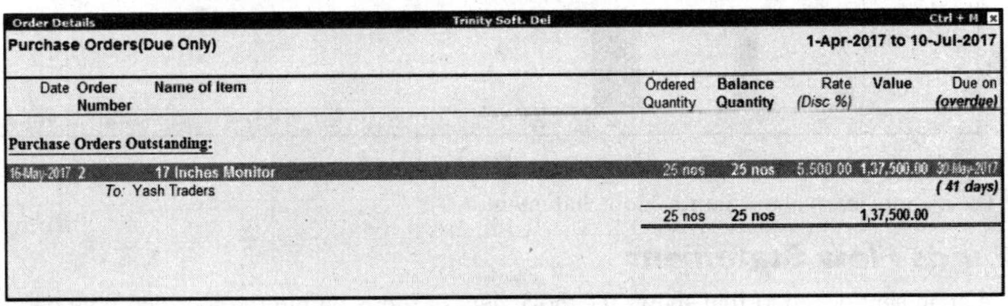

Fig.TL-11.33

Let us now learn about MIS reports.

Management Information System (MIS) Reports

MIS Reports are the reports that are used to assess the performance of the organization. These reports also allows the decision maker of organization to take decision quickly and correctly. Some of the commonly used MIS reports are as follows:

- Cash Flow statement

- Funds Flow Statement
- Ratio Analysis

Let us now learn about Cash Flow Statement.

Cash Flow Statement

Cash Flow Statement shows the inflow and outflow of cash within the specified time period. This statement is prepared to record the cash-related statement of the organization.

You can view the cash flow statement by performing the following steps:

1. *Double-click* the **Display** option under the **Reports** section on the **Gateway of Tally** menu. A **Display Menu** menu appears.
2. *Double-click* the **Cash/Funds Flow** option on the **Display Menu** menu.
   The **Cash/Funds Flow** menu appears.
3. *Double-click* the **Cash Flow** option on the **Cash/Funds Flow** menu.
   The **Cash Flow** screen appears, as shown in Fig.TL-11.34:

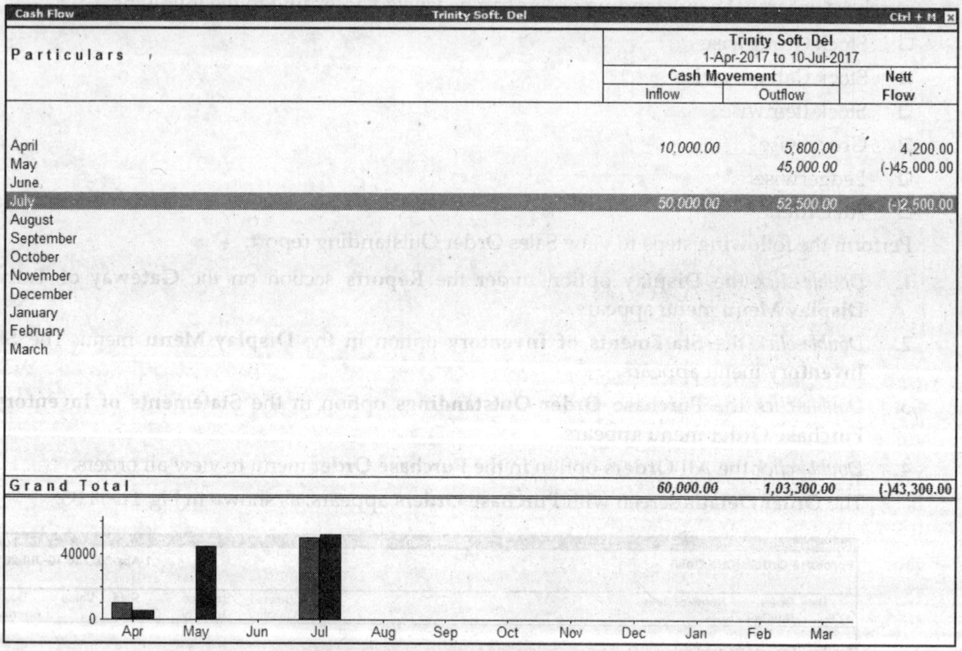

Fig.TL-11.34

Let us now learn about Funds Flow Statement.

Funds Flow Statement

A statement or report that shows the movement of funds within the specified time period is called Funds Flow Statement.

You can view the Funds Flow Statement by performing the following steps:

1. *Double-click* the **Display** option under the **Reports** section on the **Gateway of Tally** menu. A **Display Menu** menu appears.
2. *Double-click* the **Cash/Funds Flow** option on the **Display Menu** menu. The **Cash/Funds Flow** menu appears.
3. *Double-click* the **Funds Flow** option on the **Cash/Funds Flow** menu.

The **Funds Flow** screen appears, as shown in Fig.TL-11.35:

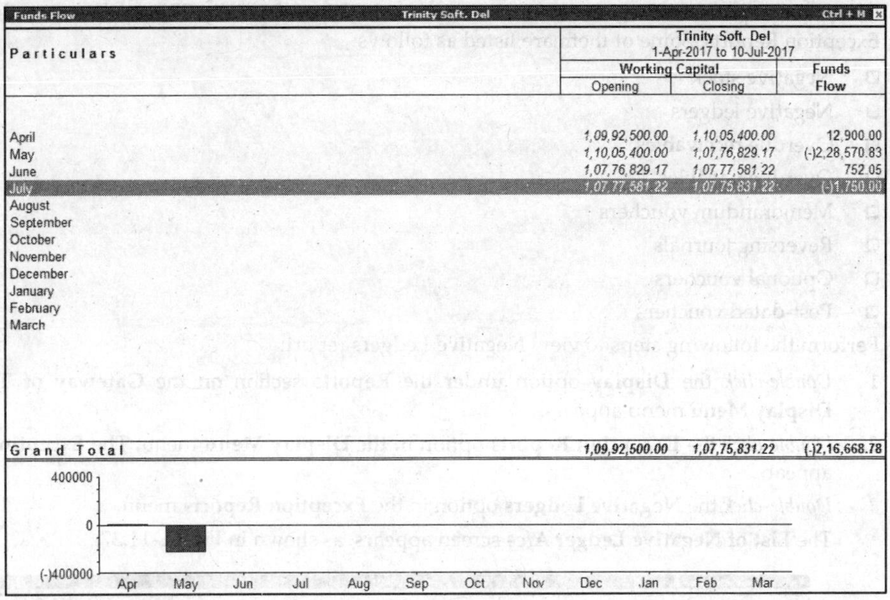

Fig.TL-11.35

Let us now learn about Ratio Analysis report.

Ratio Analysis

Ratio Analysis reports are very useful as they allow individuals to instantly assess a company or an industry by making two basic comparisons. The top management (the analyst) can compare the present and past ratios of an organization to determine if there has been an improvement in the performance of the organization over a certain period of time. Also, the ratio of one organization may be compared with similar organizations or with the industry average at the same point in time to determine how the organization is faring: whether it is average in performance or doing better or worse than others.

In Tally, you can view a Ratio Analysis report by double-clicking the **Ratio Analysis** option under the **Reports** section on the **Gateway of Tally** menu.

The **Ratio Analysis** screen appears with the needed report to view, as shown in Fig.TL-11.36:

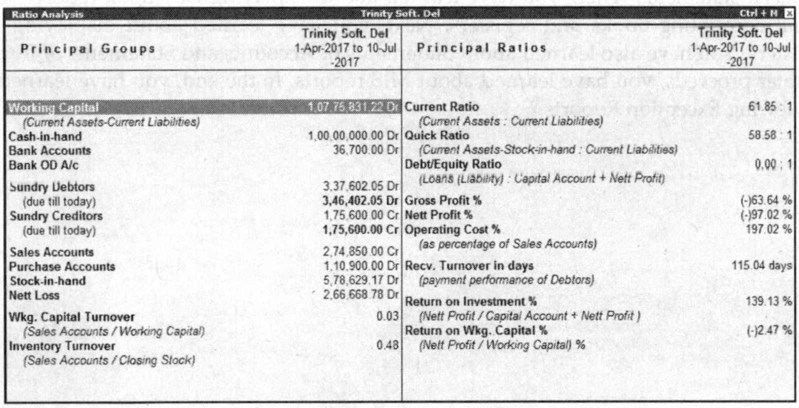

Fig.TL-11.36

Let us now learn about Exception Reports.

Exception Reports

Exception Reports track unusual transactions or balances. In Tally.ERP 9, there are different types of Exception Reports. Some of them are listed as follows:

- Negative stock
- Negative ledgers
- Overdue receivables
- Overdue payables
- Memorandum vouchers
- Reversing journals
- Optional vouchers
- Post-dated vouchers

Perform the following steps to view Negative Ledgers report:

1. *Double-click* the **Display** option under the **Reports** section on the **Gateway of Tally** menu. The **Display Menu** menu appears.
2. *Double-click* the **EXception Reports** option in the **Display Menu** menu. The **Exception Reports** menu appears.
3. *Double-click* the **Negative Ledgers** option in the **Exception Reports** menu.

   The **List of Negative Ledger A/cs** screen appears, as shown in Fig.TL-11.37:

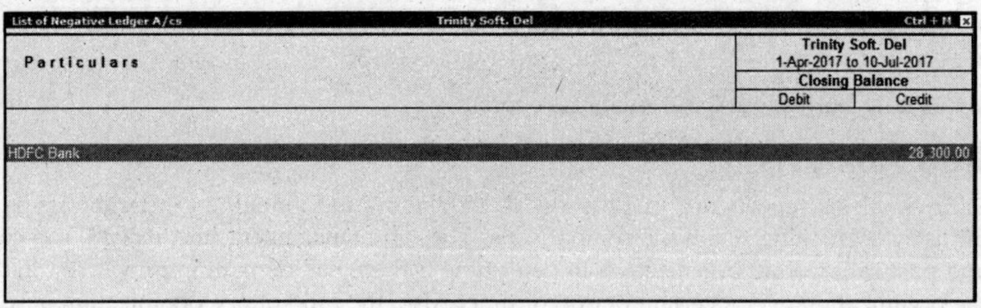

Fig.TL-11.37

With this, we come to the end of the chapter. Let us summarize the key points discussed in the chapter.

Summary

In this chapter, you have learned about displaying different types of reports. You have learned about financial statements. Then, you have learned about displaying Day Book reports. You have also learned about accounting books and registers. Next, you have learned about displaying inventory books and registers. You have also learned about Statements of Accounts and Statements of Inventory reports. As the chapter proceeds, you have learned about MIS reports. In the end, you have learned about the procedure of viewing Exception Reports.

CHAPTER

12

Introducing Tax Return Preparer (TRP)

In this Chapter:

- Understanding Tax Return Preparer (TRP)
- TRP Scheme
- Pre-requisites of a TRP
- TRP Examination and Training
- Duties of a TRP
- Incentives of a TRP
- Resource Center
- Important Points for a TRP

Introduction

The accommodations for determining the taxable income, tax liability, assessment procedure, penalties, appeals and prosecutions are provided under Income Tax Act. The powers and duties assigned to various income Tax authorities are also presented in the Income Tax act.

It is not a simple task to file income tax return (ITR). The tax return preparer (TRP) was initiated by the income tax department in the financial year 2006-2007, for reducing complications for tax assesses. The appointment of TRPs was aimed at the assistance of tax assesses in putting things together for filing of returns correctly.

The chapter begins by learning about the tax return preparer. In this chapter, you learn about the TRP scheme. You also learn about the pre-requisites to become a TRP. Next, you learn about the examination and training of TRP. After this, you learn about the duties and incentives of a TRP. Further, the chapter describes the resource center. Towards the end of the chapter, you learn about the important points that must be kept in mind by the TRPs while filing the tax returns.

Understanding Tax Return Preparer (TRP)

A TRP is a professional who is certified and trained by Income Tax department for the assistance of tax assesses in filing ITR by paying them a visit at home. The launch of TRP scheme was aimed at helping small and marginal tax payers.

The Internal Revenue Code (IRC) states that a TRP is responsible for preparing compensation, employing people for compensation, all or a part of tax return or claims for tax refund.

TRPs can be classified into two types as follows:

- **Signing tax return preparer:** A TRP whose main responsibility is to ensure the accuracy in the preparation of ITR or refund claim.
- **Non-signing tax return preparer:** Any TRP whose responsibility is to prepare the entire or a portion of ITR or refund claim.

To know about the TRPs near your area, you need to visit www.trpscheme.com. To locate TRPs, click the **Locate TRPs** link and select your state, city, and PIN code. A list of TRPs along with their identity and contact details will appear, registered near your locality.

TRP Scheme

The TRP scheme has been outlined and designed by the Government of India for the aid of the small and medium taxpayers in formulating their ITR and addressing their income tax related issues. The professionals dealing in income tax filing were authorized under this scheme. The income tax department acts as the manager of this scheme.

This scheme was launched in the financial year 2006-2007 to employ many unemployed trained graduates and partially employed graduates of disciplines such as Economics, Commerce, Mathematics, Law, Statistics, and Management/Business Administration.

The purpose of the TRP scheme is the reduction in cost of adherence for taxpayers and in encouraging them to adhere to the income tax laws. The intent of this scheme also aims at creating awareness about income tax laws among the small and marginal taxpayers, encouraging the participation of the community for improving awareness and increasing adherence. Additionally, this scheme has provided a window of opportunity to many graduates who were unemployed to help the taxpayers in preparation and filing of returns.

Pre-requisites of a TRP

The eligibility criteria to apply for TRP is as follows:

1. The age limit for the candidates applying for TRP is 21 to 35 years.
2. The candidate must possess a Bachelor degree of a recognized university in any of these subjects:
    - Law
    - Economics

- Statistics
- Mathematics
- Commerce
- Business Administration and Management

TRP Examination and Training

The examination for TRPs is conducted on a periodical basis. A candidates who will undergo the training and pass the examination will only be authorized to practice as a TRP.

NIIT will impart training to the candidates. NIIT is a recognized organization in over 42 countries in the world for its innovation in online and classroom training.

A standardized training will be delivered across 120 centers in the country by NIIT, in terms of instructors, course content and infrastructure facilities. There is a tie-up between NIIT and Taxmann (an innovator in tax education field) to develop course material and CDs for candidates enrolled in TRP training.

The skills and command of TRPs will be upgraded regularly through a web portal by NIIT, post the TRP certification.

Duties of a TRP

A TRP needs to perform the duties, mentioned as follows:

- The returns must be prepared diligently.
- His signature must be attached along with the return prepared.
- The returns must be furnished with jurisdiction of the over the concerned assese or to an officer or agency with the prior board's approval as and only directed by the Resource Centre.
- A copy of the prepared return must be given to the person whose ITR is filed.
- A copy of the acknowledgment slip must be retained from the person whose ITR is prepared.
- A monthly record of the ITRs prepared and furnished by him must be maintained which contains the following information:
  - Name of the assesses
  - PAN(Permanent Account Number) of the assesses
  - Year of the assessment
  - Date on which the ITR was furnished
  - Acknowledgment number
  - Assessing Officer's jurisdiction
  - The income amount declared in the ITR
  - The amount that is taxable
  - The amount of tax paid
  - Any amount that is disbursable to him
  - The amount of fee charged and received by him
- For every month, a statement must be furnished mentioning the particulars to the Resource Centre on or before the seventh day of the month that follows.

Incentives of a TRP

A TRP is given incentives by the Government for every ITR that he files. For example, if a tax assesse is filing the ITR for the first time, the TRP gets 3% of the income tax paid to the government. The TRP gets 2% and 3% of the tax paid as incentives, for the next two subsequent years. However, the assese will have to pay the difference amount to the TRP, if the incentive that is calculated is less than ₹250 in any particular year.

Suppose, you are filing ITR fir the first time with a TRP's help, and the tax liability is ₹15,000, then the incentive of the TRP will be ₹450 (3% of ₹15,000). You won't have to pay TRP because the amount of the incentive is ₹450. But, if the tax liability is ₹6,000, then the incentive of TRP will be ₹180 (3% of ₹6,000). You will have to pay the difference amount of ₹70 (₹250 – ₹180) in this case. If there is no tax liability for the assesse, then he will have to pay the complete amount ₹250 to the TRP. A TRP can earn a maximum of ₹1,000 per ITR.

Resource Center

The day-to-day activities of the TRP scheme are administered by the resource center. The main functions of the resource center are:

- The following things should be specified, with prior approval of the Board:
  - The number of persons that should be enrolled for TRP training in a financial year.
  - The number of training centers along with their location during a financial year.
  - The number of persons who will be trained at each center during a financial year.
- To decide the curriculum and other matters related to the TRP training.
- To maintain a record of the particulars of the TRPs.
- Other functions assigned by the board for scheme implementation.

Important Points for a TRP

Some important points to be taken care of by a TRP are as follows:

- Making sure to give a copy of the ITR to the assessee.
- Making sure to attach his signature along with the prepared ITR.
- Making sure to provide his name and unique identification number prepared ITR.
- Making sure to enter the information provided by the assesse correctly in the ITR.
- Making sure that the computation mistakes in the ITR are not repeated.
- Making sure that he does not make a wrong or fraudulent claim for disbursement.
- Making sure that he is not engaged in any financial irregularity, forgery or fraud.
- Making sure not attempting to understate the income in ITR.
- Making sure not to get involved in any other irregularities which are serious in nature, in Chief Commissioner's opinion.
- Making sure that to work in compliance with the issue directions by the Resource Centre.
- Making sure that he upgrades himself time to time on the terms of skill requirement by the Resource Centre.

A TRP shall be warned about this work deficiencies and misconduct either by the Resource Center itself or on prescribed authority's recommendation as per the rule 52 of the Income Tax Rules, 1962. The Resource Center may cancel the certificate of the TRP, if he fails to comply with the points mentioned above.

With this, we come to the end of this chapter. Let us summarize the key points of this chapter.

Summary

In this chapter, you have learned about the tax return preparer. Next, you have learned about the TRP scheme. You have also learned about the pre-requisites to become a TRP. Next, you have learned about the examination and training of a TRP. After this, you have learned about the duties and incentives of a TRP. Further, the chapter describes the resource center. Towards the end of the chapter, you have learned about some important points to be taken care of by the TRPs.

CHAPTER

13

Tax Deducted at Source (TDS)

In this Chapter:

* Basic Terminology of TDS
* Enabling TDS in Tally.ERP 9
* Creating Ledgers for TDS
* Creating TDS Vouchers
* TDS Reports

Introduction

Tax Deducted at Source (TDS) was introduced in the Income Tax Act, 1961. This tax is a mode of collecting income tax. TDS is deducted by the payer at the source of income at the rate specified under the Finance Act of that year. After deducting the tax, the payer needs to deposit the deducted amount in the government treasury. The payer also needs to issue a document to the person from whose income the tax is deducted. The person can keep this document as evidence and submit it to the income tax authorities for filing a return.

In this chapter, you learn about the basic terms used in TDS. You also learn about the process to enable TDS in Tally.ERP 9. Further, the chapter discusses the procedure to create masters for TDS. In addition, you learn about the procedure to create vouchers for TDS. Towards the end of the chapter, you learn about the procedure to view TDS reports in Tally.ERP 9.

Let us start the chapter by learning about the basic terms used in TDS.

Basic Terminology of TDS

The basic terms used in TDS are explained as follows:

- **Tax deduction Account Number (TAN):** It refers to a number issued by the Income Tax department to the people who deduct TDS.
- **Deductor:** A person who makes payments to the third parties that come under the TDS scope and applicability needs to deduct tax at source.
- **Deductee:** It refers to a third party that gives services to the deductor. The deductor then deducts the tax at source. There are various categories in which the deductee lies, which are as follows:
  - Artificial Judicial Person
  - Association of Persons
  - Body of Individuals
  - Company – Non-Resident
  - Company – Resident
  - Co-operative Society
  - Individual/HUF – Non-Resident
  - Individual/HUF – Resident
  - Local Authority
  - Partnership Firm

Let us now learn how to enable TDS in Tally.ERP 9.

Enabling TDS in Tally.ERP 9

To compute TDS in Tally, you first need to enable it.

Perform the following steps to enable TDS in Tally:

1. *Click* the **F11: Features** button on the Button Bar in the **Gateway of Tally** screen.

   The **Company Features** menu appears.
2. *Double-click* the **Statutory & Taxation** option in the **Company Features** menu.

   The **Company Operations Alteration** screen appears with the **Statutory & Taxation** options (Fig.TL-13.1).
3. *Set* the **Enable Tax Deducted at Source (TDS)** option to **Yes** (Fig.TL-13.1).

4. *Set* the **Set/alter TDS details** option to **Yes**, as shown in Fig.TL-13.1:

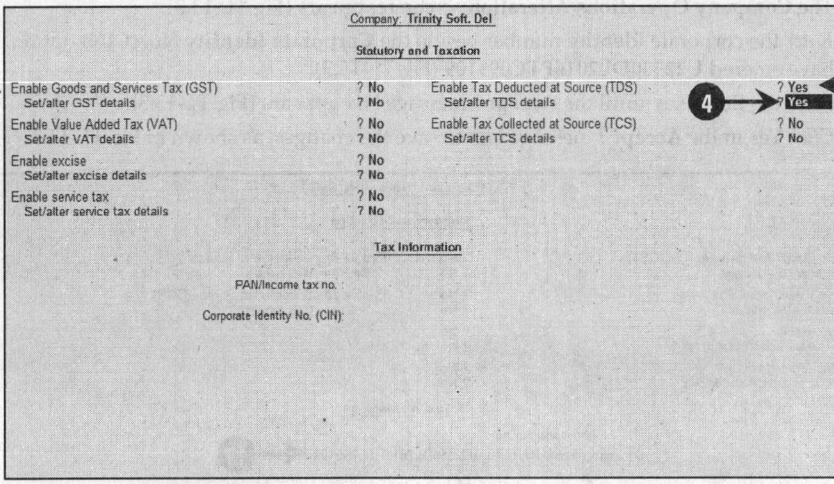

Fig.TL-13.1

5. *Press* the **Enter** key. The **TDS Deductor Details** screen appears with **Company TDS Deductor Details** options. (Fig.TL-13.2).
6. *Enter* the TAN registration number beside the **TAN registration number** option. In our case, we have entered **T20394857CYE** (Fig.TL-13.2).
7. *Press* the **Enter** key.
8. *Enter* the tax assessment number beside the **Tax deduction and collection Account Number (TAN)** option. In our case, we have entered **ATYE87562Q** (Fig.TL-13.2).
9. *Press* the **Enter** key. The **Collector/Deductor Types** menu appears.
10. *Double click* the desired deductor type from the **Collector/Deductor Types** menu for the **Deductor type** option. In our case, we have double-clicked **Company** (Fig.TL-13.2).
11. *Enter* the branch and division of deductor beside the **Deductor branch/division** option. In our case, we have entered **New Delhi** (Fig.TL-13.2).
12. *Press* the **Enter** key.
13. *Set* the **Set/alter details of person responsible** option to **No** (Fig.TL-13.2).
14. *Set* the **Ignore IT exemption limit for TDS deduction** option to **No** (Fig.TL-13.2).
15. *Set* the **Activate TDS for stock items** option to **No,** as shown in Fig.TL-13.2:

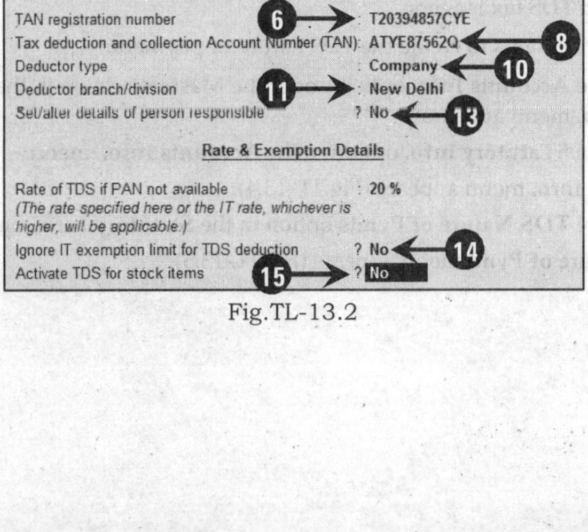

Fig.TL-13.2

16. *Press* the **Enter** key.

    The **Company Operations Alteration** screen reappears (Fig.TL-13.3).
17. *Enter* the corporate identity number beside the **Corporate Identity No. (CIN)** option. In our case, we have entered **U22550DL2016PTC099109** (Fig.TL-13.3).
18. *Press* the **Enter** key until the **Accept ?** message box appears (Fig.TL-13.3).
19. *Click* **Yes** in the **Accept ?** message box to save the changes, as shown in Fig.TL-13.3:

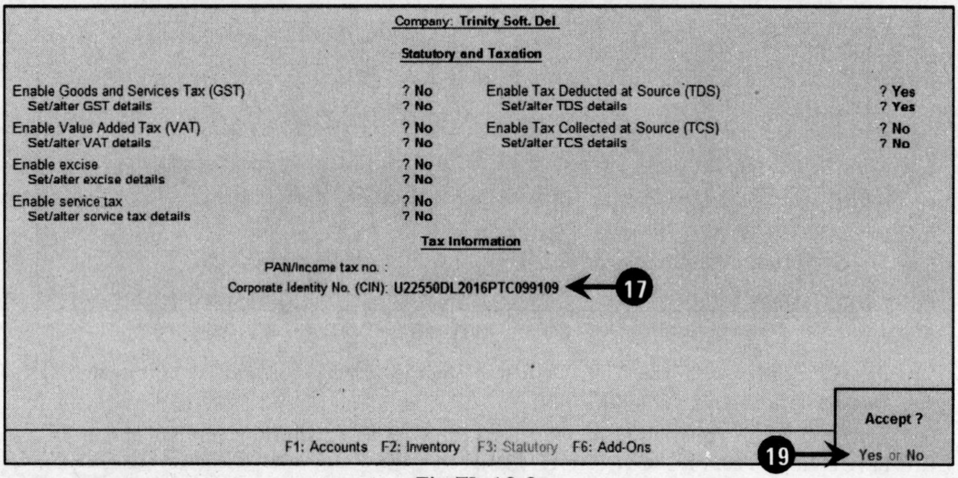

Fig.TL-13.3

Let us now learn how to create masters for TDS.

Creating Ledgers for TDS

After enabling TDS in Tally.ERP 9, you need to create the following masters:

- Creating TDS Statutory Masters
- Creating an Expense Ledger
- Creating a Party Ledger
- Creating a Tax Ledger

Let us now discuss the procedure to create these ledgers in the following sections.

Creating TDS Statutory Masters

In Tally, TDS Statutory Masters provide information about the nature of payments and deductee types. After enabling TDS in Tally, TDS statutory masters are accessible for selection at the time of creating expense, party, and TDS tax ledgers.

Perform the following steps to create the TDS nature of payment:

1. *Double-click* the **Accounts Info.** option under the **Masters** section in the **Gateway of Tally** menu. The **Accounts Info.** menu appears.
2. *Double-click* the **STatutory Info.** option in the **Accounts Info.** menu.

   The **Statutory Info.** menu appears (Fig.TL-13.4).
3. *Double-click* the **TDS Nature of Pymts** option in the **Statutory Info.** menu (Fig.TL-13.4).

   The **TDS Nature of Pymt** menu appears (Fig.TL-13.5).

4. *Double-click* the **Create** option in the **TDS Nature of Pymt** menu, as shown in Fig.TL-13.5:

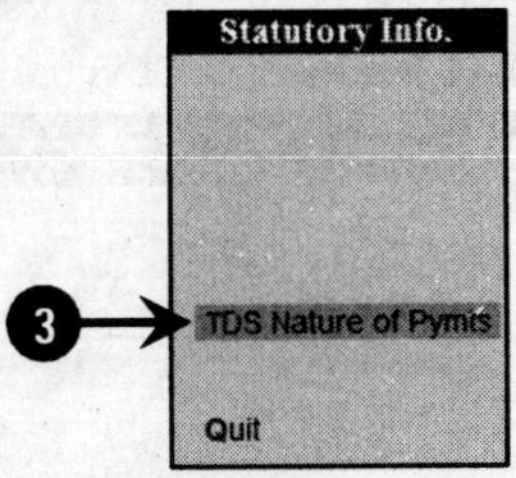

Fig.TL-13.4

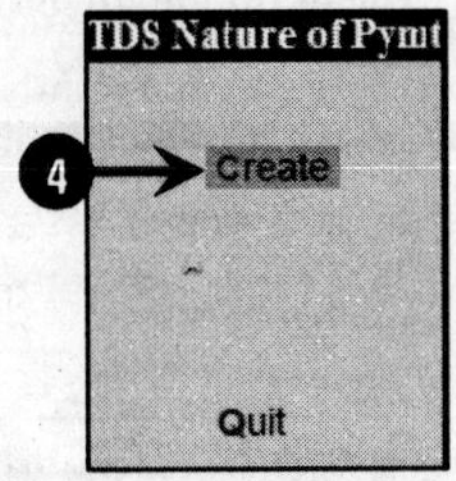

Fig.TL-13.5

The **TDS Nature of Payment Creation** screen appears (Fig.TL-13.6).

5. *Click* the **C: Helper** button on the Button Bar. The **Nature of Payment** menu appears.
6. *Double-click* the desired payment type in the **Nature of Payment** menu for the **Name** option. In our case, we have double-clicked **Commission Or Brokerage** (Fig.TL-13.6).

   The **Section** and **Payment code** options are filled automatically (Fig.TL-13.6).
7. *Press* the **Enter** key until the **Accept ?** message box appears.
8. *Click* **Yes** in the **Accept ?** message box to create the TDS nature of payments, as shown in Fig.TL-13.6:

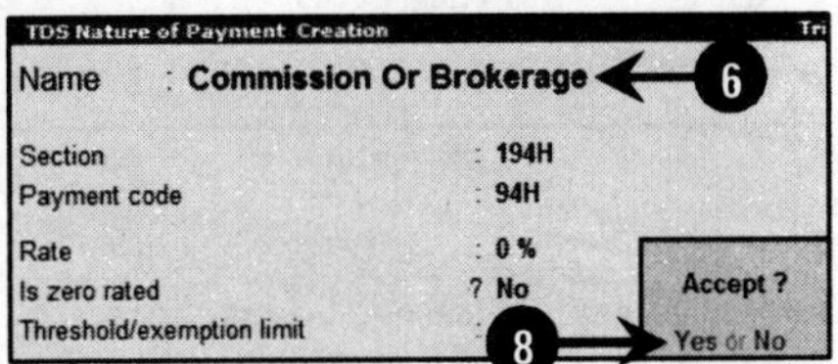

Fig.TL-13.6

Let us learn to create an expense ledger.

Creating an Expense Ledger

Perform the following steps to create an expense ledger:

1. *Double-click* the **Accounts Info.** option in the **Gateway of Tally** menu. The **Accounts Info.** menu appears.
2. *Double-click* the **Ledgers** option in the **Accounts Info.** menu. The **Ledgers** menu appears.
3. *Double-click* the **Create** option in the **Ledgers** menu. The **Ledger Creation** screen appears (Fig.TL-13.7).
4. *Enter* the name of the expense ledger beside the **Name** option. In our case, we have entered **Trinity Advertisement Expenses** (Fig.TL-13.7).
5. *Press* the **Enter** key three times. The **List of Groups** menu appears.
6. *Double-click* the **Indirect Expenses** option in the **List of Groups** menu for the **Under** option (Fig.TL-13.7).
7. *Press* the **Enter** key until **Applicability** menu appears beside the **Is TDS applicable** option.
8. *Double-click* the desired option from the **Applicability** menu for the **Is TDS applicable** option. In our case, we have double-clicked the **Applicable** option (Fig.TL-13.7).

   The **List of Nature of Payments** menu appears (Fig.TL-13.7).

9. *Double-click* the desired TDS nature of payment in the **List of Nature of Payments** menu for the **Nature of Payment** option. In our case, we have double-clicked **Payments to Contractors**, as shown in Fig.TL-13.7:

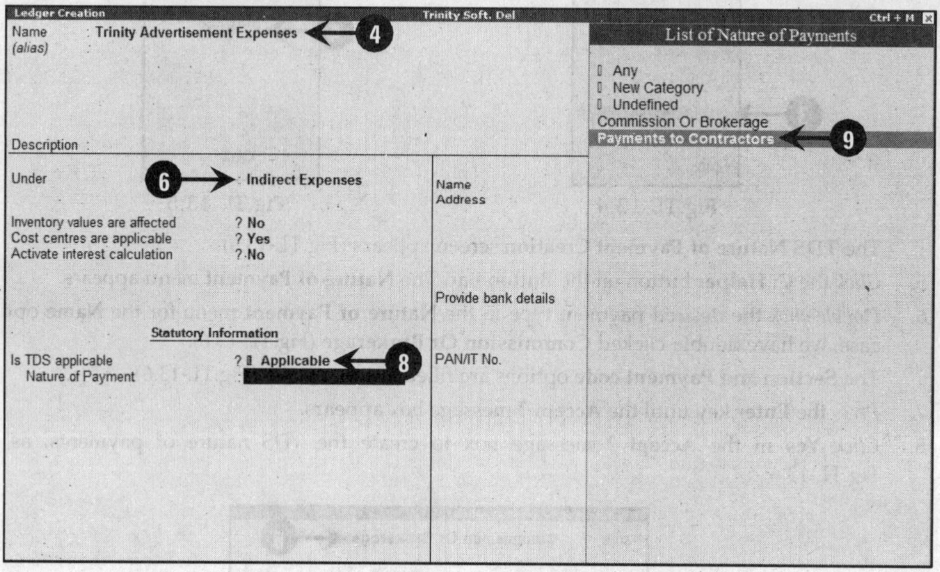

Fig.TL-13.7

10. *Press* the **Enter** key until the **Accept ?** message box appears.
11. *Click* **Yes** in the **Accept ?** message box to create the ledger.

Let us now learn to create a party ledger.

Creating a Party Ledger

Perform the following steps to create a party ledger:

1. *Double-click* the **Accounts Info.** option in the **Gateway of Tally** menu. The **Accounts Info.** menu appears.
2. *Double-click* the **Ledgers** option in the **Accounts Info.** menu. The **Ledgers** menu appears.
3. *Double-click* the **Create** option in the **Ledgers** menu. The **Ledger Creation** screen appears (Fig.TL-13.8).
4. *Enter* the name of the party ledger beside the **Name** option. In our case, we have entered **Gupta Advertising Agency** (Fig.TL-13.8).
5. *Press* the **Enter** key three times. The **List of Groups** menu appears.
6. *Double-click* the **Sundry Creditors** option in the **List of Groups** menu for the **Under** option (Fig.TL-13.8).
7. *Press* the **Enter** key until the **Is TDS Deductable** option appears.

8. *Set* the **Is TDS Deductable** option to **Yes** (Fig.TL-13.8).
9. *Press* the **Enter** key. The **Deductee Type** menu appears (Fig.TL-13.8).
10. *Double-click* the desired deductee type in the **Deductee Type** menu for the **Deductee type** option. In our case, we have double-clicked **Partnership Firm**, as shown in Fig.TL-13.8:

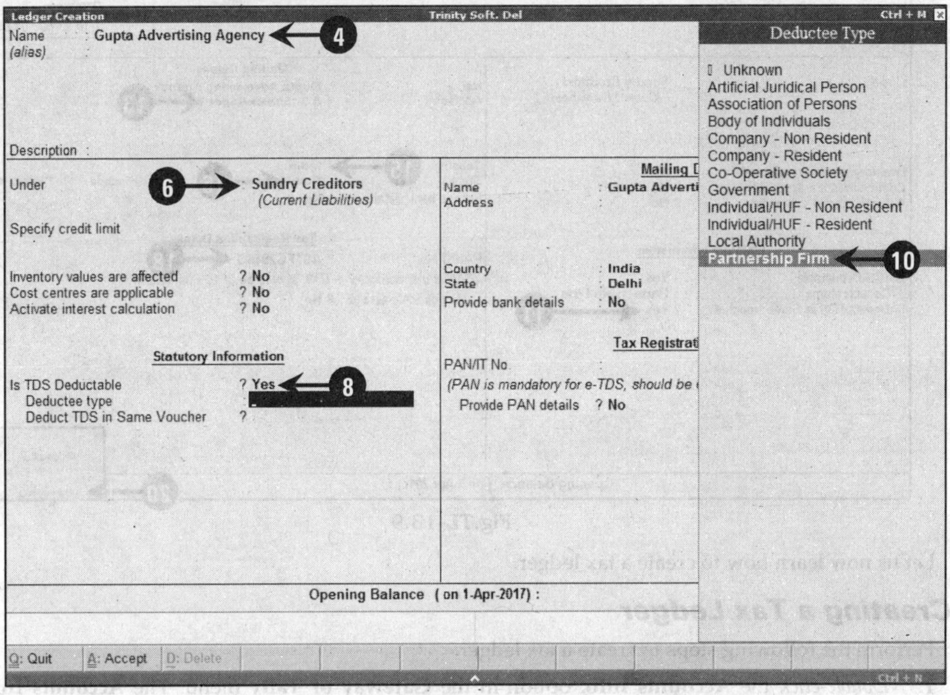

Fig.TL-13.8

11. *Set* the **Deduct TDS in Same Voucher** option to **Yes** (Fig.TL-13.9).
12. *Press* the **Enter** key.
13. *Enter* the address of the party beside the **Address** option. In our case, we have entered **A-3 Shakti Nagar** (Fig.TL-13.9).
14. *Press* the **Enter** key twice. The **List of Countries** menu appears.
15. *Double-click* the desired country for the **Country** option. In our case, we have retained with the default option (Fig.TL-13.9). The **List of States** menu appears.
16. *Double-click* the desired state for the **State** option. In our case, we have double-clicked **Delhi** (Fig.TL-13.9).
17. *Enter* the pincode beside the **Pincode** option. In our case, we have entered **110096** (Fig.TL-13.9).
18. *Enter* the PAN or IT number beside the **PAN/IT No.** option. In our case, we have entered **ASTFG2946Q** (Fig.TL-13.9).
19. *Press* the **Enter** key until the **Accept ?** message box appears.

20. *Click* **Yes** in the **Accept ?** message box to create the ledger, as shown in Fig.TL-13.9:

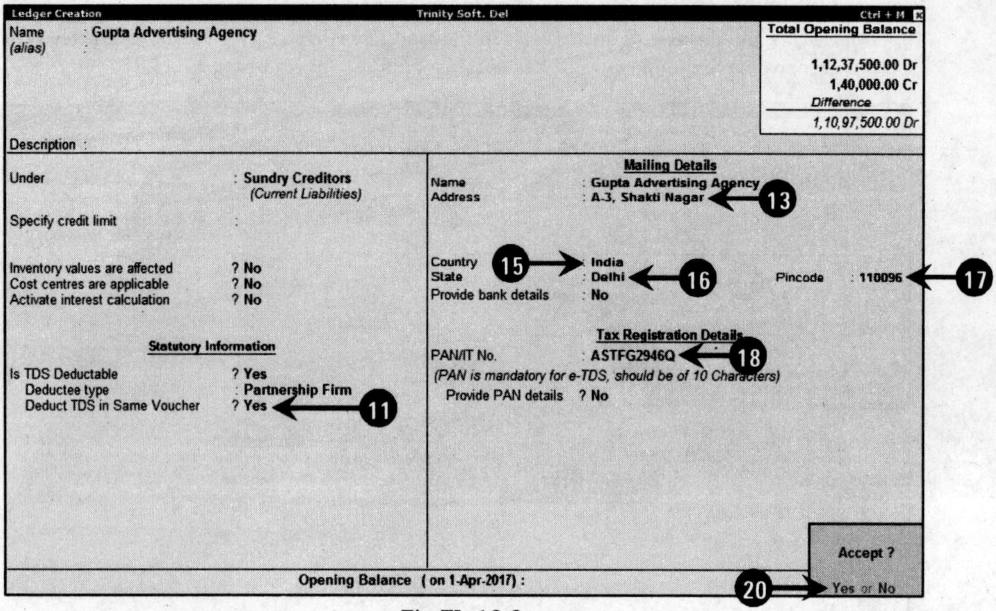

Fig.TL-13.9

Let us now learn how to create a tax ledger.

Creating a Tax Ledger

Perform the following steps to create a tax ledger:

1. *Double-click* the **Accounts Info.** option in the **Gateway of Tally** menu. The **Accounts Info.** menu appears.
2. *Double-click* the **Ledgers** option in the **Accounts Info.** menu. The **Ledgers** menu appears.
3. *Double-click* the **Create** option in the **Ledgers** menu. The **Ledger Creation** screen appears (Fig.TL-13.10).
4. *Enter* the name of the tax ledger beside the **Name** option. In our case, we have entered **Tax Ledger** (Fig.TL-13.10).
5. *Press* the **Enter** key three times. The **List of Groups** menu appears.
6. *Double-click* the **Duties & Taxes** option in the **List of Groups** menu for the **Under** option (Fig.TL-13.10).
   The **List of Duties/Taxes** menu appears.
7. *Double-click* the **TDS** option in the **List of Duties/Taxes** menu for the **Type of duty/tax** option (Fig.TL-13.10).
   The **Nature of payment** option is enabled and the **List of TDS Nature of Payments** menu appears (Fig.TL-13.10).
8. *Double-click* the desired TDS nature of payment from the **List of TDS Nature of Payments** menu for the **Nature of payment** option. In our case, we have double-clicked **Payments to Contractors** (Fig.TL-13.10).
9. *Press* the **Enter** key until the **Accept ?** message box appears.

10. *Click* **Yes** in the **Accept ?** message box to create the ledger, as shown in Fig.TL-13.10:

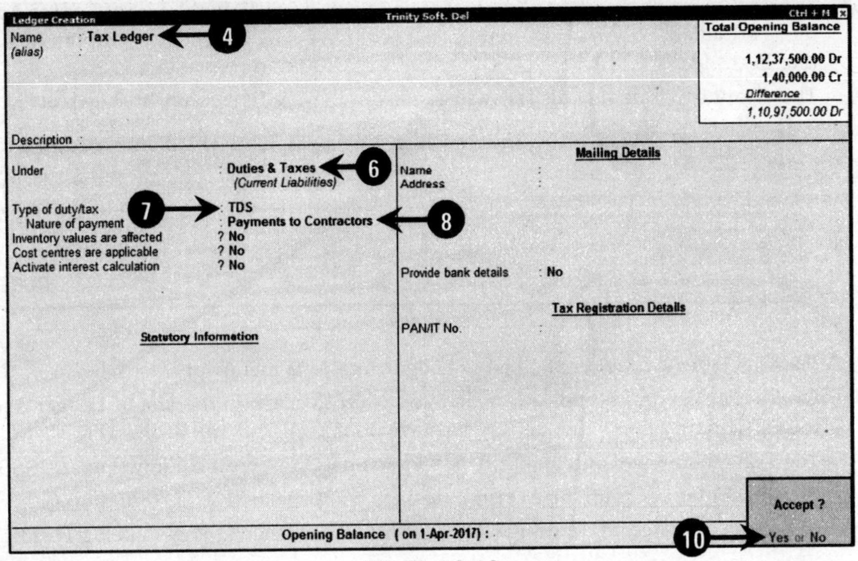

Fig.TL-13.10

Let us now learn how to create TDS vouchers.

Creating TDS Vouchers

The vouchers used to compute TDS are as follows:

- Journal voucher (TDS on Expense)
- Payment voucher

Let us now discuss the procedure to create these vouchers in the following sections.

Creating a Journal Voucher for TDS on Expense

Perform the following steps to create a journal voucher:

1. *Click* the **Accounting Vouchers** option under the **Transactions** section in the **Gateway of Tally** menu.

   The **Accounting Voucher Creation** screen appears.

2. *Click* the **F7: Journal** button on the Button Bar. The **Accounting Voucher Creation** screen for the **Journal** voucher appears with the **List of Ledger Accounts** menu.
3. *Double-click* the desired expense ledger that you want to debit in the **List of Ledger Accounts** menu for the **Particulars** column. In our case, we have double-clicked **Trinity Advertisement Expenses** (Fig.TL-13.11).
4. *Enter* the desired expense amount under the **Debit** column. In our case, we have entered **30000**, as shown in Fig.TL-13.11:

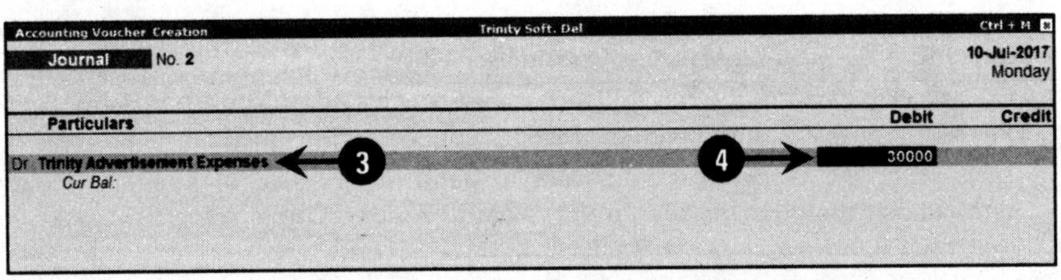

Fig.TL-13.11

5. *Press* the **Enter** key twice. The **List of Ledger Accounts** menu appears.
6. *Double-click* the desired party ledger that you want to credit in the **List of Ledger Accounts** menu for the **Particulars** column. In our case, we have double-clicked **Gupta Advertising Agency** (Fig.TL-13.12).

   The amount after deducting TDS will display in the **Credit** column, as shown in Fig.TL-13.12:

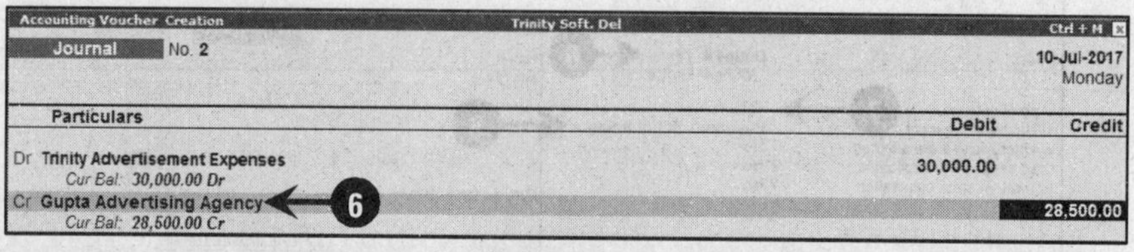

Fig.TL-13.12

7. *Press* the **Enter** key twice. The **List of Ledger Accounts** menu appears.
8. *Double-click* the desired tax ledger that you want to credit in the **List of Ledger Accounts** menu for the **Particulars** column. In our case, we have double-clicked **Tax Ledger** (Fig.TL-13.13).

   The TDS amount will automatically be displayed in the **Credit** column (Fig.TL-13.13).
9. *Press* the **Enter** key until the **Accept ?** message box appears (Fig.TL-13.13).
10. *Click* **Yes** in the **Accept ?** message box to create the voucher, as shown in Fig.TL-13.13:

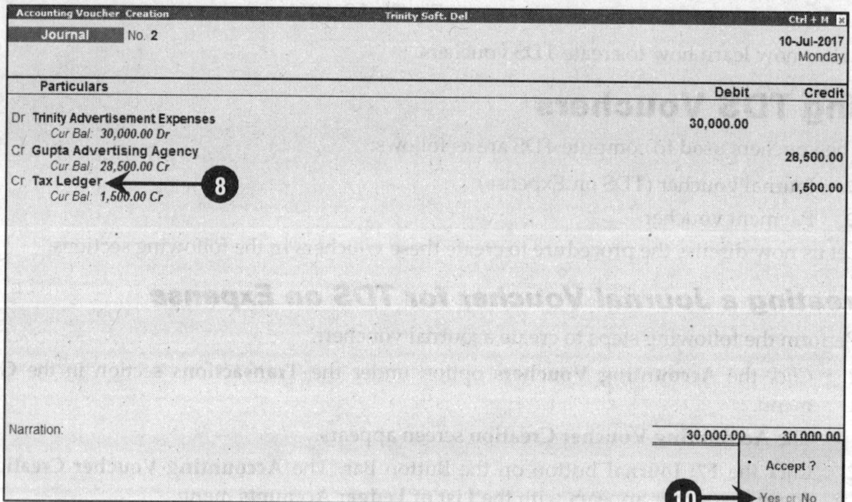

Fig.TL-13.13

Let us now learn how to create a payment voucher.

Creating a Payment Voucher

Perform the following steps to create a payment voucher:

1. *Click* the **Accounting Vouchers** option under the **Transactions** section in the **Gateway of Tally** menu. The **Accounting Voucher Creation** screen appears.
2. *Click* the **F5: Payment** button on the Button Bar. The **Accounting Voucher Creation** screen for the **Payment** voucher appears with the **List of Ledger Accounts** menu.
3. *Double-click* the ledger that you want to debit, in the **List of Ledger Accounts** menu for the **Particulars** column. In our case, we have double-clicked **Gupta Advertising Agency** (Fig.TL-13.14).

4. *Enter* the desired expense amount under the **Debit** column. In our case, we have entered **28500**, as shown in Fig.TL-13.14:

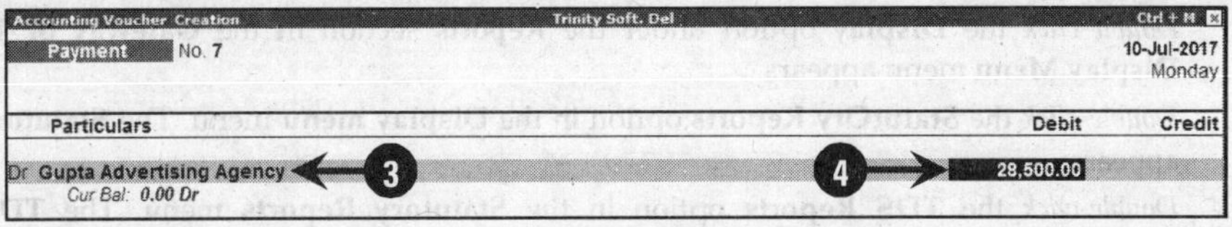

Fig.TL-13.14

5. *Press* the **Enter** key twice. The **List of Ledger Accounts** menu appears.
6. *Double-click* the ledger that you want to credit in the **List of Ledger Accounts** menu for the **Particulars** column. In our case, we have double-clicked **HDFC Bank** (Fig.TL-13.15).

   The **Credit** column gets filled automatically.
7. *Press* the **Enter** key until the **Accept ?** message box appears.
8. *Click* **Yes** in the **Accept ?** message box to create the voucher, as shown in Fig.TL-13.15:

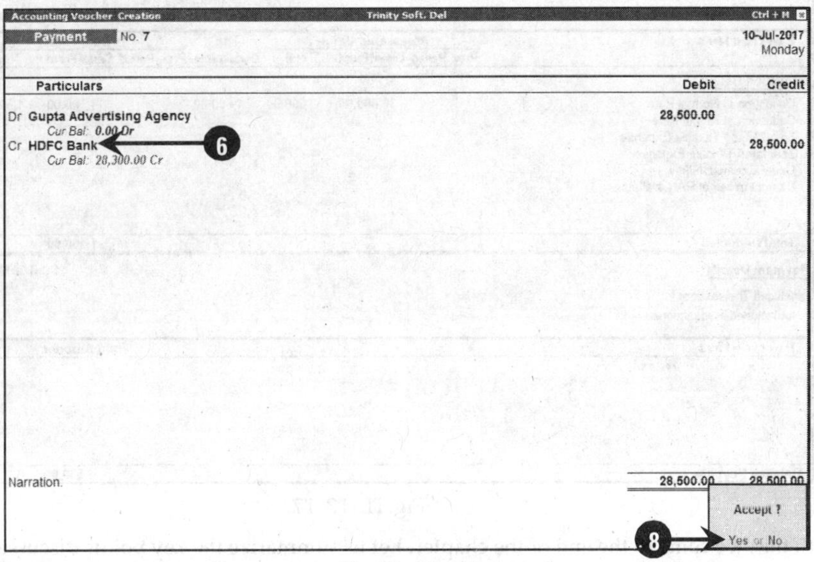

Fig.TL-13.15

Let us now learn how to view TDS reports.

TDS Reports

In Tally, you can access TDS reports by clicking **Gateway of Tally → Display → StatutOry Reports → TDS Reports.** The **TDS Return** menu appears, as shown in Fig.TL-13.16:

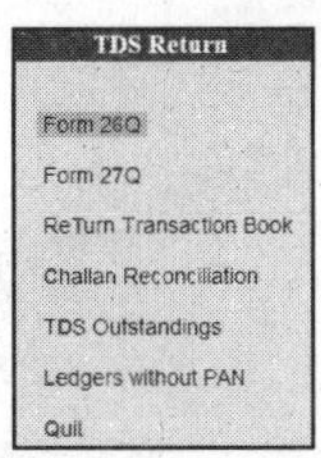

Fig.TL-13.16

You can access any report related to TDS through the TDS Return menu.

Viewing the Form 26Q Report

Perform the following steps to view the Form 26Q report:

1. *Double-click* the **Display** option under the **Reports** section in the **Gateway of Tally** menu. The **Display Menu** menu appears.
2. *Double-click* the **StatutOry Reports** option in the **Display menu** menu. The **Statutory Reports** menu appears.
3. *Double-click* the **TDS Reports** option in the **Statutory Reports** menu. The **TDS Return** menu appears.
4. *Double-click* the **Form 26Q** option in the **TDS Return** menu.

   The **Form 26Q** screen appears, as shown in Fig.TL-13.17:

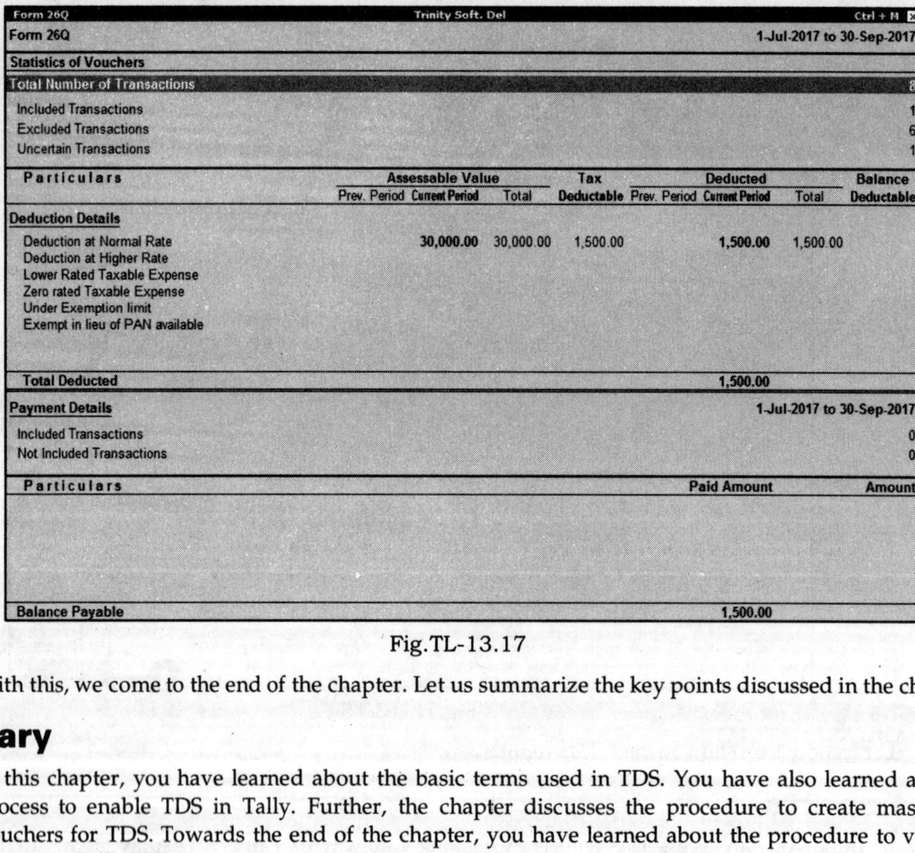

Fig.TL-13.17

With this, we come to the end of the chapter. Let us summarize the key points discussed in the chapter.

Summary

In this chapter, you have learned about the basic terms used in TDS. You have also learned about the process to enable TDS in Tally. Further, the chapter discusses the procedure to create masters and vouchers for TDS. Towards the end of the chapter, you have learned about the procedure to view TDS reports in Tally.ERP 9.

CHAPTER

14

Goods and Services Tax

In this Chapter:

- Features of GST
- Benefits of GST
- Classification of GST
- Administrative Bodies of GST
- Goods and Service Tax Network
- GST Rates in India
- GSTIN Structure
- Enrolling under GST
- Registration under GST
- Levy of GST
- Exemption from GST
- Supply of Goods
- Input Tax Credit
- Transfer of Input Tax Credit
- Payment of Tax
- Reverse Charge
- Returns
- Refund of Tax
- Offenses and Penalties
- Enabling GST in Tally.ERP 9

- Creating Masters for GST
- Creating Vouchers for GST
- Viewing the GST Rates
- Updating Party GSTIN
- Viewing GSTR-1 Report
- Viewing GSTR-2 Report
- Viewing GSTR-3B Report

Introduction

Goods and Services Tax (GST) can be defined as an indirect tax that has integrated most of the taxes that are levied on goods and services under a single realm on the national level. Presently, separate taxes are imposed on goods and services. GST is charged to the customer at the end-point of consumption. It is a consolidated form of taxes with a uniform rate of tax defined for both goods and services. The collection of tax for GST on value-added goods and services occurs at all the stages of a supply chain, i.e., sale or purchase. It is achieved through a mechanism of crediting tax.

GST was introduced in the Parliament on 8th August, 2016 as The Constitution (One Hundred and First Amendment) Act, 2016. The Government of India implemented GST finally with effect from 1st July, 2017 after four GST bills were approved in the Lok Sabha on 29th March, 2017 and Rajya Sabha on 6th April, 2017, with a clear blueprint laid down by the Ministry of Finance.

The governing body for GST is GST Council and its Chairman is the Union Finance Minister of India. GST is considered to be one of the most important reforms in the tax after independence. It is a major tax turnover that will lead to a transformation in business for a significant number of industries.

The chapter starts by explaining about the features and benefits of GST. Next, you learn about the classification of GST. You also learn about the administrative bodies of GST, and GST network. Then, you learn about the rates of GST in India, and the structure of GSTIN. You also learn about enrolling, and registering under GST. Furthermore, you learn about levy of GST, exemption from GST, and supply of goods. You also learn about ITC, and transfer of ITC. Then, you learn about tax payment, reverse charge, returns, and tax refund. In addition to this, you also learn about offenses and penalties. The chapter then discusses about the process to enable the GST feature in Tally. Further, you learn about the process to create masters and vouchers for GST. Next, you learn about the procedure to view GST rate and update party GSTIN. Towards the end of the chapter, you learn about the procedure to view GSTR-1, GSTR-2, and GSTR-3B reports.

Let us start the chapter by learning about the features of GST.

Features of GST

Salient features of GST are as follows:

- **Dual Goods and Services Tax:** GST is an indirect tax structure, dual in nature, which enables both central government and state government to levy the tax.
- **Inter-State Transactions and the IGST Mechanism:** Integrated Goods and Services Tax (IGST) is to be levied by the Centre at the inter-state level on the distribution of goods and services. The design of the IGST mechanism guarantees a coherent flow of input tax credit between any two states. IGST will have to be paid by the inter-State seller on his good's sales, post-adjustment of IGST, CGST and SGST on his purchases. The state that exports will transfer SGST's credit used in IGST's payment to the Centre. The claim of IGST's credit can be done by the dealer who imports, in his own state only, while releasing the output tax liability (CGST and SGST both). The IGST's credit used in the payment of SGST will be transferred to the state that is imported by the Centre.
- **Destination-Based Consumption Tax**: GST is a tax based on destination, which means that all the accumulated SGST will complement to the State where the consumer of the sold goods and services resides.
- **Computation of GST on the Basis of Invoice Credit Method:** Under GST, the invoice credit method will be the liability, i.e., the invoice issued by the suppliers will be the basis for allowing Cenvat credit.
- **Payment of GST:** The payment of CGST and SGST is to be done to the Central accounts and State accounts, respectively.
- **Goods and Services Tax Network (GSTN):** Goods and Services Tax Network (GSTN) is a joint non-government and not-for-profit set-up company by Central and State governments which will allocate the IT infrastructure and services shared by Central and State governments, tax payers and other stakeholders.

- **Input Tax Credit (ITC) Set-off:** For the taxes that are allowed against central and state, ITC for CGST & SGST will be levied.
- **GST on Imports:** IGST will be levied by the Centre on supply of inter-state goods and services. Centre will levy IGST on inter-state supply of goods and services. Goods that will be imported will be subject to customs duty and IGST.
- **Maintenance of Records:** To avail, utilize or refund of Input Tax Credit of CGST, SGST and IGST, separate details in accounts' books will have to be maintained by the taxpayer or the exporter.
- **Administration of GST:** GST Council will be responsible for the administration of GST and it will also act as the prime policy-making body of the GST. The council comprises the Central and State ministers, who are in-charge of the financial body.
- **Goods and Services Tax Council:** The GST Council is a union of the Centre and the States. Recommendations will be made to the Union and the States by the Council on vital issues, like rates of tax, list of exemption, threshold limits, etc. Half of the gross members of the Council form the GST Council's quorum.

Let us learn about the benefits of GST.

Benefits of GST

Some benefits of GST are as follows:

- **No more multiple taxes:** GST will eliminate multiple indirect taxes. The taxes that exist presently won't be levied after the GST is implemented. Once GST is effective, taxes like Excise duty, Octroi tax, Sales tax, CENVAT, Service tax and turnover won't be applicable. All these taxes will fall under GST only.
- **Uniformity of tax rates and structure:** GST guarantees that all indirect taxes and their structures must be common throughout the country, as this will increase the conviction and comfort of carrying out any business. Each state will come under one tax only, hence preventing any unhealthy competitions amongst states. GST proves to be beneficial for all those who do inter-state business and want to expand their business in other states.
- **Easy tax filing:** For entrepreneurs and small businessmen, GST will turn out to be a blessing. The complicacy that is associated with taxing documentation can be easily avoided, once GST comes into application. Filing returns, payment of taxes, and the process of refund will become inconvenience-free after GST applies. Tax evading and corruption will be reduced to an extent, which will make the system work more efficiently.
- **Reduction in cost:** After GST, dual charges will be eliminated. By GST, the double charges will be eliminated. The VAT on the goods that are produced like cosmetics, detergents, etc., exists currently apart from excise. GST will eliminate this. It will decrease the prices of goods and services, enabling consumers to save more money. After GST, the cost of FMCG products, small cars, cinema tickets, electrical wires and paint products, etc., is believed to reduce. GST will be advantageous for both the businessman and consumer.
- **More employment:** As a result of the reduced cost after GST, the demand of the product will increase and the supply will have to be increased to meet the demand. Hence, the employment will increase, with the increased need of more supply. GST will increase the GDP by at least 2% that will lead to generating more employment.
- **Better control on leakage:** A sturdy IT infrastructure makes GST very adaptive. The coherent transfer of input tax credit from one stage to another in the chain of value-addition is a built-in mechanism in GST's design. It will be a treat for the traders who adapt to GST.
- **From input to output:** From manufacturing till consumption, GST will apply to all the stages. Every stage of the chain is entitled to the benefit of tax credit. The margin of tax is added and the tax will be paid on the total amount at every stage. People will enjoy the tax credit benefits after GST. The tax needs to be paid on the margin amount only. There will be a reduction in the rapid effect of tax and it will also result in cost reduction.

- **Increase in GDP:** The production increases with the growing demand. It will boost the gross domestic product. There is an estimation of increase in GDP by 1-2% after GST.
- **Saving more money:** The application of GST for a consumer implies the dual charging system elimination. This will help the consumer save more money as a result of reduced prices. There is an expectation of reduction in the prices of FMCG products, small cars, cinema tickets, electrical wires, etc.
- **Increase in revenue:** The operation of GST is under the 'one country, one tax' principle. It has replaced all 17 indirect taxes with one tax only. An increase in the demand of the product will increase the tax revenue for central and state governments.
- **More competitive product:** GST addresses the rapid effect of taxes and high logistics cost. The manufacturing will become more competitive. It will be beneficial to both the businessman and the consumer.

Let us learn about the classification of GST.

Classification of GST

Broadly, the GST is categorized into four categories. These are:

- Central Goods and Services Tax (CGST)
- Integrated Goods and Services Tax (IGST)
- State Goods and Services Tax (SGST)
- Union Territory Goods and Services Tax (UTGST)

Let us learn about these categories one by one in the subsequent sections.

CGST

CGST is a constituent of GST. CGST comes under the Central Goods and Services Tax Act, 2016. CGST is levied on the migration of goods and services within a state and amendments can be made to it from time to time by a separate body. The total revenue collected under CGST is intended for the Centre. However, the states get input tax credit on CGST and it may be utilized against the Central GST's payment.

IGST

IGST is a constituent of Integrated Goods and Services Tax Act, 2016. IGST is levied on the migration of goods and services from one state to another. The share of the revenue earned on IGST is divided according to the rates fixed by the governing authorities among state government and central government.

SGST

SGST is a constituent of State Goods and Services Tax Act, 2016. SGST is introduced for easy understanding, when SGST is being introduced as the replacement of all the present taxes including Sales Tax, VAT, Luxury Tax, Entertainment tax, Taxes on lottery, betting and gambling, Entry tax. However, it has not replaced Octroi, State Cesses and Surcharges. The revenue accumulated under SGST is solely for the State Government.

UTGST

UTGST is a constituent of GST in India. GST levied on the supply of goods and services in the Union Territories like Andaman and Nicobar Islands, Chandigarh, Dadra and Nagar Haveli, Daman and Diu, Delhi (National Capital Territory of Delhi), Lakshadweep, Puducherry, etc., falls under UTGST.

There is a separate Act, namely UTGST Act implemented for Union Territories, for imposing and administering GST in India. Under this Act, the entire details of GST rates against the migration of goods and services in Union territories are stated. There is a bill named UTGST bill which has been presented in States' government to implement it as UTGST Act.

Let us learn about the administrative bodies of GST.

Administrative Bodies of GST

The following are the classes of officers under the Central Goods and Services Tax Act:

- Principal Chief Commissioners of CGST or Principal Directors General of CGST
- Chief Commissioners of CGST or Directors General of CGST
- Principal Commissioners of CGST or Principal Additional Directors General of CGST
- Commissioners of CGST or Additional Directors General of CGST
- Additional Commissioners of CGST or Additional Directors of CGST
- Joint Commissioners of CGST or Joint Directors of CGST
- Deputy Commissioners of CGST or Deputy Directors of CGST
- Assistant Commissioners of CGST or Assistant Directors of CGST

The classes of officers under the State Goods and Services Tax Act are as follows:

- Commissioner of SGST
- Special Commissioners of SGST
- Additional Commissioners of SGST
- Joint Commissioners of SGST
- Deputy Commissioners of SGST
- Assistant Commissioners of SGST

Apart from the officers mentioned above, some other class of officers can also be appointed for the purpose of CGST and SGST Act.

Goods and Service Tax Network

Goods and Service Tax Network (GSTN) is a non-government body that handles the IT system of the GST portal. It gives a shared IT infrastructure and services to both central and state governments, tax payers, and other commodities to implement GST.

The functions of GSTN are as follows:

- It gives the facility to register under GST.
- It forwards the return to both central and state authorities.
- It provides the facility to calculate and settle the amount of IGST.
- It verifies the tax payment details with concerning banks.
- It offers various MIS reports to both central and the state governments.
- It provides analysis of tax payers' profile.
- It runs the matching engine for comparing and reclaiming of input tax credit.

Let us learn about the GST rates in India.

GST Rates in India

The rates of GST in India don't come under the provision of the Act but there was a promise made by Hon. Finance Minister, Shri Arun Jaitley in the Rajya Sabha for making the upper limit of the tax rate a part of the law. Thus, 14% is fixed as the upper limit for the tax rate and 28% is fixed as the upper limit on IGST rate. Table 14.1 shows the categories of the tax rates:

Table 14.1: Tax Rate Categories

Rate of Tax	Expected bifurcation	Products
Nil (Exempted Supply)	(0% of CGST & 0% of SGST)	Milk, Kajal, Eggs, Educations Services, Curd, Health Services, Lassi, Children's Drawing & Colouring

Table 14.1: Tax Rate Categories		
Rate of Tax	**Expected bifurcation**	**Products**
		Books, Unpacked Foodgrains, Unbranded Atta, Unpacked Paneer, Unbranded Maida, Gur, Besan, Unbranded Natural Honey, Prasad, Fresh Vegetables, Palmyra Jaggery, Salt, and Phool Bhari Jhadoo etc.
5%	(2.5% of CGST & 2.5% of SGST)	Sugar, Packed Paneer, Tea, Coal, Edible Oils, Raisin, Domestic LPG, Roasted Coffee Beans, PDS Kerosene, Skimmed Milk Powder, Cashew Nuts, Footwear (< ₹500), Milk Food for Babies, Apparels (< ₹1000), Fabric, Coir Mats, Matting & Floor Covering, Spices, Agarbatti, Coal, Mishti/Mithai (Indian Sweets), Life-saving drugs, and Coffee (except instant) etc.
12%	(6% of CGST & 6% of SGST)	Butter, Computers, Ghee, Processed food, Almonds, Mobiles, Fruit Juice, Preparations of Vegetables, Fruits, Nuts or other parts of Plants including Pickle Murabba, Chutney, Jam, Jelly, Packed Coconut Water, and Umbrella etc.
18%	(9% of CGST & 9% of SGST)	Hair Oil, Capital goods, Toothpaste, Industrial Intermediaries, Soap, Ice-cream, Pasta, Toiletries, Corn Flakes, Computers, Soups, and Printers etc.
28%	(14% of CGST & 14% of SGST)	All other items that directly reach the consumer including luxury goods, i.e., white goods and beverages are covered under this category

Note that, there are three commodities which are exempted from GST, i.e., alcohol for human consumption, petroleum products and electricity.

Note

GST rates are subject to change from time to time as per the directions of Ministry of Finance. Kindly refer to the official website i.e. www.gstcouncil.gov.in.

Let us learn about the structure of GSTIN.

GSTIN Structure

Goods and Services Taxpayer Identification Number (GSTIN) is a 15 digit unique code. It is a state and PAN based code that is assigned to each taxpayer. The structure of GSTIN is as follows:

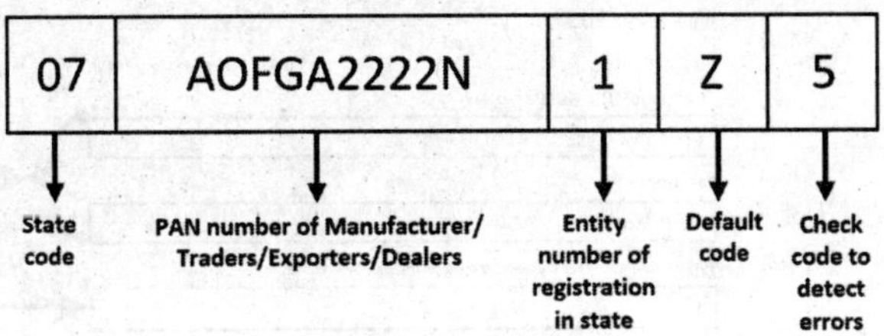

The description of the structure of GSTIN is as follows:

- The first two digits of GSTIN signifies the state code. This state code is numbered as per Indian Census 2011.
- The next ten digits of GSTIN signifies PAN number of the taxpayer.
- The thirteenth digit of GSTIN signifies the number of registration in a state.

- The fourteenth digit of GSTIN is 'Z' by default.
- The last digit of GSTIN signifies the check code, which can be an alphabet or number.

Let us learn about the procedure to enroll under GST.

Enrolling under GST

All the taxpayers, VAT payers, Service tax payers and Central Excise taxpayers are given a provisional ID and a password along with it. One will have to create his/her username and password through this provisional ID and password given through the GST common web portal – www.gst.gov.in.

Perform the following steps to enroll under GST:

1. Visit the official website of GST, i.e., **www.gst.gov.in**.
   The **GST Home** page is displayed.
2. *Click* the **Login** link. The **Login** page is displayed (Fig.TL-14.1):
3. *Click* the **here** link in the instruction at the bottom of the page, as shown in Fig.TL-14.1:

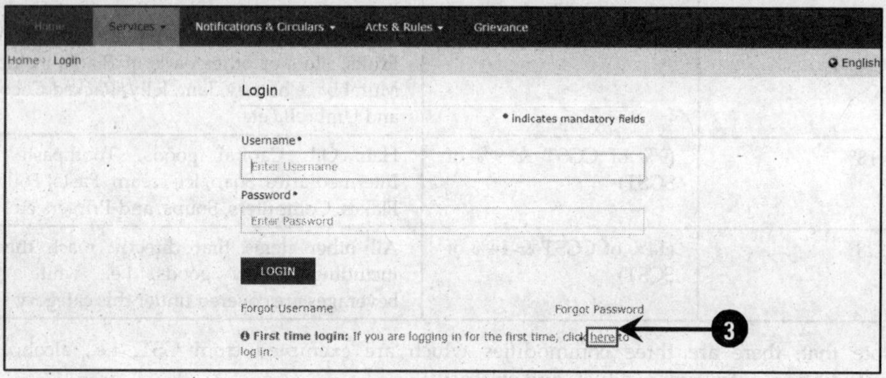

Fig.TL-14.1

   The **New User Login** page is displayed (Fig.TL-14.2).
4. *Enter* the Provisional ID and Password provided by your State VAT/Central Excise/Service Tax Authority in the **Provisional ID / GSTIN / UIN** and **Password** text boxes, respectively (Fig.TL-14.2).
5. *Enter* the captcha text in the **Type the characters you see in the image below** text box (Fig.TL-14.2).
6. *Click* the **LOGIN** button, as shown in Fig.TL-14.2:

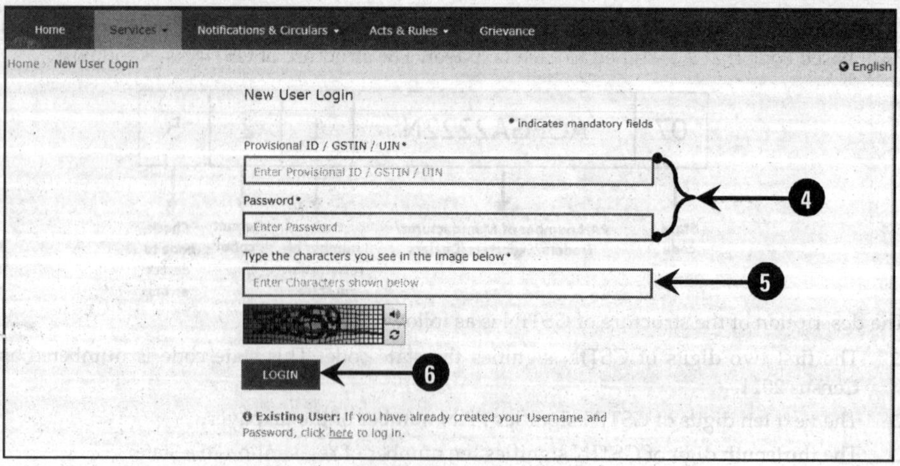

Fig.TL-14.2

The **Provisional ID Verification** page is displayed (Fig.TL-14.3).

7. *Enter* your e-mail address and mobile number in the **E-mail Address** and **Mobile Number** text boxes, respectively (Fig.TL-14.3).
8. *Click* the **CONTINUE** button, as shown in Fig.TL-14.3:

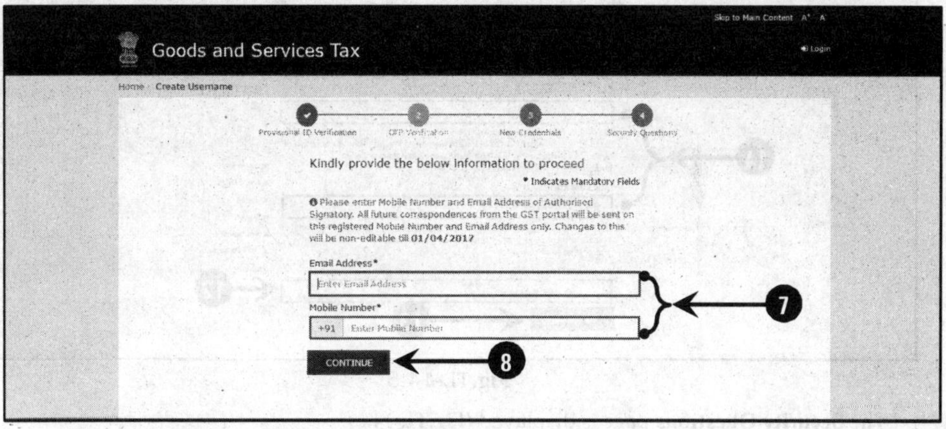

Fig.TL-14.3

The **OTP Verification** page is displayed (Fig.TL-14.4).

9. *Enter* the OTP you received in your e-mail address and mobile number in the **Email OTP** and **Mobile OTP** text boxes, respectively (Fig.TL-14.4).

Note: **In case, OTP is not received, you should click the RESEND OTP button. The OTP will be sent again to your e-mail address and mobile number. The new OTPs need to be used for the verification purpose. The OTP will be valid for a period of 10 minutes.**

10. *Click* the **CONTINUE** button, as shown in Fig.TL-14.4:

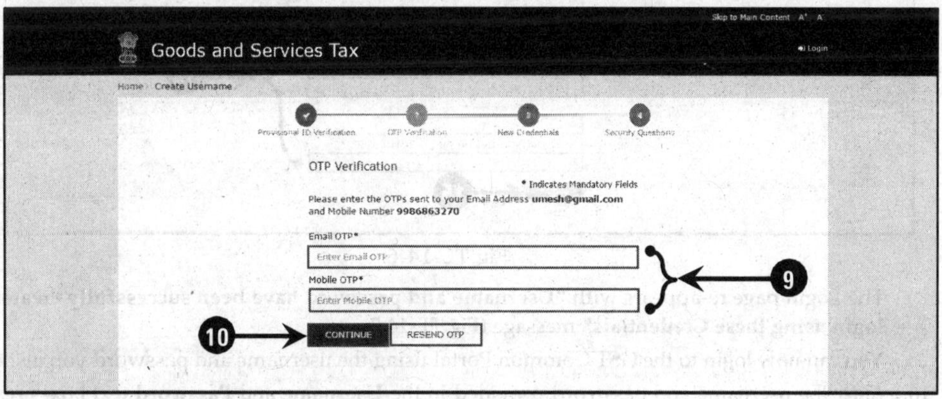

Fig.TL-14.4

The **New Credentials** page is displayed (Fig.TL-14.5).

11. *Enter* the new username and password in the **New Username** and **New Password** text boxes, respectively (Fig.TL-14.5).
12. *Re-enter* the password in the **Re-confirm Password** text box (Fig.TL-14.5).

13. *Click* the **CONTINUE** button, as shown in Fig.TL-14.5:

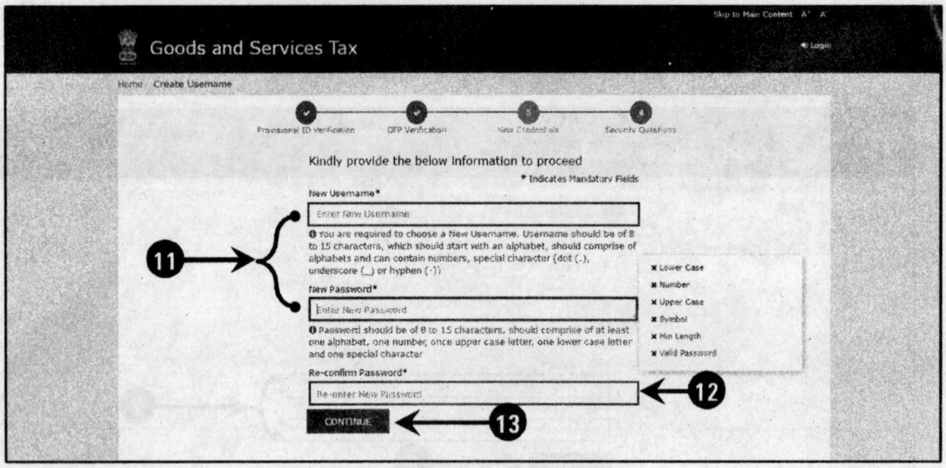

Fig.TL-14.5

The **Security Questions** page is displayed (Fig.TL-14.6).

14. *Enter* the answers for each security question in the **Security Questions** page Fig.TL-14.6.
15. *Click* the **SUBMIT** button, as shown in Fig.TL-14.6:

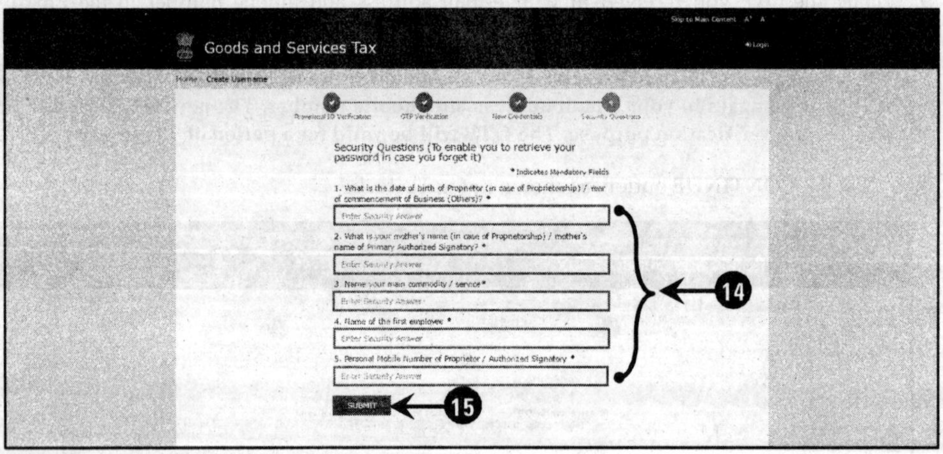

Fig.TL-14.6

The Login page re-appears with **"Username and password have been successfully created. Kindly login using these Credentials"** message (Fig.TL-14.7).

You can now login to the GST Common Portal using the username and password you just created.

16. *Enter* the username and password provided in the **Username** and **Password** text boxes respectively (Fig.TL-14.7).

17. *Click* the **LOGIN** button, as shown in Fig.TL-14.7:

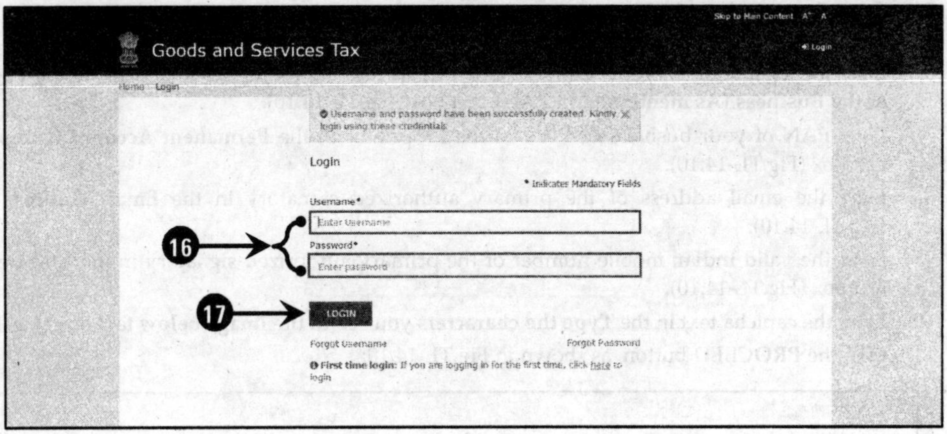

Fig.TL-14.7

The **Welcome** page is displayed (Fig.TL-14.8).

18. *Click* the **CONTINUE** button, as shown in Fig.TL-14.8:

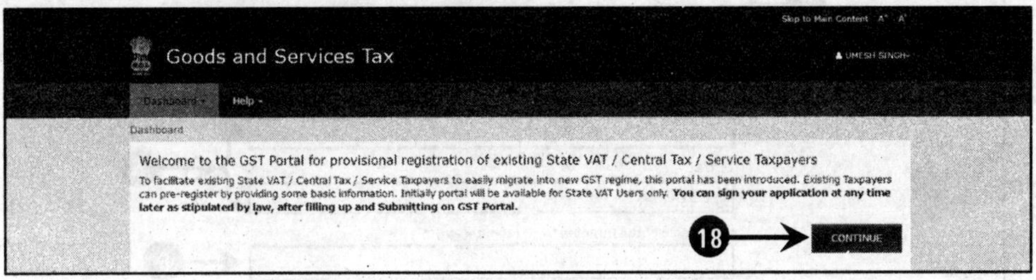

Fig.TL-14.8

Your Dashboard is displayed. The date on which you last modified the Enrolment Application will be displayed in the **Last Modified** section. You can access the enrolment application by clicking the **Dashboard → Provisional ID Enrolment**.

Let us learn about the procedure to register under GST.

Registration under GST

To register yourself as a Normal Taxpayer/Composition/Casual Taxable Person/Input Service Distributor (ISD)/SEZ Developer/SEZ Unit, at the common GST web portal, you will need to perform the following steps:

1. *Visit* the official website of GST, i.e., **www.gst.gov.in.**

   The GST Home page is displayed.

2. *Select* the **Services→ Registration→ New Registration** option, as shown in Fig.TL-14.9:

Fig.TL-14.9

   The **New Registration** page is displayed.

3. *Select* the **New Registration** radio button (Fig.TL-14.10).

4. *Select* **Taxpayer** as the type of taxpayer to be registered in the **I am a** drop-down list (Fig.TL-14.10).
5. *Select* the state for which registration is required and district in the **State / UT** and **District** drop-down lists, respectively (Fig.TL-14.10).
6. *Enter* the legal name of your business/entity as mentioned in the PAN database in the **Legal Name of the Business (As mentioned in PAN)** text box (Fig.TL-14.10).
7. *Enter* PAN of your business or PAN of the Proprietor in the **Permanent Account Number (PAN)** text box (Fig.TL-14.10).
8. *Enter* the email address of the primary authorized signatory in the **Email Address** text box (Fig.TL-14.10).
9. *Enter* the valid Indian mobile number of the primary authorized signatory in the **Mobile Number** text box (Fig.TL-14.10).
10. *Enter* the captcha text in the **Type the characters you see in the image below** text box (Fig.TL-14.10).
11. *Click* the **PROCEED** button, as shown in Fig.TL-14.10:

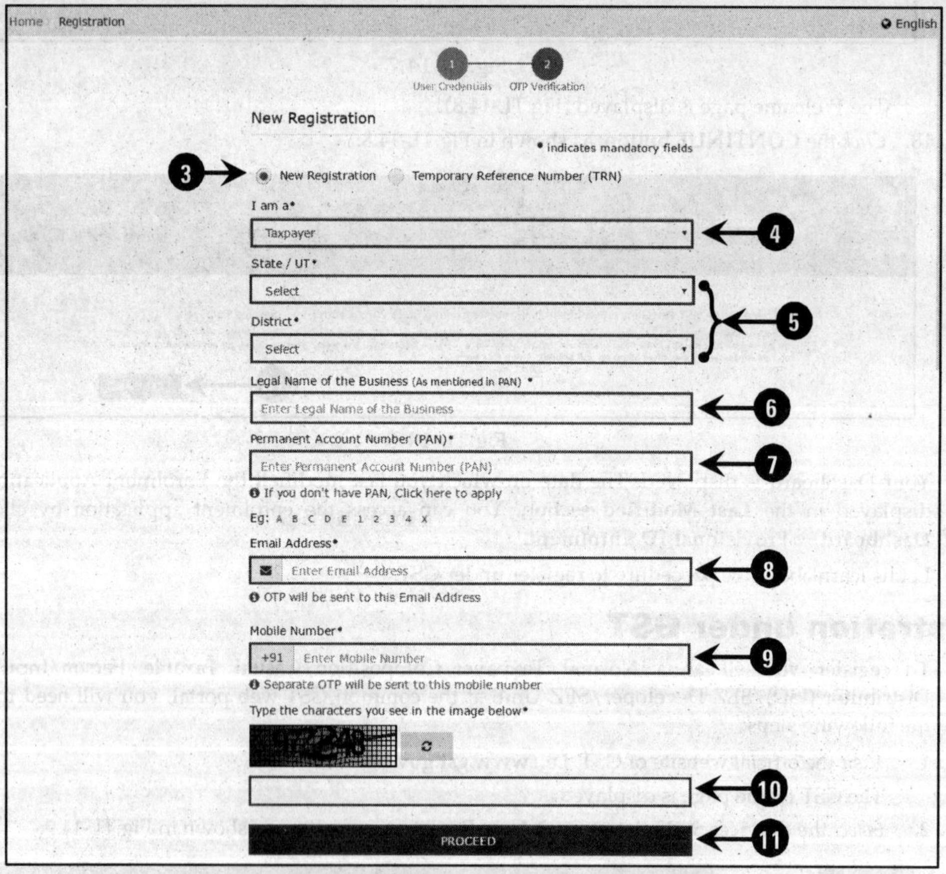

Fig.TL-14.10

The **OTP Verification** page is displayed Fig.TL-14.11.

12. *Enter* the OTP you received on your mobile number in the **Mobile OTP** field (Fig.TL-14.11).
13. *Enter* the OTP you received on your email address in the **Email OTP** text boxes (Fig.TL-14.11).

Note: **OTPs with a validity of 10 minutes are sent separately on mobile numbers and email addresses.**

14. *Click* the **PROCEED** button, as shown in Fig.TL-14.11:

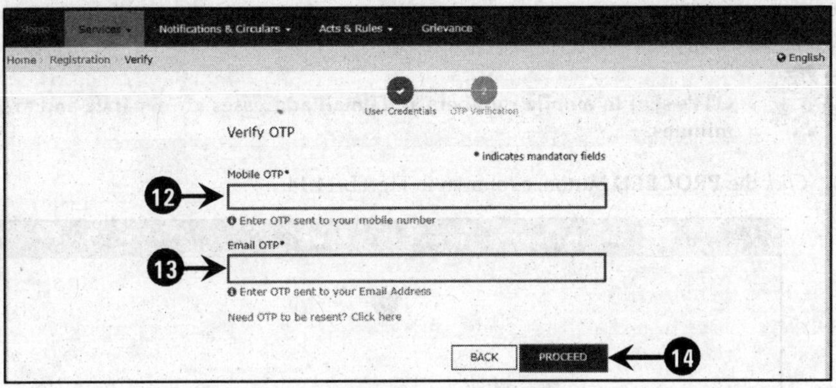

Fig.TL-14.11

The system generated **Temporary Reference Number (TRN)** is displayed (Fig.TL-14.12).

The acknowledgment information for TRN will be received on e-mail address and mobile number.

15. *Click* the **PROCEED** button, as shown in Fig.TL-14.12:

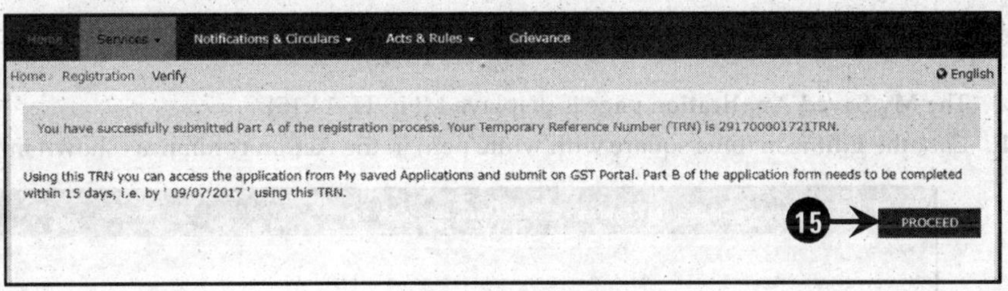

Fig.TL-14.12

Alternatively, you can also click **Services→Registration→New Registration** option and select the **Temporary Reference Number (TRN)** radio button to login using the TRN (Fig.TL-14.13).

16. *Enter* the TRN in the **Temporary Reference Number (TRN)** text box (Fig.TL-14.13).
17. *Enter* the captcha text in the **Type the characters you see in the image below** text box (Fig.TL-14.13).
18. *Click* the **PROCEED** button, as shown in Fig.TL-14.13:

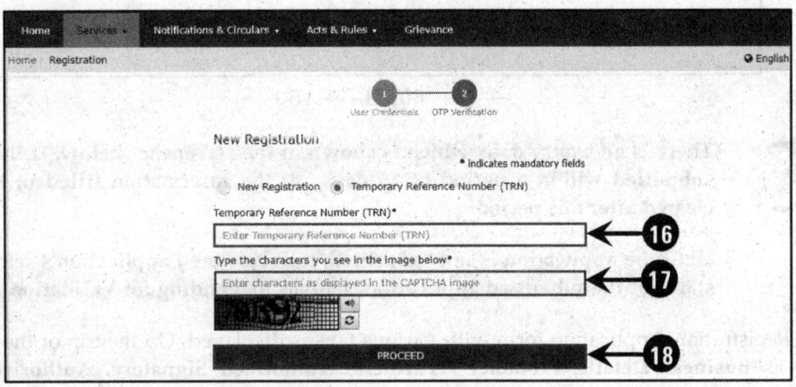

Fig.TL-14.13

The **Verify OTP** page is displayed (Fig.TL-14.14).

19. *Enter* the OTP you received on your mobile number or email address in the **Mobile / Email OTP** text box (Fig.TL-14.14).

> **Note:** **OTPs sent to mobile numbers and email addresses are separate and are valid only for 10 minutes.**

20. *Click* the **PROCEED** button, as shown in Fig.TL-14.14:

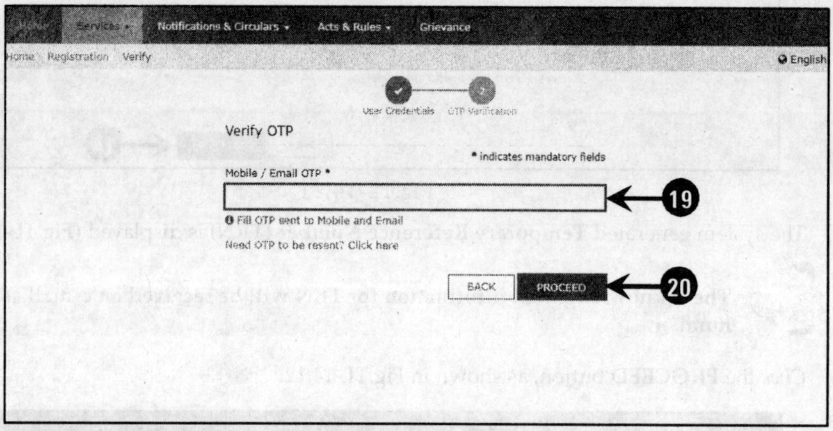

Fig.TL-14.14

The **My Saved Application** page is displayed (Fig.TL-14.15).

21. *Click* the **Edit** icon (blue square with white pen) in the **Action** column, as shown in Fig.TL-14.15:

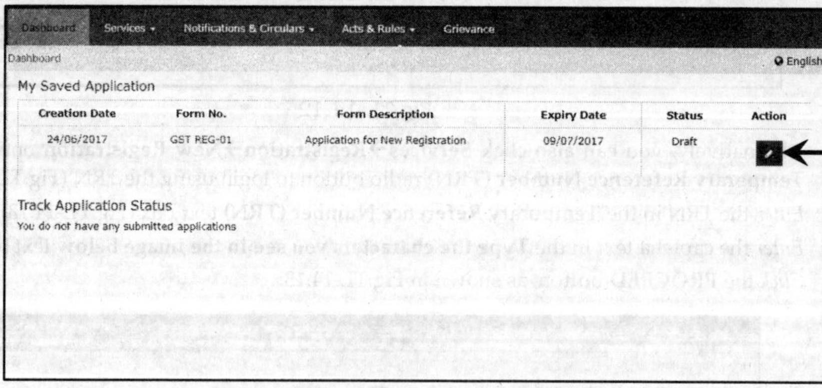

Fig.TL-14.150

> **Note:** **There is an expiry date, which is shown in the screenshot below. If the application is not submitted within a period of 15 days, all the information filled in the TRN would be cleared after this period.**
>
> **Until the application is not submitted, the registered application's remains a 'Draft'. The status of the submitted application changes to 'Pending for Validation'.**

The Registration Application form with various tabs is displayed. On the top of the page, there are ten tabs as **Business Details, Promoter / Partners, Authorized Signatory, Authorized Representative,**

Principal Place of Business, Additional Places of Business, Goods and Services, Bank Accounts, State Specific Information and **Verification**, as shown in Fig.TL-14.16:

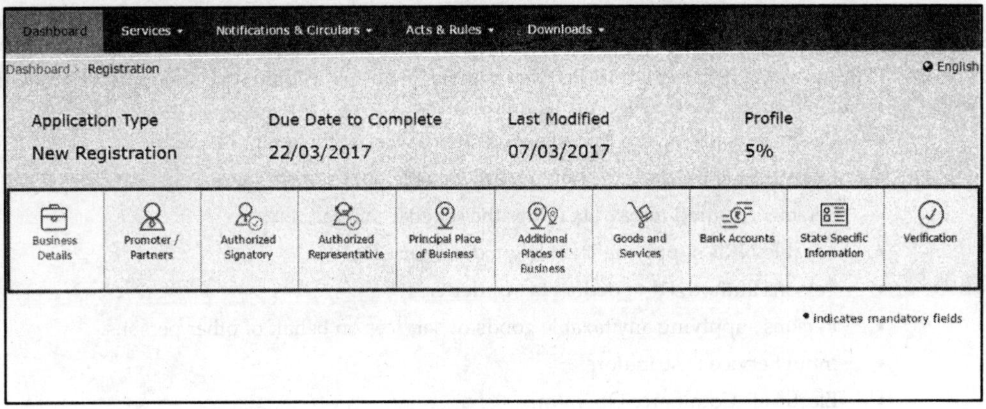

Fig.TL-14.16

Now, click each tab to enter the details required for registration. After filling the required information in each tab successfully, you will receive the **Application Reference Number (ARN)** receipt in the next 15 minutes on your registered e-mail address and mobile phone number.

Let us now learn about the levy of GST.

Levy of GST

The Section 9(1) of the Income Tax Act, 1995 states that the GST shall be levied on supply of all goods and services on inter-state and intra-state level. The rates of GST are decided by the Government on the GST Council's recommendation and shall be levied in a prescribed manner according to the Act provisions.

Taxable Person

Any person who carries out a business at any place throughout India, who is already registered or needs to get registered under the GST Act can be called a taxable person. Additionally, a person who is engaged in any kind of economic activity, involving trade and commerce will also be considered a taxable person.

The 'person' in the GST act may include any of the following:

- Individuals
- Hindu Undivided Family
- Company or Firm
- Limited Liability Partnership
- Association of Persons or Body of Individuals
- Corporation or Government company
- Body incorporated under any foreign country's laws
- Co-operative Society
- Local Authority
- Government
- Trust
- Artificial Juridical person

Criteria to Get Registered under GST

The following is the criteria to decide whether a person needs to get registered under the GST Act:

- **Aggregate Turnover**: A person whose aggregate turnover in a financial year is over 20 lakhs. This aggregate turnover criteria is over 10 lakhs for the states who fall under the special category states.
- **Compulsory GST Registration**: The persons who are required to compulsorily get themselves registered under the GST Act are as follows:
  - Persons supplying any taxable goods or services at the inter-state level.
  - Casual taxable persons supplying any taxable goods or services.
  - Persons required to pay tax under the reverse charge.
  - Taxable NRIs supplying taxable goods or services.
  - Persons authorized to deduct tax under GST.
  - Persons supplying any taxable goods or services on behalf of other persons.
  - Input Service Distributor.
  - Electronic Commerce Operator.
  - Persons supplying services related to online information, and database access or retrieval.
  - Persons supplying any goods or services through electronic commerce operators.
- **Existing Service Tax or VAT or Central Excise Registration**: It is mandatory for all persons who are registered under existing service tax or VAT or central excise license to get themselves registered under GST.
- **Transferee or Successor of a Business**: A person who carries forward a business that was run by a person who was registered under GST is required to get a GST registration.

Let us now learn about the exemption from GST.

Exemption from GST

On the basis of the kind of goods or services supplied by a person, there are some exemptions for some people from GST registration. The persons who are exempted from GST registration are:

- Agriculturists
- Persons falling under Threshold Exemption Limit
- Persons supplying good or services that are covered under Nil-Rated/Exempted category
- Persons supplying good or services that are Non-Taxable/ Non-GST
- Persons involved in activities other than supply of goods or services
- Persons supplying goods or services that are covered under the reverse charge

Let us now learn about the supply of goods.

Supply of Goods

Any activity that falls under the taxable category as per GST rules is called a supply. The government considers an activity as a supply if it meets any of the following criteria:

- Supply of goods or services
- Any taxable supply
- A taxable person making the supply
- Supply that is made in a territory that is taxable
- Supply made in exchange for cash or reward
- Supply made during business course or for growing business

Types of Supply

The supply of goods and services that fall under GST can be divided into two categories namely, Taxable supplies and Non-taxable supplies. The further classification of these supplies into different types is on the basis of the nature of the supply as follows:

- **Taxable Supplies:** These supplies refer to the taxable goods and services under GST. Taxpayers who are registered, are eligible for ITC (Input Tax Credit), i.e., they can claim for refunds on the tax paid by them during their purchases. The taxable supplies are further divided into the following:
  - **Regular taxable supplies:** The supply of goods or services whose GST rate is greater than 0% in India falls under the category of regular taxable supply.
  - **Nil-rated supplies:** The supply of goods and services whose GST rate is by default 0% in India falls under this category.
  - **Zero-rated supplies:** The supply of goods or services to a SEZ unit or exports is taken to be deemed. Whenever anything is exported, the GST rate associated with them becomes 0. However, the GST rate for such items is greater than 0%, when supplied in India.
- **Non Taxable Supplies:** These supplies refer to the goods and services that are not taxable under GST. Further, they can be divided into the following:
  - **Exempt Supplies:** There is no GST for the supply of goods or services that are exempted, even being in the purview of GST. A taxpayer who is registered cannot claim for refunds for such supplies.
  - **Non-GST supplies:** These are the supplies of goods and services that do not fall under the purview of the GST.

Components of Supply

There are three components based on which the GST tax owed by a person is calculated for a transaction. These components are described as follows:

- **Place of Supply:** The determination of the type of transaction, whether it is an inter-state, intra-state or an external trade is done through this component. It will determine the GST type associated with it.
- **Value of Supply:** The value that is taxable for the supply is determined through this component. It also determines the tax amount to be paid.
- **Time of Supply:** The date on which the taxes associated and the returns for GST are due is determined by this component.

Place of supply

To determine the right amount of tax that needs to be charged on the transaction of goods and services, one needs to understand the concept of 'place of supply'.

Place of Supply for Goods

The place from where the goods are delivered becomes the place of supply. It is the place where the ownership of the goods is changed. In case, the goods are not moved from one place to another, the location of goods at the time of delivery becomes the place of supply.

Place of Supply for Services

The location of the person who receives the service becomes the place of supply. If the services are provided to any unregistered dealer and the location information is not available, then the service provider's location will become the place of supply. The provisions specially provided to determine the place of supply are as follows:

- Services related to immovable property
- Restaurant services
- Admission to events
- Transportation of goods and passengers

- Telecom services
- Banking, financial and insurance services

If the services are associated with immovable property, then the property location becomes the place of supply.

Value of Supply

The amount of money that the seller collects for the goods and services that he supplies is considered as the value of supply. Additionally, the amount of money that a seller collects from the buyer is also considered as value of supply.

In cases, when both parties are related and the value that is reasonable may not be charged, or the transaction occurs as an exchange, the GST must be charged on the transactional value of the supplies.

The value of supply enables the parties, which are unrelated, to make transactions in the normal business course. It is responsible to ensure that GST is properly charged and collected, irrespective of the full payment of the value.

Time of Supply

The time when goods and services are supplied is considered to be the time of supply. The time of supply helps the seller to determine the due date for the tax payment.

At the time of the supply of goods and services, the GST must be paid. The time of supply is identified on the basis of goods and services which is discussed in the following subsections.

Time of Supply for Goods

For goods, the time of supply shall be the earliest of the following dates:

- Invoice issue date
- Last invoice issuing date
- Advance or payment receipt date

Time of Supply for Services

For services, the time of supply shall be the earliest of the following dates:

- Invoice issue date
- Advance or payment receipt date
- The services provision date (in case the invoice is not issued within a stipulated time)

Let us learn about Input Tax Credit.

Input Tax Credit

Input Tax Credit (ITC) allows the businesses in India to claim for reduction in the tax paid by them already while buying goods for the company and pay just the balance amount. The buyer receives credit at every stage in a supply chain for the amount of input tax paid. It can be used to claim reduction in the amount of GST needed to be paid to central and state governments. For instance, the payable amount of tax by a manufacturer of shoes is ₹500 and for that on purchases is ₹350. The manufacturer can claim for an input credit of ₹350 and only needs to pay ₹150 as tax.

Businesses can claim for ITC excluding the goods and services which are used for:

- Personal use
- Supplies exempted
- Supplies that are covered by ITC

Eligibility

For claiming ITC, the businesses must comply with the following rules:

- A buyer must have a valid tax invoice issued by a registered dealer.

- The supply must be received by the buyer. If the supply is received in installments, ITC can be claimed in the last installment's tax invoice.
- The tax due on the purchase of the buyer must have been paid by the supplier to the government in cash or through ITC.
- The returns must have been filed by the supplier. ITC can be claimed on purchases, only if the supplier of the goods complies with the rules of GST and pays tax to the government.
- The buyer must pay for the supplies received to the supplier within a time period of 180 days from invoice issue date in order to claim for ITC.

Note

ITC cannot be claimed by anyone registered under the composition scheme.

Ineligibility to Claim ITC

The cases in which a business cannot claim ITC are as follows:

- Capital goods purchased, not for the purpose of business
- Composition dealers
- Capital goods purchased for the manufacture of goods that are exempted
- Purchases for which the buyer pays tax on the basis of the reverse charge
- Credits that are blocked

Documents Requirements

The documents that are required to claim for ITC are as follows:

- Invoice provided by the supplier of the goods or services
- Invoice provided in case of reverse charge mechanism or a transaction of less than ₹200, which is alike the bill of supply
- Any debit note provided by supplier
- Bill of entry or any alike documents provided by the Customs Department
- Bill of supply provided by supplier
- Any document(invoice or credit note) provided by ISD

Time Limit to Claim ITC

Tax invoices and debit notes that are less than a year old qualify to be claimed for ITC. In other cases, ITC can be claimed by earliest of the following dates:

- The end of the financial year which applies to that invoice followed by the date of filing GST returns for September
- The date before filing an annual return that is relevant

Special cases to Claim ITC

There are some special cases apart from the ones mentioned above that are eligible for claiming ITC.

ITC Claimed on Job Work

Goods are sent to a job worker for processing by the principal manufacturer. For instance, a company that manufactures bags sends its half-made bags to the job workers for chain fitting. The manufacturer is allowed to claim ITC on purchased goods that are sent to job workers.

There are two cases in which ITC is allowed on goods sent to job workers:

- From the principal manufacturer's place of business
- From the goods supplier's place directly

To enjoy the ITC benefit, the principal manufacturer must receive the goods back within a year (within 3 years for capital goods).

ITC Claimed by Input Service Distributor (ISD)

A head office, a branch office, or a registered office can serve as an input service distributor (ISD) under GST. ITC is collected by ISD on the purchases made and thereafter, it is distributed among all the receiving branches under CGST, SGST/UTGST, and IGST.

ITC Claimed on Transfer of Business

At the time of a merger or a transfer of business, the ITC available with the transferor is passed onto the transferee.

Reversal of ITC

As already discussed, ITC cannot be claimed for non-business purposes, and on exempted supplies. There are certain conditions, in which ITC will be reversed, if claimed. ITC is reversed in the following conditions:

- If invoices are not paid within 180 days
- The seller issues a credit to ISD
- The inputs that are partially for business, and partially for supplies that are exempted or fall under the personal use category
- The capital goods that are partially for business and partially for supplies that are exempted or fall under the personal use category
- If the reversed ITC is less than required

ITC Reconciliation

ITC that is claimed by a person must match the details mentioned by the supplier of the goods in the GST return filed. If there is a mismatch, both the parties will be informed about the discrepancies.

Let us learn about the transfer of ITC.

Transfer of Input Tax Credit

In accordance with the GST law, any person who is taxable can claim for ITC for the amount of tax paid on the purchase of capital goods of the company. ITC that falls under the present tax scheme can be transferred to GST scheme during the migration process.

The Transitional Provisions rules of GST describe the procedure of moving existing ITC to GST. According to the GST Transitional Provisions, all the registered persons are required to file GST TRAN-1. GST TRAN-1 needs to be filed on GST common portal within 90 days' time from the day of enactment of GST. To simplify the migration process, the Commissioner can extend the time period of migration by another 90 days, if the Council recommends.

Procedure for Transfer

To transfer the existing ITC to GST, one needs to file the GST TRAN-1 form on GST common portal. The GST TRAN-1 form can be filed by logging into the GST portal and fill the electronic GST TRAN-1 form, which states the tax amount or duty, that needs to be claimed as ITC.

The GST TRAN-1 form will require the following details:

- Taxpayer's GSTIN
- Registered person's legal name
- Name of the trade(if any)
- A declaration that confirms that the tax returns under the existing tax scheme have been filed
- ITC amount will be taken forward as per the filed returns under the existing tax scheme
- Information about the capital goods, for which ITC is not yet claimed
- Information about the items in stock. It includes the items (with or without invoice) for which ITC is not yet claimed under the existing tax scheme.
- Information about the transferred cenvat credits by a person under the existing tax scheme

- Information about the sent goods for job work and held goods by the jobworker on registered taxpayer's behalf
- Information about the held goods by an agent on another taxpayer's behalf
- Information about the availed credits
- Information about the sent goods on the basis of approval, six months in advance to the day appointed.
- Self declaration of truth, duly signed by the registered taxpayer

The transfer of ITC to GST is same as that in the present tax scheme for the businesses that are registered under excise duty, VAT, or service tax.

Let us now learn about the payment of tax.

Payment of Tax

The taxes to be paid by a taxpayer under the GST tax scheme are classified into three categories:

- **IGST:** It should be paid to the Center in case of an intra-state supply
- **CGST:** It should be paid to the Center in case an inter-state supply
- **SGST:** It should be paid to the State in case of an inter-state supply

The tax must be paid by every 20th day of the month by every taxpayer who is registered under GST. An additional interest may be charged on the due tax if the tax is not paid by the stipulated date. The tax returns cannot be filed for for next reporting period.

Managing GST Payments

A taxpayer needs to maintain three ledgers, which are specified by the government in the GST tax scheme. In the GST common portal, there are different E-ledgers provided for management and facilitation of GST payments. E-ledger is an electronic form of statement that records all the cash and ITC transactions performed by a registered taxpayer. Additionally, the tax liability of a taxpayer is also maintained in the E-ledger. When a taxpayer registers on GST common portal, all three ledgers are opened automatically and will always be displayed on the dashboard of the portal. The GST payments can be made either through the ITC or cash available in the E-ledgers.

Cash Ledger

The cash ledger displays the total amount deposited by the taxpayer against the payment of tax, penalties, and interests charged (if any). A taxpayer can pay any payment with respect to GST through this ledger.

ITC Ledger

This ledger contains a record of the amount of ITC processed on the monthly returns of a taxpayer. Once the submitted transactions are validated, the ITC is credited. The taxpayer can make tax payments with the credit in this ledger. However, the credit cannot be adjusted with late fee or penalty.

Tax Liability Ledger

In this ledger, the entire information about the payable GST, late fees and penalties for the taxpayer can be found. At any time, the information about tax liability for a particular month can be seen by the taxpayer in this ledger.

Options for Payments

The payment of tax can be done through various options available on the GST common portal. The options available for payments are as follows:

- **Counter Payments:** If the amount of GST to be paid is less than ₹10,000, the payment can be made on the counters. The payment can be made through cash, cheque or demand draft. The payment amount that exceeds ₹10,000 shall be made by challan generation or by cards/NEFT.

- **Challan Generation:** The GST amount can be paid through an E-Challan on GST common portal by depositing the amount in the cash log. The E-Challan will be generated after the amount is deposited and it will be valid for 15 days.
- **Cards/NEFT Payments:** There is another way of online payment, which is through the Credit and Debit cards, RTGS and NEFT. Once the payment is made, a CIN (Challan identification Number) is issued to the taxpayer, which acts as a reference number.

ITC Offset with GST Amount

The taxpayer can offset the ITC received with the payable amount of GST and pay the remaining amount to the tax department.

Table 14.2 shows the provisions pertaining to the payment of tax:

Table 14.2: Different Forms for Payment of Tax

Form No.	Description
GST PMT–01	Electronic liability register of a registered person
GST PMT–02	Electronic credit ledger of a registered person
GST PMT–03	Order for re-credit of the amount to cash or credit ledger on the rejection of the refund claim
GST PMT–04	Application for intimation of discrepancy in electronic credit ledger/cash ledger/liability register
GST PMT–05	Electronic cash ledger
GST PMT–06	Challan for deposit of goods and services tax
GST PMT–07	Application for intimating discrepancy relating to payment

Let us learn about the reverse charge.

Reverse Charge

Reverse charge is a mechanism where the person who receives goods and services is responsible to pay GST rather than the supplier. Normally, the business owners collect tax from the customers and then pay it to the government. However, in reverse charge mechanism, the liability of paying tax directly to the government is of the buyer.

The accountability of reverse charge is mostly only on the buyer; however, it is also shared between the buyer and the seller in certain cases.

Applicability of Reverse Charge

The reverse charge is applicable on goods and services in the following cases:

- A business owner who is registered and receives goods and services from a vendor who is not registered
- Any service which is offered by an electronic commerce operator or an aggregator

Table 14.3 provides a list of goods that are liable to be taxable as specified by Central Board of Excise and Customs (CBEC):

Table 14.3: List of Goods Liable to be Taxable

S.No	Goods	Supplier	Recipient
1.	Cashew nuts, not shelled or peeled	Agriculturist	Registered taxable person
2.	Bidi wrapper leaves	Agriculturist	Registered taxable person
3.	Tobacco leaves	Agriculturist	Registered taxable person

Table 14.3: List of Goods Liable to be Taxable

S.No	Goods	Supplier	Recipient
4.	Silk yarn	A person who manufactures silk yarn from raw silk or silk worm cocoons.	Registered taxable person
5.	Lottery supply	State Government, Union Territory or any local authority.	Lottery distributor or selling agent

Table 14.4 provides a list of services that are taxable under the reverse charge mechanism where the recipient is liable to pay GST:

Table 14.4: List of Services Liable to be Taxable

S.No	Service	Supplier	Recipient of supply
1.	Services given in a non-taxable territory	Supplier in non-taxable territory	Registered taxpayer
2.	Goods transport via road	Goods Transport Agency	Registered taxpayer
3.	Legal services	Legal firm or advocate	Registered taxpayer
4.	Services given by an arbitral tribunal	Arbitral Tribunal	Registered taxpayer
5.	Sponsorship services	Individual or business	Corporate or partnership firms
6.	Governmental or local authority services (excluding immovable rental property, postal services, insurance and agency services, services given to an aircraft or ship in an Indian airport or port and transporting goods/passengers)	Government/Local authority	Registered taxpayer
7.	Services given by a company's director in the company itself	Director or corporate body	Company to which the services are offered
8.	Insurance agent services	Insurance agent	Insurance company
9.	Recovery agent services	Recovery agent	Banking company/Financial firm
10.	Goods transport from overseas through a vessel to an Indian customs office	Transport agency	Importer of goods
11.	Permitting to use any copyrighted content	Artist, musician or any creative person	Publishing company
12.	Taxi services given through e-commerce	Taxi driver	E-commerce operator

Reverse Charge Mechanism Requirements

The requirements to enact reverse charge mechanism are as follows:

- The person who receives goods or services must have got a GST registration.
- Accurate records must be maintained by the business owner to incur the amount of reverse charge.

- The supplier must mention on the invoice, receipt vouchers and refund vouchers that the payable amount of tax is through reverse charge.
- The advance amount paid on the supply of goods or services are taxable if they incur reverse charge.

Time of Supply for Reverse Charge

For reverse charge, the time of supply shall be the earliest of the following dates:

- Receipt of goods date
- Payment date
- Immediate date after 30 days from the goods invoice date and 60 days from the services invoice date

Note

The entry date in the receiver's book can become the date, if none of the above is applicable.

Self-Invoicing

When the owner of a business purchases any goods or services from a supplier who is not registered, self-invoicing needs to be done because the unregistered would not be able to issue an invoice.

Exemptions under Reverse Charge

Any business owner who is registered and makes intra-state purchases from an unregistered seller is exempted from GST through reverse charge, if the total amount of supply of goods or services received is less than or equal to ₹5000 per day.

Let us learn about the return of tax.

Returns

As a taxpayer, you must declare the income generated from all the transactions conducted in the business. A return refers to a document that contains particulars relating to a business activity carried out by a taxable person within a prescribed time period. Return provides a structure for paying tax that is payable in the defined time period by following the legal principles described in the GST law.

The following objectives of returns are:

1. It is a medium of transferring information to tax administration.
2. A registered taxpayer finalizes his liabilities by depositing returns and declares tax liability for a fixed period.
3. It provides the essential information to the taxpayer for making his policy decision.
4. It manages tax evasion programs and audit for tax administration.

Every person registered under GST needs to file returns. The return can be filed by the registered person on monthly or quarterly basis. The return filed by an Input Service Distributor (ISD) must contain details regarding their credit distribution for that particular month. A person who collects tax and a person who deducts tax need to file monthly return that shows the collected and deducted amount.

The return is the connecting link between the taxpayer and tax administration.

Define Annual and Final Return

Annual returns and final returns are different from each other. When a registered taxpayer applies for the cancellation of his registration, then the returns filed by that person are called final returns. Filling the last return is mandatory within three months of the cancellation date.

The annual return will be filed by every registered person who pays the tax as a general taxpayer

Filling Return by Taxpayer

A registered taxpayer can file his own GST return in different ways. A registered taxpayer can file a return of his business invoice online on the common GST portal. However, if taxpayers have a huge number of invoices then it is very difficult to file on GST portal and as it consumes a lot of time.

For such taxpayers, an offline utility is available. For using offline utility, the taxpayer first downloads auto populated details, then prepare the return statement offline by using the downloaded details and then uploading the statement on the common GST portal.

Note

GSTN has developed a systematic system of GST Suvidha Provider (GSP), which will co-ordinate with the GST common portal.

Periodicity of Return Filling

A normal period of returns for a class of taxpayers will be applied. The frequency of filing returns will be different for different classes of taxpayers.

Table 14.5 shows the provisions pertaining to the filing of various returns:

Table 14.5: Different Return Forms and their Due Date

Return Form	Description	By Whom?	By When?
GSTR-1	Information about the outgoing supplies of taxable goods or services	Registered person	10th of the succeeding month
GSTR-1A	An amendment form which is used for making corrections in GSTR-1 document that includes any mismatch between taxpayer's GSTR-1 and customer's GSTR-2	Registered person	Between 16th and 17th of the succeeding month
GSTR-2	Information about the incoming supplies of taxable goods or services	Registered person	After 10th but before 15th of the succeeding month
GSTR-2A	A tax return filed by a tax payer which is auto-drafted for purchases and incoming supplies. GSTN automatically compiles the return, on the basis of information presented in supplier's GSTR-1	GST portal	
GSTR-3	It is the monthly return which is based on a finalized detail of incoming and outgoing supplies, along with the tax payment	Registered person	20th of the succeeding month
GSTR-3A	A notice given to a tax defaulter who failed in filing monthly returns, timely	Registered person	
GSTR-3B	A temporary integrated overview of the incoming and outgoing supplies, which are introduced as moderation by the Government of India for businesses that have migrated to GST	Registered person	20th of the succeeding month
GSTR-4	Returns on quarterly basis by a compounding taxable person	Businesses registered in Composition	18th of the month that succeeds the quarter

Table 14.5: Different Return Forms and their Due Date

Return Form	Description	By Whom?	By When?
		scheme	
GSTR-4A	Returns regarding purchases for the composition dealers on quarterly basis. GST portal generates this automatically on the basis of details provided supplier's GSTR-1, GSTR-5, and GSTR-7	GST portal	
GSTR-5	Returns for a taxable person who does not reside in India	Non-Resident taxable person	20th of the succeeding month
GSTR-5A	Returns for a registered person who provides online database access or retrieval service from outside India to a taxable person in India	Non-Resident registered person	20th of the succeeding month
GSTR-6	Returns for Input Service Distributor	Input Service Distributor	13th of the succeeding month
GSTR-6A	An auto-drafted form generated on the basis of the information presented in the supplier's GSTR-1	GST Portal	
GSTR-7	Return for tax deduction authorities at source	Person deducting Tax	10th of the succeeding month
GSTR-7A	Certificate issued for tax deducted at source	GST Portal	
GSTR-8	Information related to the supplies effected by an e-commerce operator and the total tax collected	E-commerce operator/Tax collector	10th of the succeeding month
GSTR-9*	Annual returns	Registered person	31st December of the succeeding financial year
GSTR-9A	An integrated annual return for compounding vendors, which includes all filed returns for that particular year on a quarterly basis	Businesses registered in Composition scheme	31st December of succeeding financial year
GSTR-10	Final return	Taxable person with a renounced or a cancelled registration	Within three months from the cancellation date or renouncement date (whichever is later)
GSTR-11	Information regarding the incoming supplies to be provided by a person having UIN	Person possessing UIN and claiming refund	28th of the month succeeding the month for which statement is filed

*** These forms are subjected to removal.**

Table 14.6 shows the provisions pertaining to a goods and services tax practitioner:

Table 14.6: Different Forms for a Goods and Services Tax Practitioner

Form No.	Description
GST PCT-01	Application for enrolment as a GST Practitioner
GST PCT-02	Enrolment certificate of a GST practitioner
GST PCT-03	Show Cause Notice for disqualification
GST PCT-04	Order of rejection of enrolment as a GST Practitioner
GST PCT-05	Authorisation/withdrawal of authorisation for a GST practitioner

Let us learn about the refund of tax.

Refund of Tax

Generally, GST refunds would claim when the payment of GST is greater than its liabilities. For example, Mr. Ram's GST liability for the month of September is ₹50000. However, due to some mistake, Mr. Ram paid a GST of 5 lakh rupees. In such case, Mr. Ram has paid an extra GST of 4.5 lakh rupees, which can be claimed as a refund by him. An application for refunding tax will be presented in front to the appropriate officer of IGST / CGST / SGST within 2 years.

Some cases in which the refund under GST can be claimed are as follows:

- When a dealer exports goods/services under the claim of rebate
- When payment of GST tax will be made by UN bodies, embassies, para-military-fan canteens, etc.
- When a taxable person has paid an extra amount by mistake
- ITC increases due to the output being tax exempt or nil-rated
- There may be a refund after a temporary evaluation
- Refund after inquiry or conclusion by a judicial officer
- GST is subjected to refund by foreign or international tourists
- When credit is accumulated due to the lower rate of output tax than input

Refund Form

Filing of returns and claiming refund will be completely an online process under GST. We will fill up the form to claim refund, acknowledgment, and examination under GST.

Table 14.7 shows the forms fill up for claiming refunds:

Table 14.7: Forms for Claiming Refund

Sr. No	Form Number	Applicable	Title
1.	GST RFD-01	For Center Only	Refund Application form
2.	GST RFD-01 A	For Center Only	Refund Application Form (manually)
3.	GST RFD-01 B	For Center Only	Refund Order details
4.	GST RFD-02	For Center Only	Acknowledgement
5.	GST RFD-03	For Center Only	Notice of Deficiency on Application for Refund
6.	GST RFD-04	For both Center and State	Provisional Refund Order
7.	GST RFD-05	For both Center and State	Refund Sanction/Rejection Order

Table 14.7: Forms for Claiming Refund

Sr. No	Form Number	Applicable	Title
8.	GST RFD-06	For both Center and State	Order for Complete adjustment of claimed Refund
9.	GST RFD-07	For Center Only	Show cause notice for reject of refund application
10.	GST RFD-08	For both Center and State	Payment Advice
11.	GST RFD-09	For both Center and State	Order for Interest on delayed refunds
12.	GST RFD-10	For Center Only	Refund application form for Embassy/ International Organizations
13.	GST RFD-11	For Center Only	Refund of Integrated Tax Paid on Export of Goods or Services under Bond or Letter of Undertaking

Let us learn about the offenses and penalties in GST.

Offenses and Penalties

The GST tax scheme in India has brought simplicity and transparency in the taxing policies. Also, GST has less potential of evading tax than the earlier taxation schemes. To prevent the misuse and exploitation of the taxation policies, the government has laid down a list of offenses and penalties associated with GST. An offence is any non-compliant or illegal activity performed against the provisions of the GST tax scheme. A taxpayer found involved in any of such activities is likely to invoke penalties. A penalty is a form of punishment prescribed in the law that is enforced against the offense committed by the taxpayer.

Table 14.8 shows the offenses along with the penalties enforced, which are listed by the government in GST scheme:

Table 14.8: Offenses and Penalties

Offense	Activities involved	Penalty
Fraud	Giving wrong information during registration process Giving wrong information or false documents to GST officials for evading tax Acquiring tax refunds of GST through false means	₹10,000 or an equivalent amount of the evaded tax ₹10,000 for giving false information for the first time, and if it continues, then a penalty of ₹100 per day (up to maximum of ₹25,000) ₹25,000 for helping the offender
Fake invoices	Providing incorrect invoices on sale of goods or services Supply of goods or services without providing appropriate invoices Using another taxpayer's ID for supplying goods and/or services Providing an invoice without the supply of goods or services	₹10,000 or an equivalent amount of evaded tax for not issuing invoice ₹25,000 for incorrect invoice

Table 14.8: Offenses and Penalties

Offense	Activities involved	Penalty
Improper supply of goods or services	Movement of goods without suitable documents Movement of taxable goods without a GST registration Supply or storage of goods that can be confiscated	An equivalent amount of evaded tax, if the offender surrenders. Else, 50% of the value of the supply is fined
Tax evasion	Non-remittance of the collected tax to the government within a time of 3 months Acquiring refund from the government in a false manner Subduing the sales of goods or services for evading tax Fully or partial utilization of ITC without receiving goods or services	₹10,000 or an equivalent amount of evaded tax
Delay in returns filing	Failing to file returns for the monthly sales Failing to file returns for the monthly purchases Failing to file annual returns	₹100 per day (up to maximum of ₹5,000)
Tampering or destruction	Destruction of seized goods Destruction of or tampering legal documents or any material evidence Barring a tax official from performing their duty	6 months of imprisonment and an additional fine
Repeated short tax payments	Three short payments of tax in three returns during six consecutive tax period	₹10,000 or 10% of short tax payment (whichever is higher)

Common penalty

There is a fine of up to ₹25,000 for any offense covered under GST that doesn't have a penalty associated with it. In case of any fraud activities performed by a taxpayer, the following are also applicable other than the penalties mentioned in the table:

- A jail term of one year, and an amount equivalent to the evaded tax in case of evasion up to 50 lakhs
- A jail term of three years, and the penalty amount to the evaded tax in case of evasion between 50 lakhs to 100 lakhs
- A jail term of five years, and the penalty amount in case of evasion exceeding 100 lakhs

Procedure after penalty imposition

The procedure that is followed by the GST tax authority after imposing a penalty on the taxpayer is as follows:

- A legal notice will be sent to the offender, who will be given a fair chance to be heard by the tax officials.
- A summarize form of the reasons legal provisions associated with the penalty will be given to the offender.
- If the offender surrenders, the tax officials may use it as a leverage for reducing penalty imposed.

Offenses that are not penalized

The offenses that are not liable to be penalized as per the GST scheme are mentioned as follows:

- A tax amount less than ₹5000
- Unintentional or unknowingly committed offense without any back up of malicious intent
- An offense committed due to improper understanding of GST rules
- Any offense that can be rectified such as an omission of information in a document

Let us learn about the procedure to enable the GST feature in Tally.

Enabling GST in Tally.ERP 9

To compute GST in Tally, you first need to enable it. Perform the following steps to enable GST in Tally:

1. *Click* the **F11: Features** button on the Button Bar in the **Gateway of Tally** screen.

   The **Company Features** menu appears.
2. *Double-click* the **Statutory & Taxation** option in the **Company Features** menu.

   The **Company Operations Alteration** screen appears with Statutory and Taxation.
3. *Set* the **Enable Goods and Services Tax (GST)** option to **Yes**.
4. *Set* the **Set/alter GST details** option to **Yes**.
5. *Press* the **Enter** key. The **Company GST Details** screen appears with the **List of States** menu.
6. *Double-click* the desired option in the **List of States** menu for the **State** option.
7. *Enter* the desired GSTN/UIN number beside the **GSTN/UIN** option.
8. *Enter* the desired date beside the **Applicable from** option.
9. *Set* the **Set/alter GST rate details** option to **Yes**.

   The **GST Details** screen appears.
10. *Double-click* the desired type of taxability in the **Taxability** menu for the **Taxability** option.
11. *Set* the **In reverse charge applicable** option to **Yes**.
12. *Enter* the desired tax rate beside the **Integrated Tax** option.

    The **Central Tax** and **State Tax** options will be filled automatically.

Note

To enable In reverse charge applicable, Central Tax, and State Tax option, you need to set the Enable reverse charge calculation and Show all GST tax types option to Yes in the Configuration screen.

13. *Press* the **Enter** key until the **Company GST Details** screen reappears.
14. *Set* the **Enable GST Classifications** option to **Yes**.
15. *Set* the **Provide LUT/Bond details** option to **No**.
16. *Press* the **Enter** key. The **Accept ?** message box appears.
17. *Click* **Yes** in the **Accept ?** message box. The **Company Operations Alteration** screen reappears.
18. *Press* the **Enter** key until the **Accept ?** message box appears.
19. *Click* **Yes** in the **Accept ?** message box to save the changes.

Let us now learn to create masters for GST in Tally.

Creating Masters for GST

The ledgers affected by GST are as follows:

- Central tax ledger
- State tax ledger
- Purchase ledger
- Sales ledger
- Party ledger
- Stock item

Let us now discuss about the procedure to create these ledgers in the following sections.

Creating Central Tax Ledger

Perform the following steps to create a central tax ledger:

1. *Double-click* the **Accounts Info.** option in the **Gateway of Tally** menu.
   The **Accounts Info.** menu appears.
2. *Double-click* the **Ledgers** option in the **Accounts Info.** menu. The **Ledgers** menu appears.
3. *Double-click* the **Create** option under the **Single Ledger** section in the **Ledgers** menu.
   The **Ledger Creation** screen appears (Fig.TL-14.17).
4. *Type* the name of the ledger beside the **Name** option. In our case, we have typed **Central Tax @9%** (Fig.TL-14.17).
5. *Press* the **Enter** key three times. The **List of Groups** menu appears.
6. *Double-click* the desired parent group in the **List of Groups** menu for the **Under** option. In our case, we have double-clicked the **Duties & Taxes** group (Fig.TL-14.17).
   The **List of Duties/Taxes** menu appears.
7. *Double-click* the desired tax in the **List of Duties/Taxes** menu for the **Type of duty/tax** option. In our case, we have double-clicked **GST** (Fig.TL-14.17). The **Tax Types** menu appears.
8. *Double-click* the desired tax type in the **Tax Types** menu for the **Tax type** option. In our case, we have double-clicked **Central Tax** (Fig.TL-14.17).
9. *Enter* the desired percentage beside the **Percentage of calculation** option. In our case, we have entered **9%** (Fig.TL-14.17).
10. *Press* the **Enter** key. The **List of Rounding Methods** menu appears.
11. *Double-click* the desired rounding method from the **List of Rounding Methods** menu for the **Rounding method** option. In our case, we have double-clicked **Normal Rounding** (Fig.TL-14.17).
    The **Rounding limit** option appears.
12. *Enter* the desired rounding limit beside the **Rounding limit** option. In our case, we have entered **2** (Fig.TL-14.17).
13. *Press* the **Enter** key until the **Accept ?** message box appears (Fig.TL-14.17).
14. *Click* **Yes** in the **Accept ?** message box to create the ledger with the specified information, as shown in Fig.TL-14.17:

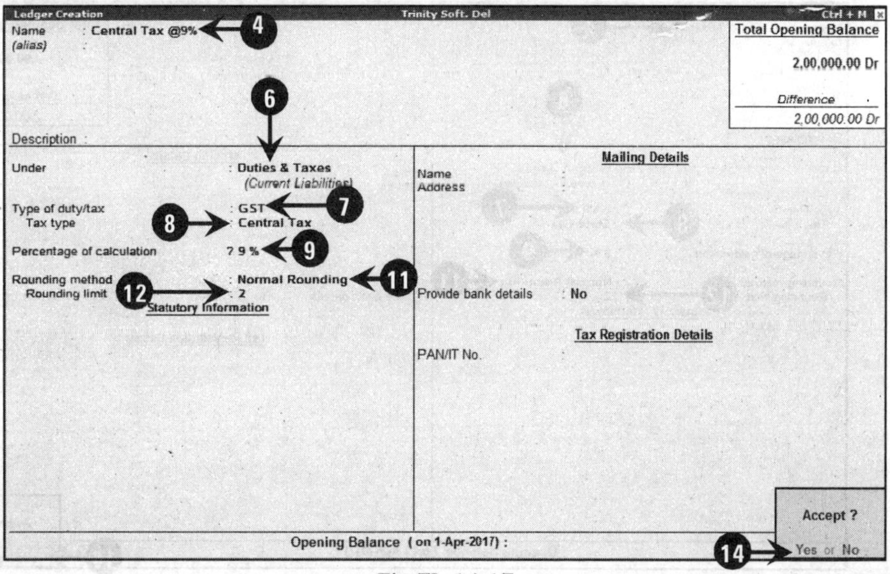

Fig.TL-14.17

Creating State Tax Ledger

Perform the following steps to create a state tax ledger:

1. *Double-click* the **Accounts Info.** option in the **Gateway of Tally** menu. The **Accounts Info.** menu appears.
2. *Double-click* the **Ledgers** option in the **Accounts Info.** menu. The **Ledgers** menu appears.
3. *Double-click* the **Create** option under the **Single Ledger** section in the **Ledgers** menu. The **Ledger Creation** screen appears (Fig.TL-14.18).
4. *Type* the name of the ledger beside the **Name** option. In our case, we have typed **State Tax@9%** (Fig.TL-14.18).
5. *Press* the **Enter** key three times. The **List of Groups** menu appears.
6. *Double-click* the desired parent group in the **List of Groups** menu for the **Under** option. In our case, we have double-clicked the **Duties & Taxes** group (Fig.TL-14.18). The **List of Duties/Taxes** menu appears.
7. *Double-click* the desired tax in the **List of Duties/Taxes** menu for the **Type of duty/tax** option. In our case, we have double-clicked **GST** (Fig.TL-14.18). The **Tax Types** menu appears.
8. *Double-click* the desired tax type in the **Tax Types** menu for the **Tax type** option. In our case, we have double-clicked **State Tax** (Fig.TL-14.18).
9. *Enter* the desired percentage beside the **Percentage of calculation** option. In our case, we have entered **9%** (Fig.TL-14.18).
10. *Press* the **Enter** key. The **List of Rounding Methods** menu appears.
11. *Double-click* the desired rounding method from the **List of Rounding Methods** menu for the **Rounding Method** option. In our case, we have double-clicked **Normal Rounding** (Fig.TL-14.18). The **Rounding limit** option appears.
12. *Enter* the desired rounding limit beside the **Rounding limit** option. In our case, we have entered **2** (Fig.TL-14.18).
13. *Press* the **Enter** key until the **Accept ?** message box appears (Fig.TL-14.18).
14. *Click* **Yes** in the **Accept ?** message box to create the ledger with the specified information, as shown in Fig.TL-14.18:

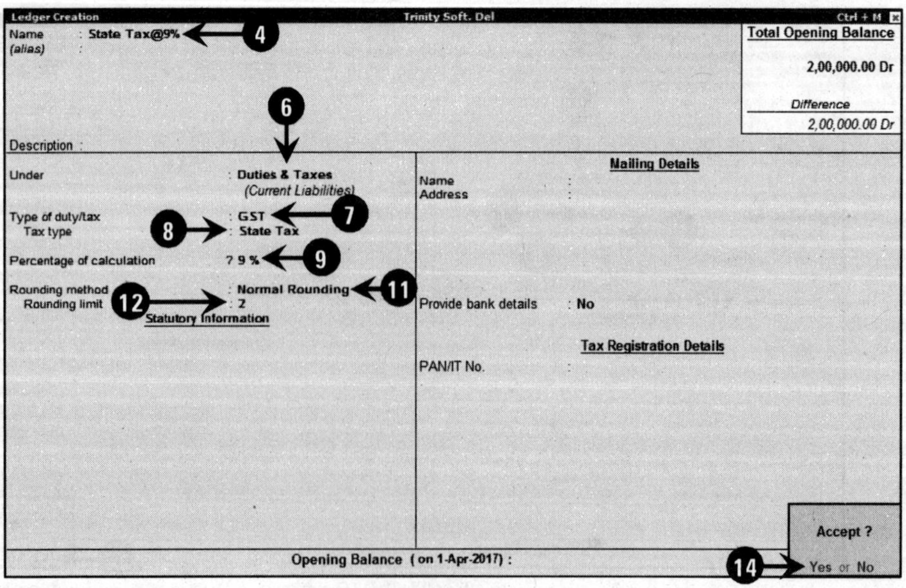

Fig.TL-14.18

Creating Party Ledger

Perform the following steps to create a party ledger:

1. *Double-click* the **Accounts Info.** option in the **Gateway of Tally** menu.
   The **Accounts Info.** menu appears.
2. *Double-click* the **Ledgers** option in the **Accounts Info.** menu.
   The **Ledgers** menu appears.
3. *Double-click* the **Create** option in the **Ledgers** menu.
   The **Ledger Creation** screen appears.
4. *Enter* the name of the party ledger beside the **Name** option. In our case, we have entered **Gupta Pvt. Ltd.**
5. *Press* the **Enter** key three times. The **List of Groups** menu appears.
6. *Double-click* the **Sundry Creditors** option in the **List of Groups** menu for the **Under** option.
   The **Maintain balances bill-by-bill** and **Default credit period** options are enabled.
7. *Set* the **Maintain balances bill-by-bill option** to **Yes**.
8. *Enter* the address of the party beside the **Address** option. In our case, we have entered **Daryaganj, New Delhi**.
9. *Press* the **Enter** key until the **List of States** menu appears.
10. *Double-click* the desired state from the **List of States** menu for the **State** option. In our case, we have double-clicked **Delhi**.
11. *Enter* the **PIN** code beside the **Pincode** option. In our case, we have entered **110002**.
12. *Enter* the **PAN** or **IT** number beside the **PAN/IT No**. option. In our case, we have entered **AOPFG2435G**.
13. *Set* the **Set/alter GST Details** option to **Yes**.
    The **GST Details** screen appears with the **Registration Types** menu.
14. *Double-click* the desired registration type in the **Registration typeS** menu for the **Registration type** option. In our case, we have double-clicked **Regular** (Fig.TL-14.19).
15. *Set* the **Is a e-Commerce operator** option to **No** (Fig.TL-14.19).
16. *Press* the **Enter** key. The **Party Type** menu appears.
17. *Double-click* the desired party type in the **Party Type** menu for the **Party Type** option. In our case, we have double-clicked **Deemed Export** (Fig.TL-14.19).
18. *Enter* the desired GSTIN/UIN number beside the **GSTIN/UIN** option In our case, we have entered 07AOPF 2435G1Z7 as shown in Fig.TL-14.19:

Fig.TL-14.19

19. *Press* the **Enter** key.
    The **Ledger Creation** screen reappears.
20. *Press* the **Enter** key until the **Accept ?** message box appears.

21. *Click* **Yes** in the **Accept ?** message box to create the ledger, as shown in Fig.TL-14.20:

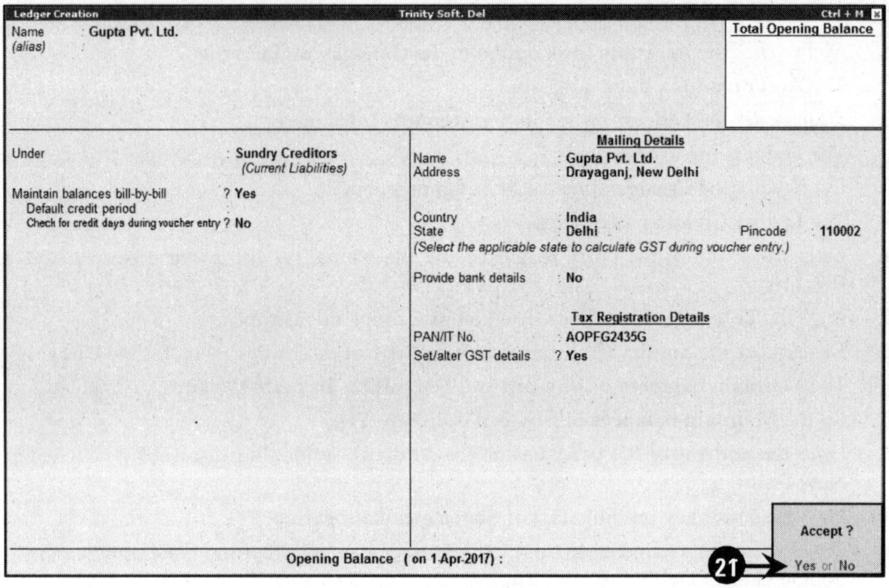

Fig.TL-14.20

Similarly, you can create more party ledgers. In our case, we have created a party ledger with the name **Jain Pvt. Ltd.** under the **Sundry Debtor** group, as shown in Fig.TL-14.21:

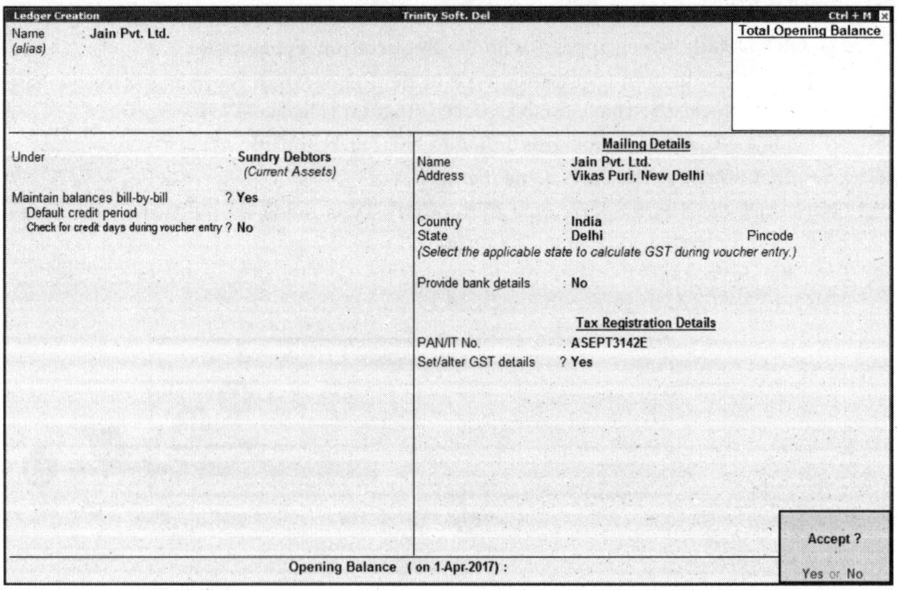

Fig.TL-14.21

Creating Purchase Ledger

Perform the following steps to create the purchase ledger:

1. *Double-click* the **Accounts Info.** option in the **Gateway of Tally** menu.

   The **Accounts Info.** menu appears.

2. *Double-click* the **Ledgers** option in the **Accounts Info.** menu.

   The **Ledgers** menu appears.
3. *Double-click* the **Create** option under the **Single Ledger** section in the **Ledgers** menu.

   The **Ledger Creation** screen appears.
4. *Type* the name of the ledger beside the **Name** option. In our case, we have typed **Purchase@18%**.
5. *Press* the **Enter** key three times. The **List of Groups** menu appears.
6. *Double-click* the desired parent group in the **List of Groups** menu for the **Under** option. In our case, we have double-clicked the **Purchase Accounts** group.
7. *Set* the **Inventory values are affected** option to **Yes**.
8. *Double-click* the **Applicable** option from the **Applicability** menu for the **Is GST Applicable** option.
9. *Set* the **Set/alter GST Details** option to **Yes**.
10. *Press* the **Enter** key.

    The **GST Details** screen appears.
11. *Double-click* the **Purchase Taxable** option from the **NatureS of Transaction** menu for the **Nature of transaction** option (Fig.TL-14.22).

    The **Taxability** option will be filled automatically.
12. *Set* the **In reverse charge applicable** option to **No** (Fig.TL-14.22).
13. *Enter* the desired tax rate beside the **Integrated Tax** option. In our case, we have entered **18%** (Fig.TL-14.22).
14. *Press* the **Enter** key.

    The **Central Tax** and **State Tax** option will be filled automatically, as shown in Fig.TL-14.22:

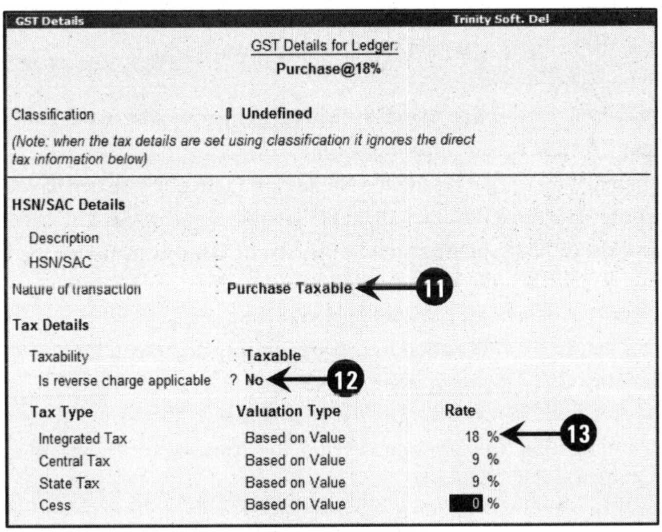

Fig.TL-14.22

15. *Press* the **Enter** key until the **Ledger Creation** reappears.
16. *Double-click* the **Goods** option from the **Supply Types** menu for the **Type of Supply** option (Fig.TL-14.23).
17. *Press* the **Enter** key until the **Accept ?** message box appears.

18. *Click* **Yes** in the **Accept ?** message box to create the ledger, as shown in Fig.TL-14.23:

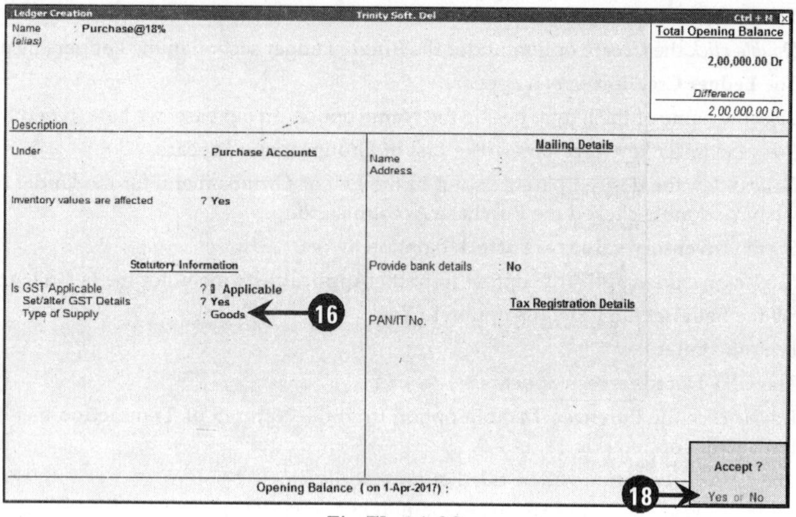

Fig.TL-14.23

Creating Sales Ledger

Perform the following steps to create the sales ledger:

1. *Double-click* the **Accounts Info.** option in the **Gateway of Tally** menu.
   The **Accounts Info.** menu appears.
2. *Double-click* the **Ledgers** option in the **Accounts Info.** menu.
   The **Ledgers** menu appears.
3. *Double-click* the **Create** option under the **Single Ledger** section in the **Ledgers** menu.
   The **Ledger Creation** screen appears.
4. *Type* the name of the ledger beside the **Name** option. In our case, we have typed **Sales@18%**.
5. *Press* the **Enter** key three times. The **List of Groups** menu appears.
6. *Double-click* the desired parent group in the **List of Groups** menu for the **Under** option. In our case, we have double-clicked the **Sales Accounts** group.
7. *Set* the **Inventory values are affected** option to **Yes**.
8. *Double-click* the **Applicable** option from the **Applicability** menu for the **Is GST Applicable** option.
9. *Set* the **Set/alter GST Details** option to **Yes.**
10. *Press* the **Enter** key. The **GST Details** screen appears.
11. *Double-click* the **Sales Taxable** option from the **Natures of Transaction** menu for the **Nature of transaction** option (Fig.TL-14.24).
    The **Taxability** option will be filled automatically.
12. *Set* the **In reverse charge applicable** option to **No** (Fig.TL-14.24).
13. *Enter* the desired tax rate beside the **Integrated Tax** option. In our case, we have entered **18%** (Fig.TL-14.24).
14. *Press* the **Enter** key.

The **Central Tax** and **State Tax** option will be filled automatically, as shown in Fig.TL-14.24:

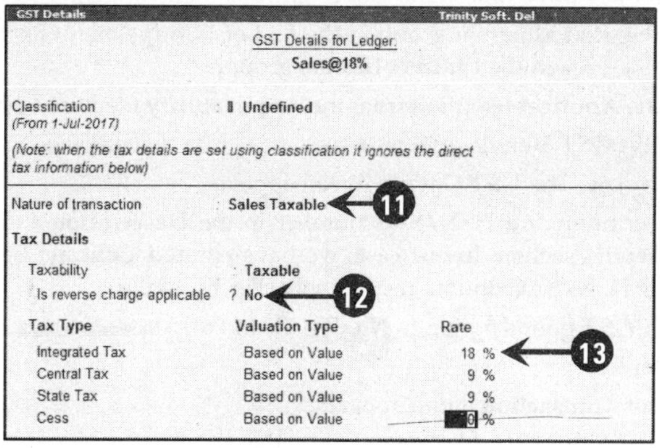

Fig.TL-14.24

15. *Press* the **Enter** key until the **Ledger Creation** reappears.
16. *Double-click* the **Goods** option from the **Supply Types** menu for the **Type of Supply** option (Fig.TL-14.25)
17. *Press* the **Enter** key until the **Accept ?** message box appears.
18. *Click* **Yes** in the **Accept ?** message box to create the ledger, as shown in Fig.TL-14.25:

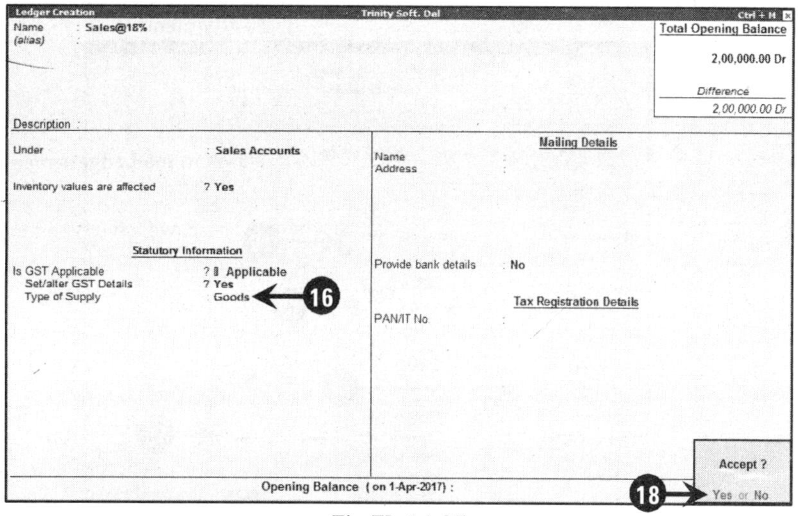

Fig.TL-14.25

Creating Service Ledger

Perform the following steps to create the service ledger:

1. *Double-click* the **Accounts Info.** option in the **Gateway of Tally** menu.

   The **Accounts Info.** menu appears.
2. *Double-click* the **Ledgers** option in the **Accounts Info.** menu.

   The **Ledgers** menu appears.
3. *Double-click* the **Create** option under the **Single Ledger** section in the **Ledgers** menu.

   The **Ledger Creation** screen appears.

4. *Type* the name of the ledger beside the **Name** option. In our case, we have typed **Contract Services**.
5. *Press* the **Enter** key three times. The **List of Groups** menu appears.
6. *Double-click* the desired parent group in the **List of Groups** menu for the **Under** option. In our case, we have double-clicked the **Indirect Income** group.
7. *Double-click* the **Applicable** option from the **Applicability** menu for the **Is GST Applicable** option.
8. *Set* the **Set/alter GST Details** option to **Yes**.
9. *Press* the **Enter** key. The **GST Details** screen appears.
10. *Enter* the description and HSN/SAC number in the **Description** and **HSN/SAC** option under the **HSN/SAC Details** section. In our case, we have entered **Contract Services** in the Description and **3102344** in the HSN/SAC option, respectively (Fig.TL-14.26).
11. *Set* the **Is non-GST goods** option to **No** (Fig.TL-14.26).
12. *Press* the **Enter** key.

    The **Natures of Transaction** menu appears.
13. *Double-click* the **Sales Taxable** option from the **Natures of Transaction** menu for the **Nature of transaction** option (Fig.TL-14.26).

    The **Taxability** option will be filled automatically.
14. *Set* the **Is reverse charge applicable** option to **No** (Fig.TL-14.26).
15. *Enter* the desired tax rate beside the **Integrated Tax** option. In our case, we have entered **12%** (Fig.TL-14.26).
16. *Press* the **Enter** key.

    The **Central Tax** and **State Tax** option will be filled automatically, as shown in Fig.TL-14.26:

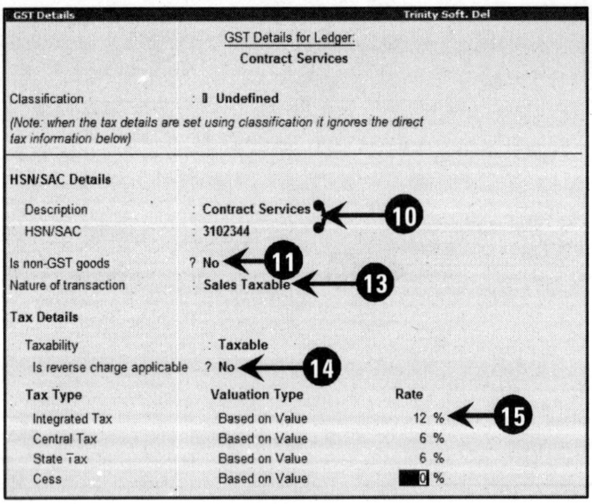

Fig.TL-14.26

17. *Press* the **Enter** key until the **Ledger Creation** screen reappears.
18. *Double-click* the **Services** option from the **Supply Types** menu for the **Type of Supply** option (Fig.TL-14.27).
19. *Press* the **Enter** key until the **Accept ?** message box appears.

20. *Click* **Yes** in the **Accept ?** message box to create the ledger, as shown in Fig.TL-14.27:

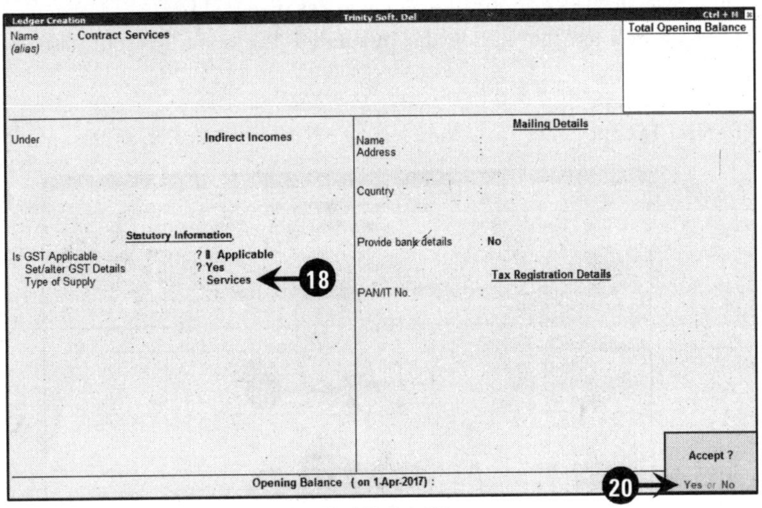

Fig.TL-14.27

Creating Stock Item

Perform the following steps to create a stock item:

1. *Double-click* the **Stock Items** option in the **Inventory Info.** menu.

   The **Stock Items** menu appears.
2. *Double-click* the **Create** option in the **Stock Items** menu.

   The **Stock Item Creation** screen appears.
3. *Type* the name of the stock item beside the **Name** option. In our case, we have entered **Casual Shoes.**
4. *Type* an alias beside the **(alias)** option.
5. *Press* the **Enter** key. The **List of Groups** menu appears.
6. *Double-click* the stock group under which you want to create a new stock item, in the **List of Groups** menu for the **Under** option. In our case, we have double-clicked **Primary**.

   The **Units** menu appears.
7. *Double-click* the measurement unit for the stock item in the **Units** menu for the **Units** option. In our case, we have double-clicked **nos**.
8. *Set* the **Is GST Applicable** option to **Applicable**.
9. *Set* the **Set/alter GST Details** option to **Yes**.

   The **GST Details** screen appears with the Tax Rate Details (Fig.TL-14.28).
10. *Enter* the description and HSN/SAC number in the **Description** and **HSN/SAC** option under the **HSN/SAC Details** section. In our case, we have entered **Casual Shoes** in the **Description** and **64042500** in the **HSN/SAC** option respectively (Fig.TL-14.28).
11. *Press* the **Enter** key.

    The Calculation Type menu appears.
12. *Double-click* the **On Value** as a calculation type in the **Calculation Type** menu for the **Calculation type** option (Fig.TL-14.28).

    The **Taxability** menu appears.

13. *Double-click* the **Taxable** option in the **Taxability** menu for the **Taxability** option (Fig.TL-14.28).
14. *Set* the **In reverse charge applicable** option to **Yes** (Fig.TL-14.28).
15. *Enter* the desired tax rate beside the **Integrated Tax** option. In our case, we have entered **18%** (Fig.TL-14.28).
16. *Press* the **Enter** key.

    The **Central Tax** and **State Tax** option will be filled automatically, as shown in Fig.TL-14.28:

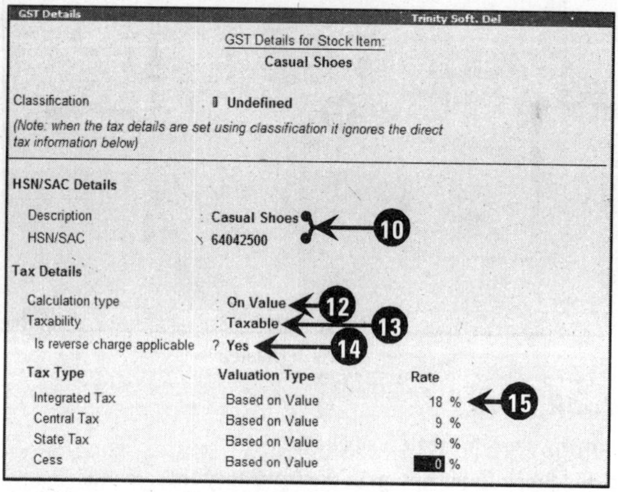

Fig.TL-14.28

17. *Press* the **Enter** key until the **Stock Item Creation** screen reappears.

    The **Supply Types** menu appears.
18. *Double-click* the **Goods** option in the **Supply Types** menu for the **Type of Supply** option (Fig.TL-14.29).
19. *Press* the **Enter** key until the **Accept ?** message box appears.
20. *Click* **Yes** in the **Accept ?** message box to create the stock item, as shown in Fig.TL-14.29:

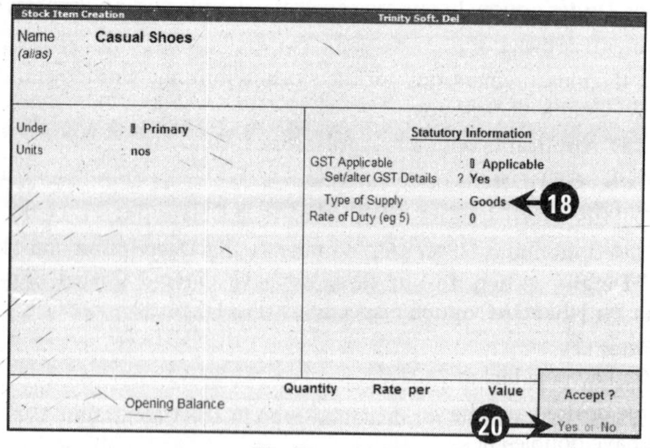

Fig.TL-14.29

Similarly, you can create the other stock items. In our case, we have created **Sport Shoes**, as shown in Fig.TL-14.30:

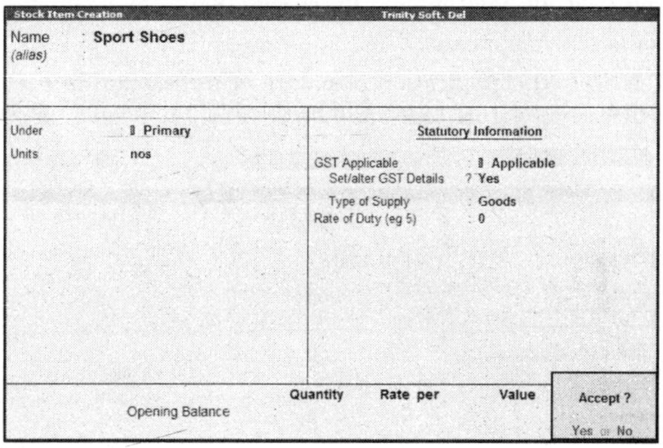

Fig.TL-14.30

Let us learn to create vouchers for GST in Tally.

Creating Vouchers for GST

The vouchers affected by VAT are as follows:

- Purchase voucher
- Sales voucher
- Creating Sales Voucher for Providing Services
- Receipt voucher
- Payment voucher
- Journal voucher

Let us now discuss the procedure to create these vouchers in the following sections.

Creating a Purchase Voucher

Perform the following steps to record the purchase transaction in Tally:

1. *Double-click* the **Accounting Vouchers** option under the **Transactions** section in the **Gateway of Tally** menu.

   The **Accounting Voucher Creation** screen appears.
2. *Click* the **F9: Purchase** button on the Button Bar.

   The **Accounting Voucher Creation** screen of the purchase voucher appears.
3. *Enter* the desired supplier invoice number beside the **Supplier invoice no.** option. In our case, we have entered **12**.
4. *Press* the **Enter** key.
5. *Enter* the date on which the voucher is created beside the **Date** option. In our case, we have entered **1-Jul-2017**.
6. *Press* the **Enter** key. The **List of Ledger Accounts** menu appears.
7. *Double-click* the desired supplier in the **List of Ledger Accounts** menu for **Party A/c name** option. In our case, we have double-clicked **Gupta Pvt. Ltd**.

   The **List of Stock Items** menu appears.
8. *Double-click* the desired stock item in the **List of Stock Items** menu for the **Name of Item** columns. In our case, we have double-clicked **Casual Shoes**.
9. *Enter* the quantity and rate of the selected item in the **Quantity** and **Rate** columns, respectively.

   The **per** and **Amount** columns will be filled automatically.

10. *Press* the **Enter** key twice. The **Accounting Details** screen appears.
11. *Double-click* the desired purchase ledger in the **List of Ledger Accounts** menu for the **Particulars** columns. In our case, we have entered **Purchase@18%**.

    The **GST Details** screen appears.
12. *Double-click* the desired classification or nature of transaction in the **Classifications/Natures** menu for the **Classification/Nature** option. In our case, we have double-clicked **Purchase Taxable** (Fig.TL-14.31).

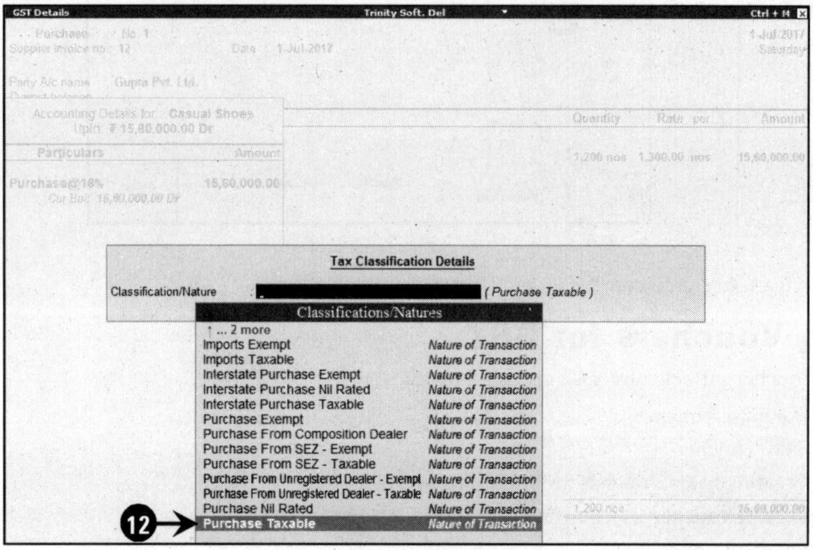

Fig.TL-14.31

The **Accounting Details** screen reappears, as shown in Fig.TL-14.32:

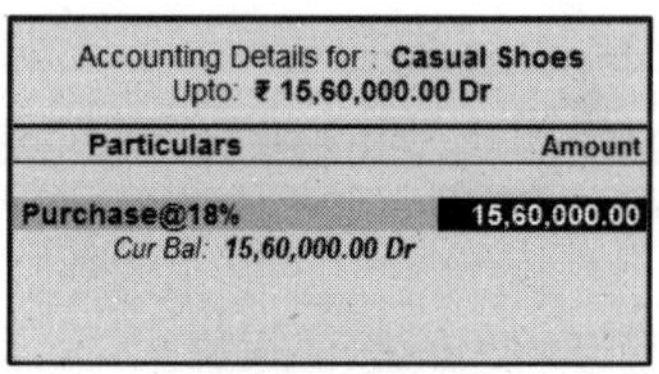

Fig.TL-14.32

13. *Press* the **Enter** key. The **Accounting Voucher Creating** screen reappears.
14. *Press* the **Enter** key. The **List of Ledger Accounts** menu appears.
15. *Select* the desired state tax ledger in the **List of Ledger Accounts** menu for the **Name of Item** column. In our case, we have double-clicked **State Tax@9%** (Fig.TL-14.33).

    The **Rate** and **Amount** columns get filled automatically.
16. *Press* the **Enter** key.

    The **List of Ledger Accounts** menu appears.
17. *Select* the desired central tax ledger in the **List of Ledger Accounts** menu for the **Name of Item** column. In our case, we have double-clicked **Central Tax @9%** (Fig.TL-14.33).

    The **Rate** and **Amount** columns get filled automatically.
18. *Press* the **Enter** key until the **Accept ?** message box appears.

19. *Click* **Yes** in the **Accept ?** message box to save the voucher, as shown in Fig.TL-14.33:

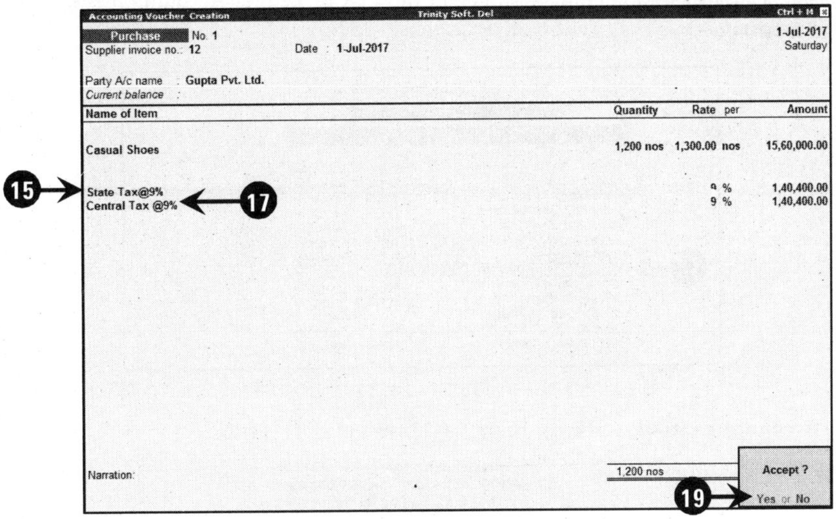

Fig.TL-14.33

Similarly, you can create more purchase vouchers to purchase items.

Creating Sales Voucher

Perform the following steps to record the sales transaction in tally:

1. *Double-click* the **Accounting Vouchers** option under the **Transactions** section in the **Gateway of Tally** menu.

   The **Accounting Voucher Creation** screen appears.

2. *Click* the **F8: Sales** button on the Button Bar.

   The **Accounting Voucher Creation** screen of the Sales voucher appears.

3. *Enter* the desired reference number beside the **Reference no.** option. In our case, we have entered **15.**

4. *Press* the **Enter** key.

   The **List of Ledger Accounts** menu appears.

5. *Double-click* the desired customer in the **List of Ledger Accounts** menu for **Party A/c name** option. In our case, we have double-clicked **Jain Pvt. Ltd**.

   The **List of Stock Items** menu appears.

6. *Double-click* the desired stock item in the **List of Stock Items** menu for the **Name of Item** columns. In our case, we have double-clicked **Sport Shoes**.

7. *Enter* the quantity and rate of the selected item in the **Quantity** and **Rate** columns.

   The **per** and **Amount** columns will be filled automatically.

8. *Press* the **Enter** key twice.

   The **Accounting Details** screen appears.

9. *Double-click* the desired sales ledger in the **List of Ledger Accounts** menu for the **Particulars** columns. In our case, we have entered **Sales@18%**.

   The **GST Details** screen appears.

10. *Double-click* the desired classification or nature of transaction in the **Classifications/Natures** menu for the **Classification/Nature** option. In our case, we have double-clicked **Sales Taxable** (Fig.TL-14.34):

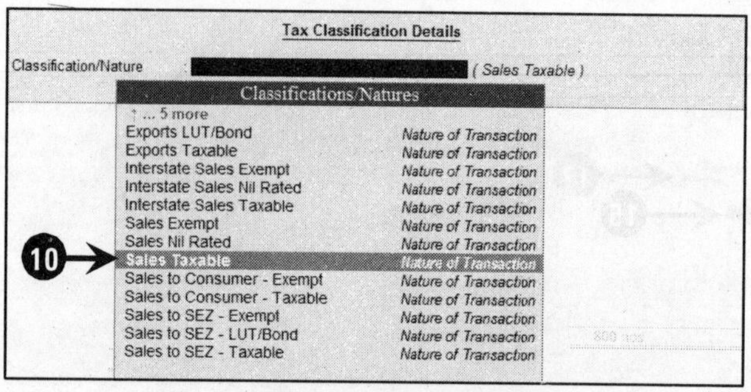

Fig.TL-14.34

The **Accounting Details** screen appears, as shown in Fig.TL-14.35:

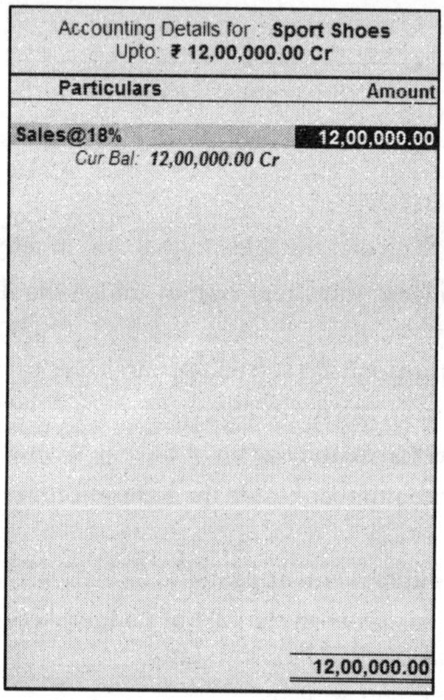

Fig.TL-14.35

11. *Press* the **Enter** key.

    The **Accounting Voucher Creation** screen reappears.

12. *Press* the **Enter** key.

    The **List of Ledger Accounts** menu appears.

13. *Select* the desired state tax ledger in the **List of Ledger Accounts** menu for the **Name of Item** column. In our case, we have double-clicked **State Tax@9%** (Fig.TL-14.36).

    The **Rate** and **Amount** columns get filled automatically.

14. *Press* the **Enter** key. The **List of Ledger Accounts** menu appears.

15. *Select* the desired central tax ledger in the **List of Ledger Accounts** menu for the **Name of Item** column. In our case, we have double-clicked **Central Tax @9%** (Fig.TL-14.36).

    The **Rate** and **Amount** columns get filled automatically.

16. *Press* the **Enter** key until the **Accept ?** message box appears.

17. *Click* **Yes** in the **Accept ?** message box to save the voucher, as shown in Fig.TL-14.36:

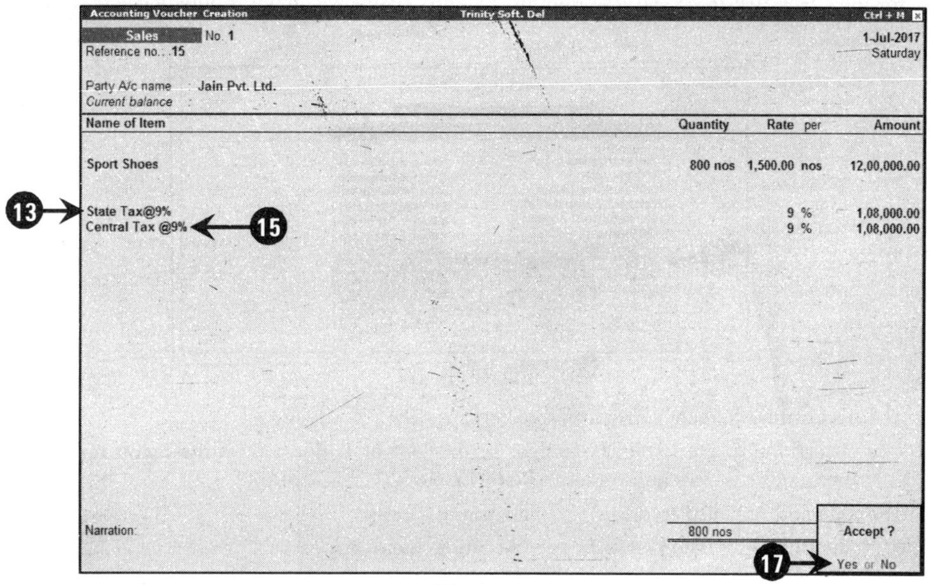

Fig.TL-14.36

Similarly, you can create more sales vouchers to sale items.

Creating Sales Voucher for Providing Services

Perform the following steps to record the sales transaction for providing services in tally:

1. *Double-click* the **Accounting Vouchers** option under the **Transactions** section in the **Gateway of Tally** menu.

   The **Accounting Voucher Creation** screen appears.
2. *Click* the **F8: Sales** button on the Button Bar.

   The **Accounting Voucher Creation** screen of the Sales voucher appears.
3. *Click* the **I: Accounting Invoice** button on the Button Bar to change the item invoice to accounting invoice.
4. *Enter* the desired reference number beside the **Reference no.** option. In our case, we have entered **15.**
5. *Press* the **Enter** key.

   The **List of Ledger Accounts** menu appears.
6. *Double-click* the desired customer in the **List of Ledger Accounts** menu for **Party A/c name** option. In our case, we have double-clicked **Jain Pvt. Ltd.**

   The **List of Ledger Accounts** menu appears.
7. *Double-click* the desired service ledger in the **List of Ledger Accounts** menu for the **Particulars** column. In our case, we have double-clicked **Contract Services.**
8. *Enter* the amount of the selected service in the **Amount** Column. In our case, we have entered **20000.**
9. *Press* the **Enter** key. The **GST Details** screen appears.

10. *Double-click* the desired classification or nature of transaction in the **Classifications/Natures** menu for the **Classification/Nature** option. In our case, we have double-clicked **Sales Taxable**, as shown in Fig.TL-14.37:

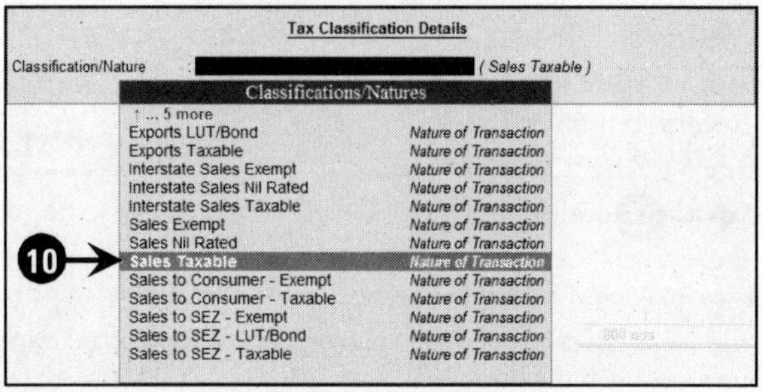

Fig.TL-14.37

The **Accounting Voucher Creation** screen reappears.

11. *Double-click* the desired state tax ledger in the **List of Ledger Accounts** menu for the **Particulars** column. In our case, we have entered **State Tax@6%** (Fig.TL-14.38).

    The **Rate** and **Amount** columns get filled automatically.

12. *Press* the **Enter** key. The **List of Ledger Accounts** menu appears.
13. *Double-click* the desired central tax ledger in the **List of Ledger Accounts** menu for the **Particulars** column. In our case, we have entered **Central Tax@6%** (Fig.TL-14.38).

    The **Rate** and **Amount** columns get filled automatically.

14. *Press* the **Enter** key until the **Accept ?** message box appears.
15. *Click* **Yes** in the **Accept ?** message box to save the voucher, as shown in Fig.TL-14.38:

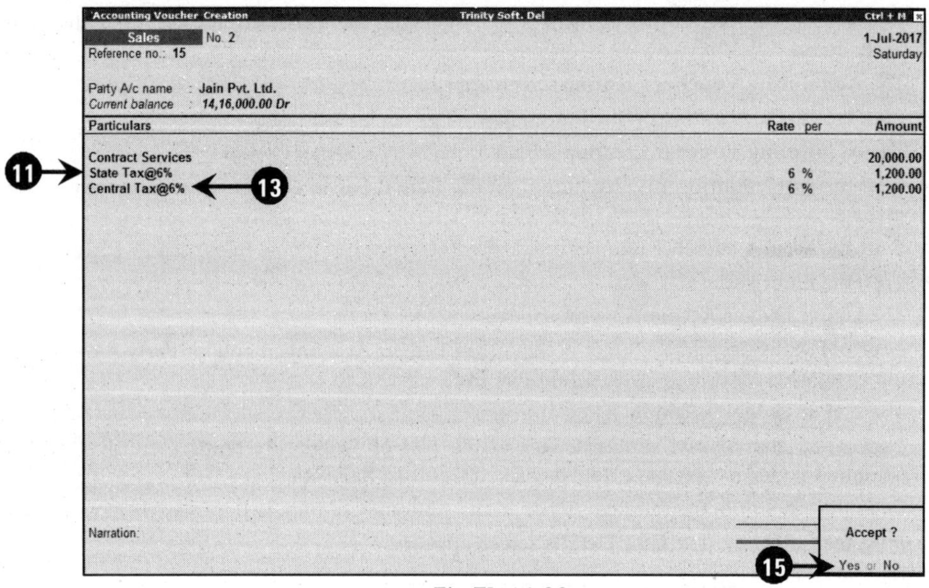

Fig.TL-14.38

Recording Voucher for Advance Receipts from Customers

Perform the following steps to record voucher for advance receipts from customers:

1. *Double-click* the **Accounting Vouchers** option under the **Transactions** section in the **Gateway of Tally** menu.

   The **Accounting Voucher Creation** screen appears.
2. *Click* the **F6: Receipt** button on the Button Bar.

   The **Accounting Voucher Creation** screen of the Receipt voucher appears.
3. *Click* the **V: Advance Receipt** button on the Button Bar to mark the voucher for advance receipt.
4. *Double-click* the desired cash or bank ledger in the **List of Ledger Accounts** menu for **Account** option. In our case, we have double-clicked **Cash**.
5. *Double-click* the desired party ledger in the **List of Ledger Accounts** menu for the **Particulars** column. In our case, we have double-clicked **Jain Pvt. Ltd.**

   The **Advance Receipt Details** screen appears with the **List of Stock Items** menu.
6. *Double-click* the desired stock item or service ledger the **List of Stock Items** menu for the **Particulars** column against which you receive the advance amount. In our case, we have double-clicked **Casual Shoes** (Fig.TL-14.39).
7. *Enter* the amount which is inclusive of GST in the **Advance Amount** Column. In our case, we have entered **1,18,000** (Fig.TL-14.39).

   Based on the amount entered, the break-up of the taxable value, central tax, and state tax is filled automatically, as shown in the Fig.TL-14.39:

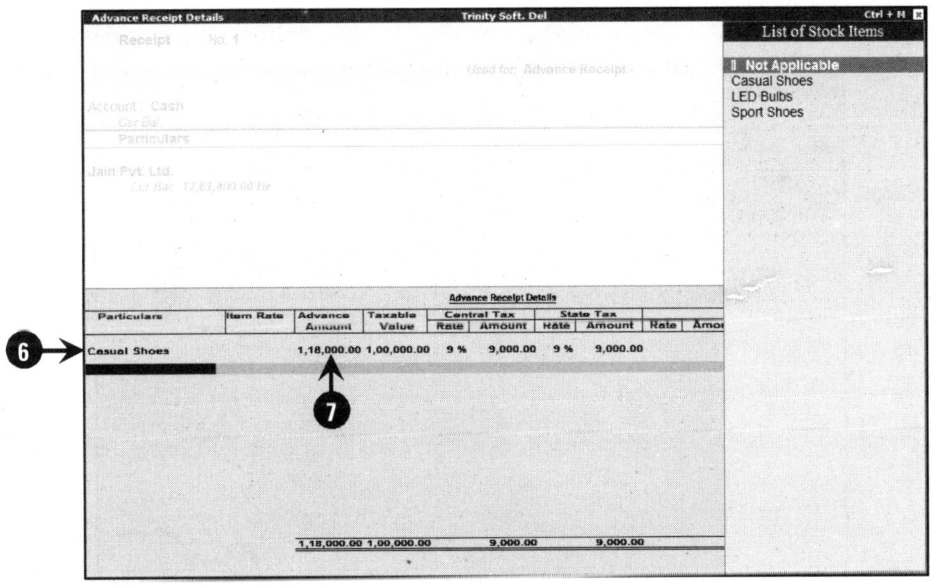

Fig.TL-14.39

8. *Double-click* the **Not Applicable** option for the **Particulars** columns to end to add more stock items or service ledger.

   The **Bill-wise Details** screen appears with the **Method of Adj.** menu (Fig.TL-14.40).
9. *Double-click* the **Advance** option on the **Method of Adj.** menu in the **Type of Ref** column (Fig.TL-14.40).
10. *Enter* the name of the bill in the **Name** column. In our case, we have entered **1** (Fig.TL-14.40).
11. *Enter* the desired due date or days in the **Due Date, or Credit Days** column.

12. *Enter* the amount in the **Amount** column, as shown in Fig.TL-14.40:

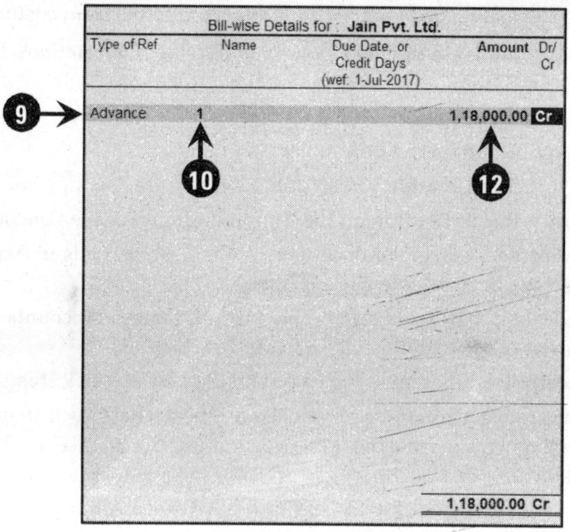

Fig.TL-14.40

13. *Press* the **Enter** key twice. The **Accounting Voucher Creation** screen reappears.
14. *Press* the **Enter** key until the **Accept ?** message box appears.
15. *Click* **Yes** in the **Accept ?** message box to save the voucher, as shown in Fig.TL-14.41:

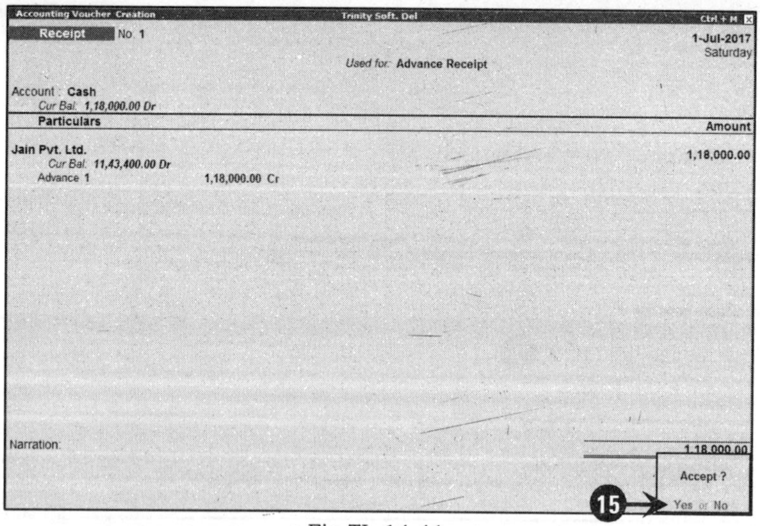

Fig.TL-14.41

Creating Payment Voucher

Perform the following steps to create a payment voucher to record the payment of tax:

1. *Double-click* the **Accounting Vouchers** option under the **Transactions** section in the **Gateway of Tally** menu.

   The **Accounting Voucher Creation** screen appears.

2. *Click* the **F5: Payment** button on the Button Bar.
   The **Accounting Voucher Creation** screen of the payment voucher appears.
3. *Click* the **S: Stat Payment** button on the Button Bar.
   The **Stat Payment Details** screen appears with the **Types of Duty/Tax** menu.
4. *Double-click* the **GST** option in the **Type of Duty/Tax** menu for the **Tax Type** option (Fig.TL-14.42).
5. *Enter* date in the **Period From** and **To** options (Fig.TL-14.42).
6. *Press* the **Enter** key.
   The **Type of Payment** menu appears.
7. *Double-click* the **Regular** option in the **Type of Payment** menu for the **Payment Type** option, as shown in Fig.TL-14.42:

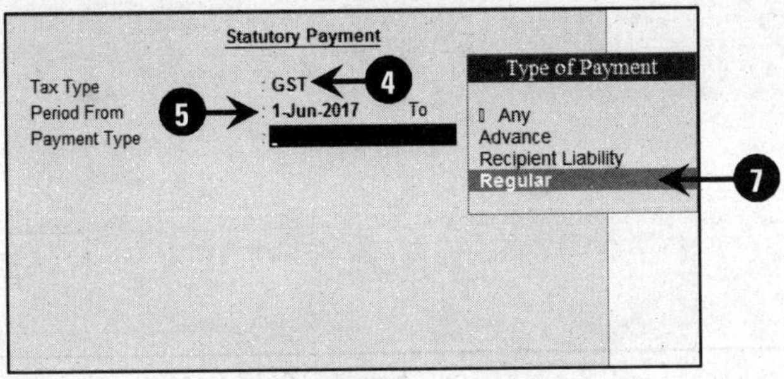

Fig.TL-14.42

The **Accounting Voucher Creation** screen reappears with the **List of Ledger Accounts** menu.

8. *Double-click* the desired cash or bank ledger from the **List of Ledger Accounts** for the **Account** option. In our case, we have double-clicked **Cash** (Fig.TL-14.43).
   The **List of Ledger Accounts** menu appears.
9. *Double-click* the GST tax ledgers (State and/or Central) from the **List of Ledger Accounts** for the **Particular** column (Fig.TL-14.43).
10. *Enter* the amount in the **Amount** column (Fig.TL-14.43).
11. *Press* the **Enter** key.
    The **Yes/No** menu appears.
12. *Double-click* the **Yes** option from the **Yes/No** menu for the **Provide GST Details** option (Fig.TL-14.43).
    The **Statutory Details** screen appears.
13. *Enter* the required information in the fields that are related to bank details.
14. *Press* the **Enter** key.
    The **Accounting Voucher Creation** screen reappears.
15. *Press* the **Enter** key.
    The **Bank Allocations** screen appears
16. *Enter* the required information in the fields that are related to bank allocations.
17. *Press* the **Enter** key.
    The **Accounting Voucher Creation** screen reappears.
18. *Press* the **Enter** key until the **Accept ?** message box appears.

19. *Click* **Yes** in the **Accept ?** message box to save the voucher, as shown in Fig.TL-14.43:

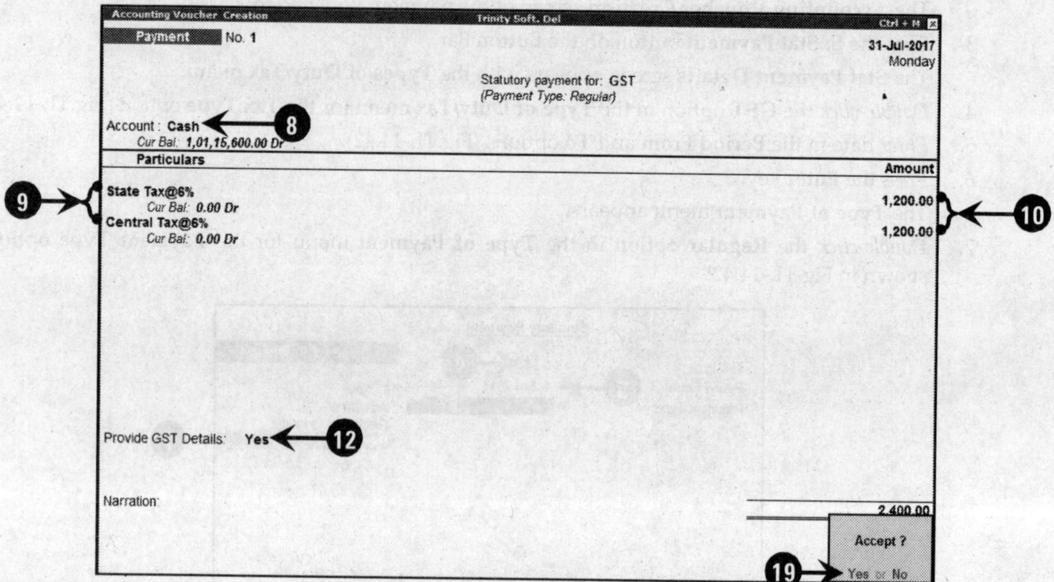

Fig.TL-14.43

Recording Voucher for Advance Payment to Supplier

Perform the following steps to record a voucher for advance receipts from customers:

1. *Double-click* the **Accounting Vouchers** option under the **Transactions** section in the **Gateway of Tally** menu.

   The **Accounting Voucher Creation** screen appears.
2. *Click* the **F6: Receipt** button on the Button Bar.

   The **Accounting Voucher Creation** screen of the Receipt voucher appears.
3. *Click* the **V: Reverse Chrg. Adv.** button on the Button Bar.
4. *Double-click* the desired cash or bank ledger in the **List of Ledger Accounts** menu for **Accounts** option. In our case, we have double-clicked **Cash**.
5. *Double-click* the desired supplier ledger in the **List of Ledger Accounts** menu for the **Particulars** column. In our case, we have double-clicked **Gupta Pvt. Ltd.**

   The **Advance Receipt Details** screen appears with the **List of Stock Items** menu.
6. *Double-click* the desired stock item or service ledger for the particulars column against which you make the payment in advance. In our case, we have double-clicked **Samsung Mobiles** (Fig.TL-14.44).
7. *Enter* the amount which is inclusive of GST in the **Advance Amount** Column. In our case, we have entered **2,00,000** (Fig.TL-14.44).

Based on the amount entered, the break-up of the taxable value, central tax, and state tax are filled automatically, as shown in Fig.TL-14.44:

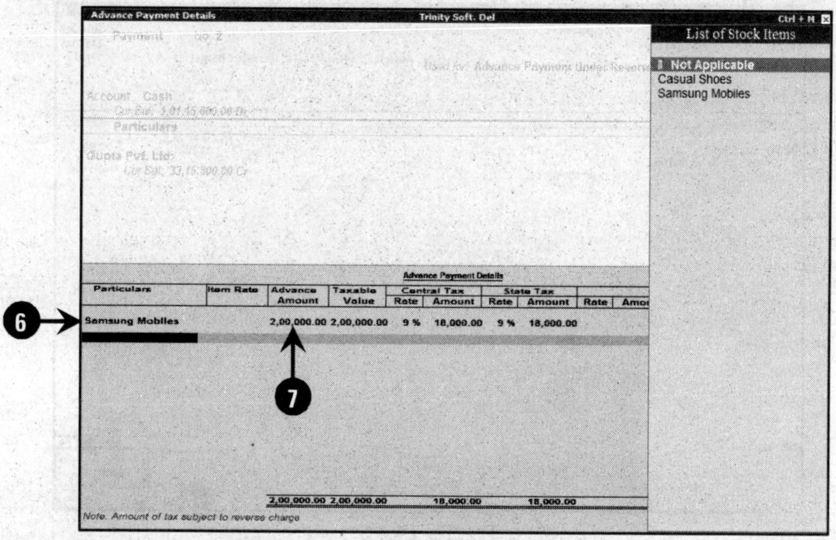

Fig.TL-14.44

8. *Double-click* the **Not Applicable** option for the **Particulars** columns to end to add more stock items or service ledger.

   The **Bill-wise Details** screen appears with the **Method of Adj.** menu.
9. *Double-click* the **Advance** option on the **Method of Adj.** menu in the **Type of Ref** column (Fig.TL-14.45).
10. *Enter* the name of the bill in the **Name** column. In our case, we have entered **2** (Fig.TL-14.45).
11. *Enter* the desired due date in the **Due Date, or Credit Days** column.
12. *Enter* the amount in the **Amount** column. In our case, we have entered **2,00,000**, as shown in Fig.TL-14.45:

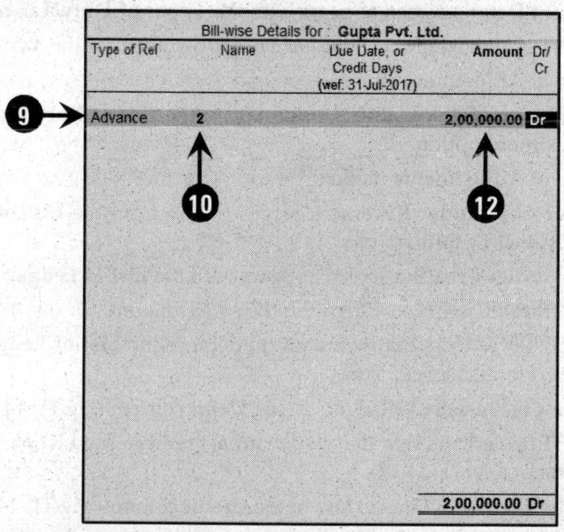

Fig.TL-14.45

13. *Press* the **Enter** key twice. The **Accounting Voucher Creation** screen reappears.

14. *Press* the **Enter** key until the **Accept ?** message box appears.
15. *Click* **Yes** in the **Accept ?** message box to save the voucher, as shown in Fig.TL-14.46:

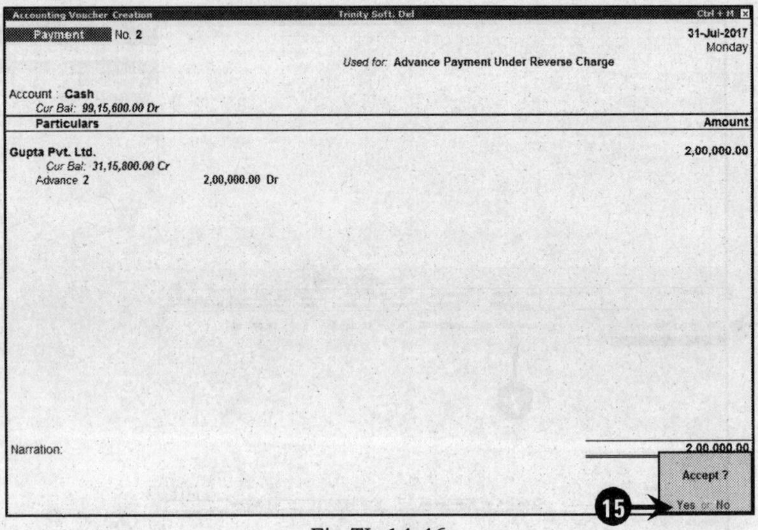

Fig.TL-14.46

Creating Journal Voucher for Tax Adjustment

Perform the following steps to record the journal voucher for tax adjustment:

1. *Double-click* the **Accounting Vouchers** option under the **Transactions** section in the **Gateway of Tally** menu.

   The **Accounting Voucher Creation** screen appears.
2. *Click* the **F7: Journal** button on the Button Bar.

   The **Accounting Voucher Creation** screen of the Journal voucher appears.
3. *Click* the **J: Stat Adjustment** button on the Button Bar.

   The **Stat Adjustment Details** screen appears with the **Types of Duty/Tax** menu.
4. *Double-click* the **GST** option from the **Types of Duty/Tax** menu for the **Types of duty/tax** option.

   The **List of Nature of Adjustments** menu appears.
5. *Double-click* the **Increase of Tax Liability** option from the **List of Nature of Adjustments** menu for the **Nature of adjustment** option.

   The **List of Nature of Adjustments** menu appears.
6. *Double-click* the **Purchase under Reverse Charges** option from the **List of Nature of Adjustments** menu for the **Additional Details** option.

   The **Accounting Voucher Creation** screen appears with the **List of Ledger Accounts** menu.

   Now, debit and credit the GST tax ledger with the same amount.
7. *Double-click* the GST tax ledgers that you want to debit in the **List of Ledger Accounts** menu in the **Particulars** column (Fig.TL-14.47).
8. *Enter* the amount for the respective ledgers in the **Debit** column (Fig.TL-14.47).
9. *Double-click* the GST tax ledgers that that you want to credit in the **List of Ledger Accounts** menu in the **Particulars** column (Fig.TL-14.47).
10. *Enter* the amount for the respective ledgers in the **Credit** column (Fig.TL-14.47).
11. *Press* the **Enter** key until the **Accept ?** message box appears (Fig.TL-14.47).

12. *Click* **Yes** in the **Accept ?** message box to save the voucher, as shown in Fig.TL-14.47:

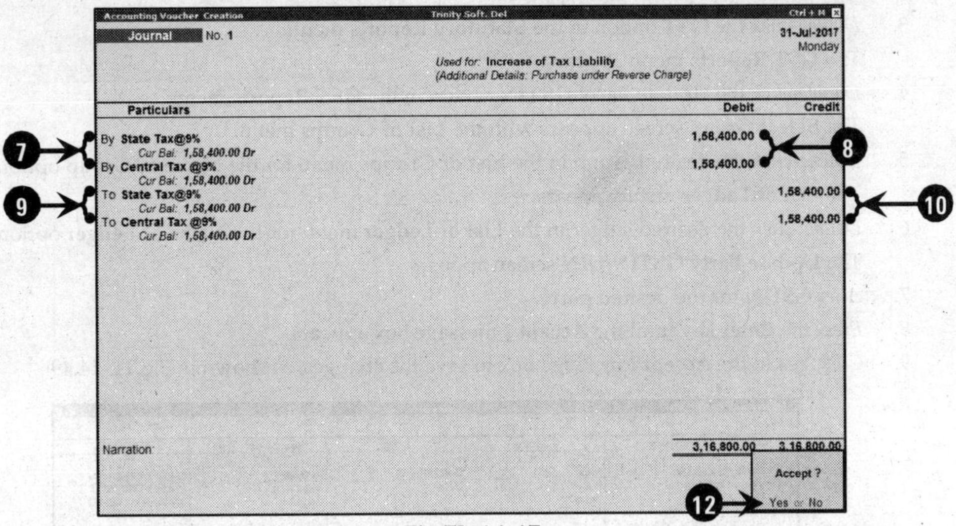

Fig.TL-14.47

Let us learn to view GST rates in Tally.

Viewing the GST Rates

You can view the GST rates on different products by performing the following steps:

1. *Double-click* the **Display** option in the **Reports** section in the **Gateway of Tally** menu.
   The **Display Menu** menu appears.
2. *Double-click* the **StatutOry Reports** option in the **Display Menu** menu.
   The **Statutory Reports** menu appears.
3. *Double-click* the **GST** option in the **Statutory Reports** menu.
   The **GST Reports** menu appears.
4. *Double-click* the **GST Rate Setup** option in the **GST Reports** menu.
   The **GST Rate Setup** screen appears and displays various GST rates applied on different products, as shown in Fig.TL-14.48:

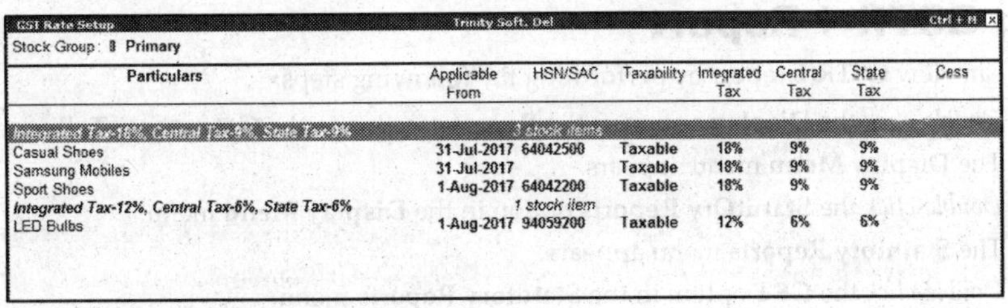

GST Rate Setup — Trinity Soft. Del — Ctrl + M

Stock Group : Primary

Particulars	Applicable From	HSN/SAC	Taxability	Integrated Tax	Central Tax	State Tax	Cess
Integrated Tax-18%, Central Tax-9%, State Tax-9%	*3 stock items*						
Casual Shoes	31-Jul-2017	64042500	Taxable	18%	9%	9%	
Samsung Mobiles	31-Jul-2017		Taxable	18%	9%	9%	
Sport Shoes	1-Aug-2017	64042200	Taxable	18%	9%	9%	
Integrated Tax-12%, Central Tax-6%, State Tax-6%	*1 stock item*						
LED Bulbs	1-Aug-2017	94059200	Taxable	12%	6%	6%	

Fig.TL-14.48

Let us learn to update Party GSTIN in Tally.

Updating Party GSTIN

You can view and update the party GSTIN by performing the following steps:

1. *Double-click* the **Display** option in the **Reports** section in the **Gateway of Tally** menu.
   The **Display Menu** menu appears.

2. *Double click* the **StatutOry Reports** option in the **Display Menu** menu.
   The **Statutory Reports** menu appears.
3. *Double-click* the **GST** option in the **Statutory Reports** menu.
   The **GST Reports** menu appears.
4. *Double-click* the **Update Party GSTIN** option in the **GST Reports** menu.
   The **Select Group** screen appears with the **List of Groups** menu.
5. *Double-click* the desired group in the **List of Groups** menu for the **Name of Group** option.
   The **List of Ledger** menu appears.
6. *Double-click* the desired ledger in the **List of Ledger** menu for the **Name of Ledger** option.
   The **Update Party GSTIN/UIN** screen appears.
7. *Alter* GSTIN for the desired party.
8. *Press* the **Enter** key until the **Accept ?** message box appears.
9. *Click* **Yes** in the **Accept ?** message box to save the changes, as shown in Fig.TL-14.49:

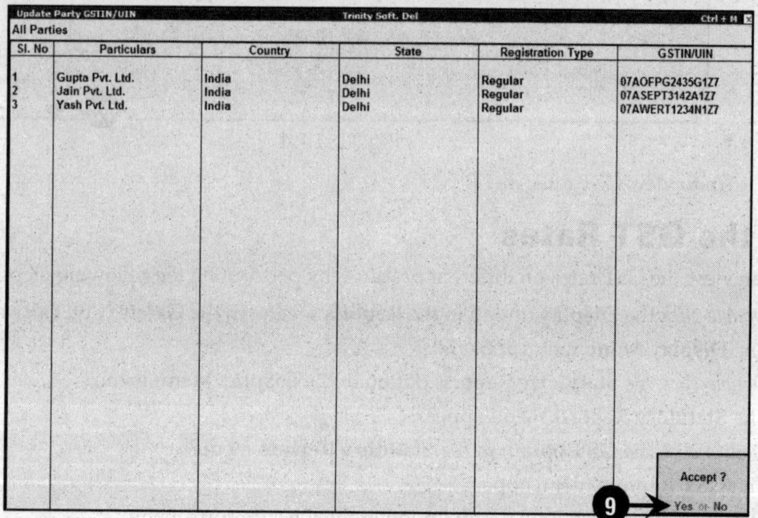

Fig.TL-14.49

Let us now learn how to view GSTR-1 report in Tally.

Viewing GSTR-1 Report

You can view GSTR-1 report by performing the following steps:

1. *Double-click* the **Display** option in the **Reports** section in the **Gateway of Tally** menu.
   The **Display Menu** menu appears.
2. *Double-click* the **StatutOry Reports** option in the **Display Menu** menu.
   The **Statutory Reports** menu appears.
3. *Double-click* the **GST** option in the **Statutory Reports** menu.
   The **GST Reports** menu appears.
4. *Double-click* the **GSTR-1** option in the **GST Reports** menu.

The **GSTR-1** screen appears that shows the return summary, as shown in Fig.TL-14.50:

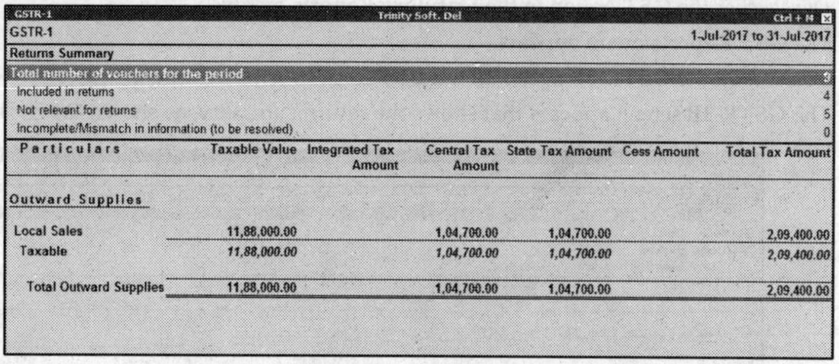

GSTR-1 — Trinity Soft. Del — Ctrl + M

GSTR-1 — 1-Jul-2017 to 31-Jul-2017

Returns Summary

Total number of vouchers for the period	9
Included in returns	4
Not relevant for returns	5
Incomplete/Mismatch in information (to be resolved)	0

Particulars	Taxable Value	Integrated Tax Amount	Central Tax Amount	State Tax Amount	Cess Amount	Total Tax Amount
Outward Supplies						
Local Sales	11,88,000.00		1,04,700.00	1,04,700.00		2,09,400.00
Taxable	*11,88,000.00*		*1,04,700.00*	*1,04,700.00*		*2,09,400.00*
Total Outward Supplies	11,88,000.00		1,04,700.00	1,04,700.00		2,09,400.00

Fig.TL-14.50

Let us learn about how to view GSTR-2 report in Tally.

Viewing GSTR-2 Report

You can view GSTR-2 report by performing the following steps:

1. *Double-click* the **Display** option in the **Reports** section in the **Gateway of Tally** menu.
   The **Display Menu** menu appears.
2. *Double-click* the **StatutOry Reports** option in the **Display Menu** menu.
   The **Statutory Reports** menu appears.
3. *Double-click* the **GST** option in the **Statutory Reports** menu.
   The **GST Reports** menu appears.
4. *Double-click* the **GSTR-2** option in the **GST Reports** menu.
   The **GSTR-2** screen appears that shows the return summary, as shown in Fig.TL-14.51:

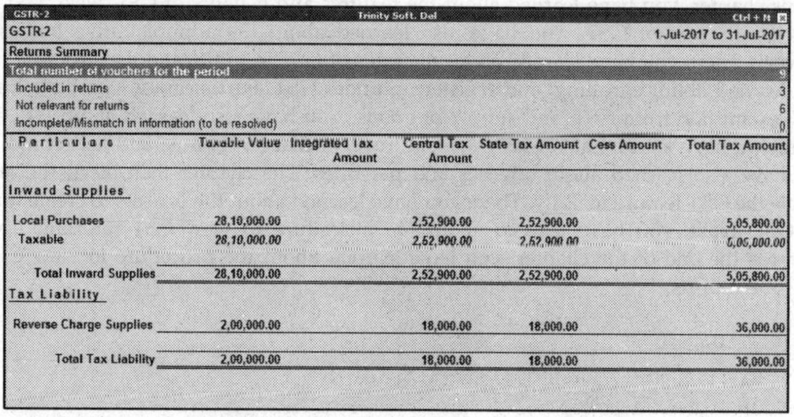

GSTR-2 — Trinity Soft. Del — Ctrl + M

GSTR-2 — 1-Jul-2017 to 31-Jul-2017

Returns Summary

Total number of vouchers for the period	9
Included in returns	3
Not relevant for returns	6
Incomplete/Mismatch in information (to be resolved)	0

Particulars	Taxable Value	Integrated Tax Amount	Central Tax Amount	State Tax Amount	Cess Amount	Total Tax Amount
Inward Supplies						
Local Purchases	28,10,000.00		2,52,900.00	2,52,900.00		5,05,800.00
Taxable	*28,10,000.00*		*2,52,900.00*	*2,52,900.00*		*5,05,800.00*
Total Inward Supplies	28,10,000.00		2,52,900.00	2,52,900.00		5,05,800.00
Tax Liability						
Reverse Charge Supplies	2,00,000.00		18,000.00	18,000.00		36,000.00
Total Tax Liability	2,00,000.00		18,000.00	18,000.00		36,000.00

Fig.TL-14.51

Let us learn to view GSTR-3B report in Tally.

Viewing GSTR-3B Report

You can view the GSTR-3B report by performing the following steps:

1. *Double-click* the **Display** option in the **Reports** section in the **Gateway of Tally** menu.
   The **Display Menu** menu appears.
2. *Double-click* the **StatutOry Reports** option in the **Display Menu** menu.

The **Statutory Reports** menu appears.

3. *Double-click* the **GST** option in the **Statutory Reports** menu.

   The **GST Reports** menu appears.

4. *Double-click* the **GSTR-3B** option in the **GST Reports** menu.

   The **GSTR-3B** screen appears that shows the return summary, as shown in Fig.TL-14.52:

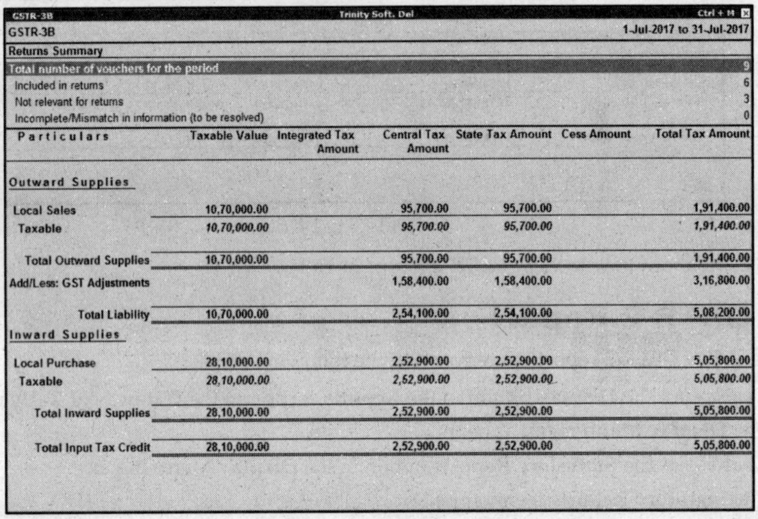

GSTR-3B — Trinity Soft. Del — Ctrl + M

GSTR-3B — 1-Jul-2017 to 31-Jul-2017

Returns Summary

Total number of vouchers for the period	9
Included in returns	6
Not relevant for returns	3
Incomplete/Mismatch in information (to be resolved)	0

Particulars	Taxable Value	Integrated Tax Amount	Central Tax Amount	State Tax Amount	Cess Amount	Total Tax Amount
Outward Supplies						
Local Sales	10,70,000.00		95,700.00	95,700.00		1,91,400.00
Taxable	*10,70,000.00*		*95,700.00*	*95,700.00*		*1,91,400.00*
Total Outward Supplies	10,70,000.00		95,700.00	95,700.00		1,91,400.00
Add/Less: GST Adjustments			1,58,400.00	1,58,400.00		3,16,800.00
Total Liability	10,70,000.00		2,54,100.00	2,54,100.00		5,08,200.00
Inward Supplies						
Local Purchase	28,10,000.00		2,52,900.00	2,52,900.00		5,05,800.00
Taxable	*28,10,000.00*		*2,52,900.00*	*2,52,900.00*		*5,05,800.00*
Total Inward Supplies	28,10,000.00		2,52,900.00	2,52,900.00		5,05,800.00
Total Input Tax Credit	28,10,000.00		2,52,900.00	2,52,900.00		5,05,800.00

Fig.TL-14.52

With this we come to the end of the chapter. Let us summarize the key points discussed in the chapter.

Summary

In this chapter, you have learned about the features and benefits of GST. Next, you have learned about the classification of GST. You have also learned about the administrative bodies of GST, and GST network. Then, you have learned about the rates of GST in India, and the structure of GSTIN. You have also learned about enrolling, and registering under GST. Furthermore, you have learned about levy of GST, exemption from GST, and supply of goods. You have also learned about ITC, and transfer of ITC. Then, you have learned about tax payment, reverse charge, returns, and tax refund. In addition to this, you have also learned about offenses and penalties. The chapter then discussed about the process to enable the GST feature in Tally. Then, you have learned about the process to create masters and vouchers for GST. Next, you have learned about the procedure to view GST rate and update party GSTIN. Towards the end of the chapter, you have learned about the procedure to view GSTR-1, GSTR-2, and GSTR-3B reports.

CHAPTER

15

E-Way Bill

In this Chapter:

* Purpose of E-way Bill
* Objectives of E-way Bill
* Features of E-way Bill
* Benefits of E-way Bill
* E-way Bill under GST
* People Who Need E-way Bill
* Participants of E-way Bill
* Validity of E-way Bill
* Cancellation of E-way Bill
* Exceptions for E-way Bill
* Concerns of the Industry
* Safety Measures Against the Concerns
* Penalties on Issuing Wrong E-way Bill
* Implementation Dates and Document Requirements of E-way Bill

Introduction

The E-way bill provision under the GST system is defined as a distinctive bill that is generated electronically for the shipment of goods worth the value of more than ₹ 50,000 within a state or outside the state. It aims at a speedy and trouble-free movement of goods all over India, without any sort of obstacle.

It has replaced the former bill, which used to be a paper bill under the VAT system with the name of road permit, way bill, etc. It helped in monitoring the movement of goods to or from a state, to keep an eye on tax evasion. It was required while transporting goods from the supplier to the receiver. However, these bills were subjected to the rules which were specific to a state and had to be generated from the portals of different states. Earlier, the transporter issued a way bill and it acted as a receipt that provided details and directives related to the shipment of the delivery of goods. The details contained the names of the supplier and the recipient, the source and destination of the delivery, and the route.

It is obligatory for all the inter-state shipment of goods valued above ₹ 50,000 from April 1. Additionally, it would be made obligatory for intra-state movement of goods in a staged manner from April 15. Some goods including the items that are liable to rot such as milk and milk products, meat, fruits, and vegetables are out of the scope of the E-way bill. Few other items that do not need the E-way bill include gold and silver jewellery, cooking gas cylinders, raw silk, wool and handlooms.

The E-way bill can be generated through the GSTN set-up, before the goods begin to move. An E-way bill number (EBN) is allotted after the E-way bill is produced. The EBN number is available to be accessible to the transporter, supplier and recipient.

In this chapter, you learn about the purpose of E-way bill. Then, you learn about the objectives, features and benefits of E-way bill. As you move further in the chapter, you learn about the E-way bill under GST. Next, you learn about the people who need an E-way bill and the participants of E-way bill. You also learn about the validity and cancellation of E-way bill. Furthermore, you learn about the exceptions for E-way bill. Then, you learn about the concerns of the industry and safety measures against these concerns. Next, you learn about the penalties of issuing wrong E-way bill. Towards the end, you learn about the implementation dates and document requirements of E-way bill.

Let us start the chapter by understanding the purpose of E-way bill.

Purpose of E-Way Bill

The E-Way bill mechanism ensures that the goods are transported in compliance with the GST Law. It is a constructive tool that helps to track the movement of goods and keep a check on tax evasion. It is also aimed at decimating the significant delays in the transit due to the inter-state check posts set up by the tax officials. For example, a truck used to cover a distance of 400 km in a day prior to the introduction of the E-way bill mechanism, which would be doubled now and, in some cases, the driver would be able to complete the return journey on the same day itself.

When a sender or a buyer generates an E-way bill, it is updated in the outward sales return of the supplier form automatically, which, in turn, leaves minimal to no scope for evading tax on the transportation of the goods. Unlike the previous tax system, there is no need for a manual cross-check of the E-way bill by the tax officials with the returns filed by the supplier, in order to validate that the consignment falls within the tax bracket.

Additionally, an individual E-way bill would save tonnes of paper. Along with this, it helps in sidelining the multiple number of clearances for the senders, buyers, and transporters unlike the previous tax system, where each State defined their own rules for the movement of goods.

Note

E-way bill needs to be generated also in the cases where the distance to be covered in the movement of goods is less than or equal to 10 km. A relaxation in Part B of Form EWB-01 is given for the distance covered from the business place to the transporting company.

Let us learn about the objectives of an E-way bill.

Objectives of E-Way Bill

The objectives of an E-way bill as laid down by the Government of India are as follows:

- A sole E-way bill for transporting goods all over India.
- To arrest the tax evasion activities.
- Trouble-free transportation of goods across India.
- To trace the movement of goods through an E-way bill number.
- Easy validation of E-way bills by tax officials.

For example, Mr. Anuj (registered under GST) owns a manufacturing company who wants to send a consignment of goods from Jaipur city to Mr. Bipin (registered under GST), who is a distributor in Yamunanagar city. The distance between Jaipur and Yamunanagar is 450 km. Mr. Anuj hires a transporter for moving the consignment. The transporter will move the goods from Jaipur to Yamunanagar. In this case, Mr. Anuj fills Part A of the Form EWB-01 and then assigns the produced E-way bill to the transporter. Thereafter, the transporter fills the vehicle details and other related information in Part B of Form GST EWB-01 and moves the goods from Jaipur to Yamunanagar.

Note

In case the goods are transported in more than one vehicle during the transit, the transporter needs to update the vehicle details in Part B of Form EWB-01, every time the goods are loaded in another vehicle before they are moved further.

If the goods belonging to one invoice are required to be transported in different vehicles, then the supplier needs to issue a finalized invoice and separate invoices for all the consignments before the movement of goods. Additionally, all the consignments must co-exist with their corresponding invoice copies. The last consignment must carry the original invoice.

Let us learn about the features of E-way bill.

Features of E-Way Bill

The new E-way bill offers numerous features, some of which are mentioned as follows:

- The E-way bill system has a user-friendly approach with operations that are very simple to use.
- The system provides various methods which enable the user to produce E-way bills in a hassle-free manner.
- The system has introduced various checks and balances to reduce the number of errors or mistakes made by the users.
- A support is provided by the system for different modes of producing E-way bills. The users can register for a particular mode and use it for their future E-way bill productions.
- The system provides the facility of creating own masters, such as customers, suppliers, producers and transporters, and of using them while producing an E-way bill.
- The sub-users of the system for E-way bill production can be created, altered and locked by the taxpayer or the registered person. Further, these sub-users and the duties related to them can be assigned to the employees or branches according to the requirement.
- The system has a provision for the registered persons to monitor the E-way bills produced against them by the other registered persons. The users can refuse the E-way bills not belonging to them.
- The system fetches the information related to GSTR-1 and feeds it to the GSTR-1 returns of the taxpayer. Hence, it saves a taxpayer's effort and time to upload the transaction details.
- The system provides support for the preparation of a combined E-way bill which can be given to the person in-charge of the conveyance, in spite of multiple E-way bills for multiple deliveries in a single vehicle.
- This system enables the unregistered transporters for enrolling and creating users to produce E-way bill and update the number of vehicles.

- The alerts are generated by the system to notify the users via web or SMS about a number of activities, such as latest updates, rejected EWBs, verified EWBs, etc.
- The tax officials can easily verify the E-way bill through the QR scan code on the bill.
- The system can integrate with RFID for tracing the vehicle movement by the tax officials, without having to stop the vehicle.

Let us learn about the benefits of E-way bill.

Benefits of E-Way Bill

The major benefits involved with the production of E-way bill are as follows:

- There is no requirement for the traders to go to the tax office for collecting E-way bill forms, as in the earlier VAT regime.
- The time taken for the validation process has reduced drastically, as now it is done through a common portal. It further allows the vehicle to pass the mobile squads faster.
- A trader can now upload the identity details of the buying trader as well, who can automatically account the transaction.
- The new system eliminates the need to generate multiple paper copies of the bill and, hence, saving tonnes of paper each day.
- The auto-preparation of GSTR-1 returns saves the time of the supplier to upload the documents.
- The monotonous and repetitive work of the tax officials to collect and match the E-way bill with the returns filed by the taxpayers is reduced eventually.

Note: **A registered supplier can use the information available on the common portal, which he provided in the E-way bill while filing the GSTR-1 for returns.**

Let us learn about the E-way bill under GST.

E-Way Bill under GST

The E-way bill process follows the following steps:

1. The registered person provides information before the goods start moving and E-way bill is produced.

Note: **Rule 138 of the CGST Rules, 2017 states the mechanism of an E-way bill and in its context, it must be noted that 'the information is to be furnished prior to the commencement of the movement of goods' and 'is to be issued whether the movement is in relation to a supply or for reasons other than supply'.**

2. Once the E-way bill is produced on the common portal, a distinctive E-way Bill Number (EBN) is given to the supplier, the transporter and the recipient.
3. The person managing the conveyance needs to carry:
   - the invoice or supply man or delivery challan
   - a copy of E-Way bill or EBN
4. The information of the produced bill is given to the recipient (if registered on the common portal), who further accepts or rejects the delivery covered by E-way bill.
5. The E-way bill produced on the GST portal consists of two components:
   - Part A includes details of GSTIN of recipient, delivery place (PIN Code), invoice number and date, worth of goods, HSN code, transport document number (Goods Receipt Number or Railway Receipt Number or Airway Bill Number or Bill of Lading Number) and transportation reasons.
   - Part B includes the details of transporter (Vehicle number).

The above-mentioned information is provided to the supplier who is registered on the common portal. The supplier may use this information to provide details in FORM GSTR-1.

Note

As per Rule 138, every registered transporter, who initiates the movement of goods of delivery more than a value of ₹ 50,000, needs to supply the information mentioned above for part A of an E-way bill. The transporter details supplied in part B help in E-way bill generation.

6. An authorised tax officer can stop any vehicle that is transporting goods in order to validate the E-way bill or EBN in physical form at inter-state and intra-state levels.
7. An abstract report of every examination of goods can be registered online by an officer in a designed format within 24 hours of the examination. However, the finalised report in the designated format can be registered within three days of the examination.

Let us learn about the people who need E-way bill.

People Who Need E-Way Bill

The people who are required to get an E-way bill are as follows:

- **Registered Person:** Goods that are moved to or from a registered person need an E-way bill. The E-way bills may be produced and carried by the registered persons or transporters, even for the goods valued less than ₹ 50,000.
- **Unregistered Person:** Every person who is not registered also needs to produce an E-way bill. In case the supplier is unregistered and the recipient is registered, the E-way bill compliance must be ensured by the recipient considering himself as a supplier.
- **Transporter:** The transporter of the goods also needs to produce an E-way bill in case the supplier didn't generate an E-way bill, irrespective of the transport mode.

Note

A Transporter ID will be provided to the unregistered transporters when they enroll on the E-way bill portal. Thereafter, the E-way bills can be produced.

The unregistered transporters can generate an E-way bill by providing details, such as transport mode, transport ID and vehicle number.

Table 15.1 describes the time at which the above-mentioned people need to produce an E-way bill, along with the Form to be used:

Table 15.1: People who need an E-way bill

Who	When	Form
All registered persons	Prior to the movement of goods	Part A of Form EWB-01
A registered person is either a supplier or a recipient of goods (transport mode could be owned or hired)	Prior to the movement of goods	Part B of Form EWB-01
A registered person is a supplier or a recipient and goods are given to the transporter	Prior to the movement of goods	The registered person shall provide the information about the transporter in Part B of Form EWB-01
Transporter	Prior to the movement of goods	Produce an E-way bill based on the information shared by the registered person in Part A of Form EWB-01
A person not registered under GST and a registered recipient	Compliance to be ensured by the recipient	1. For the goods transported within a distance of 50 kms or less, within the same State/UT from the supplier's

Table 15.1: People who need an E-way bill

Who	When	Form
		business place to the transporter's business place for further transportation, both the parties may not provide the conveyance details in Part B of Form EWB-01. 2. For the goods transported via air, ship or railways, the information in Part A of Form EWB-01 needs to be provided by the supplier or the recipient.

Note

The value of the consignment is not defined in the rules, but it is mentioned that one invoice is to be deemed as one consignment. Hence, the invoice value becomes the value of consignment and it determines the lower limit to generate an E-way bill.

Two or more invoices cannot be combined together for generating an E-way bill because one invoice is deemed as one consignment. However, a transporter may produce an integrated E-way bill in case such goods are being transported in one vehicle.

If the goods belonging to one invoice are required to be transported in different vehicles, then the supplier needs to issue a finalized invoice and separate invoices for all the consignments before the movement of the goods. Additionally, all the consignments must co-exist with their corresponding invoice copies. The last consignment must carry the original invoice.

Let us learn about the participants of E-way bill.

Participants of E-Way Bill

The introduction of E-way bill is aimed at addressing the predictions and worries of the participants by influencing the use of ICT.

The following are the participants of the E-way bill:

- **Suppliers**: They produce E-way bills and reject the ones generated against them, which do not belong to them.
- **Recipients**: They too produce E-way bills and reject the ones generated against them, which do not belong to them.
- **Transporters**: They produce E-way bills, combined E-way bills, and update the number of vehicles for all the E-way bills assigned to them for transportation.
- **Tax Officers**: They validate the E-way bills and the deliveries corresponding to them.

Note

The supplier is primarily responsible to generate an E-way bill because he originates the movement of the goods. However, if the supplier fails in doing so, the transporter can generate the E-way bill.

Table 15.2 given below lists all the forms that are required by the participants under E-way bill system:

Table 15.2: Form Requirements under E-way bill

S.No	Form	Description	Required by
1.	GST EWB-01	E-way bill	Registered supplier or recipient
2.	GST EWB-02	Consolidated E-way bill	Transporter

Table 15.2: Form Requirements under E-way bill

S.No	Form	Description	Required by
3.	GST EWB-03	Verification report	Inspection officer
4.	GST EWB-04	Report of detention	Inspection officer
5.	GST ENR-01	Application for enrolment under section 35 (2)	Unregistered persons
6.	GST INV-01	Generation of invoice reference number	Registered taxpayer

Let us learn about the validity of E-way bill.

Validity of E-Way Bill

The validity of the E-way bill rests on the distance that needs to be travelled by the goods. Usually, the bill is valid for one day for every 100 km of distance covered by the goods. For less than 100 km of distance, the E-way bill has one-day validity from the applicable date. After that, there will be an extra one-day validity for every 100 km from the applicable date. The 'applicable date' implies the date on which the E-way bill is produced. The validity period is computed from the time of E-way bill production and a period of 24 hours is counted as one day. Generally, there is no extension of the validity. The movement of the goods must not happen, if the validity expires. Nevertheless, the Commissioner is authorized to provide an extension by issuing a notification for some specific categories of goods.

Moreover, another E-way bill can be produced in the case of an unusual situation where the goods are not shipped within the specified validity. This can be done by upgrading the relevant details in Part B of Form GST EWB-01.

Let us learn about the cancellation of E-way bill.

Cancellation of E-Way Bill

In case an E-way bill is produced but the goods are not transported or they are not transported according to the information provided in the E-way bill, then the direct cancellation or through a Facilitation Centre according to the Commissioner's notification is done electronically on the common portal within 24 hours of E-way bill production. However, the cancellation cannot be done after the validation of E-way bill while the goods are in transit, as per the provisions of Rule 138B of the CGST Rules, 2017.

Part A of Form EWB-01 cannot be altered or deleted once it is generated, but Part B of the form can be modified. Therefore, the wrong E-way bill has be cancelled within 24 hours and generated again with the right details.

An E-way bill corresponding to the goods that are not moved has to be cancelled within 24 hours. If that does not happen, the supplier can request the rejection of E-way bill from the receiver's end.

Let us learn about the exceptions for E-way bill.

Exceptions for E-Way Bill

It is not mandatory to generate an E-way bill in the following cases:

- If the carrier mode is a vehicle that is not motorable
- If the goods are carried from an airport, an air cargo complex, customs port or a land customs station to an Inland Container Depot (ICD) or a Container Freight Station (CFS) for Custom clearance
- If the goods are carried under Customs control or Customs seal

- If the goods are carried from an ICD to Customs port or from one custom station to another, under Customs bond
- If the transit cargo is carried to or from Nepal or Bhutan
- If the goods are transported due to the formation of defense under the Ministry of Defense as a supplier or recipient
- If the vacant cargo containers are being carried
- If the supplier is transporting goods to or from the business place and a weighbridge within 20 kms of distance, along with a delivery challan
- If the goods are being transported by rail where the supplier is the Central Government, the State Government or any local authority
- If the goods are exempted from E-way bill conditions under the GST rules of a respective State/Union territory
- If certain goods are transported that fall under a list of exempted supply of goods as per the Annexure to Rule 138(14) – Schedule III, in which the goods are treated as no supply

Let us learn about the concerns of the industry.

Concerns of the Industry

The industry is perturbed that the technological system might not be developed to handle an enormous volume of E-way bill and, as a result, it would cause hindrance in the trade. At the initial stage of its launch on February 1, there were long delays in E-way bill generation due to technical glitches in the system. It had led the trade to come to a dead stop, which forced the government to put off its implementation.

The industry is also bothered by the possible scope for harassment by the tax officials. The taxmen have the authority to stop goods carrying vehicles and check E-way bills, which may lead to rent-seeking.

Let us learn about the safety measures against the concerns.

Safety Measures Against the Concerns

The infrastructure of the E-way bill system has been ramped up by the GSTN and NIC (National Informatics Centre) to elude any technical glitches. The system is now able to manage 75 lakh E-way bills on a daily basis, as compared to 26 lakhs earlier. To avoid any sort of harassment from the tax officials, E-way bill rules state that the goods will be scrutinized once during the journey, excluding the cases where the department receives information about tax evasion. Last but not the least, a transporter can report the issue on the E-way portal in case a vehicle is impounded for more than 30 minutes.

Let us learn about penalties on issuing wrong E-way bill.

Penalties on Issuing Wrong E-Way Bill

The penalties that would be imposed on issuing E-way bills in non-accordance with the provisions in Rule 138 of the CGST Rules, 2017 are as follows:

- As per Section 122 of the CGST Act, 2017, a taxable person who transports goods that are taxable without covering the stated documents (E-way bill being one of them) are liable to pay a penalty of ₹ 10,000 or tax attempted to be evaded (whichever amount is higher).
- As per Section 129 of CGST Act, 2017, if a person transports goods or stores any goods while in transit against the provisions of this Act, all the goods and vehicles used for transporting are liable to be detained or seized.

Implementation Dates and Document Requirements of E-Way Bill

Table 15.3 shows the dates on which the E-way bill on inter-state and intra-state level was implemented across all the states:

Table 15.3: State-wise implementation dates and documents required for E-way bill

State	Inter-state implementation	Intra-state implementation	State-wise documents required*
Andaman and Nicobar Islands	1-April-2018	25-May-2018	GST invoice
Andhra Pradesh	1-April-2018	15-April-2018	GST invoice
Arunachal Pradesh	1-April-2018	25-April-2018	GST invoice
Assam	1-April-2018	16-May-2018	E-way bill + GST invoice + AWB
Bihar	1-April-2018	20-April-2018	Bihar E-way bill Form IX for incoming movement of more than ₹ 50000 Bihar E-way bill Form X for outgoing movement of more than ₹ 50000 Bihar E-way bill Form VIII for within-state movement of more than ₹ 2 lakhs Bihar E-way bill Form VII for out-to-out movement
Chandigarh	1-April-2018	25-May-2018	GST invoice
Chhattisgarh	1-April-2018	1-June-2018	GST invoice
Dadra and Nagar Haveli	1-April-2018	25-May-2018	GST invoice
Daman and Diu	1-April-2018	25-May-2018	GST invoice
Delhi	1-April-2018	Not notified	GST invoice
Goa	1-April-2018	1-June-2018	GST invoice
Gujarat	1-April-2018	15-April-2018	E-way bill (for inbound & outbound) + GST invoice + AWB
Haryana	1-April-2018	20-April-2018	GST invoice
Himachal Pradesh	1-April-2018	20-April-2018	Form XXVI-A along with GST invoice + AWB
Jammu and Kashmir	1-April-2018	1-June-2018	GST invoice
Jharkhand	1-April-2018	20-April-2018	GST invoice
Karnataka	1-April-2018	1-April-2018	E-way bill for the value above ₹ 50000 – GST invoice + AWB
Kerala	1-April-2018	15-April-2018	Declaration (GST-KER 3 for B2C/ unregistered person); GST KER1 for B2B along with GST invoice + AWB
Lakshadweep	1-April-2018	25-May-2018	GST invoice
Madhya Pradesh	1-April-2018	25-April-2018	GST invoice
Maharashtra	1-April-2018	25-May-2018	GST invoice

Table 15.3: State-wise implementation dates and documents required for E-way bill

State	Inter-state implementation	Intra-state implementation	State-wise documents required*
Manipur	1-April-2018	25-May-2018	GST invoice
Meghalaya	1-April-2018	25-April-2018	E-way bill along with GST invoice + AWB
Mizoram	1-April-2018	1-June-2018	GST invoice
Nagaland	1-April-2018	1-May-2018	GST invoice
Odisha	1-April-2018	1-June-2018	GST invoice
Puducherry	1-April-2018	25-April-2018	GST invoice
Punjab	1-April-2018	1 June 2018	GST invoice
Rajasthan	1-April-2018	20-May-2018	GST invoice
Sikkim	1-April-2018	25-April-2018	GST invoice
Tamil Nadu	1-April-2018	2-June-2018	GST invoice
Telangana	1-April-2018	15-April-2018	GST invoice
Tripura	1-April-2018	20-April-2018	GST invoice + AWB
Uttar Pradesh	1-April-2018	15-April-2018	GST invoice
Uttarakhand	1-April-2018	20-April-2018	GST invoice
West Bengal	1-April-2018	3-June-2018	E-way bill for the value above ₹ 50000 along with GST invoice + AWB

* The state-wise document requirements are subjected to change.

With this, we come to the end of this chapter. Let us summarize the main points of the chapter.

Summary

In this chapter, you have learned about the purpose of E-way bill. Then, you have learned about the objectives, features and benefits of E-way bill. As you moved further in the chapter, you were made familiar with the E-way bill under GST. Next, you have learned about the people who need an E-way bill and the participants of E-way bill. You have also learned about the validity and cancellation of E-way bill. Furthermore, you have learned about the exceptions for E-way bill. Then, you have learned about the concerns of the industry and safety measures against these concerns. Next, you have learned about the penalties of issuing wrong E-way bill. Towards the end, you have learned about the implementation dates and document requirements of E-way bill.

CHAPTER

16

Making Cashless Transactions

In this Chapter:

* Meaning of Cashless Transaction
* Different Ways of Making Cashless Transactions

Introduction

The campaign for making Cashless India is in boom nowadays. This campaign is sponsored by the Government of India and is presented to public by our Prime Minister Shri Narendra Modi. This campaign aims at promoting cashless modes of transactions instead of transactions in hard cash. A cashless transaction is the way of making transactions through digital devices including cards, wallets, and online banking. You can make cashless transactions through cheques, cards, demand drafts, online transactions through NEFT and RTGS, UPI apps and BHIM app.

In this chapter, you will learn about cashless transaction. First of all, you will be made familiar with the common advantages and disadvantages of cashless transactions. As the chapter progresses, you will learn about different ways of making cashless transactions, like cheque, demand draft, online transaction through NEFT and RTGS, credit card/debit card, online wallets, UPI app, BHIM app, gift cards, Aadhar Enabled Payment System, and Unstructured Supplementary Service Data.

Let us start the chapter by understanding the meaning of cashless transaction.

Meaning of Cashless Transaction

Cashless transaction is defined as the act of performing transactions through digital means including cards, wallets, and online banking. The main idea of cashless transaction is reducing the usage of money in cash. It focuses on the usage of digital transaction. Cashless transaction is the transaction made by digital means rather than the hard cash. Cashless transaction has many advantages over cash transactions. Some of these are listed below:

- **Convenience:** The cashless transactions are more convenient as you do not require carrying a large amount of cash with you. You can make the transaction sitting at your own place and at any given time. You need not be presented physically for making a transaction. In case of emergencies, it is very helpful.
- **Discounts:** The cashless transactions are given a waiver of service tax up to ₹ 2,000 to promote digital transactions. Some additional discounts are also offered on the usage of cards for making payments. This helps in cutting down the costs incurred to you. Also, mobile wallets offer exciting discounts and cashback offers such as the reward points.
- **Tracking expenditure:** It will be an effortless task for people to keep track of their expenditure, if all the transactions are digitally recorded. It will be helpful while filing the income tax returns and at the time of audits. Furthermore, it will have a great influence on the budget.
- **Disciplined budget:** The recorded transactions help you keep a tab on your expenditure and, hence, creating a better budget plan. There are various applications and software tools available in the market to track your expenditure pattern and forecast your future monetary status. There is a bigger possibility of investment, but only if you spend in a controlled manner. The latte factor will decrease, if people use mobile wallets and make cashless transactions.
- **Lower risk:** You can block a card or mobile wallet remotely in case it is stolen. However, the lost money cannot be recovered. Nowadays, cards are equipped with more security features, thereby making them a safe option. It is difficult to copy them as they are equipped with biometric ID (fingerprints, eye scan, etc.).

In addition to the advantages of cashless or digital transactions, some disadvantages are also associated with it. Some major disadvantages are listed below:

- **Higher risk of identity theft:** In the event of digital transactions, one of the biggest risks is associated with identity theft. Due to less knowledge of digital transactions, we can be at a higher risk of losing our money. The incidents of online fraud are increasing at a rapid rate that is making digital transactions not a good choice for transactions. The risk of hacking also grows with more number of users making transactions digitally. There is no easy way to approach for money if a person loses his/her identity.
- **Losing phone:** As all the digital transactions are linked with your mobile number for better security, loss of mobile phone can result in restricting you from making transactions. It may develop problems, if you are completely dependent on the digital transactions and do not carry cash. It

would be more problematic when you do not have any other payment options. You also need to keep your phone charged as the problem may be raised if the phone battery dies in the middle of an online transaction.

- **Difficult for a non-tech-savvy:** The people who are less educated or unaware of the process of making the digital transactions suffer more as they need more time to the methods of conducting transactions through online mode. The fraud cases occur more due to less knowledge of the process of digital transactions.
- **Overspending:** One of the major disadvantages of cashless transactions is overspending. The people spend more money through cashless transactions but limited money when they make any purchase through cash. This leads to an imbalance between their expenditure and budget.

After understanding the meaning of a cashless transaction, let us now learn about different ways of making cashless transactions.

Different Ways of Making Cashless Transactions

As discussed earlier, cashless transactions are meant for reducing the usage of hard cash. They are meant for motivating digital currency. There are different options available for making cashless transactions, as listed below:

- Cheque
- Demand draft
- NEFT and RTGS
- Credit card and debit card
- Online wallets
- UPI app
- BHIM app
- Gift cards
- Aadhar Enabled Payment System
- Unstructured Supplementary Service Data

In this section, we will discuss about all the ways of making cashless transactions listed above.

Cheque

Cheque is known to be the oldest method being used for cashless payments. The **Negotiable Instruments Act, 1881** defines a cheque as "a bill of exchange drawn on a specified banker and not expressed to be payable otherwise than on demand". A sample cheque is shown in Fig.TL-16.1:

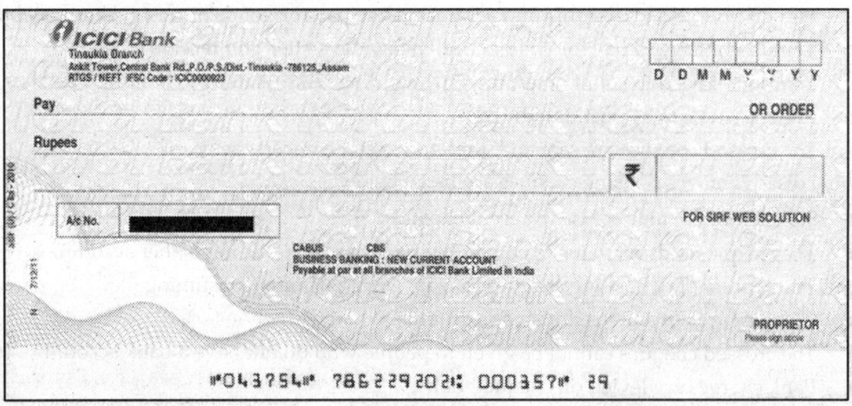

Fig.TL-16.1

In this method, you issue a cheque for the specific amount to someone else. The cheque gets deposited in the respective bank. The bank processes this payment through a clearing house.

Some of the important features of a cheque are as follows:

- A cheque must always be in written form.
- A cheque must be drawn in favor of the bank where the drawer owns his/her bank account.
- A cheque cannot be conditional, as it is invalid.
- A cheque should be meant specifically for paying a certain amount of money only. Anything other than this makes it invalid for a cheque.
- A cheque is not valid unless it is not signed by the drawer. The date on which the cheque is written must always be mentioned.
- A cheque is payable on demand, always.
- The validity of a cheque is of 3 months. And it is termed as a stale cheque, after its validity expires. A cheque that is signed for an advanced date is termed as a post-dated cheque. The validity of the cheque starts from the date mentioned on it.
- A cheque should be payable to the drawer but it may be payable to the bearer only on demand.
- The banker is liable only to the one who draws the cheque. There is no remedy against the banker, if it is a dishonored cheque.
- There is no acceptance required from the drawee in the case of a cheque. However, banks mark cheques as 'good' for clearance purpose.

There are several types of cheques. They can be classified into the following four types:

- **Open cheque:** A cheque is called 'Open Cheque' when it is possible to get cash over the counter at the bank. The holder of an open cheque can do the following:
  - Receive the payment over the counter at the bank
  - Deposit the cheque in his own account
  - Pass it to someone else by signing on the back of a cheque
- **Crossed cheque:** Crossed cheque overcomes the problem of open cheque that involves the risk of theft. The amount written on the crossed cheque is credited to the bank account of the payee. A cheque becomes a crossed cheque when you draw two parallel lines on the top-left corner, along with writing 'Account Payee' or 'Not Negotiable' on it. However, the latter part is optional.
- **Bearer cheque:** This type of cheque is payable to anyone who presents the cheque at the bank counter. It can be transferred by just delivering it.
- **Order cheque:** It is specifically payable to a person. The word 'Order' is written in place of 'Bearer' on the cheque. This cheque can be transferred to someone else by signing at the back of it.

There are several advantages and disadvantages of using cheques. Some advantages are listed below:

- You do not have to carry around a lot of cash to pay for goods or post cash to pay bills, etc.
- You do not have to pay for an item until a few days after you receive it.
- You do not need to count notes, thereby avoiding risks related to counting mistakes.
- The cheques can be post-dated.
- The crossed cheques are safe and, therefore, can be traced easily.

Some disadvantages of using cheques are listed below:

- Some creditors may refuse to accept cheques.
- The cheque holds nil value in case the drawer has no funds in his/her account.
- The process of depositing cheques into an account is time-consuming.
- Cheques are not suitable for small accounts.
- The crossed cheques cannot be given to people who do not have a bank account.
- Bank charges are levied on cheque-books.

Let us now learn about demand drafts.

Demand Draft

A payment done by draft is similar to that of a cheque, except the fact that the amount is signed up in advance. The paper used for draft is the same as that of a cheque. The money gets debited from your bank account as you get the draft. You cannot change the name of the payee on a draft once it is prepared. Fig.TL-16.2 shows a sample demand draft:

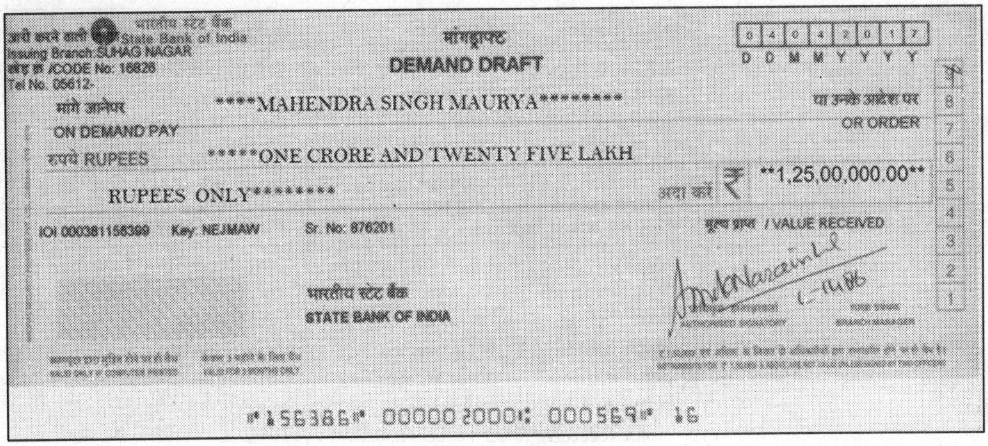
भारतीय स्टेट बैंक State Bank of India
Issuing Branch: SUHAG NAGAR
/CODE No: 16826
Tel No. 05612-
मांगड्राफ्ट
DEMAND DRAFT
0 4 0 4 2 0 1 7
D D M M Y Y Y Y
ON DEMAND PAY ****MAHENDRA SINGH MAURYA******** OR ORDER
रुपये RUPEES *****ONE CRORE AND TWENTY FIVE LAKH RUPEES ONLY********
₹ **1,25,00,000.00**
IOI 000381156399 Key: NEJMAW Sr. No: 876201
मूल्य प्राप्त / VALUE RECEIVED
भारतीय स्टेट बैंक
STATE BANK OF INDIA
AUTHORISED SIGNATORY BRANCH MANAGER
⑈156386⑈ 000002000⑆ 000569⑈ 16

Fig.TL-16.2

There are several features of a demand draft. Some of them are listed below:

- Demand draft can be issued by any person through the bank who does not have a bank account.
- It guarantees the certainty of payment to the payee.
- The bank is the only drawer who draws demand drafts for the drawees.
- The bank charges a minimal fee amount or commission for issuing a draft.
- There is no need of a clearance if the demand draft is drawn on the same bank.

Some major advantages of demand drafts are listed below:

- It is the safest option to receive money from anyone.
- It never gets defaulted as it is signed by the banker.

Some major disadvantages of demand drafts are as follows:

- You need to visit the bank for getting a demand draft issued.
- The clearance takes some additional time.

Let us now learn about the online transactions made through NEFT and RTGS.

Online Transactions through NEFT and RTGS

One of the most prominent methods to perform a cashless transaction is through NEFT or RTGS. You need a stable internet connection to transfer money online. It allows you to use your banking services from anywhere across the world. All you need is an internet connection, a username and a password to log in to your net banking account. With the help of net banking, you can check your account balance and statements. Additionally, you can pay your credit cards bills, electricity bills, make an internet recharge or a mobile recharge. It is a very secure mode for carrying out multiple transactions. The online transfer using NEFT or RTGS is way faster than the transfer through a demand draft.

RTGS stands for Real Time Gross Settlement that enables a person to transfer money on a real-time and gross basis. In simple words, 'real time' implies that the beneficiary bank will receive instructions on immediate basis to transfer the funds and 'gross' implies that the transfer is not bunched with another transaction and it is processed individually. The payments are irrevocable once performed, as these transactions take place in the RBI (Reserve Bank of India) books.

NEFT stands for National Electronic Funds Transfer and is a one-to-one funds transfer system. NEFT also initiates funds from one bank, but unlike RTGS, the NEFT settlement happens in batches during a day, rather than the individual process of the transfer. The batches are hourly based.

Table 16.1 contrasts the differences between NEFT and RTGS methods of online transaction:

Table 16.1: Differences between NEFT and RTGS

Parameter	NEFT	RTGS
Settlement Timings	NEFT is based on a Deferred Net Settlement (DNS) system which transfers funds in batches.	RTGS is based on real time system where funds are transferred on an immediate basis.
Transaction Amount	No limit.	Minimum amount defined by RBI is above ₹ 2 lakhs.
Operation Basis	Hourly based batches.	Continuous transactions.
Charges	Not exceeding ₹ 5 (+ Service Tax) per transaction for transactions up to ₹ 1 lakh. Not exceeding ₹ 15 (+ Service Tax) per transaction for transactions between ₹ 1 lakh and ₹ 2 lakhs. Not exceeding ₹ 25 (+ Service Tax) per transaction for transactions above ₹ 2 lakhs.	Not exceeding ₹ 30 per transaction for transactions between ₹ 2 lakhs and 5 lakhs. Not exceeding ₹ 55 per transaction for transactions above ₹ 5 lakhs.

Let us now learn about credit card and debit card.

Credit Card and Debit Card

A credit card is a form of plastic money that is issued to the customers to pay at a merchant's outlet for the goods he purchases and the services he is offered. The transactions on credit cards are based on the principle – buy now and pay later. The card holder is liable to pay the entire amount spent to the card issuer. The card-issuer is usually a bank or NBFC (Non-Banking Financial Company), and it grants a credit limit to the card holder, which decreases as the usage of the card increases. The card holder is basically borrowing money from the bank to pay at a merchant's outlet, make a bill payment or advance cash payment. Fig.TL-16.3 below shows a credit card:

Fig.TL-16.3

The main features of a credit card are listed below:

- A credit card gives the freedom to a card holder of travelling anywhere in the world without taking the pain to carry cash along. The possible risk of the money theft is reduced in such a case and brings peace to the card holder's mind.

- The credit card holder avails and relishes a certain credit limit that has been set on his card by the bank. The determination of the credit card limit is done on the basis of evaluating the creditworthiness of the card holder.
- The payments can be made in any currency of your choice through a credit card.
- The bank that issues you a credit card will keep the records of all your transactions that help it to create a billing statement of your credit card on a monthly or a periodical basis.
- There are regular charges applicable on the usage of a credit card, usually charged on yearly basis.
- There is a grace period given to the credit card holder and it refers to the additional number of days past the due date, within which there is no interest or late fee charged to the customer.
- In case you make any cash withdrawal transactions at an ATM outlet using your credit card, there will be an additional fee charged by the card issuer.
- The total amount due for your credit card includes the service tax as well.
- The credit card holder can also earn bonus points on a handsome number of transactions that he makes through his card. The transactions may include paying restaurant bills, shopping and purchasing petrol, etc.

A debit card is also a form of plastic money that enables the customer to pay at the merchant's outlet for the goods purchased and services availed, if any. The transactions on debit cards are based on the principle – buy now and pay now. The amount you swipe through a debit card at the merchant's outlet gets deducted from your bank account directly. The protection on financial transactions is provided by the payment processors like Visa and MasterCard. There is a daily limit set on the debit card, and doesn't let you make transactions that exceed that limit. You need to use a PIN (Personal Identification Number) when using your debit card to make a transaction. PIN is a 4-digit confidential number associated with your debit card. The transaction will not go through if the PIN entered is wrong. Fig.TL-16.4 below shows a debit card:

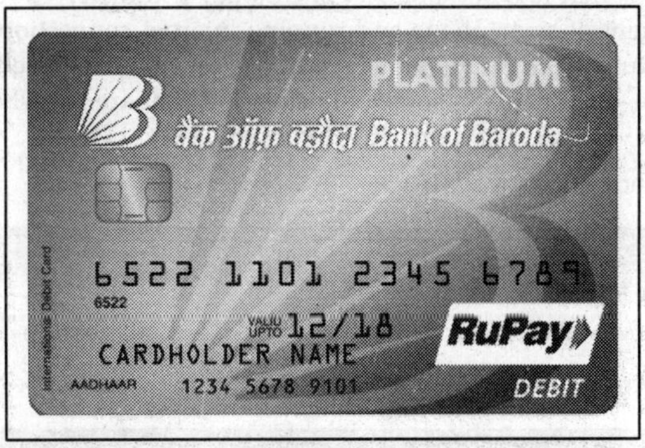

Fig.TL-16.4

Some features of a debit card are listed below:

- The material used in its making is plastic.
- There is a 16-digit unique number associated with it.
- There is a validity period of the debit card.
- There is a magnetic strip embedded in the card, which contains the confidential information about the card holder.
- There is a signature panel at the back of the card that must be signed by the card holder for authorization purpose.
- When you need to make an online transaction using your debit card, there is a CVV number that is required to be entered at the online payment gateway, which is a 3-digit number at the back of the card just adjacent to the signature panel.
- There is the customer care number written on the debit card of the bank that issued the card.

Table 16.2 below contrasts the differences between credit cards and debit cards:

Table16.2: Differences between Credit Cards and Debit Cards

Credit Cards	Debit Cards
The bill is generated every month.	There are monthly statements generated on the basis of the transactions performed on your bank account through the card.
This card is linked to the issuing bank or NBFC.	This card is linked with the bank account of the card holder.
There is a credit limit assigned to the card holder on monthly basis.	The limit of cash withdrawal and at the POS limit is assigned on a daily basis. Some of the cards may not have a limit.
If the bill is not paid after the due date passes, there is an interest charged on the card.	There is no interest associated with it.
There is a credit rating associated with it that depends on the usage of the card.	There is no effect on the credit rating.
The chances of fraud are low.	The fraud chances are high as the money is deducted immediately from your bank account.

Let us now learn about online wallets.

Online Wallets

Online wallet is a virtual wallet where you can keep your money in the digital form. The digital money can be used to make purchases of goods and availing various kinds of services, just like physical cash. The only difference is that it is not tangible. The money is transferred to the merchant's account directly. There is a requirement of smartphone and running internet connection at both the ends to perform this transaction successfully. The online wallets that are prominently used in India are Paytm, MobiKwik, Tez and FreeCharge, etc. There are some online wallets that are launched by some prominent banks like SBI State Bank Buddy, HDFC PayZapp, ICICI Pockets, Axis LIME, etc.

Fig.TL-16.5 below shows Paytm wallet:

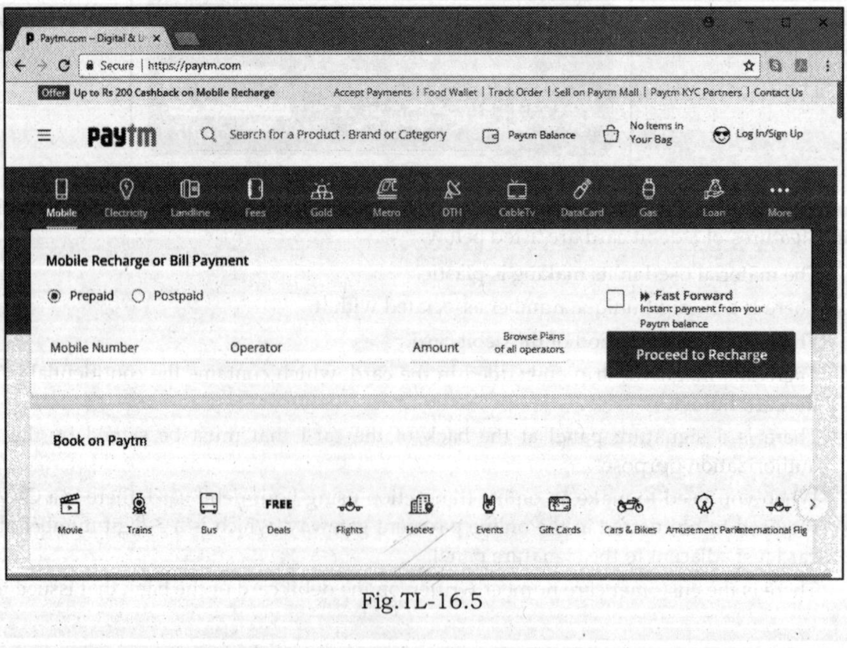

Fig.TL-16.5

To use the online wallet service, you need to add money in the wallet first. The money can be added into the wallet through NetBanking, credit card and debit card. After the money is added to the wallet, you can use it for buying goods, availing services, paying utility bills, making recharges and booking tickets, etc. The online wallet can be used to transfer money to another person's wallet or bank account. There are some merits associated with the use of online wallets for both the users and the marketeers. They are listed below:

- It serves as a cache to store the digital money.
- The user can pay instantly for any purchase that he makes.
- There are ongoing offers available on the products or services you purchase like cashback and discounts.
- The expenditure on the marketing is not very expensive.

Let us now learn about Unified Payment Interface (UPI) app.

UPI App

UPI (Unified Payment Interface) app is the latest online money transfer method that is real-time and instant. This is the latest mobile payment mode that enables a user to transfer money from one bank account to another. It is a very economical and a simple cashless transaction method, which is mobile based. The RBI (Reserve Bank of India) has kept mobile wallets out of this service.

The banks have integrated UPI in their existing mobile apps. It is compatible with the mobile apps of all the banks. UPI will act as a unique identification system for your bank, when you transfer money.

The UPI uses Aadhar ID number, mobile phone number or a virtual payment address for the authorization to perform the transaction successfully. The virtual payment address (VPA) may be your e-mail ID or your local address. It does not require a person's bank account number or IFSC code to transfer money. This service is available 24*7 and non-chargeable as of now. The SBI Pay UPI app is shown in Fig.TL-16.6 below:

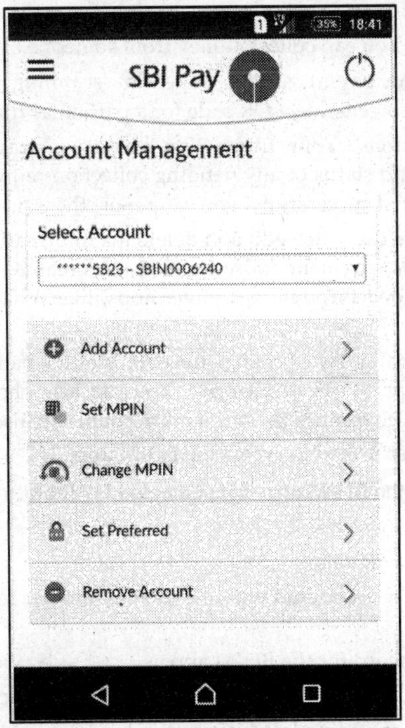

Fig.TL-16.6

Some major features of UPI app are listed below:

- There is no need to provide you bank account details and IFSC code every time you make a transaction. These details are required only once when you register for the app for the first time. Thereafter, you need only the UPI ID or VPA while transferring money.
- Unlike the online fund transfer through online banking, you don't have to wait to transfer money, before the added payee is registered successfully at the bank, which sometimes may take more than 24 hours. It provides an immediate transfer of funds.
- The limit kept for a transaction is ₹ 1 lakh.
- UPI is based on the IMPS system for money transfer that makes it available for 24 hours.
- You can make transactions between any two parties having a UPI ID.
- There is a money collector feature that is provided by UPI app. It sets a payment reminder at the debtor's end and notifies him about the due amount. As soon as the notification is approved by the debtor, the payment is done.
- The UPI app acts as a mobile wallet also that can be used to make online and offline purchases, like mobile & DTH recharges and paying utility bills.
- You may or may not use the UPI app of the bank where you own an account. You can choose from all the apps available from other banks as per your needs.

Let us now learn about the BHIM app.

BHIM App

Bharat Interface for Money (BHIM) is a mobile app that is used to perform quick and simplified financial transactions through UPI. You can make direct bank transfers instantly using BHIM app. Also you can receive payments using mobile number or Virtual Payment Address (VPA). The services that you can avail using BHIM App are listed below:

- **Sending Money:** Using VPA, bank account number & IFSC code, mobile number and QR code, money can be sent to anyone.
- **Requesting Money:** You can collect money from someone by entering the VPA.
- **Scan & Pay:** You can pay at various outlets by scanning the QR code available at the payment counter. You may also generate a QR code for a particular transaction.
- **Recording Transactions:** Your transaction history is tracked regularly. You may check your transaction history and status of any pending collection requests. In case a transaction is declined or could not be completed successfully, you can report the issue.
- **Viewing Profile:** One can view, edit and delete the information regarding your financial details, like static QR code and the payment addresses that you created. The QR code can be shared with others and can be downloaded through messenger apps, like WhatsApp, Email, etc. that are available on smartphones.
- **Bank Account:** You can view or change the details of the bank account that is linked with the BHIM app. The UPI PIN can be set or changed. You can also change the bank account linked with the BHIM in the menu. The balance in your bank account can also be checked here.

The following steps are performed to access the BHIM app:

1. *Download* and *install* the BHIM app from Google Play Store.
2. *Open* the BHIM app.
3. *Select* your preferred language.
4. *Select* the SIM which is associated with the mobile number registered with bank CBS (Core Banking Solutions).
5. *Login* by setting password for the BHIM app.
6. *Link* the BHIM app with your bank account using the bank account option.
7. *Set* your UPI PIN by providing last 6 digits of your debit card and its expiry date.

8. *Visit* **Profile** option and you can set the Virtual Payment Address (VPA).
9. *Set* a VPA as the primary VPA.

In the updated version of BHIM app, you can also scan QR codes. You can use **Scan and Pay** option for sending and collecting money.

You can perform the following steps to send money through BHIM app:

1. *Open* the app and enter the login passcode.
2. *Select* the **Send Money** option. The send request gets initiated.
3. *Enter* the mobile number of the payee in the **Mobile/Payment Address** box.
4. *Click* the **Verify** button to check the name of the payee. It fetches the name of the payee if he/she is registered on *99#/BHIM.
5. *Enter* the amount that you need to transfer in the **AMOUNT** text box.
6. *Enter* the remarks for the transaction (if any) in the **REMARKS** text box.
7. *Click* the **PAY** button. You will receive a confirmation from the app once the money is transferred.

The process is explained using screenshots as given in Fig.TL-16.7 below:

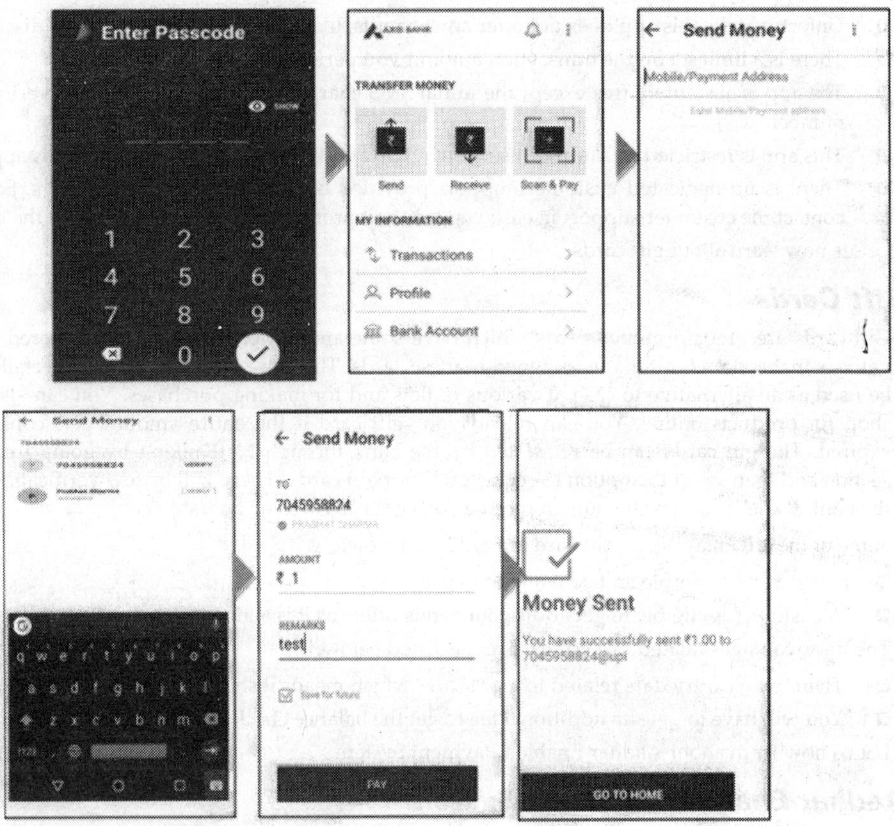

Fig.TL-16.7

The details of the transaction can be checked from the drop-down menu on the UPI PIN entry page. This page opens where the customer enters his UPI PIN.

There are some advantages of the BHIM app as listed below:

- It will not be required by the user to enter the details of the bank account over and over again in the BHIM app. The app picks up the details of the customer automatically from the corresponding bank and the phone number provided.
- There are no transaction charges involved whether the receiver has or does not have the BHIM app.
- The money transfer is instant and is between two bank accounts.
- The app does not store any other information of the user apart from his bank account number and the phone number. Hence, it is secure to use.
- The installation and set-up procedures are very easy.
- It is very simple and convenient to use.
- You can transfer money through this app 24*7*365.
- A single app is used to make all types of payments in your favorite language.

With the advantages listed as above, it is bound to have some disadvantages as well. They are as listed below:

- The app requires a stable internet connection to work smoothly.
- Unfortunately, this app does not offer any benefits, like cashback, bonus points or discounts.
- There is a limit set on the transaction amount you perform in a day.
- The app is absolutely free except the initial SMS charges of ₹ 1.25 that is sent to verify your mobile number.
- This app is restricted to Android users only. IOS and Window users cannot use this app.
- There is no dedicated customer support provided by the BHIM app developers. So, you cannot contact the customer support in case you face any problem regarding the usage of the application.

Let us now learn about gift cards.

Gift Cards

Gift cards are prepaid money cards which have some amount of monetary value stored in them. This value is that certain limit that is assigned to these cards. These are issued by banks or retailers. These can be used as an alternative to cash at various outlets and for making purchases. You can also use them to shop for products online. You can reload your gift card if the entire amount gets consumed or gets expired. The gift cards can be requested by the bank through NetBanking by going under the Cards section and then select the option to request for prepaid cards. There will be few verification checks from the bank's side, after which you will receive your gift card at your doorstep.

Some of the advantages of a gift card are as listed below:

- They are very simple and convenient to use.
- A customer is eligible to get additional bonus offers as it is a gift card.

The disadvantages related to a gift card are as listed below:

- There is an expiry date related to a gift card, which means it should be used before that time.
- You will have to give an additional fee to get the balance checked in the card.

Let us now learn about Aadhar Enabled Payment System.

Aadhar Enabled Payment System

Aadhaar Enabled Payment System (AEPS) is a method to take out money from a bank account. This method does not require your signature or your debit card to get money from your account. There is no need to visit even the branch of the bank. It uses the details of your Aadhaar ID for the authentication purpose.

No paper or card is required to perform the transaction through AEPS. However, you Aadhaar ID must be linked with your bank account to avail this service. AEPS will not work if the Aadhaar ID is not linked with the bank account. The following information is needed to perform an AEPS transaction:

- Aadhaar ID Number
- Bank IIN (Issuer Identification Number) or Name
- Fingerprint

You can make basic banking transactions as follows through AEPS:

- Checking balance
- Depositing cash
- Withdrawing cash
- Fund-to-fund transfer through Aadhaar

The following parties are involved in the transaction:

- The customer of the bank
- The one who facilitates AEPS – Banking correspondent
- The bank that is associated to the banking correspondent
- The bank where you hold your account
- NPCI (National Payments Corporation of India) which is responsible for switching, clearing and settling transactions
- UIDAI (Unique Identification Authority of India) that authenticates using fingerprint.

There are several advantages of AEPS. Some of them are listed below:

- Cash withdrawals, balance inquiry, cash deposits and funds transfers from Aadhaar to Aadhaar
- No registration is required
- Can be helpful in remote areas where transactions are carried out by banking correspondents.

Let us now learn about Unstructured Supplementary Service Data.

Unstructured Supplementary Service Data

If you do not have a running internet connection or a smartphone, you can use Unstructured Supplementary Service Data (USSD). It is a service offered by banks on the phones. All you need to do is dial *99# on your mobile phone to use this service. You will be able to use all the services that are provided to a customer using a smartphone and internet connection. The banks supporting this payment option and providing this service include SBI, ICICI, BOB, Axis Bank and PNB.

You can perform the following steps to use the USSD service on your mobile phone:

1. *Link* your mobile number with your bank account.
2. *Dial* ***99#** on the dialer of your phone.
3. *Identify* your bank by entering the first three letters or the first four letters of the IFSC code of your bank branch. A menu will appear.
4. *Select* the **Fund Transfer-MMID** option from the menu.
5. *Enter* the mobile phone number and MMID of the receiver.
6. *Enter* the amount to be transferred and your MPIN followed by a space and the last four digits of your bank account number.
7. *Click* the **Send** icon. The specified amount will be transferred to the receiver.

There are some advantages of using USSD. They are as listed below:

- No smartphone is needed to perform a transaction.
- No internet connection is required for the transaction to be performed.

With this, we come to the end of this chapter. Let us summarize the main points of the chapter.

Summary

This chapter has explored information about cashless transactions. You have understood the meaning of cashless transactions. You have also learned about the advantages and disadvantages related to the cashless transactions. Moreover, you have learned about the different ways of performing cashless transactions. You have acquainted knowledge about cheques, demand drafts, online transactions through NEFT and RTGS, credit cards/debit cards, online wallets, and UPI app. You have also learned about the procedure of setting up the BHIM app and performing transactions through it. In the end, you have learned about gift cards, Aadhaar Enabled Payment System, and Unstructured Supplementary Service Data.

MS Excel

CHAPTER

1

Introducing Excel 2013

In this Chapter:

- Exploring New Features
- Creating a New Workbook
- Saving a Workbook
- Opening an Existing Workbook
- Inserting Worksheet
- Inserting Cells, Rows, and Columns
- Decorating Worksheets
- Closing a Workbook

Introduction

A worksheet consists of large grids of rows and columns where you can enter data. In a worksheet, the intersection of a row and a column is called a cell where a user enters data in the worksheet. The data entered in a cell or a range of cells can be modified according to the user's requirements. In MS Excel 2013, a collection of worksheets is known as a workbook. Usually, a workbook contains only one worksheet, Sheet 1, by default. However, users can add more worksheets depending on their requirements.

This chapter broadly discusses the new features of MS Excel 2013. Next, the chapter discusses the procedure of creating and saving a workbook. It also describes the procedure of opening an existing workbook and inserting new worksheets. It explains how to insert cells, rows, and columns in a worksheet. You also learn about decorating worksheets in MS Excel 2013. In the end, the chapter explains the procedure to close a workbook.

Let us first learn the new features of MS Excel 2013.

Exploring New Features

MS Excel 2013 introduces various new features to help users analyze, manage, and share information in a better way. For example, MS Excel 2013 contains the instant data analysis feature to help you track important data trends. Apart from this feature, the following new features are included in MS Excel 2013:

- **Getting started quickly**: Provides templates for budgets, calendars, forms, reports, etc. In MS Excel, most of the set up and design work are done with the help of templates, thereby enabling you to perform any task quickly.
- **Flash fill data**: Allows you to enter data automatically into a worksheet, thereby saving a lot of time and efforts of users. You can use the Flash Fill feature to extract the first or the last word from the contents of a column, say the name of a person. This feature also allows you to extract the day, month, and year from a date.
- **Instant data analysis**: Helps you to convert data into a table or chart in just a single click. To use this feature, you need to click the Quick Analysis icon that appears at the bottom-right corner of the selected data. This feature speeds up the process of preparing charts, formatting, and writing formulas.
- **Save and share data online**: Helps you to save your workbooks to your own online location, such as OneDrive, and easily share them with other people.
- **Save workbook in a new file format**: Allows you to save a workbook in a file format known as Strict Open Extensible Markup Language (XML) Spreadsheet. This new file format helps you to read and write ISO8601 dates for resolving leap year concerns.
- **Enable sharing worksheet data on a webpage:** Allows you to share a worksheet on the Web, thereby allowing you to view the data on the Web page.
- **Recommended charts**: Allows you to select an appropriate chart type for representing your data. For accessing this new feature, select the desired data and click the INSERT tab first and then the **Recommended Charts** button.
- **Animation in charts**: Allows you to view an animation effect on a chart when you move a selection, create charts, and perform calculations. It also helps you in identifying the changes made in the data.
- **Insert online pictures**: Allows you to insert online pictures in a workbook to make the data more eye-catching and presentable.
- **New functions**: Provides many new functions to help you perform complex calculations with ease. The new formulas included in MS Excel 2013 are:
    - **Web functions**: Include functions such as WEBSERVICE, FILTERXML, and ENCODEURL
    - **Information functions**: Include functions such as ISFORMULA, FORMULATEXT, SHEET, and SHEETS
    - **Logical functions**: Include functions such as XOR and IFNA

- **Create a standalone PivotChart**: Provides you the flexibility to create a PivotChart without creating a PivotTable.
- **Use timeline to filter dates:** Allows you to compare your PivotChart or PivotTable over different time periods.

Let us learn how to create a new workbook.

Creating a New Workbook

Creating a workbook is the fundamental step while working with MS Excel 2013. MS Excel 2013 offers you various built-in templates that you can select to create your workbook. Apart from these templates, you can also choose templates online from the Microsoft Office website. In this section, you will learn to create a workbook using a blank template, existing templates, and online templates.

To create a new blank workbook, you need to select the **Blank workbook** template.

Perform the following steps to create a new workbook using a blank template:

1. *Click* the **Start** button (Fig.EX-1.1). The **Start** menu appears (Fig.EX-1.1).
2. *Click* the **Microsoft Office 2013** folder from the list of apps (Fig.EX-1.1).

   A list of apps related to the Microsoft Office suite appears (Fig.EX-1.2).
3. *Click* the **Excel 2013** app from the list to launch the Excel 2013 application, as shown in Fig.EX-1.2:

Fig.EX-1.1

Fig.EX-1.2

A list of different templates appears in the Backstage view (Fig.EX-1.3).

Note

Since its introduction in Excel 2010, the Backstage view is still a part of Excel 2013. It provides options to perform various operations on your workbook. The appearance of the Backstage view changes, as per the option selected.

4. *Select* the **Blank workbook** template, as shown in Fig.EX-1.3:

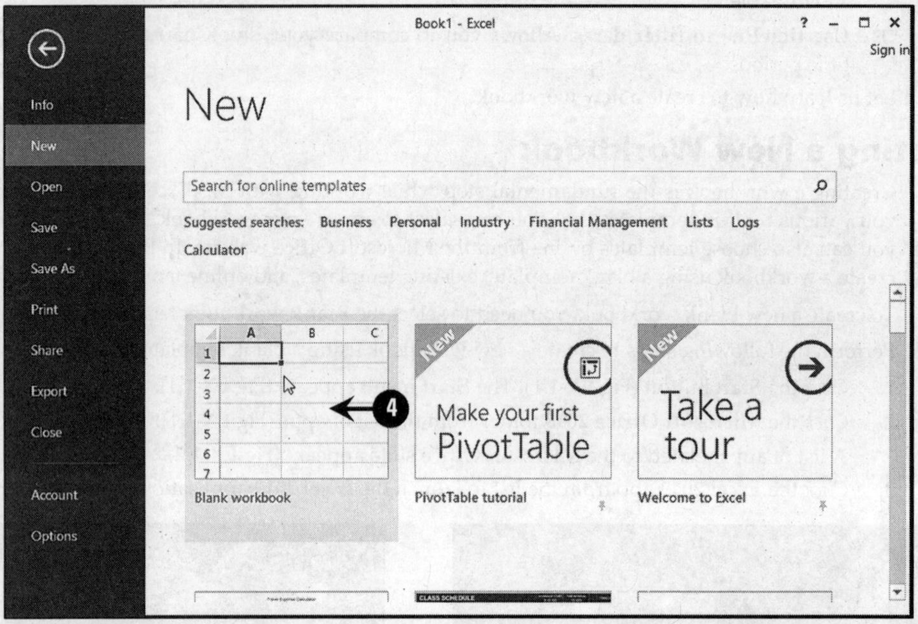

Fig.EX-1.3

A new blank workbook appears, as shown in Fig.EX-1.4:

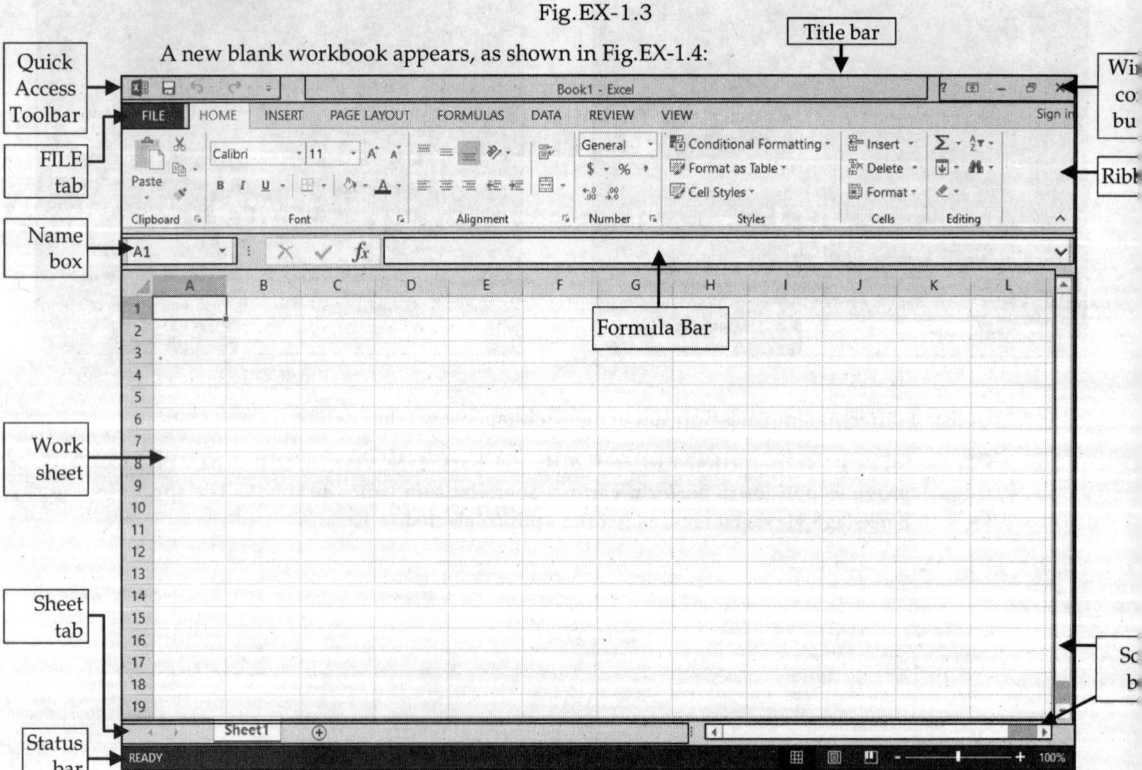

Fig.EX-1.4

You can use the templates that are already installed in the computer or available as sample templates in MS Excel 2013 to work quickly and effectively.

Perform the following steps to create a new workbook using an existing template:

1. *Launch* the **Excel 2013** application. A list of available templates appears in the Back stage view (Fig.EX-1.5).
2. *Select* the desired template from the displayed list of templates. In our case, we have selected **Travel expense log**, as shown in Fig.EX-1.5:

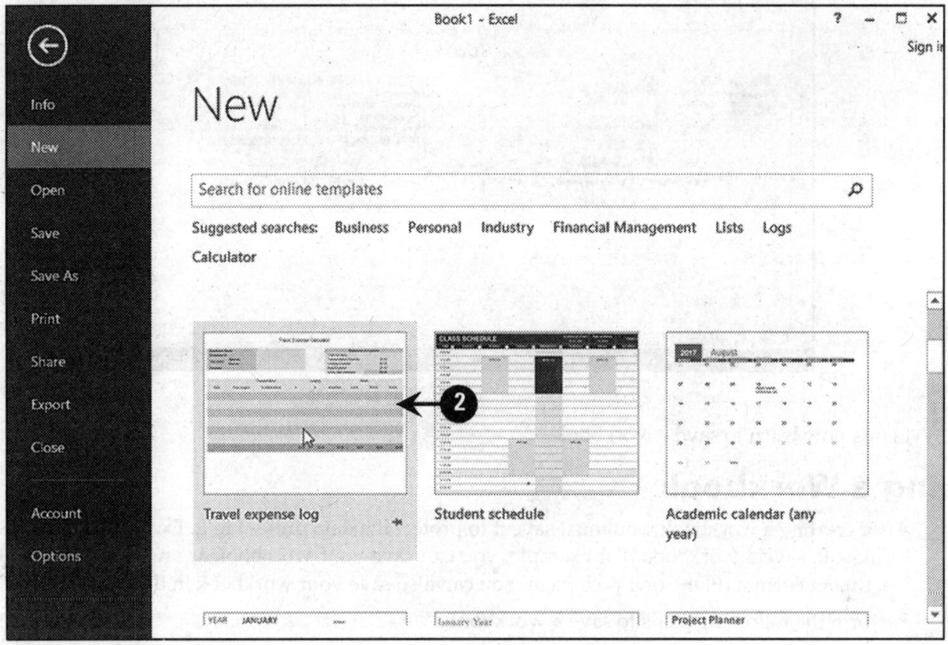

Fig.EX-1.5

The dialog box appears with the name of **Travel expense log** (Fig.EX-1.6).

3. *Click* the **Create** button, as shown in Fig.EX-1.6:

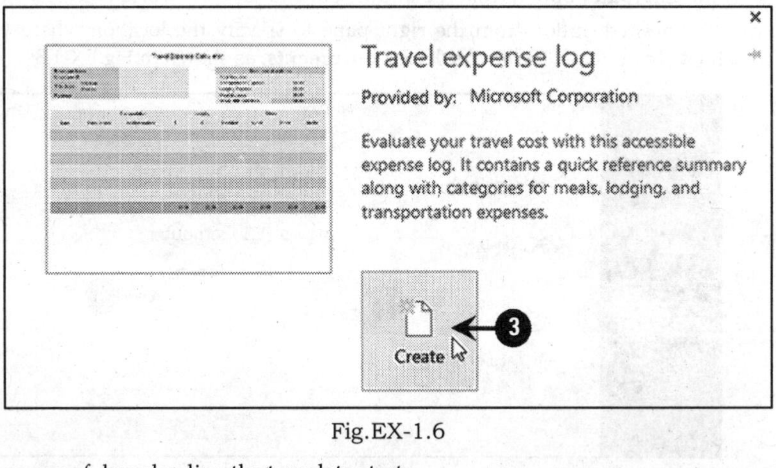

Fig.EX-1.6

The process of downloading the template starts.

After the downloading process is completed, a new workbook is created with the name **Travel expense log1**, as shown in Fig.EX-1.7:

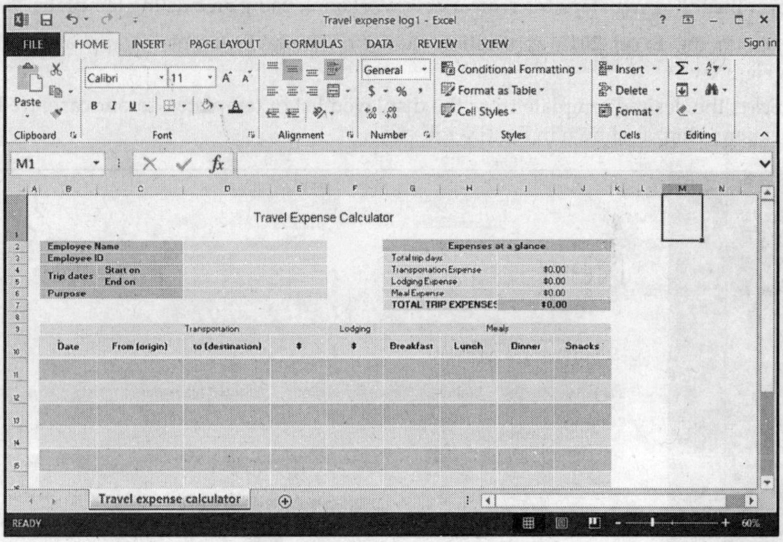

Fig.EX-1.7

Let us now learn to save a workbook.

Saving a Workbook

After creating a workbook, you must save it to protect the data present in it. Excel 2013 provides various file formats to save a workbook. For example, you can save your workbook as an Excel Workbook, a Portable Document Format (PDF), or a Web page. You can also save your workbook in the compatibility mode.

Perform the following steps to save a workbook:

1. *Click* the **FILE** tab. The Backstage view appears.
2. *Select* the **Save** option from the Backstage view.
   The **Save** screen appears (Fig.EX-1.8).
3. *Select* the **Computer** option from the middle pane to save the workbook (Fig.EX-1.8).
4. *Select* the desired option from the right pane to specify the location where you want to save the workbook. In our case, we have selected **documents,** as shown in Fig.EX-1.8:

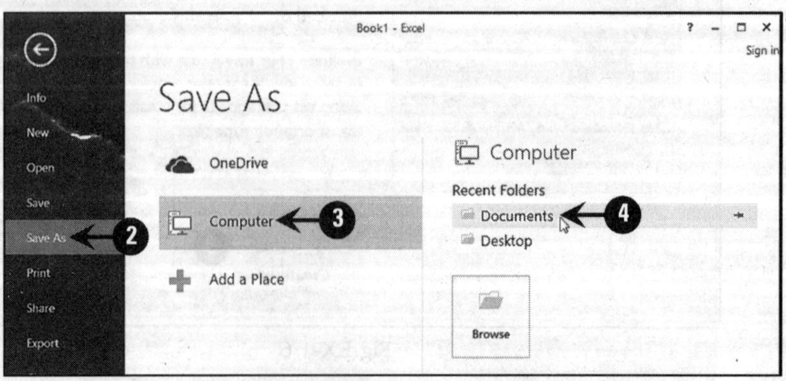

Fig.EX-1.8

The **Save As** dialog box opens (Fig.EX-1.9).

5. *Type* the desired name for the workbook in the **File name** combo box. In our case, we have typed the name **Employee** (Fig.EX-1.9).
6. *Click* the **Save** button to save the workbook, as shown in Fig.EX-1.9:

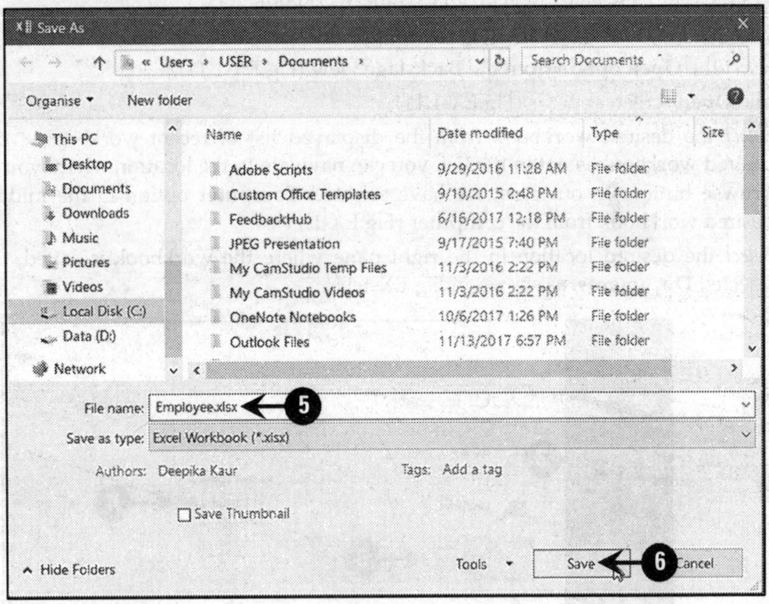

Fig.EX-1.9

By default, a workbook is saved with the .xlsx file extension. To save the workbook in a different format, click the Save as type drop-down list in the Save As dialog box and select the desired file extension from the drop-down list.

Now, the workbook is saved with the specified name, as shown in Fig.EX-1.10:

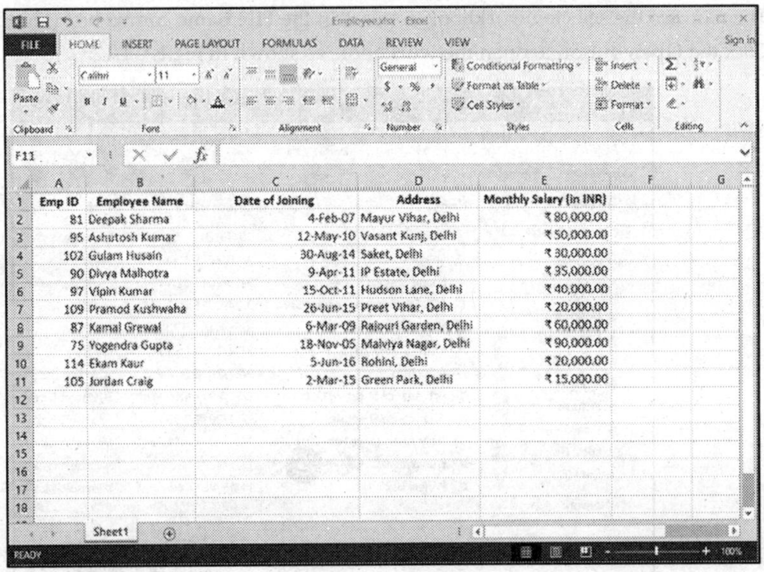

Fig.EX-1.10

Let us now learn to open an existing workbook.

Opening an Existing Workbook

In Excel 2013, you can access an existing workbook by using the Open option from the Backstage view.

Perform the following steps to open an existing workbook:

1. *Click* the **FILE** tab. The Backstage view appears.
2. *Select* the **Open** option from the Backstage view (Fig.EX-1.11).

   The **Open** screen appears (Fig.EX-1.11).
3. *Select* the desired workbook from the displayed list of recent workbooks you worked on. If the desired workbook is not in the list, you can navigate to the location where you saved it by using the **Browse** button. In our case, we have selected **Computer** option in the middle pane to open the desired workbook from the computer (Fig.EX-1.11).
4. *Select* the desired location in the right pane where the workbook is saved. In our case, we have selected **Documents**, as shown in Fig.EX-1.11:

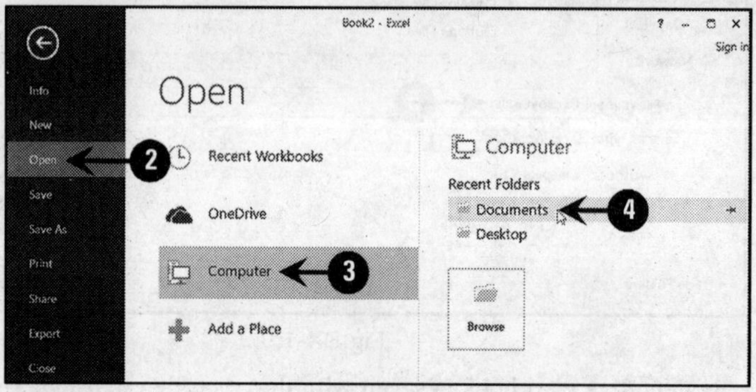

Fig.EX-1.11

The **Open** dialog box opens (Fig.EX-1.12).

5. *Select* the desired workbook that you want to open. In our case, we have selected **Employee** (Fig.EX-1.12).

   The name of the selected workbook appears in the **File name** combo box (Fig.EX-1.12).
6. *Click* the **Open** button to open the workbook, as shown in Fig.EX-1.12:

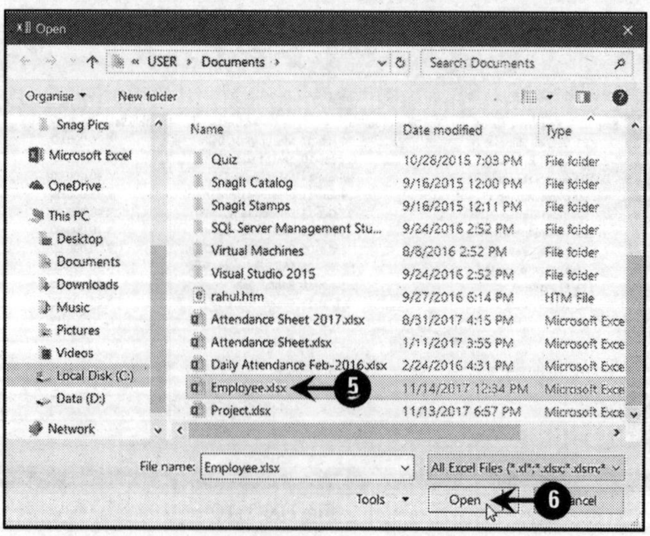

Fig.EX-1.12

The selected workbook opens, as shown in Fig.EX-1.13:

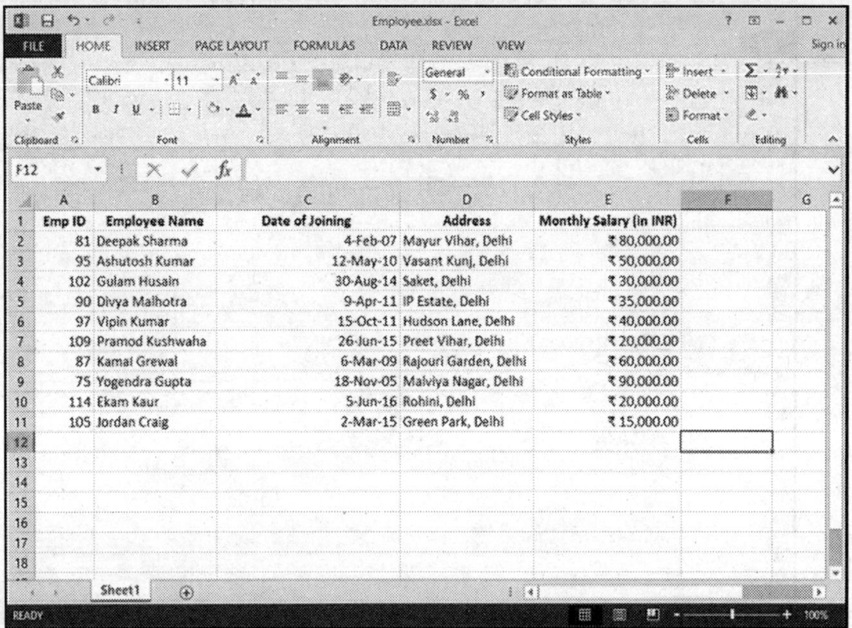

Fig.EX-1.13

Let us now learn to insert a worksheet.

Inserting Worksheet

In Excel 2013, a workbook contains single worksheet by default, which you can use to store data. However, if required, you can add more worksheets to your workbook.

Perform the following steps to add a new worksheet in an Excel workbook:

1. *Open* a new or an existing workbook.
2. *Click* the down-arrow of the **Insert** button under the **Cells** group of the **HOME** tab (Fig.EX-1.14). A drop-down list appears (Fig.EX-1.14).
3. *Select* the **Insert Sheet** option from the drop-down list, as shown in Fig.EX-1.14:

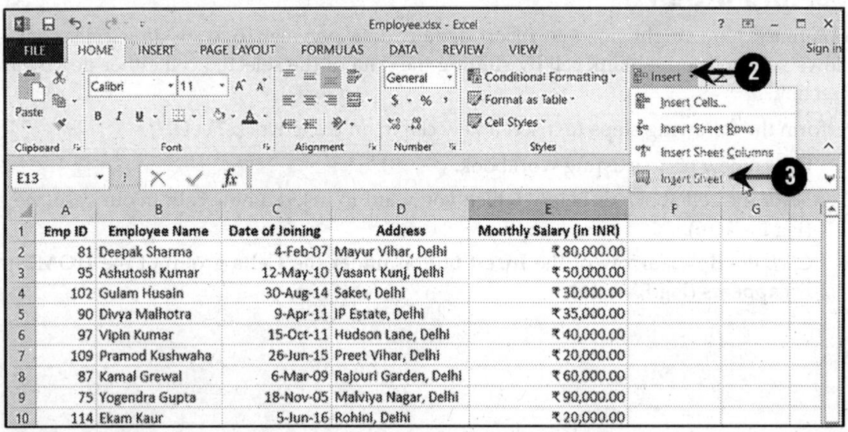

Fig.EX-1.14

A new worksheet named **Sheet2** is added before the first sheet, as shown in Fig.EX-1.15:

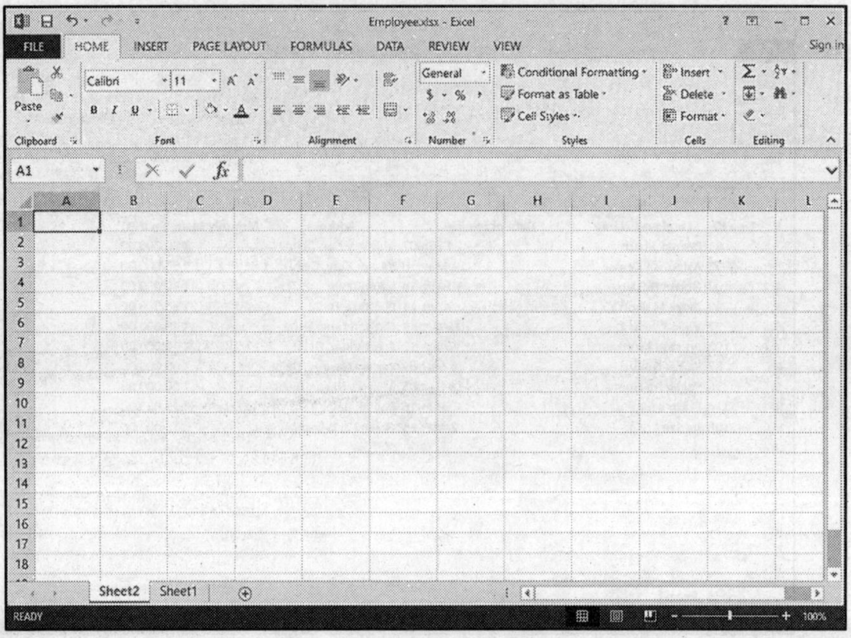

Fig.EX-1.15

Let us now insert cells, rows, and columns in a worksheet.

Inserting Cells, Rows, and Columns

You can insert cells, rows, and columns in a worksheet to accommodate more information. When you insert a new row, the row is inserted above the selected row; whereas, when you insert a new column, the column is inserted to the left of the selected column. If you insert a row and the last row of the worksheet does not contain any data, then the last row of the worksheet is removed. Similarly, when you insert a new column, the last column of the worksheet is removed if it does not contain any data. Therefore, the number of rows and columns in a worksheet remains static.

Let us learn to insert a cell.

Inserting a Cell

Sometimes, you might need to insert certain data between two existing cells containing data. Excel allows you to insert a blank cell by shifting the data of the selected cell either downwards or in the right direction.

Perform the following steps to insert a new cell in an Excel worksheet:

1. *Open* a new or an existing workbook.
2. *Select* the cell above or below which you want to insert a new cell. In our case, we have selected **E11** (Fig.EX-1.16).
3. *Click* the down-arrow of the **Insert** button under the **Cells** group of the **HOME** tab. A drop-down list appears (Fig.EX-1.16).

4. *Select* the **Insert Cells** option from the drop-down list, as shown in Fig.EX-1.16:

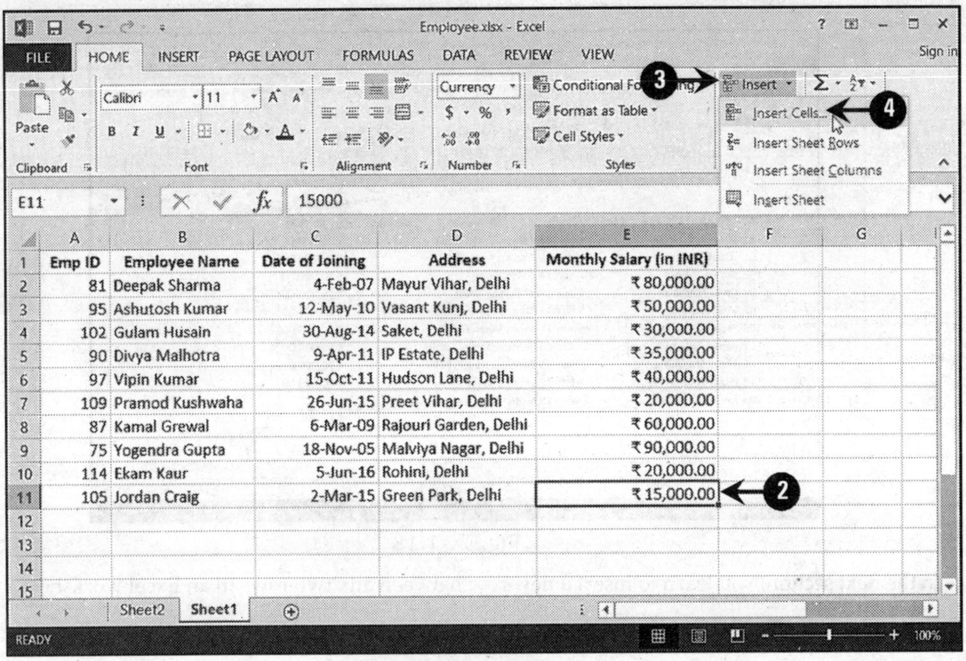

Fig.EX-1.16

The **Insert** dialog box opens (Fig.EX-1.17).

5. *Select* the **Shift cells down** radio button to shift the content of the selected cell and all other succeeding cells in the current column towards the bottom (Fig.EX-1.17).

Note: **You can select the Shift cells right radio button to shift the content of the selected cell and all other succeeding cells in the current row to the right.**

6. *Click* the **OK** button, as shown in Fig.EX-1.17:

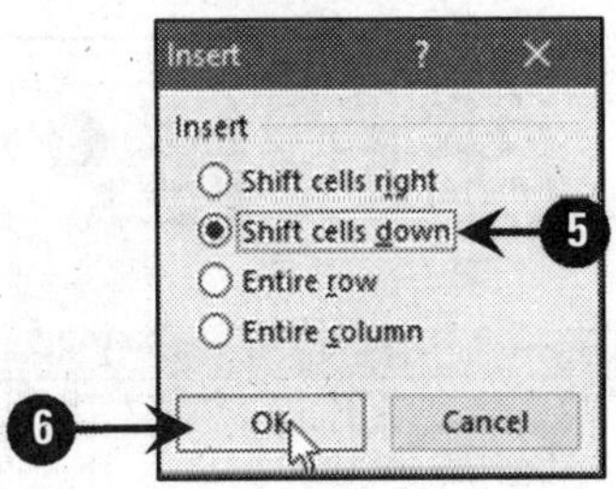

Fig.EX-1.17

The blank cell is inserted and the data of the succeeding cells in the same column is shifted down, as shown in Fig.EX-1.18:

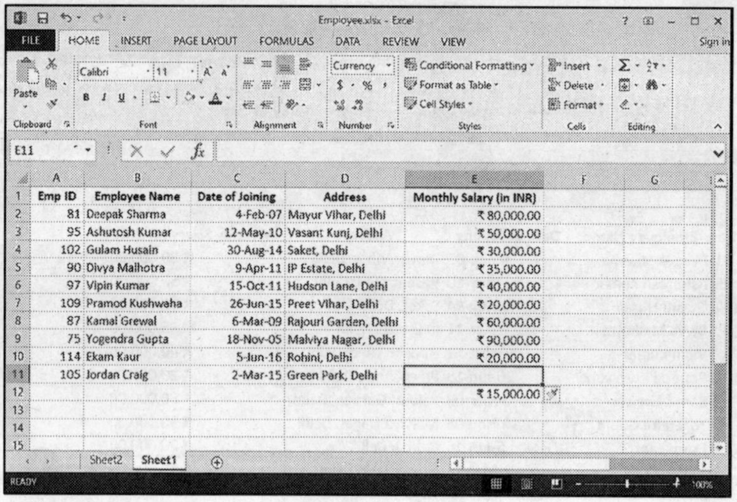

Fig.EX-1.18

In the next section, you learn to insert a new row between any two rows in an Excel worksheet.

Inserting a Row

In Excel 2013, you can add an entire row between any two rows of a worksheet containing some data. When you insert a new row, it is inserted above the selected row.

Perform the following steps to insert a new row in a worksheet:

1. *Open* a new or an existing workbook.
2. *Select* the row above which you want to insert a new row. In our case, we have selected **10th** row (Fig.EX-1.19).
3. *Click* the down-arrow button of the **Insert** button under the **Cells** group of the **HOME** tab. A drop-down list appears (Fig.EX-1.19).
4. *Select* the **Insert Sheet Rows** option from the drop-down list, as shown in Fig.EX-1.19:

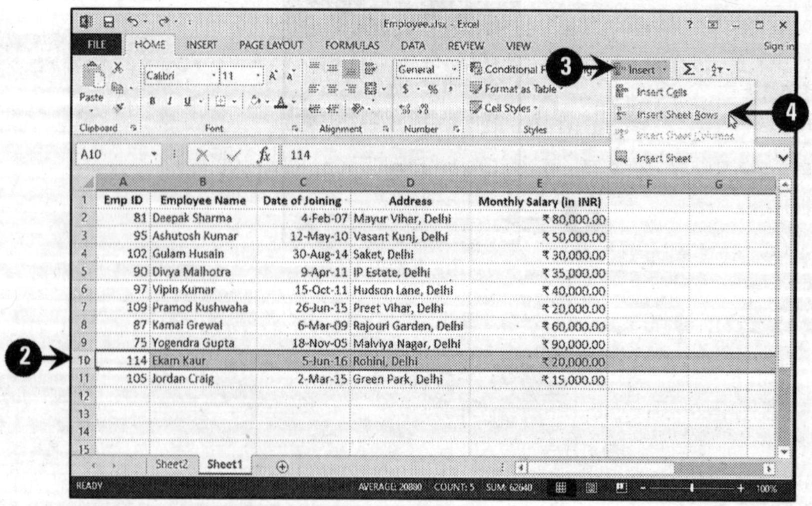

Fig.EX-1.19

A new row is inserted above the selected row, as shown in Fig.EX-1.20:

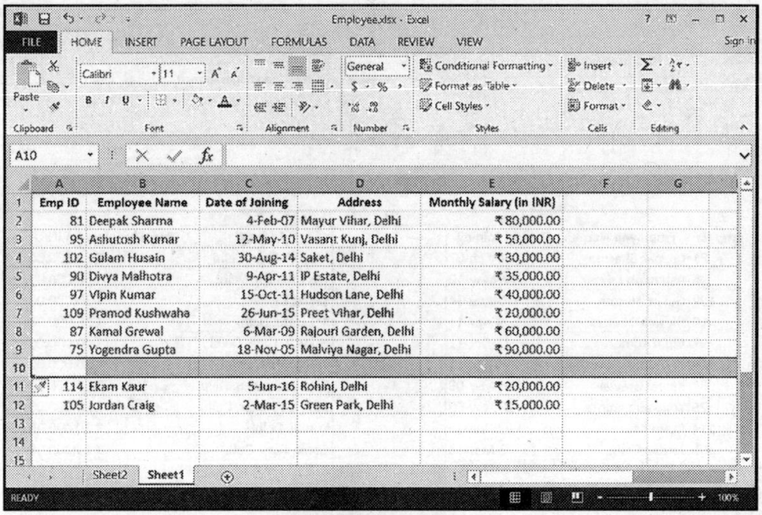

Fig.EX-1.20

Similarly, you can insert more rows in a worksheet, if required.

Let us now learn to insert a new column between any two columns in an Excel worksheet.

Inserting a Column

Apart from adding a new row in an Excel worksheet, you might also need to add a new column between any two columns in a worksheet that contains data. When you insert a new column in a worksheet, all the succeeding columns are shifted to the right of the inserted column.

Perform the following steps to insert a new column in an Excel worksheet:

1. *Open* a new or an existing workbook.
2. *Select* a column to the left of which you want to insert a new column. In our case, we have selected column **D** (Fig.EX-1.21).
3. *Click* the down-arrow button of the **Insert** button under the **Cells** group of the **HOME** tab. A drop-down list appears (Fig.EX-1.21).
4. *Select* the **Insert Sheet Columns** option from the drop-down list, as shown in Fig.EX-1.21:

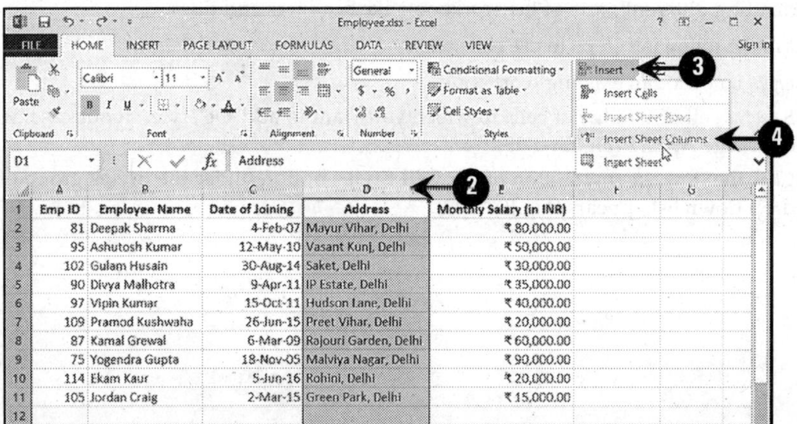

Fig.EX-1.21

A new column is inserted at the specified location, as shown in Fig.EX-1.22:

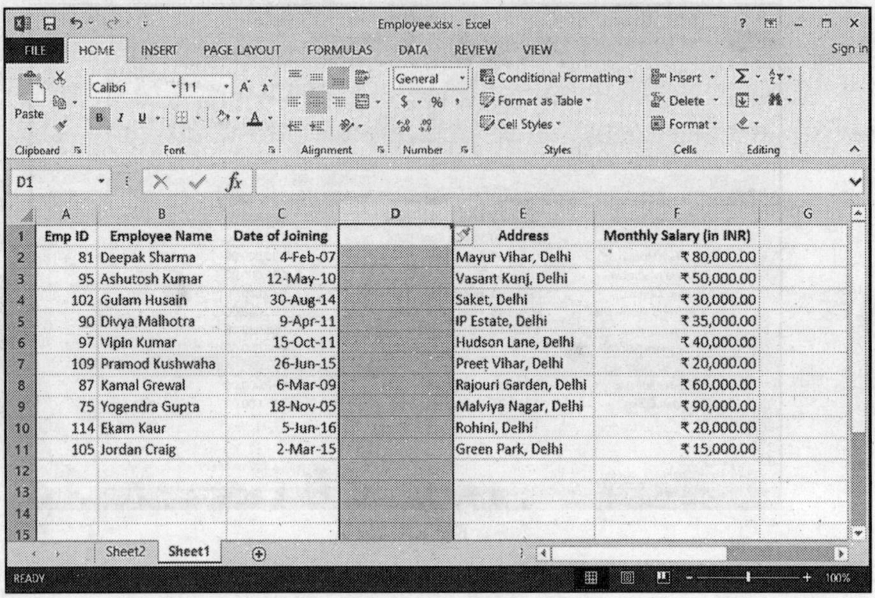

Fig.EX-1.22

Similarly, you can insert more columns, as required in, a worksheet.

Let us learn to decorate a worksheet.

Decorating Worksheets

Excel provides various tools to make your spreadsheets look professional and visually appealing. However, most Excel users are not even aware of these tools and so create plain workbooks only. Decorating worksheets helps in communicating the results clearly and reduces the risk of errors. For instance, you can fill color in the cells of the same row to identify them quickly.

Let us now learn to use cell styles.

Using Cell Styles

You can format the cells in a worksheet using Excel's predesigned cell styles. Cell styles are really helpful in formatting different parts of the workbook like headings and titles.

Perform the following steps to use cell styles:

1. *Open* a new or an existing workbook.
2. *Select* a cell or a range of cells to which you want to add the style. In our case, we have selected the cell range **A9:E11** (Fig.EX-1.23).
3. *Click* the down-arrow button of the **Cell Styles** button under the **Styles** group of the **HOME** tab. A drop-down list appears (Fig.EX-1.23).

4. *Select* a cell style from the drop-down list, as shown in Fig.EX-1.23:

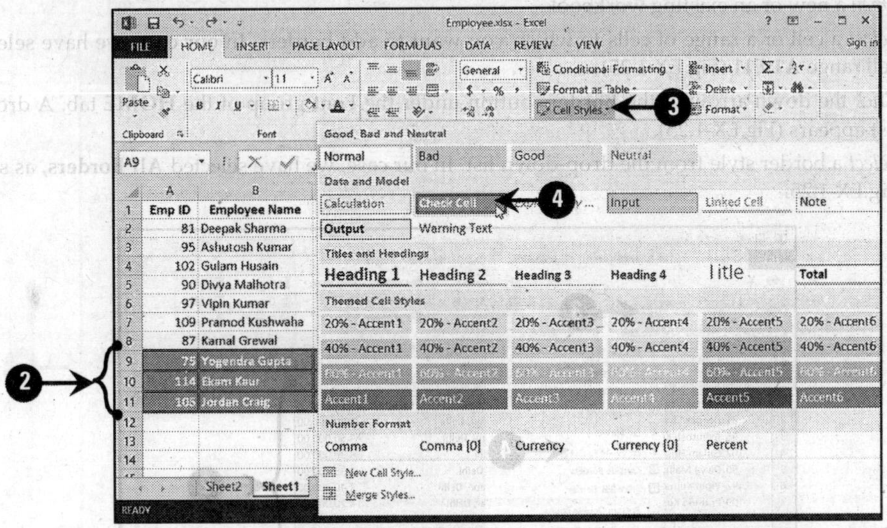

Fig.EX-1.23

As you move the mouse-pointer over different cell-styles, its preview be seen on the selected cells.

The selected cell style is applied on the selected cell, as shown in Fig.EX-1.24:

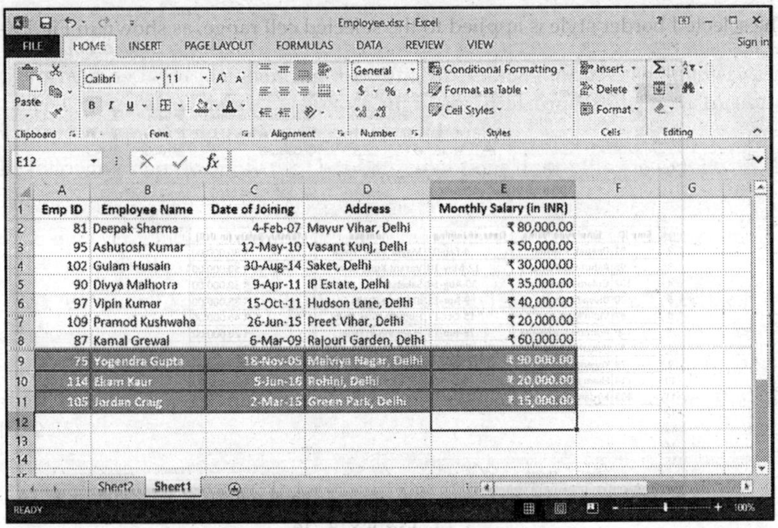

Fig.EX-1.24

Let us now learn to add borders on cells.

Adding Border on Cells

You can add border to a single cell or a range of cells in an Excel worksheet to clearly distinguish the data of a cell from the data of an adjacent cell. You can add borders to a range of cells in many ways, such as adding border to only one side of the cell range or to all its four sides. You can even draw borders manually.

Perform the following steps to add borders to a cell:

1. *Open* a new or an existing workbook.
2. *Select* a cell or a range of cells to which you want to add borders. In our case, we have selected the cell range **A1:E11** (Fig.EX-1.25).
3. *Click* the down-arrow of the **Borders** button under the **Font** group of the **HOME** tab. A drop-down list appears (Fig.EX-1.25).
4. *Select* a border style from the drop-down list. In our case, we have selected **All Borders**, as shown in Fig.EX-1.25:

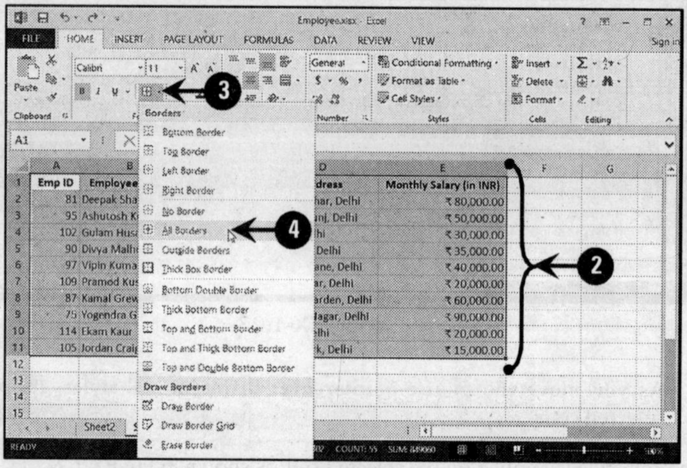

Fig.EX-1.25

The selected border style is applied to the selected cell range, as shown in Fig.EX-1.26:

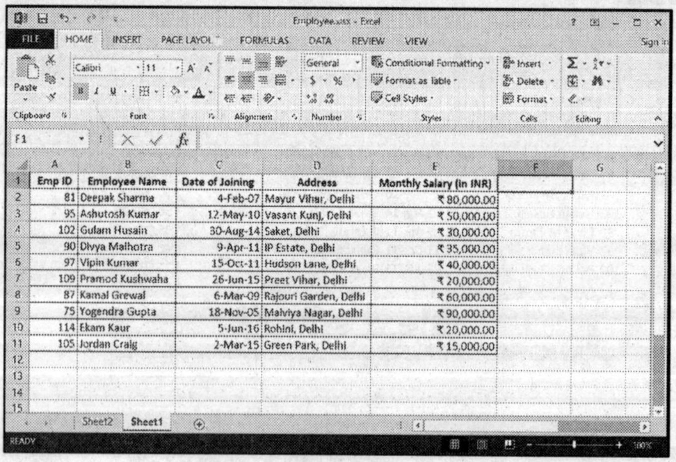

Fig.EX-1.26

It can be seen in Fig.EX-1.26 that the border is added outside the selected cell.

Let us learn to highlight cells.

Highlighting Cells

Highlighting means displaying data differently to seek the attention of the viewer. Hence, the colors are always considered as the best choice to highlight any text. In Excel 2013, you can highlight a cell or a cell range using different colors.

Perform the following steps to highlight cells in an Excel worksheet:

1. *Open* a new or an existing workbook.
2. *Select* the cell or the range of cells that you want to highlight. In our case, we have selected the cell range **A7:E8** (Fig.EX-1.27).
3. *Click* the down-arrow button of the **Fill Color** button under the **Font** group of the **HOME** tab. A drop-down list appears (Fig.EX-1.27).
4. *Select* the desired color from the list, as shown in Fig.EX-1.27:

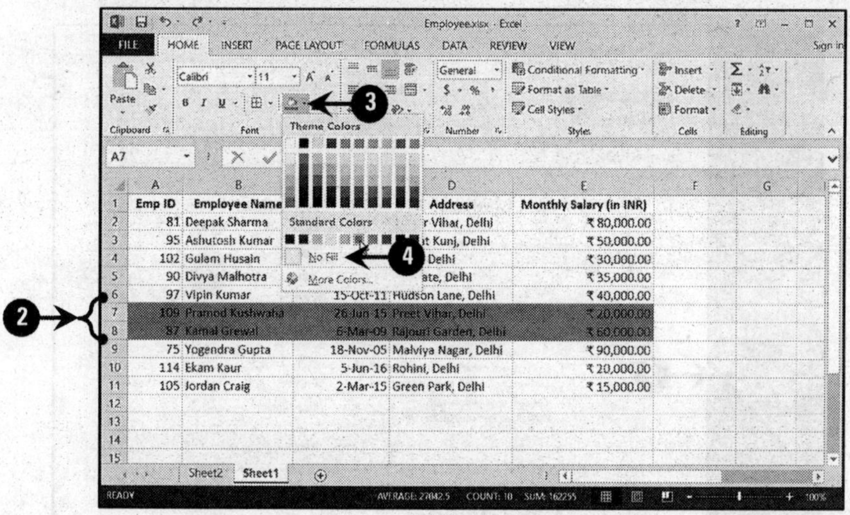

Fig.EX-1.27

> **As you move the mouse-pointer over different colors, its preview appears on the selected cells.**

The color is applied to the selected cell in the worksheet, as shown in Fig.EX-1.28:

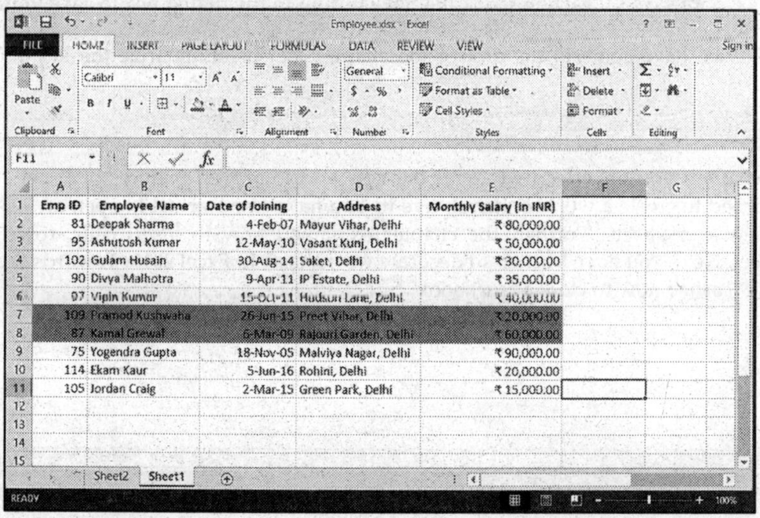

Fig.EX-1.28

Let us now learn to close a workbook.

Closing a Workbook

After completing the work in your workbook, you may need to close it. You can close a workbook by using the Close option in the Backstage view. However, the Excel application remains active. You can close the application by clicking the Close button in the upper-right corner of the Excel window.

Perform the following steps to close a workbook:

1. *Select* the **FILE** tab. The Backstage view appears (Fig.EX-1.29).
2. *Select* the **Close** option to close the current workbook, as shown in Fig.EX-1.29:

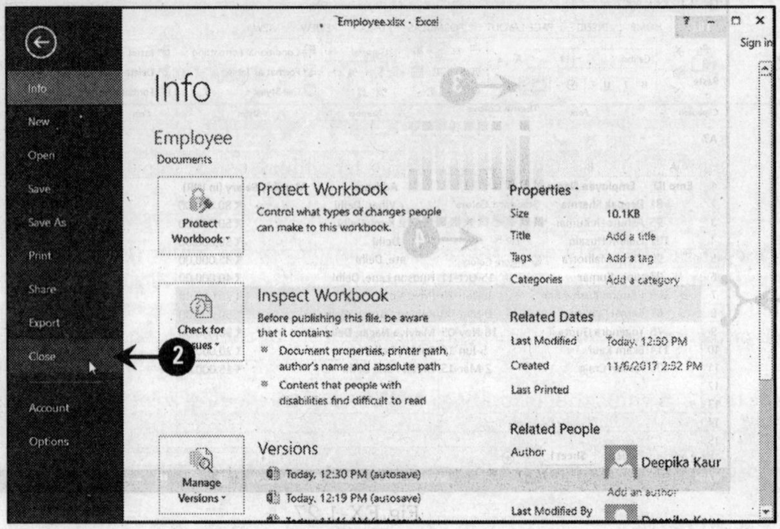

Fig.EX-1.29

The current workbook is closed, but the Excel application remains active.

The Microsoft Excel dialog box appears, prompting you to save the workbook if you have not saved it earlier. Click the Save button in the dialog box to save your workbook.

With this, we have come to the end of the chapter. Let us summarize the key points learned in this chapter.

Summary

In this chapter, you have learned about the new and improved features of Excel 2013. After this, you have learned to create a workbook and save it. You have also learned to open an existing workbook and insert new worksheets. Further, the chapter explained how to insert cells, rows, and columns in a worksheet. Next, you have learned to decorate worksheets in Excel 2013. Towards the end of the chapter, you have learned how to close a workbook.

CHAPTER

2

Working with Data

In this Chapter:

- Working with Data in a Worksheet
- Wrapping Text
- Modifying Data of a Worksheet
- Copying a Worksheet
- Working with Number Formatting
- Exploring Charts
- Working with Sparklines
- Working with Conditional Formatting
- Exploring Sort and Filter Features
- Filtering Table Data Using Slicer

Introduction

In Excel, a workbook is made up of various worksheets. You can enter different forms of data in an Excel worksheet. Excel classifies data into three types, namely, numeric, textual, and date and time data. Excel allows you to modify the content in the worksheet according to your requirement.

Excel enables you to represent the data of a worksheet through a chart and Sparkline for easy understanding. It also allows you to format the cells that meet the specific conditions with the help of the conditional formatting feature. Excel also provides various tools, such as sorting and filtering, to analyze data based on the values in one or more columns.

This chapter explains the procedure to enter data in a worksheet. Next, the chapter describes the procedure to wrap text and modify data in Excel. Then, it explains the procedure to copy a worksheet. After this, you learn how to apply number formatting. Next, you learn to work with charts and Sparkline. Moreover, the chapter explains the concept of conditional formatting. You also learn about the procedure to sort and filter data. Towards the end of the chapter, you learn to filter data in a table by using slicers.

Let us start the chapter by learning how to enter data in a worksheet.

Working with Data in a Worksheet

You can enter different forms of data in an Excel worksheet. An Excel worksheet classifies data into the following three types:

- **Numeric data**: Refers to a number representing a quantity, such as price, integer, fraction, or percentage.
- **Textual data**: Refers to the text typed in a worksheet. Textual data may represent labels used to describe values, column headings, and any descriptive text.
- **Date and Time**: Refers to data related to the date, time, or a combination of both. In Excel, you can enter date and time data in various formats, such as 3/14/17, 14-May-2017, 1:30 PM, and 1:30:55 PM.

To work with data in a worksheet, you first need to enter data in it. Data can be entered in a worksheet in two ways, manually and by using the Flash Fill feature of Excel 2013.

Let us begin by learning how to enter data manually in a worksheet.

Entering Data Manually

Suppose you want to prepare a workbook for a recently scheduled project. For doing so, you have to enter the name of the project (text-based data), total number of days allocated to the project (numeric data), the starting and ending date of the project (date-based data), and the hours spent on the project every day (time-based data). Let us now learn to enter different types of data in a worksheet.

Perform the following steps to enter text-based data manually in a worksheet.

1. *Create* a new workbook.
2. *Click* the desired cell where you want to enter the text based data.
3. *Type* the required text in the selected cell, as shown in Fig.EX-2.1:

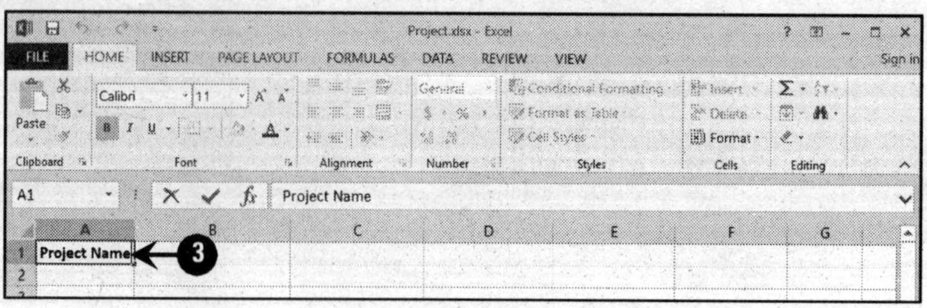

Fig.EX-2.1

Similarly, you can type the rest of the text in the worksheet, as shown in Fig.EX-2.2:

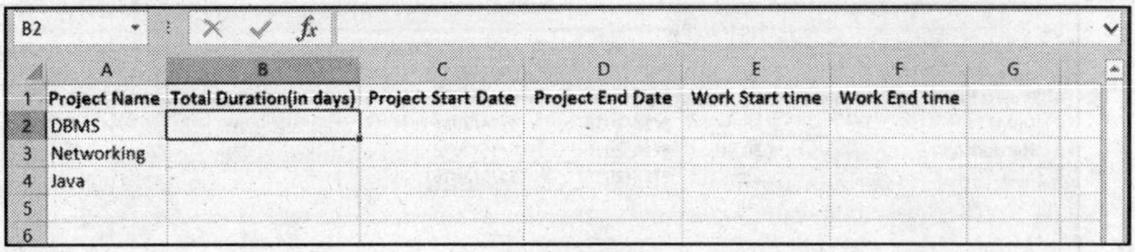

Fig.EX-2.2

Now, let us enter numeric data in a worksheet.

Perform the following steps to enter numeric data in a worksheet:

1. *Click* the cell in which you want to enter numeric data.
2. *Type* the required numeric data in the selected cell, as shown in Fig.EX-2.3:

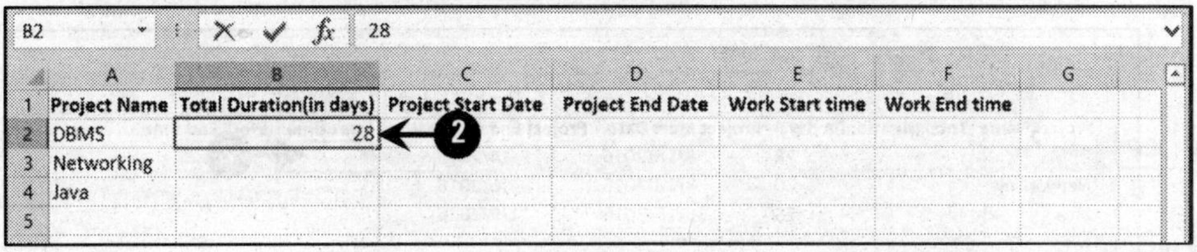

Fig.EX-2.3

Similarly, you can type rest of the numeric data in the worksheet, as shown in Fig.EX-2.4:

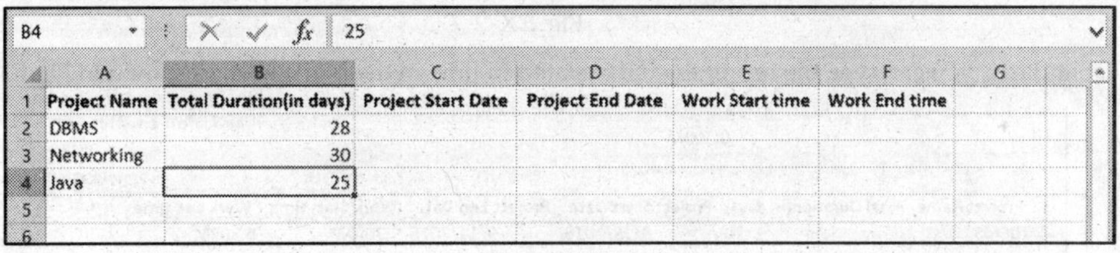

Fig.EX-2.4

Perform the following steps to enter date in a worksheet.

1. *Click* the desired cell to enter date.
2. *Type* a date in the selected cell, as shown in Fig.EX-2.5:

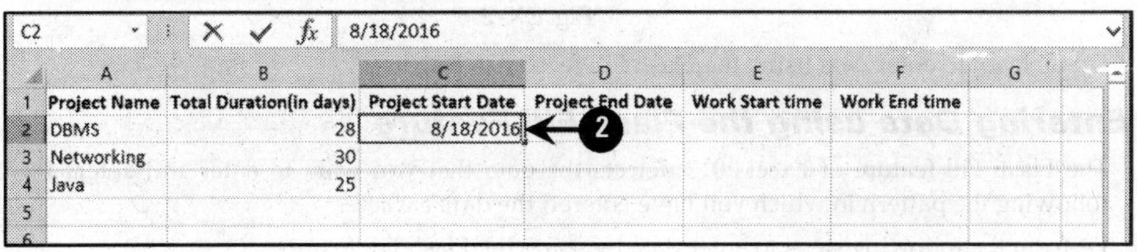

Fig.EX-2.5

Similarly, you can type the rest of the dates in the worksheet, as shown in Fig.EX-2.6:

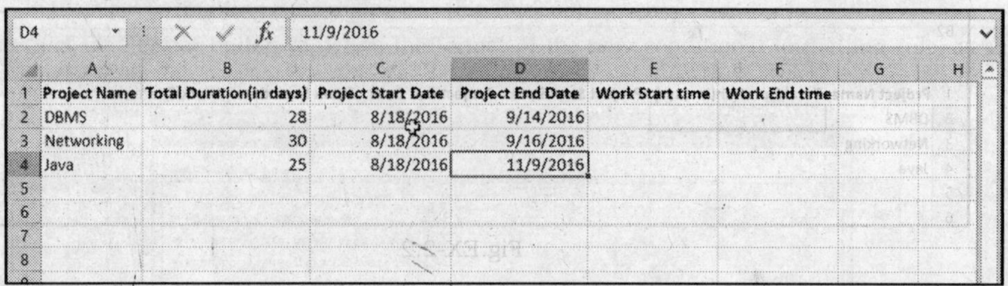

Fig.EX-2.6

Now, let us enter the time in the worksheet. For this, proceed according to the steps given as follows:

1. *Click* the desired cell to enter time.
2. *Type* a time in the selected cell, as shown in Fig.EX-2.7:

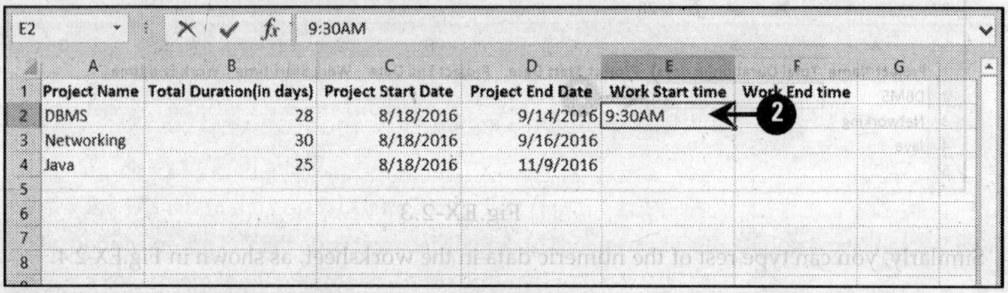

Fig.EX-2.7

Similarly, you can type the rest of the data related to time in the worksheet, as shown in Fig.EX-2.8:

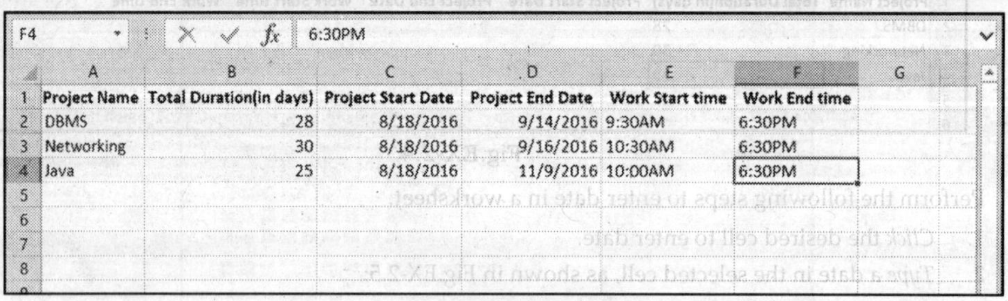

Fig.EX-2.8

Let us learn to enter data using the Flash Fill feature.

Entering Data using the Flash Fill Feature

The Flash Fill feature of Excel 2013 detects the data that you want to enter and enters it in one swipe following the pattern in which you have entered the data earlier.

Perform the following steps to enter data by using the Flash Fill feature:

1. *Open* a new workbook and enter some data manually.
2. *Type* the first name in cell **B2** (Fig.EX-2.9).
3. *Press* down-arrow key from keyboard to move the pointer to cell B3.
4. *Type* the first letter of the second name for Flash Fill to get the picture (Fig.EX-2.9).

The Flash Fill feature automatically does an AutoFill type scheme by suggesting the remaining letters of the text, as shown in Fig.EX-2.9:

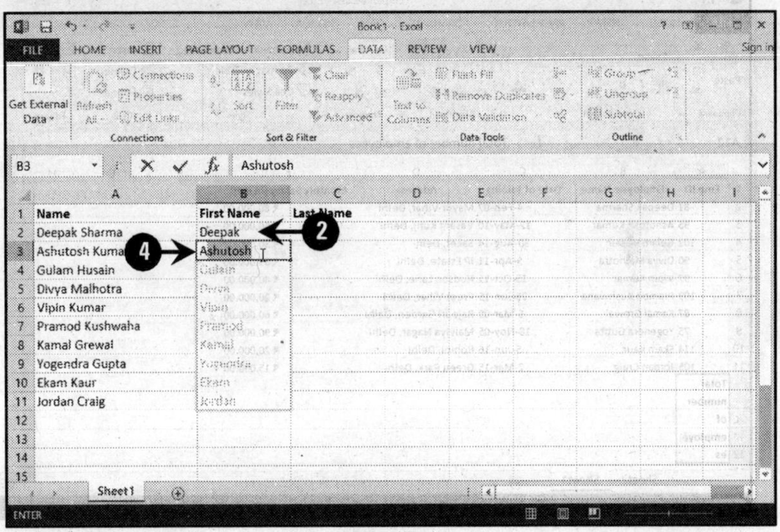

Fig.EX-2.9

Let us learn how to wrap text in Excel.

Wrapping Text

Lengthy text added to a worksheet cell appears in a single line by default even if it does not fit into the cell. The text appears to have stretched to the adjacent cells. If you want to see the entire lengthy text in the same cell, you need to wrap the text for the cell. This wrapping feature is useful especially when you have a large text string to be displayed on a cell, but do not want to increase the width of the cell.

Perform the following steps to wrap the text of a worksheet cell in a workbook:

1. *Click* the cell for which you want to wrap the text. In our case, the cell we clicked is A12 (Fig.EX-2.10).
2. *Click* the **Wrap Text** button under the **Alignment** group of the **HOME** tab, as shown in Fig.EX-2.10:

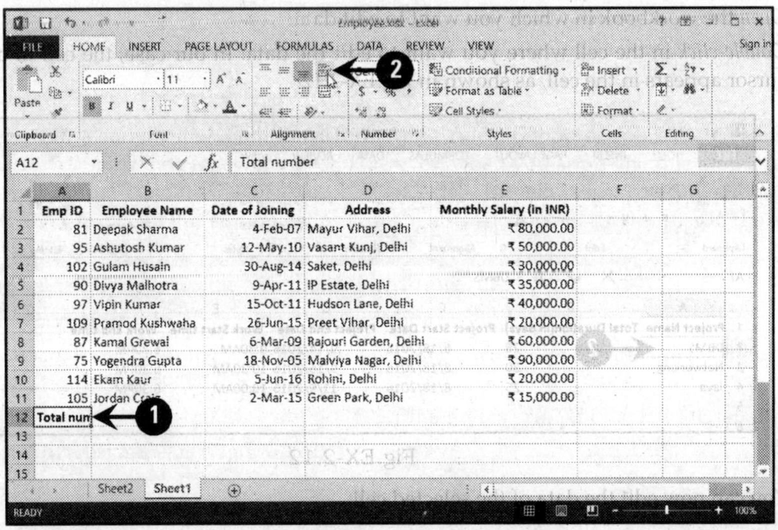

Fig.EX-2.10

The cell expands downward to display the text, as shown in Fig.EX-2.11:

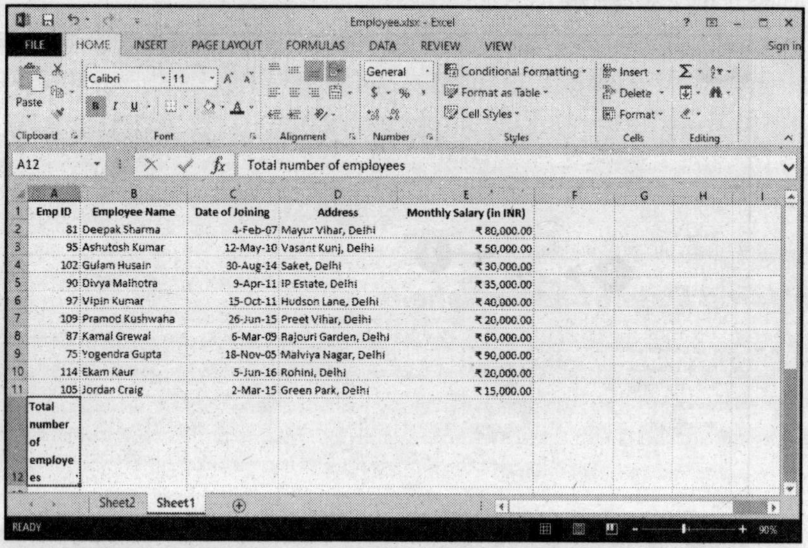

Fig.EX-2.11

Let us learn how to modify data of a worksheet.

Modifying Data of a Worksheet

Sometimes, you may find that the data entered in the cells of a worksheet is incomplete or incorrect. In such a case, you may want to make changes in the content of the worksheet. In Excel 2013, you can modify the data entered in the cells of a worksheet in different ways. You can delete the data, edit the data, or replace the data with other data according to your requirements.

Let us learn to edit data in a worksheet.

Editing Data of a Worksheet

Perform the following steps to edit data of a worksheet.

1. *Open* the workbook in which you want to edit data.
2. *Double-click* in the cell where you want to edit the data. In our case, the cell to be edited is **A2**. The cursor appears in the cell, as shown in Fig.EX-2.12:

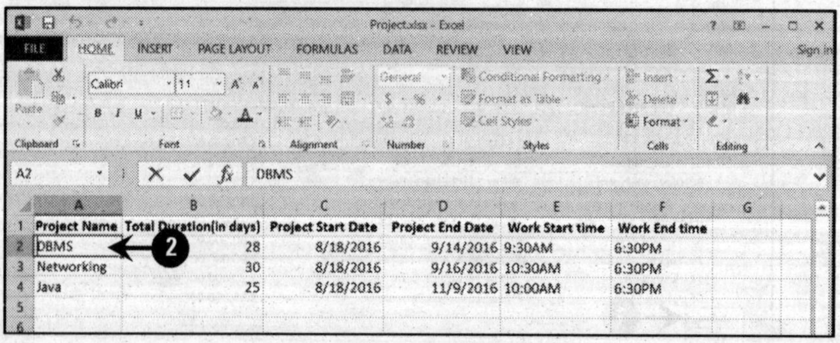

Fig.EX-2.12

You can now edit the data of the selected cell.

3. *Edit* the data in the cell, as shown in Fig.EX-2.13:

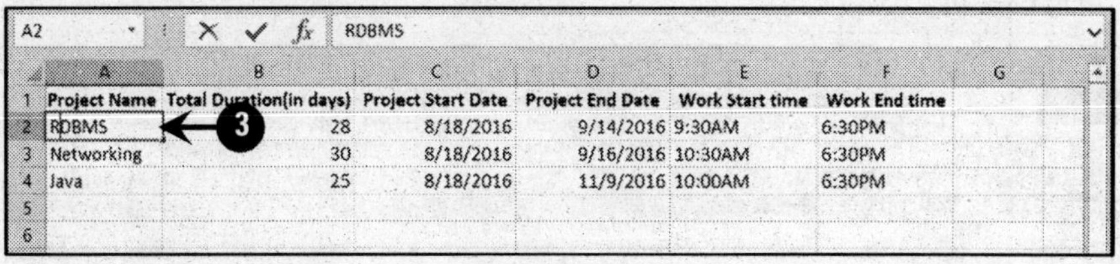

Fig.EX-2.13

Let us now learn to replace date on a worksheet

Replacing Data of a Worksheet

Apart from editing the data of an Excel worksheet, you can also replace the data of the cells. Replacing incorrect data in the cells with correct data ensures the relevancy and correctness of your worksheet.

Perform the following steps to replace data of a worksheet:

1. *Open* a workbook to replace the data.
2. *Select* the cell whose data you want to replace. In our case, we have selected **A3** as shown in Fig.EX-2.14:

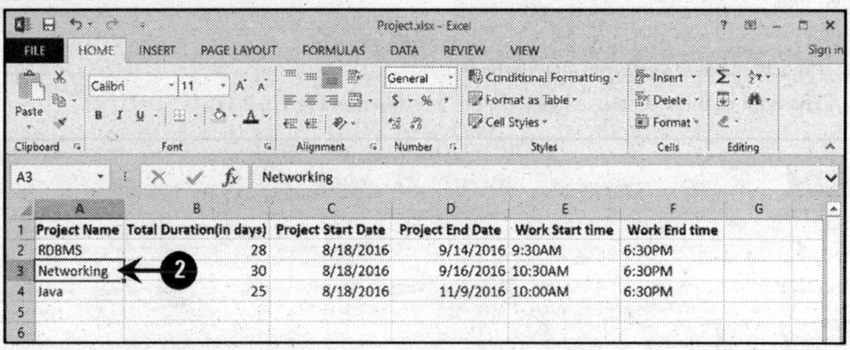

Fig.EX-2.14

3. *Type* the data to replace the existing data in the selected cell, as shown in Fig.EX-2.15:

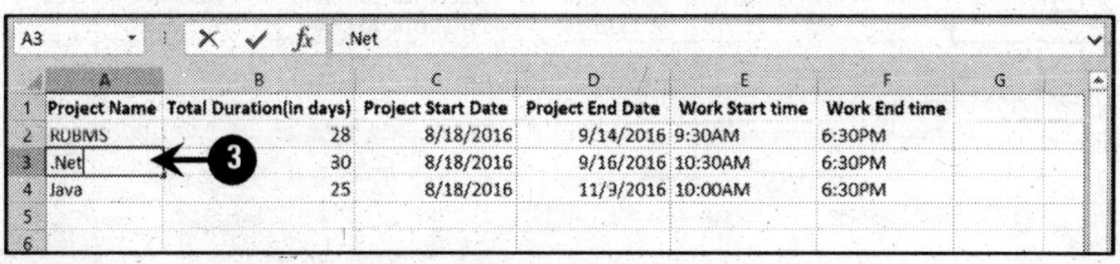

Fig.EX-2.15

Let us now learn to delete date in a worksheet

Deleting the Data of a Worksheet

You can also delete data from a worksheet if it is required no more. Simply select the data that you want to delete and press the Delete key from the keyboard.

Perform the following steps to delete data from a worksheet:

1. *Open* a workbook containing data.

2. *Select* the cell whose data you want to delete. In our case, we have selected **A4** as shown in Fig.EX-2.16:

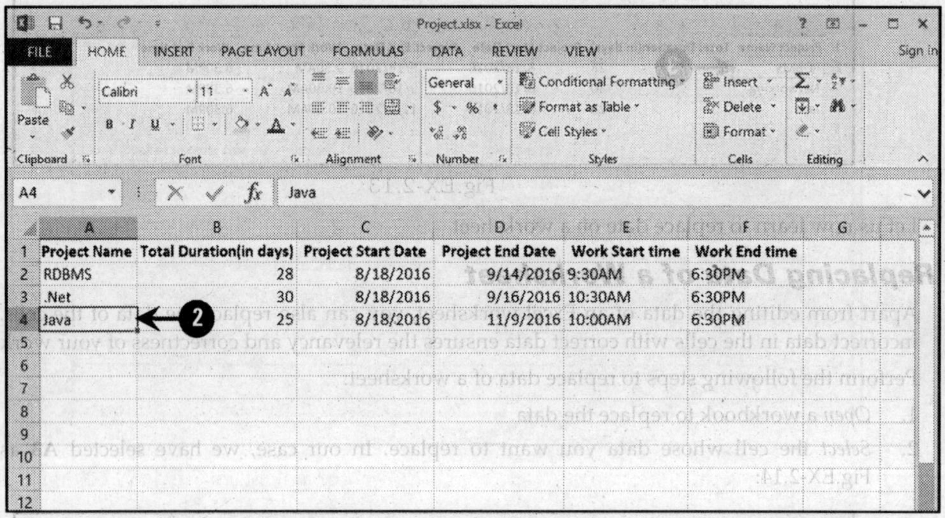

Fig.EX-2.16

3. *Press* the Delete key from the keyboard.

   The data in the selected cell is deleted, as shown in Fig.EX-2.17:

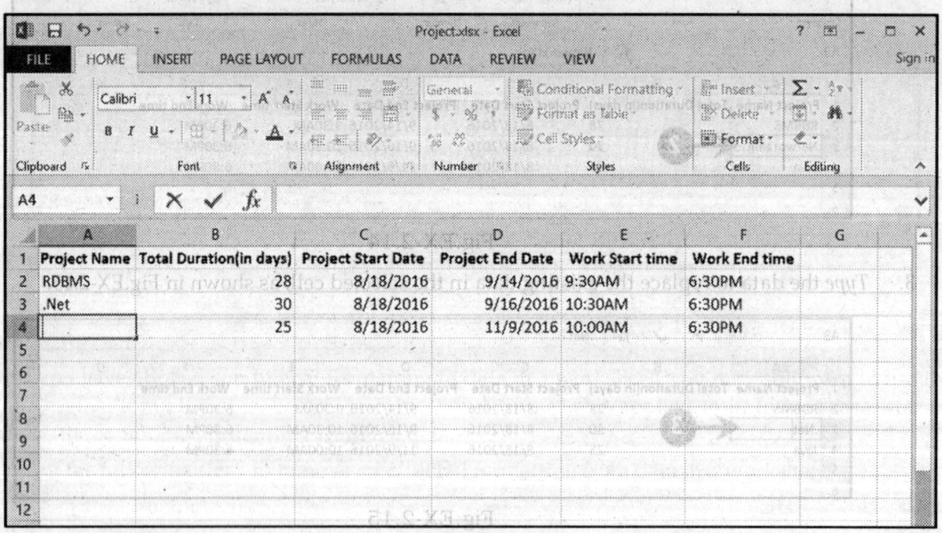

Fig.EX-2.17

Let us now learn to copy a worksheet.

Copying a Worksheet

Excel allows you to create a copy of the worksheet in the same workbook or another workbook.

Perform the following steps to copy a worksheet:

1. *Open* an existing workbook.
2. *Click* the **Format** button under the **Cells** group of the **Home** tab (Fig.EX-2.18).

   A drop-down list appears (Fig.EX-2.18).

3. *Select* the **Move or Copy Sheet** option under the **Organize Sheets** section in the drop-down list, as shown in Fig.EX-2.18:

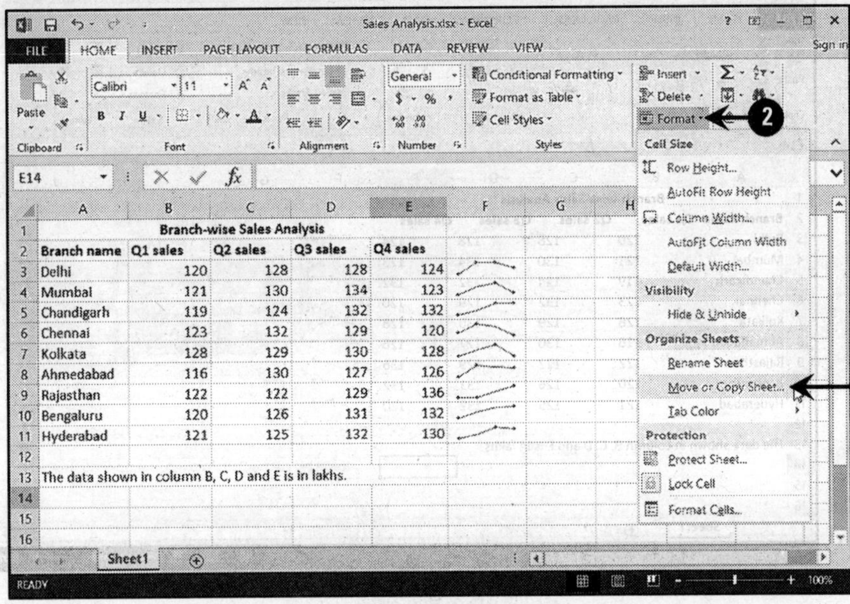

Fig.EX-2.18

The **Move or Copy** dialog box appears (Fig.EX-2.19).

4. *Select* the desired worksheet that you want to copy in the **Before sheet** list box (Fig.EX-2.19).
5. *Select* the **Create a copy** check box (Fig.EX-2.19).
6. *Click* the down arrow of the **To book** option.

   A drop-down list appears.
7. *Select* the workbook on which you want the copy of the worksheet, from the drop-down list. In our case, we have selected the **new book** option (Fig.EX-2.20).
8. *Click* the **OK** button, as shown in Fig.EX-2.20:

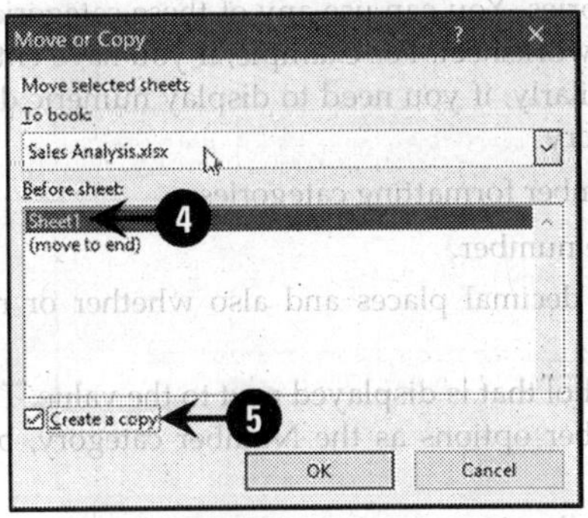

Fig.EX-2.19

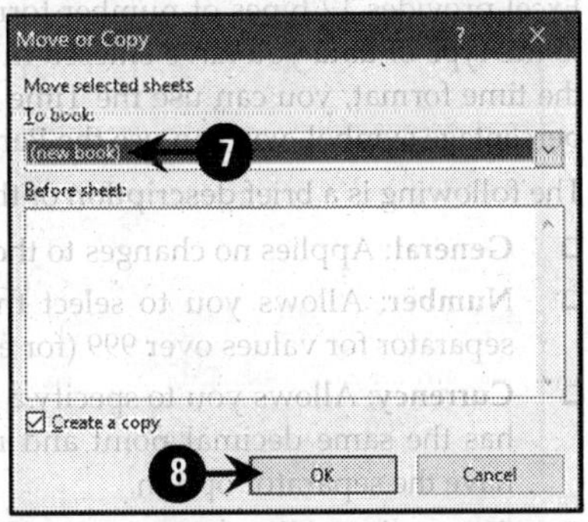

Fig.EX-2.20

A copy of the worksheet is displayed in the new workbook, as shown in Fig.EX-2.21:

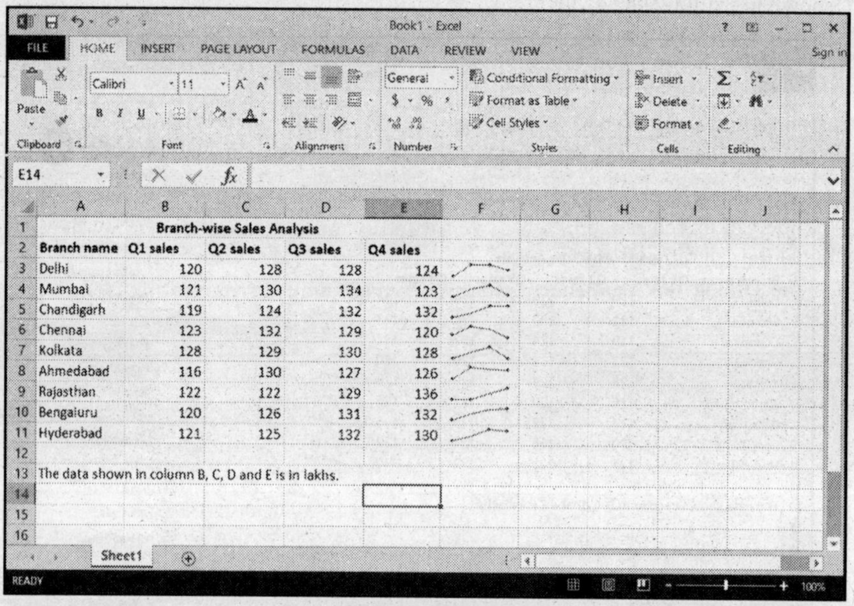

Fig.EX-2.21

Let us learn to work with number formatting in Excel 2013.

Working with Number Formatting

Number formatting is the process of changing the appearance of numbers without changing their values. In other words, number formatting does not change the actual numbers you enter, but just the way they appear in a worksheet. Number formatting is only applied on those cells that contain numbers. By formatting numeric data, you can improve the appearance of the worksheet and make the numbers easier to read and understand.

Applying Number Formatting

Excel provides 12 types of number formatting categories. You can use any of these categories according to the type of data you have entered in the cells of a worksheet. For example, if you have entered data in the time format, you can use the Time category. Similarly, if you need to display numeric data with the percentage symbol, you can use the Percentage category.

The following is a brief description of the various number formatting categories:

- **General**: Applies no changes to the format of the number.
- **Number**: Allows you to select the number of decimal places and also whether or not to use a separator for values over 999 (for example 2,500).
- **Currency**: Allows you to specify a currency symbol that is displayed next to the value. This category has the same decimal point and negative number options as the Number category, but does not have the separator option.
- **Accounting**: Aligns currency symbols and decimal points.
- **Date**: Allows you to format cell content as a date.
- **Time**: Allows you to format cell content as time.
- **Percentage**: Allows you to multiply content of cell by 100 and then display the result with a percentage symbol at the end.
- **Fraction**: Allows you to display the contents of a cell as a fraction.

- **Scientific**: Allows you to display the content of a cell in scientific notation.
- **Text**: Allows you to display the content of a cell exactly as you type it.
- **Special**: Allows you to select options according to a location. For example, selecting the United States location allows you to enter Zone Improvement Plan (ZIP) code and phone number while preserving the leading zero.
- **Custom**: Allows you to create custom number formatting.

Perform the following steps to apply number formatting:

1. *Open* an existing workbook that contains data on which you want to apply number formatting.
2. *Select* the cell or cell range in which you want to apply number formatting. In our case, we have selected the cell range **E2:E4** (Fig.EX-2.22).
3. *Click* the **Dialog Box Launcher** button under the **Number** group of the **HOME** tab, as shown in Fig.EX-2.22:

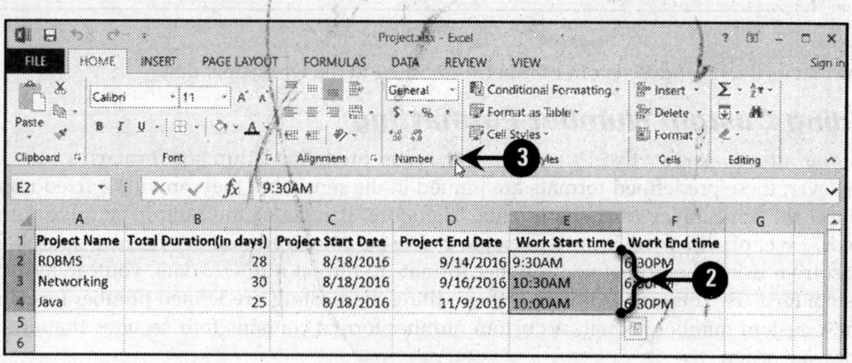

Fig.EX-2.22

The **Format Cells** dialog box appears with the **Number** tab selected by default (Fig.EX-2.23).

4. *Select* the desired category from the **Category** list box in the **Format Cells** dialog box (Fig.EX-2.23).
5. *Select* the desired format type from the **Type** list box (Fig.EX-2.23).
6. *Click* the **OK** button in the **Format Cells** dialog box, as shown in Fig.EX-2.23:

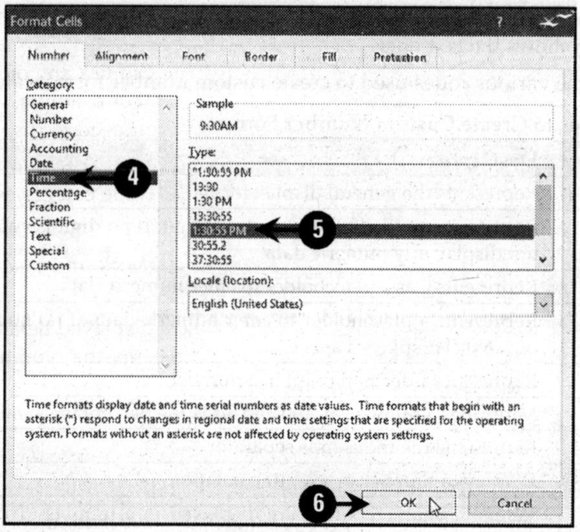

Fig.EX-2.23

The selected number formatting is applied to the selected data in the worksheet, as shown in Fig.EX-2.24:

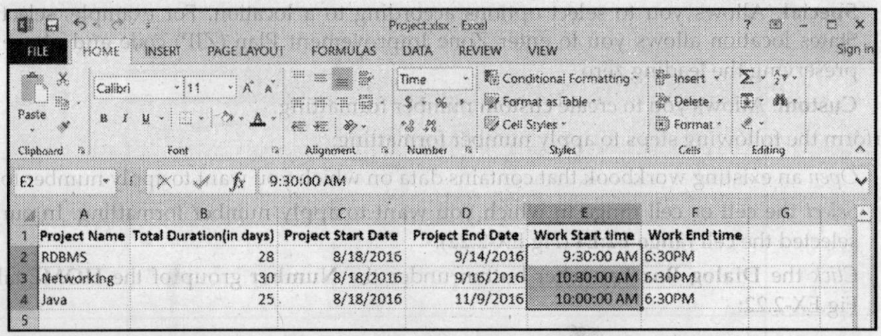

Fig.EX-2.24

Now, let us learn to add custom number formatting to the worksheet data.

Adding Custom Number Formatting

As you already know, Excel provides numerous predefined number formats to use in a workbook. However, these predefined formats are limited in the sense that they provide a fixed number of ways to control the appearance of numeric data. Therefore, if none of the built-in number formats meet your needs, Excel provides the facility to create and use customized number formats as well. In other words, apart from using the predefined number formats to format numeric data, you can also create your own custom formats. You can do this by either editing the existing predefined number formats or by creating a new custom number format. A custom number format contains four sections that are arranged in the following order:

```
positive number; negative number; zero values; text data
```

Each section in a custom number format is separated by a semi colon (;). There is no need for specifying all four sections, while creating a custom number format.

If you use only one section, the custom number format applies to all types of data entries. If you use two sections, the first section shows the positive values, the second section shows the negative values, and the third section shows the zero values. If you use all the four sections, the first section shows the positive values, the second section shows the negative values, and the third section shows the zero values, and the fourth section shows the text data.

Table 2.1 shows the various codes used to create custom number formats along with their description:

Table 2.1: Codes to Create Custom Number Formats

Code	Description
General	Represents the general display format.
#	Represents a placeholder to enter a digit. If no digit is entered in place of #, Excel does not display any numeric data.
0 (Zero)	Represents 0 as a placeholder to enter numeric data.
?	Represents a placeholder to enter numeric data. If no numeric data is entered in place of ?, Excel displays a space.
.	Represents a decimal point in a number.
%	Multiplies a number by 100 and adds the percentage symbol.
,	Represents the thousands separator.
E-E+e-e+	Displays a number in scientific notation.
$ - + / ( ) : space	Refers to characters that are displayed in a number. To display any other character, enclose the character in quotation marks or precede it with a backslash.
\	Displays a given number as a fraction.

Table 2.1: Codes to Create Custom Number Formats

Code	Description
-(Underscore)	Allows a space that is equal to the width of the character that follows this code.
"text"	Shows text inside double quotation marks, for example, "Shyam".
@	Refers to the placeholder to enter textual data.
[Color]	Shows characters in the specified color. The available colors are Black, Blue, Green, Cyan, Red, White, Magenta, and Yellow.
[Color n]	Displays a color value picked from the color palette (available in Excel)
[condition value]	Specifies the condition for each section of a number format. For example, the format [Red] [<=100]; [Blue] [>100] condition displays numbers that are less than or equal to 100 in the red font and numbers that are greater than 100 in a blue font.

Apart from using custom number formatting to display text with numbers, you can also customize date and time to control the way the data appear in a worksheet.

Table 2.2 shows the various codes used to create custom date and time formats along with their description:

Table 2.2: Codes to Create Custom Date and Time Formats

Code	Description
m	Shows a month number without leading zeros, for example, 1-12
mm	Shows a month number with leading zeros, for example, 01-12
mmm	Shows a month as an abbreviation, for example, Jan-Dec
mmmm	Shows the full name of a month, for example, January-December
mmmmm	Shows the first letter of a number of a month, for example, J-D
d	Shows a day without leading zeros, for example, 1-31
dd	Shows a day with leading zeros, for example, 01-31
ddd	Shows the name of a day as an abbreviation, for example, Sun-Sat
dddd	Shows the full name of a week day, for example, Sunday-Saturday
yy	Shows a year as a two-digit number, for example, 00-99
yyyy	Shows a year as a four-digit number, for example, 1900-2013
h	Shows the hour without leading zeros, for example 0-24
hh	Shows the hour with leading zeros, for example 00-24
s	Shows the seconds without leading zeros, for example0-59
ss	Shows the seconds with leading zeros, for example 00-59
[]	Shows the hours greater than 24 and minutes and seconds greater than 60. For example, you use this code to represent a flight that has been delayed by say, 72 hours.
AM/PM	Shows the time in the 2-hour format.

After learning about various codes used to customize the number format in Excel, let us learn to use these codes in an Excel worksheet.

Perform the following steps to apply custom number formatting codes:

1. *Open* an existing workbook that contains numeric data.

2. *Select* the numeric data in which you want to add text. In our case, we have selected the cell range **E2:E11** (Fig.EX-2.25).
3. *Click* the **Dialog Box Launcher** button under the **Number** group of the **HOME** tab, as shown in Fig.EX-2.25:

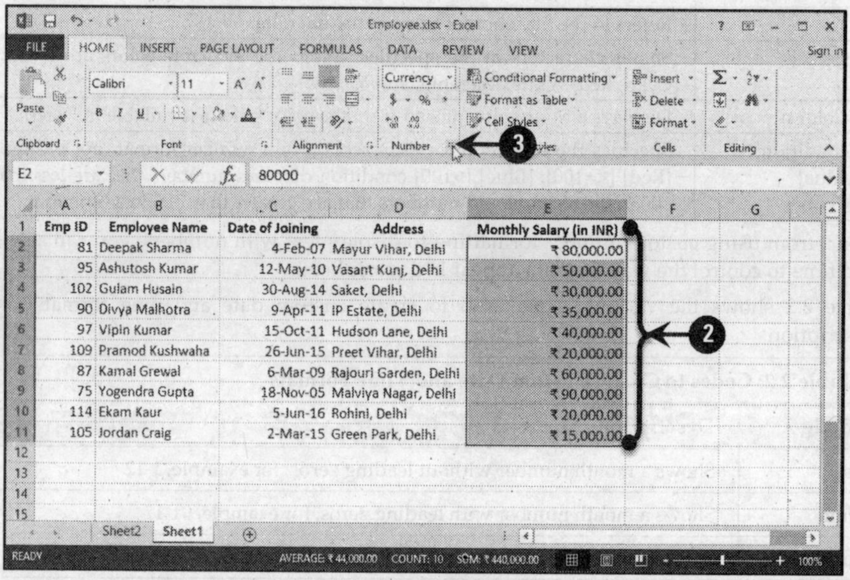

Fig.EX-2.25

The **Format Cells** dialog box appears with the Number tab selected by default (Fig.EX-2.26).

4. *Select* the **Custom** category from the **Category** list box in the **Format Cells** dialog box (Fig.EX-2.26).
5. *Type* the custom format in the **Type** text box (Fig.EX-2.26).
6. *Click* the **OK** button, as shown in Fig.EX-2.26:

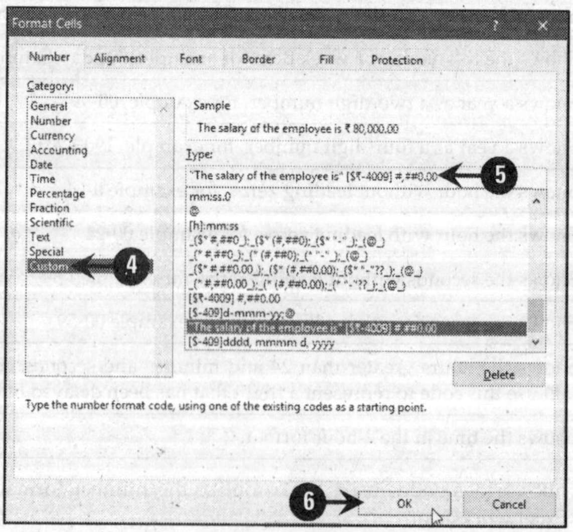

Fig.EX-2.26

The custom formatting is applied to the selected data, as shown in Fig.EX-2.27:

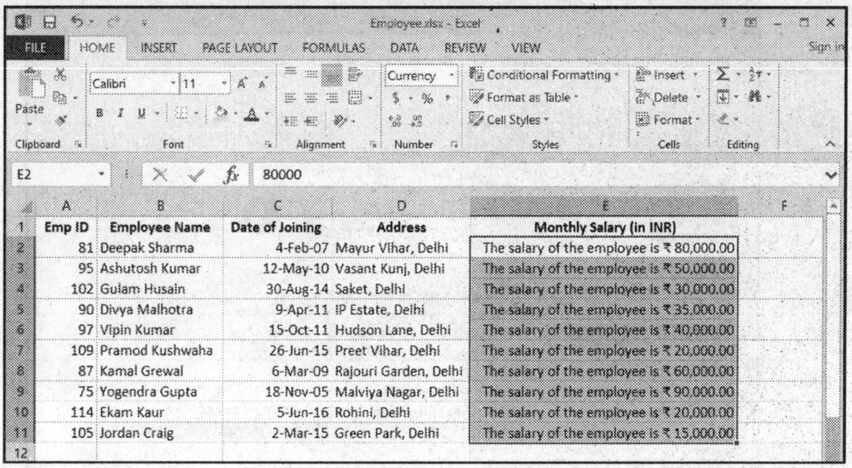

Fig.EX-2.27

Now, perform the following steps to apply custom number formatting on date and time data:

1. *Open* an existing workbook containing data in the date and time format (Fig.EX-2.28).
2. *Select* the data on which you want to apply custom formatting. In our case, we have selected the cell range **C2:C11** (Fig.EX-2.28).
3. *Click* the **Dialog Box Launcher** button under the **Number** group of the **HOME** tab, as shown in Fig.EX-2.28:

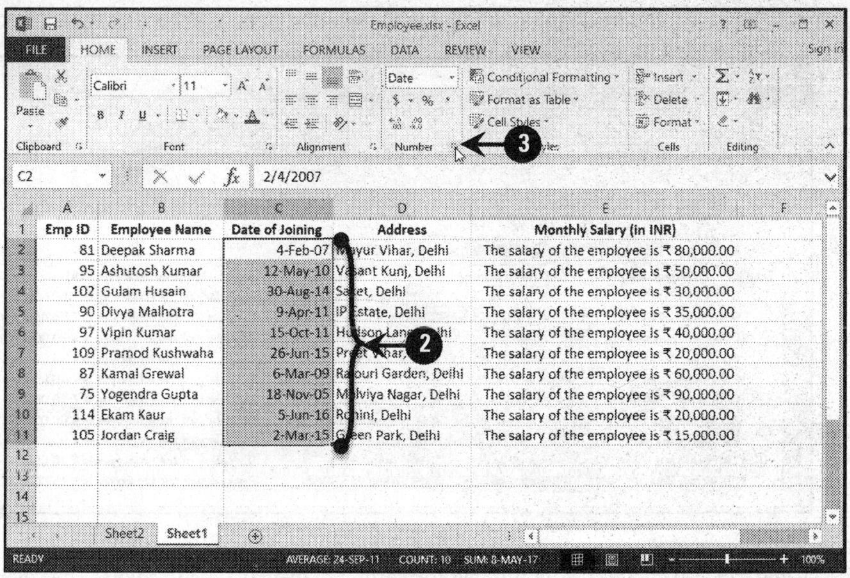

Fig.EX-2.28

The **Format Cells** dialog box appears (Fig.EX-2.29).

4. *Select* the **Custom** category from the category list box in the **Format Cells** dialog box (Fig.EX-2.29).
5. *Type* the custom format for the date and time format in the **Type** text box (Fig.EX-2.29).

6. *Click* the **OK** button in the **Format Cells** dialog box, as shown in Fig.EX-2.29:

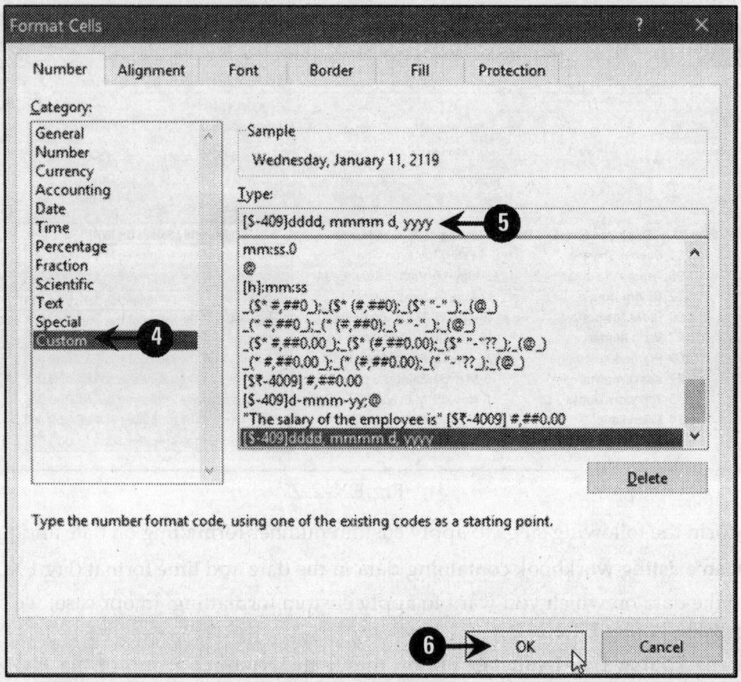

Fig.EX-2.29

The defined custom formatting is applied to the selected data, as shown in Fig.EX-2.30:

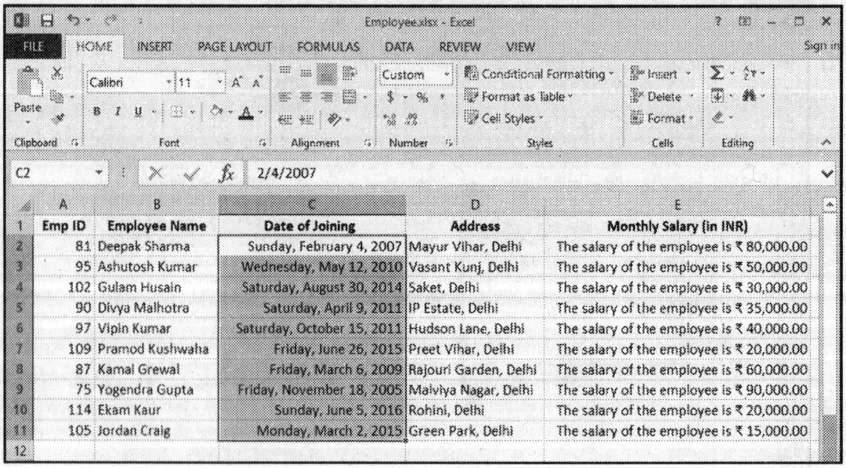

Fig.EX-2.30

In Excel, you can also create custom number formatting to display data in colors. The coloring of the data is entirely based on the conditions you specify. For example, suppose you want to display salary greater than ₹20000 in red color and the salary less than or equal to ₹20000 in blue color. In such a case, you can apply color-based formatting to display the salary in the desired color format.

Perform the following steps to apply color-based formatting on data:

1. *Open* a new or existing workbook with data.

2. *Select* the data on which you want to apply color-based formatting. In our case, we have selected the cell range **E2:E11** (Fig.EX-2.31).
3. *Click* the **Dialog Box Launcher** button under the **Number** group of the **HOME** tab, as shown in Fig.EX-2.31:

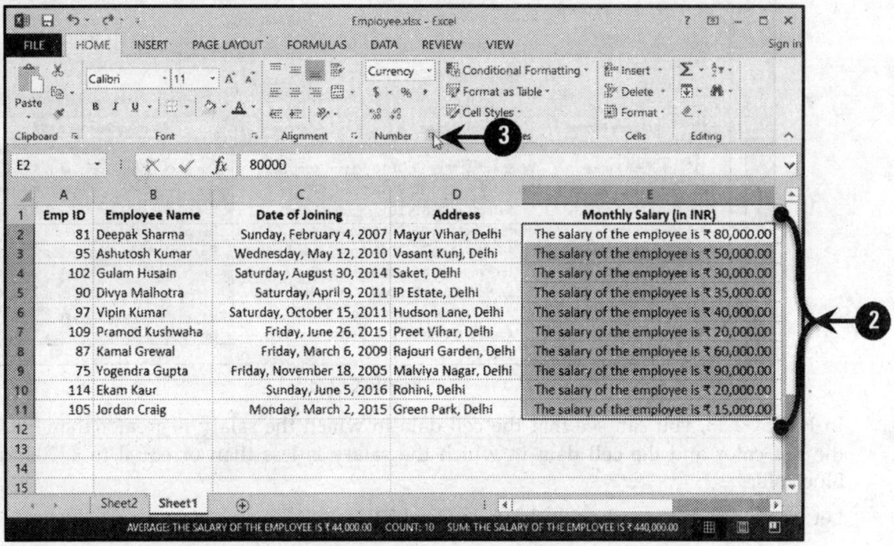

Fig.EX-2.31

The **Format Cells** dialog box appears with the **Number** tab selected by default (Fig.EX-2.32).

4. *Select* the **Custom** category from the **Category** list box in the **Format Cells** dialog box (Fig.EX-2.32).
5. *Type* a custom format code in the **Type** text box (Fig.EX-2.32).
6. *Click* the **OK** button in the **Format Cells** dialog box, as shown in Fig.EX-2.32:

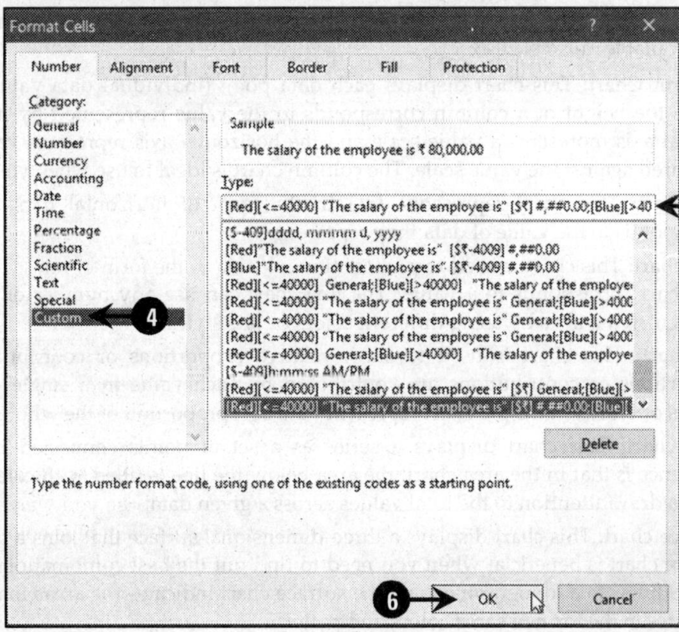

Fig.EX-2.32

The defined custom formatting is applied to the selected data, as shown in Fig.EX-2.33:

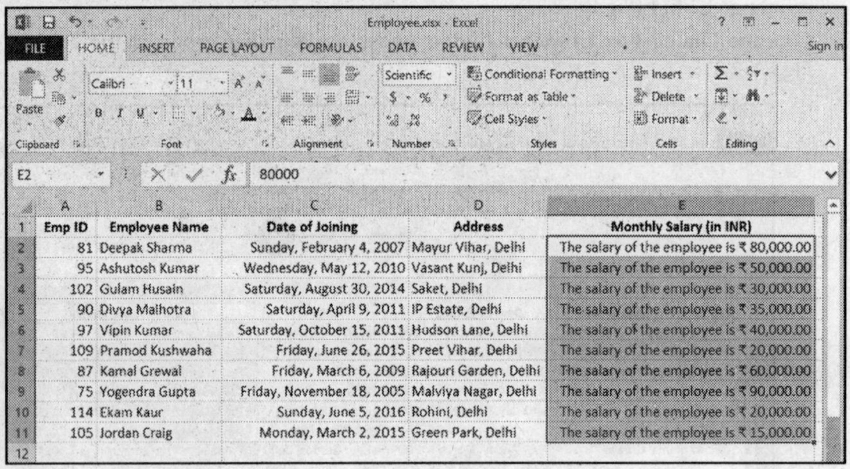

Fig.EX-2.33

In Fig.EX-2.33, you can see that the cell data in which the salary is greater than ₹20000 is displayed in the red color and the cell data in which the salary is less than or equal to ₹20000 is displayed in the blue color.

Let us now learn to work with charts in Excel 2013.

Exploring Charts

Excel provides you with various types of charts that you can use to represent your data. You can also create a wide range of customizable charts, such as column charts, pie charts, surface charts, and bubble charts. In addition, Excel provides various options that you can use to change the appearance of a chart by adding elements, such as a chart title, an axis title, and a legend. You can also select a suitable chart type depending on the data you want to represent. For this, you first need to select the data and then select the type of chart that you want to use to represent your data. The following are the different types of charts available in Excel 2013:

- **Column Chart:** This chart displays each data point (individual data values) as a vertical column, where the height of a column corresponds to the value represented by it. In a column chart, the vertical axis represents a value scale and the horizontal axis represents various categories that are measured against the value scale. The column chart is ideal to use when you want to compare data.
- **Bar chart:** This chart represents data in the form of horizontal bars. The length of the bars corresponds to the value of data they represent.
- **Line chart:** This chart is used to plot continuous data in the form of lines. Therefore, each point on a line chart corresponds to a value. The line chart can use any number of data series and you can distinguish the lines by using different colors or line styles.
- **Pie chart:** This chart is used to show relative proportions or contributions to a whole. These proportions or contributions are contributed by each value in a single data series. The various sectors or blocks in the pie chart represent data as a proportion of the whole.
- **Area chart:** This chart displays a series as a set of points connected by a line. However, the difference is that in the area chart, the area below the line is filled with color of the line. Area charts help to draw attention to the total values across a given data.
- **Surface chart:** This chart displays a three-dimensional surface that joins a group of data points. The surface chart is beneficial when you need to find out the best combinations between two groups of data. Similar to a topographic map, the surface chart indicates the areas that contain the same range of values in the form of same colors and patterns.

- **Radar chart:** This chart, also known as a star chart, plots the values of each category along a separate axis that starts from the center of the chart and ends on the outer ring.
- **Doughnut chart:** This chart is used to show the relationship of parts as a whole. However, unlike a pie chart, the doughnut chart contains more than one data series.
- **X, Y (Scatter) chart:** This chart is used to show the relationship between the numerical values in two data series. This type of chart represents one data series on X-axis and the other data series on Y-axis.
- **Bubble chart:** This chart is similar to an X, Y (scatter) chart with the only difference that the bubble chart displays bubbles instead of data points. You can use the bubble chart in place of the X, Y (Scatter) chart if your data has three data series, which contain a set of values. The size of the bubbles in the bubble chart is determined by the values of the third data series.
- **Stock chart:** This chart is used to show the fluctuations of stock prices. However, this chart can also be used to represent scientific data. It is important to organize the data of the stock chart very carefully.
- **Combo chart:** This chart represents the data by using the combination of two or more charts.

Let us learn about the Recommended Charts feature introduced in Excel 2013.

Introducing Recommended Charts

Excel 2013 provides you with a new feature known as Recommended Charts. It recommends the most appropriate charts for representing your data. You can also preview what your data would look like in different charts and then select the desired chart.

Perform the following steps to use the Recommended Charts feature in your worksheet:

1. *Open* a new or an existing workbook that contains data.
2. *Select* the data that you want to represent in a chart. In our case, we have selected the cell range **A1:D7** (Fig.EX-2.34).
3. *Click* the **Recommended Charts** button under the **Charts** group of the **INSERT** tab, as shown in Fig.EX-2.34:

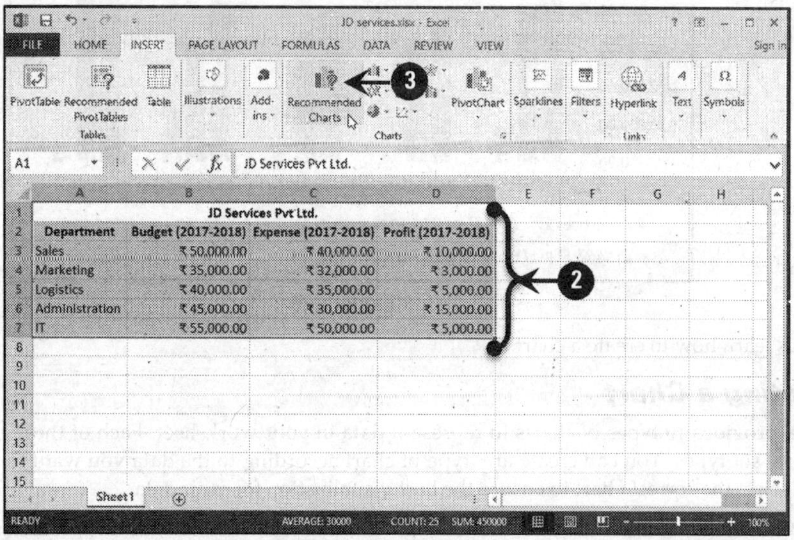

Fig.EX-2.34

The **Insert Chart** dialog box appears (Fig.EX-2.35).

4. *Select* the desired chart type for representing your data (Fig.EX-2.35).

5. *Click* the **OK** button, as shown in Fig.EX-2.35:

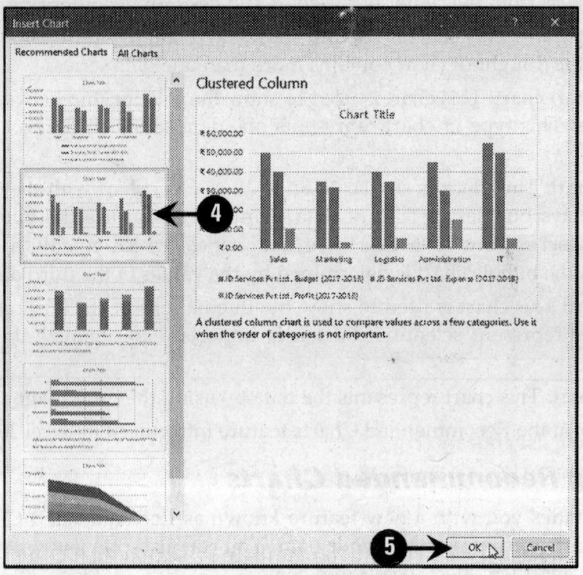

Fig.EX-2.35

Fig.EX-2.36 displays the stacked column chart based on the data given in Fig.EX-2.34:

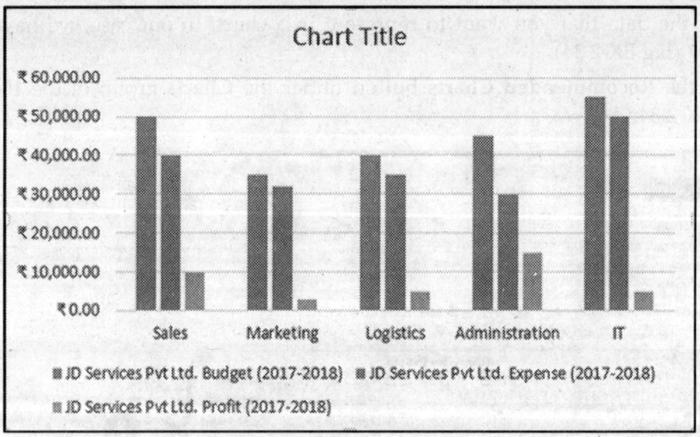

Fig.EX-2.36

Let us learn how to create a chart.

Creating a Chart

Excel provides 10 types of charts to represent data in your worksheet. Each of these chart types contains several subtypes. You can create any type of chart according to the data you want to represent. The idea is to select the correct chart to ensure the best visualization for your data.

Perform the following steps to create a chart:

1. *Open* a new or an existing workbook whose data you want to represent in a chart.
2. *Select* the data that you want to represent in a chart. In our case, we have selected the cell range **A1:D7** (Fig.EX-2.37).

3. *Click* the desired chart type under the **Charts** group of the **INSERT** tab, as shown in Fig.EX-2.37:

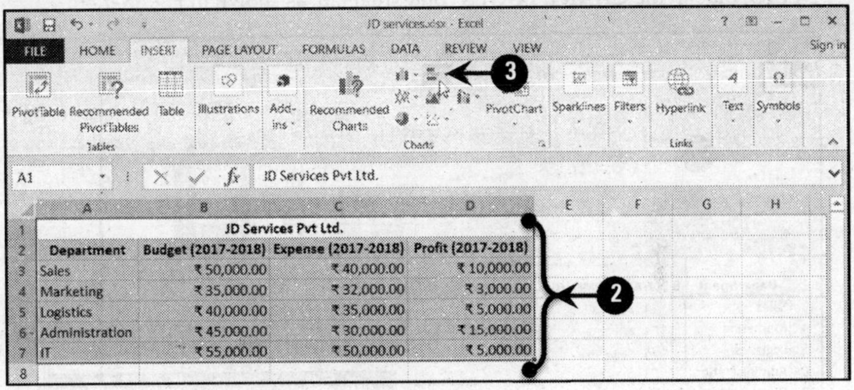

Fig.EX-2.37

A drop-down list appears (Fig.EX-2.38).

4. *Select* the desired chart from the drop-down list (Fig.EX-2.38).

The selected chart is created on the worksheet, as shown in Fig.EX-2.39:

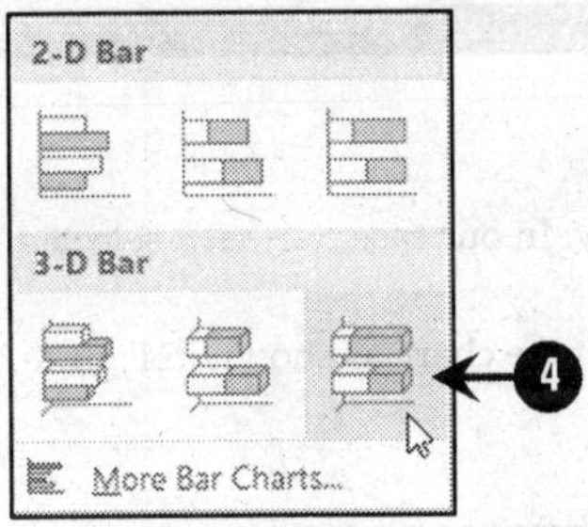

Fig.EX-2.38

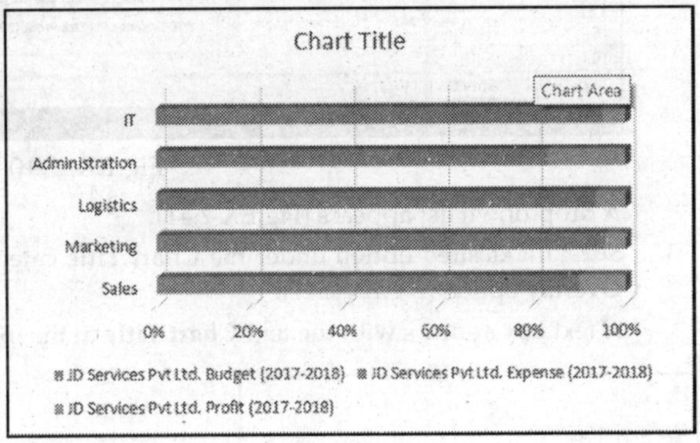

Fig.EX-2.39

Let us now discuss the various options to work with charts.

Working with Chart Options

After selecting an appropriate chart type for your data, you can use the various options to work with the chart and add various elements to it. A chart element enhances the look of the chart and also helps in making its content easily readable. Chart elements can be selected through the various chart options available for a particular chart. In this section, you learn to set the chart title, and axis title of the chart.

Let us learn how to set a chart title.

Setting the Chart Title

A chart title can be defined as a label that represents the type of information your chart contains. The title of the chart should be short and describe its main purpose.

Perform the following steps to set a title for a chart:

1. *Select* the chart whose title you want to set (Fig.EX-2.40).

2. *Click* the down arrow of the **Add Chart Element** button under the **Chart Layouts** group of the **DESIGN** tab in the **CHART TOOLS** contextual tab, as shown in Fig.EX-2.40:

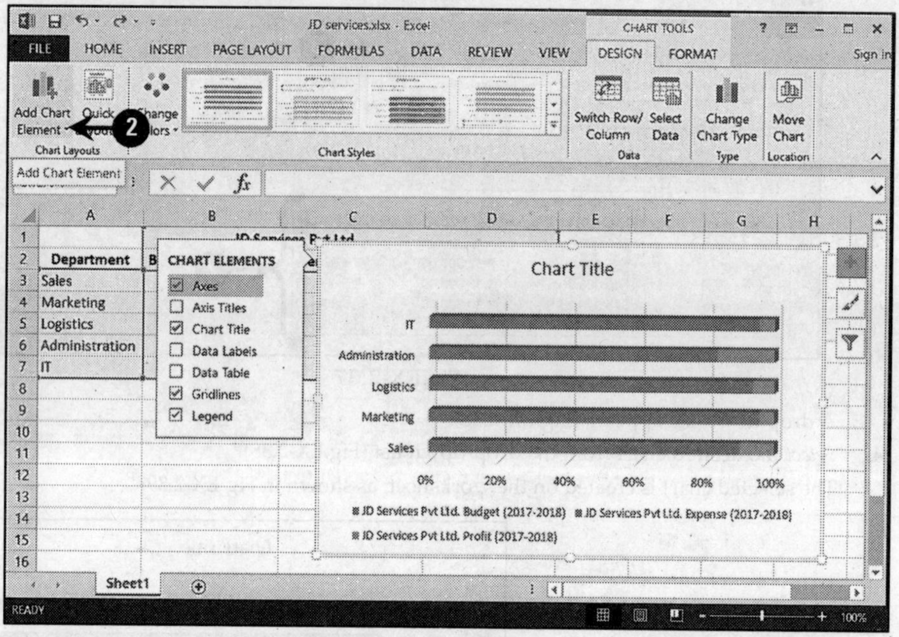

Fig.EX-2.40

A drop-down list appears (Fig.EX-2.41).

3. *Select* the desired option under the **Chart Title** category. In our case, we have selected the **Centered Overlay** option (Fig.EX-2.41).

A text box appears with the text **Chart Title** at the top of the chart, as shown in Fig.EX-2.42:

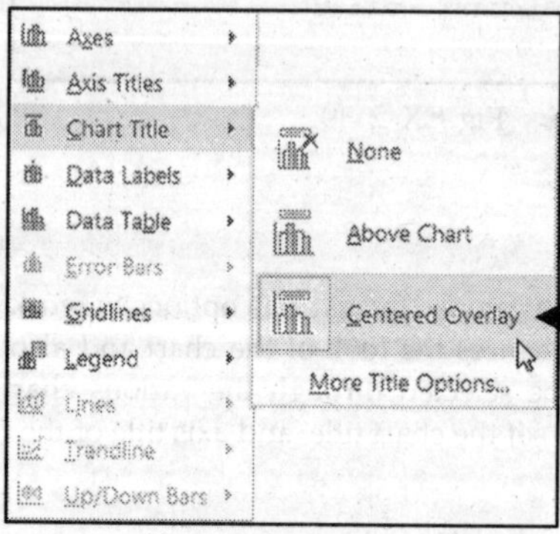

Fig.EX-2.41

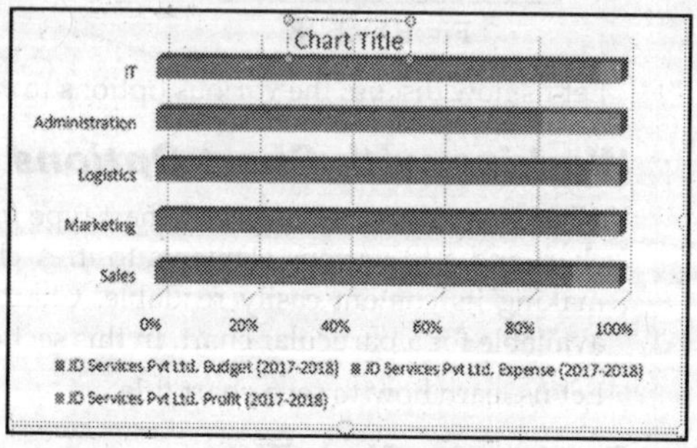

Fig.EX-2.42

4. *Type* the title of the chart in the **Chart Title** text box, as shown in Fig.EX-2.43:

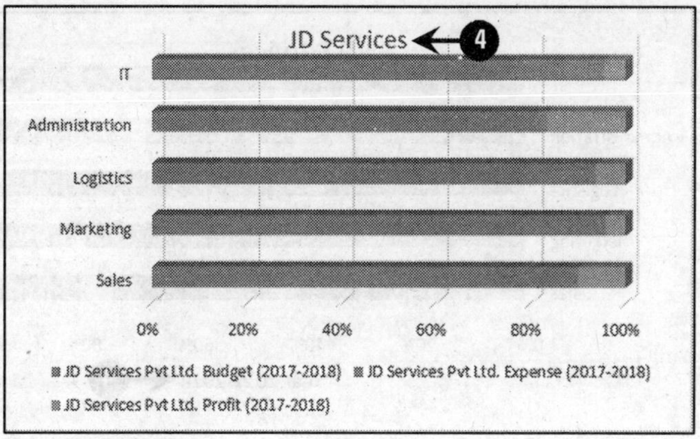

Fig.EX-2.43

Let us learn about the set axis title.

Setting the Axis Title

The charts that you create in Excel can be either two-dimensional (2D) or three-dimensional (3D). 2D charts consist of the X-axis and Y-axis, where the X-axis is the horizontal axis that shows the categories of data, and the Y-axis is the vertical axis that shows the numerical values against which the data categories are measured. 3D charts have an additional axis called Z-axis that is used to show the depth of the third dimension in the chart.

Perform the following steps to set an axis title for a chart:

1. *Select* the chart whose axis title you want to set.
2. *Click* the down arrow of the **Add Chart Element** button under the **Chart Layouts** group of the **DESIGN** tab in the **CHART TOOLS** contextual tab.

   A drop-down list appears (Fig.EX-2.44).
3. *Select* the desired option under the **Axis Titles** category. In our case, we have selected **Primary Horizontal** option (Fig.EX-2.44).

   The **Axis Title** text box appears below the chart, as shown in Fig.EX-2.45:

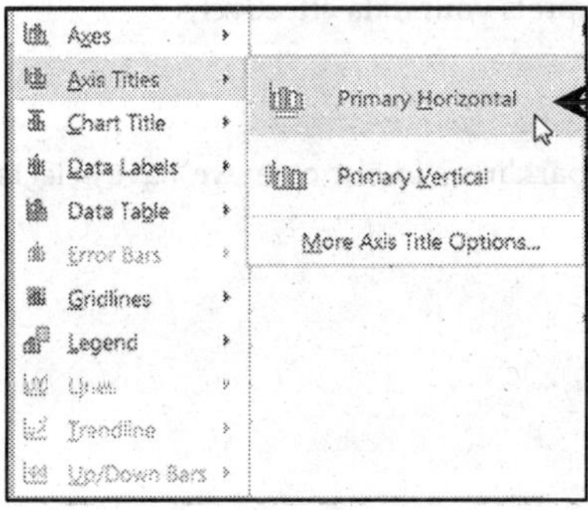

Fig.EX-2.44

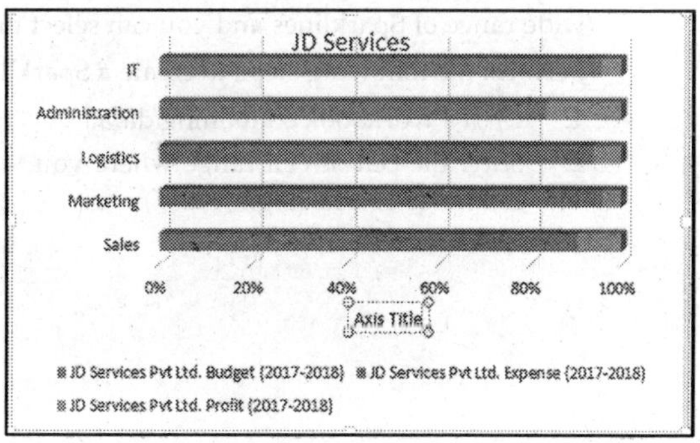

Fig.EX-2.45

4. *Type* the axis title of the chart in the **Axis Title** text box, as shown in Fig.EX-2.46:

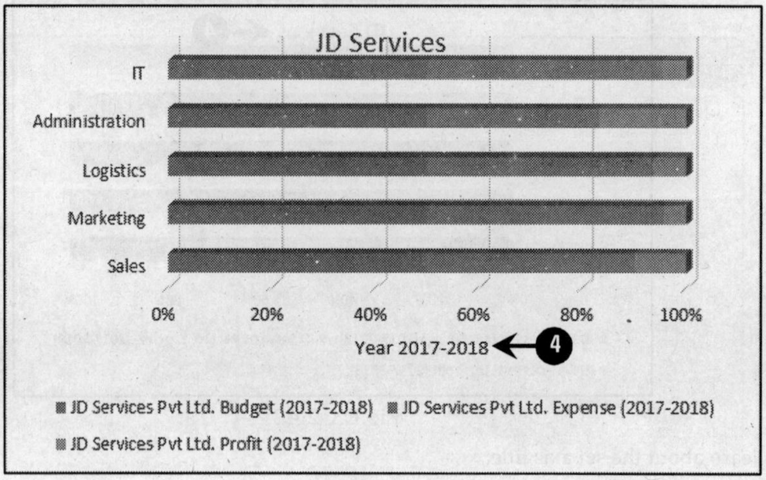

Fig.EX-2.46

Let us learn to work with sparklines.

Working with Sparklines

Sparklines are mini charts that you can place inside a cell of a worksheet to represent numerical data. They are intended to give you a quick look at the trends or changes that may not be easily spotted in the data itself. There are three types of Sparklines, which are as follows:

- **Line:** Displays the values of the selected data in a worksheet in the form of a line
- **Column:** Displays the values of the selected data in a worksheet in the form of small columns
- **Win/Loss:** Displays the data in binary form by showing each point as high or low

Let us now learn to create a Sparkline.

Creating Sparklines

You can create Sparklines to make your data easily understandable. Sparklines appear next to the data they interpret, thereby allowing you to get a clear idea of the data easily and quickly. Excel provides a wide range of Sparklines and you can select the one that interprets your data effectively.

Perform the following steps to create a Sparkline:

1. *Open* a workbook containing data.
2. *Select* the cell or cell range where you want to create Sparklines. In our case, we have selected the cell range **F3:F11** (Fig.EX-2.47).

3. *Select* the type of Sparkline that you want to create, under the **Sparklines** group of the **INSERT** tab. In our case, we have selected **Line**, as shown in Fig.EX-2.47:

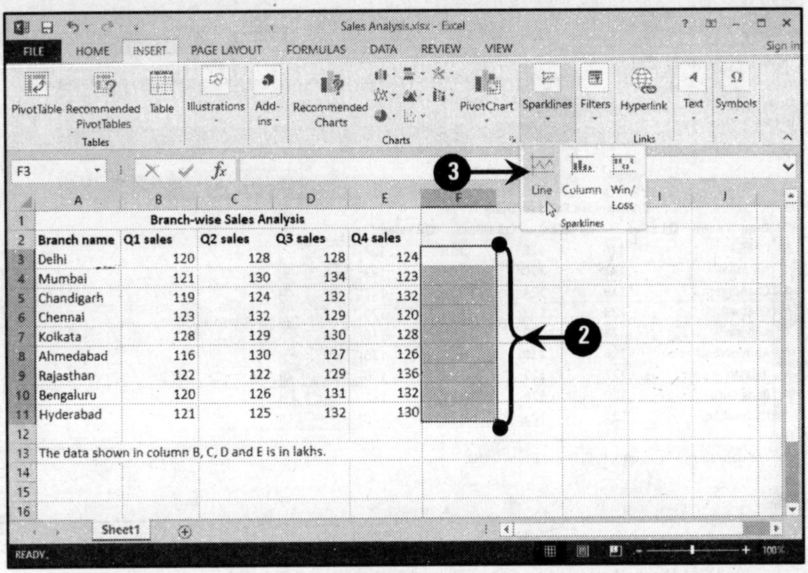

Fig.EX-2.47

The **Create Sparklines** dialog box appears, which displays the cell range that you selected in the worksheet (Fig.EX-2.48).

4. *Select* the data range for which you want to create Sparklines in the worksheet. In our case, we have selected **B3:E1** (Fig.EX-2.48).

   The selected data range appears in the **Data Range** text box in the **Create Sparklines** dialog box (Fig.EX-2.48).

5. *Click* the **OK** button to create Sparklines, as shown in Fig.EX-2.48:

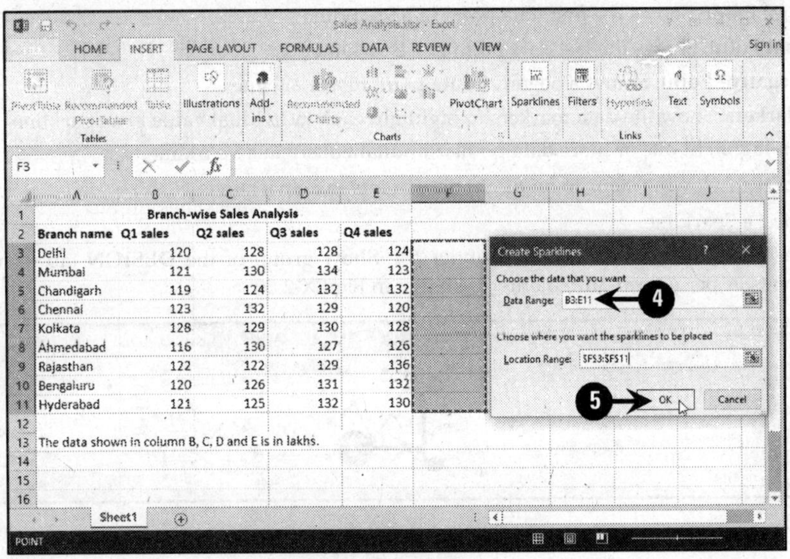

Fig.EX-2.48

The Sparklines appear in the worksheet, as shown in Fig.EX-2.49:

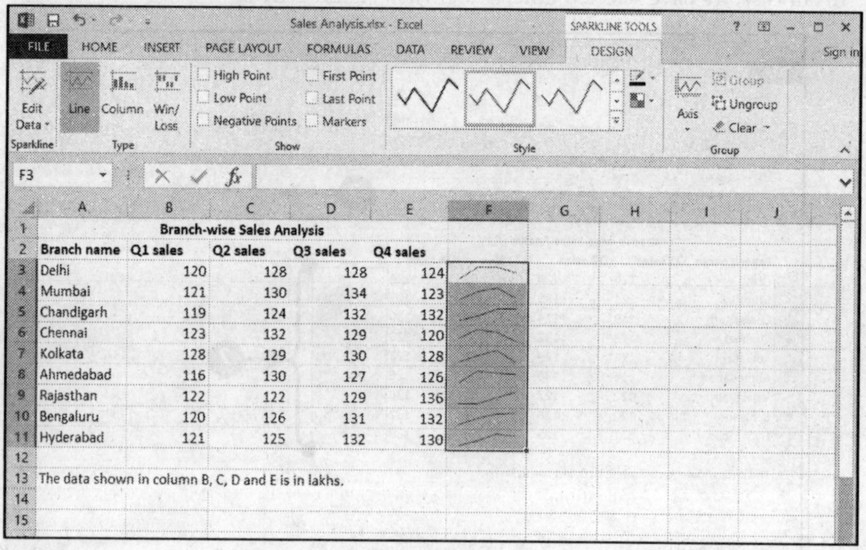

Fig.EX-2.49

Let us learn to highlight data points in a sparkline.

Highlighting Data Points

Apart from changing the color and type of Sparklines, you can also highlight the data points of Sparklines. Highlighting data points allows you to show important values, such as the highest, lowest, first, and last data values, in Sparklines. Excel provides the following options to highlight data points in a Sparkline:

- **High Point**: Shows the highest data point in a Sparkline
- **Low Point:** Shows the lowest data point in a Sparkline
- **First Point:** Shows the first data point in a Sparkline
- **Last Point:** Shows the last data point in a Sparkline
- **Negative Point**: Shows a negative data point in a Sparkline
- **Markers:** Show the data markers to highlight each individual value in a Sparkline.

You can highlight one or more data points simultaneously in a Sparkline.

Perform the following steps to highlight data points in a Sparkline:

1. *Select* a Sparkline.
2. *Select* one or more check boxes under the **Show** group of the **DESIGN** tab to highlight the data points as per your requirements, as shown in Fig.EX-2.50:

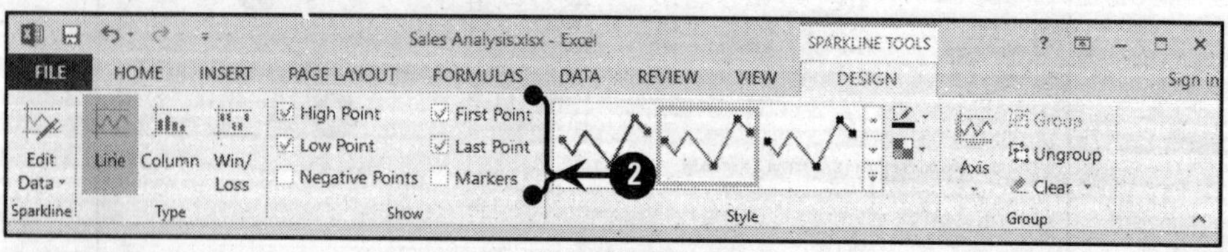

Fig.EX-2.50

The selected data points are highlighted in the Sparklines, as shown in Fig.EX-2.51:

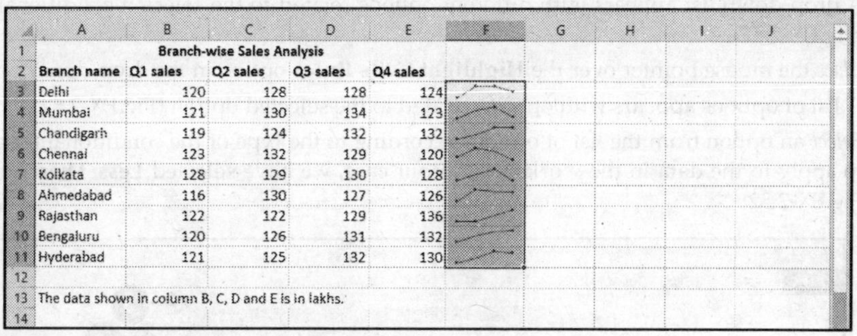

Branch-wise Sales Analysis				
Branch name	Q1 sales	Q2 sales	Q3 sales	Q4 sales
Delhi	120	128	128	124
Mumbai	121	130	134	123
Chandigarh	119	124	132	132
Chennai	123	132	129	120
Kolkata	128	129	130	128
Ahmedabad	116	130	127	126
Rajasthan	122	122	129	136
Bengaluru	120	126	131	132
Hyderabad	121	125	132	130

The data shown in column B, C, D and E is in lakhs.

Fig.EX-2.51

Let us learn about the conditional formatting.

Working with Conditional Formatting

The concept of conditional formatting can be best understood with an example. Let us suppose you have a large workbook that contains data spread over several worksheets. However, you want to highlight the important data so that it can easily stand out from the rest of the information in a workbook. In such a case, conditional formatting is used to automatically apply a defined format to cells that meet the specific conditions.

Let us learn to apply conditional formatting in Excel 2013.

Applying Conditional Formatting

You can also apply conditional formats within cells to identify data in a worksheet by setting specific criteria for the cells. In Excel, the conditions set to format cell data are known as conditional formatting rules. There are five types of conditional formatting in Excel: Highlight Cells Rules, Top/Bottom Rules, Data Bars, Color Scales, and Icon Sets. Each of these conditional formatting types includes various options related to respective conditional formatting type.

Let us discuss the different types of conditional formatting available in Excel 2013 and use them in a worksheet.

Using the Highlight Cells Rules Conditional Formatting

The Highlight Cells Rules conditional formatting is used to highlight data based on a defined condition. To set a condition, you need to select the appropriate Highlight Cells Rules conditional formatting option. The Highlight Cells Rules conditional formatting includes the following options:

- **Greater Than**: Highlights the cells whose value is greater than the specified value
- **Less Than**: Highlights the cells whose value is less than the specified value
- **Between**: Highlights the cells whose value occurs between the specified values
- **Equal To**: Highlights the cells whose value is equal to the specified value
- **Text that Contains**: Highlights the cells that contain textual data
- **A Date Occurring**: Highlights the cells whose data meets the specified date condition
- **Duplicate Values**: Highlights the values that are unique or occur multiple times in a worksheet

Perform the following steps to apply the Highlight Cells Rules conditional formatting in a worksheet:

1. *Open* a workbook that contains data.
2. *Select* the data on which you want to apply the conditional formatting. In our case, we have selected the cell range **B3:E7** (Fig.EX-2.52).

3. *Click* the **Conditional Formatting** button under the **Styles** group of the **HOME** tab (Fig.EX-2.52).

   A drop-down list appears with different options related to the selected conditional formatting type (Fig.EX-2.52).

4. *Place* the mouse pointer over the **Highlight Cells Rules** option in the drop-down list (Fig.EX-2.52).

   A list of options appears with options related to the selected option (Fig.EX-2.52).

5. *Select* an option from the list of options according to the type of the conditional formatting you want to apply to the data in the worksheet. In our case, we have selected **Less Than** option as shown in Fig.EX-2.52:

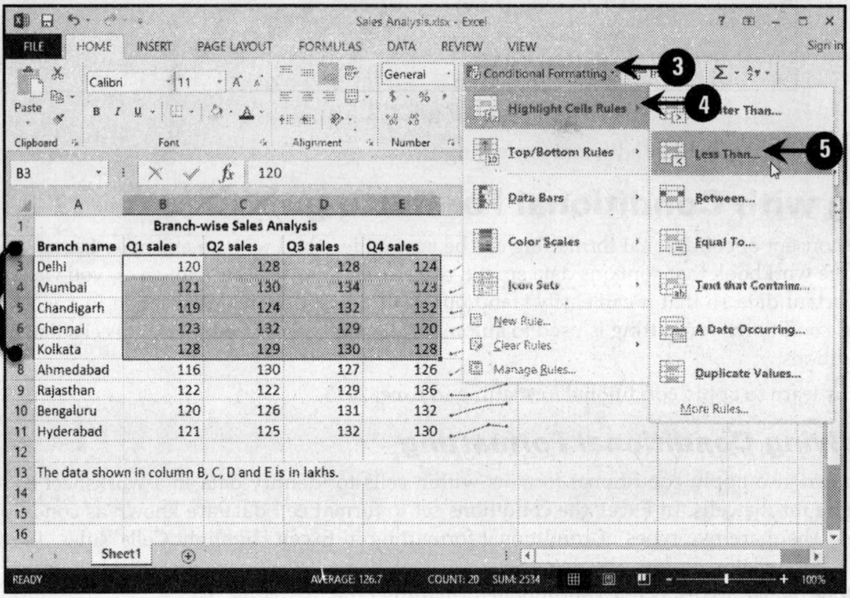

Fig.EX-2.52

   The **Less Than** dialog box appears (Fig.EX-2.53).

6. *Type* a value that you want to set as the less than formatting condition in the textbox under the **Format cells that are LESS THAN** section. In our case, we have typed 125 (Fig.EX-2.53).

7. *Click* the down arrow button under the **Format cells that are LESS THAN** section to select a color to highlight the values that fulfill the specified condition in the selected cell range (Fig.EX-2.53).

   A drop-down list appears (Fig.EX-2.53).

8. *Select* the desired option from the drop-down list. In our case, we have selected **Yellow Fill with Dark Yellow Text** as shown in Fig.EX-2.53:

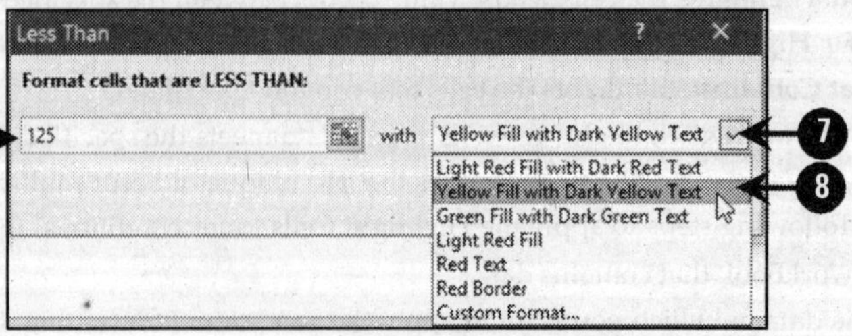

Fig.EX-2.53

9. *Click* the **OK** button in the **Less Than** dialog box.

The cells whose value is less than 125 in the worksheet are highlighted with the color you have specified in the **Less Than** dialog box, as shown in Fig.EX-2.54:

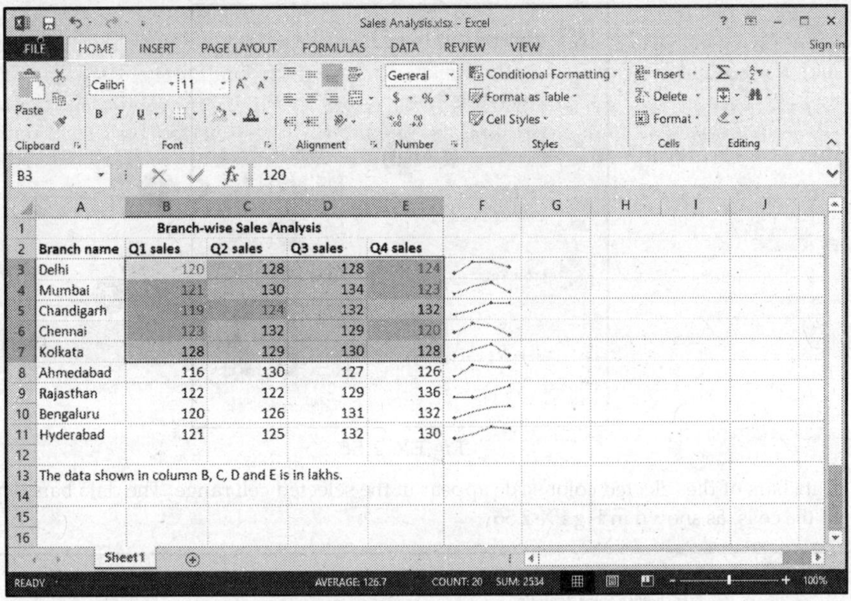

Fig.EX-2.54

Let us learn to use the Data Bars conditional formatting in Excel 2013.

Using the Data Bars Conditional Formatting

You can use the Data Bars conditional formatting when you want to show bars in a cell range along with values. This formatting helps in enhancing the visual appeal of your data and allows you to compare the values in a cell range at a glance. Therefore, it is an ideal formatting type to use if you want to understand large volumes of numeric data quickly and easily.

Perform the following steps to apply the Data Bars conditional formatting in Excel worksheet:

1. *Open* a workbook.
2. *Select* the data on which you want to apply the Data Bars conditional formatting. In our case, we have selected the cell range **B3:E7.**
3. *Click* the **Conditional Formatting** button under the **Styles** group of the **HOME** tab.

   A drop down-list appears (Fig.EX-2.55).
4. *Place* the mouse pointer over the **Data Bars** option in the drop-down list (Fig.EX-2.55).

   A list of options appear displaying several types of color schemes to use in the data bars (Fig.EX-2.55).

5. *Select* a color scheme from the list of options according to the type of conditional formatting you want to apply to the data in the worksheet, as shown in Fig.EX-2.55:

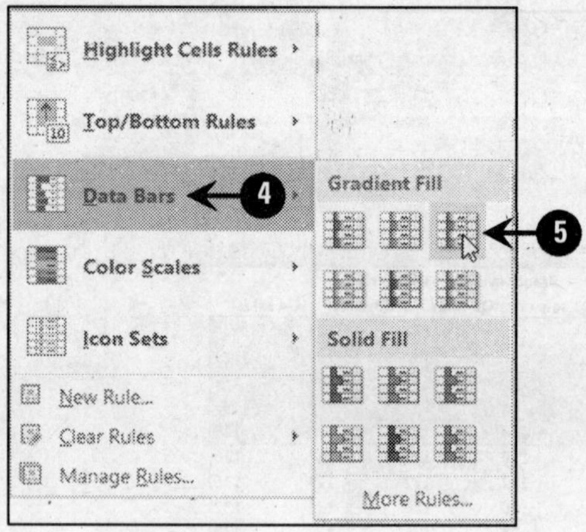

Fig.EX-2.55

Data bars of the selected color scale appear in the selected cell range. The data bars depict the values of the cells, as shown in Fig.EX-2.56:

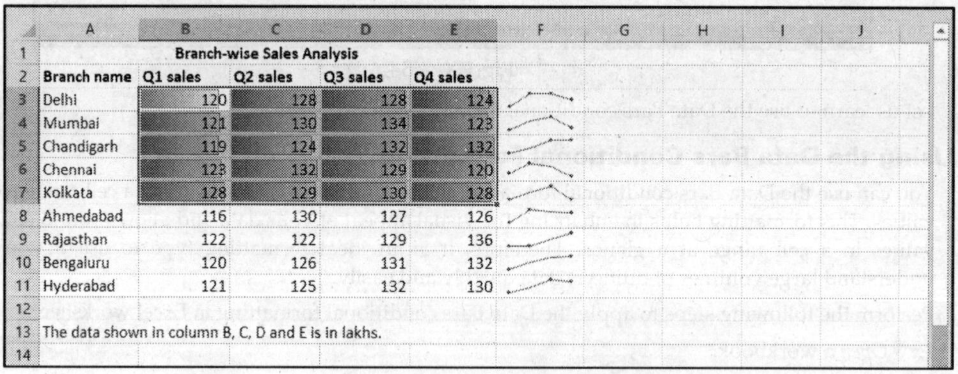

	A	B	C	D	E	F	G	H	I	J
1		Branch-wise Sales Analysis								
2	Branch name	Q1 sales	Q2 sales	Q3 sales	Q4 sales					
3	Delhi	120	128	128	124					
4	Mumbai	121	130	134	123					
5	Chandigarh	119	124	132	132					
6	Chennai	123	132	129	120					
7	Kolkata	128	129	130	128					
8	Ahmedabad	116	130	127	126					
9	Rajasthan	122	122	129	136					
10	Bengaluru	120	126	131	132					
11	Hyderabad	121	125	132	130					
12										
13	The data shown in column B, C, D and E is in lakhs.									
14										

Fig.EX-2.56

Now, let us learn to use the Top/Bottom Rules conditional formatting.

Using the Top/Bottom Rules Conditional Formatting

The Top/Bottom Rules conditional formatting is used to highlight the top (highest) or bottom (lowest) values, percentages, or averages in a cell range. Excel displays ten values of the selected formatting type by default; however, you can change this count according to your requirements. The Top/Bottom Rules conditional formatting includes the following options:

- **Top 10 Items**: Highlights the 10 highest values in the selected cell range
- **Bottom 10 Items**: Highlights the lowest 10 values in the given cell range
- **Top 10%:** Highlights the highest 10% values in the selected cell range
- **Bottom 10%:** Highlights the lowest 10% values in the selected cell range
- **Above Average**: Highlights the values that are more than the average value in the selected cell range
- **Below Average**: Highlights the values that are less than the average value in the selected cell range

Perform the following steps to apply the Top/Bottom Rules conditional formatting in a worksheet:

1. *Open* a workbook.
2. *Select* the data on which you want to apply conditional formatting. In our case, we have selected the cell range **B3:E7.**
3. *Click* the **Conditional Formatting** button under the **Styles** group of the **HOME** tab.
   A drop-down list appears (Fig.EX-2.57).
4. *Place* the mouse pointer over the **Top/Bottom Rules** option in the drop-down list (Fig.EX-2.57).
   A list of options appears with options related to the **Top/Bottom Rules** option (Fig.EX-2.57).
5. *Select* an option from the list of options according to the type of conditional formatting you want to apply to the data in the worksheet. In our case, we have selected **Top 10 Items** option as shown in Fig.EX-2.57:

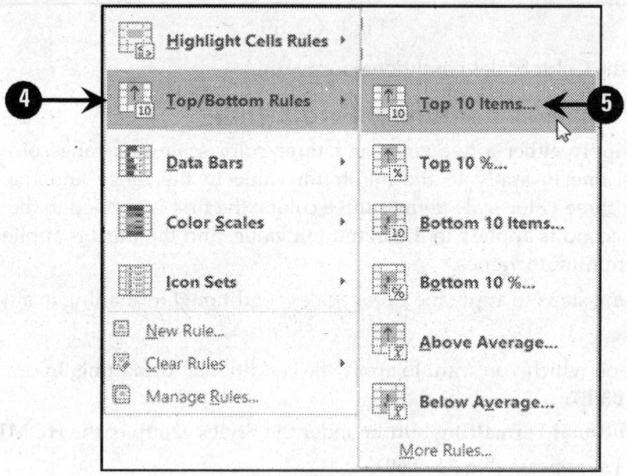

Fig.EX-2.57

   The **Top 10 Items** dialog box appears (Fig.EX-2.58).

6. *Click* the down arrow button of the list box under the **Format cells that rank in the TOP** section to select a color to highlight the top values in the selected cell range(Fig.EX-2.58).
7. *Select* the desired option from the drop-down list. In our case, we have selected **Green Fill with Dark Green Text** as shown in Fig.EX-2.58:

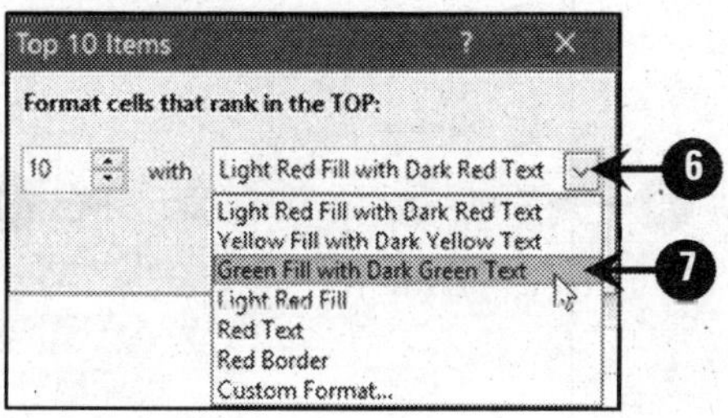

Fig.EX-2.58

8. *Click* the **OK** button in the dialog box.

The worksheet displays the top 10 values highlighted in specified color, as shown in Fig.EX-2.59:

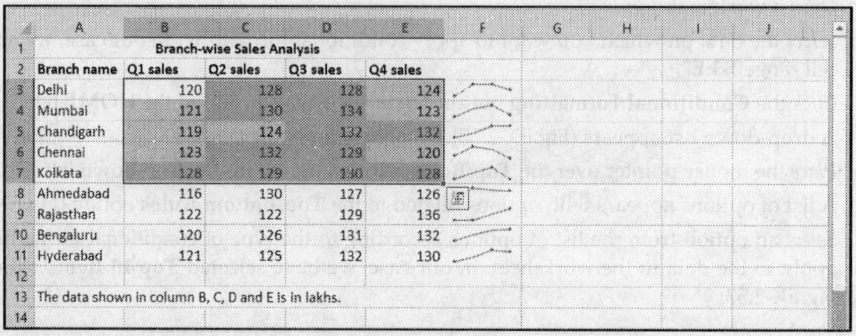

Fig.EX-2.59

Let us learn to use the Color Scales conditional formatting.

Using the Color Scales Conditional Formatting

In Excel, you can apply either a two color or a three color scale to a range of cells. A two-color scale defines two colors, one to apply to the minimum value in the range and the other to apply to the maximum value. A three-color scale defines three colors: the first is applied to the maximum value in the range of cells, the second is applied to the minimum value, and the third is applied to the average of the maximum and the minimum values.

Perform the following steps to apply the Color Scales conditional formatting in a worksheet:

1. *Open* a workbook.
2. *Select* the data on which you want to apply the conditional formatting. In our case, we have selected the cell range **B3:E7**.
3. *Click* the **Conditional Formatting** button under the **Styles** group of the **HOME** tab.

   A drop-down list appears (Fig.EX-2.60).
4. *Place* the mouse pointer over the **Color Scales** option in the drop-down list (Fig.EX-2.60).

   A list of options appears displaying several types of color scales (Fig.EX-2.60).
5. *Select* a color scale from the list of options, which you want to apply to the selected cell range, as shown in Fig.EX-2.60:

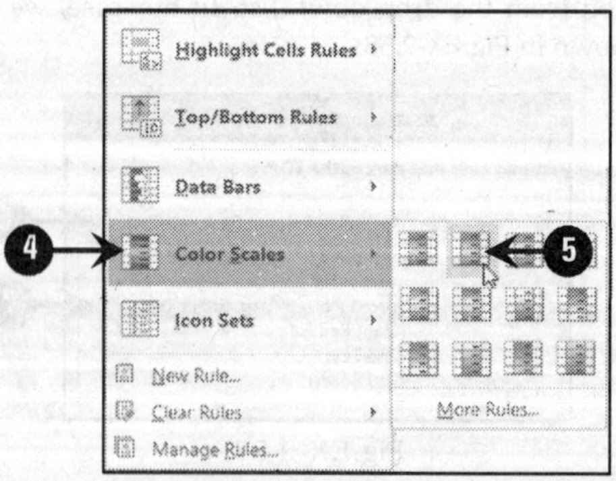

Fig.EX-2.60

The selected color scale is applied on the selected worksheet data, as shown in Fig.EX-2.61:

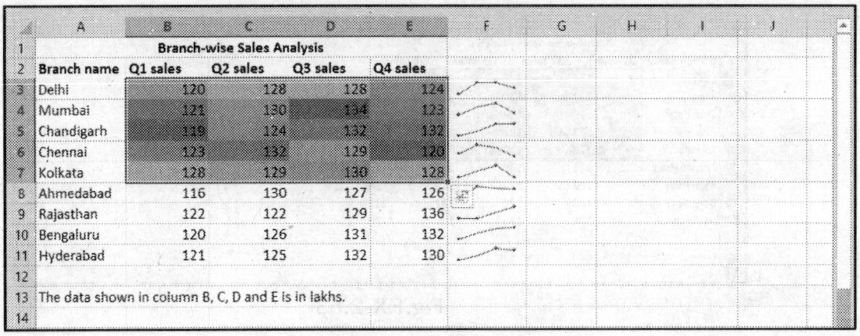

Fig.EX-2.61

Let us learn to use the Icon Sets conditional formatting.

Using the Icon Sets Conditional Formatting

You can use the Icon Sets conditional formatting to enhance the visual appeal of your data and to see how the value of a cell compares with the values of the other cells in a cell range. In the Icon Sets conditional formatting, icons are reused to represent data in the cells based on the values of cells. Icon sets make it easy for user to know how the values of a given cell range relate to each other.

Perform the following steps to apply the Icon Sets conditional formatting in a worksheet:

1. *Open* a workbook.
2. *Select* the data on which you want to apply the conditional formatting. In our case, we have selected the all range **B3:E7.**
3. *Click* the **Conditional Formatting** button under the **Styles** group of the **HOME** tab.

   A drop-down list appears (Fig.EX-2.62).
4. *Place* the mouse pointer over the **Icon Sets** option in the drop-down list (Fig.EX-2.62).

   Another drop-down list appears (Fig.EX-2.62).
5. *Select* an icon set from the drop-down list, which you want to apply to the selected cell range, as shown in Fig.EX-2.62:

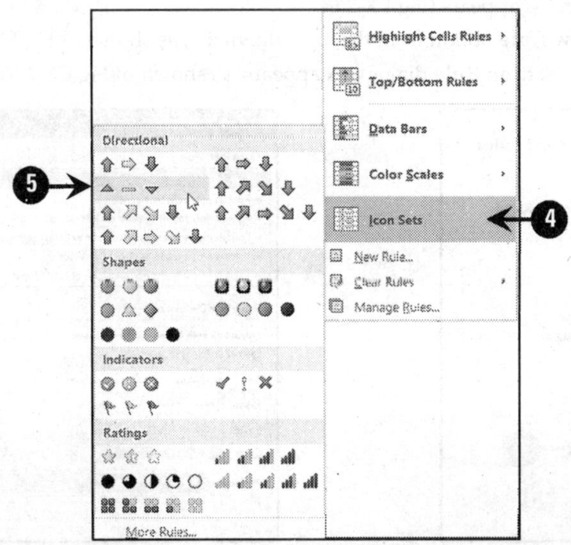

Fig.EX-2.62

The selected icon set is applied on the selected worksheet data, as shown in Fig.EX-2.63:

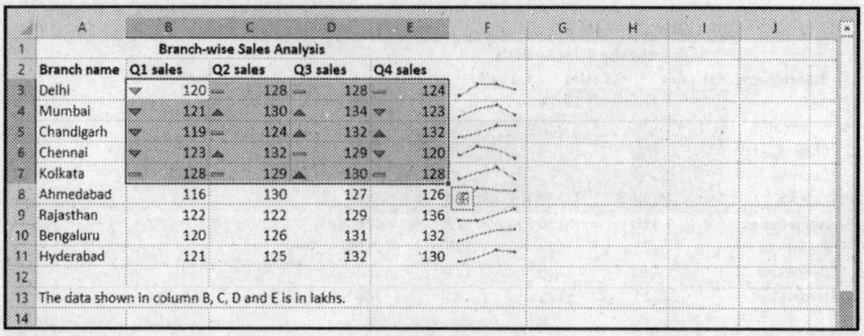

Fig.EX-2.63

After learning about the various types of conditional formatting applied on a worksheet data, let us learn to manage rules in conditional formatting.

Manage Rules in Conditional Formatting

As you know, the criteria or conditions set in conditional formatting are known as rules. You learned to work with the various built-in conditional formatting types in Excel. However, sometimes, you may want to format your data in your own style. You can do this by creating conditional formatting rules so that the data is formatted exactly the way you want. You can also edit the rules of either the built-in conditional formatting types or the rules that you create.

Let us begin this section by learning to create a new conditional formatting rule.

Creating New Rules for Conditional Formatting

As you have seen, conditional formatting offers one of the best ways to make key data stand out in a worksheet. However, you do not need to limit your choice to the built-in conditional formatting types. In Excel, you can create your own conditional formatting type by creating new rules.

Perform the following steps to create a new conditional formatting rule in Excel:

1. *Open* a workbook.
2. *Select* the data on which you want to apply the new conditional formatting rule.
3. *Click* the **Conditional Formatting** button under the **Styles** group of the **HOME** tab.

   A drop-down list appears (Fig.EX-2.64).
4. *Select* the **New Rule** option from the drop-down list, as shown in Fig.EX-2.64:

   The **New Formatting Rule** dialog box appears, as shown in Fig.EX-2.65:

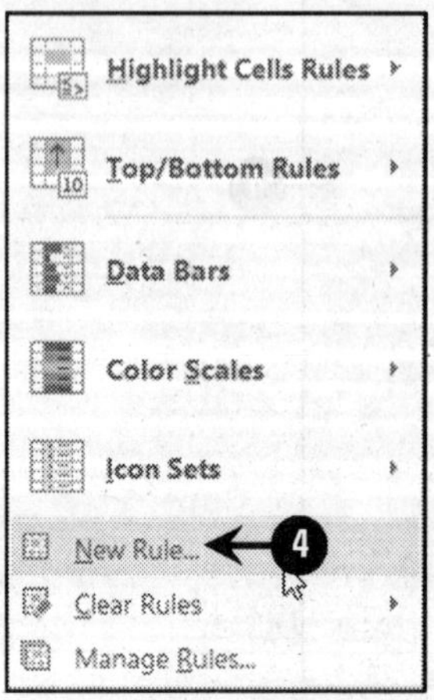

Fig.EX-2.64

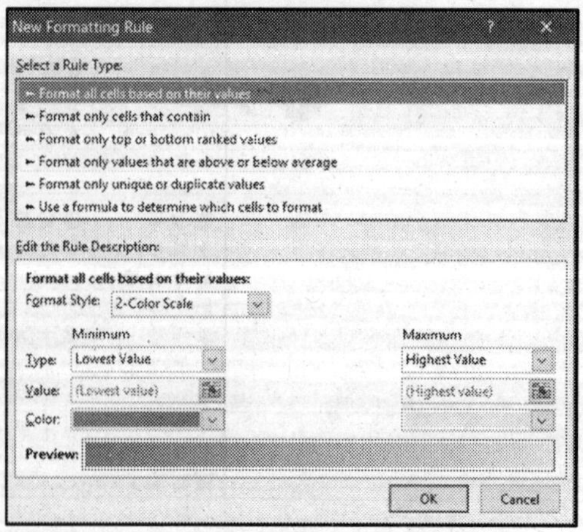

Fig.EX-2.65

5. *Select* an option in the **Select a Rule Type** list box to specify the type of conditional rule type you want to create. In our case, we have selected **Format only cells that contain** option (Fig.EX-2.66).

   The options in the **Edit the Rule Description** section of the **New Formatting Rule** dialog box change according to the type of conditional formatting rule you select in the **Select a Rule Type** list box (Fig.EX-2.66).
6. *Click* the first down arrow button of the **Format only cells with** option (Fig.EX-2.66).

   A drop-down list appears (Fig.EX-2.66).
7. *Select* the desired option from the drop-down list to specify where the conditional formatting rule is to be applied. In our case, we have selected **Cell Value** option as shown in Fig.EX-2.66:

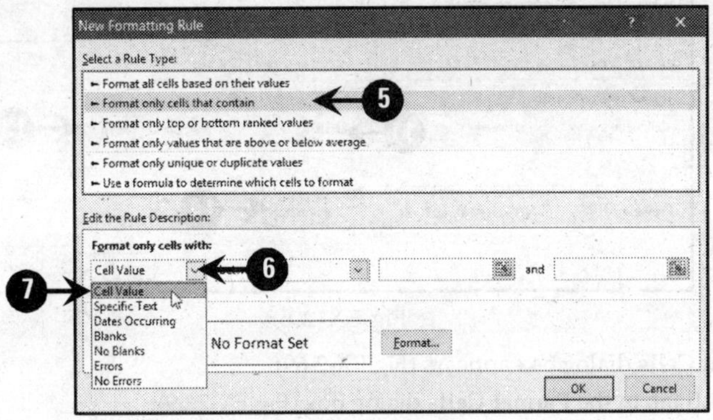

Fig.EX-2.66

8. *Click* the second down arrow button of the **Format only cells with** option.

   A drop-down list appears (Fig.EX-2.67).
9. *Select* the desired option from the drop-down list of the **Format only cells with** option to specify where the conditional formatting rule is to be applied. In our case, we have selected **between** option as shown in Fig.EX-2.67:

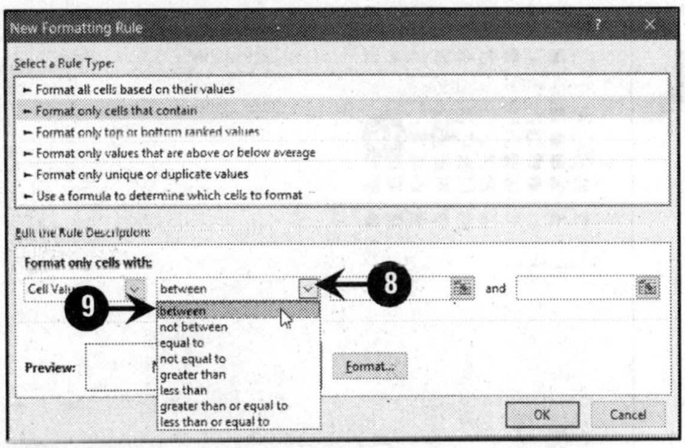

Fig.EX-2.67

10. *Click* the first text box under the **Format only cells with** option.
11. *Select* the cell in the worksheet whose value you want to set as the start value for the criteria of the rule (Fig.EX-2.68).

    The address of the selected cell appears in the first text box of the **Format only cells with** option in the **New Formatting Rule** dialog box (Fig.EX-2.68).
12. *Click* the second text box of the **Format only cells with** option.
13. *Select* the cell in the worksheet whose value you want to set as the end value for the criteria of the rule (Fig.EX-2.68).

The address of the selected cell appears in the second text box of the **Format only cells with** option in the **New Formatting Rule** dialog box (Fig.EX-2.68).

14. *Click* the **Format** button to define the format of the new conditional formatting rule, as shown in Fig.EX-2.68:

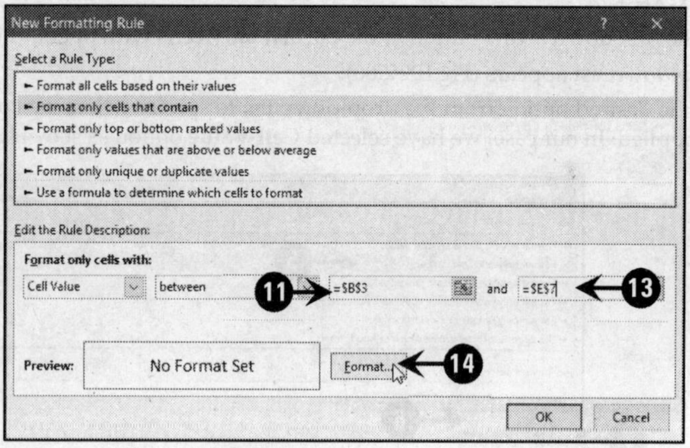

Fig.EX-2.68

The **Format Cells** dialog box appears (Fig.EX-2.69).

15. *Select* the **Fill** tab in the **Format Cells** dialog box (Fig.EX-2.69).

    The options of the **Fill** tab appear under the tab in the **Format Cells** dialog box (Fig.EX-2.69).

16. *Select* a color from the **Background Color** option (Fig.EX-2.69).

17. *Click* the **OK** button, as shown in Fig.EX-2.69:

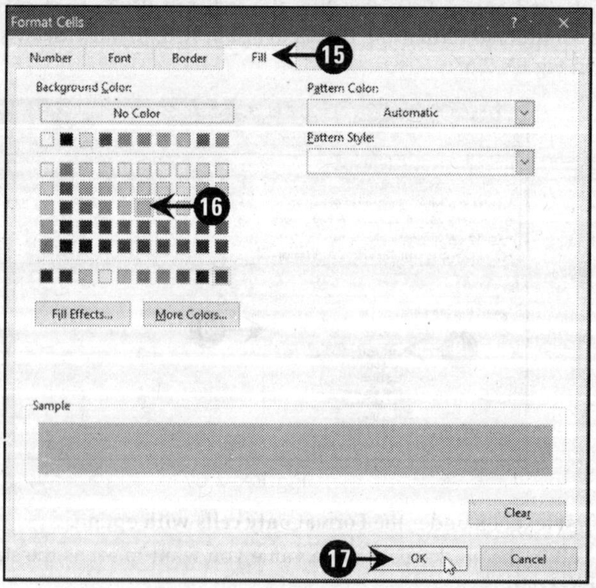

Fig.EX-2.69

The **New Formatting Rule** dialog box is activated (Fig.EX-2.70).

18. *Click* the **OK** button, as shown in Fig.EX-2.70:

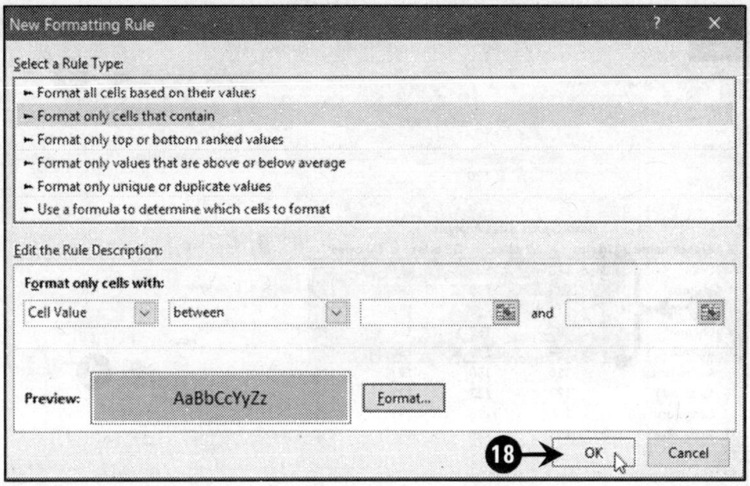

Fig.EX-2.70

The new conditional formatting is applied to the selected data in the worksheet, as shown in Fig.EX-2.71:

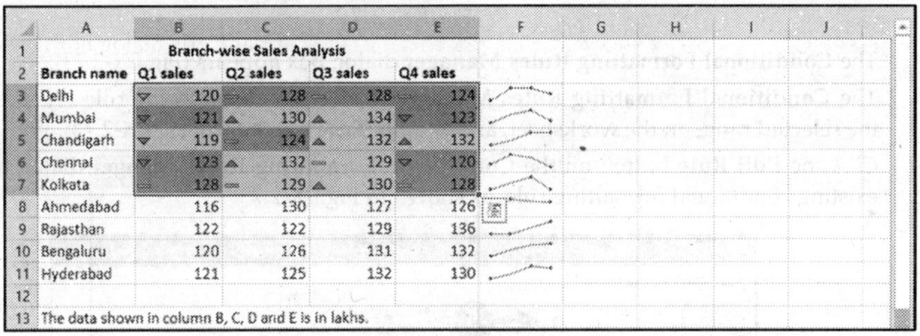

Fig.EX-2.71

Now, let us learn to edit conditional formatting rules.

Editing Conditional Formatting Rules

In Excel, you can also edit the conditional formatting rules. Suppose, you have created a conditional formatting rule for some data in a worksheet. However, when you apply the rule on the data you realize that it does not format the data the way you had expected. In such cases, you can edit he particular rule according to your needs. In this section, let us pick the three color icon used earlier in the chapter to learn how to edit a conditional formatting rule.

Perform the following steps to edit conditional formatting rule:

1. *Open* a workbook.
2. *Select* the required cell range to make changes in the conditional formatting. In our case, we have selected the all range **B3:E7** (Fig.EX-2.72).
3. *Click* the **Conditional Formatting** button under the **Styles** group of the **HOME** tab (Fig.EX-2.72).

   A drop-down list appears (Fig.EX-2.72).

4. *Select* the **Manage Rules** option from the drop-down list, as shown in Fig.EX-2.72:

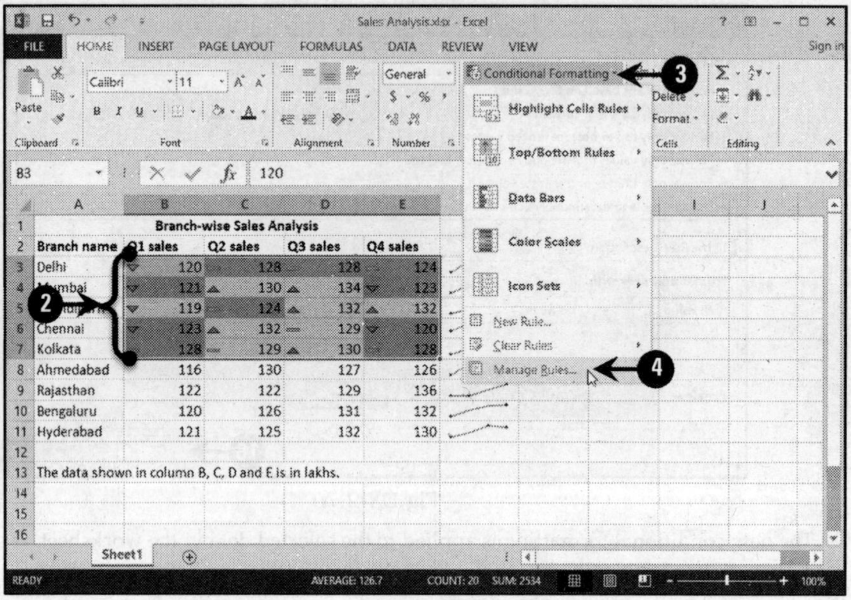

Fig.EX-2.72

The **Conditional Formatting Rules Manager** dialog box appears (Fig.EX-2.73).

The **Conditional Formatting Rules Manager** dialog box displays the rule type, format, address of the selected range in the worksheet, and **Stop If True** check box (Fig.EX-2.73).

5. *Click* the **Edit Rule** button on the **Conditional Formatting Rules Manger** dialog box to modify the existing conditional formatting rule, as shown in Fig.EX-2.73:

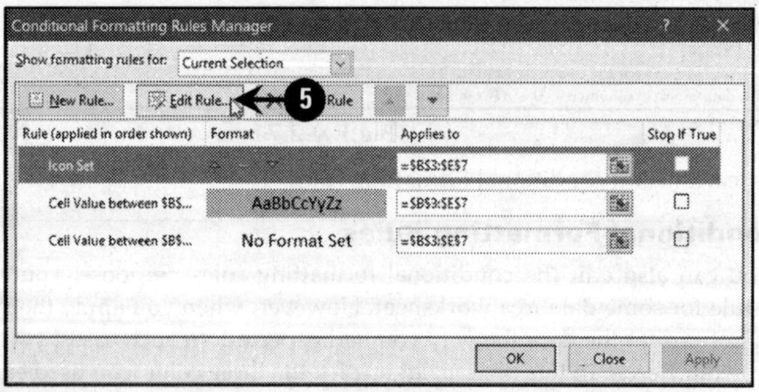

Fig.EX-2.73

The **Edit Formatting Rule** dialog box appears (Fig.EX-2.74).

6. *Click* the down arrow button of the **Icon Style** option under the **Edit the Rule Description** section (Fig.EX-2.74).

A drop-down list appears (Fig.EX-2.74).

7. *Select* the icon style that you want to apply to the selected cell range. In our case, we have selected the **3 Traffic Lights** icon style from the drop-down list, as shown in Fig.EX-2.74:

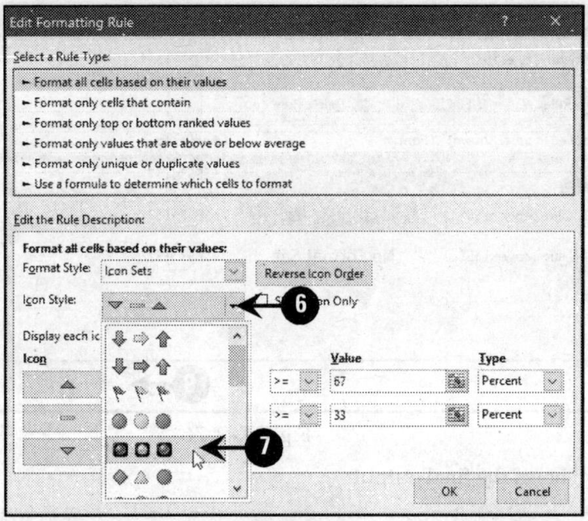

Fig.EX-2.74

The selected icon set replaces the existing icon set in the **Edit Formatting Rule** dialog box. In addition, the values for these icons are automatically set by Excel based on their existing values. If required, you can set the condition of each type of icon in its respective list box and the value in the respective **Value** text box under the **Display each icon according to these rules** section in the **Edit Formatting Rule** dialog box. In our case, we are using the existing conditions, values, and types for the icons (Fig.EX-2.75).

8. *Click* the **OK** button to close the **Edit Formatting Rule** dialog box, as shown in Fig.EX-2.75:

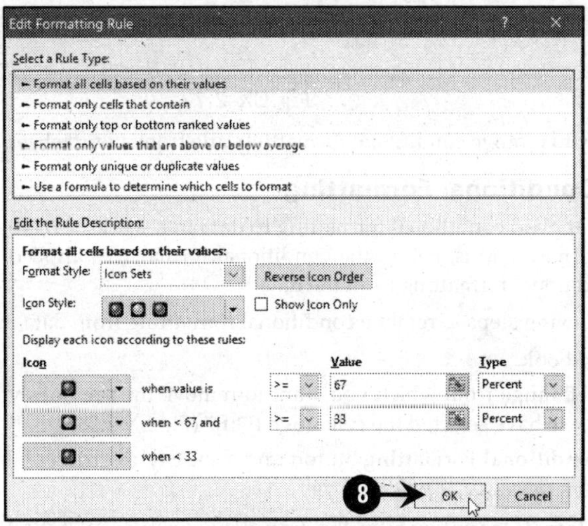

Fig.EX-2.75

The **Conditional Formatting Rules Manager** dialog box reappears (Fig.EX-2.76).

9. *Click* the **OK** button to close the **Conditional Formatting Rules Manager** dialog box, as shown in Fig.EX-2.76:

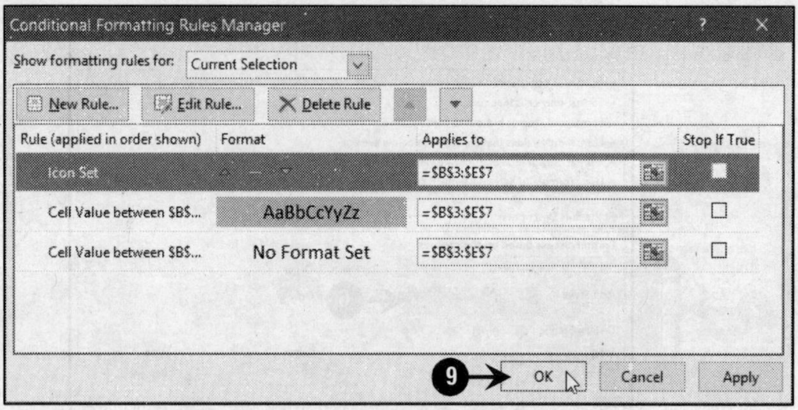

Fig.EX-2.76

Fig.EX-2.77 shows the final output:

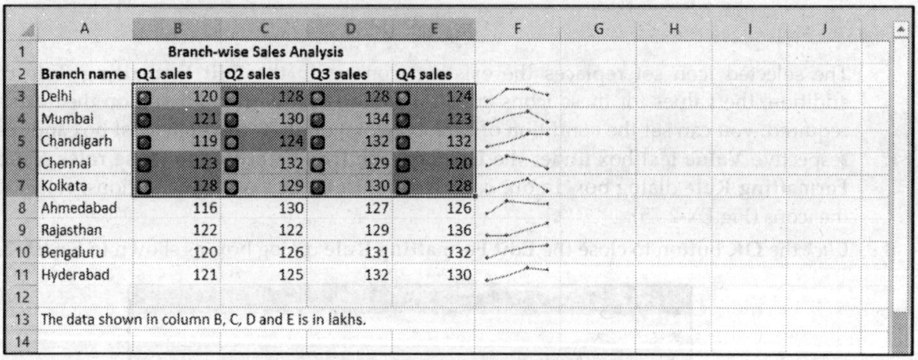

Fig.EX-2.77

Let us learn how to remove conditional formatting rule from a worksheet.

Removing a Conditional Formatting

After you have applied conditional formatting to data in a worksheet, you may still want to use the data in its original format, that is, before the conditional format was applied to it. In that case, you need to remove the conditional formatting from the data.

Perform the following steps to remove conditional formatting from data in a worksheet:

1. *Open* a workbook.
2. *Select* the cell range from which you want to remove the previously applied conditional formatting In our case, we have selected the cell range **B3:E7** (Fig.EX-2.78).
3. *Click* the **Conditional Formatting** button under the **Styles** group of the **HOME** tab (Fig.EX-2.78).

   A drop-down list appears (Fig.EX-2.78).
4. *Select* the **Clear Rules** option from the drop-down list (Fig.EX-2.78).

   Another drop-down list appears (Fig.EX-2.78).

5. *Select* an option of your choice from the drop-down list. In our case, we have selected the **Clear Rules from Selected Cells** option, as shown in Fig.EX-2.78:

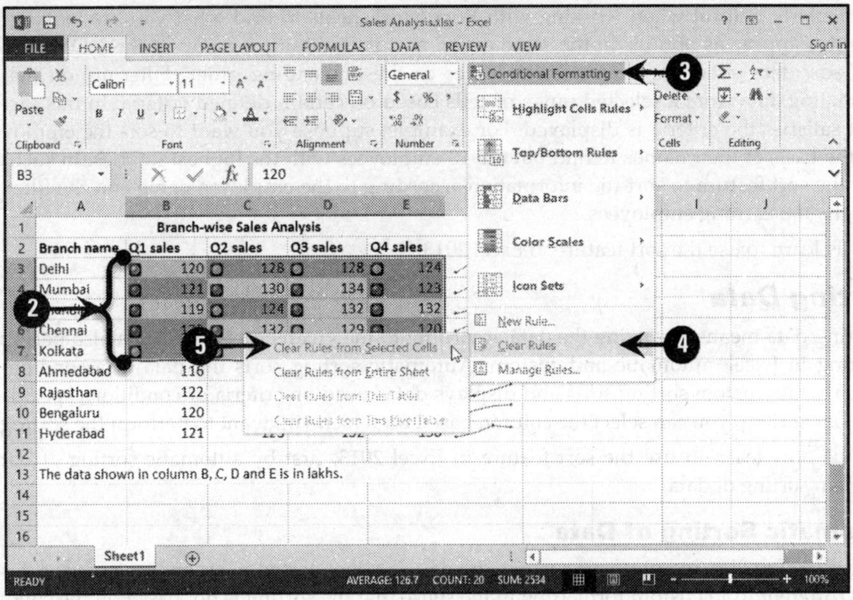

Fig.EX-2.78

The conditional formatting is removed from the selected cell range, as shown in Fig.EX-2.79:

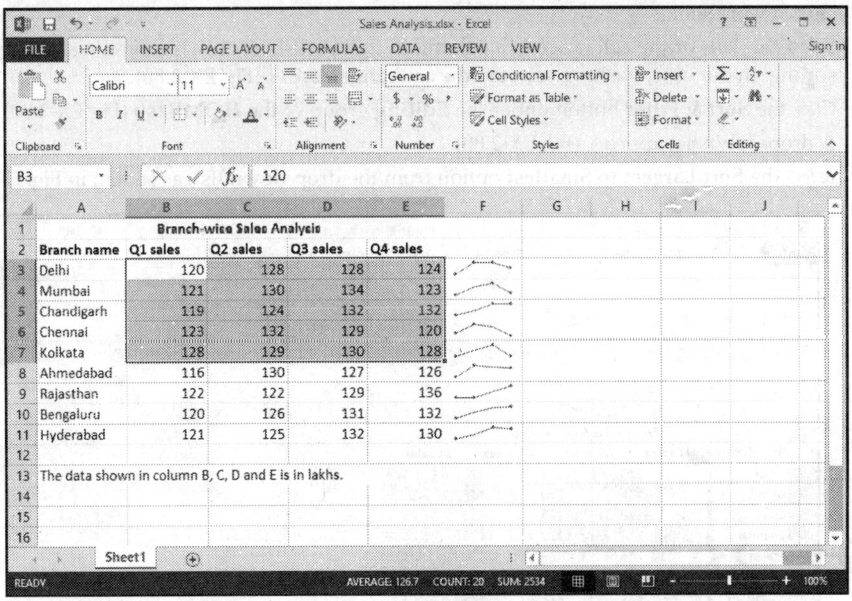

Fig.EX-2.79

Let us learn about the sort and filter features in Excel.

Exploring Sort and Filter Features

The sort and filter features of Excel help to arrange and retrieve specific data. These features are particularly helpful when working with large worksheets to find what you are looking for. Both these features appear as options in the same group that is the Editing group of the HOME tab. In Excel, you can sort data either in the ascending order or the descending order. Filtering, on the other hand, is extracting data from a selected range of cells based on certain defined criteria. In this case, only the data that satisfies the criteria is displayed. For example, suppose you want to sort the employee information on the basis of their names to find out the 10 employees with the highest salaries. In such a case, you can use the sort feature to sort the information according to the employee name and the filter feature to find out the top earning employees.

Let us learn to use the sort feature in Excel 2013.

Sorting Data

Sorting data means arranging the data according to the given criteria. You can also perform two types of sorting in Excel, automatic and custom. Automatic sorting sorts the data in ascending or descending order while custom sorting sorts and displays data based on criteria or conditions specified by a user. In custom sorting, you can select the column based on which you want to perform the sorting.

Let us now learn to use the sort feature in Excel 2013, first by automatic sorting of data and then by custom sorting of data.

Automatic Sorting of Data

As learned earlier, in automatic sorting, the data is either sorted in ascending order or descending order. It is different from custom formatting in the sense that the sorting is not based on the conditions specified by the user.

Perform the following steps to apply the automatic sorting on data:

1. *Open* a workbook.
2. *Select* the cells or the cell range in a column in the worksheet on which you want to apply automatic sorting. In our case, we have selected the cell range **B3:E11** (Fig.EX-2.80).
3. *Click* the **Sort & Filter** button under the **Editing** group of the **HOME** tab (Fig.EX-2.80).
   A drop-down list appears (Fig.EX-2.80).
4. *Select* the **Sort Largest to Smallest** option from the drop-down list, as shown in Fig.EX-2.80:

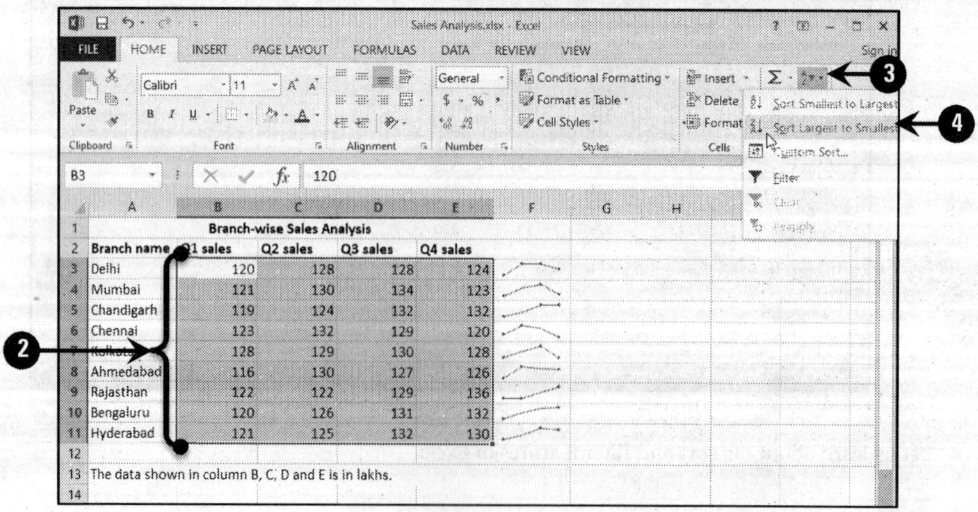

Fig.EX-2.80

The sorting is applied to the data in the worksheet, as shown in Fig.EX-2.81:

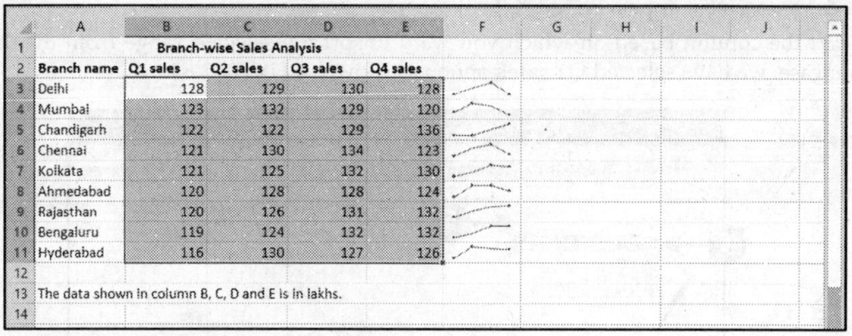

Fig.EX-2.81

As shown in Fig.EX-2.81, the data of the column containing the selected cell range is sorted in the descending order. In addition, the values in the other cells of the rows corresponding to that column are also affected.

Let us learn to apply custom sorting of data in Excel 2013.

Custom Sorting of Data

Sometimes, you want to sort the data in some other criterion other than the ascending or descending order. Excel provides you the facility to apply the custom sorting on the data so that it is sorted specifically according to your requirements.

Perform the following steps to apply custom sorting on data:

1. *Open* a workbook.
2. *Select* the data on which you want to apply the custom sorting. In our case, we have selected the cell range **B3:E11** (Fig.EX-2.82).
3. *Click* the **Sort & Filter** button under the **Editing** group of the **HOME** tab.

   A drop-down list appears (Fig.EX-2.82).
4. *Select* the **Custom Sort** option from the drop-down list, as shown in Fig.EX-2.82:

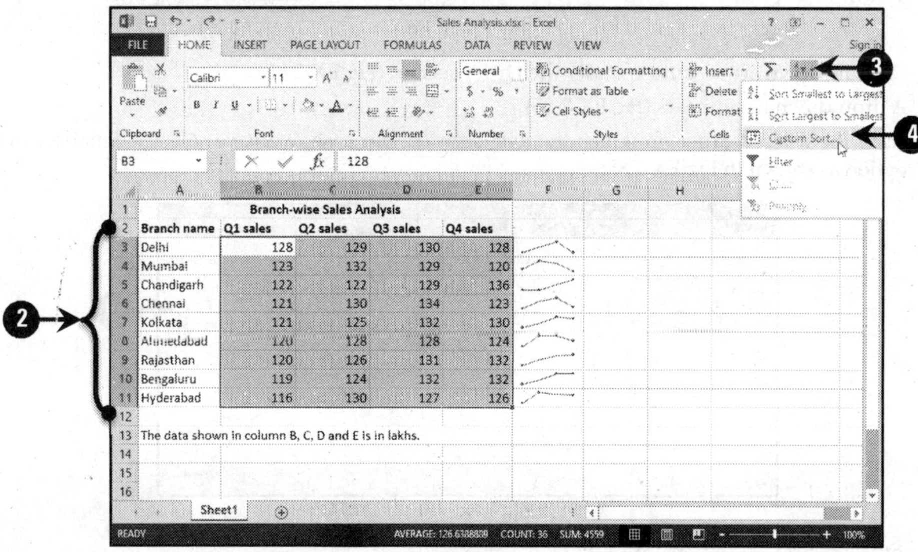

Fig.EX-2.82

The **Sort** dialog box appears (Fig.EX-2.82).

5. *Click* the down arrow button under **Column** section (Fig.EX-2.83).

   A drop-down list appears (Fig.EX-2.83).

6. *Select* the column based on which you want to sort the selected range from the drop-down list. In our case, we have selected **Q1 sales** option as shown in Fig.EX-2.83:

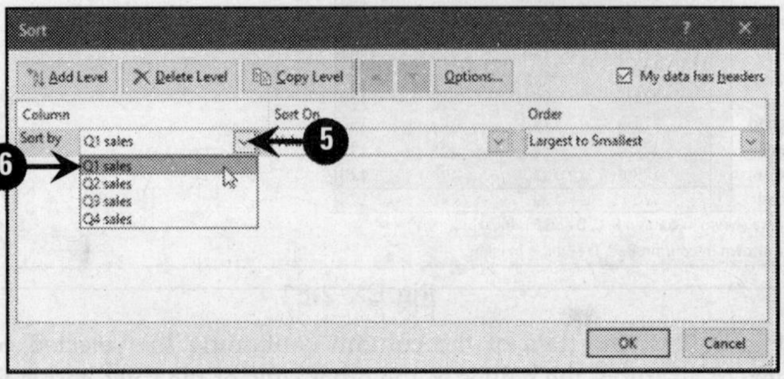

Fig.EX-2.83

7. *Click* the down arrow button under the **Sort On** section (Fig.EX-2.84).

   A drop-down list appears (Fig.EX-2.84).

8. *Select* the desired option based on the sorting type. In our case, we have selected **Values** as shown in Fig.EX-2.84:

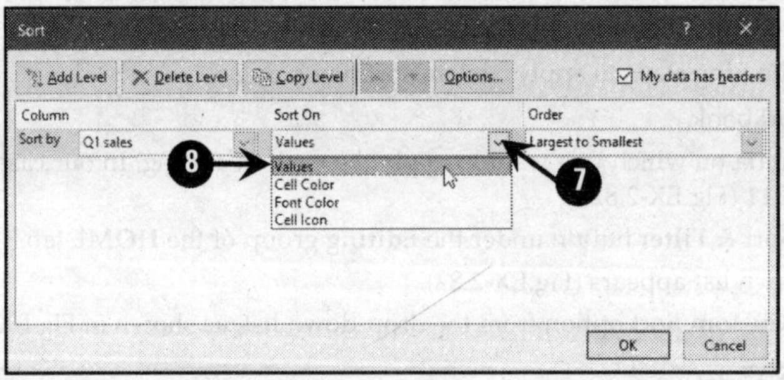

Fig.EX-2.84

9. *Click* the down arrow button under the **Order** section (Fig.EX-2.85).

   A drop-down list appears (Fig.EX-2.85).

10. *Select* the desired order on which the data sorts. In our case, we have selected **Smallest to Largest** option as shown in Fig.EX-2.85:

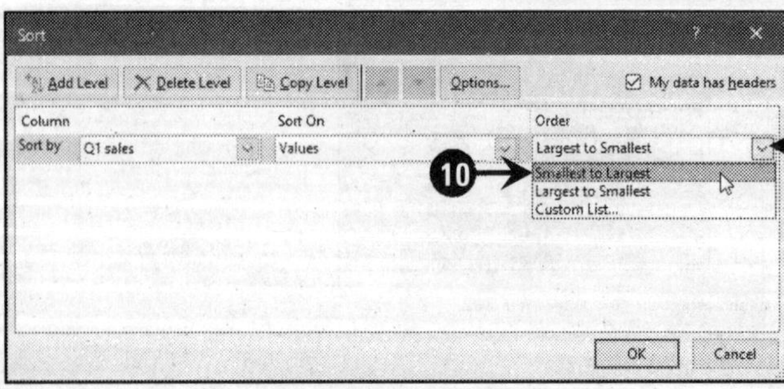

Fig.EX-2.85

11. *Click* the **OK** button in the **Sort** dialog box.

The sorting is applied to the selected data on a worksheet, as shown in Fig.EX-2.86:

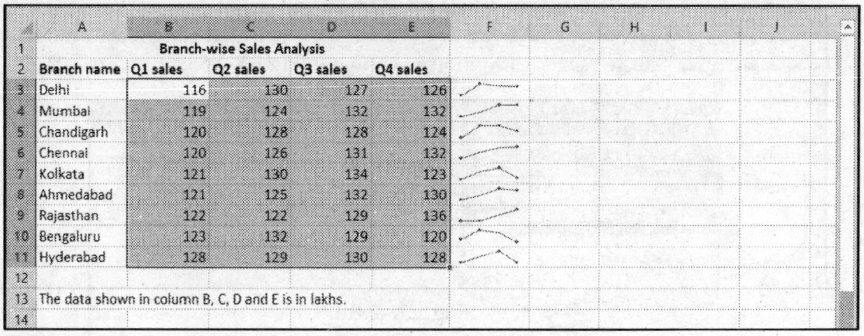

Fig.EX-2.86

As shown in Fig.EX-2.86, the data is sorted in ascending order according to the Q1 sales column. In addition, the values in the other cells of the rows corresponding to that column are also affected.

Now, let us learn to use the filter feature in Excel 2013.

Filtering Data

Filtering data refers to the process of retrieving specific data from a worksheet, which meets the criteria specified by a user. When you have a large chunk of data in a worksheet and want to display specific parts of it, you can do so by applying it from the worksheet. Filtering can be applied on textual as well as numeric data. When you apply filtering on a single or multiple columns in a worksheet, down arrow buttons appear on each head of the selected columns. You can filter data in two ways: by using the automatic filtering feature and by using the built-in filtering feature.

Perform the following steps to apply automatic filtering on the worksheet data:

1. *Open* a workbook.
2. *Select* a cell range on which you want to apply the automatic filtering. In our case, we have selected cell range **B3:E11** (Fig.EX-2.87).
3. *Click* the **Sort & Filter** button under the **Editing** group of the **HOME** tab (Fig.EX-2.87).
   A drop down list appears (Fig.EX-2.87).
4. *Select* the **Filter** option from the drop-down list, as shown in Fig.EX-2.87:

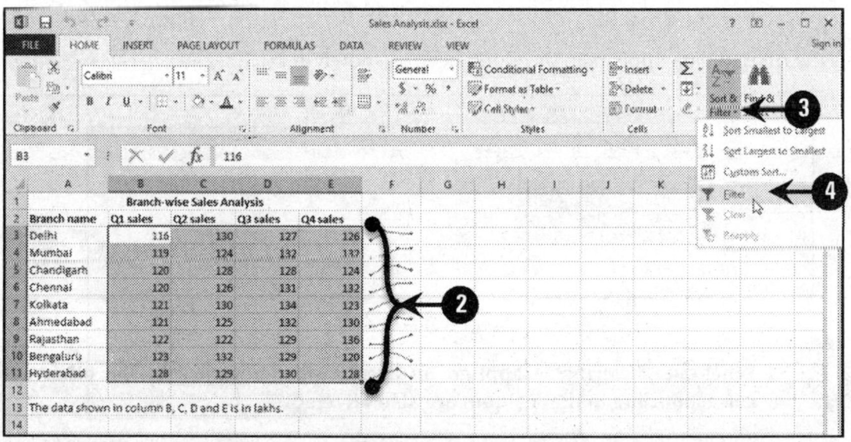

Fig.EX-2.87

A down arrow appears on the head of the selected columns (Fig.EX-2.88).

5. *Click* any of the down arrow button, as shown in Fig.EX-2.88:

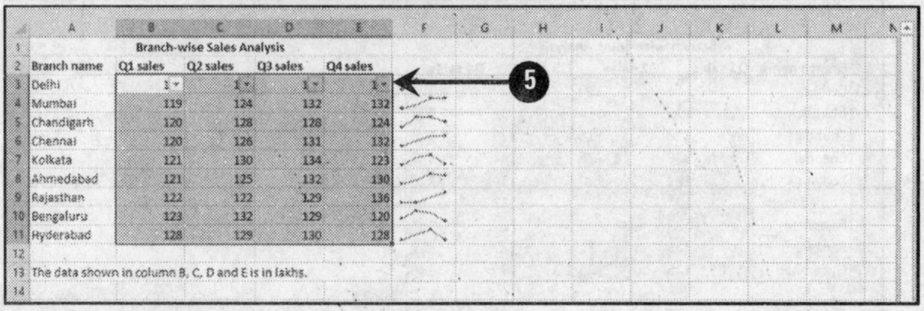

Fig.EX-2.88

A drop-down list appears, displaying various sort and filter options, as well as the check boxes with the values of the selected column. All the check boxes are selected by default. You can filter the data in the columns by selecting or clearing the respective check boxes (Fig.EX-2.89).

6. *Clear* the check boxes based on the data you want to filter (Fig.EX-2.90).
7. *Click* the **OK** button, as shown in Fig.EX-2.90:

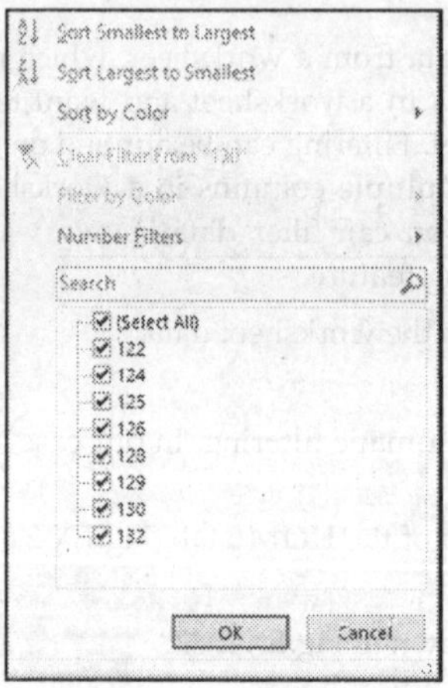

Fig.EX-2.89

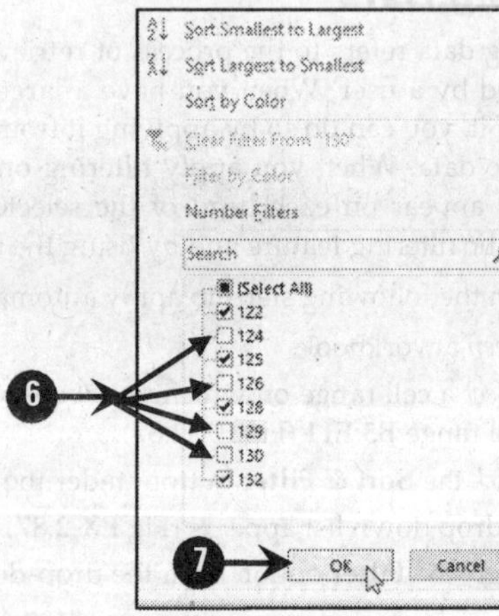

Fig.EX-2.90

The filtered data appears in the worksheet, as shown in Fig.EX-2.91:

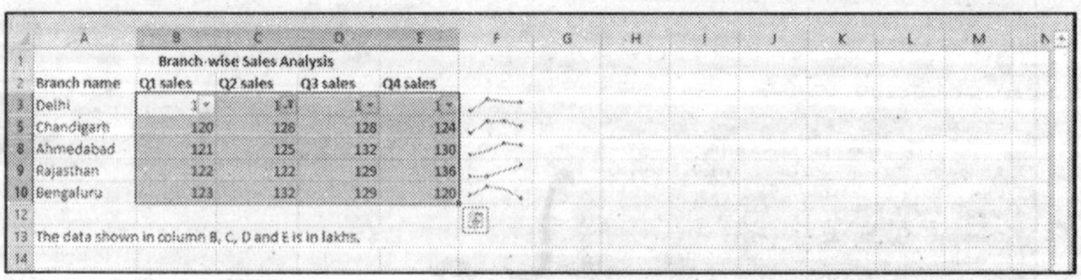

Fig.EX-2.91

Note: **Whenever filtering is applied on a column, the values in the other cells of the rows corresponding to that column are also affected.**

Apart from automatic filtering, you can also use the built-in filtering types available in Microsoft Excel.

Perform the following steps to filter data by using the built-in filtering:

1. *Open* a workbook containing the data you want to filter.

2. *Select* the cell range in a column.
3. *Click* the **Sort & Filter** button under the **Editing** group of the **HOME** tab.
   A drop-down list appears.
4. *Select* the **Filter** option from the drop-down list.
   A down arrow button appears on the head of the selected column (Fig.EX-2.92).
5. *Click* the down arrow button (Fig.EX-2.92).
   A drop-down list appears, displaying various sort and filter options, as well as the check boxes, with the values of the selected column (Fig.EX-2.92). You can filter data in the column by selecting or clearing the check boxes (Fig.EX-2.92).
6. *Place* the mouse pointer over desired filtering option in the drop-down list. In our case, we have placed the mouse pointer over **Number Filters** option (Fig.EX-2.92).
   A list of options appears (Fig.EX-2.92).
7. *Select* the desired option from the list of options to specify the condition based on which you want to filter the data. In our case, we have selected the **Above Average** option as shown in Fig.EX-2.92:

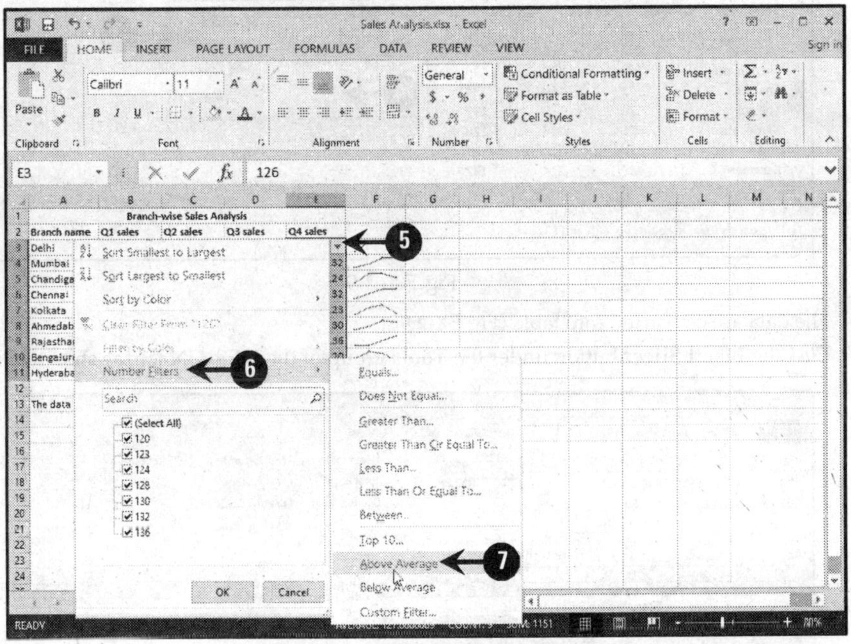

Fig.EX-2.92

The worksheet displays the filtered values based on the selected column, as shown in Fig.EX-2.93:

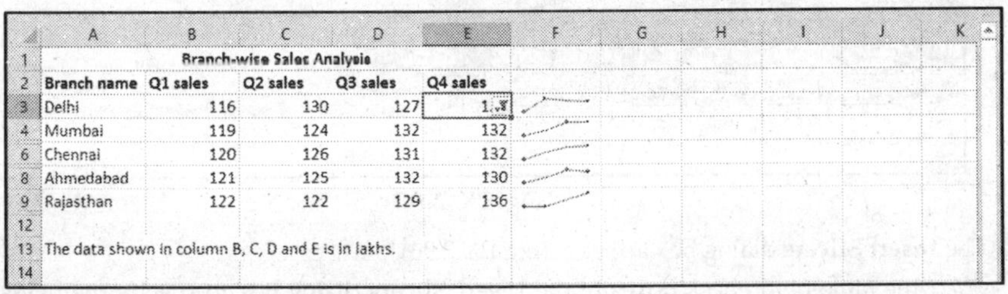

Branch name	Q1 sales	Q2 sales	Q3 sales	Q4 sales
Delhi	116	130	127	1...
Mumbai	119	124	132	132
Chennai	120	126	131	132
Ahmedabad	121	125	132	130
Rajasthan	122	122	129	136

Branch-wise Sales Analysis

The data shown in column B, C, D and E is in lakhs.

Fig.EX-2.93

Let us learn to filter table data by using slicer.

Filtering Table Data Using Slicer

The slicer tool allows you to filter the data of a table in the Excel worksheet. This tool provides interactive visual controls with a user-friendly interface. In Excel 2013, you can use slicers to not only quickly filter the data of a table, but also to indicate the current filtering state, which makes it easy to understand what exactly is shown in a filtered table data.

Perform the following steps to filter table data by using slicer:

1. *Open* a workbook containing the data you want to filter.
2. *Click* the **Table** button under the **Tables** group of the **INSERT** tab.

   The **Create Table** dialog box appears (Fig.EX-2.94).
3. *Select* the cell range that you want to convert into a table. In our case, we have selected the cell range **A2:E11** (Fig.EX-2.94).
4. *Click* the **OK** button, as shown in Fig.EX-2.94:

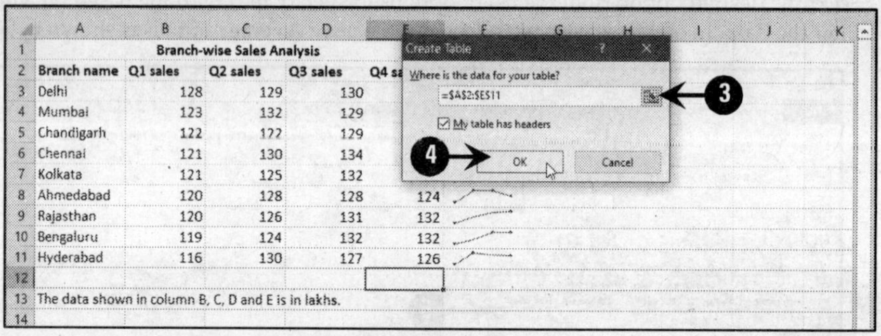

Fig.EX-2.94

   The data are converted into table (Fig.EX-2.95).
5. *Click* the **Insert Slicer** button under the **Tools** group of the **DESIGN** tab, as shown in Fig.EX-2.95:

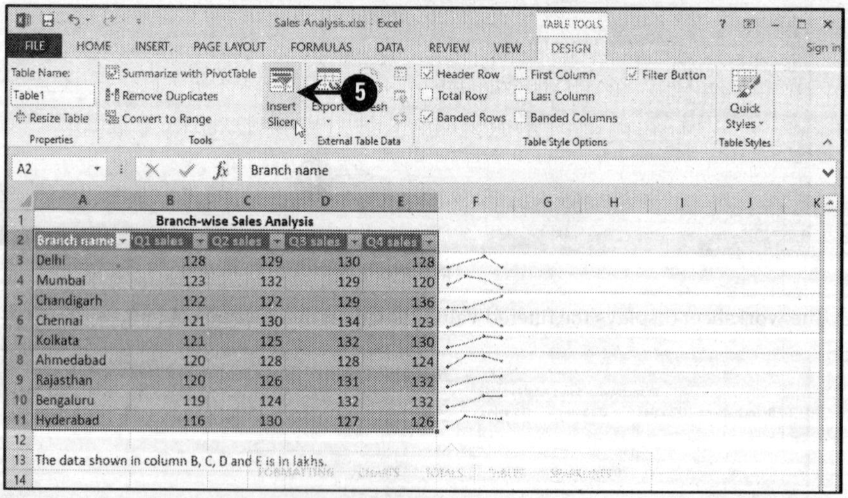

Fig.EX-2.95

   The **Insert Slicers** dialog box appears (Fig.EX-2.96).
6. *Select* the table field check boxes in the **Insert Slicers** dialog box to specify the fields for which you want to create slicers (Fig.EX-2.96).

7. *Click* the **OK** button to insert the slicers, as shown in Fig.EX-2.96:

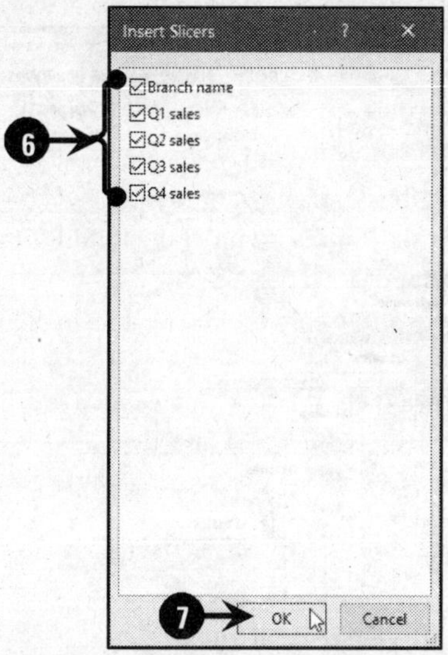

Fig.EX-2.96

Slicers are displayed with the fields you selected in the **Insert Slicers** dialog box along with the items of the fields (Fig.EX-2.97).

8. *Select* the item in the slicer based on which you want to filter the data of the table, as shown inFig.EX-2.97:

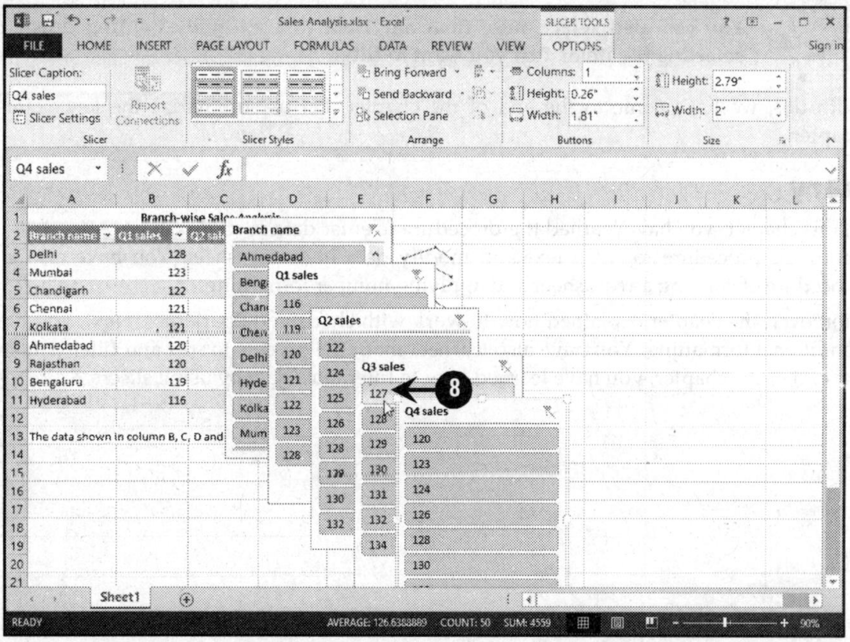

Fig.EX-2.97

Even though a value appears more than one time in a column, the slicer shows it only once.

The items in all the other slicers (that is, **Branch, Q1 sales, Q3 sales**, and **Q4 sales**) related to the **Q3 sales** item become active while the other slicer items remain inactive, as shown in Fig.EX-2.98:

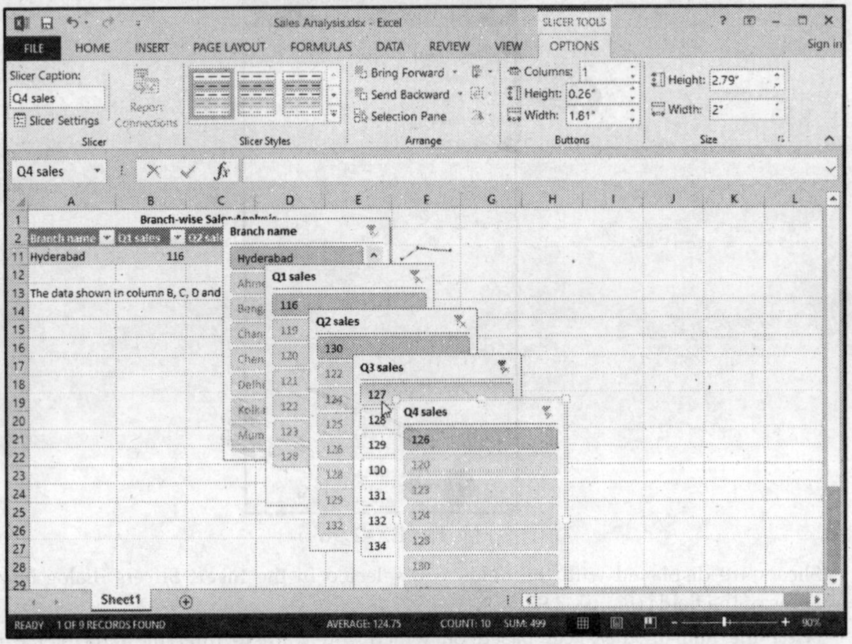

Fig.EX-2.98

You can also select more than one item in a slicer by holding down the ctrl key and selecting the items that you want to filter.

With this, we have come to the end of the chapter. Let us summarize the key points learned in this chapter.

Summary

In this chapter, you have learned the procedure to enter data in a worksheet. After this, you have learned about the procedure to wrap text and modify data in a worksheet. You have also learned about the procedure of copying a worksheet and applying number formatting.

Moreover, the chapter explained how to work with charts and Sparklines. Next, you have learned about conditional formatting. You have also learned about the process to sort and filter data in Excel. Towards the end of the chapter, you have learned how to filter table data by using slicers.

CHAPTER

3

Working With Formulas and Functions

In this Chapter:

* Understanding Formulas
* Exploring Cell Referencing
* Defining the Basic Concepts used in a Function
* Using Mathematical and Statistical Functions
* Working with Logical Functions
* Working with Lookup and Reference
* Working with Auditing Tools

Introduction

In Excel 2013, formulas and functions are important applications. These applications are useful in performing complex mathematical calculations on a large amount of data and derive accurate results easily and quickly. A formula is an equation or an expression, which is used to perform calculations on data; whereas, a function is a predefined formula that takes a value, performs calculation on the value, and returns a value as a result. The values that are used in a function are called arguments, and must appear in a specific order. The functions are used for simplifying formulas, especially those formulas that are used for performing long and complex calculations.

In this chapter, you learn about the basic concepts used in formulas. Next, you learn about the concept of cell references and the basic concepts of a function. Besides this, you learn to use mathematical, logical, lookup and reference functions. Finally, you learn to check errors in a function using the auditing tools.

Understanding Formulas

Formulas are the integral part of Excel. A formula is a set of symbols and values that performs calculations and returns a result. The symbols used in formulas are known as operators. In Excel, a formula always starts with an equal sign (=), followed by an equation or an expression. The formulas are used to perform basic calculations, such as addition, subtraction, or finding the average, as well as complex calculations, such as finding the standard deviation of sample data or the hyperbolic tangent of a number. To understand the formulas more clearly, a basic understanding of some of the terms, such as operators, operator precedence, and cell referencing, is needed.

Let us first discuss how to create a simple formula.

Create a Simple Formula

In Excel 2013, you can create a simple formula in your worksheet for performing operations, such as addition, subtraction, multiplication, or division. Note that a simple formula starts with an equal sign (=) followed by constants, such as numeric values and calculation operators. Perform the following steps to create a formula in Excel:

1. *Open* an Excel workbook.
2. *Select* the cell where you want to create the formula. In our case, we have selected the cell **B2**.
3. *Type* the = (equal sign) operator in the selected cell (Fig.EX-3.1).
4. *Type* the calculation constants and operators in the selected cell (Fig.EX-3.1).
5. *Press* the **Enter** key.

   Excel computes the formula and displays the result in the selected cell, as shown in Fig.EX-3.2:

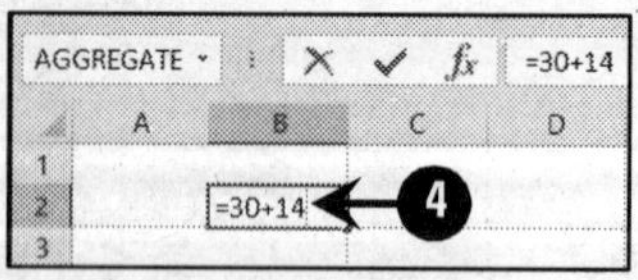

Fig.EX-3.1

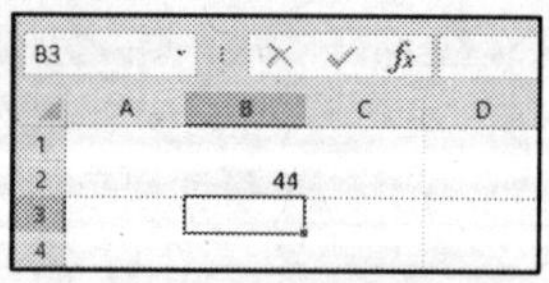

Fig.EX-3.2

Similarly, you can create other formulas using mathematical operators such as addition, multiplication, division, and subtraction.

Let us now learn about cell referencing.

Exploring Cell Referencing

A cell reference refers to a cell or a range of cells in an Excel worksheet, where the values or data used in a formula, function, chart, and Excel commands, are displayed. These cells are referenced by their addresses, which consist of a number that specifies the row of the cell and a letter that specifies the column of the cell. With cell referencing, one formula can use the data held in different parts of a worksheet, or several formulas can use the value of one cell. The following three types of cell references are used in Excel:

- Absolute cell references
- Relative cell references
- Mixed cell references

Let us discuss the types of cell referencing in detail.

Absolute Cell References

In Excel, an absolute cell reference determines the location of a cell or cell range. In absolute cell reference, the address of the cell consists of a column letter and a row number enclosed by dollar signs ($), for example, A2 and B4. Absolute cell reference is used when the cell reference is needed to remain fixed on a specific cell.

Fig.EX-3.3 shows an example of absolute cell reference:

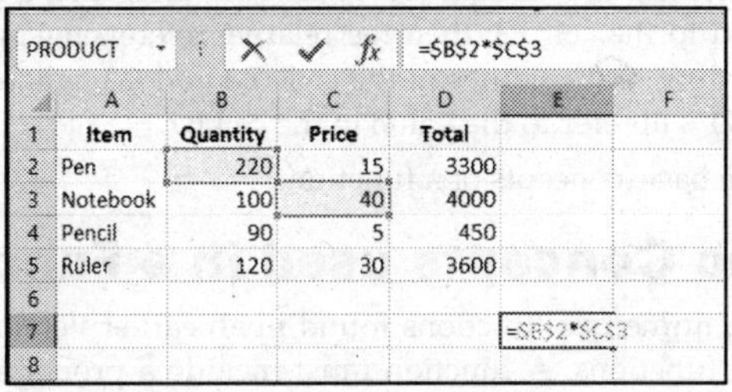

Fig.EX-3.3

In Fig.EX-3.3, the cell addresses **B2** and **C3** are represented as **B2** and **C3**, respectively, which indicate that they are absolute references.

Let us discuss relative cell referencing.

Relative Cell References

In relative cell referencing, the reference of a cell is based on the relative position of the cell that contains the formula. In this case, changing the location of a formula changes the address of the referenced cells. Fig.EX-3.4 and Fig.EX-3.5 show an example of relative cell referencing:

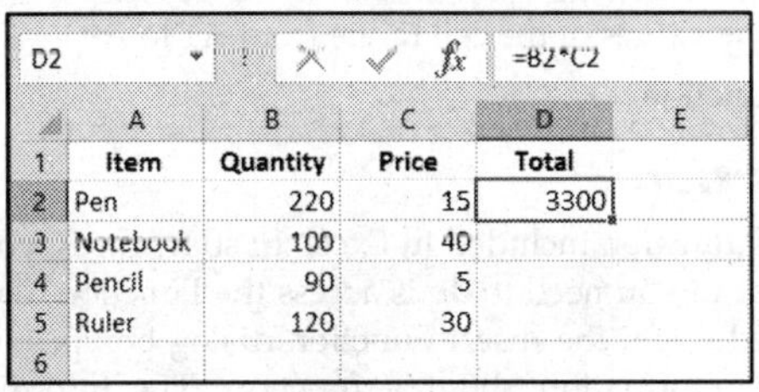

Fig.EX-3.4

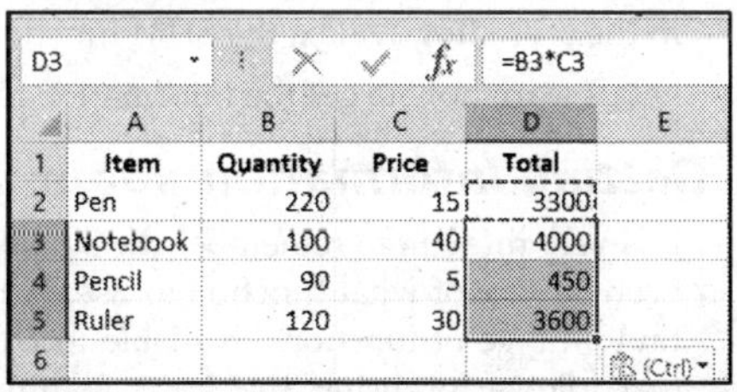

Fig.EX-3.5

In Fig.EX-3.4, the cell **D2** contains a formula **B2*C2**. In Fig.EX-3.5, when the formula of the cell **D2** is copied and applied to the cell **D3**, relative referencing ensures that the formula is adjusted according to the values in the cells **B3** and **C3**. This is because the result in the cell **D3** reflects the product of the corresponding values of the cells **B3** and **C3**.

Let us now learn about mixed cell referencing.

Mixed Cell References

As the name suggests, mixed cell references use both absolute and relative referencing. Fig.EX-3.6 shows an example of mixed referencing:

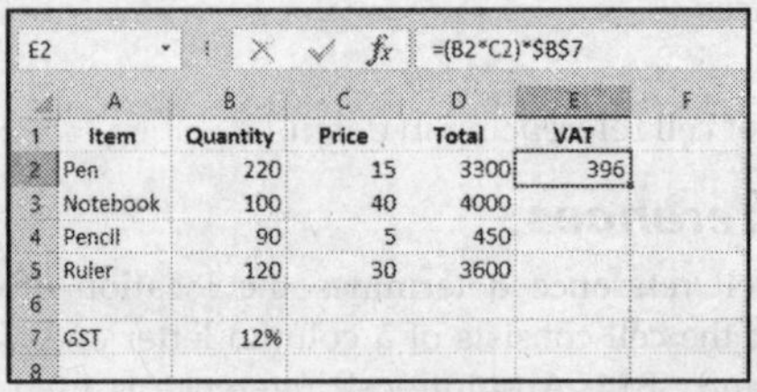

Fig.EX-3.6

In Fig.EX-3.6, we have entered the formula **(B2*C2)*B7** in the cell **E2**. In other words, the formula uses both relative cell referencing **(B2*C2)** as well as absolute referencing **B7**. This means that if the formula of the cell **E2** is copied to the cell **E3**, then the relative referencing will ensure that the formula **(B2*C2)** will be adjusted according to the values in the cells **B3** and **C3**; whereas absolute referencing will ensure that the formula **(B7)** will refer to the value in the cell **B7**.

Let us now discuss the basic concepts of a function.

Defining the Basic Concepts used in a Function

Apart from providing numerous functions found in an earlier version of Excel, the new Excel 2013 also provides several new functions. A function must include a proper syntax and proper arguments to be able to perform an operation. If the proper syntax is not used or incorrect arguments are passed, then the function generates an error.

Let us learn the function syntax.

Explaining the Function Syntax

A function begins with the equal sign (=), followed by the name of the function and its arguments. The name of the function indicates the operation it will perform. The arguments in a function are present inside round brackets. For example, one of the most commonly used functions in Excel, SUM, is used for adding up the data in the cells. The syntax of the SUM function is as follows:

```
=SUM (A1:A9)
```

In the preceding syntax, the SUM function adds the values of the cell range from A1 to A9.

Let us learn how to get the information about a function.

Getting Information about a Function

It is very difficult to remember the syntax of each function included in Excel. In some cases, you may not even be sure of what function to use. In that case, all you need to do is access the Function dialog box to find a range of functions available in Excel. In addition, the Insert Function dialog box provides a link that allows for using the Help feature to get information about a function. The information is a description of what the function does as well as its syntax.

Perform the following steps to get information about a function in Excel:

1. *Open* a new or existing workbook.
2. *Click* the **Insert Function** button, as shown in Fig.EX-3.7:

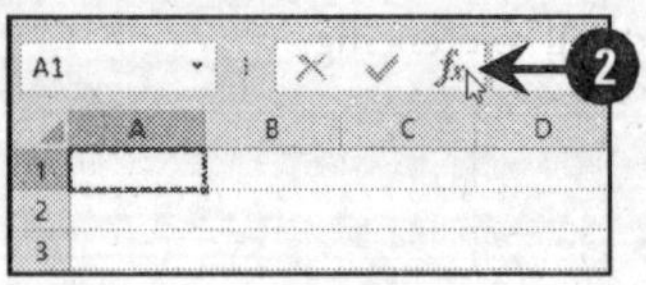

Fig.EX-3.7

The **Insert Function** dialog box appears (Fig.EX-3.8).

3. *Click* the down-arrow button of the **Or select a category** option in the **Insert Function** dialog box (Fig.EX-3.8). A drop-down list appears (Fig.EX-3.8).
4. *Select* the desired function category from the drop-down list. In our case, we have selected **Date & Time** category (Fig.EX-3.8).

   The functions in the **Select a function** list box change according to the selected function category.
5. *Select* the desired function from the **Select a function** list box. In our case, we have selected the **Day** function (Fig.EX-3.9).
6. *Click* the **Help on this function** link in the **Insert Function** dialog box, as shown in Fig.EX-3.9:

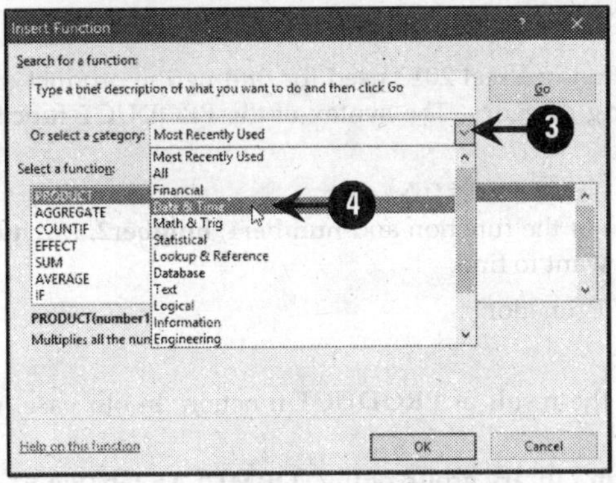

Fig.EX-3.8

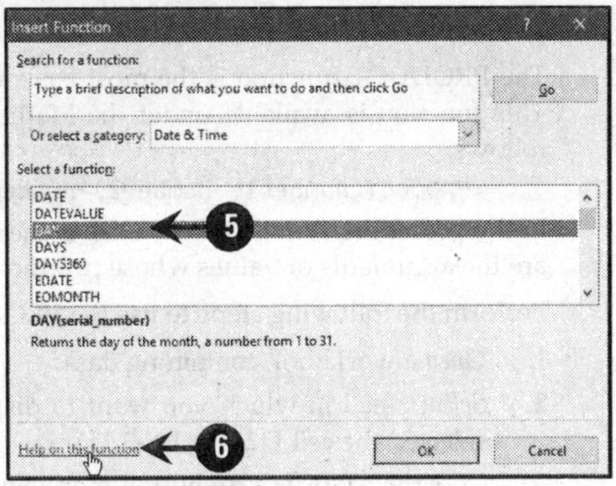

Fig.EX-3.9

The **Excel Help** window appears, as shown in Fig.EX-3.10:

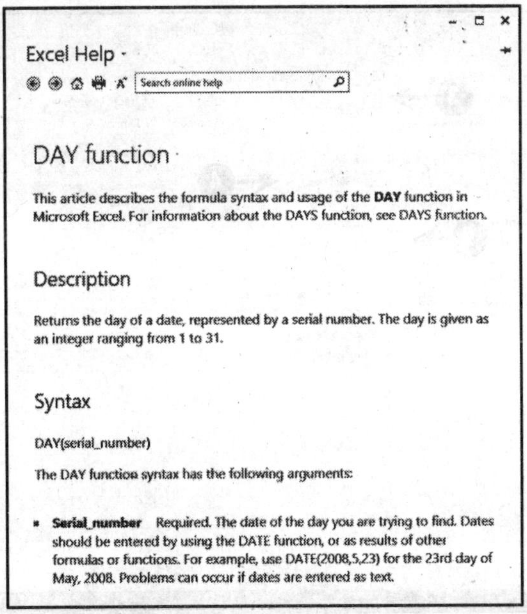

Fig.EX-3.10

As shown in Fig.EX-3.10, the **Excel Help** window contains all the necessary information of the selected function, including its syntax.

Let us learn to work with various types of built-in functions available in Excel, starting with the mathematical and statistical functions.

Using Mathematical and Statistical Functions

Mathematical functions in Excel are used to perform calculations such as the sum, average, and product of the values in a cell range. Statistical functions, on the other hand, are used to analyze values. For example, you can use statistical functions to find out the greatest or smallest value in a range. In Excel 2013, the mathematical functions can be accessed by clicking the Math & Trig button and the statistical functions by selecting the Statistical option from the drop-down list that appears when the More Functions button is clicked. Both these buttons are located in the Function Library group under the Formulas tab of the ribbon. These options can also be accessed from the Insert Function dialog box. This dialog box appears when the Insert Function button is clicked.

The PRODUCT Function

The PRODUCT function is the most basic function in Excel 2013 used for finding the product of values. This function is available under the Math & Trig category. The syntax of the PRODUCT function is as follows:

```
=PRODUCT(number1, number2, number 3, ........, number N)
```

In the preceding syntax, **PRODUCT** is the name of the function and **number1, number2, …., number N** are the arguments or values whose product you want to find.

Perform the following steps to use the PRODUCT function:

1. *Open* a workbook containing data.
2. *Select* a cell in which you want to display the result of **PRODUCT** function. In our case, we have selected the cell **D2** (Fig.EX-3.11).
3. *Click* the **Math & Trig** button in the **Function Library** group of the **FORMULAS** tab (Fig.EX-3.11). A drop-down list appears (Fig.EX-3.11).
4. *Select* the **PRODUCT** option from the drop-down list, as shown in Fig.EX-3.11:

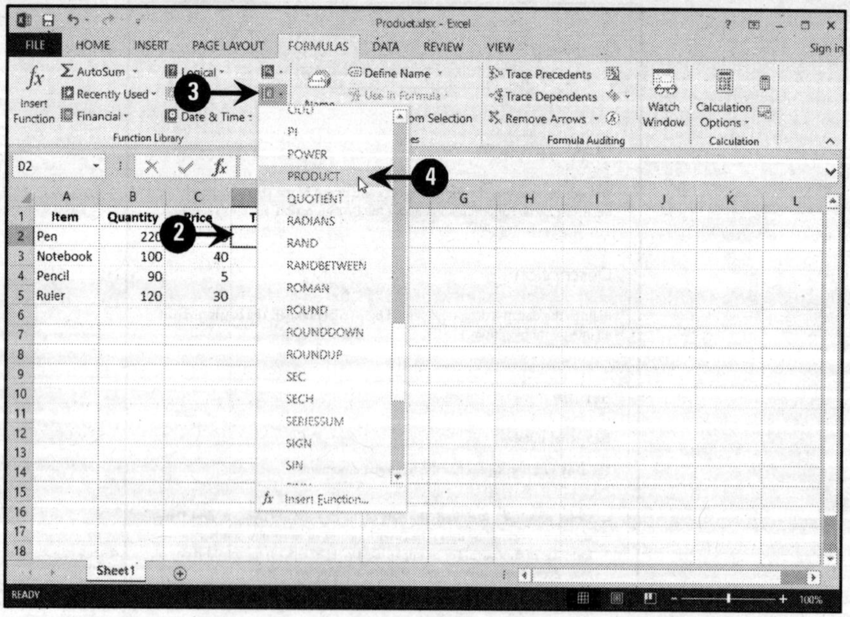

Fig.EX-3.11

The **Function Arguments** dialog box appears (Fig.EX-3.12).

5. *Select* a cell range in the worksheet on which you want to apply the **PRODUCT** function. In our case, we have selected the cell range **B2:C2** (Fig.EX-3.12).

6. *Click* the **OK** button, as shown in Fig.EX-3.12:

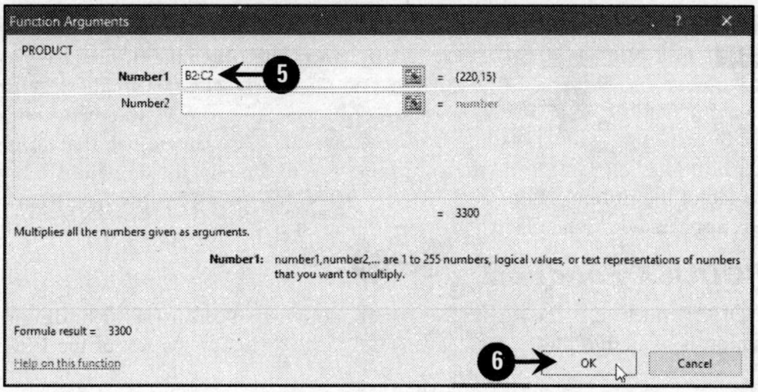

Fig.EX-3.12

The values of the selected cell range are multiplied and the result appears in the **D2** cell (Fig.EX-3.13). Similarly, you can calculate the multiplication of other fields, as shown in Fig. EX-3.14:

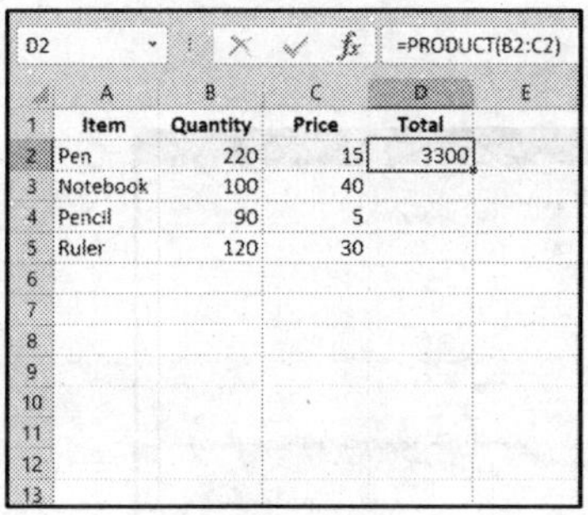

Fig.EX-3.13

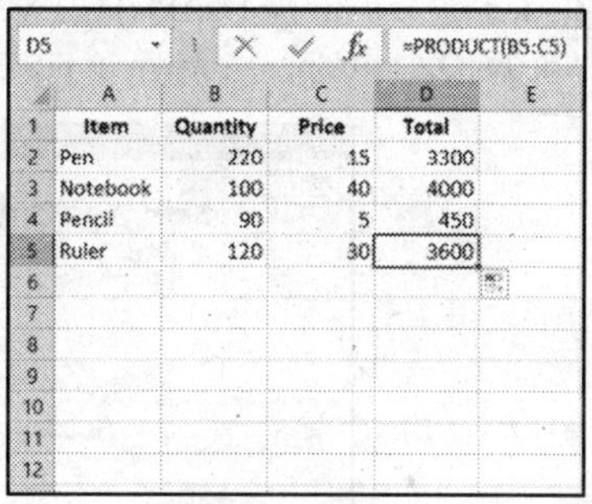

Fig.EX-3.14

The SUM Function

The SUM function is the most basic function in Excel that is used to add the values in a range of cells. The syntax of the SUM function is as follows:

```
=SUM(number1, number2, number 3, ........, number N)
```

In the preceding syntax, **SUM** is the name of the function and **number1, number2, ..., number N** are the arguments or values whose sum you want to find.

Perform the following steps to add values by using the SUM function in a worksheet:

1. *Open* a new or an existing workbook.
2. *Select* the cell in which you want to display the result of the **SUM** function. In our case, we have selected the cell **D6** (Fig.EX-3.15).
3. *Click* the **Math & Trig** button in the **Function Library** group of the **FORMULAS** tab (Fig.EX-3.15). A drop-down list appears (Fig.EX-3.15).

4. *Select* the **SUM** option from the drop-down list, as shown in Fig.EX-3.15:

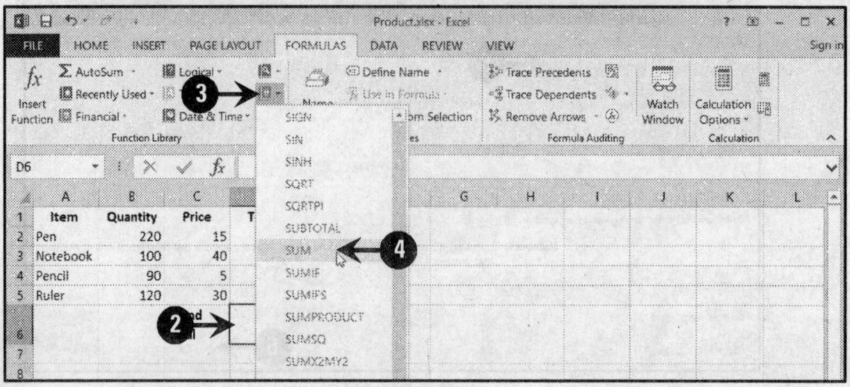

Fig.EX-3.15

The **Function Arguments** dialog box appears (Fig.EX-3.16).

5. *Select* the cell range whose sum you want to find in the **Number1** text box. In our case, we have selected the cell range **D2:D5** (Fig.EX-3.16).
6. *Click* the **OK** button, as shown in Fig.EX-3.16:

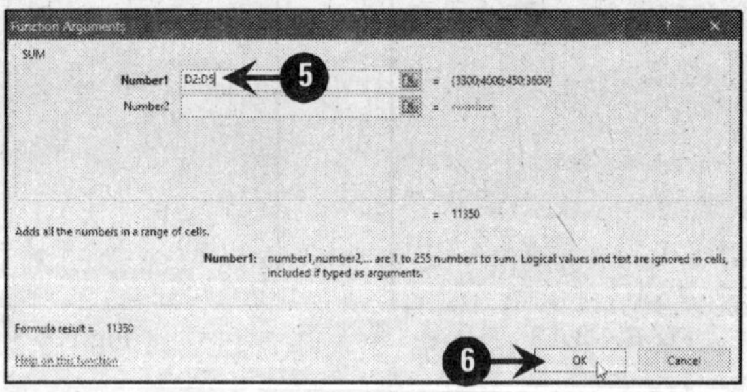

Fig.EX-3.16

The sum of the selected cell range is displayed in the active cell, as shown in Fig.EX-3.17:

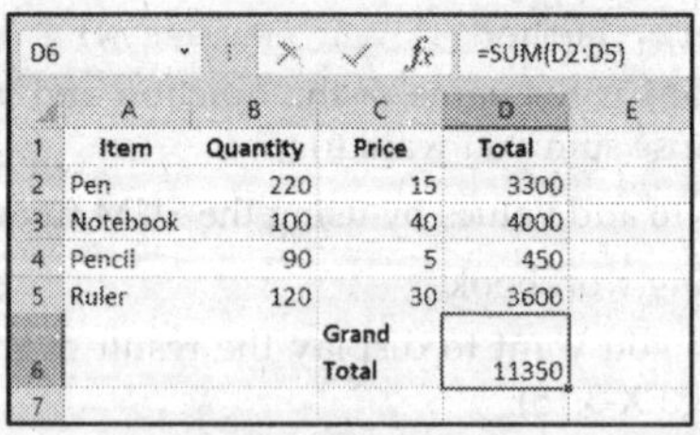

Fig.EX-3.17

The ROUND Function

The ROUND function is used to round a value or a number to a specified number of digits. The syntax of the ROUND function is as follows:

```
=ROUND(number, num_digits)
```

In the preceding syntax, **ROUND** is the name of the function, **number** specifies the number that you want to round, and **num_digits** specifies the number of places to which you want to round the number.

Perform the following steps to round a number by using the ROUND function in a worksheet:

1. *Open* a workbook that contains some decimal data.
2. *Select* the cell in which you want to display the result after applying the **ROUND** function. In our case, we have selected the cell **E7** (Fig.EX-3.18).
3. *Click* the **Math & Trig** button in the **Function Library** group of the **FORMULAS** tab (Fig.EX-3.18). A drop-down list appears (Fig.EX-3.18).
4. *Select* the **ROUND** option from the drop-down list, as shown in Fig.EX-3.18:

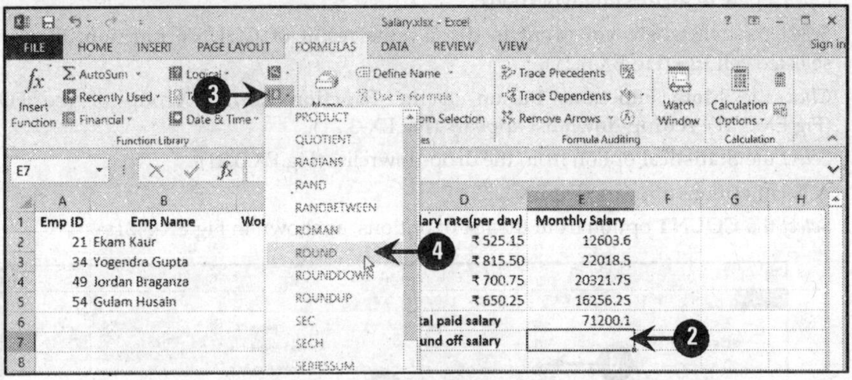

Fig.EX-3.18

The **Function Arguments** dialog box appears (Fig.EX-3.19).

5. *Enter* the cell address or cell range that contains the number you want to round in the **Number** text box. In our case, we have typed the cell address **E6** (Fig.EX-3.19).
6. *Type* the number in the **Num_digits** text box to specify the number of digits to which you want to round the number. In our case, we have typed **0** (Fig.EX-3.19).
7. *Click* the **OK** button, as shown in Fig.EX-3.19:

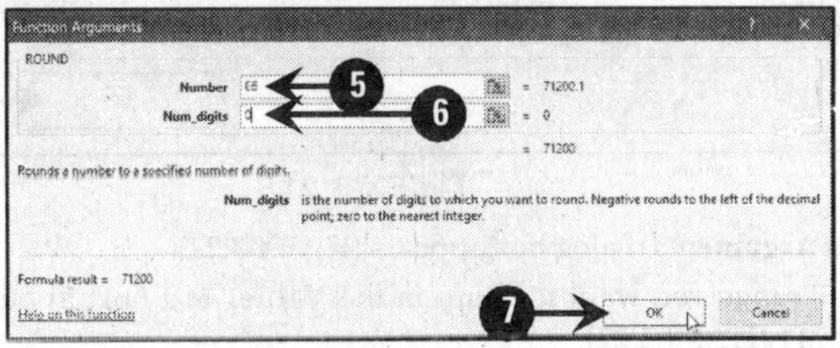

Fig.EX-3.19

The selected number is rounded to the specified number of digits and displayed in the active cell, as shown in Fig.EX-3.20:

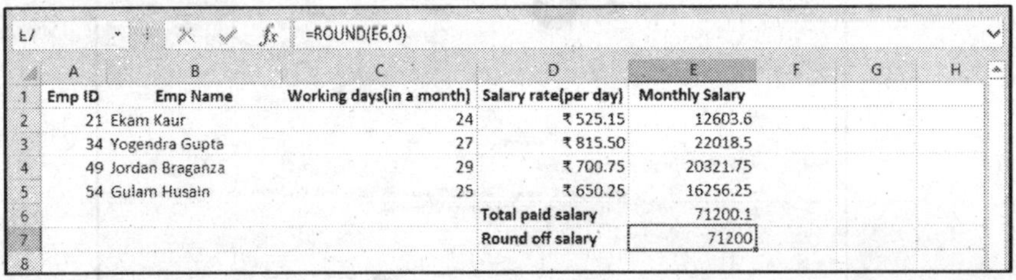

Fig.EX-3.20

The COUNT Function

The COUNT function is used to count the number of entries in the selected range of cell. The COUNT function does not count the blank entries and text data. The syntax of the COUNT function is:

```
=COUNT(number1, number2, number3,..........)
```

In the preceding syntax, **COUNT** is the name of the function and **number1, number2, number3, ...** are the arguments or values on which you want to apply the COUNT function.

Perform the following steps to count the entries in a specified range by using the COUNT function:

1. *Open* a new or an existing workbook.
2. *Select* the cell where you want to display the result of **COUNT** function. In our case, we have selected cell **E13** (Fig.EX-3.21).
3. *Click* the **More Functions** button in the **Function Library** group of the **FORMULAS** tab (Fig.EX-3.21). A drop-down list appears (Fig.EX-3.21).
4. *Select* the **Statistical** option from the drop-down list (Fig.EX-3.21).

   A list of options appears (Fig.EX-3.21).
5. *Select* the **COUNT** option from the list of options, as shown in Fig.EX-3.21:

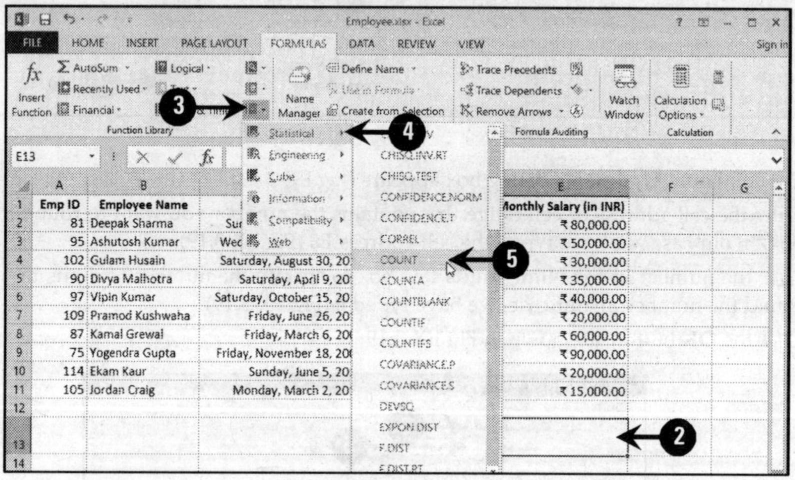

Fig.EX-3.21

The **Function Arguments** dialog box appears (Fig.EX-3.22).

6. *Specify* the cell range you want to count in the **Value1** text box. In our case, we have specified the cell range **E2:E11** (Fig.EX-3.22).
7. *Click* the **OK** button, as shown in Fig.EX-3.22:

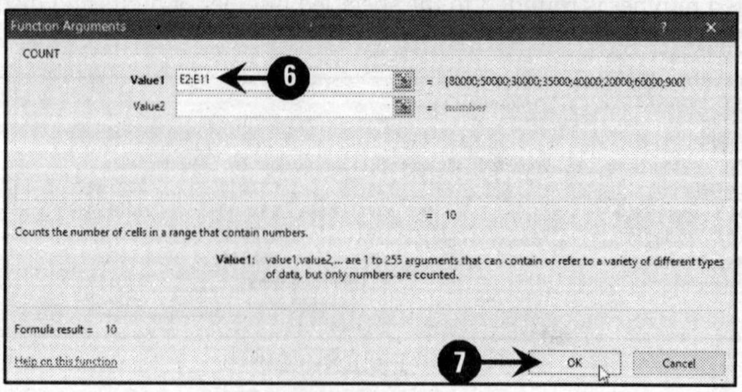

Fig.EX-3.22

The number of entries of the selected cells is displayed in the active cell, as shown in Fig.EX-3.23:

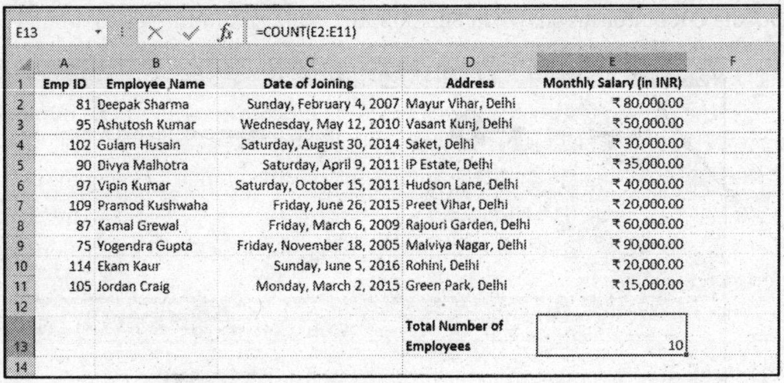

Fig.EX-3.23

The AVERAGE Function

The AVERAGE function calculates the average or mean value of the group of numbers. The average value can be obtained by adding the selected values and dividing the sum by the number of values. The syntax of the AVERAGE function is as follows:

```
=AVERAGE(number1, number2, number3,........)
```

In the preceding syntax, **AVERAGE** is the name of the function and **number1, number2, number3, ...** are the arguments or values on which you want to apply the AVERAGE function.

Perform the following steps to calculate the average of numbers by using the AVERAGE function:

1. *Open* a new or an existing workbook.
2. *Select* the cell in which you want to display the result after applying the **AVERAGE** function. In our case, we have selected the cell **E12** (Fig.EX-3.24).
3. *Click* the **More Functions** button in the **Function Library** group of the **FORMULAS** tab (Fig.EX-3.24). A drop-down list appears (Fig.EX-3.24).
4. *Select* the **Statistical** option from the drop-down list (Fig.EX-3.24).

   A list of options appears (Fig.EX-3.24).
5. *Select* the **AVERAGE** option from the list of options, as shown in Fig.EX-3.24:

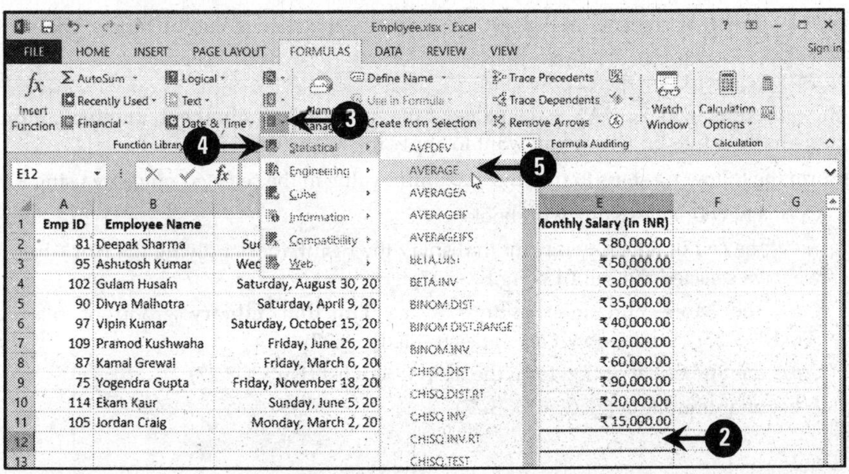

Fig.EX-3.24

The **Function Arguments** dialog box appears (Fig.EX-3.25).

6. *Specify* the cell range whose average you want to obtain in the **Number1** text box. In our case, we have specified the cell range **E2:E11** (Fig.EX-3.25).
7. *Click* the **OK** button, as shown in Fig.EX-3.25:

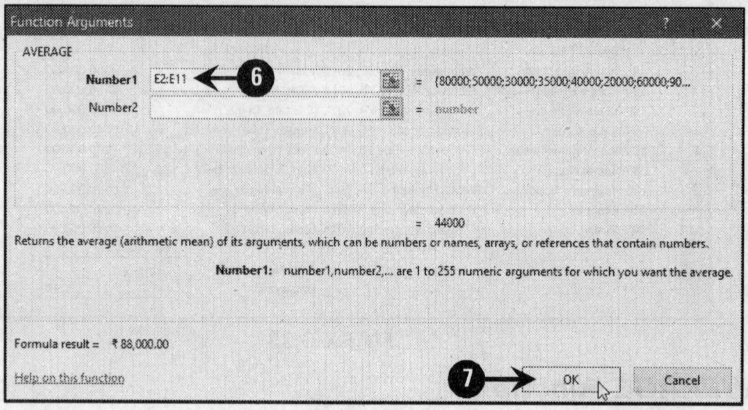

Fig.EX-3.25

The average value of the selected cell range is displayed in the active cell, as shown in Fig.EX-3.26:

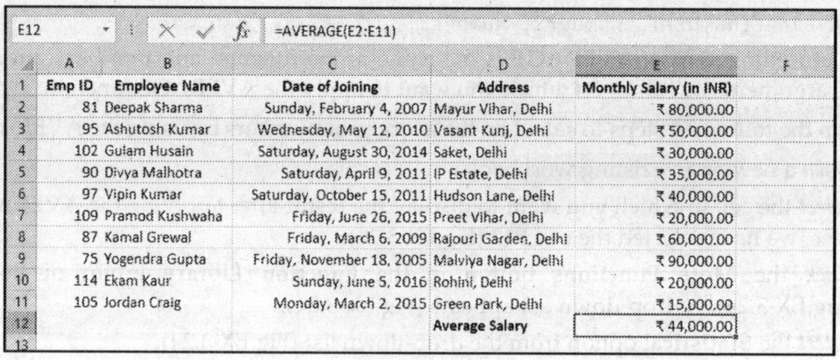
E12 =AVERAGE(E2:E11)

	A	B	C	D	E
1	Emp ID	Employee Name	Date of Joining	Address	Monthly Salary (in INR)
2	81	Deepak Sharma	Sunday, February 4, 2007	Mayur Vihar, Delhi	₹ 80,000.00
3	95	Ashutosh Kumar	Wednesday, May 12, 2010	Vasant Kunj, Delhi	₹ 50,000.00
4	102	Gulam Husain	Saturday, August 30, 2014	Saket, Delhi	₹ 30,000.00
5	90	Divya Malhotra	Saturday, April 9, 2011	IP Estate, Delhi	₹ 35,000.00
6	97	Vipin Kumar	Saturday, October 15, 2011	Hudson Lane, Delhi	₹ 40,000.00
7	109	Pramod Kushwaha	Friday, June 26, 2015	Preet Vihar, Delhi	₹ 20,000.00
8	87	Kamal Grewal	Friday, March 6, 2009	Rajouri Garden, Delhi	₹ 60,000.00
9	75	Yogendra Gupta	Friday, November 18, 2005	Malviya Nagar, Delhi	₹ 90,000.00
10	114	Ekam Kaur	Sunday, June 5, 2016	Rohini, Delhi	₹ 20,000.00
11	105	Jordan Craig	Monday, March 2, 2015	Green Park, Delhi	₹ 15,000.00
12				Average Salary	₹ 44,000.00

Fig.EX-3.26

The MAX Function

The MAX function returns the largest value in the specified value or range. The syntax of the MAX function is:

```
=MAX(number1, number2, number3, ..........)
```

In the preceding syntax, **MAX** is the name of the function and **number1, number2, number3, ...** are the arguments or values on which you want to apply the MAX function.

Perform the following steps to find the maximum value in the selected range by using MAX function:

1. *Open* a new or an existing workbook.
2. *Select* the cell in which you want to display the result after applying the **MAX** function. In our case, we have selected the cell **E13** (Fig.EX-3.27).
3. *Click* the **More Functions** button in the **Function Library** group of the **FORMULAS** tab (Fig.EX-3.27). A drop-down list appears (Fig.EX-3.27).
4. *Select* the **Statistical** option from the drop-down list (Fig.EX-3.27).
   A list of options appears (Fig.EX-3.27).

5. *Select* the **MAX** option from the list of options, as shown in Fig.EX-3.27:

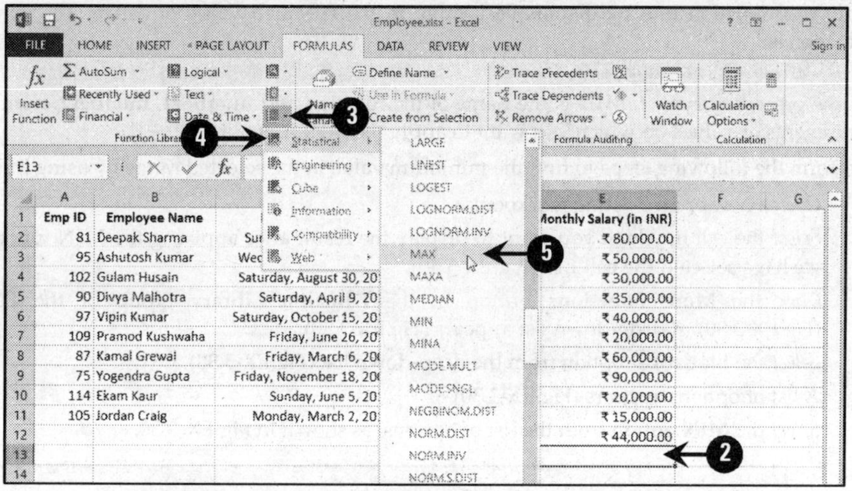

Fig.EX-3.27

The **Function Arguments** dialog box appears (Fig.EX-3.28).

6. *Specify* the cell range from which you want to find the maximum value. In our case, we have specified the cell range **E2:E11** (Fig.EX-3.28).
7. *Click* the **OK** button, as shown in Fig.EX-3.28:

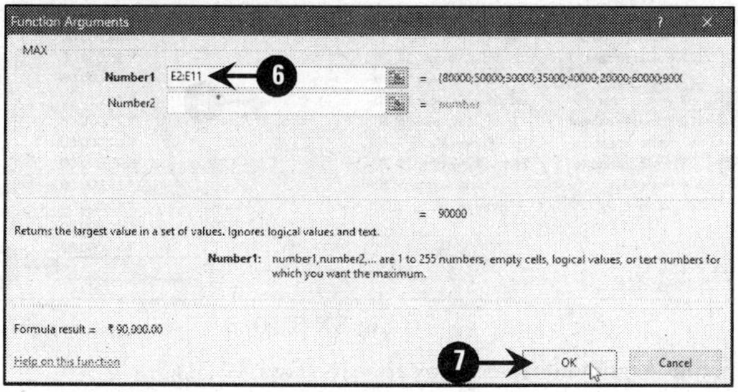

Fig.EX-3.28

The largest value of the selected cell range is displayed in the active cell, as shown in Fig.EX-3.29:

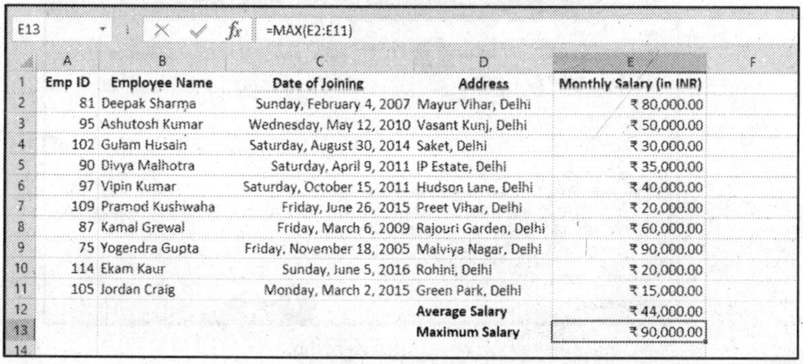

Fig.EX-3.29

The MIN Function

The MIN function returns the smallest value in the specified value or range. The syntax of the MIN function is:

```
=MIN(number1, number2, number3, ..........)
```

In the preceding syntax, **MIN** is the name of the function and **number1, number2, number3, ...** are the arguments or values on which you want to apply the MIN function.

Perform the following steps to find the minimum value in the selected range by using MIN function:

1. *Open* a new or an existing workbook.
2. *Select* the cell in which you want to display the result after applying the **MIN** function. In our case, we have selected the cell **E14** (Fig.EX-3.30).
3. *Click* the **More Functions** button in the **Function Library** group of the **FORMULAS** tab (Fig.EX-3.30). A drop-down list appears (Fig.EX-3.30).
4. *Select* the **Statistical** option from the drop-down list (Fig.EX-3.30).

   A list of options appears (Fig.EX-3.30).
5. *Select* the **MIN** option from the list of options, as shown in Fig.EX-3.30:

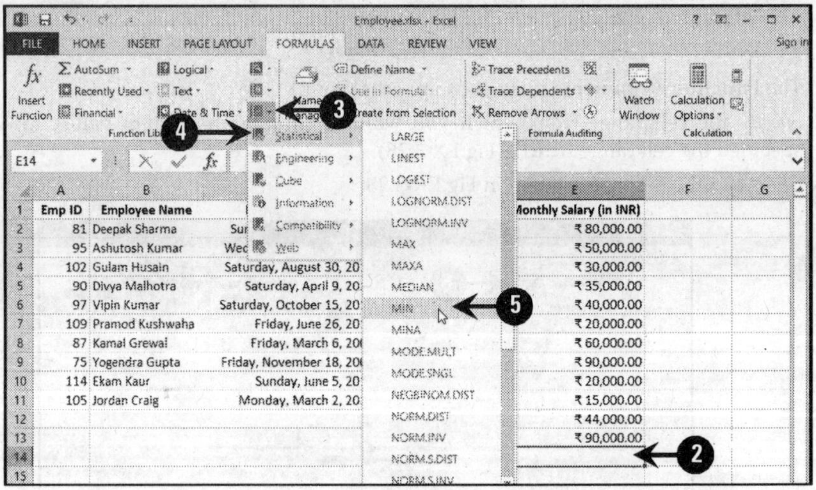

Fig.EX-3.30

   The **Function Arguments** dialog box appears (Fig.EX-3.31).
6. *Specify* the cell range. In our case, we have specified the cell range **E2:E11** (Fig.EX-3.31).
7. *Click* the **OK** button, as shown in Fig.EX-3.31:

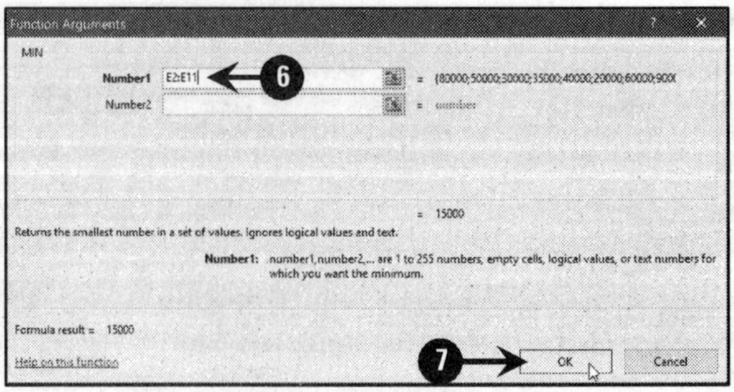

Fig.EX-3.31

The smallest value of the selected cell range is displayed in the active cell, as shown in Fig.EX-3.32:

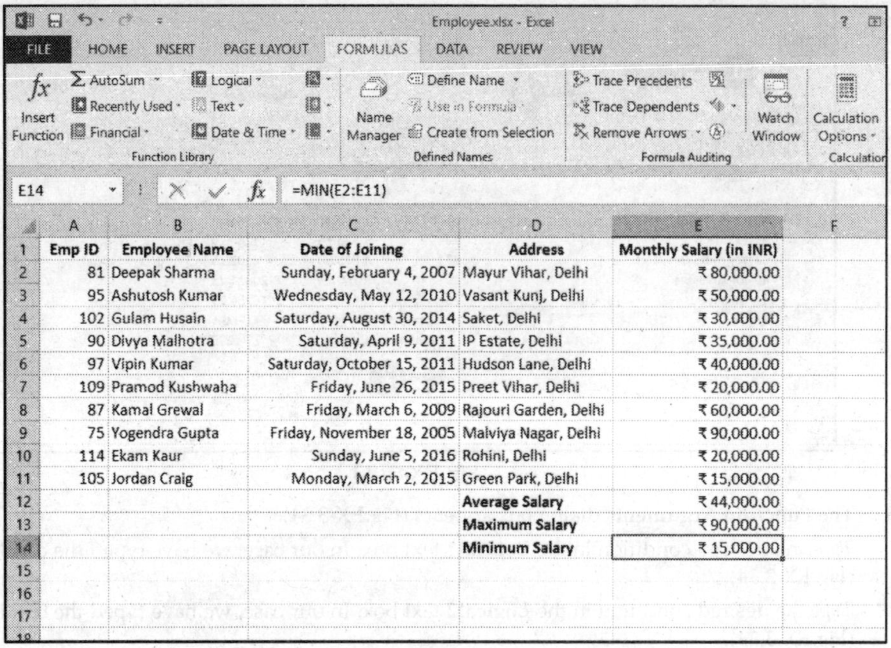

Fig.EX-3.32

Let us now discuss logical functions.

Working with Logical Functions

In Excel, logical functions are used to introduce decision making into a worksheet. In other words, these functions enable us to test a condition for logical TRUE or FALSE. They are usually used in making comparisons and finding out whether the specified values in a formula are equal to each other or not, or which value is higher or lower, and return TRUE or FALSE based on the evaluation of the formula.

Let us now learn to work with some major logical functions.

The AND Function

The AND function returns TRUE if all the arguments used in the function are true; otherwise, it returns FALSE. The syntax of AND function is as follows:

```
=AND(logical1, logical2,…)
```

In the preceding syntax, **AND** is the name of the function; **logical1** is the first condition that you want to test; and **logical2** is an additional condition that you want to test. These conditions can be evaluated to either TRUE or FALSE.

Perform the following steps to use the AND function:

1. *Open* a new or an existing workbook.
2. *Select* the cell in which you want to display the result after applying the **AND** function. In our case, we have selected the cell **C9** (Fig.EX-3.33).
3. *Click* the **Logical** button in the **Function Library** group of the **FORMULAS** tab (Fig.EX-3.33).

   A drop-down list appears (Fig.EX-3.33).

4. *Select* the **AND** option from the drop-down list, as shown in Fig.EX-3.33:

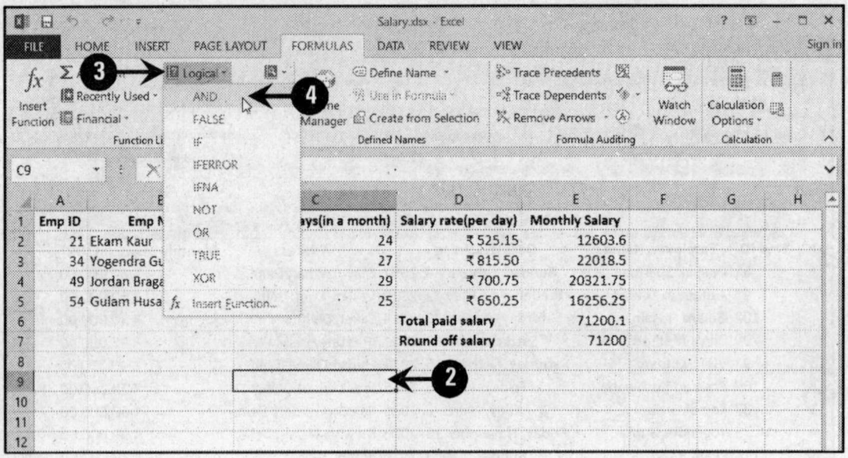

Fig.EX-3.33

The **Function Arguments** dialog box appears (Fig.EX-3.34).

5. *Type* the desired condition in the **Logical1** text box. In our case, we have typed the condition **D2<D3** (Fig.EX-3.34).
6. *Type* the desired condition in the **Logical2** text box. In our case, we have typed the condition **D4>D2** (Fig.EX-3.34).
7. *Click* the **OK** button, as shown in Fig.EX-3.34:

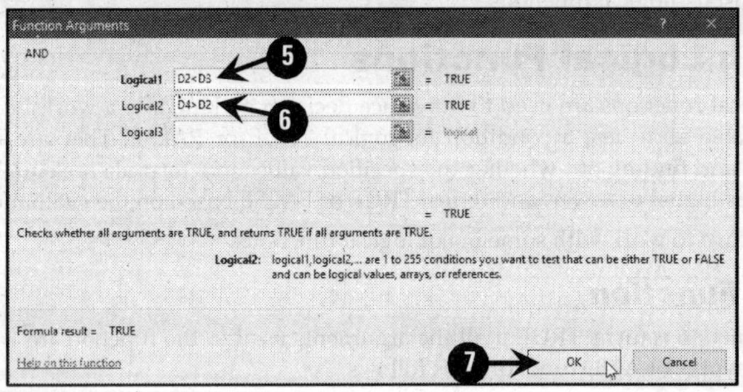

Fig.EX-3.34

The result is displayed in the active cell, as shown in Fig.EX-3.35:

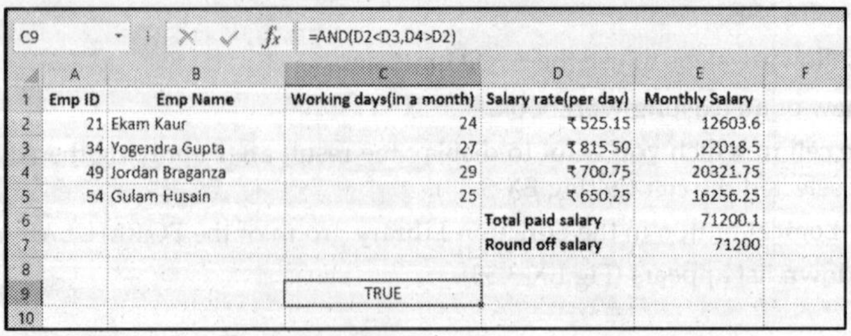

Fig.EX-3.35

The OR Function

The OR function returns TRUE, if any condition is TRUE; and returns FALSE, if all the arguments are FALSE. The syntax of the OR function is as follows:

```
=OR(logical1, logical2, …)
```

In the preceding syntax, **OR** is the name of the function; **logical1** is the first condition that you want to test; and **logical2** is an additional condition that you want to test. These conditions can be evaluated to either TRUE or FALSE.

The main difference between the OR and AND functions is that the OR function returns TRUE if any one of the specified conditions in it is satisfied, and the AND function returns TRUE only when all the specified conditions are satisfied.

Perform the following steps to use the OR function:

1. *Open* a new or an existing workbook.
2. *Select* the cell in which you want to display the result after applying the **OR** function. In our case, we have selected the cell **C9** (Fig.EX-3.36).
3. *Click* the **Logical** button in the **Function Library** group of the **FORMULAS** tab. A drop-down list appears (Fig.EX-3.36).
4. *Select* the **OR** option from the drop-down list, as shown in Fig.EX-3.36:

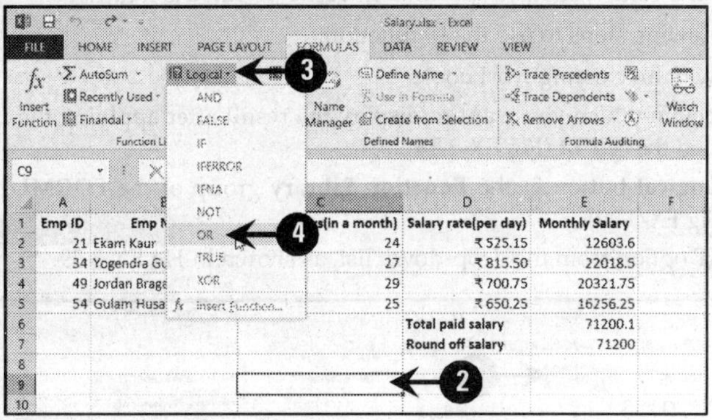

Fig.EX-3.36

The **Function Arguments** dialog box appears (Fig.EX-3.37).

5. *Enter* the desired condition that you want to test in the **Logical1** text box. In our case, we have typed the condition **D4<D5** (Fig.EX-3.37).
6. *Enter* the desired condition that you want to test in the **Logical2** text box. In our case, we have typed the condition **D2<D3** (Fig.EX-3.37).
7. *Click* the **OK** button, as shown in Fig.EX-3.37:

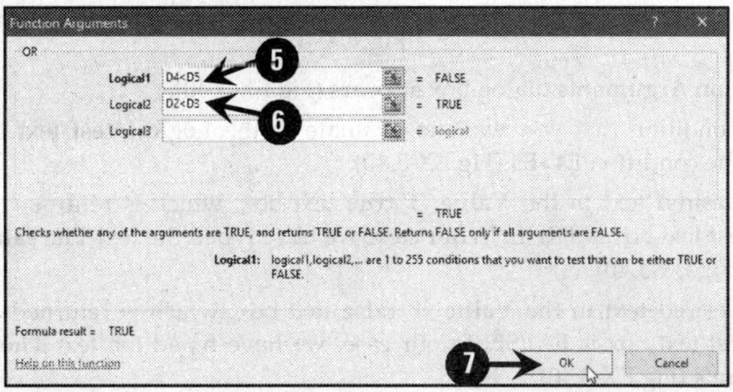

Fig.EX-3.37

The result is displayed in the active cell, as shown in Fig.EX-3.38:

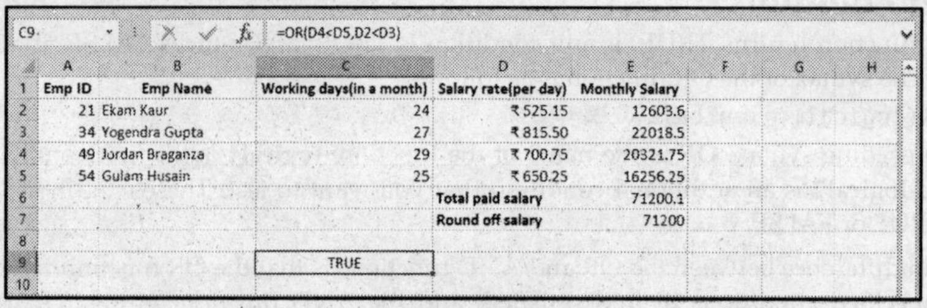

Fig.EX-3.38

The IF Function

The IF function checks to see whether a certain condition is true or false. The function returns one value if the condition evaluates to TRUE, and another value if it evaluates to FALSE. The syntax of the IF function is as follows:

```
=IF(logical_test, [value_if_true], [value_if_false])
```

In the preceding syntax, **IF** is the name of the function and **logical_test** is the condition you want to test. If the condition is satisfied, the value you have specified in **value_if_true** is returned; and if the condition is not satisfied, the value you have specified in **value_if_false** is returned.

Perform the following steps to use the IF function:

1. *Open* a new or an existing workbook.
2. *Select* the cell in which you want to display the result after applying the **IF** function. In our case, we have selected the cell **F4** (Fig.EX-3.39).
3. *Click* the **Logical** button in the **Function Library** group of the **FORMULAS** tab. A drop-down list appears (Fig.EX-3.39).
4. *Select* the **IF** option from the drop-down list, as shown in Fig.EX-3.39:

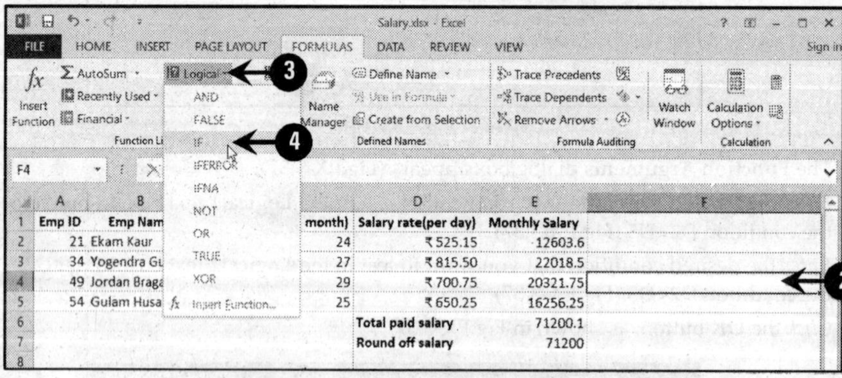

Fig.EX-3.39

The **Function Arguments** dialog box appears (Fig.EX-3.40).

5. *Specify* a condition that you want to evaluate in the **Logical_test** text box. In our case, we have specified the condition **E4>E5** (Fig.EX-3.40).
6. *Type* the desired text in the **Value_if_true** text box, which is returned if the condition set in the **Logical_test** text box is TRUE. In our case, we have typed the text **The salary of Jordan is more than Gulam's** (Fig.EX-3.40).
7. *Type* the desired text in the **Value_if_false** text box, which is returned if the condition set in the **Logical_test** text box is FALSE. In our case, we have typed the text **The salary of Gulam is more than Jordan's** (Fig.EX-3.40).

8. *Click* the **OK** button, as shown in Fig.EX-3.40:

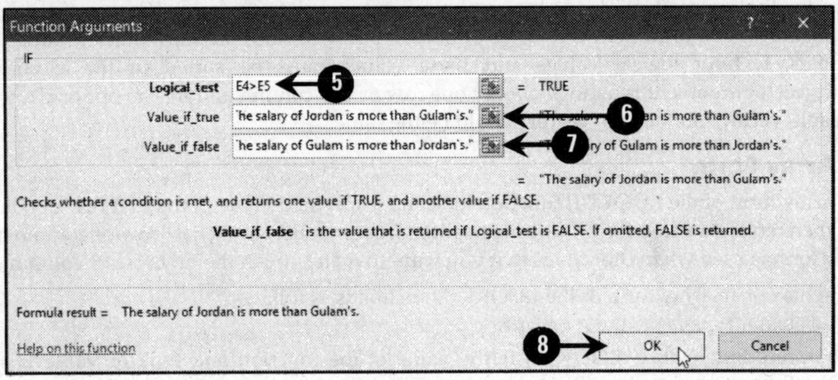

Fig.EX-3.40

The result is displayed in the active cell, as shown in Fig.EX-3.41:

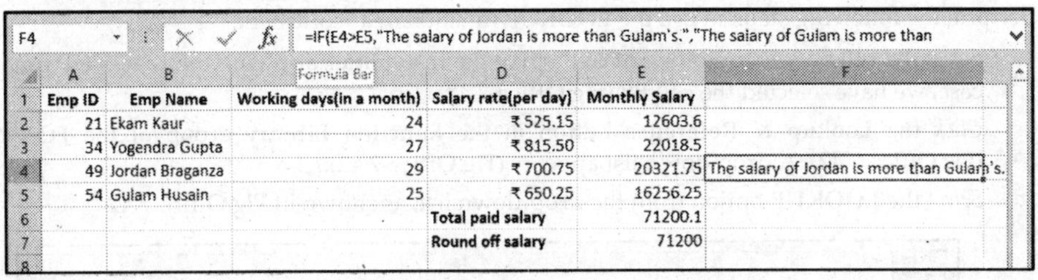

Fig.EX-3.41

Let us now learn about Lookup functions.

Working with the Lookup & Reference Functions

The Lookup & Reference functions in Microsoft Excel are used to simplify the process of retrieving specified data from a cell range in a worksheet. The Lookup functions return a value from a table (that is, a cell range, also known as an array) by looking up columns and rows in the worksheet. The Reference functions are used to retrieve general information from a cell range, such as total number of rows or columns in a specified cell range. The Lookup function return the actual content of a cell and the Reference function returns the reference of the cell whose data you want to use.

Using the LOOKUP Function

The LOOKUP function returns a value either from a single row or column range or from an array. The LOOKUP function works correctly when the data that is looked up needs to be sorted in the ascending order. The LOOKUP function has two forms:

- The vector form
- The array form

The Vector Form

The vector form of LOOKUP searches a value in a one-row or one-column range (known as a vector) and returns a value from the same position in a second one-row or one-column range.

The syntax of a vector form of the LOOKUP function is as follows:

```
=LOOKUP(lookup_value, lookup_vector, [result_vector])
```

In the preceding syntax, **LOOKUP** is the name of the function and **lookup_value** is a value to be looked up in the **lookup_vector**. This value can be a number, text, a logical value, a range name, or reference. The lookup vector argument is a range of only one row or one column. Values in **lookup_vector** can be numbers, text, or logical values and these values must be sorted in the ascending order. The **result_vector** argument is a range of only one row or one column and it is an optional argument. The size of **result_vector** and **lookup_vector** should be the same.

The Array Form

The array form of the LOOKUP function looks up a specified value in the first row or column of an array and then returns a value from the same position (row number) in the last row or column of the array. The array form is used when the values that you want to match are in the first row or column of the array.

The syntax of an array form of the LOOKUP function is as follows:

```
=LOOKUP(lookup_value, array)
```

In the preceding syntax, **LOOKUP** is the name of the function and **lookup_value** is a value that the LOOKUP function searches for in an array. This value can be a number, text, a logical value, a range name, or a reference that refers to a value; **array** is a range of cells that contains text, numbers, or logical values that you compare with **lookup_value**.

Perform the following steps to use the LOOKUP function in a worksheet:

1. *Select* the cell on which you want to display the result after applying the **LOOKUP** function. In our case, we have selected the cell **B8** (Fig.Office-7.42).
2. *Click* the **Lookup & Reference** button in the **Function Library** group of the **FORMULAS** tab (Fig.Office-7.42). A drop-down list appears (Fig.Office-7.42).
3. *Select* the **LOOKUP** option from the drop-down list, as shown in Fig.Office-7.42:

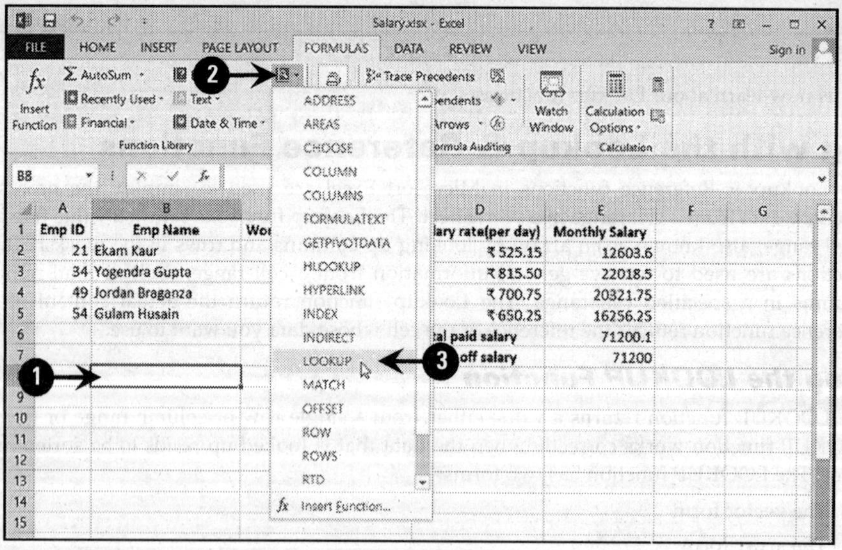

Fig.Office-7.42

The **Select Arguments** dialog box appears (Fig.Office-7.43).

4. *Select* the argument type for the **LOOKUP** function from the **Arguments** list box. In our case, we have selected **lookup_value,array** (Fig.Office-7.43).
5. *Click* the **OK** button (Fig.Office-7.43).

   The **Function Arguments** dialog box appears (Fig.Office-7.44).
6. *Select* the cell that you want the **LOOKUP** function to search in the array. In our case, we have selected the cell **A4** (Fig.Office-7.44).

7. *Select* the cell range or array in the **Array** text box, in which the **Lookup_value** is to be searched. In our case, we have selected the cell range **A1:E5** (Fig.Office-7.44).
8. *Click* the **OK** button, as shown in Fig.Office-7.44:

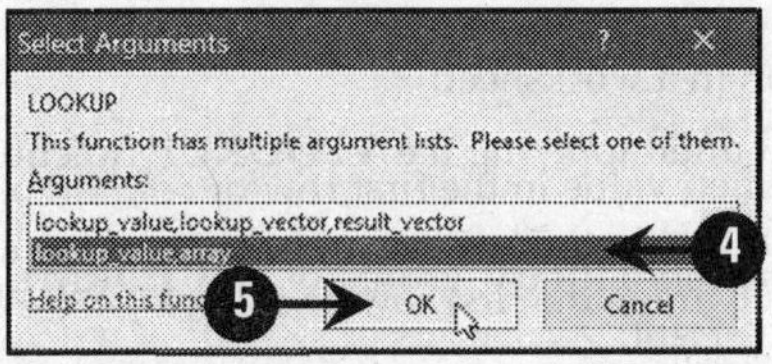

Fig.Office-7.43

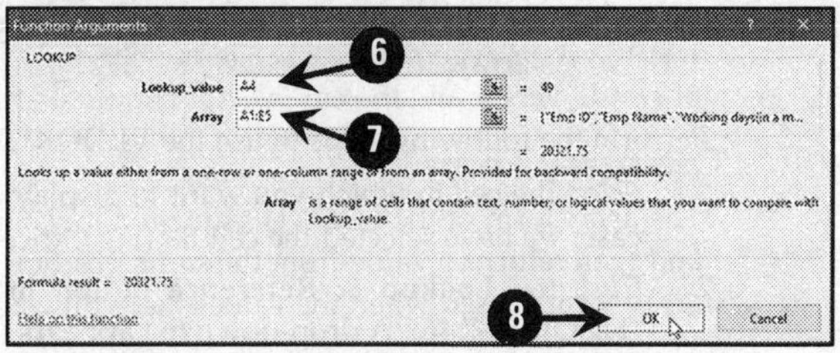

Fig.Office-7.44

The result is displayed in the active cell, as shown in Fig.Office-7.45:

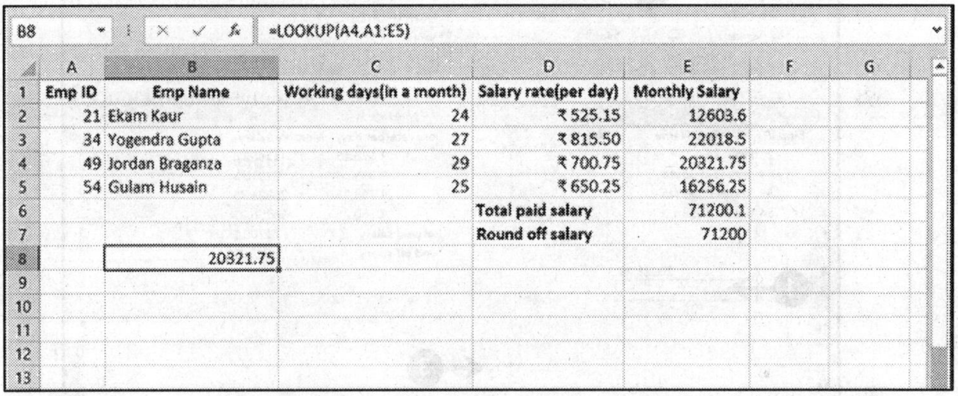

Fig.Office-7.45

Using the VLOOKUP Function

The VLOOKUP function searches a value in the first column of a table array and returns a value in the same row (that is, the row in the first column in which the value is searched) from another column in the table array. The syntax of the VLOOKUP function is as follows:

```
=VLOOKUP(lookup_value, table_array, col_index_num, [range_lookup])
```

In the preceding syntax, **VLOOKUP** is the name of the function, and the various arguments used in the syntax can be described as follows:

- **lookup_value:** Refers to the value that you want to search in the first column of a table array. It can be a value or a reference. If lookup_value is smaller than the smallest value in the first column of the table array, the VLOOKUP function returns the #N/A error.
- **table_array:** Refers to two or more columns of data. The values in the first column of table_array are searched by lookup_value. These values can be text, numbers, or logical values. These values are not case sensitive.
- **col_index_num:** Refers to a column number in table_array from which the matching value is returned. A col_index_num argument of 1 returns the value in the first column in table_array and col_index_num argument of 2 returns the value in the second column in table_array. The VLOOKUP function returns the # VALUE error when the value of col_index_num is less than 1, and returns the #REF error when the value of col_index_num is greater than the total number columns in table_array.
- **range_lookup:** Refers to a logical value that specifies whether you want to find an exactor estimated match. It is an optional argument.

The VLOOKUP function always considers the first selected column of a table array as the starting point to find a value within the table array. It is not mandatory to consider column A or cell A1 as the starting point when using the VLOOKUP function. The starting point for the VLOOKUP function can start from any cell of the first column of the array.

Perform the following steps to use the VLOOKUP function in a worksheet:

1. *Select* the cell in which you want to display the result after applying the **VLOOKUP** function. In our case, we have selected the cell **B9** (Fig.Office-7.46).
2. *Click* the **Lookup & Reference** button in the **Function Library** group of the **FORMULAS** tab (Fig.Office-7.46). A drop-down list appears (Fig.Office-7.46).
3. *Select* the **VLOOKUP** option from the drop-down list, as shown in Fig.Office-7.46:

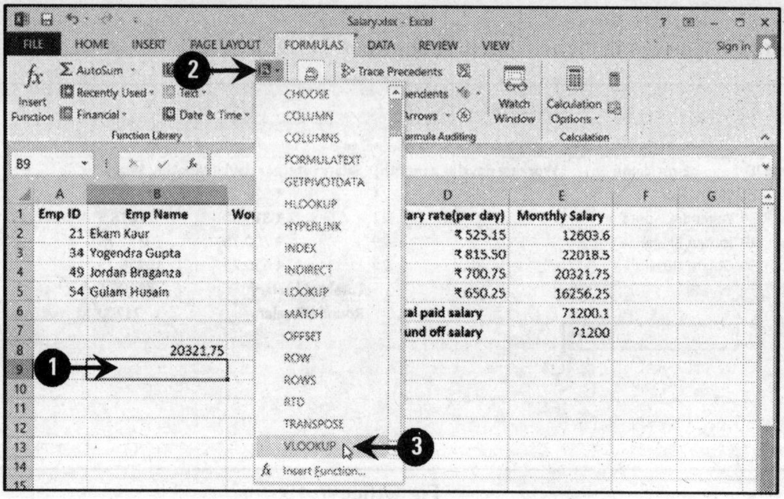

Fig.Office-7.46

The **Function Arguments** dialog box appears (Fig.Office-7.47).

4. *Select* the cell whose value you want to search in the **Lookup_value** text box. In our case, we have selected the cell **A4** (Fig.Office-7.47).
5. *Select* the cell range or array in which **Lookup_value** is to be searched. In our case, we have selected the cell range **A1:E5** (Fig.Office-7.47).
6. *Enter* the column number in the **Col_index_num** text box from which the matching value is to be returned. In our case, we have entered the value 4 (Fig.Office-7.47).
7. *Click* the **OK** button, as shown in Fig.Office-7.47:

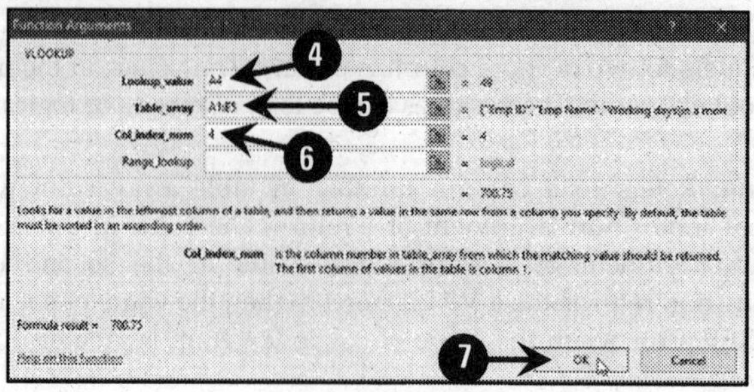

Fig.Office-7.47

The result is displayed in the active cell, as shown in Fig.Office-7.48:

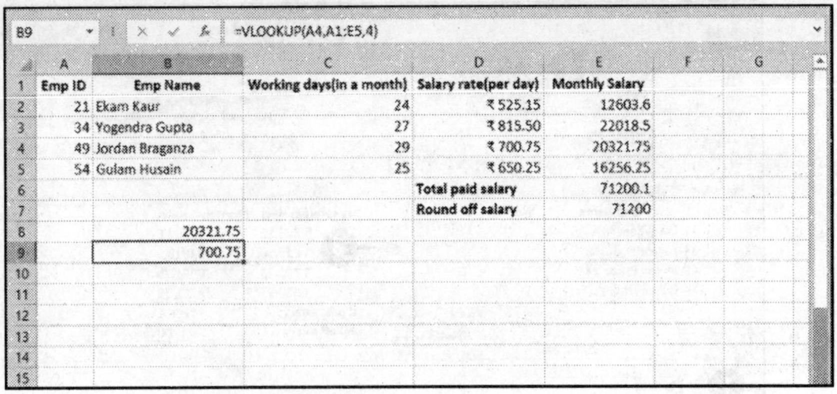

B9 =VLOOKUP(A4,A1:E5,4)

	A	B	C	D	E	F	G
1	Emp ID	Emp Name	Working days(in a month)	Salary rate(per day)	Monthly Salary		
2	21	Ekam Kaur	24	₹ 525.15	12603.6		
3	34	Yogendra Gupta	27	₹ 815.50	22018.5		
4	49	Jordan Braganza	29	₹ 700.75	20321.75		
5	54	Gulam Husain	25	₹ 650.25	16256.25		
6				Total paid salary	71200.1		
7				Round off salary	71200		
8		20321.75					
9		700.75					
10							
11							
12							
13							
14							
15							

Fig.Office-7.48

Using the HLOOKUP Function

The HLOOKUP function searches a value in the first row of a table array and returns a value in the same column (that is, the column in the first row in which the value is searched) from another row in the table array. The syntax of HLOOKUP function is as follows:

```
=HLOOKUP(lookup_value, table_array, row_index_num, [range_lookup])
```

In the preceding syntax, **HLOOKUP** is the name of the function and the various arguments used in the syntax can be described as follows:

- **lookup_value:** Refers to the value that you want to search in the first row of a table array. It can be a value or a reference.
- **table_array:** Refers to a range of cells that contains values. These values can be text, numbers, or logical values. These values are not case sensitive.
- **row_index_num:** Refers to the row number in table_array from which the matching value is returned. A row_index_numargument of 1 returns the value in the first row of table_array and a row_index_numargument of 2 returns the value in the second row from the table array. The HLOOKUP function returns the #VALUE!error value when row_index_num is less than 1 and returns the #REF error value when row_index_num is greater than the total number of rows in the table array.
- **range_lookup:** Refers to a logical value that indicates whether you want to find an exact or an estimated match. It is an optional argument.

The HLOOKUP function always considers the first selected row of a table array as the starting point to find a value within the table array. It is not mandatory to consider row 1 of column A as the starting point when using the HLOOKUP function. The starting point for the HLOOKUP function can start from any cell of the first row of the table array.

Perform the following steps to use the HLOOKUP function in a worksheet:

1. *Select* the cell in which you want to display the result after applying the **HLOOKUP** function. In our case, we have selected the cell **B10** (Fig.Office-7.49).
2. *Click* the **Lookup & Reference** button in the **Function Library** group of the **FORMULAS** tab (Fig.Office-7.49). A drop-down list appears (Fig.Office-7.49).

3. *Select* the **HLOOKUP** option from the drop-down list, as shown in Fig.Office-7.49:

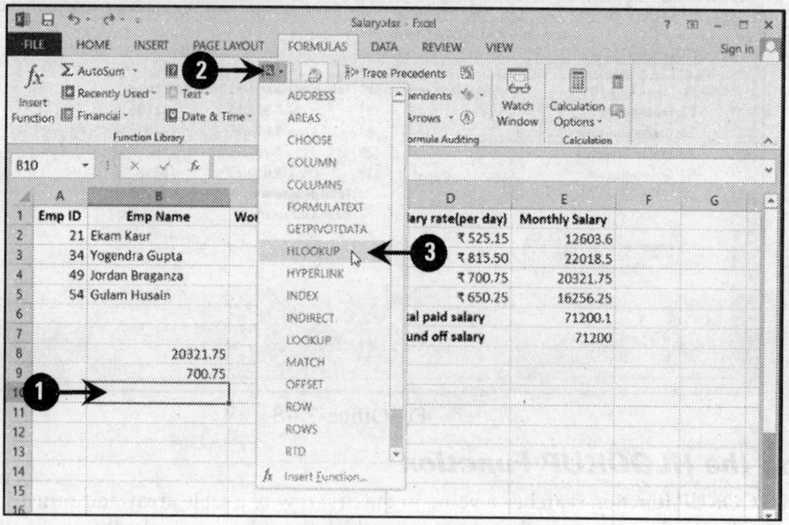

Fig.Office-7.49

The **Function Arguments** dialog box appears (Fig.Office-7.50).

4. *Select* a cell containing the value you want to search in the **Lookup_value** text box. In our case, we have selected the cell **B4** (Fig.Office-7.50).
5. *Select* the cell range or array in the **Table_array** text box. In our case, we have selected the cell range **A1:E5** (Fig.Office-7.50).
6. *Enter* a number in the **Row_index_num** text box to specify the row from which the matching value is to be returned. In our case, we have entered **5** (Fig.Office-7.50).
7. *Click* the **OK** button, as shown in Fig.Office-7.50:

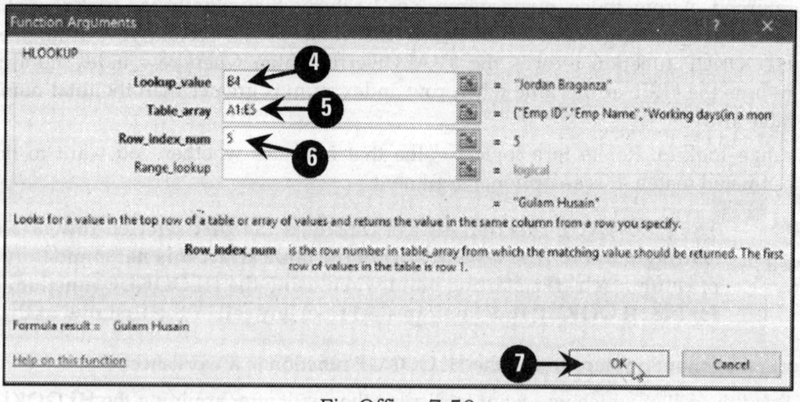

Fig.Office-7.50

The result is displayed in the active cell, as shown in Fig.Office-7.51:

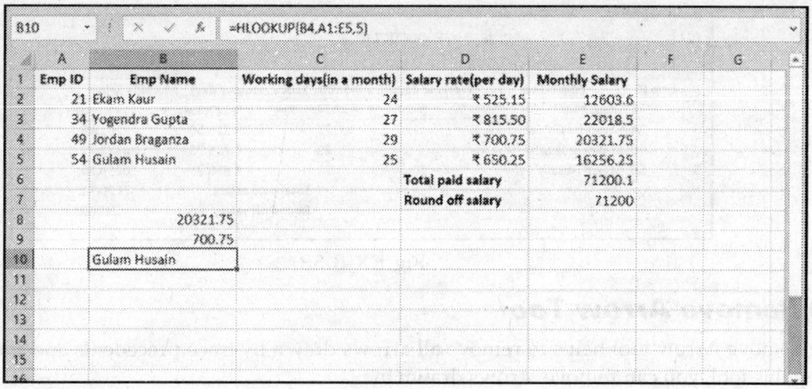

Fig.Office-7.51

Let us now learn about auditing tools.

Working with Auditing Tools

Microsoft provides Formula Auditing Tools that help you to find errors in your worksheet and formulas. By using auditing tool, you can understand, visualize, and troubleshoot the relationship among cell references, formulas, and data. One of the main advantages of these tools is that they allow you trace the flow of data in a worksheet.

Let us now discuss the working of some of these tools.

The Trace Precedents Tool

The Trace Precedents tool selects the cell containing the formula and helps in tracing the source. The arrows show the relationship between the active cell and its related cells that integrate it into their formula.

Perform the following steps to trace precedents:

1. *Open* an existing worksheet in which the data is stored.
2. *Select* the cell that contains the formula. In our case, we have selected the cell **E2** (Fig.EX-3.52).
3. *Click* the **Trace Precedents** option under the **Formula Auditing** group of the **FORMULAS** tab, as shown in Fig.EX-3.52:

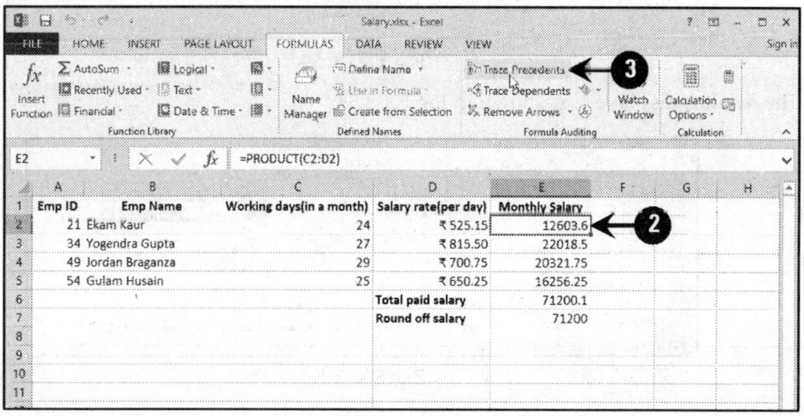

Fig.EX-3.52

The result is displayed, as shown in Fig.EX-3.53:

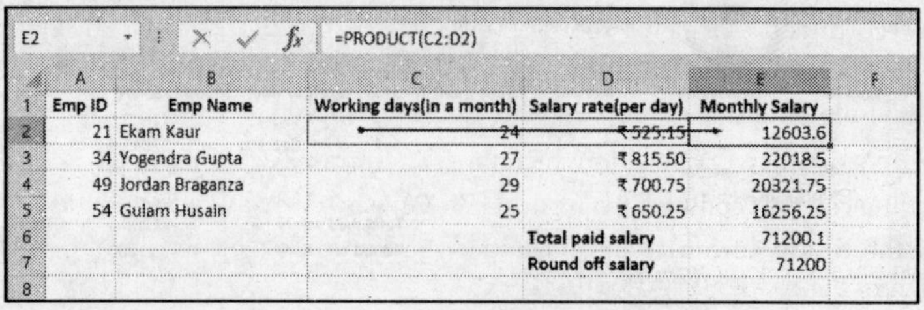

	A	B	C	D	E	F
1	Emp ID	Emp Name	Working days(in a month)	Salary rate(per day)	Monthly Salary	
2	21	Ekam Kaur	24	₹525.15	12603.6	
3	34	Yogendra Gupta	27	₹815.50	22018.5	
4	49	Jordan Braganza	29	₹700.75	20321.75	
5	54	Gulam Husain	25	₹650.25	16256.25	
6				Total paid salary	71200.1	
7				Round off salary	71200	
8						

Fig.EX-3.53

The Remove Arrow Tool

The Remove Arrow tool helps to remove all arrows drawn by trace precedents and trace dependents. By using this tool, you can remove arrows drawn by:

- Only trace precedents arrow
- Only trace dependents arrow
- Both trace precedents and trace dependents arrows

Perform the following steps to use the Remove Arrow tool:

1. *Open* an existing worksheet in which trace precedents or trace dependents are applied.
2. *Click* the down arrow button in the **Remove Arrows** option under the **Formula Auditing** group of the **FORMULAS** tab. A drop-down list appears (Fig.EX-3.54).
3. *Select* the desired option from the drop-down list to remove the trace precedents or trace dependents, or both. In our case, we have selected **Remove Precedent Arrows** option, as shown in Fig.EX-3.54:

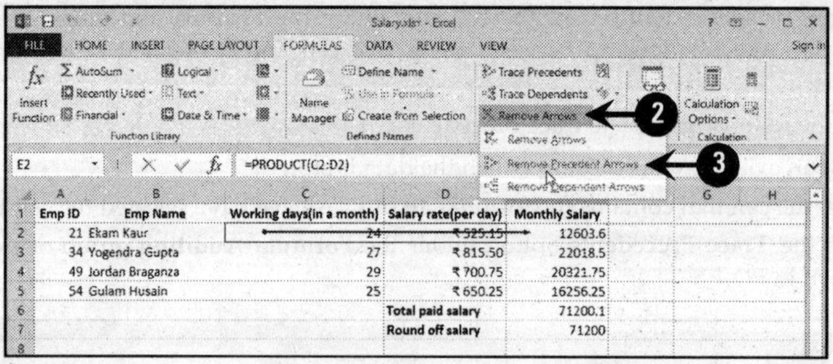

	A	B	C	D	E	F	G	H
1	Emp ID	Emp Name	Working days(in a month)	Salary rate(per day)	Monthly Salary			
2	21	Ekam Kaur	24	₹525.15	12603.6			
3	34	Yogendra Gupta	27	₹815.50	22018.5			
4	49	Jordan Braganza	29	₹700.75	20321.75			
5	54	Gulam Husain	25	₹650.25	16256.25			
6				Total paid salary	71200.1			
7				Round off salary	71200			
8								

Fig.EX-3.54

The result is displayed, as shown in Fig.EX-3.55:

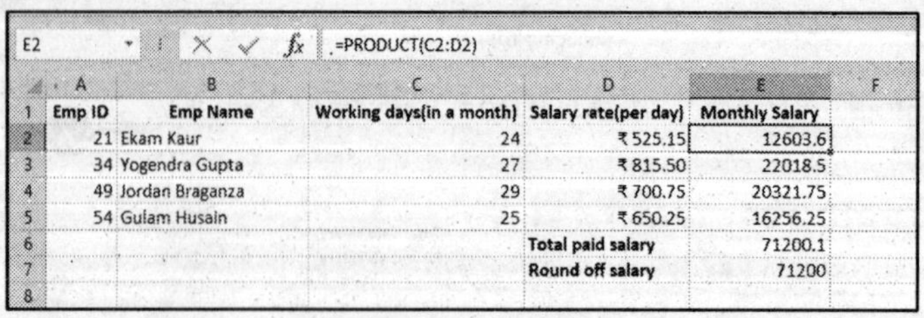

	A	B	C	D	E	F
1	Emp ID	Emp Name	Working days(in a month)	Salary rate(per day)	Monthly Salary	
2	21	Ekam Kaur	24	₹525.15	12603.6	
3	34	Yogendra Gupta	27	₹815.50	22018.5	
4	49	Jordan Braganza	29	₹700.75	20321.75	
5	54	Gulam Husain	25	₹650.25	16256.25	
6				Total paid salary	71200.1	
7				Round off salary	71200	
8						

Fig.EX-3.55

The Show Formulas Tool

The Show Formulas tool helps to trace the cells in the worksheet that contains formulae. This tool displays the formula used in each cell instead of the resulting value.

Perform the following steps to use the Show Formulas tool:

1. *Open* an existing worksheet in which the data are stored.
2. *Select* the cell that contains the formula. In our case, we have selected the cell **E6** (Fig.EX-3.56).
3. *Click* the **Show Formulas** button under the **Formula Auditing** group of the **FORMULAS** tab, as shown in Fig.EX-3.56:

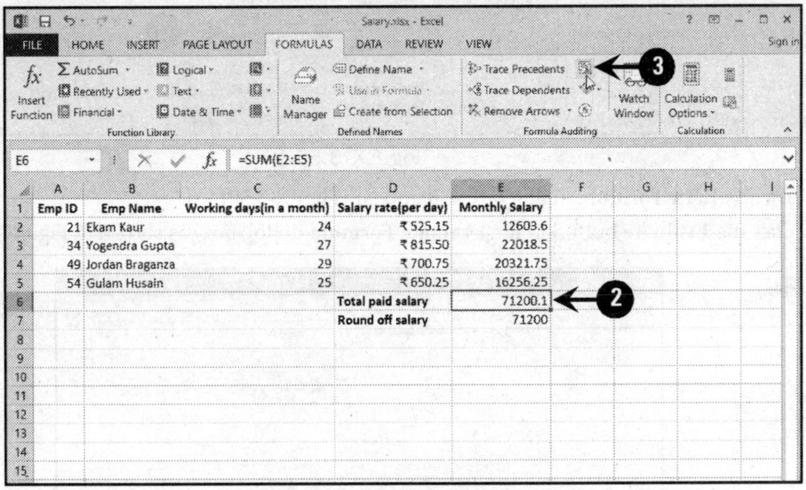

Fig.EX-3.56

The result is displayed as shown in Fig.EX-3.57:

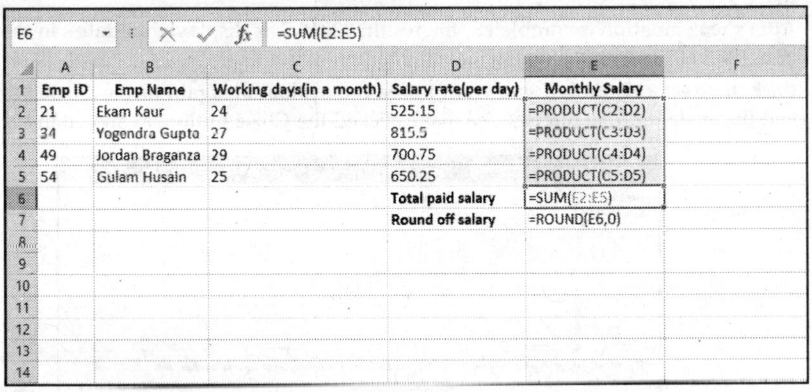

Fig.EX-3.57

The Evaluate Formula Tool

The Evaluate Formula tool is used to debug a formula by evaluating its part individually. This feature in Microsoft enables you to notify the step by step calculations performed within a formula.

Perform the following steps to evaluate formula in Excel:

1. *Open* an existing worksheet in which the data is stored.
2. *Select* the cell that that you want to evaluate. In our case, we have selected the cell **E3** (Fig.EX-3.58).

3. *Click* the **Evaluate Formula** button under **Formula Auditing** group of the **FORMULAS** tab, as shown in Fig.EX-3.58:

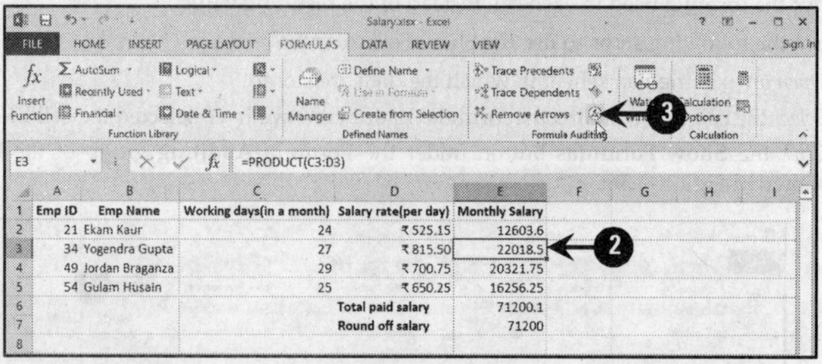

Fig.EX-3.58

The **Evaluate Formula** dialog box will appear (Fig.EX-3.59).

4. *Click* the **Evaluate** button in the **Evaluate Formula** dialog box, as shown in Fig.EX-3.59:

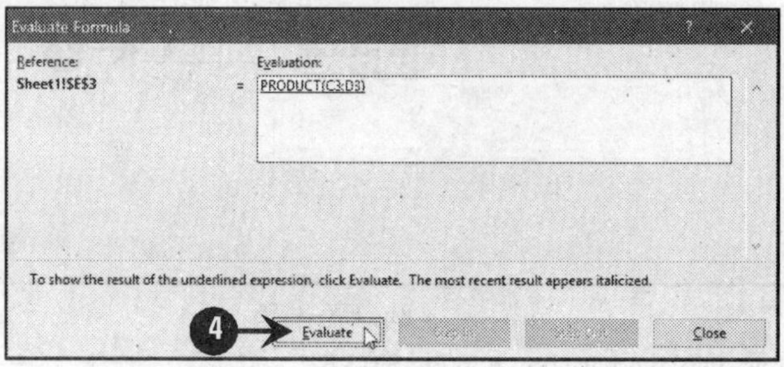

Fig.EX-3.59

After the evaluation is completed, the result, **22018.5,** is displayed in Italics in the text box as shown (Fig.EX-3.60).

5. *Click* the **Restart** button if you want to see the evaluation again or the **Close** button if you want to end the evaluation. In our case, we have clicked the **Close** button, as shown in Fig.EX-3.60:

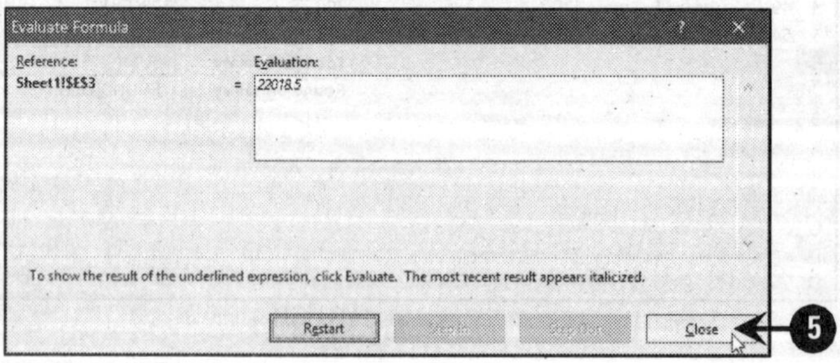

Fig.EX-3.60

The **Evaluate Formula** dialog box is closed.

Sometimes, when functions are used incorrectly in a worksheet, they can generate different types of errors. Let us discuss these errors and how they can be rectified to obtain the correct output.

Checking Errors

In Excel 2013, an error generated by a function can be easily corrected by understanding the different error values. For example, suppose Excel displays a value that begins with a hash mark (#). This means that the function has returned an error, which needs to be rectified. However, if an entire cell is filled with hash mark, it means that the column in which the cell is located is not wide enough to display the data or value in the cell. This problem can be solved by either increasing the width of the column or changing the number format of the value in the cell to view the value clearly.

The following types of errors can occur while working with formulas in Microsoft Excel:

- **#DIV/0!:** Occurs when a value is divided by zero in a formula. This error also occurs when the formula attempts to divide a value by an empty cell (that is, a cell that has no value).
- **#NAME?:** Occurs when Microsoft Excel does not recognize the text specified in a formula. This can happen if the text used in a formula is deleted.
- **#N/A:** Occurs when a value is not available to a function or formula. Some functions, such as VLOOKUP, can return #N/A.
- **#NULL!:** Occurs when an intersection of two ranges that do not intersect is specified.
- **#NUM!:** Occurs when there is an invalid numeric value in a function, for example, assigning a negative value where a positive value is expected.
- **#REF!:** Occurs when an invalid cell is referenced. This can also happen if the referenced cell is deleted from the worksheet.
- **#VALUE!:** Occurs when a formula includes an argument or operand of the wrong type. An operand is a value or cell reference that a formula uses to calculate a result.

To obtain the correct output, an error in a function must be removed. This can be done by simply double-clicking the cell containing the function, and correcting the function in the cell itself or by selecting the cell and making the required corrections from the Formula Bar that displays the function.

Perform the following steps to check and correct errors in the formulas present in a worksheet:

1. *Open* a workbook that has an error you want to correct.
2. *Select* the cell containing the error (Fig.EX-3.61).
3. *Click* the **Error Alert** button. The error type is displayed with the different error checking options, as shown in Fig.EX-3.61:

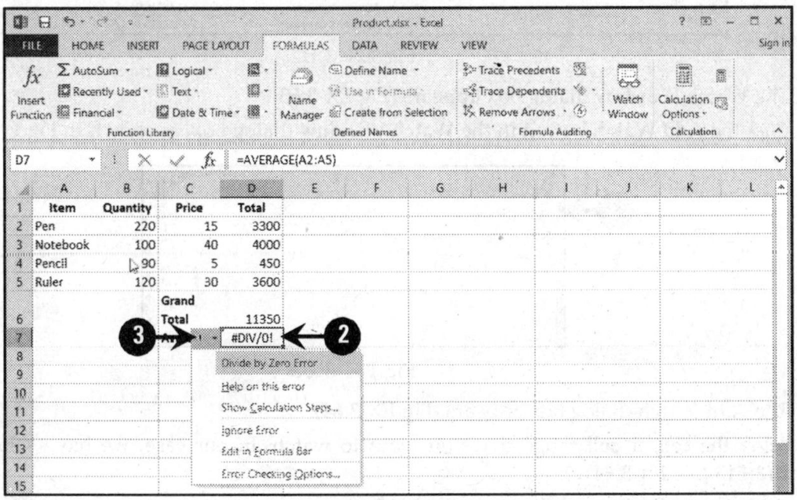

Fig.EX-3.61

The error checking options are briefly described as follows:

- **Help on this error:** Opens the Excel Help window with information pertaining to the specific error type as well as information on how to correct the error
- **Show Calculation Steps**: Opens the Evaluate Formula dialog box where you can check all steps leading to the error

- **Ignore Error:** Allows you to accept the formula as it is
- **Edit in Formula Bar:** Allows you to edit the formula in the Formula Bar to remove the error
- **Error Checking Options:** Opens the Excel Options dialog box, where you can set the rules for error checking

The Watch Window Tool

There are many instances when the whole view of some cells is not visible on a worksheet. Excel 2013 provides a tool named, Watch Window, to overcome this problem. In Watch Window tool, you can view those cells and their formulas that are not visible in the worksheet.

Perform the following steps to understand the working of Watch Window tool:

1. *Open* a new or an existing workbook.
2. *Click* the **Watch Window** button under the **Formula Auditing** group of the **FORMULAS** tab, as shown in Fig.EX-3.62:

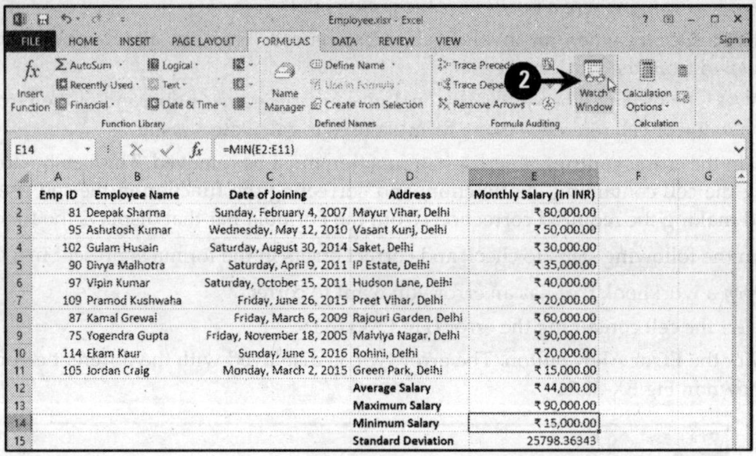

Fig.EX-3.62

The **Watch Window** dialog box appears (Fig.EX-3.63).

3. *Click* the **Add Watch** button in the **Watch Window** dialog box, as shown in Fig.EX-3.63:

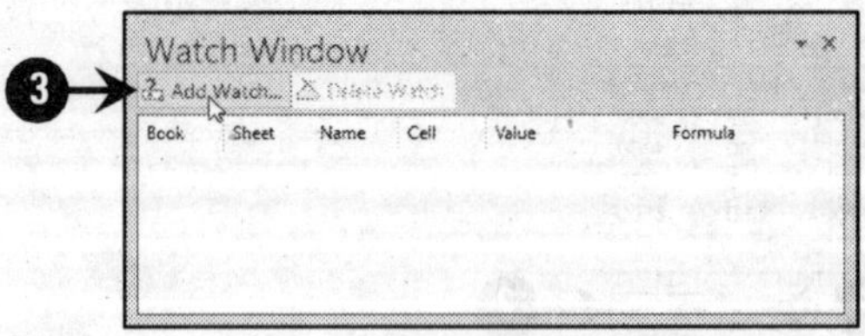

Fig.EX-3.63

The **Add Watch** dialog box appears (Fig.EX-3.64).

4. *Select* the cell or cell range that you want to watch. In our case, we have selected the cell range **E13:E15** (Fig.EX-3.64)
5. *Click* the **Add** button, as shown in Fig.EX-3.64:

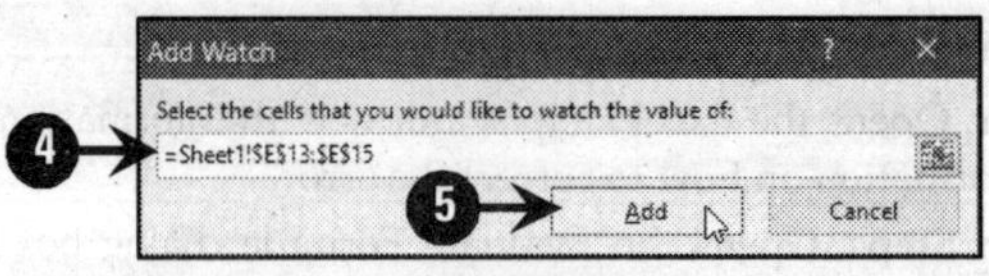

Fig.EX-3.64

The cell is added in the **Watch Window** dialog box, as shown in Fig.EX-3.65:

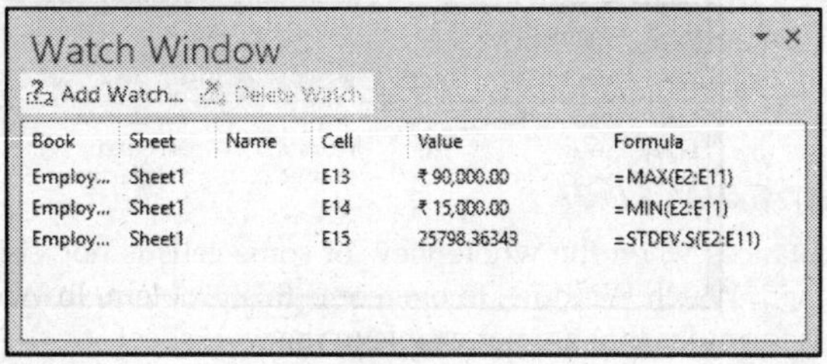

Fig.EX-3.65

6. *Double-click* the entry in **Watch Window** dialog box, to display the cell in the worksheet. In our case, we have double-clicked on the cell **E14** entry (Fig.EX-3.66).

   The related cell in the worksheet is highlighted, as shown in Fig. EX-3.66:

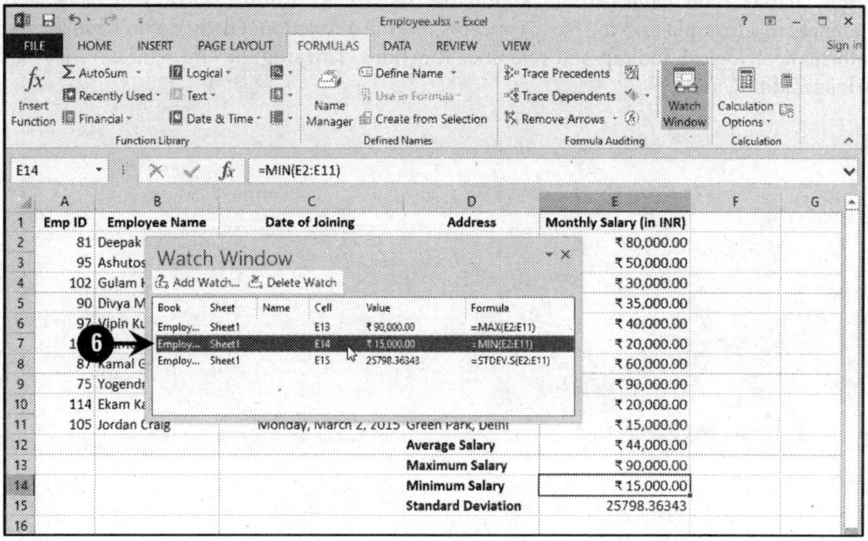

Fig.EX-3.66

You can also delete an entry from the **Watch Window**.

7. *Select* the entry in the **Watch Window** dialog box. In our case, we have selected cell **E15** (Fig.EX-3.67).
8. *Click* the **Delete Watch** button in the **Watch Window** dialog box, as shown in Fig.EX-3.67:

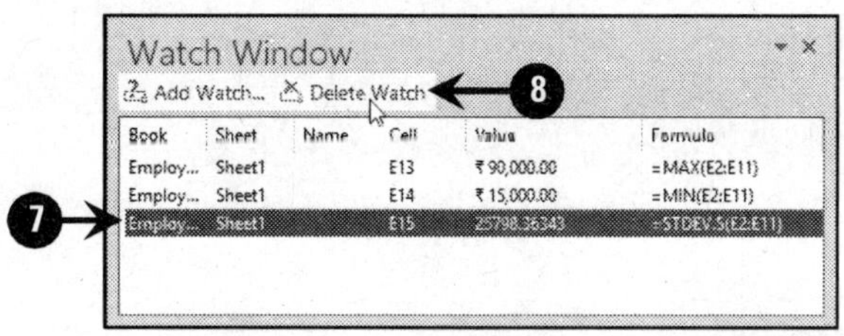

Fig.EX-3.67

The entry is deleted from the **Watch Window** dialog box, as shown in Fig.EX-3.68:

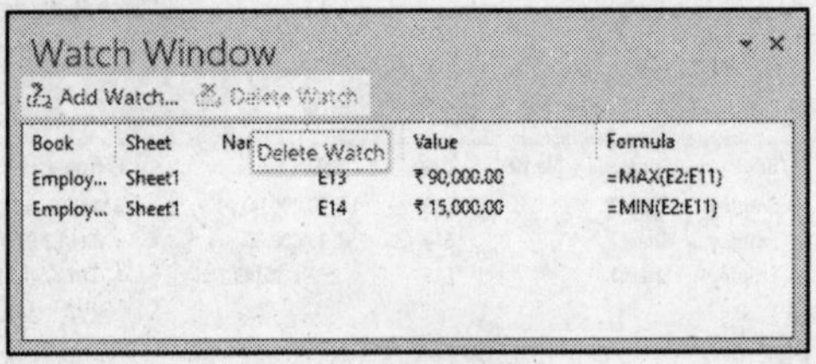

Fig.EX-3.68

With this, we have come to the end of the chapter. Let us summarize the key points learned in this chapter.

Summary

In this chapter, you have learned about the basic of a formula. Next, you have learned about cell references in a formula and the basic concepts used in a function. Further, you have learned to work with mathematical, logical, lookup and reference functions. Towards the end, you have learned to work with various auditing tools.

CHAPTER

4

Working with Data Analysis Tools and Data Protection

In this Chapter:

* Working with a PivotTable
* Creating Power View
* Understanding What-if Analysis Tool
* Protecting Data in Excel
* Linking Worksheets and Workbooks
* Consolidating Worksheet

Introduction

Data analysis and data protection are two crucial features of Excel. Data analysis is an integral function of Excel and refers to the process of collecting data from a source, summarizing the data, and extracting useful information from it. A data source may be a range of cells in a worksheet, a table, or data imported into a worksheet from an external source, such as Access or SQL Server. Excel provides special tools to perform data analysis, such as the PivotTable tool, Data Model tool, Power View tool, and What-if Analysis tool.

On the other hand, data protection safeguards the workbook from any unauthorized access. At the time of protecting the worksheet, you can lock specific range of cells and restrict user from altering values. You can also set password to open the workbook or make it read-only. Thus, you can insure that no one makes changes to the workbook without seeking permission.

This chapter will explain the PivotTable tool, wherein you learn to create a PivotTable report and use slicers to filter the PivotTable report. Next you learn the procedure to create power view in Excel. In addition, you learn the use of What-if Analysis tool as well as its related tools, such as Data Table, Scenario Manager and Goal Seek. Towards the end of the chapter, you study about the concept of data protection in Excel. Then, you learn to link worksheets and workbook. Towards the end, you learn to consolidate worksheets..

Let us learn about PivotTable.

Working with a PivotTable

A PivotTable reorganizes and summarizes the data to generate a dynamic summary report (called PivotTable report) from a database. The database can reside in a worksheet or an external file, such as Access or SQL Server. PivotTables are used to extract data from a database and present it in a meaningful and understandable format. For example, you may want to view the salary details of all the employees in a company. In such case, you can use the PivotTable tool on the company database to retrieve the required information and present it as a PivotTable report. You can also perform the same task by using the functions available in Excel, but when there is a lot of information to be retrieved, a PivotTable is generally preferred. This is because it helps in retrieving information quickly and easily.

In the next sub-sections, you learn to create a recommended PivotTable, create a PivotTable, and filter PivotTable data by using the Slicer tool.

Creating Recommended PivotTable

Excel 2013 provides a new feature known as Recommended PivotTable that recommends you the appropriate PivotTable to analyze the data. You can also preview what your data would look like in the Recommended PivotTable and then you can select the desired PivotTable to represent your data.

Perform the following steps to create a recommended PivotTable:

1. *Open* a new or existing workbook that contains data.

2. *Click* the **Recommended PivotTables** button under the **Tables** group of the **INSERT** tab, as shown in Fig.EX-4.1:

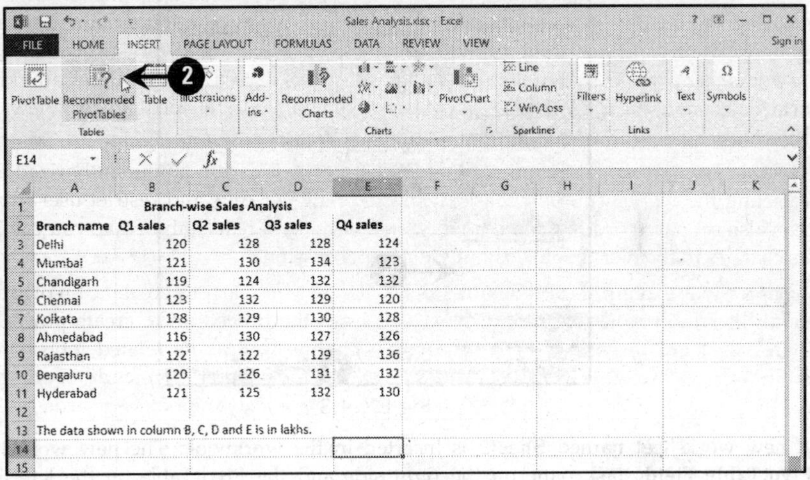

Fig.EX-4.1

The **Choose Data Source** dialog box appears.

3. *Select* a cell range from the worksheet on which you want to apply the PivotTable tool. In our case, we have selected the cell range **A2:E11** (Fig.EX-4.2).

Note: **When you select a table or cell range from the worksheet, the Choose Data Source dialog box changes to the Create PivotTable dialog box appears with the selected data.**

4. *Click* the **OK** button, as shown in Fig.EX-4.2:

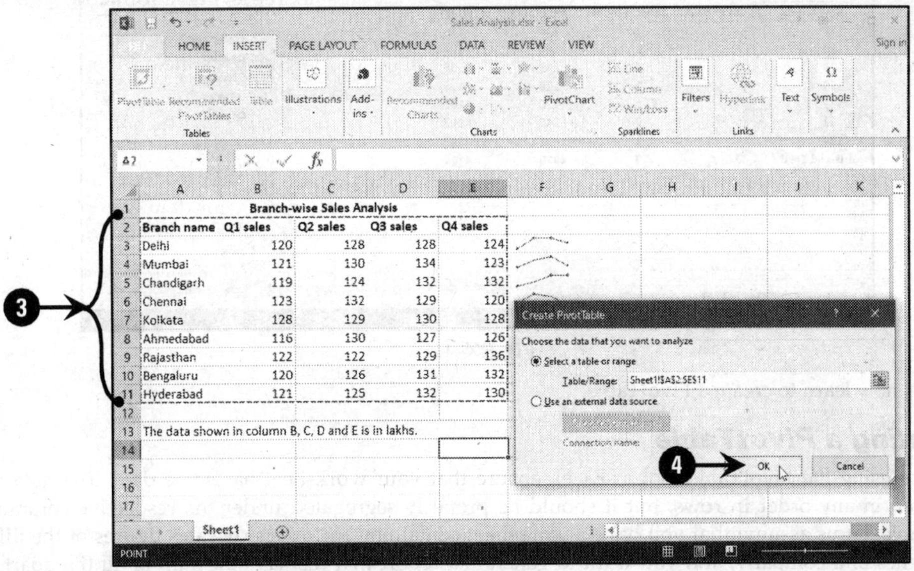

Fig.EX-4.2

The **Recommended PivotTables** dialog box appears (Fig.EX-4.3).

5. *Select* the desired recommended PivotTable from the list of PivotTables (Fig.EX-4.3).

6. *Click* the **OK** button, as shown in Fig.EX-4.3:

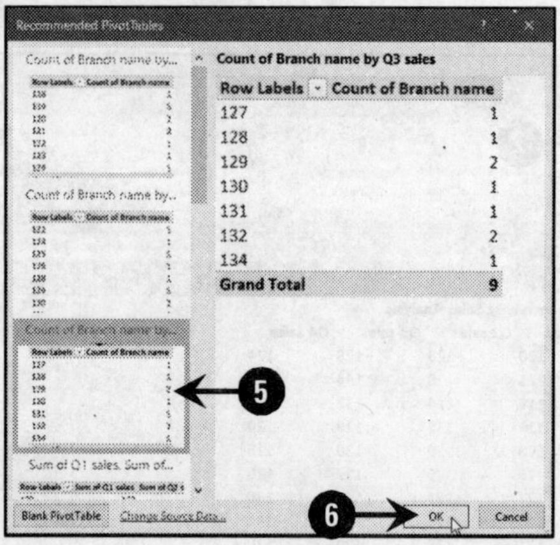

Fig.EX-4.3

A new worksheet named **Sheet2** is inserted in the workbook. The new worksheet contains the **PivotTable Fields** task pane on the right side and the PivotTable on the left side, as shown in Fig.EX-4.4:

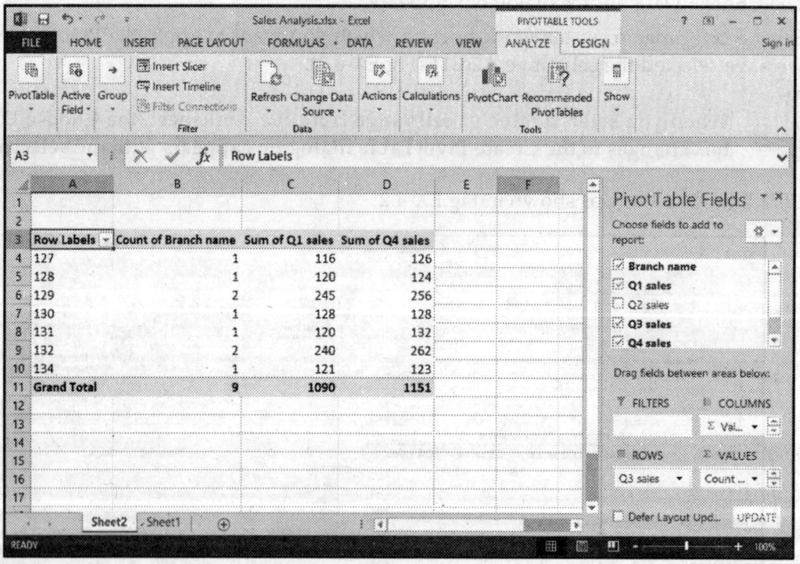

Fig.EX-4.4

Let us now learn to create a PivotTable.

Creating a PivotTable

Before using the PivotTable tool in Excel, ensure that your worksheet has some data. The data can be entered in any order in rows, but it should be properly segregated under the respective columns. For example, let us assume that you have a worksheet containing the quarterly sales figures of the different branches of a company, and you want to generate a report that displays the sum of all the quarters for each branch. You can easily perform this task by creating a PivotTable by using the PivotTable tool.

Perform the following steps to create a PivotTable in a worksheet:

1. *Open* a new or existing workbook that contains data.

2. *Click* the **PivotTable** button under the **Tables** group of the **INSERT** tab, as shown in Fig.EX-4.5:

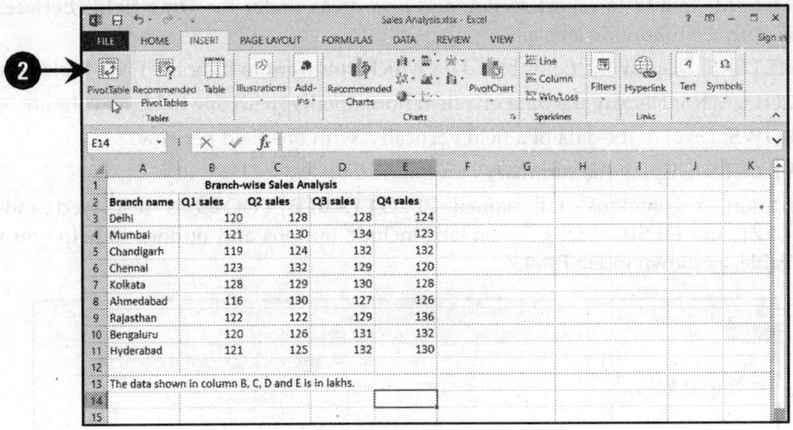

Fig.EX-4.5

The **Create PivotTable** dialog box appears (Fig.EX-4.6).

In Fig.EX-4.6, the location where the PivotTable is to be placed in the worksheet is displayed in the **Location** text box by default.

3. *Select* a cell range from the worksheet on which you want to apply the **PivotTable** tool. In our case, we have selected the cell range **A2:E11** (Fig.EX-4.6).

4. *Select* a radio button to specify the location where you want to place the PivotTable. In our case, we have selected the **New Worksheet** as the location (Fig.EX-4.6).

> Note: **If you want to place the PivotTable in the current worksheet of the opened workbook, select the Existing Worksheet radio button, and if you want to place the PivotTable in a new worksheet, select the New Worksheet radio button in the Create PivotTable dialog box.**

5. *Click* the **OK** button, as shown in Fig.EX-4.6:

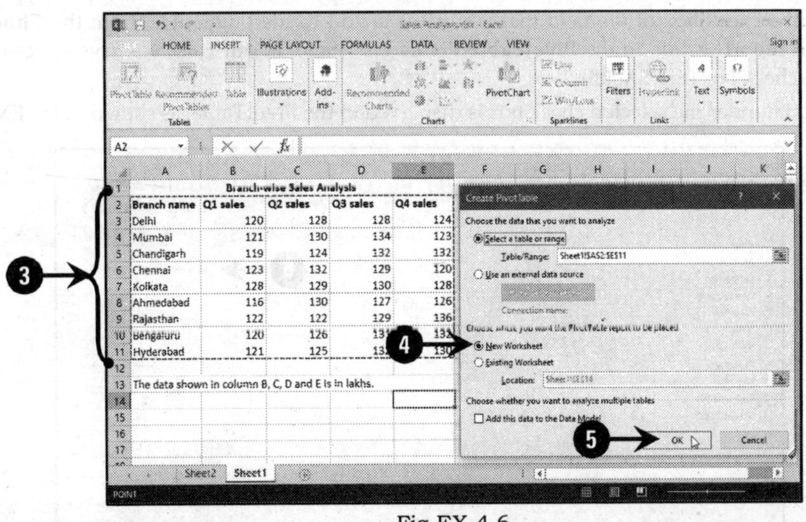

Fig.EX-4.6

A new worksheet named **Sheet3** is inserted in the workbook. The new worksheet contains the **PivotTable Fields** task pane on the right side and the PivotTable on the left side. The **PivotTable**

Fields task pane displays the column headings (fields) present in the selected range under the **Choose fields to add to report** section and four areas under the **Drag fields between areas below** section with the following labels:

- **FILTERS:** Display the fields based on which you want to filter the PivotTable report
- **COLUMNS:** Display the data of a field horizontally, with one field per column
- **ROWS:** Display the data of a field vertically, with one field per row
- **VALUES:** Display the summary of numeric data

In addition, a contextual tab named **PIVOTTABLE TOOLS** is displayed and contains the **ANALYZE** and **DESIGN** tabs. These tabs include buttons and options to help you work with the PivotTable, as shown in Fig.EX-4.7:

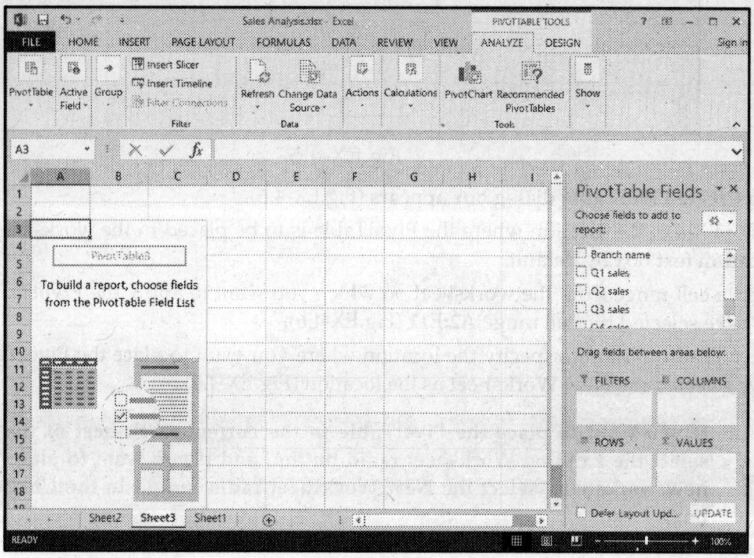

Fig.EX-4.7

6. *Select* the check box of the field that you want to add to the PivotTable, from the **Choose fields to add to report** section in the **PivotTable Fields** task pane. In our case, we have selected the **Branch name** check box (Fig.EX-4.8).

   The data under the selected check box is displayed in the PivotTable, as shown in Fig.EX-4.8:

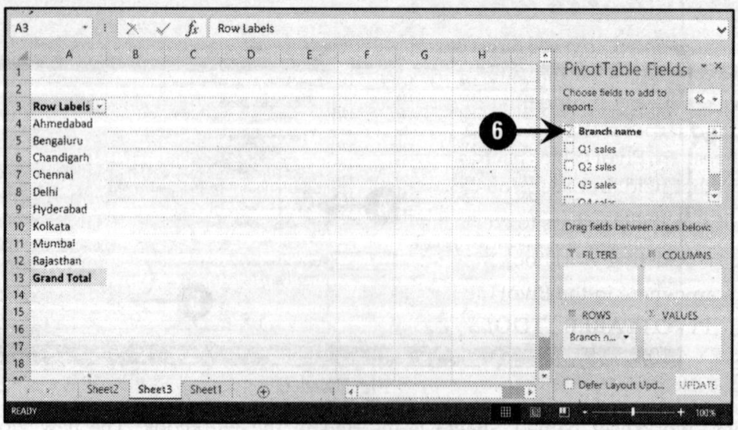

Fig.EX-4.8

Similarly, you can select check boxes of the other fields that you want to add to the PivotTable. In our case, we have selected the **Q1 sales, Q2 sales, Q3 sales**, and **Q4 sales** check boxes, as shown in Fig.EX-4.9:

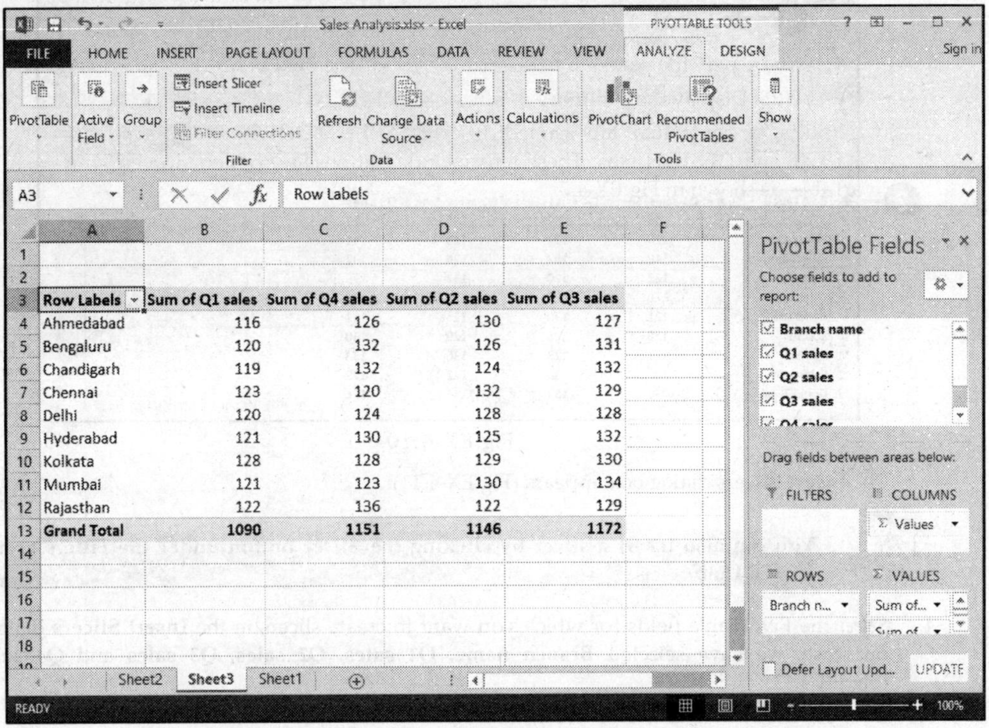

Fig.EX-4.9

You can also create a PivotTable by dragging the fields present under the Choose fields to add to report section to the respective areas under the Drag fields between areas below section, in the PivotTable Fields task pane.

Let us learn to use the slicer to filter PivotTable reports.

Using the Slicer to Filter PivotTable Reports

Slicer provides interactive visual controls with a user friendly interface and is used to filter the data in a PivotTable. In Excel, slicers filter a PivotTable report quickly and indicate the current filtering state, which makes it easy to understand what exactly is shown in it. Using slicers, you can easily isolate the relevant and important parts of the data in a worksheet, and analyze and evaluate the data in different perspectives. In PivotTable, each slicer represents an individual field and displays the list of items present in that field. In Excel, you can create one or more slicers at the same time.

Perform the following steps to create a slicer for filtering a PivotTable report:

1. *Open* an existing workbook in which you have created a PivotTable report.
2. *Click* anywhere in the PivotTable report to create a slicer (Fig.EX-4.10).

   The **PIVOTTABLE TOOLS** contextual tab appears with **ANALYZE** and **DESIGN** tabs (Fig.EX-4.10).

3. *Click* the **Insert Slicer** button in the **Filter** group of the **ANALYZE** tab, as shown in Fig.EX-4.10:

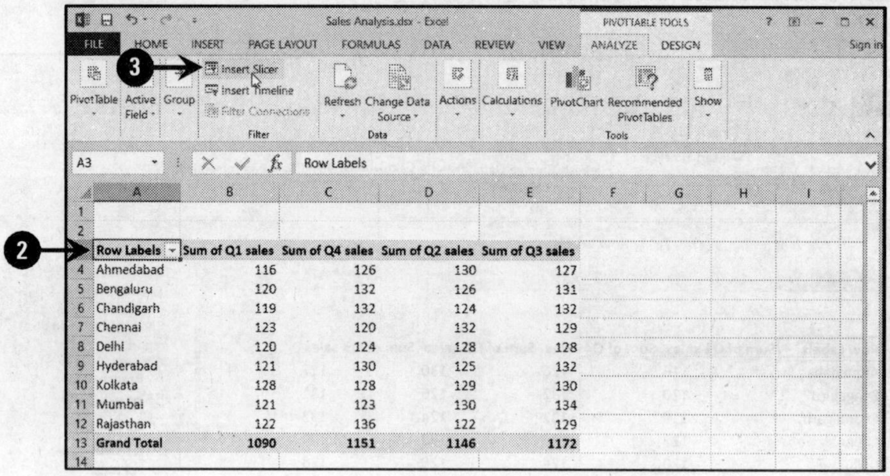

Fig.EX-4.10

The **Insert Slicers** dialog box appears (Fig.EX-4.11).

Note: **You can also insert a slicer by clicking the Slicer button under the Filters group of the INSERT tab.**

4. *Select* the PivotTable fields for which you want to create slicers in the **Insert Slicers** dialog box. In our case, we have selected **Branch name, Q1 sales, Q2 sales, Q3 sales** and **Q4 sales** fields (Fig.EX-4.11).
5. *Click* the **OK** button, as shown in Fig.EX-4.11:

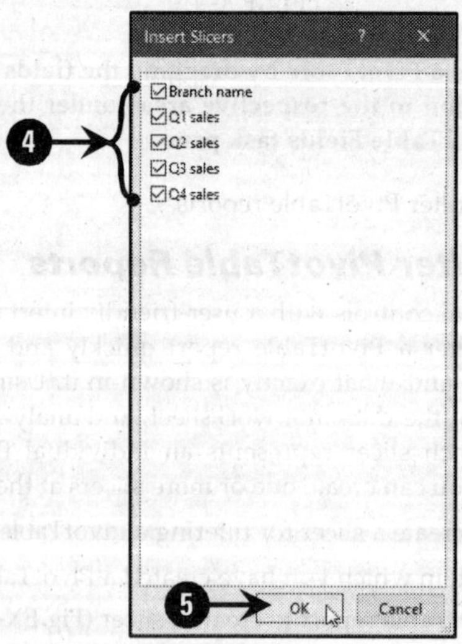

Fig.EX-4.11

The slicers are displayed with the selected fields and their items (Fig.EX-4.12).

6. *Select* an item in the slicer based on which you want to filter the **PivotTable** report. In our case, we have selected the item **Delhi** as shown in Fig.EX-4.12:

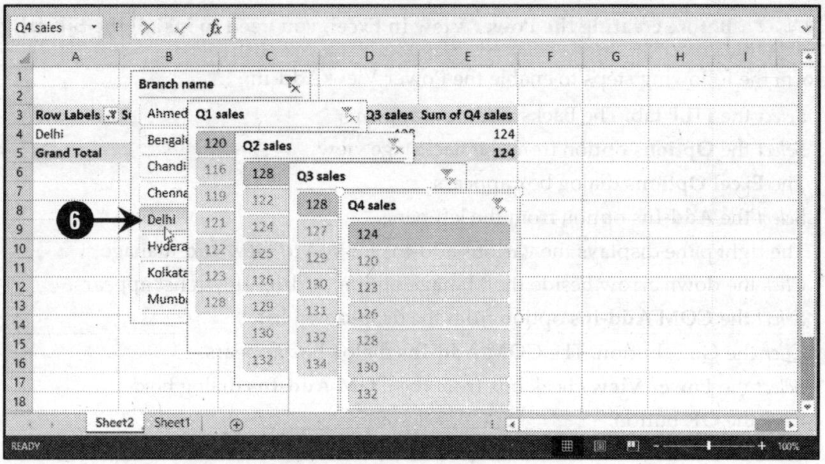

Fig.EX-4.12

The items in all the other slicers (i.e., **Q1 sales, Q2 sales, Q3 sales,** and **Q4 sales**) related to the **Delhi** item become active, while the other slicer items remain inactive, as shown in Fig.EX-4.13:

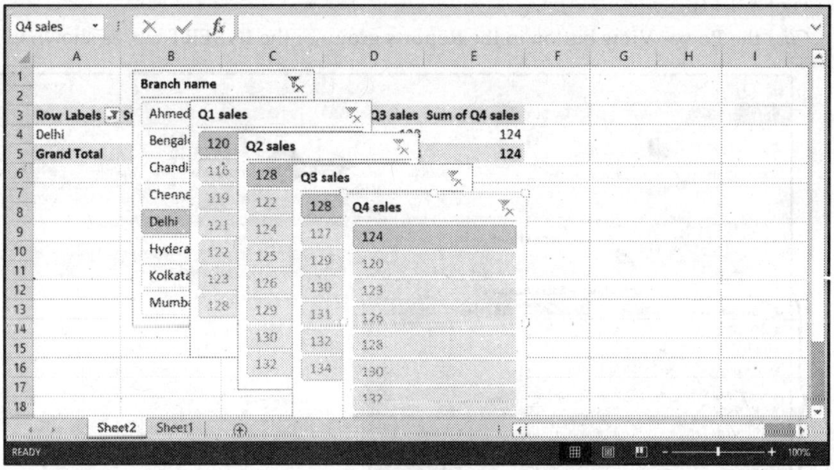

Fig.EX-4.13

You can also select more than one item in a slicer by holding down the **Ctrl** key and selecting the items that you want to filter.

Note: **You cannot select items from multiple slicers at a time.**

Let us now learn to create a Power View in Excel.

Creating Power View

In Excel, the Power View tool allows you to analyze an interactive data as well as provides the facility to make data more attractive by creating data visualization, such as tables, charts, and slicers. The Power View tool enhances the visualization and presentation of the data. Office Professional Plus and Office 365

Professional Plus editions only, provide the Power View feature. In Excel, the Power View button is turned off by default, so you need to enable the Power View Add-in.

Before creating the Power View in Excel, you need to install the Silverlight application.

Perform the following steps to enable the Power View Add-in:

1. *Select* the **FILE** tab. The Backstage view appears.
2. *Select* the **Options** option from the Backstage view.
   The **Excel Options** dialog box appears.
3. *Select* the **Add-Ins** option from the left pane.
   The right pane displays the various add-ins for you to view and manage.
4. *Click* the down arrow beside the **Manage** option. A drop-down list appears.
5. *Select* the **COM Add-ins** option from the drop-down list.
6. *Click* the **Go...** button. The **COM Add-Ins** dialog box appears.
7. *Select* the **Power View** check box from the **COM Add-Ins** dialog box.
8. *Click* the **OK** button.
   The Power View command is enabled in the Excel.

Now, perform the following steps to create a power view:

1. *Open* a new or existing workbook that contains data.
2. *Select* the data from the worksheet. In our case ,we have selected the cell range **A2:E11...** Fig.EX-4.14).
3. *Click* the **Power View** button in the **Reports** group of the **INSERT** tab, as shown in Fig.EX-4.14:

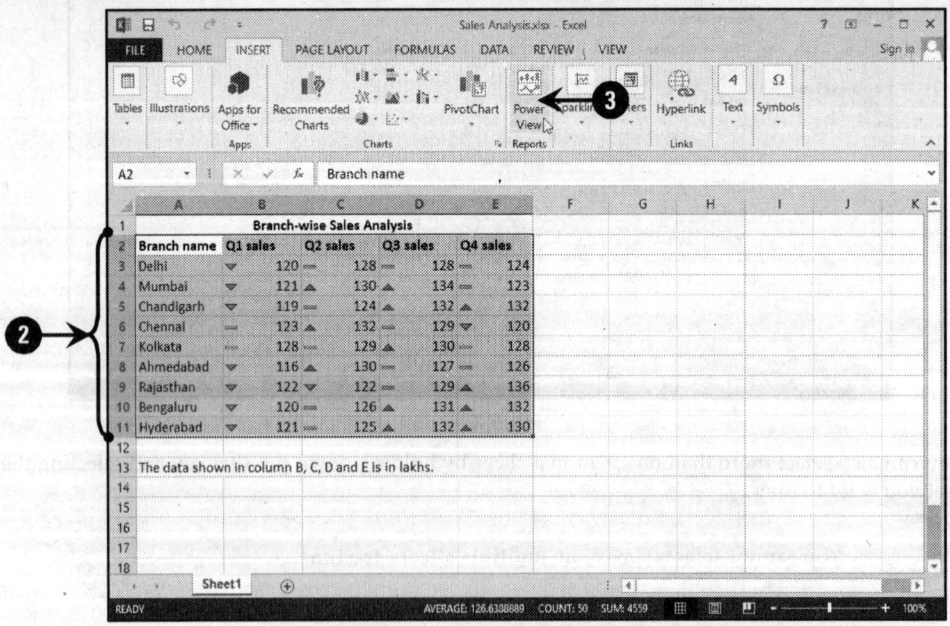

Fig.EX-4.14

A worksheet named **Power View1** appears, displaying the Power View of the selected data, as shown in Fig.EX-4.15:

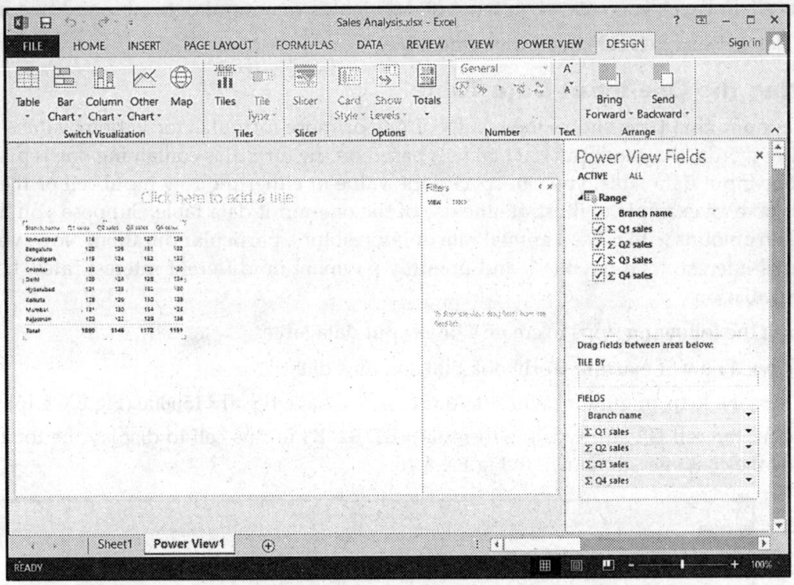

Fig.EX-4.15

You can filter the data of the Power View by selecting or clearing the check boxes under the Range section in the Power View Fields task pane.

Let us discuss the What-if Analysis tool.

Understanding What-if Analysis Tool

The What-if Analysis tool allows you to make changes to values in the cells of a worksheet and see the effect of these changes on the final result or outcome of a calculation. In this section, we discuss the entire process of using the What-if Analysis tool in the worksheet. However, before discussing it, let us learn about different tools included in the What-if Analysis tool. These tools are described as follows:

- **Data Table:** Allows you to see how changes made in the input values in a table affect the result. You can use data tables to calculate and compare the outcome of different inputs of a formula. The different combinations of input values and results are presented in a table format for easy comparison. Depending on your requirements, you can change one or two variables (input values) in a data table.
- **Scenario Manager:** Allows you to create, manipulate, and save scenarios that use different input variables to produce results. A scenario is a set of values that Excel saves and can substitute automatically in your worksheet so that you can perform what-if analysis on a set of data. You can use scenarios to predict the outcome of different situations in your worksheet. The Scenario Manager tool allows you to change multiple cells in order to see the effect of the changes.
- **Goal Seek:** Allows users to find the correct input to produce the desired output. If you know the result that you want from a formula, but not the input value the formula needs to get that result, then you can use the Goal Seek feature..

Let us discuss these three tools in detail.

Using the Data Table Tool

A data table shows how changing one or two variables in a formula will affect the result of the formula. Data tables provide a shortcut for calculating the results of multiple scenarios in one operation and storing the results of these scenarios in one table. This allows you to analyze the results and select the optimum scenario according to your requirements. The cell in which each input value from a data table is substituted is known as an input cell. There are two types of input cells: Row input cell and Column input cell. In Excel, you create two types of data tables, one-input data table and two-input data table.

Now, let us learn to create one-input data table.

Creating the One-Input Data Table

A one-input data table shows the results of one or more formulas for various values of a one-input cell. In other words, the one-input data table is based on the formulas containing one replaceable input value. In a one-input data table, you can specify the value of either the row input cell or the column input cell. Let us take an example to illustrate the use of the one-input data table. Suppose you have taken a loan of a certain amount with a fixed annual rate of interest for a particular duration. Now, you want to calculate the total interest, total payment, and monthly payment on different interest rates. Let us learn to make this calculation.

Perform the following steps to create a one-input data table:

1. *Open* a new or existing workbook that contains data.
2. *Type* the loan amount in cell **F2.** In our case, we have typed **₹150000** (Fig.EX-4.16).
3. *Click* the cell **G2** and type the formula **=B1*B2*B3** in this cell to display the total interest to be paid by the customer, as shown in Fig.EX-4.16:

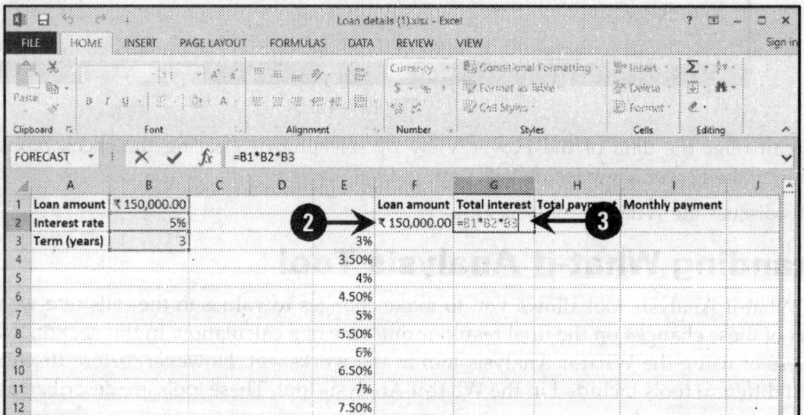

Fig.EX-4.16

4. *Press* the **Enter** key. The total interest (**₹ 22,500.00**) appears in the cell **G2**, as shown in Fig.EX-4.17:

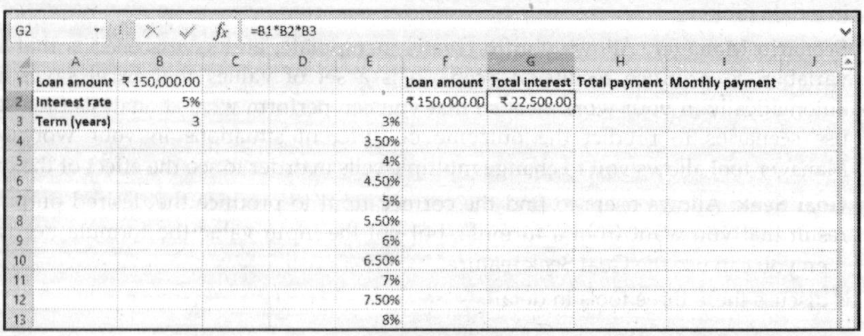

Fig.EX-4.17

5. *Click* the cell **H2** and type the formula **=F2+G2** in this cell to display the total amount to be paid by the customer, as shown in Fig.EX-4.18:

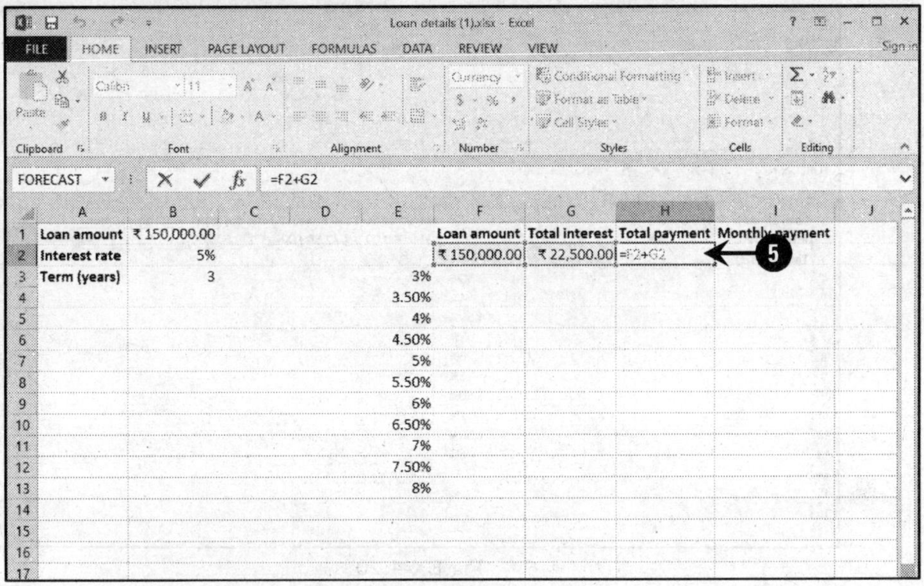

Fig.EX-4.18

6. *Press* the **Enter** key. The total amount **(₹ 172,500.00)** appears in the cell **H2**, as shown in Fig.EX-4.19:

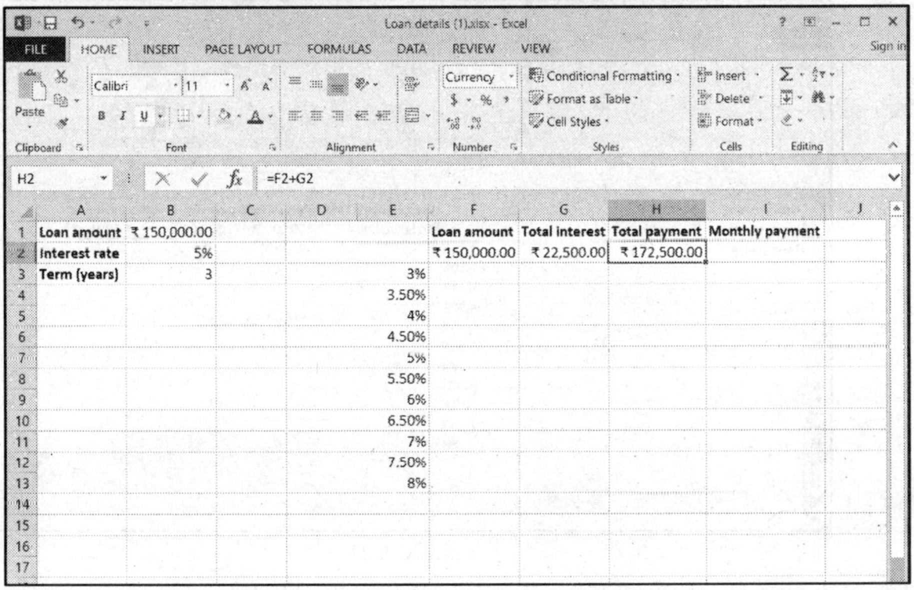

Fig.EX-4.19

7. *Click* the cell **I2** and type the formula **=H2/(B3*12)** to display the monthly amount to be paid by the customer, as shown in Fig.EX-4.20:

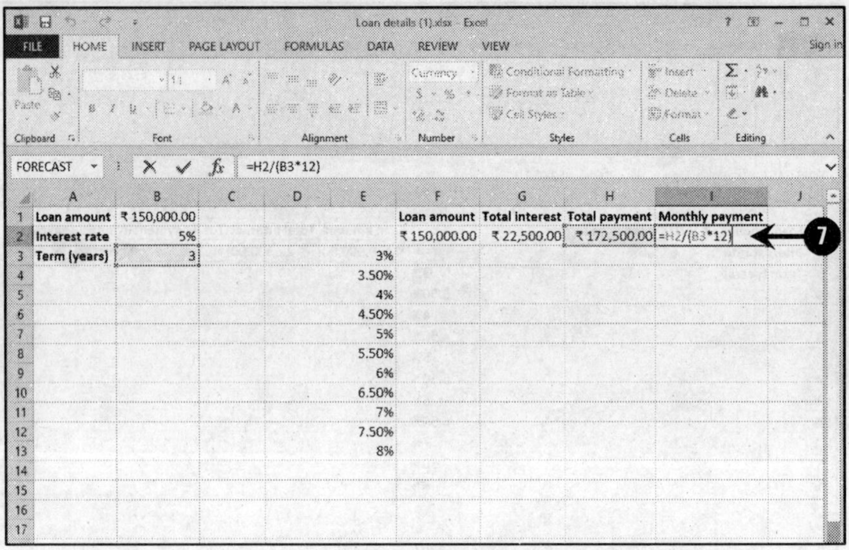

Fig.EX-4.20

8. *Press* the **Enter** key. The amount for monthly payment **(₹ 4,791.67)** appears in the cell **I2**, as shown in Fig.EX-4.21:

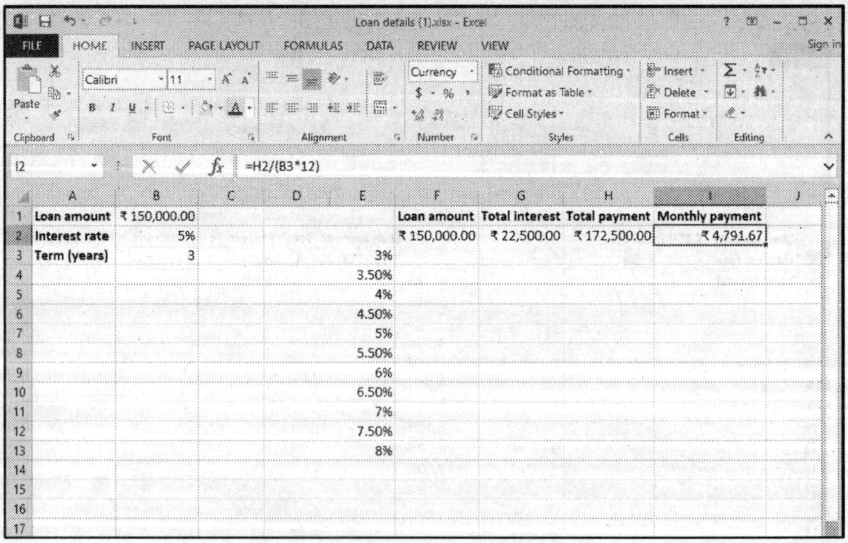

Fig.EX-4.21

9. *Select* the cell range on which you want to perform the calculation. In our case, we have selected the cell range **E2:I13** (Fig.EX-4.22).
10. *Click* the **What-if Analysis** button under the **Data Tools** group of the **DATA** tab (Fig.EX-4.22).

    A drop-down list appears (Fig.EX-4.22).

11. *Select* the **Data Table** option from the drop-down list, as shown in Fig.EX-4.22:

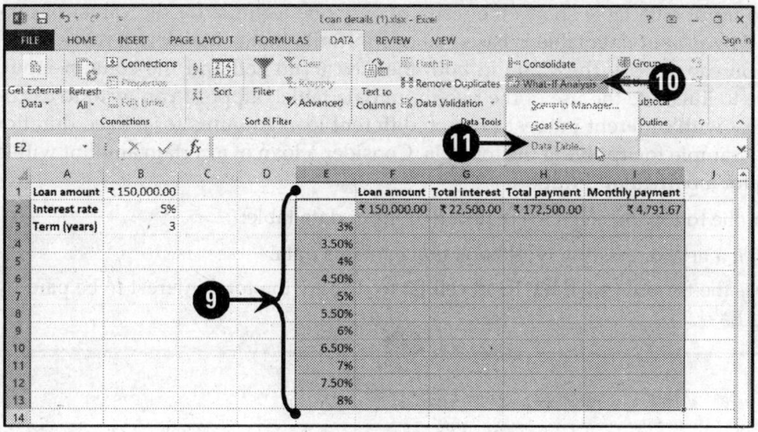

Fig.EX-4.22

The **Data Table** dialog box appears, and the cursor appears in the **Row input cell** text box (Fig.EX-4.23).

12. *Press* the **Tab** key. The cursor now shifts to the **Column input cell** text box.
13. *Select* the cell based on which you performed the calculation initially to specify the column input value. The address of the selected cell appears in the **Column input cell** text box. In our case, we have selected **B3** (Fig.EX-4.23).
14. *Click* the **OK** button, as shown in Fig.EX-4.23:

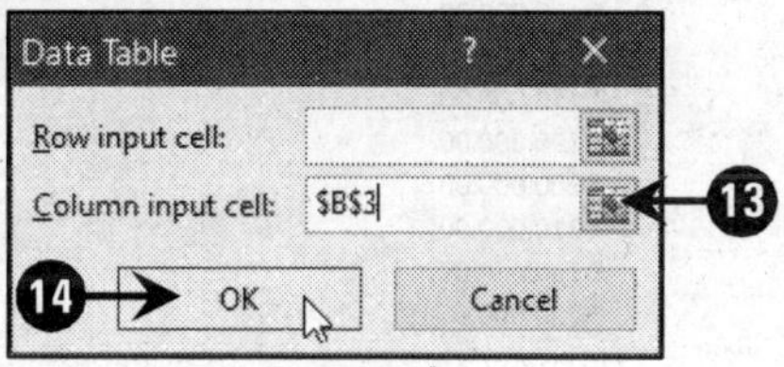

Fig.EX-4.23

The calculations are performed in the selected cells, as shown in Fig.EX-4.24:

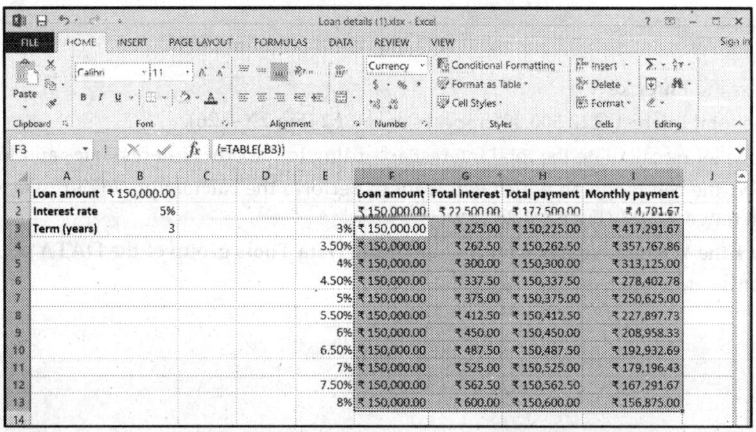

Fig.EX-4.24

Let us create the two-input data table.

Creating the Two-Input Data Table

The two-input data table shows the result of only one formula for the values of two input cells. In other words, a two-input data table is based on one formula that contains two replaceable input values. In this table, you can specify the value in both the row input cell and the column input cell. Let us take an example to illustrate the use of the two-input data table. Suppose you want to calculate the total amount of interest with different interest rates on different loan amounts for a fixed duration. For this, you need to take a sample for applying the formula. Consider a loan of a certain amount with a fixed annual rate of interest for a particular duration.

Perform the following steps to create a two-input data table:

1. *Open* a new or existing workbook that contains data.
2. *Type* the formula **=B1*B2*B3** in cell **E2** to display the total interest to be paid by a user, as shown in Fig.EX-4.25:

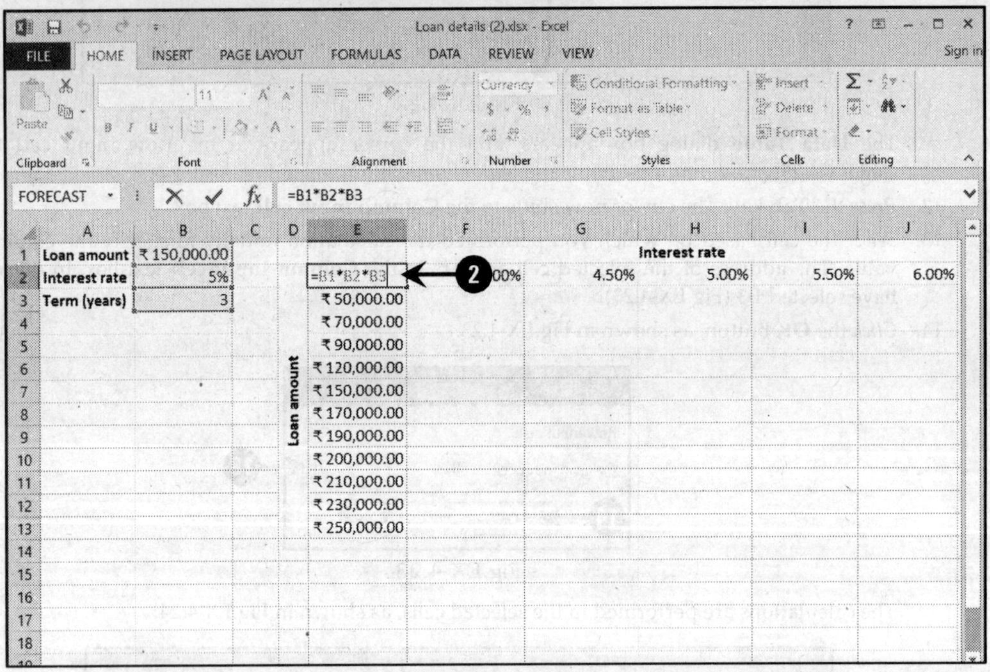

Fig.EX-4.25

3. *Press* the **Enter** key.

   The total interest (**₹22,500.00**) appears in cell **E2** (Fig.EX-4.26).

   Now, let us calculate the total interest according to the other interest rates and loan amounts.
4. *Select* the cell range on which you want to perform the calculation. In our case, we have selected the cell range **E2:J13** (Fig.EX-4.26).
5. *Click* the **What-if Analysis** button under the **Data Tools** group of the **DATA** tab.

   A drop-down list appears (Fig.EX-4.26).

6. *Select* the **Data Table** option from the drop-down list, as shown in Fig.EX-4.26:

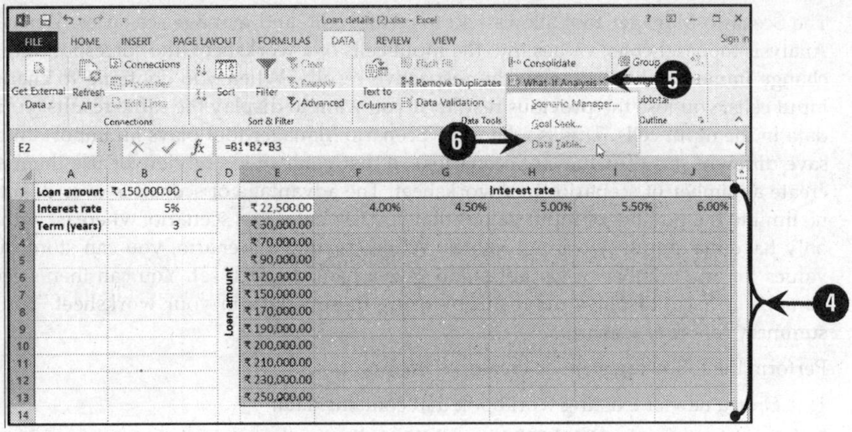

Fig.EX-4.26

The **Data Table** dialog box appears (Fig.EX-4.27).

7. *Select* the cell based on which you performed the calculation initially to specify the row input value. The address of the cell appears in the **Row input cell** text box. In our case, we have selected the cell **B2** (Fig.EX-4.27).
8. *Press* the **Enter** key.
9. *Select* the cell based on which you performed the calculation initially to specify the column input value. The address of the cell appears in the **Column input cell** text box. In our case, we have selected the cell **B1** (Fig.EX-4.27).
10. *Click* the **OK** button, as shown in Fig.EX-4.27:

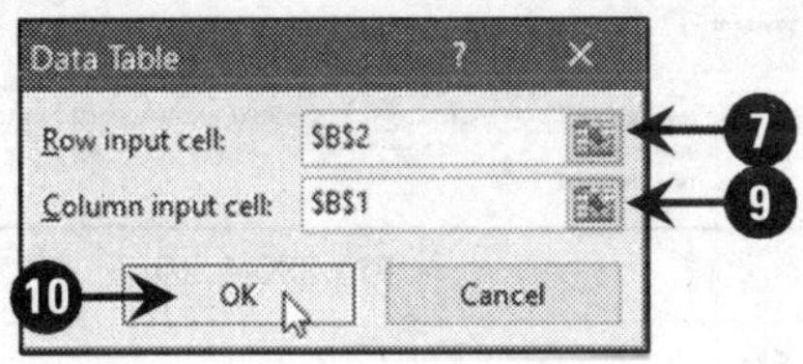

Fig.EX-4.27

The calculations are performed in the selected cells, as shown in Fig.EX-4.28:

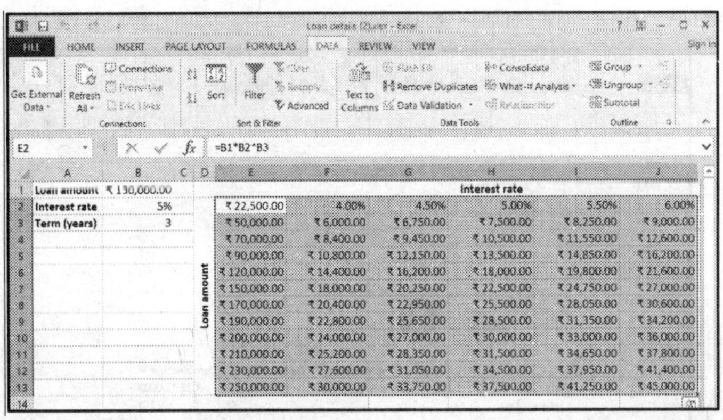

Fig.EX-4.28

Now, let us learn to use scenario manager tool.

Using the Scenario Manager Tool

The Scenario Manager tool allows you to create, edit, and manage scenarios. When you use the What-if Analysis tool and enter values into the input cells of a worksheet, the corresponding values in other cells change immediately to display the respective results. When you continue to change the values in the input cells, you lose the previous results; if you want to display the same results, you have to re-enter the data in the input cells. This is where the Scenario Manager tool plays an important role. It allows you to save different sets of values (or scenarios) so that you can easily view or use them at any time. You can create a number of scenarios in a worksheet. The advantage of scenarios over data tables is that there is no limit to the number of input values that you can enter in a scenario; whereas, with data tables, you can only have maximum two input values. While creating a scenario, you can store different sets of input values for any number of variables and give a name to each set. You can then select a set of values by name, and Excel displays the result by using those values in your worksheet. You can also generate a summary report of scenarios.

Perform the following steps to create a scenario:

1. *Open* a new or existing workbook that contains data.
2. *Type* the formula **=B1*B2*B3** in cell **B5** to display the total interest to be paid by a user for a loan, as shown in Fig.EX-4.29:

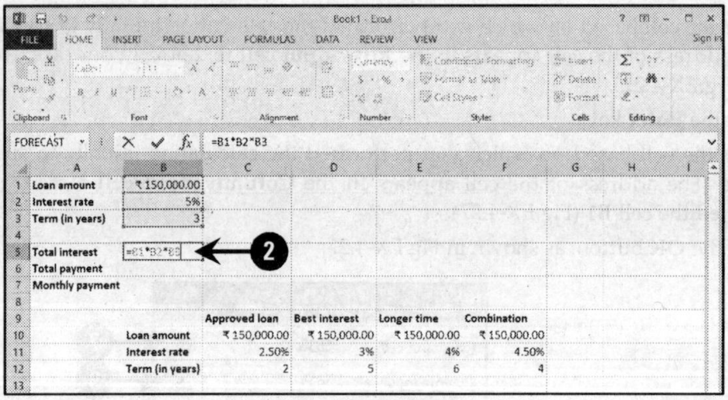

Fig.EX-4.29

3. *Press* the **Enter** key.

   The total interest (**₹22,500.00**) appears in cell **B5** (Fig.EX-4.30).
4. *Type* the formula **=B1+B5** in cell **B6** to display the total payment to be paid by the user, as shown in Fig.EX-4.30:

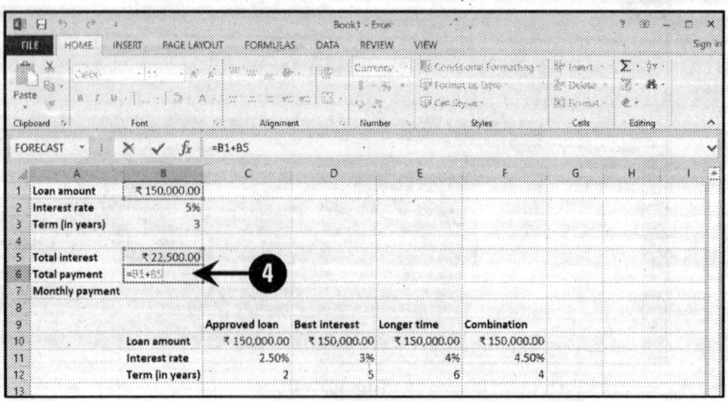

Fig.EX-4.30

5. *Press* the **Enter** key.

   The total payment to be paid (**₹ 172,500.00**) appears in cell **B6** (Fig.EX-4.31).

6. *Type* the formula **=B6/(B3*12)** in cell **B7** to display the monthly payment to be paid by the user, as shown in Fig.EX-4.31:

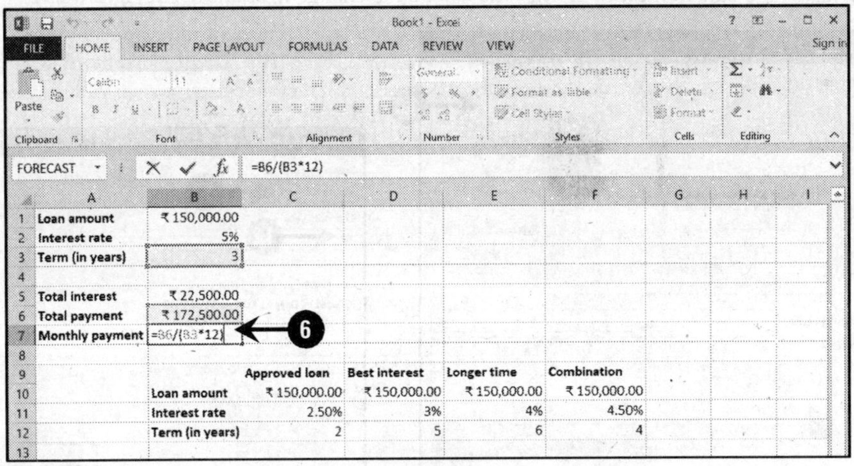

Fig.EX-4.31

7. *Press* the **Enter** key.

   The monthly payment to be paid (**₹ 4,791.67**) appears in cell **B7** (Fig.EX-4.32).

   After completing the various calculations for the loan, now, let us use the Scenario Manager tool to create a scenario.

8. *Click* the **What-if Analysis** button under the **Data Tools** group of the **DATA** tab (Fig.EX-4.32).

   A drop-down list appears (Fig.EX-4.32).

9. *Select* the **Scenario Manager** option from the drop-down list, as shown in Fig.EX-4.32:

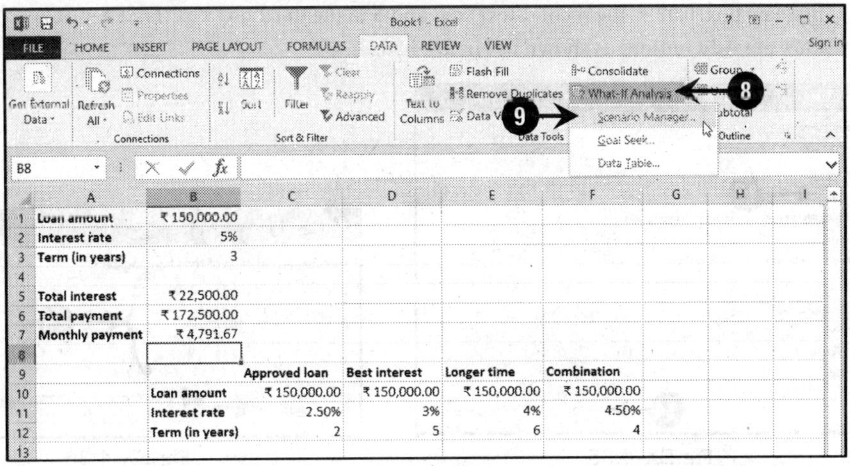

Fig.EX-4.32

   The **Scenario Manager** dialog box appears (Fig.EX-4.33).

10. *Click* the **Add** button in the **Scenario Manager** dialog box (Fig.EX-4.33).

    The **Add Scenario** dialog box appears with the address of the currently selected cell in the **Changing cells** text box and the name of the user in whose system the scenario is being created as well as the date of the creation of the scenario in the **Comment** text area (Fig.EX-4.34). For creating scenarios, we will use the data already given in the worksheet.

11. *Type* the name of the scenario in the **Scenario name** text box. In our case, we have typed **Approved loan** in the text box (Fig.EX-4.34).
12. *Select* the data in the **Changing cells** text box to change it, as shown in Fig.EX-4.34:

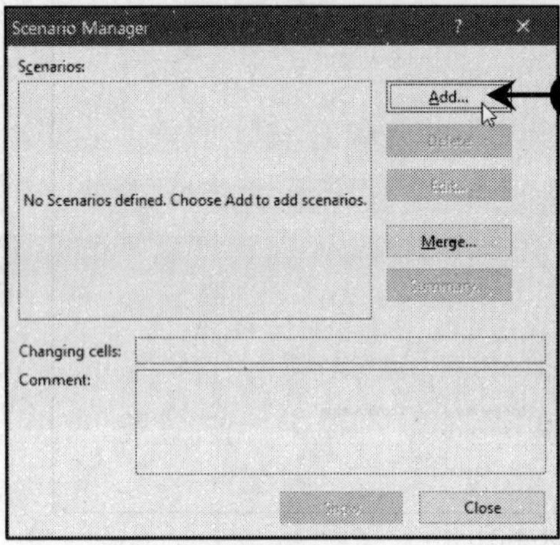

Fig.EX-4.33

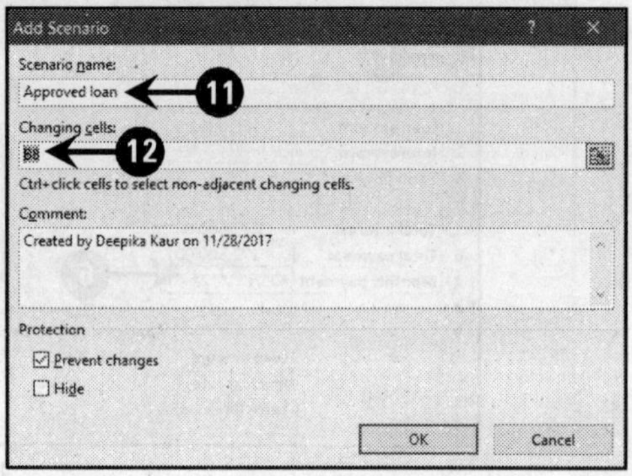

Fig.EX-4.34

13. *Select* the cell range that you want to include in the scenario. The data in the **Changing cells** text box changes according to your selection. In our case, we have selected the cell range **B1:B3** (Fig.EX-4.35).
14. *Click* the **OK** button in the **Edit Scenario** dialog box (Fig.EX-4.35).

    The **Scenario Values** dialog box appears, displaying the values of the scenario in the respective text boxes (Fig.EX-4.36).

    You can change these values according to your requirements.
15. *Type* the desired values for the **Approved loan** scenario. In our case, we have typed **150000** in the first text box, **0.07** in the second text box, and **5** in the third text box (Fig.EX-4.36).
16. *Click* the **Add** button, as shown in Fig.EX-4.36:

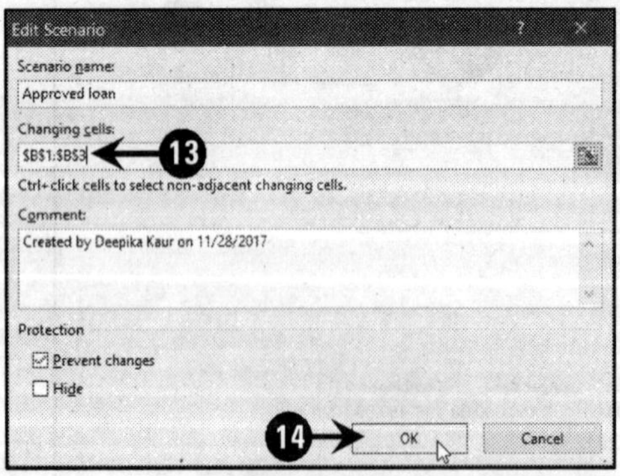

Fig.EX-4.35

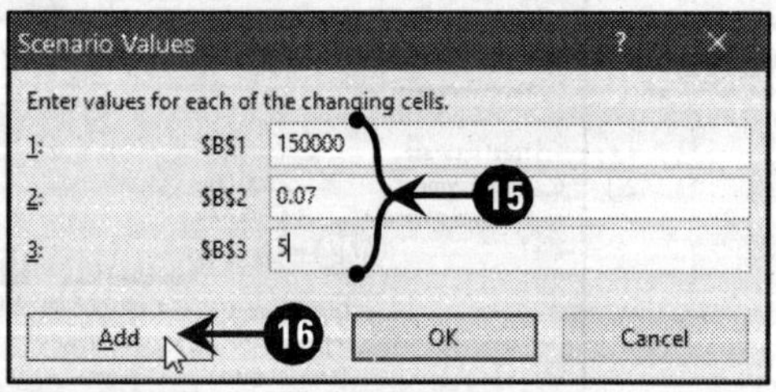

Fig.EX-4.36

The **Add Scenario** dialog box reappears (Fig.EX-4.37).

You can now set the values for the second scenario in the **Add Scenario** dialog box.

17. *Type* the name of the second scenario in the **Scenario name** text box. In our case, we have typed **Best interest** in the text box (Fig.EX-4.37).
18. *Click* the **OK** button (Fig.EX-4.37).
    The **Scenario Values** dialog box appears (Fig.EX-4.38).
19. *Type* the desired values for the **Best interest** scenario. In our case, we have typed **150000** in the first text box, **0.02** in the second text box, and **4** in the third text box (Fig.EX-4.38).
20. *Click* the **Add** button, as shown in Fig.EX-4.38:

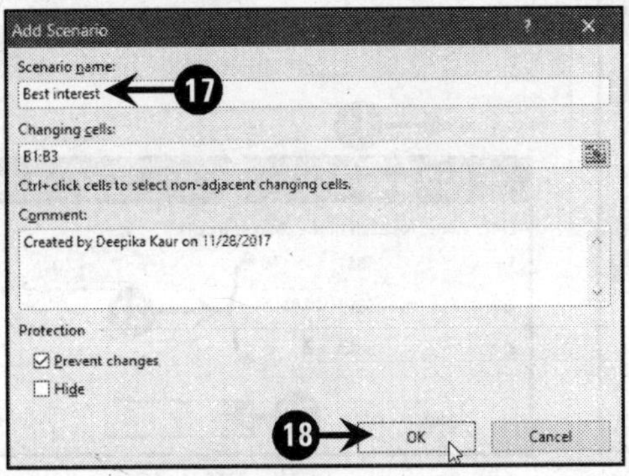

Fig.EX-4.37

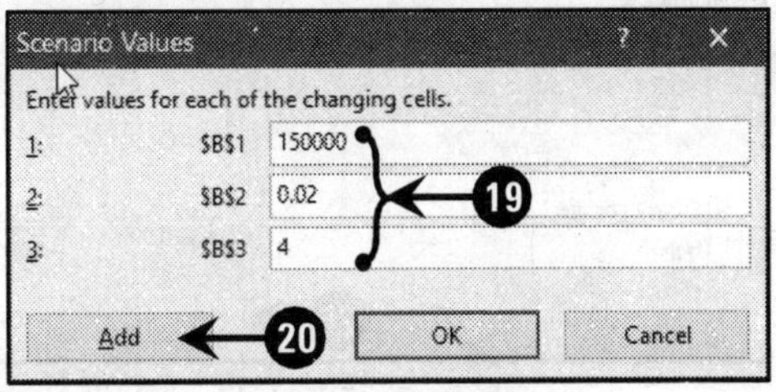

Fig.EX-4.38

The **Add Scenario** dialog box reappears (Fig.EX-4.39).

21. *Type* the name of the third scenario in the **Scenario name** text box. In our case, we have typed **Longer time** in the text box (Fig.EX-4.39).
22. *Click* the **OK** button (Fig.EX-4.39).
    The **Scenario Values** dialog box appears (Fig.EX-4.40).
23. *Type* the desired values for the **Longer time** scenario. In our case, we have typed **150000** in the first text box, **0.06** in the second text box, and **2** in the third text box (Fig.EX-4.40).
24. *Click* the **Add** button, as shown in Fig.EX-4.40:

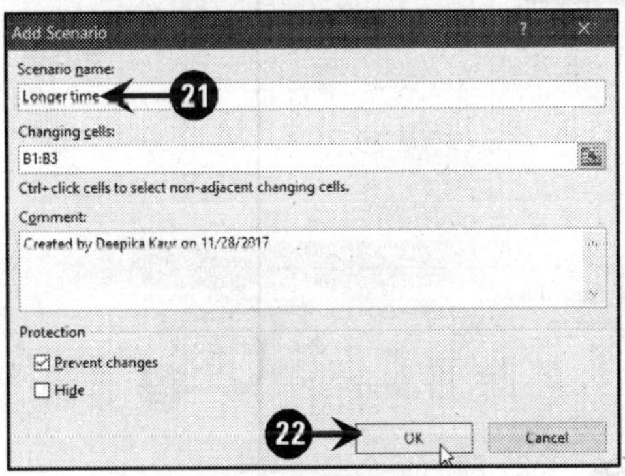

Fig.EX-4.39

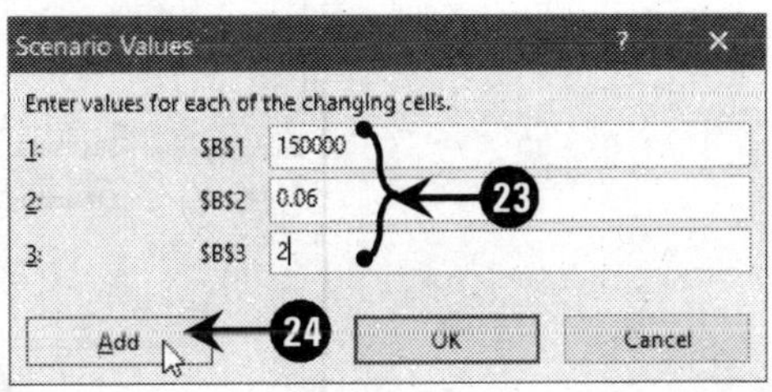

Fig.EX-4.40

The **Add Scenario** dialog box reappears (Fig.EX-4.41).

25. *Type* the name of the fourth scenario in the **Scenario name** text box. In our case, we have typed **Combination** in the text box (Fig.EX-4.41).

26. *Click* the **OK** button (Fig.EX-4.41).

    The **Scenario Values** dialog box appears (Fig.EX-4.42).

27. *Type* the desired values for the **Combination** scenario. In our case, we have typed **150000** in the first text box, **0.03** in the second text box, and **2** in the third text box (Fig.EX-4.42).

28. *Click* the **OK** button after creating all the scenarios, as shown in Fig.EX-4.42:

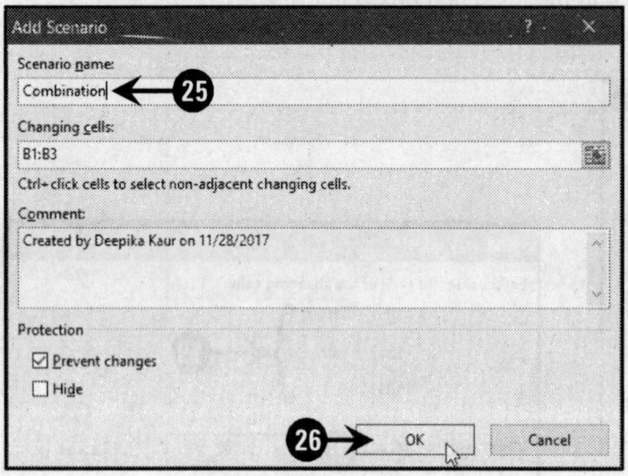

Fig.EX-4.41

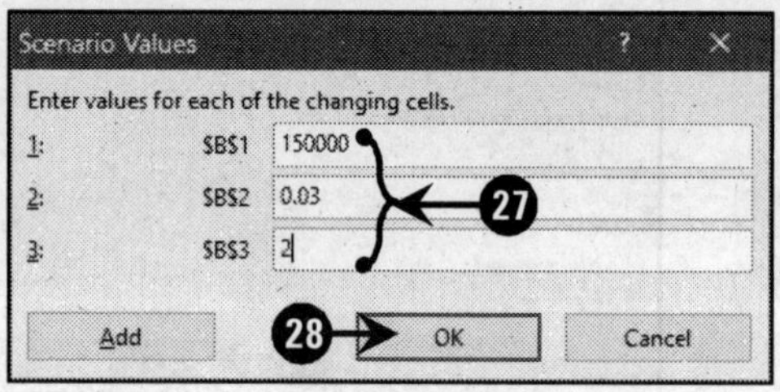

Fig.EX-4.42

The **Scenario Manager** dialog box appears, displaying the list of scenarios created in the preceding steps (Fig.EX-4.43).

29. *Select* a desired scenario name in the **Scenario Manager** dialog box to view it. In our case, we have selected **Best interest** scenario (Fig.EX-4.43).

30. *Click* the **Show** button, as shown in Fig.EX-4.43:

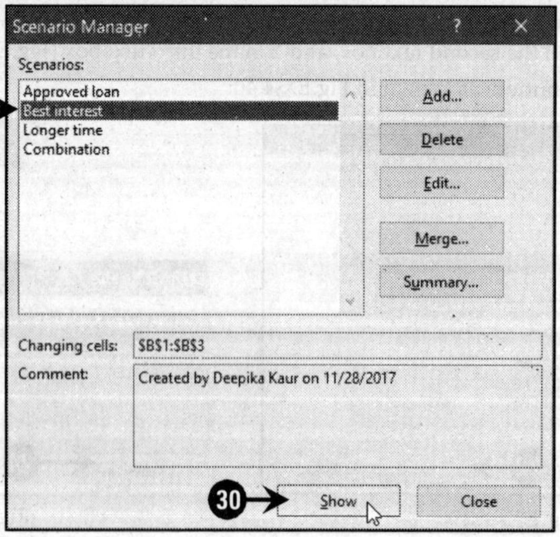

Fig.EX-4.43

The values of the selected scenario appear in the worksheet. In other words, the values in cells **B1**, **B2**, and **B3** change, and the corresponding changes are made in the values of cells **B5**, **B6**, and **B7**, as shown in Fig.EX-4.44:

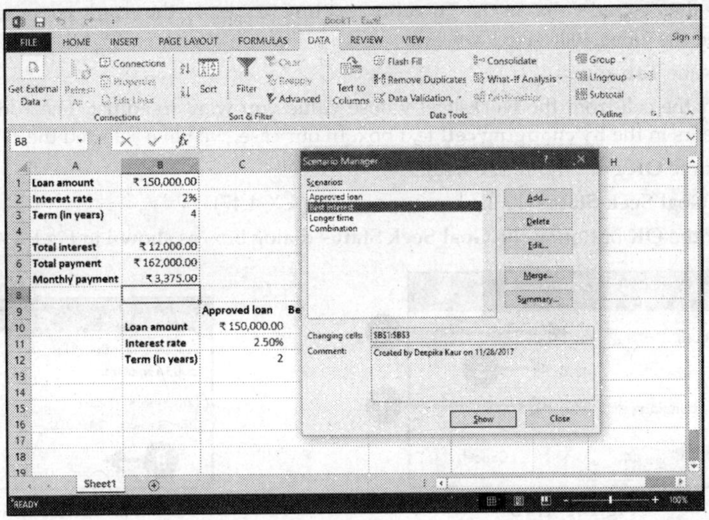

Fig.EX-4.44

Similarly, you can view the values of other scenarios by using the **Scenario Manager** dialog box.

Let us learn about the goal seek tool.

Using the Goal Seek Tool

Goal Seek tool is used when you know the result of the formula you are using but not the input value that the formula needs to obtain the result. Let us consider an example to better understand the working of the Goal Seek tool. Suppose the monthly payment of a loan of ₹150000 for a time period of 3 years at an annual interest rate of 5% is ₹4,791.67. In this case, you can use the Goal Seek tool to calculate the total amount of loan with different monthly payments and with the same interest rate and time period. For example, let us calculate the total amount of loan if the monthly payment is ₹4000.

Perform the following steps to calculate the total loan amount by using the Goal Seek tool:

1. *Open* a new or existing workbook that contains the information about the loan.
2. *Click* the **What-if Analysis** button under the **Data Tools** group of the **DATA** tab (Fig.EX-4.45).

   A drop-down list appears (Fig.EX-4.45).
3. *Select* the **Goal Seek** option from the drop-down list, as shown in Fig.EX-4.45:

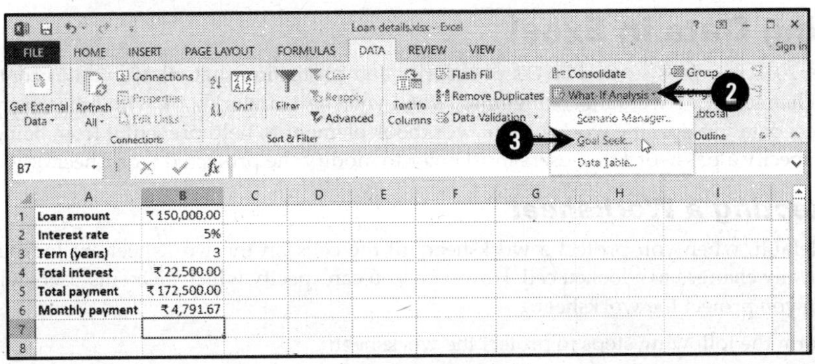

Fig.EX-4.45

The **Goal Seek** dialog box appears (Fig.EX-4.46).

4. *Select* the cell from the worksheet that contains the formula you want to resolve. The address of the selected cell appears in the **Set cell** text box. In our case, we have selected the cell **B6** (Fig.EX-4.46).
5. *Type* the desired value in the **To value** text box to specify the result you want. In our case, we have typed the value **4000** (Fig.EX-4.46).
6. *Press* the **Tab** key.
7. *Select* the cell from the worksheet whose value you want to adjust. The address of the selected cell appears in the **By changing cell** text box. In our case, we have selected the cell **B1** (Fig.EX-4.46).
8. *Click* the **OK** button (Fig.EX-4.46).

   The **Goal Seek Status** dialog box appears (Fig.EX-4.47).
9. *Click* the **OK** button in the **Goal Seek Status** dialog box, as shown in Fig.EX-4.47:

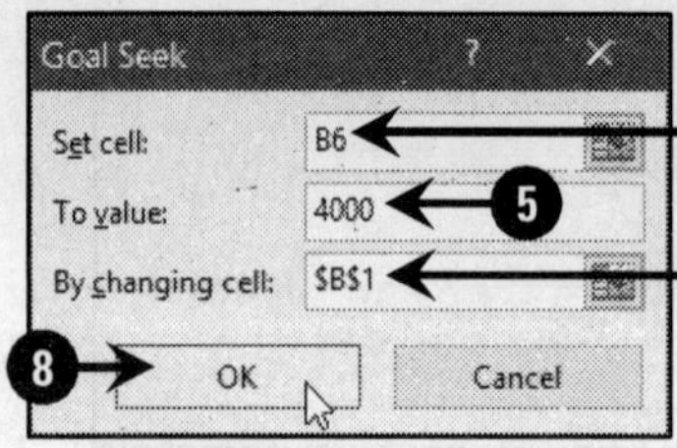

Fig.EX-4.46

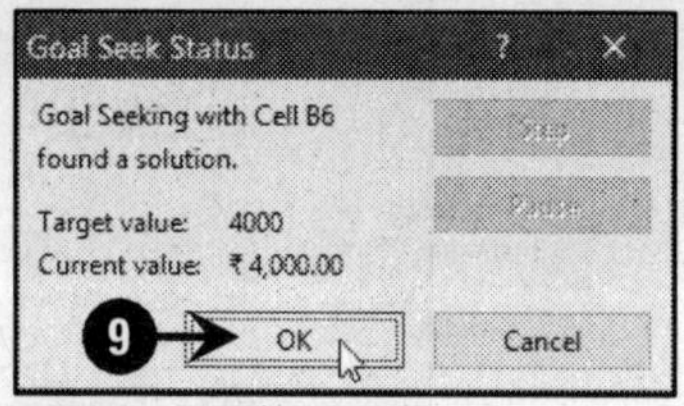

Fig.EX-4.47

The amount of the loan changes from ₹150000 to ₹125,217.39 according to the monthly amount you want to pay, i.e., ₹4000 as shown in Fig.EX-4.48:

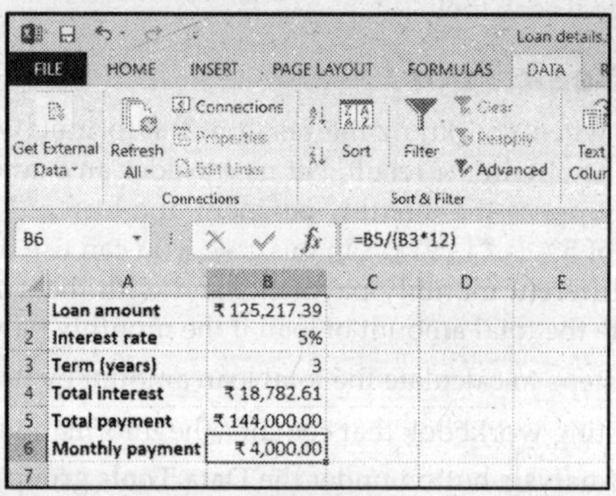

Fig.EX-4.48

Let us now learn the concept of protecting data in Excel.

Protecting Data in Excel

Excel 2013 provides several layers of security and protection that allows you to control who can access and change your Excel data. Sometimes, when you share a workbook with other users, you may want to protect data in a specific worksheet or workbook element to help prevent it from being changed. You can also specify a password that users must enter to modify the protected worksheet or workbook element.

Protecting a Worksheet

By default, when you protect a worksheet, all the cells on the worksheet are locked, and users cannot make any changes to a locked cell. However, you can specify which elements users will be able to change when you protect the worksheet.

Perform the following steps to protect the worksheet:

1. *Select* the worksheet that you want to protect.

2. *Click* the **Format** button under the **Cells** group of the **HOME** tab.

   The drop-down list appears (Fig.EX-4.49).

3. *Select* the **Protect Sheet** option under the **Protection** section from the drop-down list, as shown in Fig.EX-4.49:

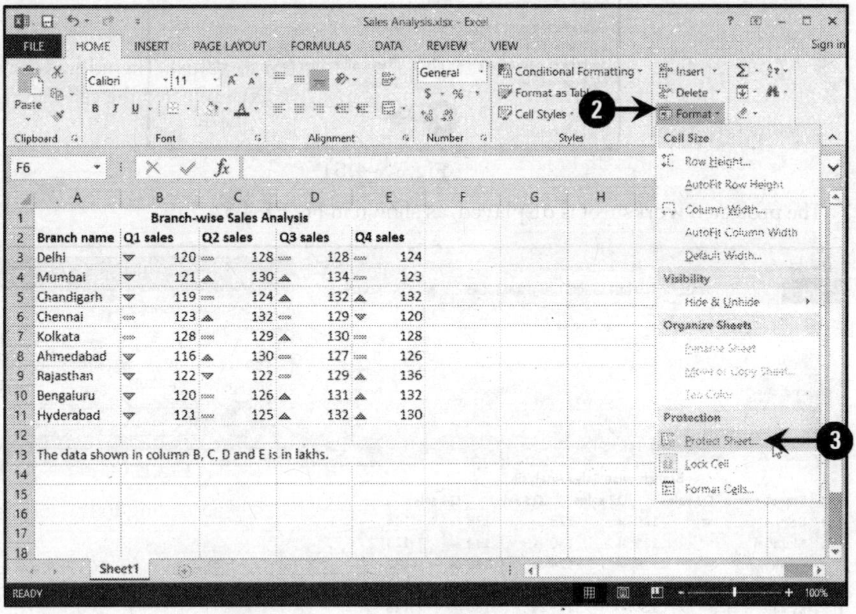

Fig.EX-4.49

The **Protect Sheet** dialog box appears (Fig.EX-4.50).

4. *Type* the password in the **Password to unprotect sheet** textbox. In our case, we have typed the password **protect123** (Fig.EX-4.50).
5. *Click* the **OK** button, as shown in Fig.EX-4.50:

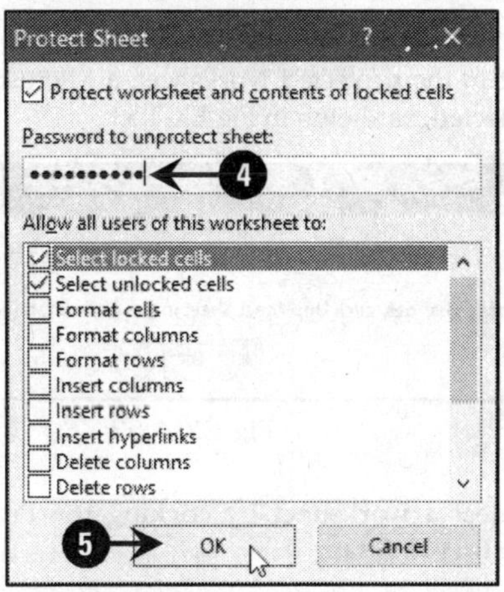

Fig.EX-4.50

The **Confirm Password** dialog box appears (Fig.EX-4.51).

6. *Type* the same password in the **Reenter password to proceed** textbox that you typed in **Password to unprotect sheet** textbox under **Protect Sheet** dialog box (Fig.EX-4.51).

7. *Click* the **OK** button, as shown in Fig.EX-4.51:

Fig.EX-4.51

The protected worksheet is displayed, as shown in Fig.EX-4.52:

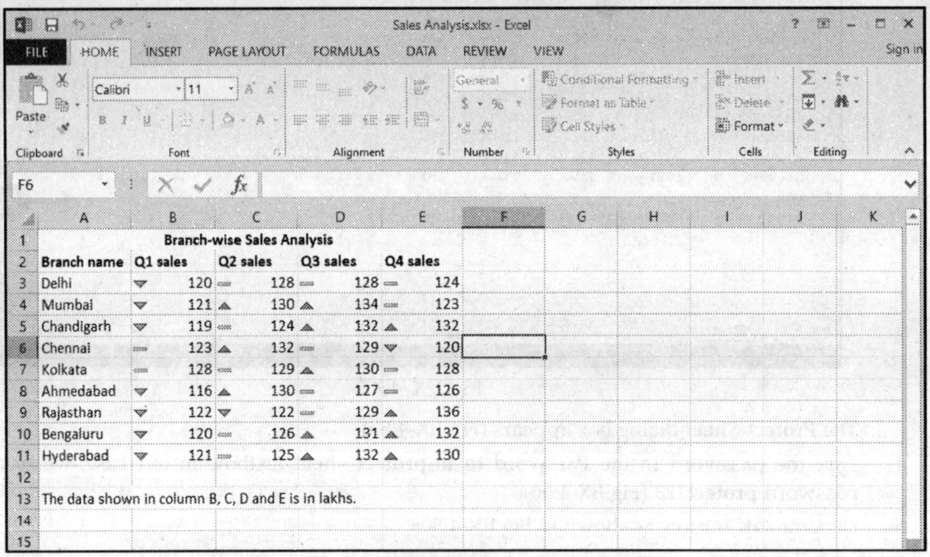

Fig.EX-4.52

If you type anything in the protected worksheet, a Microsoft Excel dialog box appears that shows the worksheet is protected, as shown in Fig.EX-4.53:

Fig.EX-4.53

Note

You can protect a worksheet by clicking the Protect Sheet button under the Changes group, of the REVIEW tab.

Perform the following steps to access the protected worksheet:

1. *Open* the protected worksheet.
2. *Click* the **Format** button under the **Cells** group in the **HOME** tab.

   A drop-down list appears (Fig.EX-4.54).

3. *Select* the **Unprotect Sheet** option under the **Protection** section from the drop-down list, as shown in Fig.EX-4.54:

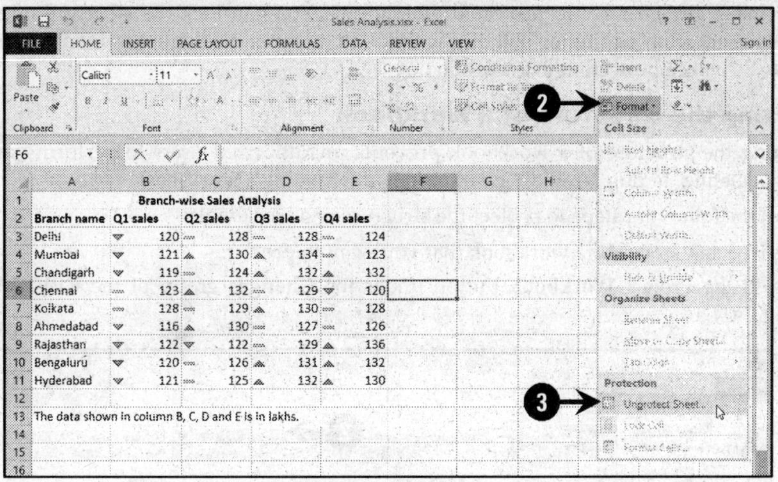

Fig.EX-4.54

The **Unprotect Sheet** dialog box appears (Fig.EX-4.55).

4. *Type* the password in the **Password** textbox that you entered at the time of protecting the worksheet. In our case, we have typed **protect123** (Fig.EX-4.55).
5. *Click* the **OK** button, as shown in Fig.EX-4.55:

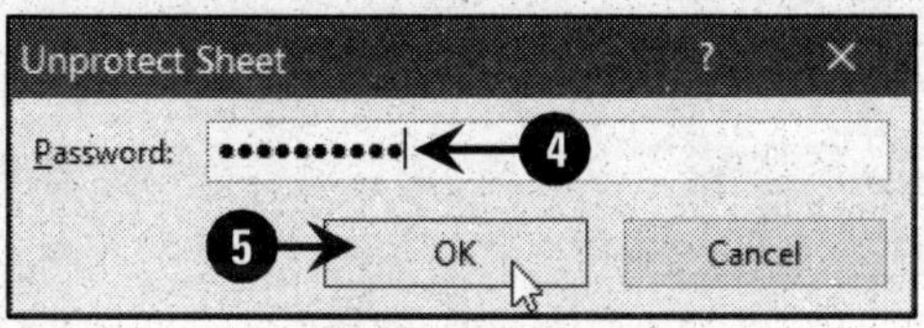

Fig.EX-4.55

The protected worksheet gets unprotected and you can perform any task on the worksheet, as shown in Fig.EX 4.56:

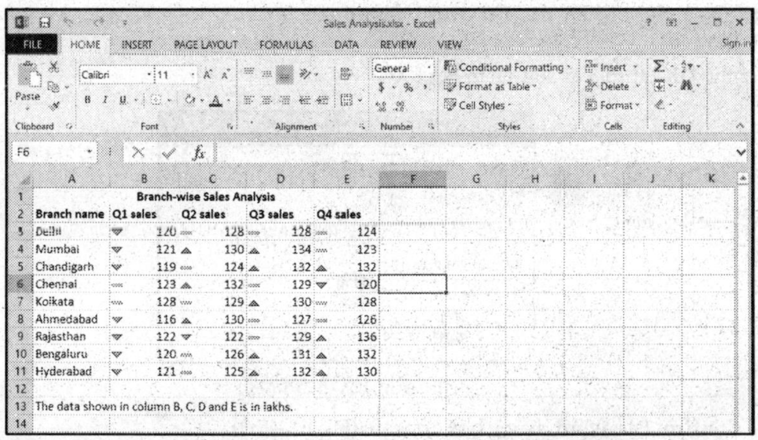

Fig.EX-4.56

Let us now learn to protect a workbook.

Protecting a Workbook

By default, when you protect a workbook, all the worksheet under the workbook is protected, and users cannot make any changes to protected worksheets. You can lock the structure of a workbook, which prevents users from adding or deleting worksheets or from displaying hidden worksheets. Let us learn to apply Structure protection to a workbook.

Protecting the Structure of a Workbook

Protecting the structure of a workbook prevents unauthorized users to perform various tasks such as adding, deleting, hiding, un-hiding, renaming, and moving a worksheet.

Perform the following steps to protect the structure of a workbook:

1. *Open* a new or existing workbook that you want to protect.
2. *Select* the **Protect Workbook** button under the **Changes** group of the **REVIEW** tab, as shown in Fig.EX-4.57:

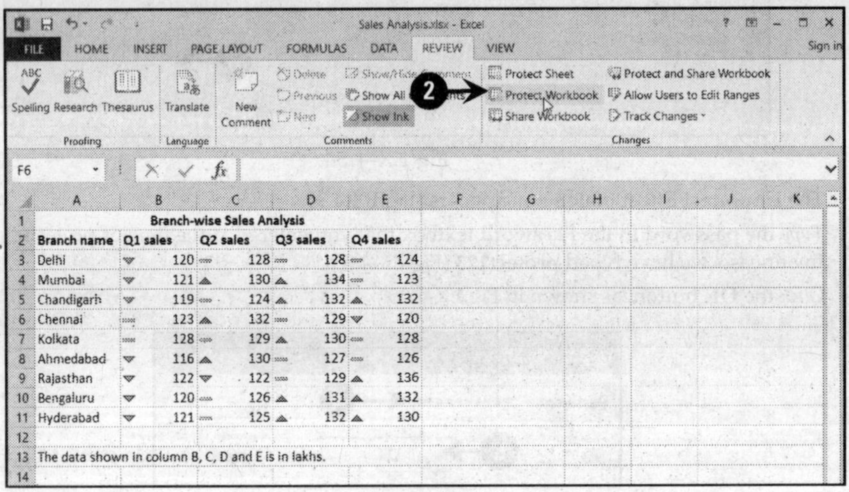

Fig.EX-4.57

The **Protect Structure and Windows** dialog box (Fig.EX-4.58).

3. *Check* the **Structure** checkbox in **Protect Structure and Windows** dialog box (Fig.EX-4.58).
4. *Type* the password in the **Password (optional)** textbox. In our case, we have typed **protect123** (Fig.EX-4.58).
5. *Click* the **OK** button, as shown in Fig.EX-4.58:

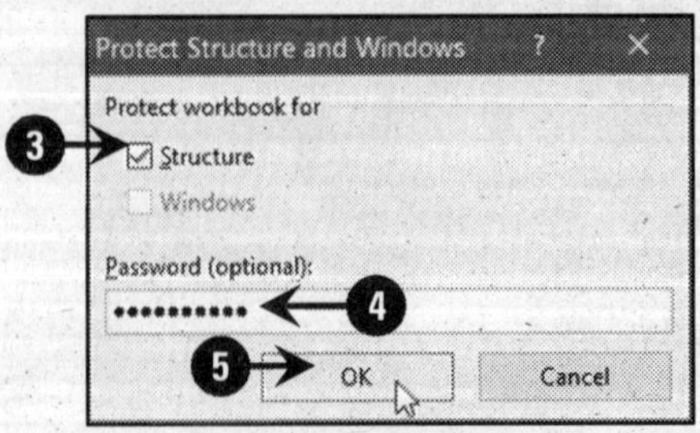

Fig.EX-4.58

The **Confirm Password** dialog box appears (Fig.EX-4.59).

6. *Type* the same password in the **Reenter password to proceed** textbox (Fig.EX-4.59).

7. *Click* the **OK** button, as shown in Fig.EX-4.59:

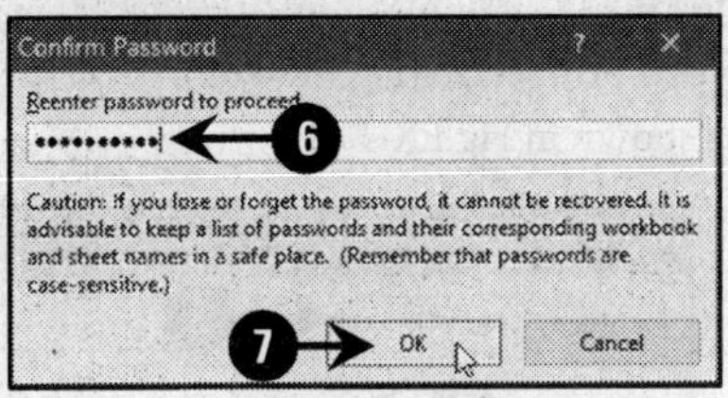

Fig.EX-4.59

The protected workbook is displayed, as shown in Fig.EX-4.60:

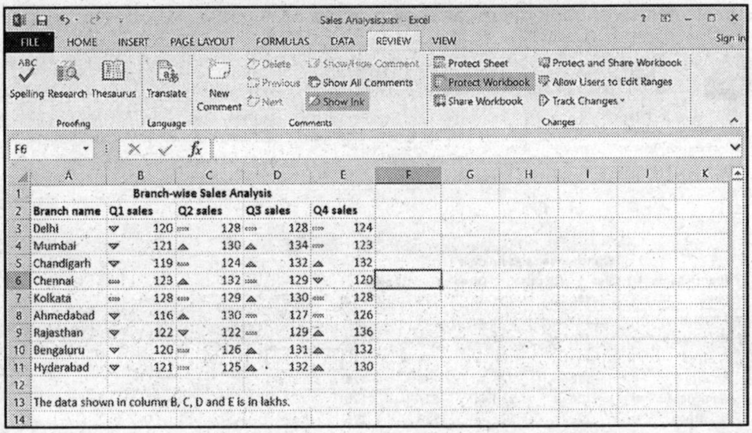

Fig.EX-4.60

Now, let us access a protected workbook by performing the following steps:

1. *Open* the protected workbook.
2. *Click* the **Protect Workbook** button under the **Changes** group of the **REVIEW** tab, as shown in Fig.EX-4.61:

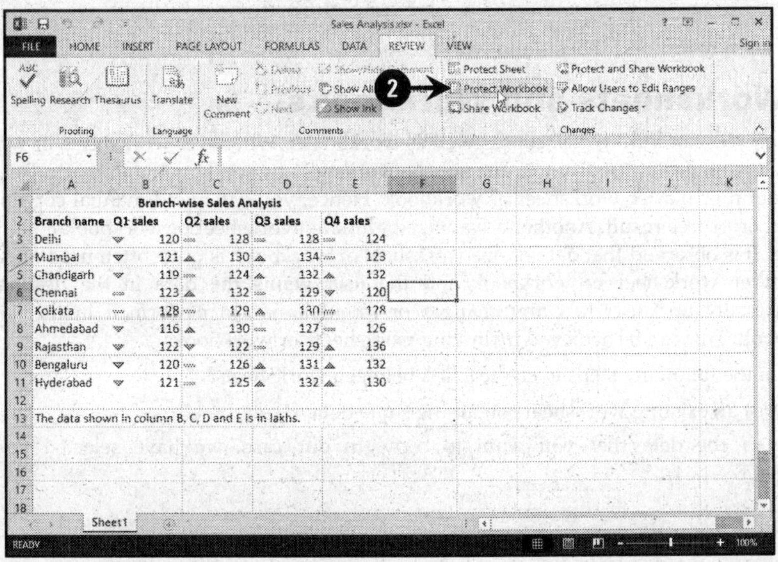

Fig.EX-4.61

The **Unprotect Workbook** dialog box appears (Fig.EX-4.62).

3. *Type* the password in the **Password** textbox that you entered at the time of protecting the worksheet In our case, we have typed **protect123** (Fig.EX-4.62).
4. *Click* the **OK** button, as shown in Fig.EX-4.62:

Fig.EX-4.62

The protected workbook opens, as shown in Fig.EX-4.63:

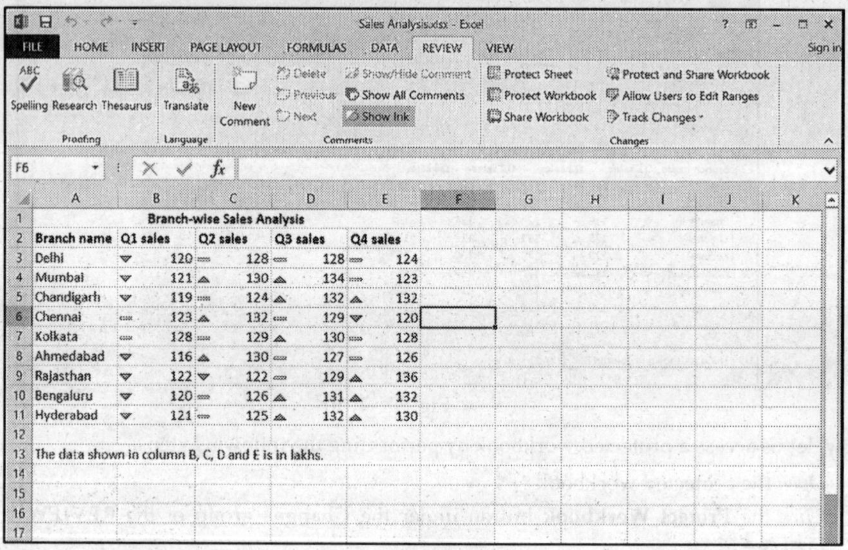

Fig.EX-4.63

Let us learn to link worksheets and workbooks.

Linking Worksheets and Workbooks

In Excel, you can link worksheets as well as workbooks. Whenever worksheets or workbooks are linked together, changes carried out in the source worksheet or workbook automatically get reflected in the destination or master worksheet or workbook. Hence, you can avoid manual copying and pasting data and get error free result. Another advantage of linking worksheet or workbook is calculation and update of data. It is observed that data of one worksheet or workbook is quite often used or related with the data of another worksheet or workbook and the user wants the data in the destination worksheet to automatically update when any changes or calculations are performed in the source worksheet or workbook. This can be achieved by linking worksheets or workbooks.

Perform the following steps to create a link between worksheets:

1. *Open* an existing worksheet containing some data.
2. *Select* the data that you want to copy. In our case, we have selected the cell range **A1:E5** (Fig.EX-4.64).

3. *Click* the **Copy** button under the **Clipboard** group of the **HOME** tab, as shown in Fig.EX-4.64:

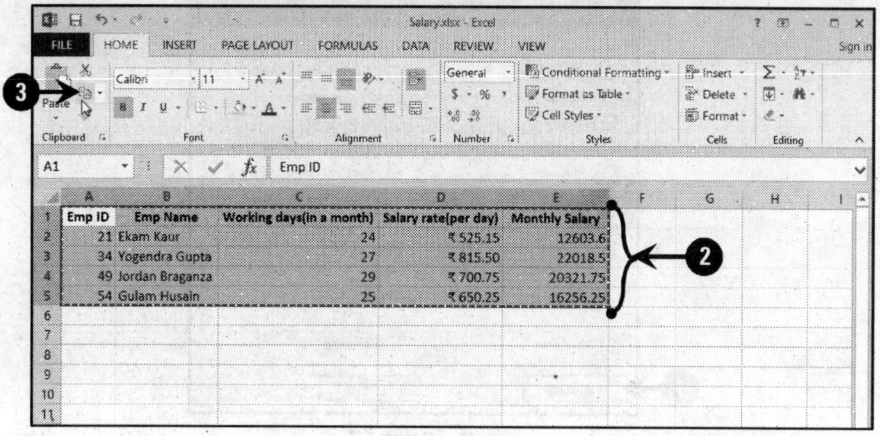

Fig.EX-4.64

4. *Select* another worksheet in **Sheet** tab where you want to paste the data. In our case, we have selected **Sheet2** as shown in Fig.EX-4.65:

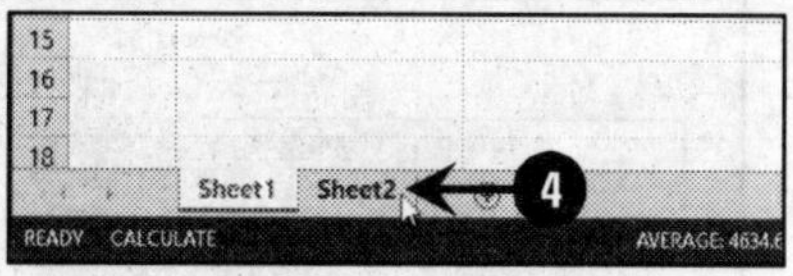

Fig.EX-4.65

The **Sheet2** is active in the workbook (Fig.EX-4.66).

5. *Click* the lower part of the **Paste** button under the **Clipboard** group of the **HOME** tab. The drop-down list appears (Fig.EX-4.66).
6. *Select* the **Paste Special** option from the drop-down list, as shown in Fig.EX-4.66:

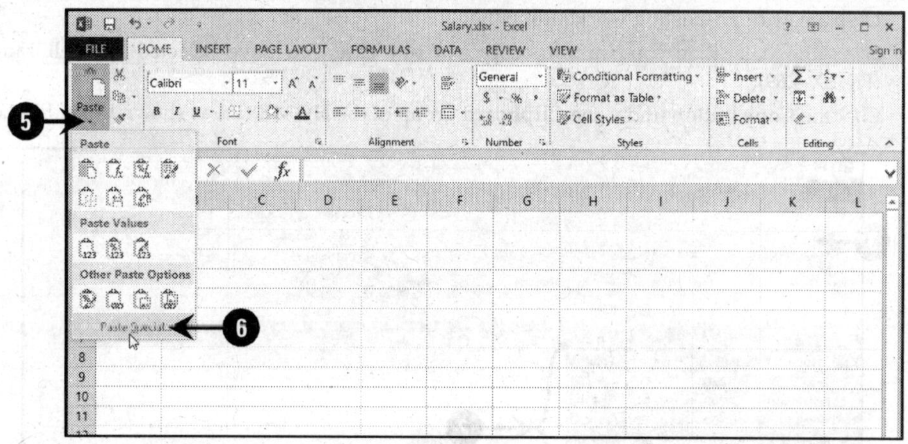

Fig.EX-4.66

The **Paste Special** dialog box appears (Fig.EX-4.67).

7. *Click* the **Paste Link** button in the **Paste Special** dialog box as shown in Fig.EX-4.67:

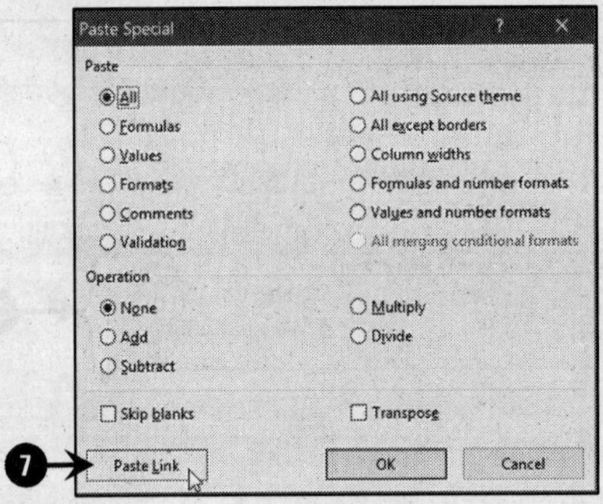

Fig.EX-4.67

The data is copied as a link and the formula bar displays the reference of the original worksheet, a shown in Fig.EX-4.68:

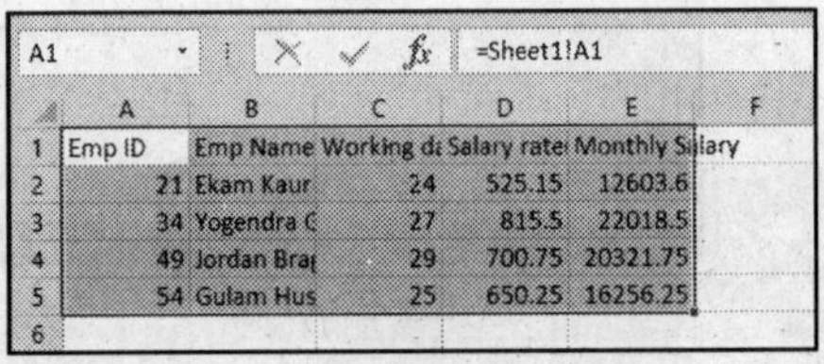

Fig.EX-4.68

If you make any changes in **Sheet1**, they simultaneously appear in **Sheet2**.

After learning the process of linking worksheets, let us proceed and learn to link two workbooks b performing the following steps:

1. *Open* a new or an existing workbook.
2. *Select* the data that you want to copy. In our case, we have selected the cell range **A1:D** (Fig.EX-4.69).
3. *Click* the **Copy** button under the **Clipboard** group of the **HOME** tab, as shown in Fig.EX-4.69:

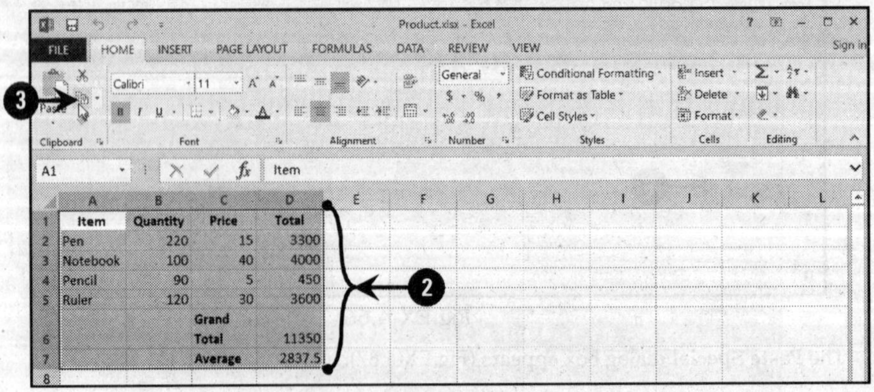

Fig.EX-4.69

4. *Open* another workbook in which you want to create a link. In our case, we have opened a nev workbook (Fig.EX-4.70).

5. *Click* the lower part of the **Paste** button in the **Clipboard** group of the **HOME** tab.
   The drop-down list appears (Fig.EX-4.70).
6. *Select* the **Paste Special** option from the drop-down list, as shown in Fig.EX-4.70:

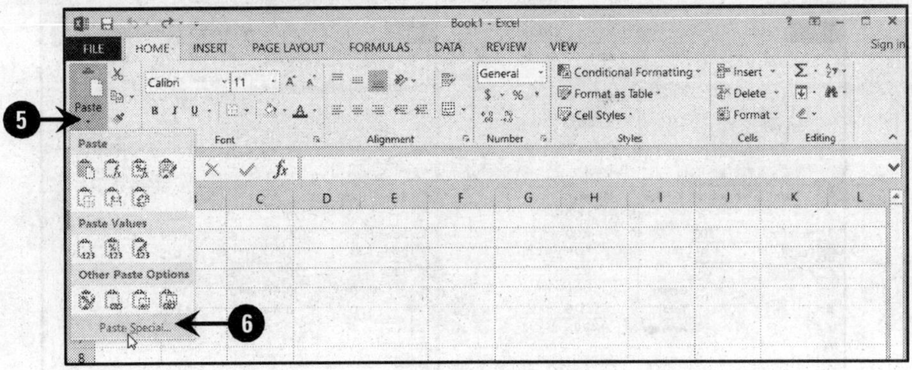

Fig.EX-4.70

The **Paste Special** dialog box appears (Fig.EX-4.71).

7. *Click* the **Paste Link** button in the **Paste Special** dialog box, as shown in Fig.EX-4.71:

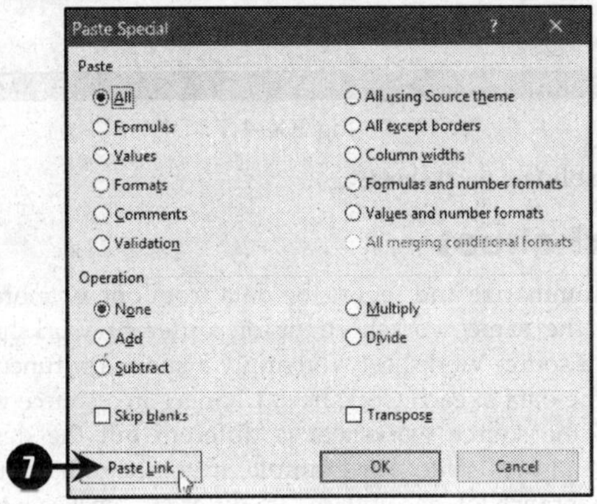

Fig.EX-4.71

The data is copied as a link and the formula bar displays the reference of the original workbook, as shown in Fig.EX-4.72:

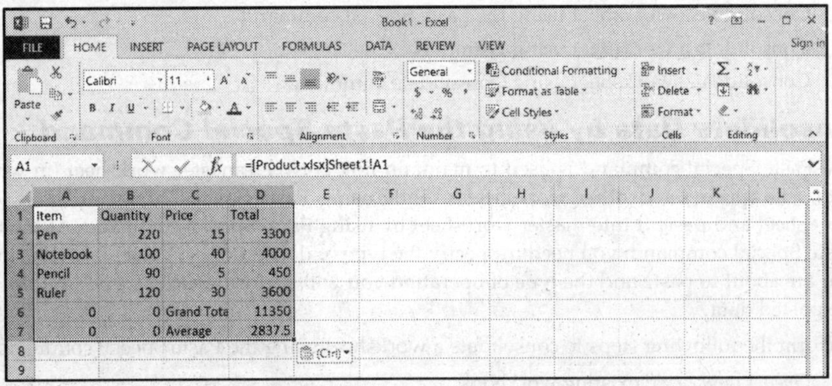

Fig.EX-4.72

If you make any changes in the source workbook, the data in the destination workbook is also changed. In our case, we have changed the data of cell B3 in the source workbook and the changes done in the source workbook also reflect in the destination workbook, as shown in Fig.EX-4.73:

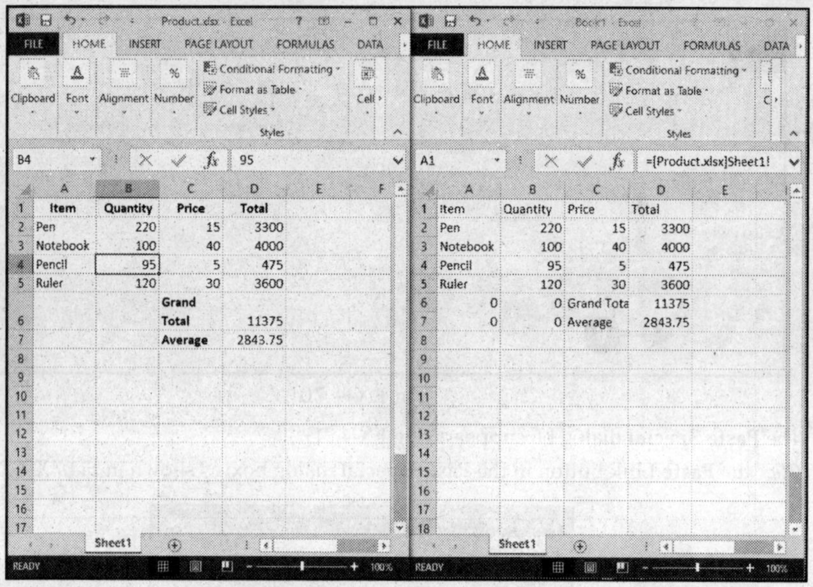

Fig.EX-4.73

Let us now learn to consolidate worksheets.

Consolidating Worksheet

Consolidate means to summarize and report the data from one or more source worksheets. The source worksheets can be in the same worksheet, or on different worksheets or workbooks. When you consolidate the data of a source worksheet, you apply a summary function to generate a summary data. You can easily update the data of each worksheet. Changes in a source worksheet affect the consolidated data. In consolidating, the source worksheet is different but the destination worksheet where you consolidate the data are always same. For example, if you have half yearly sales data of Jaipur, Delhi, Mumbai, and Chennai branch of a company in different worksheets, then you can consolidate or summarize the sales from each worksheet into a company's master worksheet.

In Excel, you can consolidate data of different worksheets into a single worksheet by using any of the following methods:

- Consolidate a worksheet using the Paste Special command
- Consolidate a worksheet using Formulas
- Consolidate a worksheet using Consolidate command

Consolidate Data by using the Paste Special Command

The Paste Special command is used to maintain link between master worksheet (in which consolidated data will appear) and other worksheets. While using Paste Special command, you copy data from a worksheet and paste it into master worksheet by using Paste Special command. At the time of executing Paste Special command, you need to specify the type of data (such as, value, formula, and comment) that you are about to paste and the type of operation you will perform (such as, add, multiply, and divide) on the pasted data.

Perform the following steps to consolidate a worksheet using the Paste Special command:

1. *Open* a new or an existing workbook.

2. *Select* the data that you want to consolidate. In our case, we have selected cell range **B3:B8** (Fig.EX-4.74).
3. *Click* the **Copy** button under the **Clipboard** group of the **HOME** tab, as shown in Fig.EX-4.74:

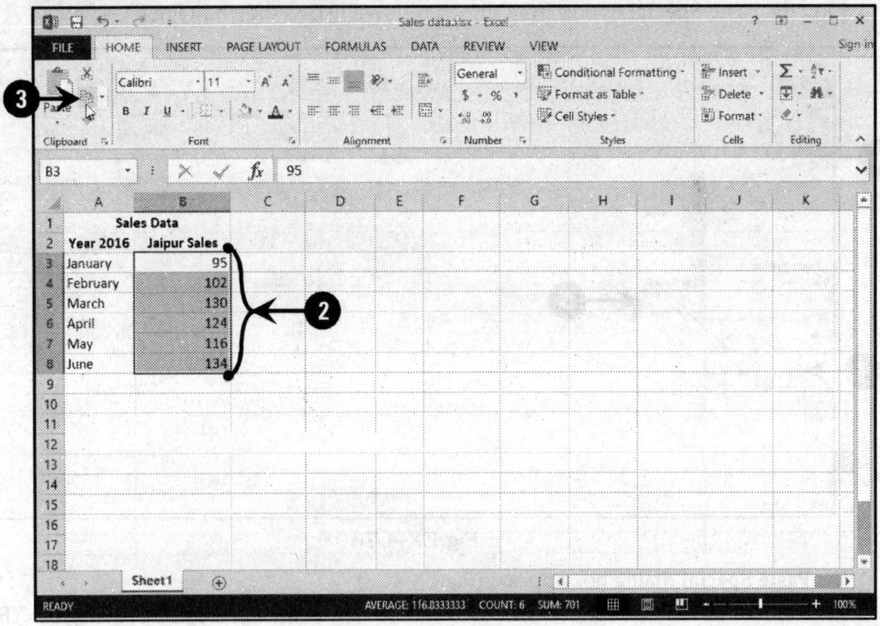

Fig.EX-4.74

4. *Select* the worksheet in the Sheet tab, where you want to consolidate the data. In our case, we have selected **Sheet5**, as shown in Fig.EX-4.75:

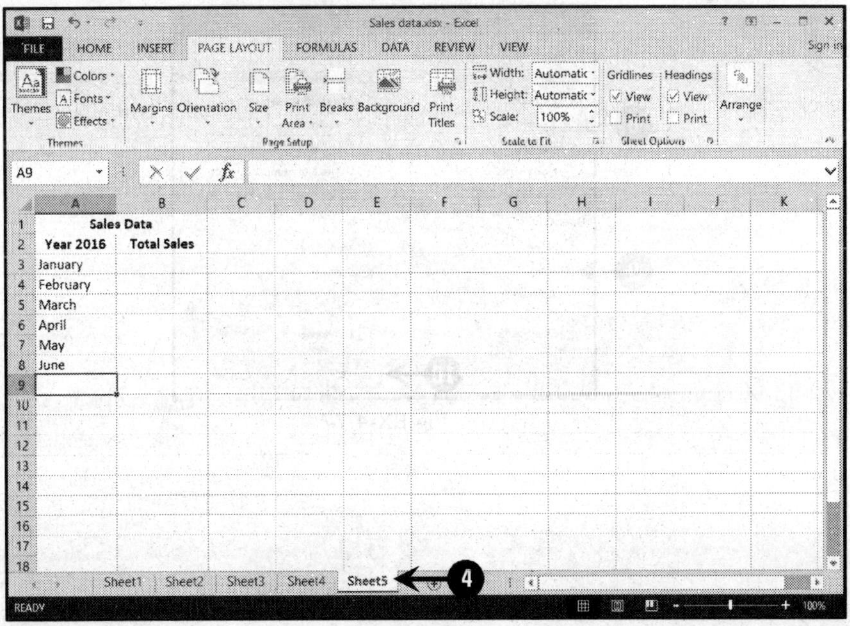

Fig.EX-4.75

5. *Select* the cell where you want to paste the data. In our case, we have selected cell **B3** (Fig.EX-4.76).
6. *Click* the lower part of the **Paste** button under the **Clipboard** group of the **HOME** tab. The drop-down list appears (Fig.EX-4.76).
7. *Select* the **Paste Special** option from the drop-down list, as shown in Fig.EX-4.76:

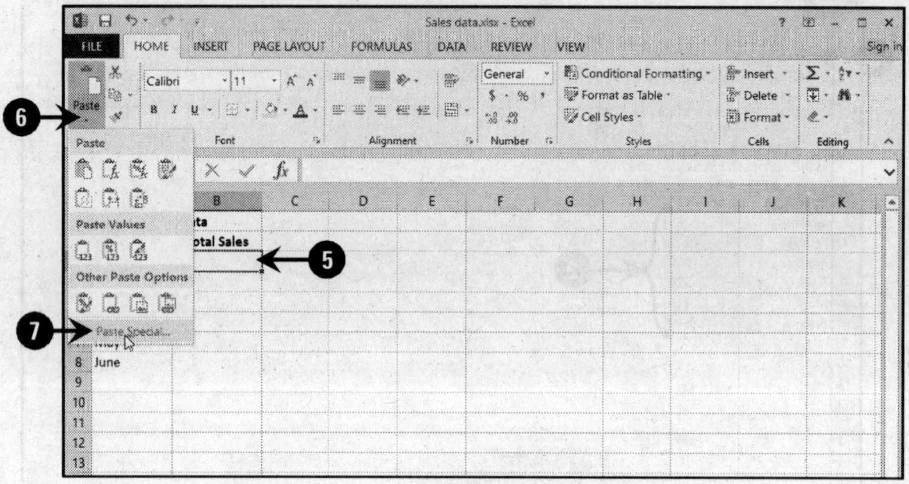

Fig.EX-4.76

The **Paste Special** dialog box appears (Fig.EX-4.77).

8. *Select* the **Values** radio button under the **Paste** section in the **Paste Special** dialog box (Fig.EX-4.77).
9. *Select* the **Add** radio button under the **Operation** section in the **Paste Special** dialog box (Fig.EX-4.77).
10. *Click* the **OK** button, as shown in Fig.EX-4.77:

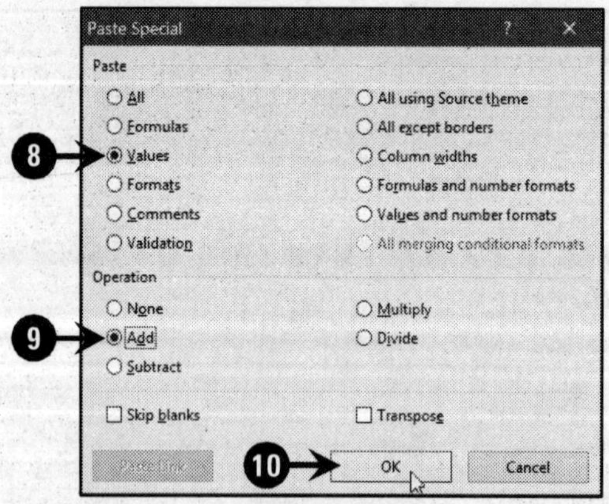

Fig.EX-4.77

The data is copied in the **Sheet5** worksheet, as shown in Fig.EX-4.78:

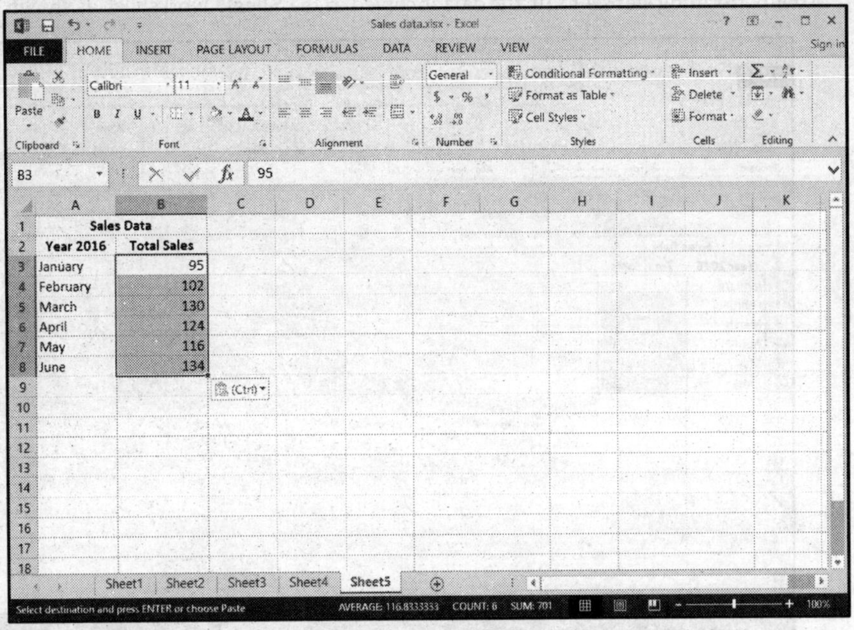

Fig.EX-4.78

11. *Select* the worksheet in the **Sheet** tab of data you want to consolidate. In our case, we have selected **Sheet2** (Fig.EX-4.79).
12. *Select* the data that you want to consolidate. In our case, we have selected cell range **B3:B8** (Fig.EX-4.79).
13. *Click* the **Copy** button under the **Clipboard** group of the **HOME** tab, as shown in Fig.EX-4.79:

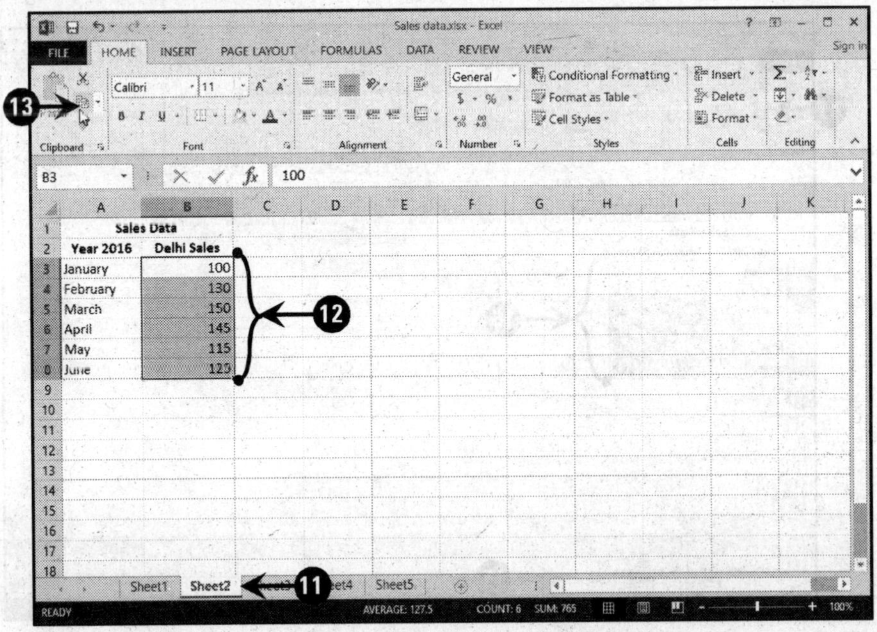

Fig.EX-4.79

14. *Repeat* steps **4** to **10.**
    After performing steps 4 to 10, the data is copied in the **Sheet5** worksheet, as shown in Fig.EX-4.80:

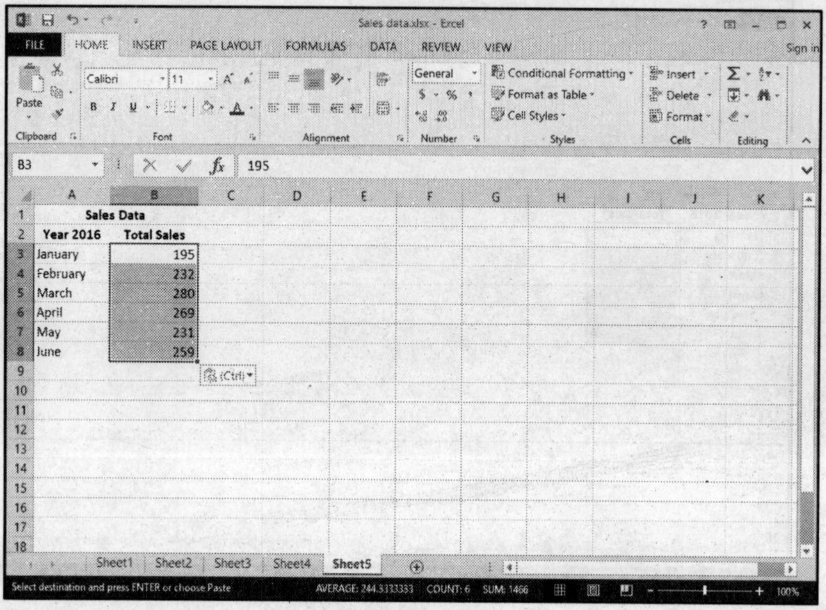

Fig.EX-4.80

15. *Select* the worksheet in the Sheet tab of data you want to consolidate. In our case, we have selected **Sheet3** (Fig.EX-4.81).
16. *Select* the data that you want to consolidate. In our case, we have selected cell range **B3:B8** (Fig.EX-4.81).
17. *Click* the **Copy** button under the **Clipboard** group of the **HOME** tab, as shown in Fig.EX-4.81:

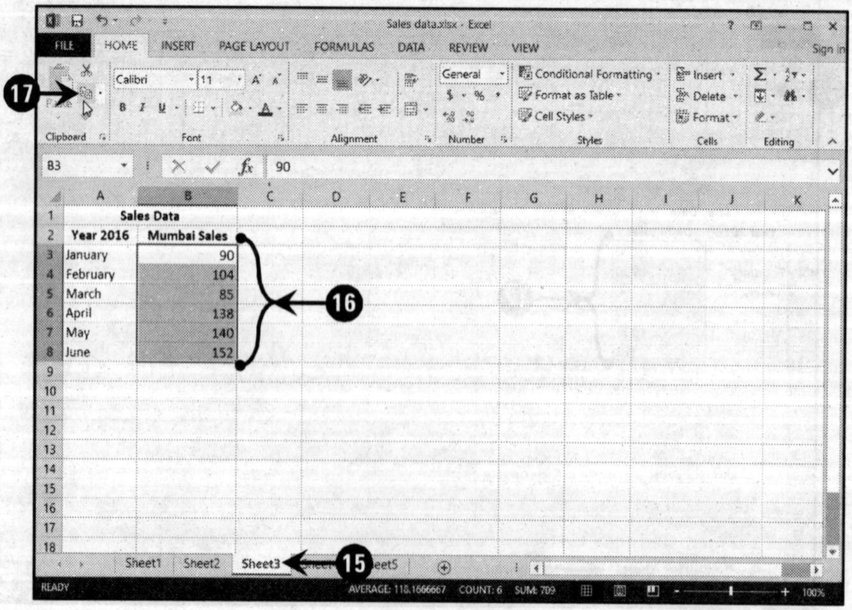

Fig.EX-4.81

18. *Repeat* steps **4** to **10**.

    After performing steps 4 to 10, the data is copied in the **Sheet5** worksheet, as shown in Fig.EX-4.82:

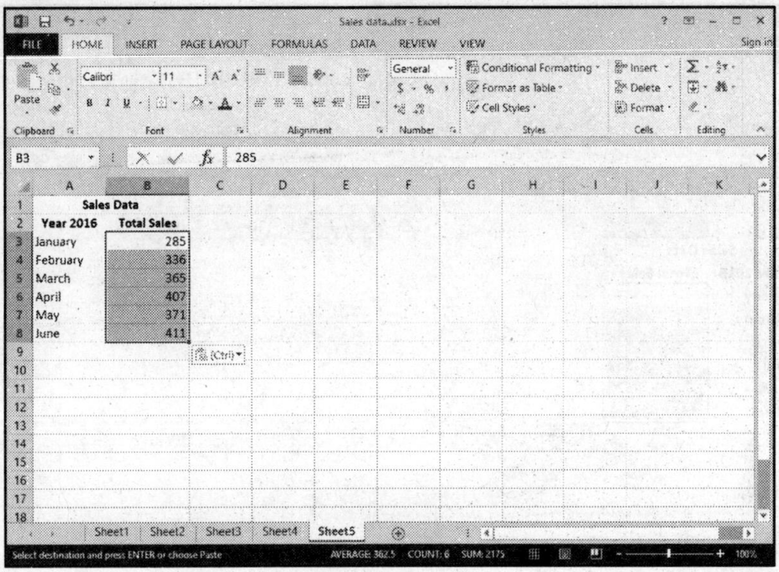

Fig.EX-4.82

19. *Select* the worksheet in the **Sheet** tab of data you want to consolidate. In our case, we have selected **Sheet4** (Fig.EX-4.83).
20. *Select* the data that you want to consolidate. In our case, we have selected cell range **B3:B8** (Fig.EX-4.83).
21. *Click* the **Copy** button under the **Clipboard** group of the **HOME** tab, as shown in Fig.EX-4.83:

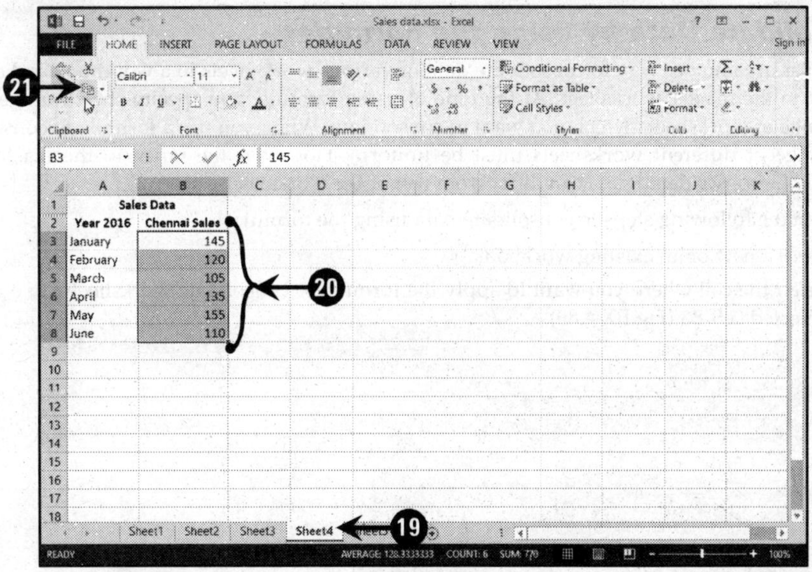

Fig.EX-4.83

22. *Repeat* steps **4** to **10**.

    After performing steps 4 to 10, the data is copied in the **Sheet5** worksheet, as shown in Fig.EX-4.84:

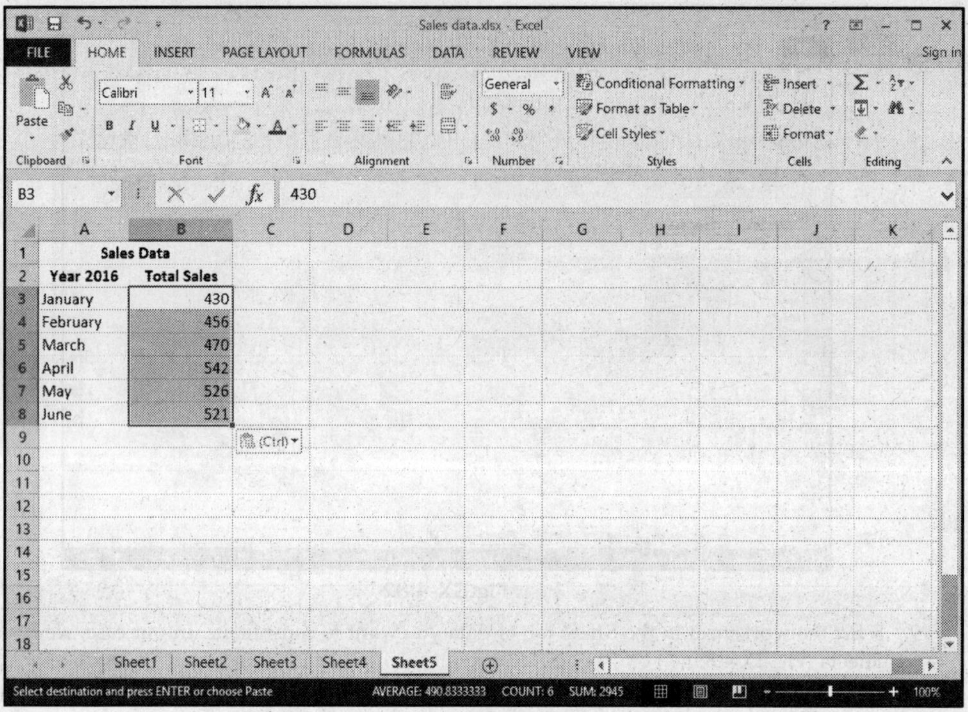

Fig.EX-4.84

Let us now learn to consolidate data by using formula.

Consolidate Data by using the Formulas

Formulas are another way to consolidate data of various worksheets in a workbook and display the final output in the master worksheet. At the time of using formula, you specify sheet number or names and cell range of worksheets which you want to consolidate. When you use a formula to consolidate data, the cell range of different worksheets must be uniform. However, the range in the master worksheet to display the consolidated data can differ from rest of the worksheets.

Perform the following steps to consolidate data using the formulas:

1. *Open* a new or an existing workbook.
2. *Select* the cell where you want to apply the formula to consolidate worksheets. In our case, we have selected cell **B3** (Fig.EX-4.85).

3. *Type* the formula in the selected cell. In our case, we have typed **=SUM(Sheet1:Sheet4!B3)**, as shown in Fig.EX-4.85:

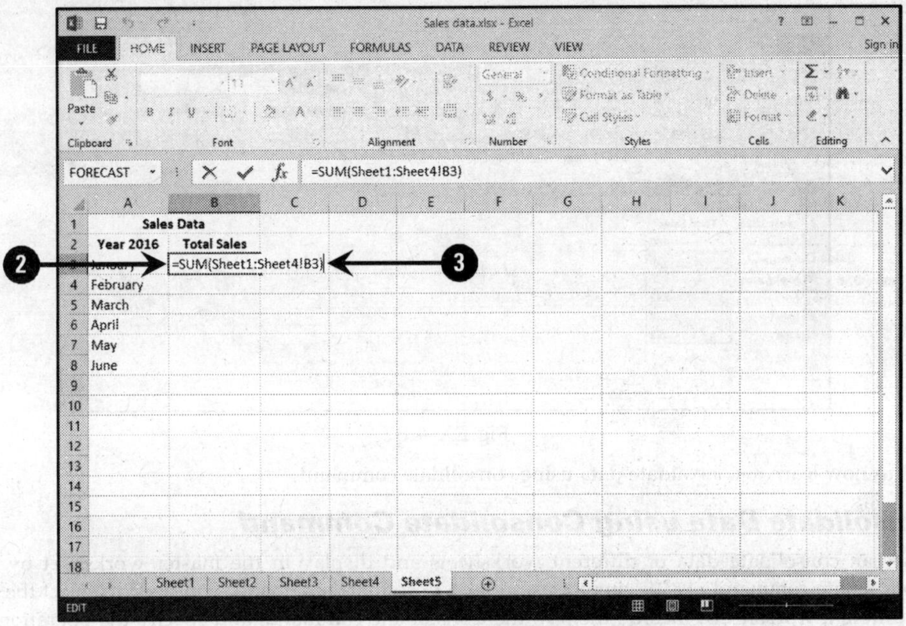

Fig.EX-4.85

4. *Press* the **Enter** key.

   The consolidated data is displayed in worksheet, as shown in Fig.EX-4.86:

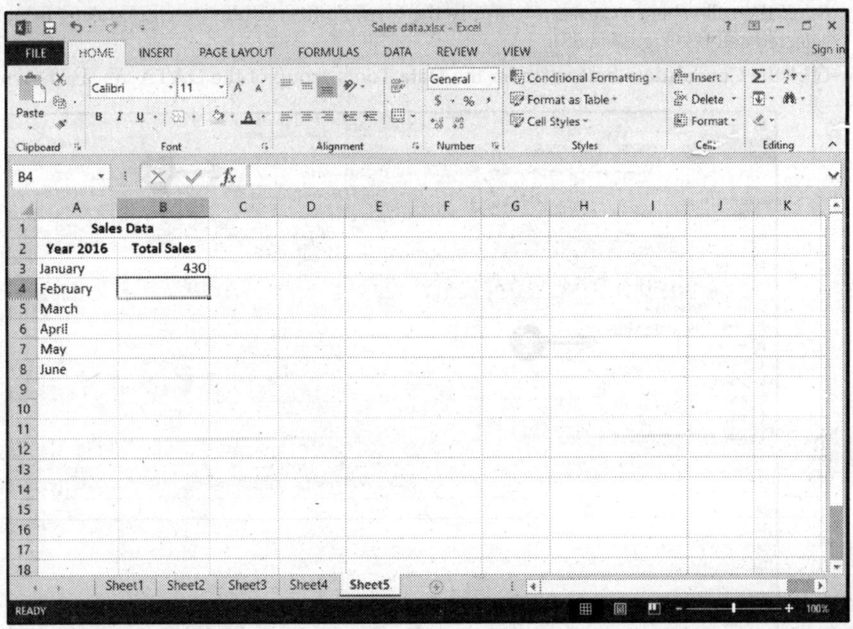

Fig.EX-4.86

Similarly, you can consolidate the data of the each month of the branches of the company. In our case, we have consolidated **February**, **March**, **April**, **May**, and **June**, as shown in Fig.EX-4.87:

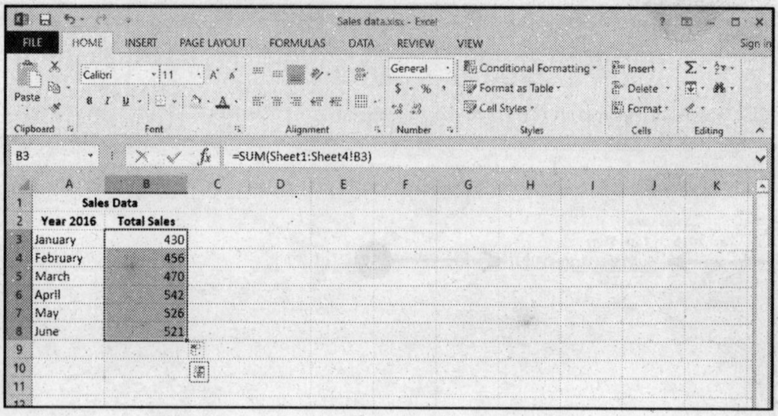

Fig.EX-4.87

Let us now learn to consolidate data using consolidate command

Consolidate Data using Consolidate Command

You can consolidate data of different worksheets and display in the master worksheet by using the Consolidate command. At the time of using the Consolidate command, you need to select the cell range in different worksheets, include them in the Consolidate command, and specify the operation (such as, add, multiply, and divide) you want to perform on cell ranges selected from different worksheet.

Perform the following steps to consolidate data using consolidate command:

1. *Open* a new or an existing workbook.
2. *Select* the cell where you want to apply the formula to consolidate worksheets. In our case, we have selected cell **B3** (Fig.EX-4.88).
3. *Click* the **Consolidate** button under the **Data Tools** group of the **DATA** tab, as shown in Fig.EX-4.88:

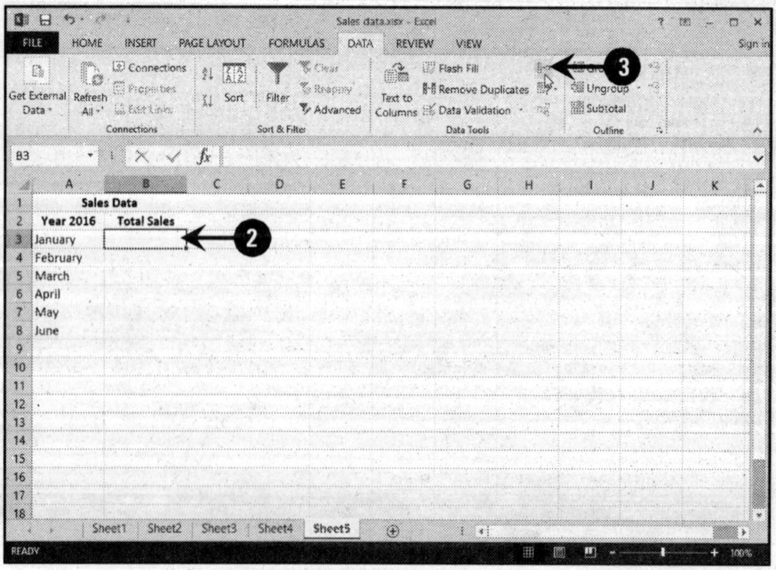

Fig.EX-4.88

The **Consolidate** dialog box appears (Fig.EX-4.89).

4. *Select* the worksheet in the **Sheet** tab of data you want to consolidate. In our case, we have selected **Sheet1** (Fig.EX-4.89).
5. *Select* the data that you want to consolidate. In our case, we have selected cell range **B3:B8** (Fig.EX-4.89).

   The reference of the data is displayed in the **Reference** range box (Fig.EX-4.89).
6. *Click* the **Add** button in the **Consolidate** dialog box, as shown in Fig.EX-4.89:

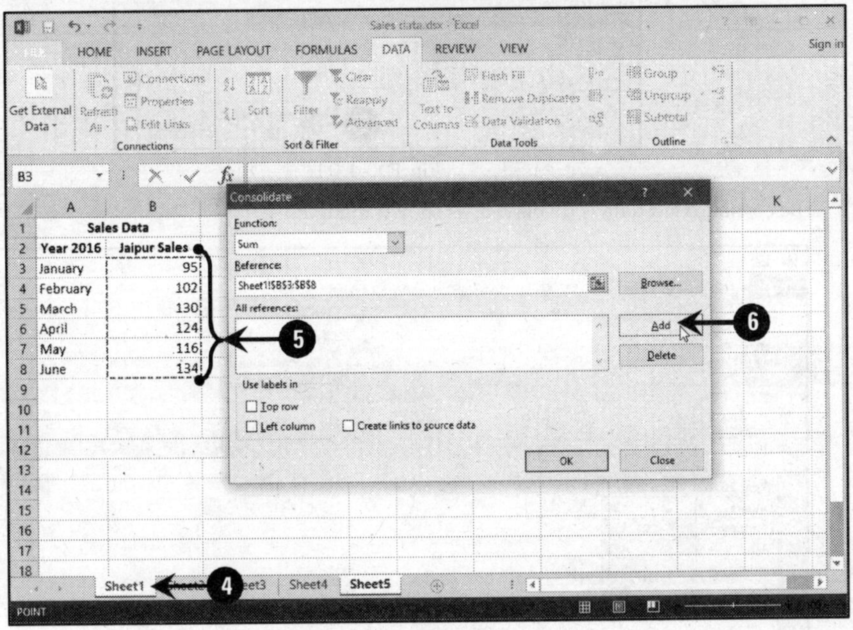

Fig.EX-4.89

The reference in **Reference** range box is highlighted and displayed in **All references** list box, as shown in Fig.EX-4.90:

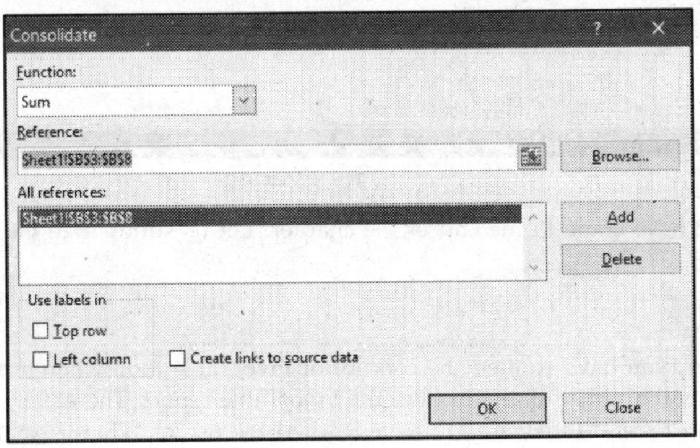

Fig.EX-4.90

Similarly, you can add the data that you want to consolidate in the **Consolidate** list box. In our case, we added the **Sheet2**, **Sheet3**, and **Sheet4** data (Fig.EX-4.91).

7. *Click* the **OK** button in the Consolidate dialog box, as shown in Fig.EX-4.91:

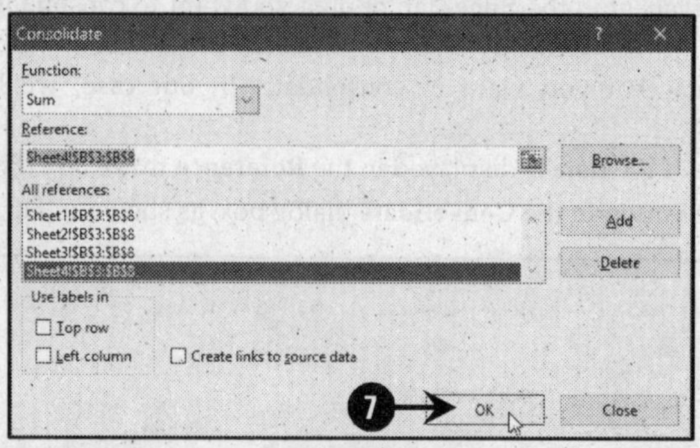

Fig.EX-4.91

The consolidated data is displayed, as shown in Fig.EX-4.92:

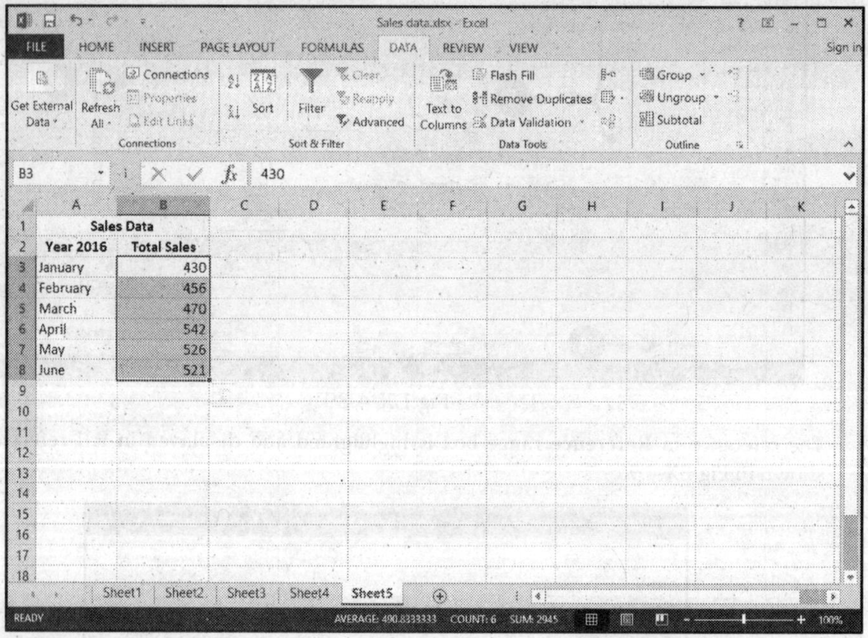

Fig.EX-4.92

With this, we have come to the end of the chapter. Let us summarize the key points discussed in this chapter.

Summary

In this chapter, you have studied the concept of PivotTable tool, wherein you have learned to create a PivotTable report and use slicers to filter the PivotTable report. Thereafter, you have learned to create a power view in Excel. Moreover, you have learned the use of What-if-Analysis tool, wherein you have learned to use Data Table, Scenario Manager and Goal Seek tools. Next, you have learned to protect a worksheet and a workbook. Furthermore, you have learned link worksheets and workbooks. Finally, you have learned to consolidate worksheets using Paste Special command, Formulas, and Consolidate command.

CHAPTER

5

Working with Google Sheets

In this Chapter:

* Features of a Google Sheet
* Creating a Google Sheet
* Entering Data in a Google Sheet
* Importing and Exporting Data in a Google Sheet
* Putting Comments on a Google Sheet
* Sharing a Google Sheet

Introduction

Google Sheet is a Web-based spreadsheet app, which is a part of Google's free online office suite. It lets you create, modify, and format a spreadsheet in the web browser, without the need to install any additional software. There are many other tasks that you can perform using Google Sheet, like data analysis, carrying out calculations, and tracking a project's progress. Multiple users can work on a single spreadsheet simultaneously and all the changes that are made to it are saved automatically. The changes made by other users will be visible to you while you work on the spreadsheet.

This chapter discusses the features of a Google Sheet. Next, the chapter discusses the procedure of creating a Google Sheet. It also describes the procedure of entering data in a sheet. The chapter also describes the procedure to import and export date from Google Sheet. Next, you learn the procedure of putting comments on the sheet. Then, you learn the procedure to import and export data from a google sheet. Towards the end; you learn it to share a sheet.

Let us first learn about the features of a Google Sheet.

Features of a Google Sheet

Google Sheet is an advanced online spreadsheet software, which is fast, real-time, efficient and flexible. It comes with various other striking features to help users analyze, manage, and share information in a better way. For example, Google Sheet provides a multi-user environment. Let us discuss all other features:

- **Simplified processing of data**: The calculations can be performed effortlessly with the help of the powerful functions and formulas provided by the spreadsheet. You may also add charts, pivot tables and filters to make the representation of data look better.
- **Compatibility with all the common file types**: The spreadsheets in other file formats can be imported and converted to edit them instantly without any hassle. One can also export a Google Sheet in various file formats.
- **Independency of working from any device**: You can work on your spreadsheets from any device (computer, tablet or phone), irrespective of your location. One can work in offline mode also.
- **Real-time editing and commenting**: More than one user can work simultaneously on the spreadsheet and changes made to the spreadsheet are visible to one another. You can add comments to the spreadsheet and chat with other users.
- **Form integration**: Forms can be created and embedded into a website. The information that is fed in the forms will go straight into the spreadsheet for further reviewing and creating analysis report.
- **Add-on tools**: There are third-party add-on tools available that enhance the functionality, data-flow and presentation of the spreadsheet.

Let us learn about the way of creating a google sheet.

Creating a Google Sheet

This is the first step to start working with a Google Sheet. Google Sheet offers various in-built templates for creating a spreadsheet. You may choose from these templates or choose a blank template. In this section, you will learn to create a spreadsheet using a blank template or an existing template.

To create a new blank spreadsheet, you need to select the Blank workbook template.

Perform the following steps to create a new spreadsheet using a blank template:

1. *Open* the Web browser.
2. *Type* **www.docs.google.com** in the address bar.
3. *Press* the **Enter** key. The login page for the **Google Docs** opens.
4. *Type* your username and password that you use to access your **Gmail** account.
5. *Press* the **Enter** key. The **Google Docs** home page opens.
6. *Click* the **Main menu** button. The options in the **Main menu** appear (Fig.EX-5.1).

7. *Select* the **Sheets** option, as shown in Fig.EX-5.1:

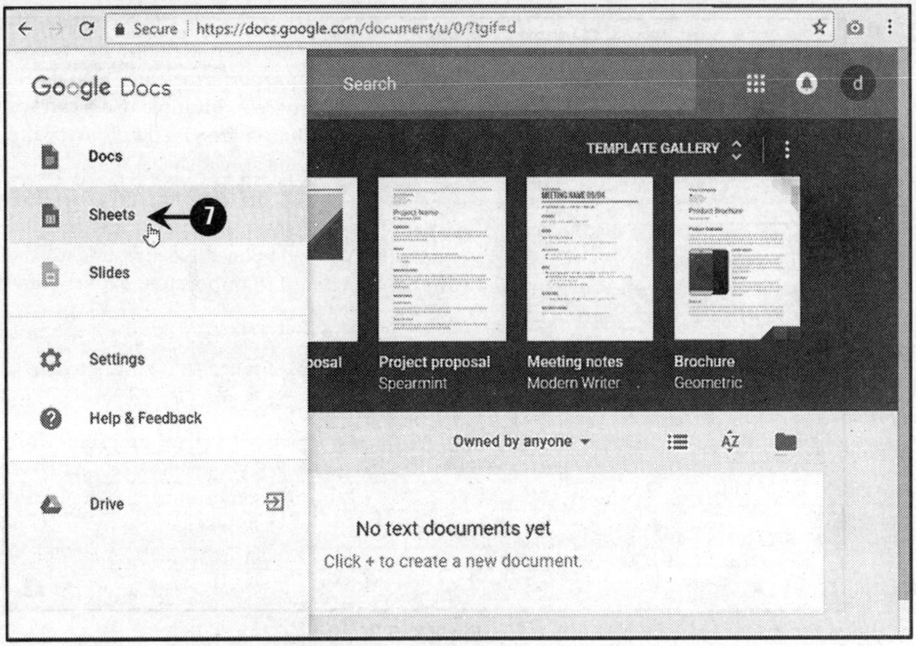

Fig.EX-5.1

The **Google Sheets** page opens (Fig.EX-5.2).

8. *Click* the **Blank** template in the **TEMPLATE GALLERY**, as shown in Fig.EX-5.2:

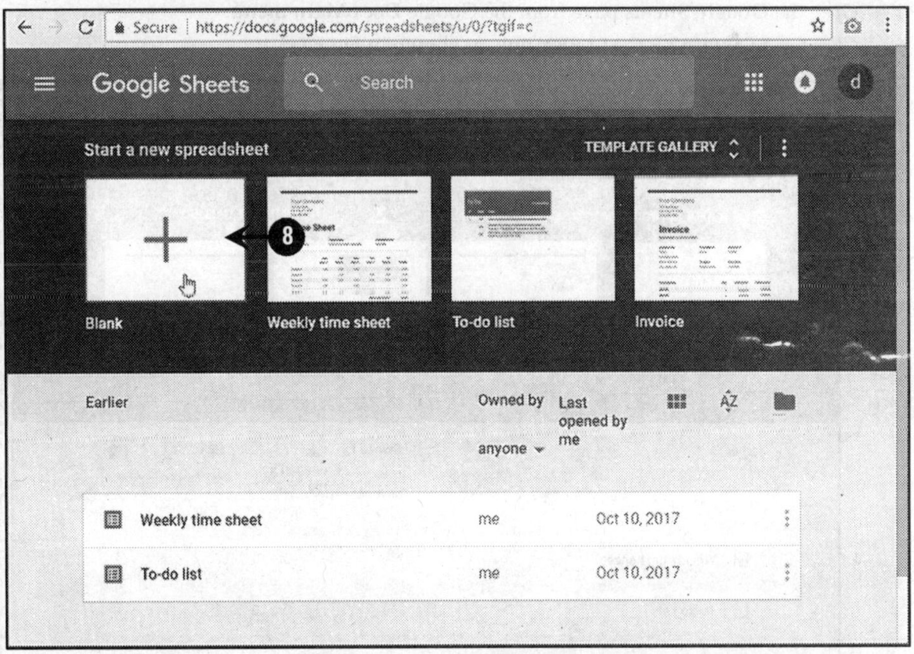

Fig.EX-5.2

The new blank Google Sheet appears, as shown in Fig.EX-5.3:

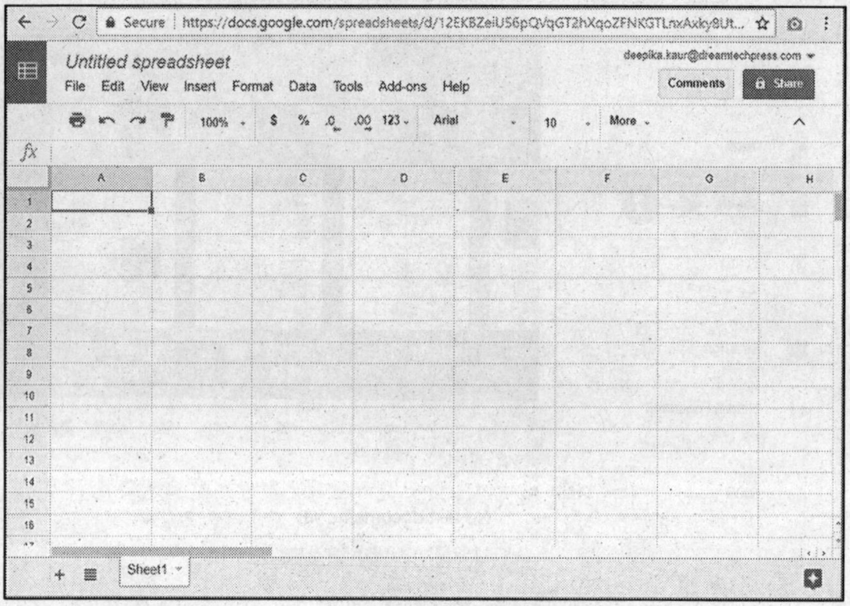

Fig.EX-5.3

You can use the templates that are available as sample templates in Google Sheets to create spreadsheets faster and efficiently.

Perform the following steps to create a new spreadsheet using an available template:

1. *Open* the **Google Sheets** page from the Google Docs **Main menu**.
2. *Click* the **TEMPLATE GALLERY** link, as shown in Fig.EX-5.4:

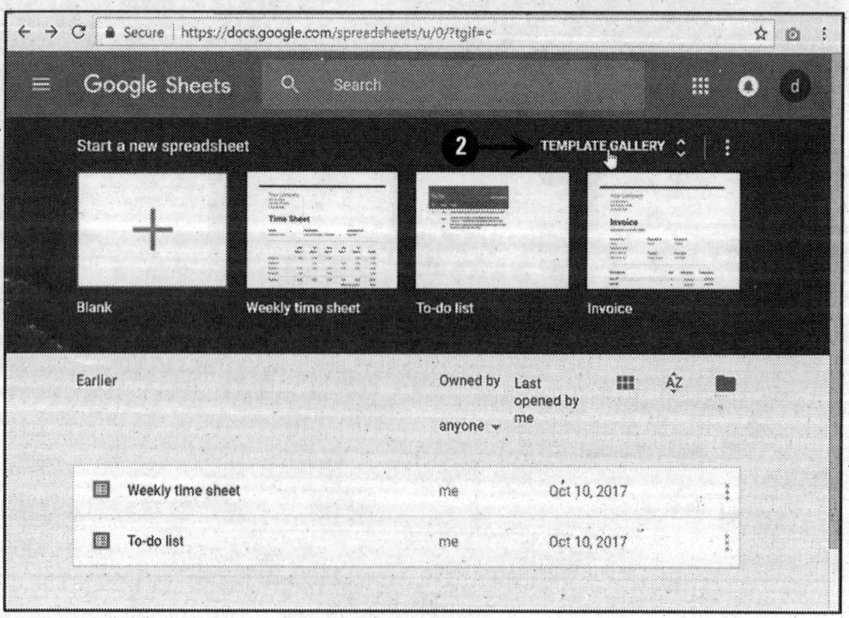

Fig.EX-5.4

A list of all the available templates appears on the screen, as shown in Fig.EX-5.5:

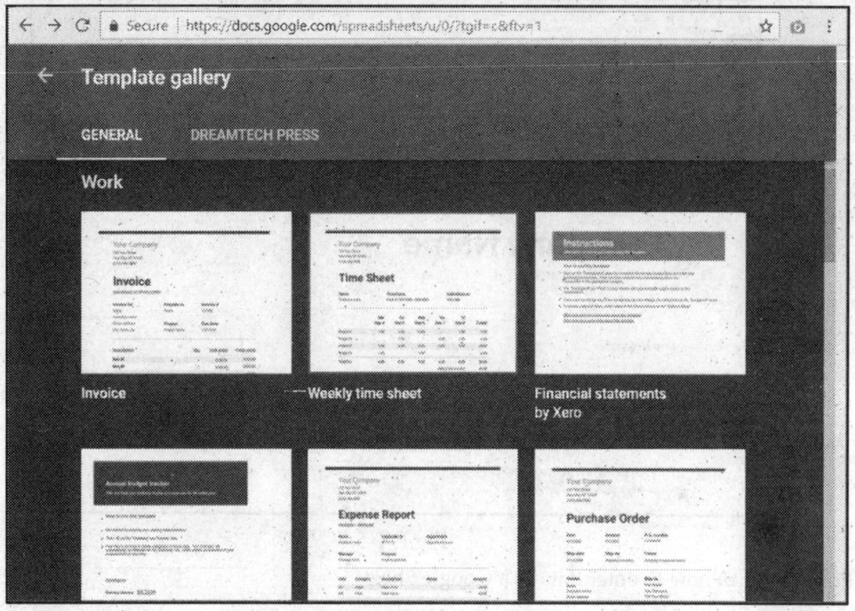

Fig.EX-5.5

3. *Select* the desired template from the list of templates. In our case, we have selected the **Employee shift schedule** template, as shown in Fig.EX-5.6:

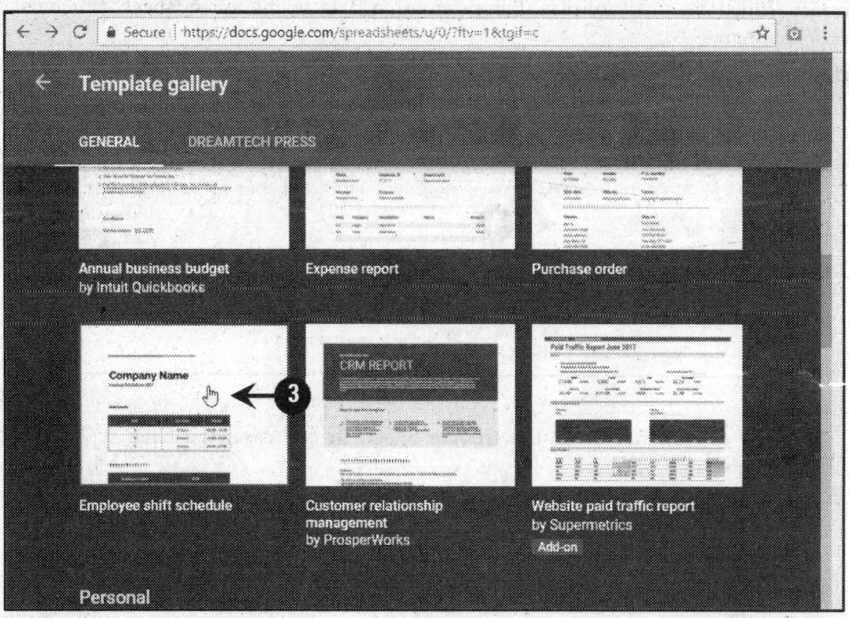

Fig.EX-5.6

A new Google Sheet is created using the **Employee shift schedule** template, as shown in Fig.EX-5.7:

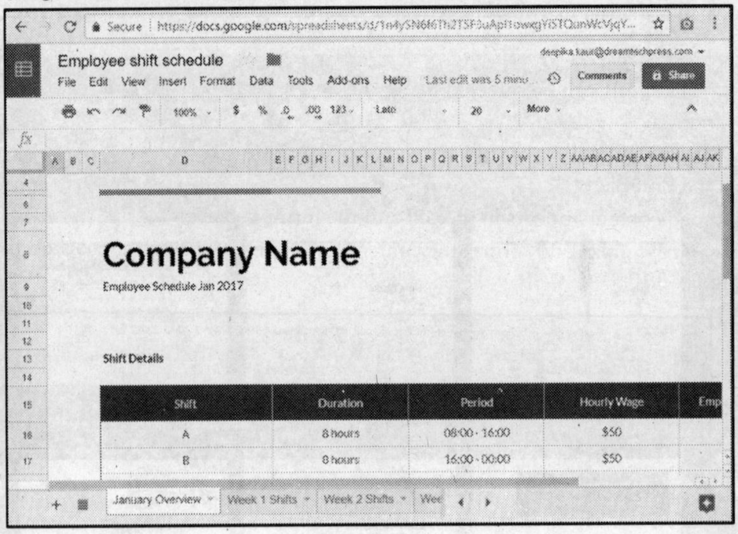

Fig.EX-5.7

Let us now learn how to enter data in a Google Sheet.

Entering Data in a Google Sheet

After creating the Google Sheet, you can start working on it by adding content to it. The data that you enter is stored in the cells. Cells may contain different kinds of content, like text, numbers, dates, currency, functions and formulas. Before entering data in the spreadsheet, you must save it with an appropriate name.

Perform the following steps to rename your spreadsheet:

1. *Click* the **Untitled spreadsheet** label. It will change into a textbox and the text will get selected, as shown in Fig.EX-5.8:

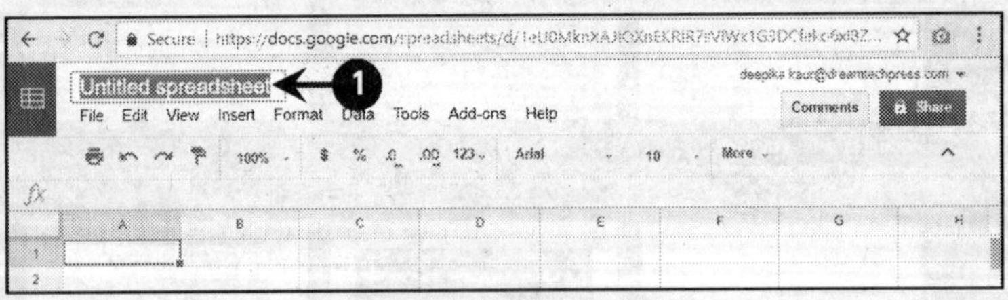

Fig.EX-5.8

2. *Type* the desired name for the Google Sheet. In our case, we have typed the name as **Books Catalogue** (Fig.EX-5.9).
3. *Press* the **Enter** key. The new name will appear on the label, as shown in Fig.EX-5.9:

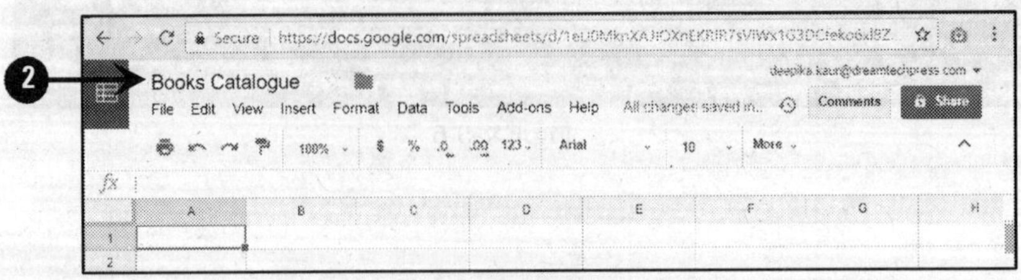

Fig.EX-5.9

After renaming the spreadsheet, you may start adding data into it.

4. *Click* a cell to select it. You will see a blue outline highlighting the cell.

The cells can be selected using the down arrow key on your keyboard.

5. *Type* the content in the selected cell.
6. *Press* the **Enter** key.

The typed content appears in the cell and the formula bar.

You can customize and format the content you typed by using the tools on the menu bar, as shown in Fig.EX-5.10:

Fig.EX-5.10

Let us learn how to import and export data in a Google Sheet.

Importing and Exporting Data in a Google Sheet

Google Sheet allows you to import and export spreadsheets in a very convenient manner. It imports the spreadsheet created in other programs with different formats and then converts it into Google Sheets.

Let us start learning how to import data in Google Sheet.

Perform the following steps to import data into your Google Sheet:

1. *Open* a new blank Google Sheet.
2. *Click* the **File** menu (Fig.EX-5.11). A drop-down menu appears.
3. *Select* the **Import** option from the drop-down menu, as shown in Fig.EX-5.11:

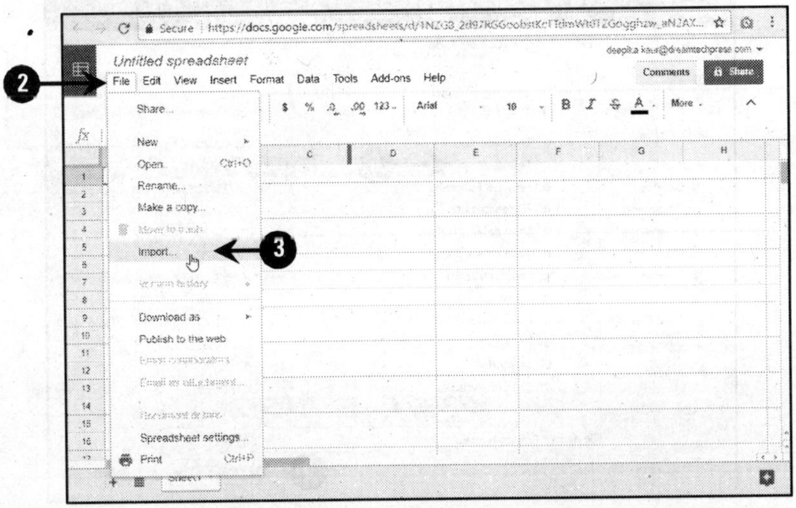

Fig.EX-5.11

The **Import file** dialog box appears, which gives you various location options from where you can import a spreadsheet (Fig.EX-5.12). You can choose your desired location from the following tabs:

- **My Drive:** You can choose from the spreadsheets stored in your Google Drive.
- **Shared with me:** These are the spreadsheets that are shared with you by other Google drive users.
- **Recent:** The spreadsheets that you have worked upon recently will be listed here.
- **Upload:** You can choose to upload a spreadsheet from your computer.

4. *Select* the desired location from where you want to import the spreadsheet. In our case, we have selected the **Upload** tab to import a file from the computer (Fig.EX-5.12).
5. *Click* the **Select a file from your computer** button, as shown in Fig.EX-5.12:

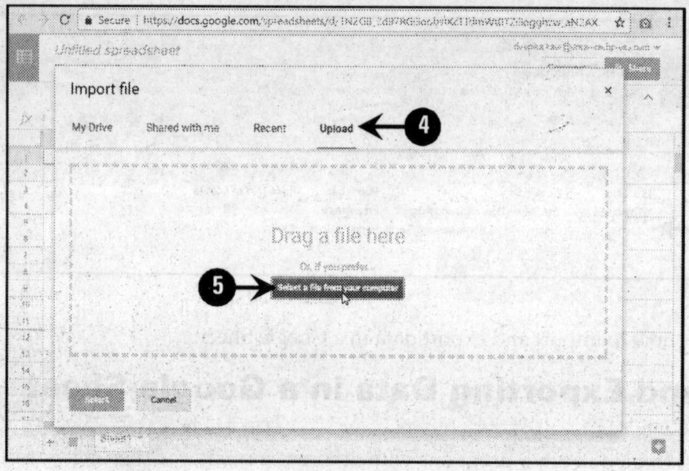

Fig.EX-5.12

The **Open** dialog box appears (Fig.EX-5.13).

6. *Select* the spreadsheet you want to import from your computer. In our case, we have selected **Employee** spreadsheet (Fig.EX-5.13).
7. *Click* the **Open** button, as shown in Fig.EX-5.13:

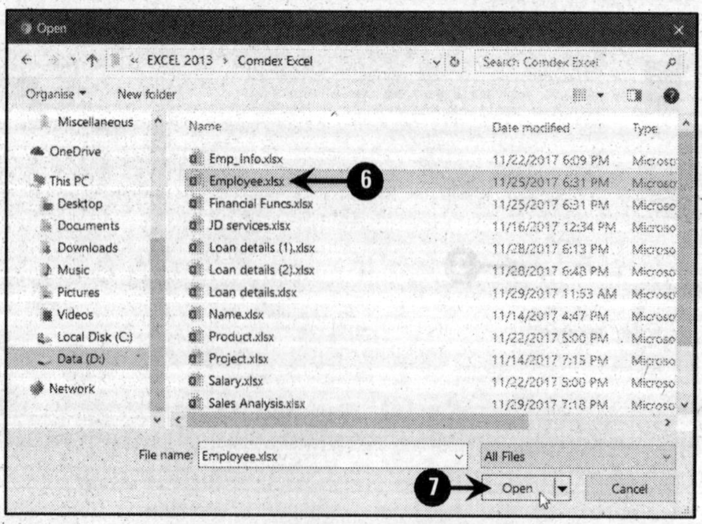

Fig.EX-5.13

The **Import file** dialog box re-appears (Fig.EX-5.14).

8. *Select* the desired radio button for **Import action** to specify where the imported sheet will appear. In our case, we have selected the **Create new spreadsheet** radio button (Fig.EX-5.14).
9. *Click* the **Import** button, as shown in Fig.EX-5.14:

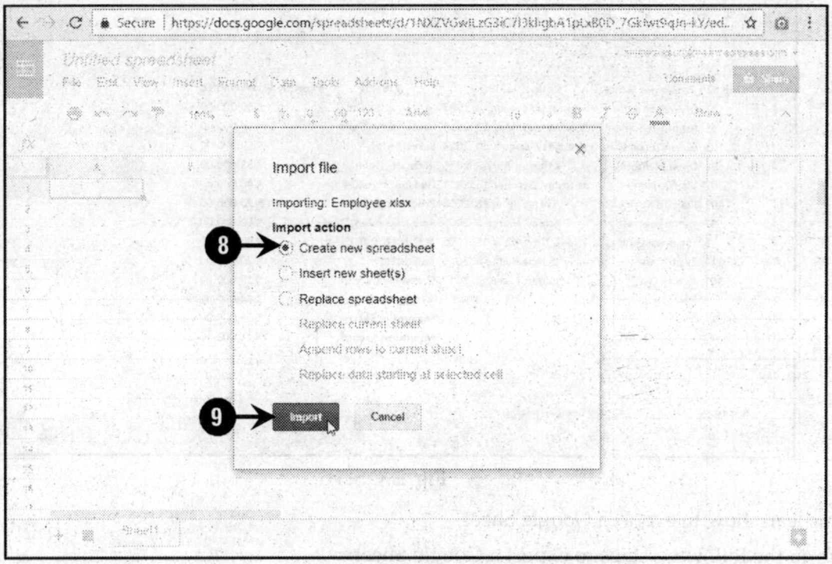

Fig.EX-5.14

The **File imported successfully** message appears (Fig.EX-5.15).

10. *Click* the **Open now >>** link to open the imported spreadsheet, as shown in Fig.EX-5.15:

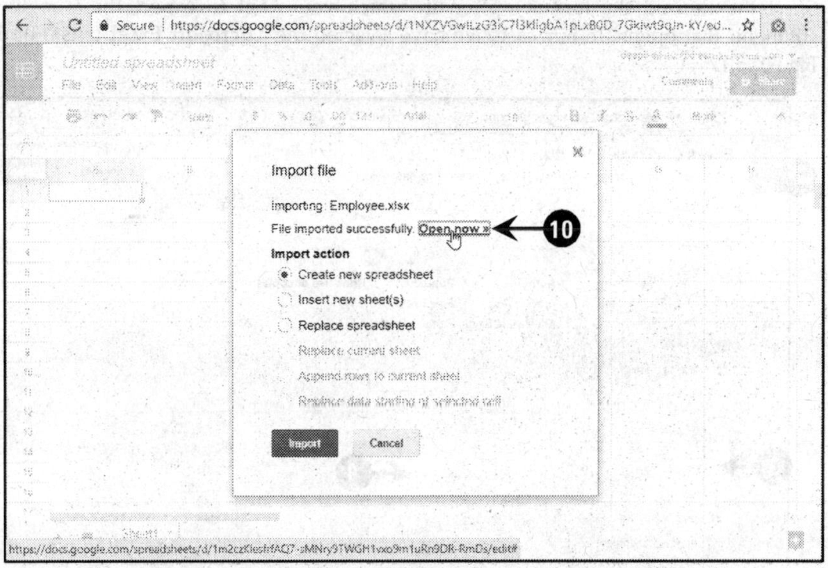

Fig.EX-5.15

The imported spreadsheet appears in a new spreadsheet, as shown in Fig.EX-5.16:

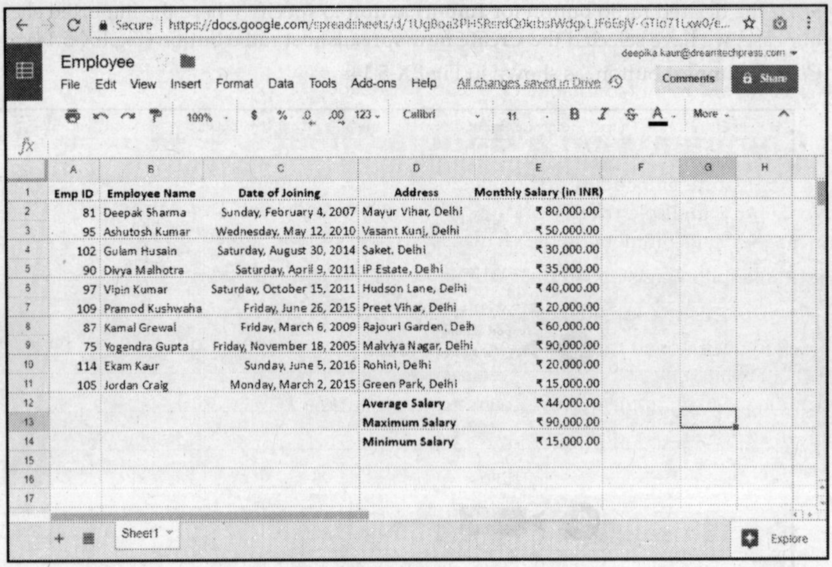

Fig.EX-5.16

Let us learn how to export a Google Sheet.

Perform the following steps to export a Google Sheet:

1. *Open* an existing spreadsheet that you want to export.
2. *Click* the **File** menu (Fig.EX-5.17) A drop-down menu appears.
3. *Select* the **Download as** option from the drop-down menu (Fig.EX-5.17).
4. *Select* the desired the format option in which you want to export the Google Sheet, from the submenu that opens. In our case, we have selected the **Microsoft Excel (.xlsx)** option, as shown in Fig.EX-5.17:

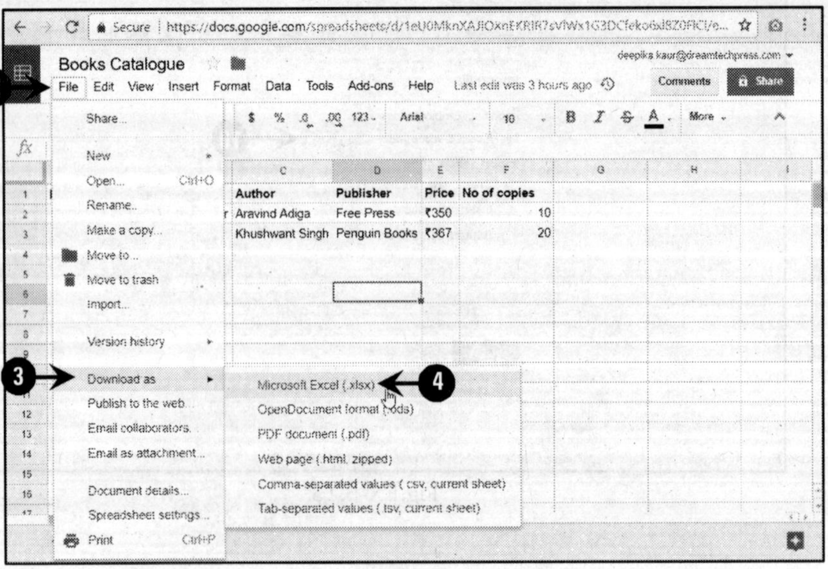

Fig.EX-5.17

The Google Sheet will be downloaded in the selected file format at the default download location that is set for your browser.

Additionally, you can also export your Google Sheet in several different file formats including Excel, OpenOffice, PDF, Text, HTML*, and CSV.

Let us learn how to put comments on a Google Sheet.

Putting Comments on a Google Sheet

There is a feature embedded in Google Sheet to put comments on the spreadsheet. It proves to be very convenient for multiple users working on a single spreadsheet. This enhances the collaboration between them, as they can comment on the changes they make in the spreadsheet.

Perform the following steps to put comments on your spreadsheet:

1. *Open* an existing spreadsheet on which you want to put comment.
2. *Select* a cell or cell range on which you want to comment. In our case, we have selected the cell **E3** (Fig.EX-5.18).
3. *Click* the **Comments** button next to the **Share** button (Fig.EX-5.18).
4. *Click* the **Comment** button from the notification area that opens, as shown in Fig.EX-5.18:

Fig.EX-5.18

A comment box appears with the name that you have specified in your Google account (Fig.EX-5.19).

5. *Type* your comment in the comment box. In our case, we have typed, **Incorrect price!!**. (Fig.EX-5.19).
6. *Click* the **Comment** button to post the comment, as shown in Fig.EX-5.19:

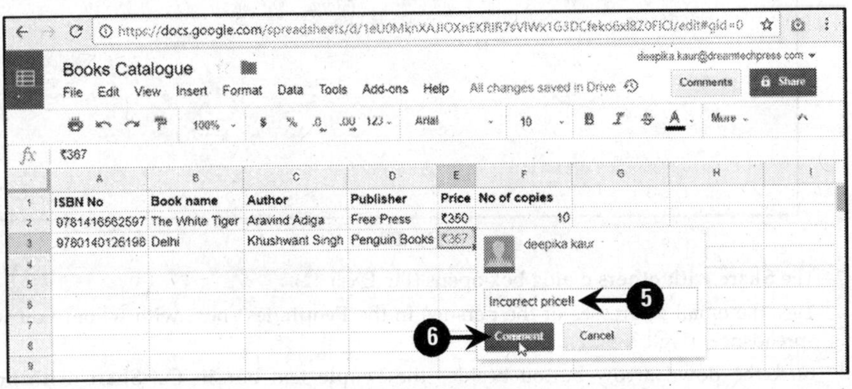

Fig.EX-5.19

The comment appears on the specified cell of the spreadsheet, as shown in Fig.EX-5.20:

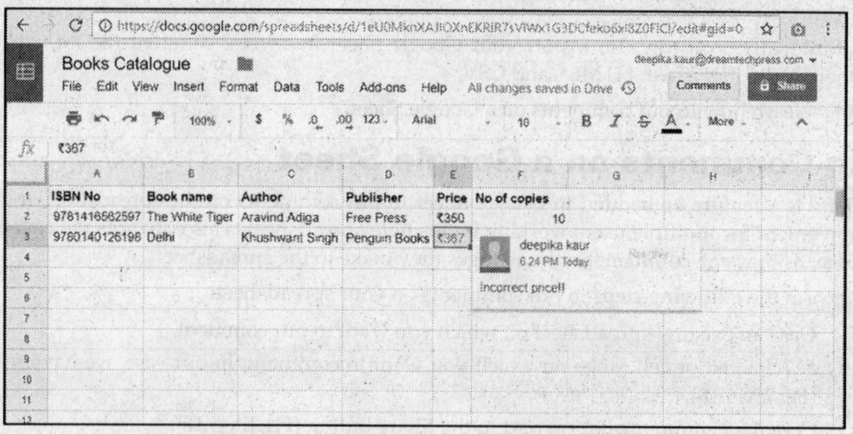

Fig.EX-5.20

Let us learn how to share a Google Sheet with others.

Sharing a Google Sheet

You may need to share your Google Sheet with other people in your contacts. It just takes a few seconds to do so.

Perform the following steps to share your spreadsheet:

1. *Open* the spreadsheet that you want to share.
2. *Click* the **Share** button, as shown in Fig.EX-5.21:

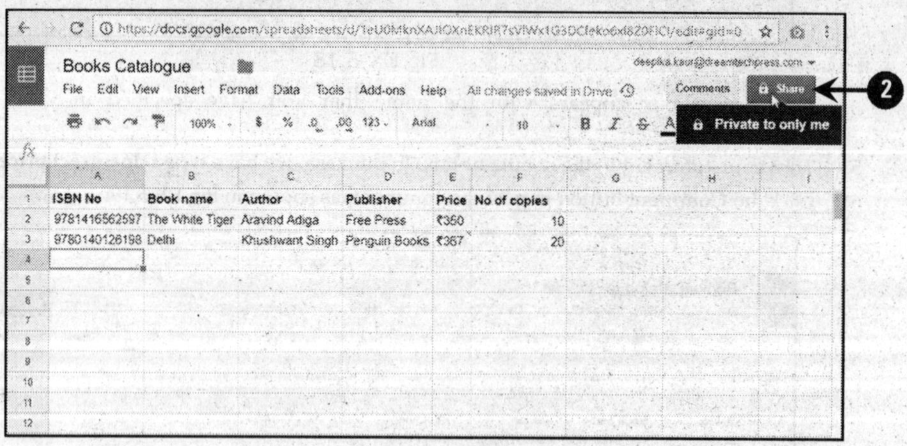

Fig.EX-5.21

   The **Share with others** dialog box opens (Fig.EX-5.22).

3. *Type* the email addresses of the persons in the **People** text box, with whom you want to share the spreadsheet (Fig.EX-5.22).
4. *Click* the down arrow button besides the **People** text box in the **Share with others** dialog box (Fig.EX-5.22).

   A drop down list appears.

5. *Set* the permission that you wish to grant to the user who accesses the spreadsheet. By default, the permission is set to **Can edit.** In our case, we have set the **Can view** permission, as shown in Fig.EX-5.22:

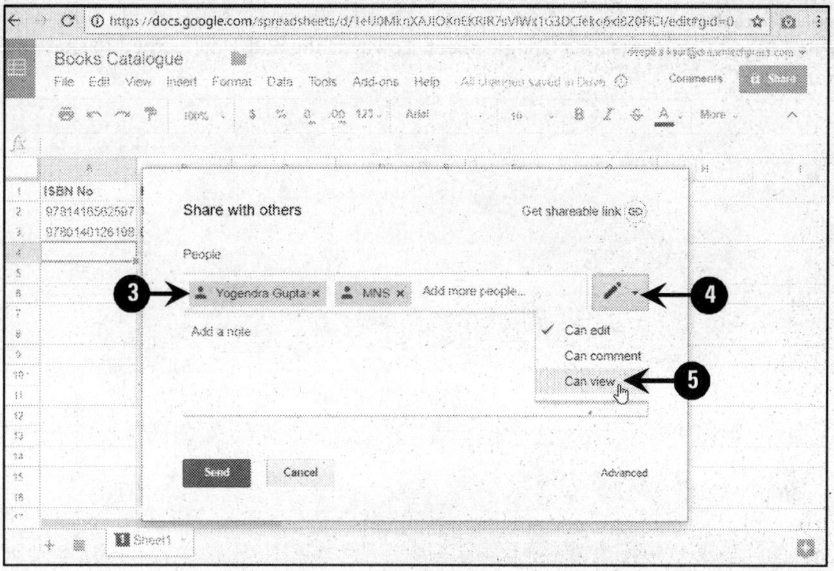

Fig.EX-5.22

6. *Add* a note for the people if you want (Fig.EX-5.23).
7. *Click* the **Send** button, as shown in Fig.EX-5.23:

Fig.EX-5.23

The Google Sheet is shared with people whose email addresses were specified.

With this, we come to the end of the chapter. Now, let us summarize the key points we have learned in this chapter.

Summary

In this chapter, you have learned about the features of a Google Sheet. You have learned to create a Google Sheet and enter data into it. Next, you learned to import an external spreadsheet into a Google Sheet. Thereafter, you learned to export a Google Sheet in different file formats. Furthermore, you learned to put comments on a Google Sheet. Towards the end, you learned to share a Google Sheet with other people.